REAL ESTATE PRINCIPLES

NINTH EDITION

CHARLES F. FLOYD AND MARCUS T. ALLEN

Dearborn™
Real Estate Education

This publication is designed to provide accurate and authoritative information in regard to the subject matter covered. It is sold with the understanding that the publisher is not engaged in rendering legal, accounting, or other professional service. If legal advice or other expert assistance is required, the services of a competent professional should be sought.

President: Mehul Patel
Vice President of Product Development & Publishing: Evan M. Butterfield
Editorial Director: Kate DeVivo
Development Editor: Leah Strauss
Director of Production: Daniel Frey
Senior Managing Editor, Production: Jack Kiburz
Production Artist: Virginia Byrne
Creative Director: Lucy Jenkins
Senior Product Manager: Melissa Kleeman

Published by Dearborn™ Real Estate Education
30 South Wacker Drive
Chicago, Illinois 60606-7481
(312) 836-4400
www.dearbornRE.com

Printed in the United States of America

08 09 10   10   9   8   7   6   5   4   3   2   1

The Library of Congress has cataloged the eighth edition as follows:

Floyd, Charles F.
  Real estate principles / Charles F. Floyd and Marcus T. Allen. 8th ed.
    p. cm.
  Includes index.
  ISBN 0-7931-9624-8
  Real estate business—United States. I. Allen, Marcus T. II. Title.
  HD255.F57 2005
  333.33'0973—dc22   2004028205

Ninth edition ISBN-13: 978-1-4277-6279-5
Ninth edition ISBN-10:   1-4277-6279-1

DEDICATION

This book is dedicated to
R. W. Barber
a man of the land
and
C. O. Floyd
a man of business.
—*Charles F. Floyd*

This book is dedicated to
Rhonda, Melanie, and Issabella.
—*Marcus T. Allen*

CONTENTS

CHAPTER 3

Private Restrictions on Ownership   48

CHAPTER 4

Public Restrictions on Ownership   70

PART TWO

Real Estate Service Industries   169

PART FOUR

Real Estate Finance and Investment Analysis   355

CHAPTER 16

Residential and Commercial Property Financing   356

CHAPTER 17

Risk, Return, and the Time Value of Money   392

Welcome to the ninth edition of *Real Estate Principles*! As one of the most popular and well-respected texts in college-level real estate education, this book has served as the framework for a practical and rigorous learning experience for introductory real estate students at schools across the nation since its first edition was published in 1981. This ninth edition continues that tradition by incorporating the latest industry advances and education technologies into a comprehensive, student-friendly presentation of the real estate "body of knowledge." We are absolutely convinced that students who master the material presented in this text will become better-informed real estate market participants whether their primary real estate interests lie in consumption, investment, brokerage, appraisal, law, property and asset management, or any combination of these disciplines.

In addition to an overall updating of the material from previous editions, readers will find substantive application of many cutting-edge topics in the real estate realm, including residential and commercial property financing, Wall Street's influence, innovative land-use control measures, and recent trends in real estate development, brokerage, property management, and appraisal.

PEDAGOGICAL DEVICES

For students, the book contains the following pedagogical devices designed to enhance their learning experience:

- Each chapter begins with a Chapter Preview that clearly sets forth the learning objectives.

- The Key Terms discussed in each chapter appear in boldface for emphasis. These terms are succinctly defined in the end-of-book Glossary.

- Many tables, figures, and photographs are provided throughout the text to help readers visualize the topics and incorporate them in their knowledge base.

- Each chapter ends with a Chapter Review that concisely summarizes the key concepts.

- Thought-provoking review exercises are provided at the end of each chapter.

■ Suggested reading lists for each chapter are included to direct students who wish to learn more about specific concepts to additional sources of information, including books, academic journals, practitioner journals, newspapers, magazines, and Internet sites.

INSTRUCTOR SUPPORT

For instructors, we have developed an extensive collection of support materials that can be easily downloaded (with the proper password) from the publisher's Web site at *www.dearbornRE.com*. The materials include

■ detailed lecture notes in Microsoft PowerPoint and Microsoft Word format for each chapter (for use with a computer display projector or as transparency slides);

■ assignment exercises for each chapter (with answers);

■ an extensive multiple-choice, true-false, and short-answer test bank for creating customized assignments and examinations; and

■ ready-made examinations for each part of the text, including

   ■ real estate legal analysis,

   ■ real estate market analysis,

   ■ real estate services analysis, and

   ■ real estate finance and investment analysis.

Readers familiar with previous editions of this text will be pleased to find that this edition continues to incorporate many of the special features from previous editions that enhance the students' learning experiences. Close-Ups, Legal Highlights, People Profiles, and Case Studies are liberally sprinkled throughout the book to demonstrate how real estate principles can be observed and applied in the "real world."

FLEXIBLE PATHWAYS THROUGH THE TEXT

Because real estate is such a dynamic and diverse discipline, we have purposefully designed this edition of *Real Estate Principles* in such a way that instructors who wish to approach the material from their own preferred direction can do so with relative ease. Each chapter can be treated as a stand-alone learning module within the real estate body of knowledge. While we recommend presenting the material in the chapter order provided for general business students, an instructor who wishes to focus on finance and investment analysis issues can easily shift Chapters 16 through 20 to the beginning of the semester (after Chapter 1) to allow adequate time for in-depth coverage. Or an instructor who wishes to focus on real estate economics might consider following the first chapter with Chapters 11 through 15. We would be pleased to get feedback from instructors describing how they choose to sequence the chapters in their courses.

ACKNOWLEDGMENTS ————————————————————————

No project of the magnitude of this book can be accomplished without a spirit of teamwork and mutual respect between all the parties involved. We wish to sincerely thank all of the people who provided comments, suggestions, and other invaluable forms of support in the research, writing, and production process, especially Edward L. Prill of Colorado State University; Jeffrey J. Rymaszewski of Sheldon B. Lubar School of Business; and Dr. Ronald Throupe of Burns School of Real Estate and Construction Management at Daniels College of Business/University of Denver.

In addition, special thanks are due to the students in our classrooms who served as guinea pigs for the new material.

Finally, we hope that everyone who reads this book will be able to use the lessons contained herein to improve their real estate decision-making skills and, ultimately, to enrich their lives with respect to real estate resources.

Charles F. Floyd, PhD
University of Georgia

Marcus T. Allen, PhD
Florida Atlantic University

Why Study Real Estate?

CHAPTER PREVIEW

Why study **real estate**? Why is it important? What are the characteristics that make real estate different from other types of assets? Fundamentally, people must have places to live and businesses must have locations for their activities. As a result, real estate is a vital resource that touches the economic lives of all people. A thorough understanding of the complexities of real estate resources and the markets in which they are traded enables us to make informed choices regarding real estate for either personal or business use. The objective of this book is to present the general principles necessary for effective real estate decision making. The text also serves as a starting point for more advanced study of the concepts and issues facing real estate market participants.

REAL
ESTATE
TODAY

CASE STUDY
The Importance
of Location

CASE STUDY
The Gestation
of Park Springs

1

THE ROLE OF REAL ESTATE STUDIES IN BUSINESS EDUCATION

When you first learned that your college or university offers a real estate principles course as part of its business school curriculum, you may have thought that the focus of the course would be to prepare for a career as a real estate broker. While real estate brokerage is an excellent career choice for many people, this book does not assume that a career in brokerage is your motivation for taking a real estate course. Instead, we present the principles of real estate from the perspective of the user of real estate resources. These principles provide a foundation for effective real estate decision making, whether you intend to manage a sizable real estate portfolio or simply to become more knowledgeable about your personal real estate transactions.

In most universities and colleges, real estate is regarded as a specialty area under the general umbrella of business studies. As such, a real estate principles course covers issues and topics unique to the real estate discipline and much too specific for adequate coverage in other areas of academic study. Because of the specialized knowledge required for effective real estate decision making, real estate issues deserve independent attention in a business curriculum. The intricacies of real estate resources and markets can baffle the ill-prepared decision maker, but a solid foundation in real estate principles will help you make effective business and personal real estate decisions throughout your career. In addition, the topics covered in this text will serve as a springboard for those students who wish to pursue a more detailed study of real estate in subsequent courses.

PERSONAL AND BUSINESS-RELATED REAL ESTATE DECISIONS

A thorough understanding of real estate principles is extremely important for real estate decision making in both personal and business-related venues. As individuals, all of us will probably face the following questions several times over the years:

- Should I buy a house or a condo or should I lease an apartment for my personal or family residence?
- What neighborhood do I want to live or invest in?
- What type of financing should I use, and how do I arrange it?
- Should I use a broker to sell my property or try to sell it myself?
- How should I structure the sales contract to get the best deal?
- How do I decide which property I should invest in?

The same issues that face us as individuals also apply in the business environment. Consider a company that requires additional office space to expand its operations and compete effectively in its product market. Such a company faces many questions that can be addressed only with the knowledge of real estate principles. The following are examples:

- Should the company buy or lease additional space? If the company leases space, how should it structure the details of the lease agreement to best serve its objectives?

- If the company decides to buy more real estate, should it build a new property or purchase an existing one?

- How should the company finance the purchase or development?

- Should the company acquire a larger building than it currently requires and lease the additional spaced to tenants until the company needs it?

- Should the company consider relocating the corporate headquarters to a more central location, either in its current city or in another city altogether?

Appropriate answers to these and other important questions require familiarity with the overall operation of real estate markets, as well as specific knowledge of legal issues, transaction details, and the financial framework of real estate resources. For this reason, real estate principles are a fundamental component of undergraduate business education, regardless of your chosen field of study.

ORGANIZATION OF THIS BOOK

Our goal is to present some of the basic principles of real estate in such a manner that you will be well prepared to anticipate and evaluate changing market conditions and make real estate decisions that best serve your personal and business objectives. We have divided the topics considered in the text into four categories:

1. **Part One, Real Estate Legal Analysis** (Chapters 2–7) considers issues related to the legal concept of real estate ownership. We define various ownership interests one can obtain in real estate, deed and legal description methods, and private and public limitations on ownership.

2. **Part Two, Real Estate Service Industries** (Chapters 8–10) discusses the real estate services industry, including brokerage, property management, and appraisal.

3. **Part Three, Real Estate Market Analysis** (Chapters 11–15) considers the dynamics of real estate markets as a result of national, regional, and local influences on property values and uses. In addition, we review the classic models of urban growth and discuss various aspects of the land development process. We also examine the residential, commercial, and industrial development process.

4. **Part Four, Real Estate Finance and Investment Analysis** (Chapters 16–19) examines the financing of real estate investment and ownership, and real estate investment analysis.

The remainder of this introductory chapter sets the stage for the topics to be addressed throughout this text by describing the special economic characteristics of real estate, the economic importance of real estate, and various career opportunities in the real estate industry.

SPECIAL CHARACTERISTICS OF REAL ESTATE

What is real estate? Simply defined, *real estate* is property in land and buildings. Technically, real estate consists of the physical land and structures, while **real property** consists of the legal interests associated with ownership of the physical real estate. In practice, however, the two terms are virtually synonymous. All other movable property such as automobiles, furniture, boats, and clothing is known as **personal property**. As an economic resource, real estate has some distinct characteristics that distinguish it from other types of resources. These characteristics are

- fixed location;
- uniqueness;
- interdependence of land uses;
- long life;
- long-term commitments;
- large transactions; and
- long gestation period.

Fixed Location

The characteristic of real estate that distinguishes it from all other types of economic resources is its fixed location. If there is an oversupply of wheat in Kansas, or of automobiles in Michigan, they can be moved to areas of relative scarcity. This is not true of real estate resources. If there is an oversupply of condominiums in Miami, office space in Manhattan, or shopping centers in Minneapolis, they cannot be transported to other communities where the demand is stronger. A tract of land, of course, cannot be moved a few feet up the street to help meet demand for space at that site. Thus, the success of real estate acquisition, development, and investment decisions is directly affected by the forces of supply and demand in a local area.

Uniqueness

Because real estate is fixed in location, every parcel is unique or, to use a fancy term, heterogeneous. Even subdivision lots located side by side are not perfect substitutes for each other because of differences in such factors as topography, tree cover, and view. These factors often create large differences in property values. For example, lots fronting on a lake will probably sell for much more than lots just across the street; lots with a spectacular mountain view may sell for many times more than nearby ones without the view.

The Importance of Location

How important is location to the value of real estate? Very important in the case of a 77-square-foot "studio apartment" in the exclusive Knightsbridge neighborhood of London. The former storage closet, originally conceived as a maid's room, is only slightly larger than a prison cell, but is priced at $335,000, or about $4,500 per square foot. Moreover, the room has no electricity or heat, which would cost an additional $59,000 to make it habitable. Rather pricey, but the tiny apartment is located in one of the wealthiest neighborhoods in the world and is within walking distance to exclusive stores such as Harrod's and the city's iconic Hyde Park.

Almost unbelievably, other ultra high-end London properties have been selling for even higher prices, sometimes as much as $6,000 per square foot. The average house price in the area where the studio is located rose to over $2.2 million in 2006. By comparison, the closet-sized apartment is a bargain. The old real estate axiom that the three most important factors in real estate are location, location, and location certainly applies in this case.

Interdependence of Land Uses

Real estate's fixed location leads to another economic characteristic: interdependence of land uses. The use of real property depends greatly on the provision of public serves, the uses made of nearby land, and the general economic vitality of the neighborhood and community.

It is extremely difficult to use land to its full economic potential, particularly in an urban setting, unless adequate public services are provided and neighboring land is used appropriately. Even agricultural lands need to be served by roads, and such basic utilities as electricity and telephone serve are necessary for practical homestead use. As we move to denser residential development, public water and sewerage systems are essential as are such governmental services as education, police and fire protection, and various social services. Land must be converted to public use for parks, schools, and other governmental services, particularly transportation facilities. If adequate governmental services and public land uses are not available, it will be difficult or even impossible to develop land for residential, commercial, or industrial use.

The use of land is also affected greatly by nearby land use. If a large tract of vacant land is located near areas of expanding residential and commercial development, this location should increase both the land's potential use and its value in the marketplace. Conversely, the value of land may be affected adversely by its proximity to "undesirable" uses. It would probably be difficult, for example, to develop a single-family housing development next to a chemical plant or slaughterhouse. Such uses, however, particularly if served by transportation facilities and other public services, may make nearby land valuable for industrial purposes.

The economic vitality of a neighborhood, community, or region greatly affects the demand for real property and its value. If the economy of the area is expanding, the population also will increase, bringing about a corresponding increase in the demand for residential, commercial, and industrial land. Conversely, if the economy of the area is in temporary or long-term decline, the demand for real estate and real estate value also will tend to decline.

It is the interdependence of land uses that leads to the necessity of both private and public land-use controls, topics we will study in Chapters 3 and 4. The use of land affects the owners of other land more than the use of almost any other type of private property and may create costs to the public at large. For example, the filling of floodplain lands (the low-lying land near streams) to make them suitable for high-density residential use may cause other owners of land on the floodplain to be affected adversely in periods of heavy rainfall. If other landowners also fill in their portion of the floodplain, a flood hazard may be created that will require large public expenditures to alleviate.

Long Life

Although its ability to generate income may change over time, land is virtually indestructible. Additionally, *real estate improvements*—that is, buildings on the land—generally have very long lives. For example, a family would expect a new home to last as long as they wanted to live there and beyond, and many houses last for a century or more when maintained properly. Apartment houses, shopping centers, and other types of income-producing property also have very long lives.

Long-Term Commitments

The long lives of real estate improvements mean that investment decisions are, by their very nature, long-term commitments. Although the immediate prospects for the production of income are very important in real estate investment analysis, the factors that influence income generation over the long term are equally critical. For example, the proximity of a motel to a heavily traveled highway is a predominant factor in the financial success of the motel. If the motel is built in a location that soon will be bypassed by a new freeway, it probably will not be a successful investment during much of its life. Conversely, shopping centers are often built somewhat ahead of the market to gain advantageous location in advance of expected population growth.

The characteristics of long life and long-term commitments force the real estate investor and developer to establish realistic, long-term outlooks if they want to make successful investment decisions. The real estate investor who merely assumes that favorable economic trends will continue will probably be unsuccessful. For example, most of the problems that arose during the recent decline in real estate prices occurred because investors and financial institutions regarded the future with unbridled optimism. Investors should analyze carefully the factors that have caused economic trends to be favorable in the past and try to ascertain what will happen to these factors for some years into the future.

Large Transactions

Another important economic characteristic is the relatively large size of real estate transactions. Because they involve large expenditures, real estate transactions are not entered into either lightly or frequently. A home is by far the average family's largest single purchase. Investment in income-producing real estate requires large outlays beyond the financial means of most investors.

The large size and long-term nature of real estate transactions mean that buyers usually have to rely at least partially on some type of outside financing. This economic characteristic has led to the rise of the real estate brokerage industry. Both buyers and sellers generally need assistance to analyze the marketplace, evaluate long-term investment decisions, arrange financing and, in general, deal with the complexities of these transactions.

Long Gestation Period

A final economic characteristic of real estate is the long **gestation period** of real property improvements. The time between the conception of a real estate project and its actual completion and subsequent entry into the available supply may be several years. Suppose a group of investors decides to build an apartment complex. To complete this project, they first must acquire the land, then have engineering and architectural plans drawn for the site and buildings, secure zoning and other regulatory approvals, and arrange the financing before they can begin to build the project.

Long delays may occur at any of these steps. For example, it may be difficult to secure approval for the zoning board, or it may be necessary to wait several months for the completion of a new sewer line, or bad weather may delay construction.

The long gestation period makes the supply of real estate slow to respond to increases or decreases in demand. Because the supply cannot be increased quickly, increases in demand often results in rapid upward price movements unless an excess supply exists. Conversely, demand may decline during a project's gestation period, leaving it to face a much reduced market when completed. This is yet another reason the real estate developer must analyze factors affecting future demand and supply. There may be a strong market for, say, office space in a certain area at present. This does not necessarily mean that the strong demand will continue. Many investors and financial institutions have discovered, to their immense sorrow, that by the time the project was completed, demand for the products had declined. Or they may not have fully considered the impact of other projects that were being built at the same time. Successful real estate investment requires a thorough, long-term economic analysis.

The Gestation of Park Springs

The development history of the Park Springs continuing care retirement community provides an excellent example of the long gestation period for real estate development: ten years from conception to generating income.

In 1994, developers Andy and Kevin Isakson bought a 110-acre former private airport site that straddled two county lines in suburban Atlanta in order to obtain the two acres needed to complete the assemblage for a Super Target shopping center site. They then sold part of the remainder for a parking lot for the 1996 Atlanta Olympics but were left with 54 acres that had limited access and no utilities. In order to make the tract suitable for development they worked with the two counties involved and the state department of transportation to relocate an adjoining road to make the site more accessible. This also meant that the site would be surrounded on three sides by 3,500-acre Stone Mountain State Park. In order to gain utilities they had obtain water from one county and sewerage from the other. Finally, after four years of effort the site was ready for development. Now came the need to obtain zoning.

The plan was for a mixed-use development including apartments. This proposal was met with considerable community opposition based on a fear of an influx of school children and an increase of traffic in the already congested area. Thus, the initial zoning proposal failed. Then one of the community leaders suggested an age-restricted senior retirement community. This was attractive to the community because there wouldn't be additional local school children and the retired

residents would generate lower traffic, particularly at busy hours. The developers responded with a proposal that included 398 residences restricted to persons 62 years of age and older. This proposal gained overwhelming community support and was approved after two more years of effort. This brings us to the year 2000, six years after purchase, with nothing but expense and no income from the property.

The developers saw the market for a continuing care retirement community, one where seniors could purchase the right to occupy an independent living residence with the option of moving to assisted living or skilled care nursing facilities on the same site as their health needs changed. They offered a variety of units, ranging from an 800-square-foot one-bedroom apartment for $135,000 to a 2,400-square-foot detached two- to three-bedroom home for $600,000. For this entry fee the purchaser obtained the right to occupy the unit for his or her lifetime and the use of the development's facilities, including a fitness center, library, woodworking shop, pottery shop, and three restaurants. A monthly fee covered all utilities, biweekly cleaning, all maintenance, and taxes. At owners' death, 90 percent of the entry fee would be refunded to their estate.

The concept met with great market acceptance, and finally in 2004, ten years after the property was purchased, the first units were sold and the project began generating a cash flow—not yet a profit, but at least a cash flow. By 2007, all but 16 of the units had been sold, and entry fees had risen by 45 percent, generating a healthy profit for the developers upon resale of these units. Even

(continued)

The Gestation of Park Springs

so, the development won't begin to really show an overall profit until 2009. Park Springs has been a resounding success, but only with developers who were able to surmount the many obstacles inherent in the site and absorb the large development costs during the more than ten-year gestation period.

THE ECONOMIC IMPORTANCE OF REAL ESTATE

Real estate is a vital component of the national economy and constitutes a large portion of national wealth. Land and structures make up approximately two-thirds of the wealth of the United States; the remainder consists of equipment and inventories. As individuals and businesses borrow against real estate assets, their borrowing activities give rise to the real estate finance industry. In 2007, mortgage debt in the United States was more than $13.6 trillion.

Real estate is also vital to the economy as a resource for current production. Expenditures for housing, housing operation, and furniture and household equipment comprised 25 percent of all personal consumption expenditures in year 2007, and investment in structures and related equipment accounted for 53 percent of gross private domestic investment.

Although these figures give some indication of the impressive contributions of real estate to the national economy, they still underrepresent its total impact. Portions of the "real estate industry," notably real estate finance, are not included as part of "real estate" in the national income and product accounts. In addition, the industry generates a significant portion of the business of many other industries by creating a demand for products such as furniture and electrical appliances.

▌ THE REAL ESTATE INDUSTRY: THE PRIVATE SECTOR ─────────

The real estate industry is diverse, offering many career opportunities. To some students a career in real estate means selling homes, and, indeed, this is a significant part of the real estate brokerage industry. But many other fascinating careers in real estate exist, and one of the purposes of this book is to introduce these career opportunities, as well as to provide the basic knowledge needed to become a part of the real estate industry.

Real Estate Brokerage

In 2007 the largest real estate brokerage trade association, the National Association of REALTORS®, had over 1.3 million members, including brokers and salespersons. The compensation earned by participants in the brokerage industry fluctuates with the ups and downs of the real estate market, but the U.S. Bureau of Labor Statistics estimated that in 2006 real estate brokers earned an annual average of $80,230, and salespersons $54,350.

Real Estate Brokerage Specialties

Five principal classifications of real estate exist in the private marketplace: owner-occupied residential, renter-occupied residential, commercial, industrial, and farm and other open land. Because it is difficult to be an expert in all aspects of the real estate market, most brokers specialize in certain types of property. The extent of specialization depends on a number of factors, particularly the size of the local market. The real estate broker in a small city may deal in several or all types of properties. In larger cities, brokers may sell one type of real estate or properties located in only one part of a city. Quite commonly, some brokers and salespersons sell only owner-occupied houses, while others deal only in the sale of leasing of income-producing properties.

Property Management

Many people who invest in such income-producing real estate as apartments and shopping centers have neither the inclination nor the expertise to take care of the properties' day-to-day operating activities, such as leasing, rent collection, building repairs, and building services. These tasks—and, indeed, the general objective of maximizing the value of a property—are delegated to the property manager. Some small brokers manage real estate as a supplementary activity, while many larger firms have a separate property management department. Still other property managers may be hired directly by the firm that owns the properties. If the property manager does a good job, this function can add considerable value to a property. It can also earn a good income for the property manager.

Real Estate Finance

Several characteristics of real property, principally the long-term nature of real estate investment and the consequent need for large amounts of money over a long period of time, make mortgage credit both necessary for most purchasers and attractive to many lenders. In turn, this has given rise to the real estate finance industry.

Real estate loans are made by many types of institutions and even by individuals, and major employment opportunities are found in savings associations, savings banks, commercial banks, mortgage banking firms, and life insurance companies. Savings associations and savings banks specialize in residential loans and do most of their lending locally. Commercial banks also lend money on real estate, particularly for relatively short-term construction loans, and they also purchase many mortgages for mortgage bankers.

The mortgage bank and mortgage brokerage industries also play large roles in the financing of real estate. Mortgage bankers do not collect deposits from savers and have only a small amount of their own capital to lend.

After originating loans to borrowers, mortgage bankers sell the loans in the secondary mortgage market, but they continue to service (collect payments, mail late notices, etc.) the loans for a fee. Mortgage brokers do not originate loans themselves but instead bring lenders and borrowers together in exchange for on-time fees. Both mortgage bankers and brokers are essential parts of the financial mechanism that shifts funds from capital surplus to capital deficit areas.

Appraisal

Estimates of value are needed in almost every aspect of real estate and development. Sellers need to know what their potential purchases are worth in comparison with other properties in the market. Mortgage lenders need estimates of value, **appraisal,** before they make lending decisions. Appraisals also are essential for tax assessors, insurance adjusters, right-of-way agents, and other government officials. Accordingly, many appraisers are employed by financial institutions, other private firms, and government organizations, while many others work as *independent fee appraisers*—that is, they offer their services to the public for a fee.

Counseling

Closely related to real estate appraisal is real estate counseling. The real estate appraiser makes estimates of value, while the real estate counselor advises individuals and firms regarding their real estate investments. Though the two specialties require similar kinds of knowledge, the counselor must have even more extensive knowledge than the appraiser of all phases of real estate, tax laws, and other aspects of investment.

Development and Construction

Real estate development certainly is one of the most fascinating aspects of real estate and one that offers greater potential return—and greater potential risk—than perhaps any other field within the industry. Real estate development involves the subdivision of land and the construction of improvements such as roads, utilities, and buildings ranging from individual homes to multi-million-dollar office building and shopping centers.

Asset Management

Although real estate makes up a large portion of corporate assets, most corporations have not placed adequate emphasis on managing these assets efficiently. Increasingly, however, firms are establishing corporate real estate departments, and this has led to many new opportunities in the real estate field. As might be expected, utilities and other firms with very large percentages of their assets in real estate have been leaders in the field, and other companies as well are realizing that efficient management of their real estate can add significantly to corporate profits.

Land-Use Planning

Also closely related to real estate development is land-use planning. This is a diverse field: Many planners are engaged in physical design, others are concerned primarily with the economic and investment aspects of development, while still others are employed by governmental agencies concerned with land-use policies and regulations.

THE REAL ESTATE INDUSTRY: THE PUBLIC SECTOR

In addition to those located in the private sector, many real estate–related jobs are found at the various levels of government. Such jobs generally are related to acquisition and management of property, real property taxation, land-use planning, and land-use and housing policy.

Federal, state, and local governments acquire real property for public building, parks, transportation projects, and other government functions. Such land acquisition requires the services of many real estate specialists, including appraisers and right-of-way agents.

Many appraisers are engaged in valuing real property for taxation purposes. Most such appraisers are property tax assessors at the local government level, but many are employed by other levels of government.

Land-use planning has grown in importance with the increase in both urbanization and concern for the environment. Planners are employed by local government planning agencies, regional planning districts, and state development offices. In addition, various federal agencies—in particular those in the U.S. Department of

Housing and Urban Development and the U.S. Department of Commerce—employ planners to help formulate economic development, land-use, and housing policies.

Many real estate specialists also work in government and in quasi-government financial agencies such as the Federal Home Loan Mortgage Corporation and the Federal National Mortgage Association.

CHAPTER REVIEW

- The five broad categories that comprise the real estate "body of knowledge" considered in this text include real estate market analysis, the legal framework of real estate, real estate services, the real estate transaction process, and investment analysis.

- Simply defined, *real estate* is property in land and buildings.

- The special economic characteristics of real estate are (1) fixed location, (2) uniqueness, (3) interdependence of land uses, (4) long life, (5) long-term commitments, (6) large transactions, and (7) long gestation period.

- The characteristic of real estate that distinguishes it from all other types of economic resources is its fixed location. Fixity of location means that every parcel of real estate is unique, and this factor can create large difference in property values.

- Land is indestructible, and real estate improvements generally have long lives. Thus, investment decisions are by their very nature long-term decisions.

- Because real estate purchases involve large expenditures committed for long periods of time, outside financing is essential for most transactions.

- The use of land depends greatly on (1) the provision of public services, (2) nearby land uses, and (3) the general economic vitality of the neighborhood and community.

- The *gestation period* for real estate improvements—that is, the time between conception of a real estate project and its actual completion and subsequent entry into the available supply—may be several years. This long gestation period makes the supply of real estate slow to respond to increases in demand.

- Land and structures make up approximately two-thirds of the national wealth of the United States, with the remainder consisting of equipment and inventories. Expenditures for housing and household operation constituted 25 percent of all personal consumption expenditures in year 2007, while investment in structures and related furniture and fixtures account for 53 percent of gross private domestic investment.

- Five principal classifications of real estate exist in the private marketplace: (1) owner-occupied residential, (2) renter-occupied residential, (3) commercial, (4) industrial, and (5) farm and other open land.

■ The general objective of the real estate property manager is to maximize the income flowing to the owners from income-producing property.

■ Mortgage loans now total about $13.6 trillion and have led to the development of a major sector of the real estate and finance industries. Major employment opportunities related to real estate are found in savings banks, commercial banks, mortgage banking and mortgage brokerage firms, and life insurance companies.

■ Real estate appraisers estimate the value of real property. Their services are used by buyers and sellers, financial institutions, tax assessors, and many others.

■ Real estate counselors advise individuals and firms about their real estate investments. They must have extensive knowledge of all aspects of real estate, tax law, and investment.

■ Real estate development offers greater potential return and greater potential risk than perhaps any other field within the real estate industry.

■ Land-use planners are engaged in physical design, economic and investment aspects of development, and land-use policies and regulations.

■ Many real estate specialists are employed at various levels of government in property acquisition, tax administration, land-use and housing policy development, and other operations of government.

▌ KEY TERMS

appraisal   real estate
gestation period   real property
personal property

PART ONE

Real Estate
Legal Analysis

Property Rights and Legal Descriptions

CHAPTER PREVIEW

REAL ESTATE TODAY

CLOSE-UP
The Last Chance
Ditch

LEGAL HIGHLIGHT
Who Can Use
the Shore?

CLOSE-UP
The Empire State
Building

LEGAL HIGHLIGHT
How Did an Acre
Get to Be an Acre?

Perhaps you own or lease some real estate. What exactly are the rights that come with owning or leasing this property? These can be difficult questions because real property rights associated with real estate can be quite complex. Real property rights can be divided in many ways. For example, one party may own the right to use the surface of the land, another may hold the right to subsurface minerals, and yet another party may hold the right to use the water that flows across or under the land. Or two or more owners may hold unique and specific rights to exactly the same parcel of real estate, perhaps jointly, perhaps separately. This chapter examines these and other property rights issues that every market participant should understand to ensure effective real estate decisions.

After reading this chapter, you should be familiar with how property rights are divided among various claimholders. The objectives of this chapter are to

- define the concepts of real property and personal property;

- demonstrate how property rights are physically divided;

- consider how property rights are bundled into "estates in land";

- describe how properties can be jointly owned by two or more owners; and

- examine the three methods for legally and uniquely identifying individual parcels of real estate.

REAL VERSUS PERSONAL PROPERTY

In the previous chapter, we defined **real estate** as land and things attached to the land. Another important term real estate market participants need to understand is **property.** Although the term *property* can be used in several ways, we generally think of property as any objects that can be owned or possessed—buildings, vehicles, books, clothing, furniture, stocks, or bonds, for example. Legally, the concept of property can be divided into two broad classes: real property and personal property. **Real property** consists of legal interests in land and things permanently attached to the land. **Personal property** includes legal interests in all other types of property. Stated more simply, real property refers to real estate—land and things attached to that land—while personal property refers to movable property such as automobiles, furniture, clothing, and business equipment. Personal property is also called **chattel.**

Generally speaking, the requirements to transfer real property from one owner to another are much more complex than are those for personal property. To buy a book at a store, for example, the purchaser simply tenders the funds and receives the book and perhaps (but not always) a written receipt or "bill of sale." But when real property is transferred, a written document must be prepared with language that uniquely identifies the property being transferred, the specific rights and interests being transferred, the parties to the transfer, and any other important details involved in the transfer. There are a few exceptions to the rule requiring a written document as evidence of real property transfers (such as a lease for less than one year in some states), but it is always a good idea to specify the details of transactions involving real property in written form to prevent misunderstandings and disputes even if such a document is not absolutely required.

When ownership rights to real property (often called **title**) are transferred, the document normally used to convey the rights from one party to another is called a **deed.** When a tenant acquires property rights to leased property, the document used to convey the rights from the property owner to the tenant is called a **lease.** Leases convey the rights of use and possession of real property under the agreed-on terms, but leases do not transfer ownership rights to the property. Both deeds and leases are considered in detail later in this book.

FIXTURES

Whether a particular item of property is considered real or personal property cannot always be readily determined. For example, an air-conditioning unit clearly is movable personal property at the time it is purchased. However, when it becomes attached to land as part of a building, it is treated as part of the real estate and considered real property. Personal property that becomes part of the real property when it is attached to the land or a building is termed a **fixture.**

For example, the antique chandelier you inherited from Aunt Matilda and hung in your dining room is a fixture and part of your house. Unless it is specifically excluded when the house is sold, the new buyer becomes the proud owner of the chandelier along with the rest of the real estate. Other items generally considered fixtures include landscaping, automatic garage door openers, water heating or filtering systems, window treatments (such as blinds and drapes), and appliances installed in the house (such as built-in dishwashers and central air conditioners). It is important to remember that if you are selling a home and want to retain ownership of Aunt Matilda's chandelier or your prized rose bushes, you must specifically exclude them from the transaction. Likewise, if you are purchasing a property, you should be careful to specify what items are to be included when negotiating the terms of the transaction.

Tests for Fixture Status

Whether an item of personal property has become a fixture can be critically important in determining (1) the value of real property, (2) whether a real estate transaction includes the item, (3) whether the item is part of the security given to the mortgagee (lender), and (4) whether the item remains with the landlord or can be removed by the tenant when the lease terminates.

Intent of the Parties

The most crucial test used to determine whether something is a fixture or personal property is the **test of intent of the parties.** The best way to indicate intent, of course, is by a written agreement that states clearly which items are to be considered part of the real estate and which are to be considered personal property. For instance, a sales contract for a house might specify that the satellite television antenna may be removed by the seller. Or a lease agreement for a factory or warehouse building might state that the tenant may attach **trade fixtures** (personal property used in a trade or business) such as machinery, office equipment, and counters to the building without losing the right to remove these items at the termination of the lease. (Notice that trade fixtures are, by definition, personal property, not real property.) As long as the intent of the parties is made clear, there should be no confusion about whether the item in question is considered a fixture or personal property.

Other Tests of Fixture Status

Unfortunately, the intent of the parties often is unclear, so other tests of fixture status must be applied. If an item of personal property becomes attached to the real estate, it usually is considered a fixture, and the damage caused to the land or building by the item's removal is a crucial element in the **test of attachment.** For example, while a portable window air conditioner would be personal property, an air conditioner that is built into a wall would be considered a fixture because the building would be damaged if the air conditioner were removed. Another method for determining whether an item is a fixture is the **test of adaptability.** Under this test, items that have been specifically adapted to the real estate are generally considered fixtures. The issue considered in this test is whether removal of the item would substantially alter the usefulness of the remaining real estate. For example, kitchen cabinets and a built-in entertainment center would probably be considered fixtures, while free-standing, noncustom cabinets would be classified as personal property.

Because these last two tests for fixtures do not necessarily provide clear-cut distinctions between real and personal property, the parties involved always should indicate their clear intent by a written agreement. This, of course, helps avoid disputes in *all* business matters.

MINERAL AND AIR RIGHTS

Real property rights are not limited to the surface of the earth; they also include the space above the earth's surface (**air rights**) and minerals or other useful materials that exist below the surface (collectively called **mineral rights**). Historically, a landowner's real property interests have been conceptualized as pie-shaped, beginning at the earth's center and extending through the surface indefinitely into outer space. In modern thought, the property rights associated with the surface of the land, minerals, or other useful material that may exist under the surface of the land and air-space above the land are often separated among several different owners. Similarly, the rights to water that may flow over the land or adjacent to the land are sometimes considered separately from the land itself.

Ownership of airspace is limited to a reasonable distance above the earth's surface. Obviously, an airplane flying over a property at an altitude of several thousand feet rarely interferes with the owner's use or enjoyment of the land. But when aircraft fly so low that a reasonable use of the land is prevented (for example, near a lengthened airport runway), the owner of the land may be entitled to compensation on the basis that the plane is interfering with the owner's property rights.

Mineral rights and air rights may be owned by someone other than the owner of the surface of the land. It is common, for example, for a surface owner to sell to a third party the rights to any oil, gas, coal, and other materials that may be located below the surface. The air rights, likewise, may be transferred to persons other than the owner of the surface. For example, office buildings and parking decks have been constructed over the tracks of railroads, with the owner of the building owning only the air rights.

WATER RIGHTS

Water rights—who has the right to withdraw water from the land—is a question of considerable importance, particularly in the more arid western states, and increasingly in the eastern states. These rights vary from state to state and depend primarily on what type of water the land touches.

Rights Relating to Navigable Bodies of Water

The owner whose land joins a navigable body of water, such as an ocean, a sea, or certain rivers, generally owns the land to the high-water mark (the government

The Last Chance Ditch

 To most living in the eastern United States, the availability of water is taken for granted. Not so in the arid West, and water rights can be a very important factor in land value.

As engineering structures go, the Last Chance Ditch is not very imposing, but it has provided an essential element in the economic lifeblood of a part of the Truckee Meadows area near Reno, Nevada, for more than a century. It also provides an example of just how important water rights can be.

The Last Chance Ditch was begun by land developers in 1874 and extends approximately ten miles southward from the Truckee River in Reno. Under a 1943 court decree that clarified area water rights, the ditch company may draw 8,644 acre-feet of water each year from the river (an acre-foot is enough water to cover an acre of land with one foot of water). The company may draw this amount of water from the river if available after the Pioneer Ditch and the Steamboat Ditch companies, which have priority because they started earlier, have received their allocations.

The Last Chance Ditch's share is then suballocated to property owners holding agricultural water rights along its length, most having the right to about four acre-feet of "consumptive" water per acre. This means that shareholders normally receive this much water flowing onto their properties during a year. They cannot dam up the water; any "waste," about one-third of the flow, returns to the ditch for use downstream. These rights provide a benefit to the landowner that can be sold separately, recently bringing $2,500 per acre-foot, or $10,000 per acre for shareholders in the Last Chance Ditch.

If agricultural land is developed for residential use, additional water rights are required, usually from a utility company that holds water rights and provides water services. For homes on one-third-acre lots, about 6.5 acre-feet are needed per acre. For land that holds no water rights, it costs around $16,250 per acre just to acquire them. For shareholders in the Last Chance Ditch, the cost would be reduced to $6,250 because they already have rights to four acre-feet. So, the Last Chance Ditch is not a very impressive structure, but it provides quite impressive economic benefits to those holding rights to its water.

usually owns the land underneath the water). The owners of such adjoining lands are called *littoral proprietors*. Disputes regarding the use of water from these waterways seldom occur because there usually is sufficient water to be shared. The principal issue involving navigable waters has been pollution. Laws exist at both the federal and state levels to hold polluters of such waters responsible for their actions.

Who Can Use the Shore?

Littoral rights affect the use of water, but they also relate to the use of land. For example, does a landowner's right to control his land extend to the waterline of an adjoining lake, or does the public have the right to walk along the shoreline?

This was the issue involved in a dispute between across-the-street neighbors on Lake Huron in Michigan. Richard and Kathleen Goeckel own property on the lake. Joan Glass owned the house across the street and had a fifteen-foot easement on the Goeckel property that allowed her to go to the beach. The Goeckels objected to her use of the trail and walking the shoreline in front of their home. Glass's right to use the trail on the easement was easily established, but the issue of whether the public has a right to walk the shoreline went all the way to the Michigan Supreme Court. The appeals court had ruled that citizens have the right to walk along the beach as long as they remain in the water. Property owners, the court said, have exclusive right down to where dry land begins and may bar access to the beach.

The Michigan Supreme Court disagreed, ruling that although landowners may own to the water's edge, under the public trust doctrine inherent in the common law, the public has a right to walk along the shore to the ordinary high water mark. Joan Glass can continue her strolls along the shore. [*Glass v. Goeckel*, 703 NW2d 1 (2005)]

Rights to Nonnavigable Bodies of Water

The rights of a landowner to use water from a nonnavigable lake or stream that flows across the land are more complex. If an upstream owner uses too much water, for example, there may be too little water left for landowners downstream to use as they wish. How should the water be allocated among the competing owners? The laws that answer this question have developed in a way that reflects the abundance or scarcity of water within the geographic area. The two dominant theories with regard to an owner's rights to nonnavigable bodies of water are the **riparian rights doctrine** and the **prior appropriation doctrine.** The dominant theory in the eastern United States is the riparian rights doctrine. Under this theory, all owners whose land underlies or borders the water have equal rights to the water. This concept allows all riparian landowners to use all the water needed as long as the use does not deprive other landowners who are also entitled to some of the water.

In contrast, many states west of the Mississippi are extremely arid and, consequently, have rejected the theory of riparian rights and adopted the prior appropriation doctrine. Under this concept, the first person to use a body of water for some beneficial economic purpose has a right to use all the water needed, even if landowners who later find a use for the water may be precluded from using it. This "first-come, first-served" concept is based on the premise that there is an insufficient supply of water to satisfy everyone's needs; therefore, the first landowner(s) using the water for some worthwhile purpose should be allowed to use all of the water. Prior appropriation states usually establish a permit system whereby a governing authority can control the water's use.

Underground Water

There are two types of underground water. Water that flows in a defined channel is called an *underground* or *subterranean stream,* while water in pockets not clearly located is known as *percolating water.* Issues involving underground streams generally are resolved by applying the same principles that would be used if the body of water existed on the earth's surface. In the case of percolating waters, states generally apply a reasonable use test: A landowner may use the water beneath the land for industrial, agricultural, or other purposes necessary to the beneficial use of the land. However, if withdrawing the water depletes the underground water supply of adjoining landowners, the courts may restrict such action.

ESTATES IN LAND

Collections or bundles of ownership interests in real property often are described as **estates in land.** These are divided into two basic types: **freehold estates,** or ownership, and **leasehold estates,** or the right to use and possess (but not own) property owned by someone else. Homebuyers normally purchase a freehold estate; renters have a leasehold estate. Figure 2.1 summarizes the different types of estates. When discussing estates in land, the terms *grantor, grantee, lessor,* and *lessee* often are used. The **grantor** is the party who transfers (by sale or gift) a real property interest; the **grantee** is the party who receives the interest. In the case of leasehold estates, the landlord is known as the **lessor,** and the tenant is known as the **lessee.**

Freehold Estates

Freehold estates are separated into presently possessed interests and those that may be possessed in the future. Presently possessed interests are classified as fee simple absolute estates, qualified fee estates, or life estates. Future interests that accompany qualified fee estates and life estates include reversion and remainder interests. We discuss each of these ownership interests below.

Fee Simple Absolute Estates

The **fee simple absolute estate** is the fullest and most complete set of ownership rights one can possess in real property. Also known as a *fee estate* or a *fee simple estate,* this estate is the one most commonly associated with "owning real estate" and is the type of estate acquired in a typical transaction.

FIGURE 2.1 | Types of Estates in Land

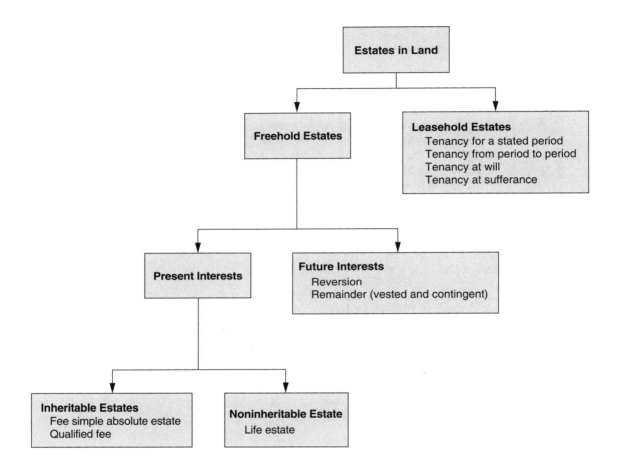

The property owner receiving a fee simple absolute title has an unlimited right to transfer the property to another during his or her lifetime or at death. Legally stated, the fee simple absolute estate is alienable, devisable, and descendible. *Alienable* means the owner can transfer any interest in the property while living. *Devisable* means interests can be transferred by a will on the death of the owner. *Descendible* means the interest passes to the owner's legal heirs if he or she dies without a valid will.

In addition to the ability to transfer a fee simple absolute estate without restriction, the owner has the right of unlimited use and even abuse of the land, constrained only by liens and other encumbrances, public land-use controls, and restrictive covenants. These restrictions are discussed in Chapters 3 and 4.

Qualified Fee Estates

In a **qualified fee estate,** the owner's rights can be "defeased" or lost in the future, should a stated event or condition come to pass. For example, the University of Georgia holds a qualified estate in an old rock house located on the campus in the midst of its modern buildings. Many years ago, the Lumpkin family donated a large tract of land to the university with the qualification in the deed that the family house had to be "forever maintained." If the university were to destroy the building or let it fall to ruin, a large portion of the campus (with many modern buildings) would revert to the donor's heirs.

Qualified fee estates are present interests in real property, but each qualified fee estate must also be accompanied by a future interest in the property. The future interests that follow qualified fee estates are known as **reversions.** If the condition specified is ever violated (for example, removal of the Lumpkin house), ownership in the property reverts to the grantor (or the grantor's heirs). Depending on the language used to initially create the qualified fee estate, the reversion may happen automatically if the stated condition is violated or may require the holder of the reversion interest to initiate legal action to enforce the condition.

Many qualified fee estates are set up to protect a grantor's personal preferences or wishes. A landowner once sold a parcel of land with the qualification that the property never be used for the distribution of alcoholic beverages (the grantor was a recovering alcoholic). If this condition were ever violated, the property would revert back to the grantor. The grantee accepted this condition because he had no intention of using the property in that fashion. After some years went by, the current owner decided to sell the land and was approached by a national convenience store chain about the property. Upon learning the condition the previous owner had placed on the land when he sold the land to the current owner, the convenience store chain quickly lost interest in the property. Had the chain bought the property, built a store, and sold a six-pack of beer or a bottle of chardonnay, the property rights purchased by the chain would have terminated immediately, and the original grantor of the land would once again be the owner.

Life Estates

A **life estate** is a type of freehold estate that terminates automatically and immediately upon the death of a named person. The named person may or may not be the holder of the life estate. For example, a father may leave a last will and testament that creates a life estate in a property he owned at the time of his death for his daughter Sarah with the words "To Sarah, for her life" or "To Sarah, for Ann's life." In the first case, Sarah would be the owner of the property for as long as she lives. In the second case, Sarah would own the property as long as Ann lives. In both cases, Sarah is known as the **life tenant.** When the life tenant is someone other than the person whose life the life estate is tied to, the life estate is known as an **estate pur autre vie** (estate for the life of another).

Because it is impossible to know how long the named person will live, life estates have an indeterminable duration, but all life estates will eventually terminate (everyone dies sooner or later). Therefore, all life estates must have a future interest associated with them. If the grantor of the life estate does not specify to whom the property will belong on termination of the life estate, then the future interest is the reversion interest we described earlier in our discussion of qualified fee estates, and the property will revert back to the grantor (or the grantor's heirs, if the grantor is dead) on the death of the named person. On the other hand, the grantor of the life estate may specify that a party other than the original grantee will become the owner of the property upon the termination of the life estate.

For example, the grantor could create a life estate with the words "To Sarah, for her life, and then to Robert." In this situation, Robert holds the **remainder** interest in the property while Sarah is alive. The party who holds the remainder interest associated with a life estate is known as the **remainderman.** Notice that on Sarah's death, the life estate terminates, and Robert will own all of the rights to the property originally held by the grantor of the life estate *and* the remainder interest. If the grantor had a fee simple absolute estate, then Robert will own a fee simple absolute estate upon Sarah's death. If the grantor had a qualified fee estate, then Robert will own only a qualified fee estate upon Sarah's death.

Remainder interests can take the form of a **vested remainder** or a **contingent remainder.** A vested remainder exists when the remainderman is guaranteed ownership of the property at some time in the future, but a contingent remainder exists when there are conditions attached to the remainder interest that could prevent the remainderman from receiving a present interest in the property. For example, Alan could grant a life estate to "Nell for her life, then to Billy if he is married at the time of Nell's death, otherwise to Clyde." In this situation, both Billy and Clyde hold contingent remainder interests in the property. If Billy is married when Nell dies, then Billy will own the land on Nell's death. If Billy is not married when Nell dies, then Clyde will own the land on Nell's death.

The life estate is a very useful technique in estate planning. John might, for example, put the family home and farm in trust for his children Sue and Sally but give his wife Mary a life estate. Estate taxes have to be paid on John's death. Mary may use the property during the remainder of her lifetime, but at her death, no additional taxes are due because she possessed only a life estate. This often can reduce taxes greatly, particularly if the property has increased dramatically in value since John's death.

Leasehold Estates

The term *leasehold estate* refers to the rights of use and possession (but not ownership) held by a tenant as a result of a lease agreement with a property owner. The lease agreement may specify that the leasehold estate will last for a specific time period, or it may specify that the leasehold estate will last for as long as the lessor and lessee are willing to continue their relationship. In either case, the tenant possesses or occupies the land or building for the duration of a lease with the understanding that the landlord retains full ownership of the real property. In other words, the landlord has a reversionary interest at the termination of the leasehold estate, often referred to as the **right of reentry.** While the tenant's leasehold estate is in place, the landlord can be said to hold a **leased fee estate,** meaning that the landlord is the owner of the property, but the property is currently leased to a tenant.

Leases, or tenancies, can be divided into the following four categories:

1. Tenancy for a stated period
2. Tenancy from period to period
3. Tenancy at will
4. Tenancy at sufferance

A **tenancy for a stated period** occurs when a landlord and a tenant enter into an agreement for a specified term. The stated period may be six months, a year, ten years, or any mutually acceptable time period. In most states, leases that exceed one year must be written and signed by the parties. Of course, it is advisable always to have a written agreement even if the law does not require one.

A **tenancy from period to period** is created when landlord and tenant agree to continue their relationship from year to year or month to month, or some other period length. The agreement may establish an original term of one year, for example, with the provision that the lease is to continue yearly unless terminated at the end of a period with proper notice by either party. The method of giving proper notice should be set forth in the lease agreement. It is common to require notice of termination 30 to 60 days prior to the expiration of a period, depending on state law.

When parties enter into a lease agreement without specifying either a termination date or a period length, the parties have created a **tenancy at will.** As the name implies, this lease lasts as long as both tenant and landlord desire and can be terminated at any time. Many states have statutes that specify the amount of time required in the termination notice for tenancies at will. A 30-day notice is most typical for tenants; some states require, however, that the landlord give 60 days' advance notice of termination.

A **tenancy at sufferance** occurs when a tenant is in possession of a landlord's property against the wishes of the landlord. Such a situation may occur when a tenant refuses to re-lease the premises at the termination of the lease but continues to possess the property until evicted by the landlord. A tenancy at sufferance also might occur when a property owner's existing mortgage is foreclosed. The foreclosure terminates the borrower's rights to the property, but the borrower may remain in possession of the property until evicted by the new owner. **Eviction** is the legal process used by lessors to terminate leasehold estates when lessees fail to abide by the lease terms or refuse to return possession of the property at the termination of a leasehold estate. Eviction laws vary from state to state, but the laws generally require that the lessor notify the lessee of the violated lease terms and give the lessee a prescribed amount of time to remedy the violation or return possession of the property to the lessor. If the lessee fails to remedy the violation or return possession of the property, the lessor can seek the court system's assistance to recover damages and/or have the tenant physically removed from the property.

The Empire State Building

We speak of the "bundle of sticks" to describe the various elements of real estate ownership. The Empire State Building saga provides a vivid example of how real estate ownership can be subdivided into leased fee and leasehold interests, how the terms of the lease can affect the division of value between the two elements of ownership, and how they can be recombined.

The Empire State Building is a legendary property, for four decades the tallest building in the world, and celebrated in movies and legend. With its 2.24 million square feet housing 20,000 workers and its office space 95 percent occupied, the building is worth up to $1 billion. Then why did it sell in 2002 for only $57.5 million? Here's a hint. Only the leased fee was sold. Almost all the value was in the leasehold interest.

In 1961 a partnership bought the building for $68 million. An insurance company provided $29 million financing and was given ownership of the fee interest in order to receive tax advantages that reduced the cost of financing for the partnership. The other partners received a 114-year master lease that allowed them to control the building until the year 2075.

After the insurance company had exhausted the tax benefits, it sold the building, but the sale brought only $40 million because the fee owner received only $1.72 million in lease payments per year plus regaining control of the building when it would be 123 years old. All the rental income went to the leasehold interest.

Finally, the investor group that holds the lease purchased the building for $57.5 million, once again combining the leased fee and leasehold interests into a simple fee ownership. The group did this because it felt this would enable the building to be sold more easily and would ensure better financing terms.

CONCURRENT ESTATES

The preceding discussion of property interests was based on the assumption that only one person owns each interest. These interests are known as **estates in severalty,** that is, estates "standing alone." Nevertheless, most of the real property interests discussed above may be owned simultaneously by more than one person.

Perhaps you want to buy a house with your spouse, another relative, or even an unrelated person; perhaps your Aunt Matilda left you and your sister Bess a farm to be owned jointly; perhaps you want to make a real estate investment with business associates. All these situations involve the ownership of property simultaneously by two or more persons or entities and are examples of **concurrent estates** or, more simply, joint ownership. The most common types of concurrent estates are

- tenancy in common,
- joint tenancy,
- tenancy by the entirety, and
- community property.

Note that although the word *tenancy* is used here, it should not be confused with a tenant's relationship with a landlord.

Tenancy in Common

The traditional form of concurrent ownership is **tenancy in common.** Each of the joint owners holds an undivided, proportional interest in the entire property. For example, if Jack and Bob own a warehouse as tenants in common, each owns a portion of the entire property, but neither knows which portion is his. Each owner can dispose of his or her portion of ownership through sale or will.

Tenants in common who become unhappy with the joint relationship can demand a *partition* of the property. Voluntary partitions result when cotenants agree how to divide the property. If they cannot agree, however, a court may order a compulsory partition.

Joint Tenancy

Joint tenancy is similar to tenancy in common except it carries with it the **right of survivorship.** If a co-owner should die, the other owner or owners automatically divide the share owned by the deceased. This type of ownership often is used to ensure the continued operation of an investment property should one of the owners die. The joint tenancy ends if any tenant sells his or her share of the property to a third party. The joint tenancy then converts to a tenancy in common.

Historically, to establish a valid joint tenancy, the four unities of time, title, interest, and possession had to be present. To satisfy the *unity of time,* the joint tenants' ownership had to be created at the same time by the same conveyance. The *unity of title* exists when the owners have the same estate in the land, such as a fee simple estate, a life estate, or another estate discussed in this chapter.

Joint tenants meet the *unity of interest* requirement only when they have the same percentage interest in the real estate. For example, two joint tenants must each own 50 percent of the undivided property, three must own 33.33 percent each, four must own 25 percent each, and so forth. Finally, joint tenants have *unity of posses-sion* only when each owner has the right to possess all of the real estate subject to the other owners' rights of possession.

Originally, due to the unity of time requirement, a grantor who was the sole owner of real estate could not create a joint tenancy with the right of survivorship between himself and another person. To get around this problem, the grantor had to deed the property to a friendly third party, known as a "straw man," who would then transfer that property to the grantor and the other party as joint tenants. Some states have abolished the need to use a straw man in the above situation and thus have relaxed the unity of time requirement under particular circumstances.

Tenancy by the Entirety

A **tenancy by the entirety** is a specialized type of joint tenancy that can be cre-ated only between husbands and wives. The spouses share ownership equally, shares automatically pass to the surviving spouse, and individual interests cannot be sold without the consent of the other spouse or without division by a court in case of divorce. Some states do not recognize tenancy by the entirety.

Community Property

Some states recognize a system of property rights between husbands and wives generally called **community property.** In these states, all property acquired during the marriage, whether real or personal, is considered property of the "marital com-munity." In other words, property ownership is divided equally between husband and wife. This division may disregard the financial contribution each spouse actu-ally made to the property's acquisition. Real property in community-property states cannot be transferred without the consent of both parties. Thus, a purchaser of real community property must obtain the signatures of both husband and wife on the sales contract and deed.

It is possible for married couples in one of these community-property states to acquire property not subject to a spouse's interest. Examples of this separate prop-erty include property owned prior to the marriage or property received by one of the spouses as a gift or an inheritance. Generally, any income derived from a spouse's separate property also is separate income.

CONDOMINIUM OWNERSHIP

In addition to the traditional forms of concurrent ownership, the *condominium* and *cooperative* are two other ways to own real estate jointly. In a **condominium** (condo) all owners typically have fee simple titles to their personal units, while com-mon areas such as sidewalks, yards, entrances, hallways, pools, tennis courts, and other recreational facilities are jointly owned in a tenancy in common or some other form of concurrent ownership. (If the condominium is built on land that is leased with a ground lease, the unit owners hold a leasehold interest in the land rather than a fee interest.) A condominium association handles the maintenance of the common areas, and each unit pays a mandatory fee to cover the expenses of the association. The officers or directors of the association are typically elected by majority vote from all of the unit owners. Condos are also common for commercial and industrial uses.

All states have laws governing the formation of condominiums. These statutes require that three basic documents be filed—the condominium declaration, the bylaws, and deeds conveying the individual units. The purchase of a condominium interest is legally more complex and potentially more demanding than the typical single-family home purchase. In most states, this complexity and past abuses have led to more rigorous disclosure of information to prospective buyers of condominium homes. In Florida, for example, where condos abound, condo developers are required to give potential buyers 15 days to rescind a contract to purchase a new condo. Sales of existing condos require a rescission period of 3 days. The clock for these rescission periods starts ticking when the buyer is given copies of condominium documents to examine rather than the effective date of the contract, so most developers and sellers give such documents to potential buyers in advance of signing a contract.

Condominium Declaration

The condominium declaration describes the individual units and all common areas, assigns a specific share of the common areas to each unit, creates an association to govern the project and maintain the common areas, and sets forth restrictions on use. These restrictions usually are quite extensive and often deal with such details as the color of curtains in the windows and whether pets must be kept on a leash.

The declaration also may grant the association the **right of first refusal** to help it screen prospective purchasers. If an individual property owner decides to sell his or her unit and locates a willing buyer, the association has a limited time either to approve of the purchaser or to purchase the unit from the current owner under the same terms. This right of first refusal cannot be used to exclude prospective purchasers on the basis of race, creed, color, or national origin, although this type of discrimination often is hard to prove.

Bylaws

The bylaws represent a private contract among property owners regarding the operation of the condominium. They provide for the selection of the board of directors, the powers and duties of the directors, meetings, regulations for the common areas, assessment and collection of association fees, and other relevant matters.

Individual Unit Deed

Deeds for condominium units are similar to other deeds conveying real property. These deeds are described in Chapter 5.

▌ COOPERATIVE OWNERSHIP

In the **cooperative** form of ownership (often abbreviated to co-op), the land and building usually are owned by a nonprofit corporation specifically created for the purpose of owning the property. Individual residents own stock in the corporation that owns the property and thus have the right to occupy a particular unit in the property. Rather than a fee simple ownership of real property, owners in a co-op have a **proprietary lease** for a specific unit. The lease period is typically indefinite because it is tied to the tenant's interest in the cooperative corporation. The lease does not require the tenant to pay rent, but the tenant must pay a periodic fee to the co-op for the tenant's proportionate share of maintenance, repairs, mortgage payments, taxes, and so on. The tenants vote for and elect a board of directors or officers for the cooperative pursuant to the organization's bylaws.

▌ TIME-SHARES

Time-share, or interval ownership, is a type of concurrent estate that splits ownership by time. Most of the activity in the time-share is vacation oriented, with several large companies such as Disney and Marriot expanding into this market. There are two basic categories of time-sharing interests, a fee interest time-share and a right-to-use time-share. A **fee interest time-share** divides the ownership of a unit, usually a resort condominium, into 52 separate, weekly intervals. Owners receive a fee simple title to their particular ownership period. A **right to use time-share,** on the other hand, basically is a lease arrangement with a leasehold interest for a specific period of time and often with more restrictions regarding resale.

Whether or not it is deserved, the time-share industry is sometimes regarded as having a less than stellar reputation because of the high-pressure sales tactics used by some developers and promoters. Potential buyers often are lured to the property on the pretense of a free vacation, only to find that the time they planned to lie in the sun by the pool is eaten up with relentless sales seminars and guilt-producing pitches from aggressive sales agents. The entry into the time-share market by larger, more stable companies may be a signal that the reputation of the time-share industry is poised for improvement.

▌ LEGAL DESCRIPTIONS

A proper legal description of the property involved is essential in all documents that affect title to real estate. When it comes to the actual transfer of title to real estate through a deed, for example, a precise legal description is necessary. Specification of the exact boundaries of the land being conveyed is essential for a valid transfer. In the United States, three methods commonly are used to obtain a precise legal description of land—the metes-and-bounds system, the rectangular survey system, and reference to recorded plats. Each property has a unique legal description.

Preparing the Legal Description

For existing properties, a proper legal description of a property often can be obtained from the tax office or other public records. A new, original legal description will be needed, however, for a property that is being subdivided from an existing parcel or created by combining multiple existing parcels. New, original legal descriptions should be prepared by an attorney and a certified land surveyor. This avoids potential risks for buyer, seller, and real estate professional (broker, appraiser, etc.) that can result from an improperly drafted legal description. A correctly drafted legal description is important, particularly in deeds, mortgages, and other instruments directly affecting title to land.

Metes and Bounds

The original way to achieve a formal legal description of the exact boundaries of any piece of land was to refer to its corners and boundary lines in a **metes-and-bounds description.** *Metes* are the distances used in a description, and *bounds* are the directions of the boundaries that enclose a piece of land. A metes-and-bounds description starts at a designated point of beginning and, through specific distances, directions, and reference points, locates the boundary lines and corners of the parcel of land. When a surveyor uses the legal description to identify the exact boundaries of a parcel of land, he or she usually drives an iron pin or stake deep into the ground at each corner of the property. These pins serve as the reference points in the legal

FIGURE 2.2 | Angles in a Circle

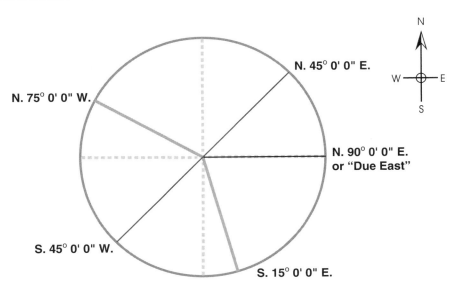

description and can easily be located (perhaps with a metal detector) many years after they are placed in the ground.

In modern metes-and-bounds descriptions, distances are measured in feet to the nearest one-tenth or one-hundredth of a foot, and the angles are measured in degrees, minutes, and seconds. Recall that there are 360 degrees in a circle and that a circle can be divided into four quadrants: northeast, southeast, southwest, and northwest. Each quadrant contains 90 degrees (90°); each degree contains 60 minutes (60'); and each minute contains 60 seconds (60"). Figure 2.2 demonstrates various angles using this system.

The following metes-and-bounds description describes the property depicted in Figure 2.3.

> Beginning at an iron pin on the northern side of Lava Street 95.0 feet due East of the northeastern corner of the intersection of Sixth Avenue and Lava Street, as measured along the northern side of Lava Street; running thence N. 8° 0' 0" E. 200.0 feet to an iron pin; running thence due East 100.0 feet to an iron pin; running thence S. 8° 0' 0" W. 200.0 feet to an iron pin; running thence due West 100.0 feet to the point of beginning.

FIGURE 2.3 | Metes-and-Bounds Description

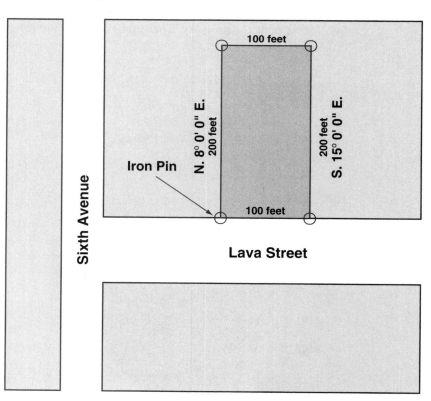

While a metes-and-bounds description may look a bit cryptic at first glance, it simply describes the boundary lines and corners of the parcel of a particular parcel of land. Each metes-and-bounds description must start with a point of beginning (POB). Thereafter, each boundary is detailed—its length, its direction, and the points where it begins and ends. It is vital that the boundaries described actually enclose the property involved. In other words, each boundary must begin at the preceding boundary's end and end at the next boundary's beginning. The description of the last side always must conclude at the original POB.

The metes-and-bounds method easily addresses irregular shaped parcels of land, even those with curved boundary lines. Curved boundary lines are described by referring to the length of the curve and its radius. With this system, land surveyors can accurately identify the corners of a parcel of real estate and the boundary lines that connect them.

By now, it should be obvious that reference points are crucial to the metes-and-bounds description. Before developers began to use iron pins to mark these points, natural monuments often were used. Such a monument might be "the large oak tree," "the spring-fed stream," or "the old Indian rock mound." Although reference to such natural objects could cause some confusion because they are subject to change over time, they still are used today to describe some rural land. The following land description, found in an old deed in North Carolina, demonstrates an interesting use of natural monuments as reference points in a standard metes-and-bounds description.

Beginning at an ash bush on the North bank of Withrow's Creek above the bridge, corner to the lands of R. N. Barber, and running thence North 14 degrees West 17.50 chains [one chain equals 66 feet] to a stone pile, in the line of Mrs. E. M. Summerell; running thence North 68 degrees East 6.56 chains to a post oak, corner to the lands of Elias Barber; running thence South 27 degrees East 8.80 chains to a hickory on the North bank of Withrow's Creek, corner to the lands of Jane Barber; running thence Southwesterly up said creek 13.75 chains to the point of beginning, containing 12 acres, more or less.

Legal descriptions do not describe "the side of the hill"; they define a flat plane that may or may not have a mountain in it. In mountain states, many sellers will tell you they have, say, 20 fenced acres, thinking they are really selling 20 acres—not their actual smaller number of surveyed acres. For example, suppose a tract of land measures 1,000 feet by 1,000 feet, or approximately 23 acres. If the property contains a steeply sloped hill within its boundaries, the actual ground area of this tract could be much more than 23 acres.

Rectangular Survey System

Shortly after the end of the Revolutionary War, when the westward movement from the original states began, a method of describing wilderness land was required. The U.S. Congress approved a description method known as the **rectangular survey system** (also called the *congressional survey system* or *government survey system*). With the exception of Texas, land descriptions in all states west of the Mississippi,

REAL ESTATE TODAY

LEGAL HIGHLIGHT

How Did an Acre Get to Be an Acre?

 Unlike the rational metric system, the English system of land measurement that the United States inherited does not seem to make much sense. It does, however, but only if related to experience rather than to mathematics. Village farmland in medieval England was laid out in long rows so that plows drawn by oxen would not have to turn around often. A strip of land a furrow long and wide enough to be plowed in a day was called an *acre*. Its actual size varied from one part of the country to another, however, until a standard measure was introduced by one Edmond Gunter during the time of King James I. Gunter defined a *chain* as 66 feet and a *furlong* (the length of furrow for an ox-drawn plow) as ten chains. An acre was defined as the length of a furlong by the width of one chain (660 feet by 66 feet), or 43,560 square feet). Eight furlongs stretch 5,280 feet, or one mile, and 650 rectangular acres fit in a square mile. It is all very logical, but only if your frame of reference is medieval England.

the five states formed from the Northwest Territory, and most of Alabama, Florida, and Mississippi are based on this method.

Principal Meridians and Base Lines

The rectangular survey system is based first on **principal meridians** running north and south and **base lines** running east and west. Placement of these meridians and base lines generally coincides with an established landmark, such as the mouth of the Ohio River. The principal meridian was drawn north-south through the river's mouth, and the base line was drawn east-west to intersect the meridian at the landmark. The principal meridians and base lines around the United States are shown in Figure 2.4. Because the earth is round, lines that are drawn to run north and south eventually converge at the north and south poles. Surveyors use reference points created by "guide meridians" and "standard parallels" to account for this convergence when locating the corners of a property using the rectangular survey method.

Townships

The land on each side of the principal meridian is divided into six-mile-wide strips by **range lines,** which run north and south and are numbered consecutively east or west of the principal meridian. For example, the first range line to the east of the principal meridian is numbered 1 East, the second is numbered 2 East, and so forth. Similarly, the land above and below the base line is divided into six-mile wide strips by **township lines,** which run east and west and are numbered consecutively north and south of the base line. For example, the first township line north of the base

FIGURE 2.4 | Principal Meridians and Base Lines in the United States

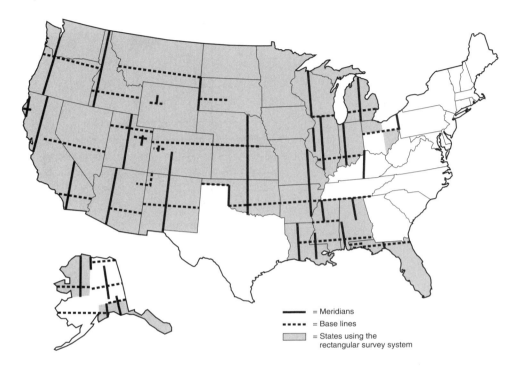

= Meridians
= Base lines
= States using the rectangular survey system

line is numbered 1 North, the second is numbered 2 North, and so forth. The range and township lines form the basic unit of the rectangular survey, the **township,** an area of land six miles square.

To identify a specific township, reference is made to the intersection of the township and range lines. For example, the shaded township in Figure 2.5 is Township 3 North, Range 2 West, abbreviated as T3N, R2W. It's often useful to count the spaces (the townships) rather than the township and range lines when locating townships on maps.

Townships are not only the basic unit of the rectangular survey system, they often are the basis of political subdivisions as well. Somewhat confusingly, however, the term is also used to describe political subdivisions in states that were not surveyed under the rectangular system.

Sections

The rectangular survey system divides each township into 36 equal-sized **sections.** Within any given township, sections are numbered beginning in the northeast corner, moving westerly, then southerly one section, and back easterly. The process

FIGURE 2.5 | Principal Meridians and Base Lines in the United States

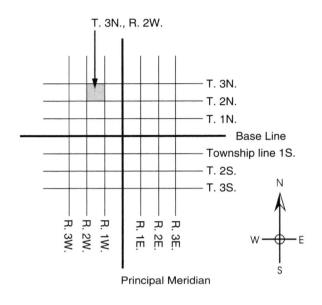

FIGURE 2.6 | A Township Divided into Sections

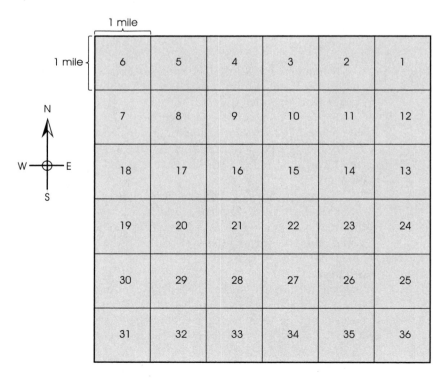

continues until all sections are numbered. Figure 2.6 demonstrates this numbering process. Each section consists of one square mile, or 640 acres.

In the states covered by the rectangular survey, rural land is generally sold in patchwork pieces. Of course, farms in these states may be smaller than the sectional size of 640 acres. For example, farms claimed under the Homestead Act were one-quarter section, or 160 acres. As another example, a buyer might purchase the land indicated in Figure 2.7, the northwest quarter of the southeast quarter of the northeast quarter of the Section. How many acres did the buyer purchase? The answer is ten.

Aerial photographs clearly show the effect a particular method of land survey has on rural areas. Under the metes-and-bounds survey system, farmlands are laid out in the random pattern illustrated in Figure 2.8, a photograph of farmland in the eastern United States. A comparable rural area that was surveyed under the rectangular system, with its even patchwork pattern, is shown in Figure 2.9. This photograph of land in Kansas is typical of the midwestern and western United States.

FIGURE 2.7 | Subdivision of a Section (640 Acres)

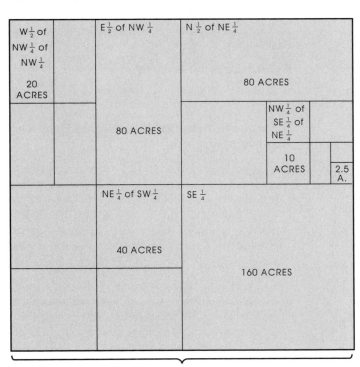

Combined Use of Metes-and-Bounds and Rectangular Survey Systems

The rectangular survey system describes very accurately the extensive acreage involved in farmland. It becomes difficult to use, however, when one wishes to describe the small subdivision lots found in most communities. Subdividing a section of 640 acres into lots of one-half acre or less is an all but endless task. Therefore, metes-and-bounds descriptions become vital to clear legal descriptions. Many properties are described by some combination of the metes-and-bounds and rectangular survey methods. For example, a combined description might appear as follows:

> Part of SW ¼ of the SE ¼ of Section 14, T43S,R34E., Tallahassee Principal Meridian, Hendry County, State of Florida, beginning at a point being 202 feet East of the SW corner of the SE ¼ of said Section 14; running thence North 8 degrees East 200 feet to an iron pin; running thence due East 100 feet to an iron pin; running thence South 8 degrees West 200 feet to an iron pin; running thence due West 100 feet to the point of beginning.

FIGURE 2.9 | Aerial Photograph of Land Surveyed under the Rectangular Survey System

FIGURE 2.9 | Aerial Photograph of Land Surveyed under the Rectangular Survey System

Figure 2.10 shows the parcel described above. The parcel is located within the southwest quarter of the southeast quarter of Section 14 in Township 43 South, Range 34 East of the Tallahassee Principal Meridian.

Figure 2.11 shows a residential development that has grown up in and around farmland that was surveyed under the rectangular survey system. Here, we see the combined use of the metes-and-bounds system applied on the rectangular survey system. Notice that the undeveloped tracts still appear rectangular, but the newer subdivided tracts reflect irregularly shaped lots on curving streets.

References to Recorded Plats

A common alternative and supplement to these methods of legally describing real estate is to refer to engineers' drawings of parcels of real estate called **plats** that have been recorded as part of the official public record. Plats show the streets, blocks, and lots as they actually exist. A plat of a subdivision appears in Figure 2.12. Notice that the plat contains the precise distances and directions (metes and bounds) of each property boundary. Once this document is part of the official public record, properties can be described simply by reference to the numbers of the lots as they

FIGURE 2.10   Parcel Indicated by Combined Description

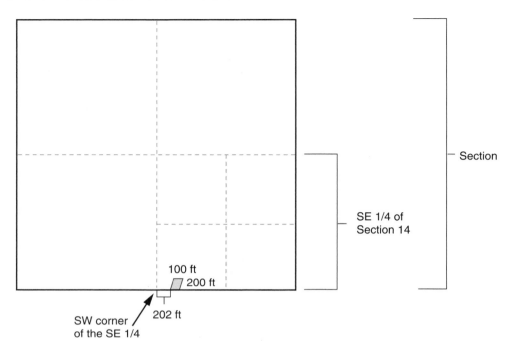

appear in the plat of the block of the subdivision in which the lot is located. For example, we could identify the parcel highlighted in Figure 2.12 as "Lot 4 of Block G" of this subdivision as recorded in the public records of the county where the subdivision is located.

In the case of a condominium, each individual unit of the complex is described separately by referring to a previously recorded plat of the complex. In addition, a condominium description includes a reference to the fractional share (based on the number of units) of the common areas within the complex.

An interesting problem of legal description arises when the property involves an **air lot,** which means the property does not actually touch the ground. In these cases, vertical distances are measured from a point of known vertical height. The most common vertical reference is mean sea level, but official benchmarks that can be used as reference points for both horizontal and vertical distances have been established throughout the United States by the Coast and Geodetic Survey. Thus, the air lot of a 32nd-floor condominium might be described by identifying the parcel of land underneath and the vertical measurements of the airspace above the ground.

FIGURE 2.11 | Aerial Photograph of Land Surveyed by the Combined Metes-and-Bounds and Rectangular Survey System

CHAPTER REVIEW

- *Real estate* refers to land and things attached to the land. *Real property* refers to the legal interests associated with real estate. *Personal property* refers to all movable items (not real estate) and the rights associated with them.

- Items that were once considered personal property but have become part of the real property are called *fixtures*.

- Real estate can be physically divided into surface rights, mineral rights, air rights, and water rights.

- Real property can be divided into different bundles of property rights called *estates in land*.

FIGURE 2.12 | Plat of a Subdivision

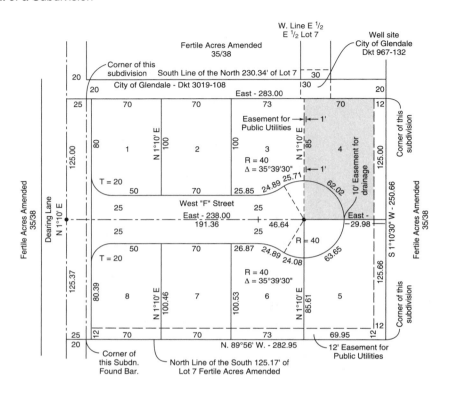

- Estates in land can be divided into freehold (ownership) and leasehold estates.

- Freehold estates include the fee simple absolute estate, qualified fee estates, life estates, and reversion and remainder interests.

- Leasehold estates include tenancy for a stated period, tenancy from period to period, tenancy at will, and tenancy at sufferance.

- Freehold estates are generally transferred by a legal document called a *deed.* Leasehold estates are transferred by a legal document called a *lease.*

- When more than one owner has rights to the same real estate, the ownership is referred to as concurrent ownership.

- Examples of concurrent ownership include tenancy in common, joint tenancy, and tenancy by the entirety.

- Other ways the rights to real property can be divided among multiple owners include condominiums, cooperatives, and time-shares.

■ Three different methods are used to describe individual parcels of real estate: metes and bounds, rectangular survey, and references to recorded plats.

KEY TERMS

air lot

air rights

base lines

chattel

community property

concurrent estates

condominium

contingent remainder

cooperative

deed

estate pur autre vie

estates in land

estates in severalty

eviction

fee interest time-share

fee simple absolute estate

fixture

freehold estates

grantee

grantor

joint tenancy

lease

leased fee estate

leasehold estates

lessee

lessor

life estate

life tenant

metes-and-bounds description

mineral rights

personal property

plats

principal meridians

prior appropriation doctrine

property

proprietary lease

qualified fee estate

range lines

real estate

real property

rectangular survey system

remainder

remainderman

reversions

right of first refusal

right of reentry

right of survivorship

right to use time-share

riparian rights doctrine

sections

tenancy at sufferance

tenancy at will

tenancy by the entirety

tenancy for a stated period

tenancy from period to period

tenancy in common

test of adaptability

test of attachment

test of intent of the parties

time-share

title

township

township lines

trade fixtures

vested remainder

water rights

STUDY EXERCISES

1. What is the difference between the terms *real estate* and *real property?*

2. What are *fixtures* and why is it important to be able to identify them?

3. What are the three general physical divisions of property rights?

4. Fred leases a building from George for his new restaurant. To increase his business, Fred installs an antique bar in the center of the restaurant,

complete with water and drain lines. A year later, Fred's business is so successful he decides to move to a larger building. He plans to remove the bar and take it to the new location, but George protests, claiming the bar is a fixture and cannot be removed. Does Fred have the right to remove the bar? Why or why not?

5. Distinguish between the riparian rights doctrine and the prior appropriation doctrine of water rights.

6. If Bob buys a parcel of land from Sarah, who is the grantor and who is the grantee?

7. Define each of the following terms with respect to the fee simple estate: *alienable, devisable, descendible.*

8. What is the primary difference between a fee simple absolute estate and a qualified fee estate?

9. What is the difference between a life estate and an estate pur autre vie?

10. Mabel, a senior citizen, has a life estate in the home in which she lives that was willed to her by her brother. Mabel's grandson holds the remainder interest in the property. Mabel wishes to move to a warmer climate, so she offers her interest in the house to a neighbor for $10,000. The house has a total value of $100,000. Under what circumstances would the neighbor buy Mabel's interest?

    a. If the neighbor declines to purchase her property, Mabel will offer it to her grandson, who has the remainder interest. Would he be likely to buy her estate?

    b. If Mabel's grandson declines to purchase her property, Mabel plans to leave it to her friend Betty in her will. What interest will Betty have upon Mabel's death?

11. Lisa and Anne were business partners who owned real estate as joint tenants with the right of survivorship, not as tenants in common. At the time of Lisa's death, a dispute arose between Lisa's heirs and Anne as to who was the rightful owner of Lisa's one-half interest in the property. Who is entitled to the property interest that Lisa owned?

12. Madeline has an opportunity to invest in either a cooperative or a condominium. What are the differences between these types of ownership?

13. Dick agrees to rent a two-bedroom house from Larry for a two-year period with monthly rent payments. What type of leasehold estate is involved in this transaction?

14. Charles rents a home from Woodley on a month-to-month basis. On June 1, Woodley gives proper notice to Charles that he wishes to terminate the tenancy on August 31. On September 2, Charles has still has not vacated the property. Under what kind of tenancy is Charles now holding possession?

15. According to the rectangular survey system, if a buyer purchases the south half of the northeast quarter of a section of land, how many acres has he or she purchased?

16. How many square feet are in an acre? How many acres are in a section? How many sections are in a township?

17. Use a simple sketch to show the location of T5S, R6E. Appropriately label the principal meridian, base line, and each of the range and township lines in the sketch.

18. Use a simple sketch to show the location of section 17 in a township.

19. Use a simple sketch to show the location of the parcel described as "the NW 1/4 of the NE 1/4 of the SE 1/4 of the SE 1/4" of a section. How many square feet does the parcel contain?

20. Use a simple sketch to show the boundaries and reference points of a property described as follows:

    "Beginning at a point 200 feet due North of the southwest corner of Section 11; running thence 100 feet N. 45° E to an iron pin; running thence 100 feet S. 45° E. to an iron pin; running thence 100 feet S. 45° W. to an iron pin; running thence 100 N. 45° W. to the point of beginning."

21. Internet Exercise: Visit the Web site for National Public Radio at *www.npr .org* and enter the words "Water in the West" in the search box. Listen to the audio stories in the four-part series (especially part three). Do you think the prior appropriation doctrine should be reconsidered, or do you think the free market should be allowed to work out its own solution to the problems described in the series?

FURTHER READING

Jennings, Marianne M. *Real Estate Law,* 7th ed. Mason, Ohio: West Thomson South-Western, 2005.

Karp, James, and Elliot Klayman. *Real Estate Law*, 6th ed. Chicago: Dearborn Real Estate Education, 2006.

McCormak, Jack C. *Surveying,* 4th ed. New York: John Wiley and Sons, 1999.

Private Restrictions on Ownership

CLOSE-UP
Meadow Brook
Ranch Use
Covenants

LEGAL HIGHLIGHT
Validity of
Restrictive
Covenants

LEGAL HIGHLIGHT
Restrictive
Covenant Disputes

LEGAL HIGHLIGHT
A Cautionary Tale
on Mechanics' Liens

LEGAL HIGHLIGHT
Prescriptive
Easement

LEGAL HIGHLIGHT
The Case of the
Landlocked Parcel

CLOSE-UP
Use of
Conservation
Easements

LEGAL HIGHLIGHT
Adverse Possession

CHAPTER PREVIEW

Even though someone may own the entire fee simple ownership rights in a parcel of real estate, this interest is often limited by certain restrictions placed on the property by public or private entities. These restrictions and limitations, known collectively as **encumbrances**, generally run with the land; in other words, they are binding on anyone who gains a subsequent interest in the property. In some cases, encumbrances may adversely affect both the use and the value of the property. In extreme cases, the land may be so encumbered that it would be valueless for a potential purchaser. Conversely, some public or private land-use restrictions may enhance the value of a property by protecting it from detrimental actions by others.

We consider several forms of *private* restrictions on ownership in this chapter, and we will consider *public* restrictions on ownership in the next chapter. The private restrictions we will consider in this chapter include

- covenants, conditions, and restrictions (CC&Rs);

- liens;

- easements;

- profit a prendre;

- adverse possession; and

- encroachments.

■ COVENANTS, CONDITIONS, AND RESTRICTIONS

Covenants, conditions, and restrictions, often abbreviated as **CC&Rs,** are private encumbrances that limit the way a property owner can use a property. The CC&Rs are essentially promises made by a landowner about how the property will or will not be used that are enforceable through the court system by the parties who expect to benefit from the promises. These promises are typically found in the deed or plat associated with the property and are recorded in the public record system. Once attached to a property, these covenants "run with the land" and are binding on successive owners of the property. For example, a developer who wants to limit the uses of the properties in the project may attach covenants to the deeds for each parcel that prohibit or require certain uses of the property. The developer's goal is to increase the value of the property to prospective purchasers by assuring them that they will be protected from detrimental uses of the properties by their neighboring property owners. Of course, the use of CC&Rs is not limited to developers. Individual property owners may also attach limitations on how their properties can be used by subsequent owners. For example, the seller of a property may attach restrictions that prohibit any commercial use of the property or that preserve a scenic view available to other properties.

It is increasingly common for developers to attach covenants that subject each parcel in the development project to the authority of a property owners' association that is empowered by a majority vote of all property owners (with each parcel getting one vote) to adopt rules and restrictions that all property owners must adhere to. Because the developer owns all of the properties in the project when the association is first created, the developer will establish the initial rules and restrictions. As the parcels in the project are sold to individual property owners, the owners will eventually gain majority control of the property owners' association and can change the rules as they collectively see fit. Such rules can be very specific. For example, the CC&Rs for a residential subdivision may restrict the use of the properties in the project to single-family uses only, may require that houses be a certain minimum size, and/or may prohibit business enterprises, nondomestic animals, or large antennas. The CC&Rs may also require the approval by the association of all buildings and landscaping plans, prohibit the use of certain building materials, and even mandate the painting of homes at regular intervals with approved paint colors. It is important to note that CC&Rs cannot create unreasonable or unlawful limitations on an owner's use of land. For example, restrictions preventing the sale of property to a person of a particular ethnic or racial group clearly are unenforceable because they violate the laws and the Constitution of the United States.

The Real Estate Close-Up on the next page shows some of the CC&Rs in a rural subdivision called Meadow Brook Ranch.

CC&Rs are particularly important to the owners of attached condominium dwellings. Suppose, for example, that the owners of one unit in a condominium project paint their unit in their college's colors—a brilliant orange and green. Or suppose they decide that bright pink plastic flamingos would be just the thing for the front lawn. Not only might these actions have definite detrimental aesthetic impacts, they would have economic impacts on fellow property owners and, therefore, could be

Meadow Brook Ranch Use Covenants

1. All lots in Meadow Brook Ranch are restricted to use for residential purposes only. No signs shall be placed on any part of these residential lots indicating a commercial or nonresidential use thereof.

2. No animals or fowl shall be permitted other than those types of animals or fowl normally found on rural property that are raised for personal family use and/or pleasure on a strictly noncommercial basis. Permitted types of animals shall include horses, chickens, and household pets. No swine shall be permitted. A maximum of two (2) dogs per lot shall be permitted. Exotic Game shall be allowed upon the property, with the exception of those that would affect the health, safety, and/or welfare of any of the landowners within the subdivision. Any and all animals, including household pets, require appropriate fencing to confine them to their lot. No animal shall be permitted until this appropriate fencing is completed.

3. No junk or junkyards of any kind or character shall be permitted, nor shall accumulation of scrap, used materials, inoperative automobiles, or machinery, or other unsightly storage of personal property be permitted.

4. No portion of the property shall be used in a manner that adversely affects adjoining property owners or creates an annoyance or nuisance to other property owners. This shall include noise pollution such as barking dogs, loud music, or any animal or fowl that causes a nuisance.

5. No hunting with firearms shall be permitted on any lot. Bow hunting shall be allowed on lots of at least 10 acres. No discharging of any firearms or fireworks shall be permitted on any lot.

6. No residence shall be erected on any part of said property or building site having less than 1,700 square feet of floor space livable area in the main building with one-half (½) thereof of masonry construction, with the exception of log homes, which will not require one-half (½) masonry construction.

7. All buildings erected on the premises shall be of new construction and materials. No buildings or portion of buildings of old material may be moved into said subdivision.

8. It is the intent of the undersigned that all dwellings and other structures have a neat and attractive appearance. No metal walls or walls of temporary sheeting will be allowed. The entire exterior walls of all dwelling units or other buildings hereafter constructed must be completed within one year after the commencement of work thereon or the placing of materials therefore on said property, whichever occurs the earliest, and in connection therewith it is understood that the use of the word "completed" also means the finishing of all such exterior walls.

(continued)

REAL ESTATE TODAY

CLOSE-UP

Meadow Brook Ranch Use Covenants

9. No more than one residence shall be erected per each two and one-half (2.5) acres.

10. No outside toilets, privies, or cesspools will be permitted, and no installation of any type of sewage disposal device shall be allowed that would result in raw or untreated or unsanitary sewage being carried into any water body; all septic tanks must conform to the regulations of the State and County concerning septic systems.

11. No tents, campers, or trailers shall be used on any of the property for residential purposes, on a temporary or permanent basis. No premanufactured, modular, trailer, or any other structure not built on the site shall be permitted.

12. All tracts shall be kept in a clean and orderly condition at all times, and all trash, garbage, and other waste shall be kept in sanitary containers.

13. No structures used for storage purposes shall be erected or placed upon any parcel that will be visible from any roadway, unless placed within the most rear one-third (1/3) of the parcel, that being such portion farthest away from any roadway. All such structures shall be neatly maintained.

14. No resubdivision of any tract of less than two and one-half (2.5) acres shall be permitted.

prevented through CC&Rs (stating, for instance, that outside paint colors must meet the approval of a homeowners' association and that no statuary or other furniture may be placed in front yards).

Because CC&Rs are a type of contractual agreement, parties to the agreement may enforce it through the court system. To recover damages or obtain an injunction, the nonbreaching party (usually the property owners' association) must be able to show that some damage has been suffered. In other words, to be justified in enforcing the CC&Rs, the party must be able to show how the intended benefit has been denied.

Suppose, for example, that Mary violates the covenants in the deed to her home by erecting a 12-foot satellite dish antenna in her front yard. Either the developer or other property owners could secure a court injunction to force the removal of the offending antenna. If the covenant violation were even more severe, they could seek monetary damages.

Covenants generally run with the land, from owner to owner. They may exist only for a stated period of time—say, 20 years—or they can be terminated by the agreement of all affected parties should the right of enforcement be waived or abandoned or if the restricted land is condemned for a public use. Alternatively, an owner

Validity of Restrictive Covenants

Salma Worthington purchased a home in the Mains Farm subdivision near Sequim, Washington, for the purpose of establishing an adult-care facility. She knew restrictive covenants limited land use in the subdivision to "single-family residential purposes only," but contended that the proposal use did not violate the covenants. She and her daughter moved into the home, along with four elderly residents. The homeowners' association sued to endorse the deed restrictions. The association won.

The court held that Worthington's use of her home was not for "single-family residential purposes only" because of the business elements involved. Since Worthington provided 24-hour care for fees of $500 to $1,000 per person per month, the property's use was essentially commercial, a use that was inconsistent with a residential purpose.

Worthington also contended that even if her use violated the restrictive covenants, the covenants could not prevent a home-care facility because the state legislature had adopted legislation permitting such facilities in all areas zoned for residential or commercial purposes, including areas zone for single-family dwellings. She contended that this enactment established the fact that maintaining disabled persons outside institutions is of greater value to the public than is the right to restrict the use of land through restrictive covenants.

Again, the court disagreed, holding that unlike covenants that might attempt to restrict ownership by race, creed, color, national origin, or handicap, the covenants in question served the legitimate public purpose of protecting residential neighborhoods from the effect of business uses. Although the legislature has restricted local governments from zoning adult family homes out of residential areas, it did not limit the right of private homeowners to adopt restrictive covenants that prohibit certain uses of land in residential areas.

[*Mains Farm Homeowners Association v. Worthington*, 824 P.2d 495]

could place a permanent restriction on the land. CC&Rs can supersede public land use regulations if they are more restrictive than the public regulations, as the Legal Highlight shown above illustrates.

LIENS

A **lien** is a claim on a property as either security for a debt or fulfillment of some monetary charge or obligation. For example, an owner might give a mortgage on a property in order to borrow money, thus creating a lien on the property. The lien does not represent right of ownership for the creditor; rather, it amounts to a financial security interest in the property, a claim the creditor holds against the property to help ensure the debt will be repaid. If the creditor is a private individual or

REAL ESTATE TODAY
LEGAL HIGHLIGHT

Restrictive Covenant Disputes

 Protective restrictive covenants sometimes lead to controversy when they are enforced. As these examples illustrate, some of these controversies involve very substantive issues, while others reflect rather trite neighborhood disputes.

The Case of the Unapproved Garage

After Don and Carolyn Colliver bought a house in the Stonewall Equestrian Estates, they wanted to build a detached two-car garage on their lot. Under the restrictive covenants this had to be approved by the community association, but it turned down the plans. Subsequently, the parties could not reach agreement, and the Collivers began constructing the garage without approval. The association took legal action to enforce the covenants. Even so, the Collivers continued the construction, which when finished cost almost $70,000.

In court, the Collivers challenged the validity of the covenants and the right of the community association to enforce them. Unfortunately for them, the court disagreed and ordered that the garage be removed:

"Despite the pending litigation and relief sought, the Collivers continued with the construction of the garage at their own peril. They took an unwise risk and expended a large amount of money in spite of this litigation and the Association's clear disapproval of their garage. We require the Collivers to remove the structure in its entirety immediately."

[*Colliver v. Stonewall Equestrian Estate Assoc.*, 134 SW3d 521, Court of Appeals of Kentucky]

Is a Church a Residential Use?

Eddie Chan and Fat Fan Cheung bought adjacent houses in the Kingsbridge Park subdivision. Cheung sought and received permission from the Architectural Control Committee to add a "game room" to his house. When it was constructed it became apparent the room was designed and furnished not as a game room, but for worship.

Chan and Cheung deeded their houses to the Tien Tao Association, a nonprofit religious corporation. Tien Tao erected three 30-foot flagpoles in the backyard of one of the homes, paved the back lawn, and repainted the home's shutters an unapproved color. They did not seek advance approval for these changes as required in the restrictive covenants. Tien Tao housed Cheung and another priest in one of the houses and provided accommodations for followers who gathered to worship. The unauthorized changes, plus the apparent use of the properties for other than single-family residential use as required by the covenants, led the community association to sue for compliance.

The court ruled that the flagpole and other alterations violated the covenants, as did the use of the properties for religious purposes. Tien Tao also argued that the purpose of the covenants was to restrict their members' religious freedom in violation of the Fair Housing Act. The court disagreed, ruling that the association sought to abate a nuisance, not to exclude Taoist believers from the community: "That the nuisance stemmed from a gathering of a religious nature does not exclude it from coverage by the restrictions."

[*Tien Tao Association v. Kingsbridge Park Community Association*, 953 SW2d 525, Texas Court of Appeals, 1st District]

(continued)

REAL ESTATE TODAY

LEGAL HIGHLIGHT

Restrictive Covenant Disputes

The Case of the Too-Large Plaque

When Sol and Renee Silberman bought their home in Lakewood Greens they hung a 45" by 25" terra-cotta plaque that depicted three cherubs pouring water from a pail. During a routine property inspection the community association's property manager noticed the plaque and told the Silbermans that under the restrictive covenants it required the approval of the architectural control board. After their application was denied, the Silbermans still refused to remove the plaque, contending it was hung with only two screws and did not require any architectural changes or modifications, that the model home had three terra-cotta urns, and that many other homeowners had similar plaques or hangings. The association then filed suit to force removal of the plaque.

The appeals court found that the Silbermans' plaque was much larger than those hung by other homeowners, and that the other homeowners who had similar but smaller plaques complied with the covenants. The Silbermans were ordered to remove the plaque, and the community was again safe from too-large terra-cotta cherubs.

[*Lakewood Greens Homeowners Assoc. v. Silberman*, 765 So.2d 95, Florida Court of Appeals, 4th District]

---

business, the mortgage lien creates a private restriction on ownership. If the creditor is a government, the resulting encumbrance is a public restriction on ownership. The property tax lien is a common example of a public restriction and will be considered in the next chapter.

Real estate liens may be either voluntary or involuntary. Voluntary liens are those placed on property by the owner, usually in the form of a mortgage to secure repayment of long-term debt. Involuntary liens protect the interest of persons who have valid claims against the owner of real property—such as those resulting from a judgment in a lawsuit, from not being paid for some service, or from unpaid taxes.

Liens are also classified as specific or general. A **specific lien** is created to secure debts that are associated with a particular parcel of real estate. A **general lien**—for example, a judgment lien or an income tax lien—is placed on all of the property that might be owned by an individual, including any real estate.

Specific Liens

The two types of specific liens that are created to protect creditors using real estate as their security for repayment of debts are mortgages and mechanics' liens.

A Cautionary Tale on Mechanics' Liens

Most homeowners have never heard of a mechanic's lien, but every year some learn in a very painful way. Howard Krish had paid the final bill on his $9,600 roofing job, and he had the receipt. Even so, he was being sued by a building supply company for $3,100 to pay for the felt and shingles that were used on his Boynton Beach, Florida, home. Johnston Roofing had accepted his check but had not paid its suppliers. Krish, along with ten of his neighbors who had paid in full for new roofs, had to pay the building supply company to avoid having their homes sold to satisfy the mechanic's lien.

Or consider the sad case of Maria Ghiran, a Chicago resident who decided to move to Florida. She hired a contractor to build her house and paid him two installments totaling $57,000. When she flew down to inspect the work, she found a slab of concrete—and nothing more. The contractor had gone bankrupt after taking her money, and the subcontractors and suppliers placed mechanics' liens on the property.

The moral of this story is clear. Homeowners need to check the mechanic's lien law in their state before paying contractors for work on their property. In some states, homeowners can avoid paying twice if they can prove they paid the general contractor for the work. To avoid this painful surprise in other states, such as Florida in our sad tales, homeowners need to get signed lien releases before paying their general contractor.

Mortgages

Because few people choose to buy real estate without borrowing money, a **mortgage** is the most common encumbrance on an owner's title. In return for a loan to buy real property, purchasers often pledge the property as collateral for the debt. In other words, the borrower creates a lien in favor of the lender. The borrower who pledges real estate as security or collateral against a loan is the **mortgagor;** the lender that receives the benefits of this lien is the **mortgagee.** (A helpful hint for keeping the "ors" and "ees" straight in all real estate terms: the "ors" give property rights or interests in property and the "ees" receive them.) Although mortgage liens put a restriction on a mortgagor's ownership interest, they make it possible for purchasers to obtain long-term financing for relatively large real estate purchases.

A mortgage lien acts as a private restriction on ownership. If the loan is not repaid on schedule, or if other requirements of the loan contract are not met, the mortgagee may instigate **foreclosure** proceedings. In some states, the foreclosure process results in the property being sold at public auction with the proceeds of the auction being used to satisfy the debt. In other states, foreclosure results in the transfer of ownership from the mortgagor to the mortgagee. The mortgagee can then use or sell the property at it sees fit. Mortgage lending is discussed more fully in Chapter 16.

Mechanics' Liens

A **mechanic's lien** (also known as a *construction lien* in some states) protects those who provide labor or materials for real estate improvements, including suppliers, architects, engineers, landscapers, carpenters, plumbers, and similar workers. Any such suppliers of materials and labor who are not paid can file a mechanic's lien on the property. If payment still is not made, foreclosure proceedings can result, with the property being sold to satisfy the debt.

Mechanics' liens are not just a concern to persons who fail to pay for work done to their real property; they also can create problems for subsequent purchasers. Suppose, for example, that Marty and Carole Teem purchase a home from Potts Development. Some weeks after closing on the house, they are dismayed to learn that several subcontractors have filed mechanics' liens on their home because they were not paid by the general contractor. Even though the Teems have already paid for the house, they may have to pay twice for the same work if the claims are valid. Needless to say, it is vital to see that all suppliers of material and labor are paid before the general contractor is fully paid or the house purchase completed.

General Liens

Like specific liens, general liens do not represent property ownership; they are, however, creditors' claims against a property owner's title. Unlike special liens, general liens normally may be filed on either personal or real property.

A common general lien is a **judgment lien.** The winner in a lawsuit who has not been paid may collect the debt by claiming an interest in the loser's property, including any real estate. If the judgment debt still is not paid, the property can be sold to satisfy the creditor's claim. Such a sale, commonly referred to as a *judicial sale,* is conducted as an auction by a sheriff or another legal authority. In some states, the debtor-owner of the real property may redeem ownership interest within a year of the sale by reimbursing the purchaser for the sales price and paying all costs of the sale.

Other general liens that could result in similar ownership limitations are public liens for delinquent taxes: federal income, federal estate, state income, and state estate or inheritance. As in a court-awarded judgment, such unpaid tax debts can be levied on real property. Ultimately, if the lien is not satisfied and removed, the land can be sold at public auction.

EASEMENTS

An **easement** is a right given to one party by a landowner to use the land in a specified manner. The landowner does not have to give up his or her land, but rather coexists with the holder of the easement. For example, property owners may grant a utility company the right to run a power line across their land, or one landowner may allow an adjoining owner to build a driveway across her property. From the perspective of the property that is subject to the easement, easements are restrictions of property rights.

FIGURE 3.1 | Easement Appurtenant Created by a Joint Driveway

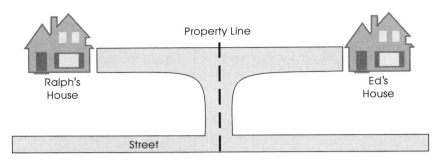

Types of Easements

There are two types of traditional easements: an easement appurtenant and an easement in gross. An **easement appurtenant** exists when an easement is legally connected to an adjoining property. Suppose, for example, that Bill pays Susan to grant him an easement to run a sewer line from his house across her property to the city's trunk sewer line. In this case, Bill's land is being served or benefited by the easement and is known as the **dominant estate.** Susan's land, on the other hand, is burdened by the easement and is known as the **servient estate.** Susan can continue to use her land, but she cannot do anything that would interfere with Bill's use of the sewer line.

As with almost all encumbrances, this easement "runs with the land"; in other words, it continues when ownership changes unless specifically terminated using one of the methods to be discussed below. Even though the new owners of Susan's land may not want Bill's sewer line to remain on their property, they have little choice in the matter.

In some cases, adjoining properties are both dominant and servient. Suppose that Ralph and Ed are neighbors, and each wants a paved driveway. To save money, they decide to share the building costs of one driveway that will serve both lots, as shown in Figure 3.1. Each grants the other an easement appurtenant to use the portion of the driveway on each other's land. Both lots are simultaneously the servient estate and the dominant estate.

With an **easement in gross** there is no dominant estate, only a servient estate. For example, a utility company that acquires an easement to run its power line or pipeline across a property or the highway department that acquires an easement for a road right-of-way has acquired an easement in gross. The easements have been granted to the utility company or the highway department, not to parcels of land. The land over which the utility line or road crosses is the servient estate, and the easement binds all future owners of the property.

FIGURE 3.2 | Easement Created by Express Grant

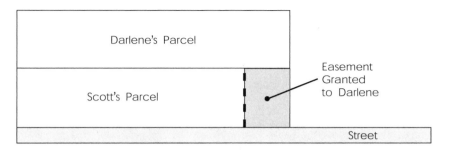

Creation of Easements

Both appurtenant easements and easements in gross may be established in a number of ways. The most common method is by an express grant or reservation, but easements also may be established by implication and by prescription.

Express Grant or Reservation

Most easements are created by either **express grant** or **express reservation.** Suppose Scott sells half of his ten-acre lot to Darlene. If the property Darlene is purchasing has no road frontage, Scott may expressly grant her the right to use a portion of his remaining property for a driveway. In this case, Scott owns the servient estate, and Darlene owns the dominant estate. The deed Scott gives Darlene should specify the easement appurtenant that has been created. This easement is shown in Figure 3.2.

An easement also may be established by an express reservation. If Sam were to sell the front half of his land to Bob, the remainder of Sam's property would be landlocked because it does not front on a public road. In the deed that transferred ownership of the frontage land to Bob, Sam could reserve a right of passageway through Bob's newly acquired land. Sam owns the dominant estate, and Bob owns the burdened (servient) estate. By this express reservation in the sale of land, an easement appurtenant has been created, as shown in Figure 3.3.

Implication

Sometimes, when one or more parcels are severed from a larger tract under common ownership, the right to use the land may be implied from the factual circumstances even when an easement is not expressly created. The easement supposedly reflects the intentions of the parties and is called an **easement by implication.**

Suppose no mention of an easement was made in the previous examples. If Scott sold the land illustrated in Figure 3.2 to Darlene, and he allowed her to use the road on the property he retained, an easement by **implied grant** would be established.

FIGURE 3.3   Easement Appurtenant Created by Implied Reservation

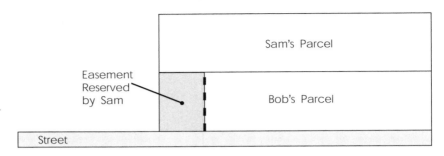

Likewise, as depicted in Figure 3.3, Sam's continued use of the passageway over the land granted to Bob would create an easement by **implied reservation.**

In both of these situations, the implied easement arises from necessity. In the absence of the easements, the properties would have no access and virtually no value. Of course, even when an easement can be implied, it is best that all easements be stated expressly in writing.

Prescription

An **easement by prescription** may be created when someone other than the owner uses the land "openly, hostilely, and continuously" for a statutory time period. To use the land openly means that the user comes onto the land and acts entitled to be there. Such a user does not use the land secretly, as if to hide the use. Hostile use means the user treats the land as if he or she is the true owner of an easement. If the landowner has given specific permission for the use of land, hostility does not exist. To be continuous, the use must be uninterrupted for the time period provided by the applicable statute, usually between 7 and 20 years. These elements of prescription are very similar to those required for gaining title by adverse possession, a topic discussed later in this chapter.

Suppose, for example, that college students begin driving across kindly farmer Hodge's land to reach a swimming hole on the river. Being a good fellow, he says nothing about it, and the use continues for many years. Later, when Mr. Hodge attempts to close the road, he is sued successfully to keep it open because of the prescriptive easement. This may seem to be unfair, but it is the law.

The lesson of all this for property owners is clear: They should not allow anyone to use their property without specific permission, and they should make certain the use is interrupted at intervals. Otherwise, these property owners may find that a prescriptive easement has been created.

Prescriptive Easement

After property has been used by another for a period of years, the owners may be forced to give up some of their property rights. This the Nicholsons discovered.

For more than 50 years two houses had shared a common driveway that provided access to each property's carport. When bad blood developed between the two neighbors, one of the owners, the Nicholsons, started construction of a fence along a portion of the common driveway that would have denied access to Dean Wells's carport. Mr. Wells sued to stop them, and he won.

The court held that continuous use of the driveway for more than 50 years created a prescriptive easement through adverse possession. Mr. Wells had acquired a property interest to use the driveway, even though part of it was on the Nicholsons' lot.

[*Nicholson v. Wells*, Ct. of Appeals of Arkansas, Div. 2, 2004]

Nature of Easements

Easements are considered to be *permanent in nature*—that is, easements "run with the land" from owner to owner. Under an easement appurtenant, both the benefit to the dominant estate and the burden on the servient estate are transferred to the new owner if either of the properties is transferred. Owners Scott and Bob, represented in Figures 3.2 and 3.3, own their respective lots subject to an easement of passageway over their land. If ownership of these lots were to change, the easement would still exist, as the passageway continues to be necessary for both Darlene and Sam to have access to the highway.

The burden on the servient estate also runs with the land in easements in gross. If Susan grants a utility company an easement to use her land for its electrical lines, then sells her land to Wilbur, the transfer does not destroy the utility company's right to use the land. The easement, therefore, is just as valid under Wilbur's ownership as it is under Susan's. In some states, the utility company normally can pass this right to another organization as long as the burden on the servient estate is not increased. For example, an electric company could permit a cable television company to run its cable alongside those of the utility. In other states, additional users would have to negotiate their own easements with the landowner.

It is important to distinguish between the concepts of easement and **license.** A *license* is a revocable personal privilege to use land for a particular purpose. Whereas easements are permanent in nature, licenses are generally temporary and can be revoked at will. A landowner might, for example, allow a friend to park his car on her land anytime he wishes, as long as his doing so doesn't inconvenience her. The

The Case of the Landlocked Parcel

 It is an established principle of real estate property law that a parcel of land that has no access to a public road must be granted an easement across adjacent lands to gain access. This does not mean, however, that the easement must be provided wherever the landlocked property owner desires.

Douglas Culpepper owned a 58-acre parcel of land in rural Louisiana that was landlocked, a fact he knew when he purchased the property. An old logging trail had been used in the past for access, as well as a second logging road across land owned by a wood products company.

Two years before Culpepper bought his property, the adjacent property owner, John Davis, replanted his property, including the old logging trail, in pine seedlings. He also put up a fence where the logging trail started at the public road. Subsequently, Culpepper tore down the fence and bulldozed a new road across Davis's land following the old trail. He destroyed the then seven-foot-high pines, and he also installed a water line down the center of the new road. Davis re-erected the fence, but Culpepper promptly tore it down again.

Davis sued, seeking damages for trespass, and Culpepper countersued, claiming ownership of the road. Culpepper lost.

The court held that although under Louisiana law the owner of property that has no access to a public road may claim a right of passage over neighboring property, he may not demand an easement anywhere he chooses. The passage has to be along the shortest route from the enclosed estate to the public road at the location that is least injurious to the intervening lands unless this route is totally impractical due to adverse terrain. In this case, there was the second and shorter logging trail from the Culpepper property across land owned by the forest products company. The court ruled this road provided sufficient access for Culpepper and rejected his claim for right of passage across Davis's land. Davis was awarded $21,845 in damages and attorney's fees. Culpepper was also ordered to remove the water line.

[*Davis v. Culpepper*, La. App. 2 Cir. 794 SO2d 68]

benefits under a license and the burdens to the grantor's land are temporary in nature and do not pass to successive owners.

Termination of Easements

Even though easements are considered permanent and pass from owner to owner, the rights and restrictions of an easement may be terminated under certain circumstances. Methods of terminating an easement include agreement, merger, and abandonment.

Agreement

Parties affected by the easement may expressly agree to terminate their respective rights in the easement. Such an agreement should be written and recorded so that notice is given to everyone interested that a prior easement no longer exists. Because easements are valuable, convincing the owner of the dominant estate can be quite expensive. If an easement is created by an express grant or reservation that specifies it will last for a limited term only, the easement automatically ceases at the end of that term.

Merger

An easement can also be terminated by the merger of the dominant and servient estates. If Bill's land is burdened by an easement that permits Sarah, the adjoining landowner, to travel across a portion of his property, Bill could persuade Sarah to sell him the land and thereby terminate the easement. Bill could then sell the land to another party without granting an easement, provided the property has another access route. Such a strategy is used when an agreement to terminate an easement cannot be reached.

Abandonment

A third method of terminating an easement is abandonment. If the benefited party does not exercise his or her rights to use the servient estate over an extended period of time, the easement may be terminated. The length of time an easement may remain in effect without being used varies from state to state and from case to case. Some states require that the holder of a servient estate perform some act to block the easement's use before any abandonment is possible. In essence, these states say that the easement must be terminated by the burdened owner's prescriptive use or adverse possession.

A RELATIVELY NEW TYPE OF EASEMENT

While the easements discussed so far are "affirmative easements" that allow specific uses of real estate by nonowners of the property, a **conservation easement** is a type of "negative easement" that prevents specific uses of the real estate by the owner. For example, suppose a property owner is seeking to gain approval for a new development project. Rather than clearing the trees and natural vegetation from the whole parcel and constructing buildings, the developer might elect to commit some portion of the property to a natural area by creating a conservation easement. Such a decision might improve the marketability of the development project (having a natural area nearby might be pleasing to potential purchasers of the project), and it might also help persuade the development approval authorities to grant the development permit for the project. Conservation easements are an increasingly popular way for property owners to protect land from future development. Conservation easements are almost always created by express grant or reservation.

R E A L   E S T A T E   T O D A Y

CLOSE-UP

Use of Conservation Easements

 Those desiring to preserve historic buildings or open space often make use of restrictive covenants and easements.

Historic buildings sometimes are sold with covenants that limit the use of the building or the ways in which it can be altered. An owner may give a facade easement to a historic preservation organization to ensure that the facade of a building will remain. Conservation easements are often used to protect open space and farmland.

John and Faye McCune owned a 200-acre farm that had been in Faye's family for more than 200 years. They wanted to preserve the farm rather than sell it for development, a fate that had befallen most farms in their area because the city was rapidly expanding in their direction. Property taxes, which were based on the developmental potential of the land in commercial use, were also increasing rapidly, and the McCunes were concerned that the increased tax burden might force them to sell the farm. A conservation easement on the land offered them many advantages.

The McCunes donated a conservation easement on the farm to the Central Piedmont Land Trust. The easement restricted use of the land to agriculture and permitted the building of no more than three additional houses for family members. None of these could be built closer than 800 feet to the existing 200-year-old farmhouse and were required to be built in a style compatible with the old farmhouse.

Because the McCunes had given up the ability to sell the land for commercial development, the conservation easement constituted a sizable charitable donation, the difference between the value of the land in its highest and best use and its value in agricultural and limited family residential use. Appraiser Steve Gaultney valued this donation at $800,000, or $4,000 per acre. This constituted a very sizable income tax deduction for the McCunes. They were able to take a deduction from their taxable income for federal income taxes up to 30 percent of their "adjusted gross income," and they were able to spread this deduction over six years. They were also fortunate to live in a state that allows an income tax credit for a conservation easement donation, so, essentially, they did not have to pay any state income taxes for six years.

Because the potential use of the land was reduced from commercial to agricultural, the property tax assessment on the farm was also reduced to reflect this lower value. Even though estate taxes had been reduced by the Congress, the lowered value also ensured that the McCune children would not be facing a large estate tax burden on the farm. The easement in no way prevented the McCunes in giving the farm to their children or in selling the property. It only restricted its potential use.

For this family in this situation, the conservation easement was clearly a "win-win" proposition. The community also gained because it was assured of continued open space.

(This case is a slightly fictionalized account of an actual event.)

PROFIT A PRENDRE

A *profit,* more correctly known as a **profit a prendre,** is a nonpossessory interest in real property that permits the holder to remove part of the soil or produce of the land. It is similar to an easement, although the holder of a profit has the right to remove specified resources, such as soil, produce, wild animals, coal or other minerals, or timber, but the holder of an easement does not. A profit a prendre runs with the land unless terminated using one of the methods similar to those of terminating easements.

ENCROACHMENTS

An **encroachment** is an unauthorized invasion or intrusion of a fixture, a building, or other improvement onto another person's property. Examples are a fence that strays across the property line and a driveway or patio that is constructed partially on the adjoining property. Although most of these intrusions are the result of carelessness or poor planning rather than intent, they should not be taken lightly. The owner of the property being encroached on has the right to force the removal of the encroachment; however, if that owner fails to force removal, the other party may claim the legal right to continue encroaching by adverse possession (discussed below). Encroachments can have a detrimental impact on property value.

The best way to detect encroachments is to have a boundary survey prepared for the property. The surveyor will locate the boundary lines and corners of the property as well as any encroachments onto the property from adjoining properties.

ADVERSE POSSESSION

Perhaps nothing in real estate law is so upsetting to property owners as **adverse possession,** which allows individuals to acquire title to land they do not own because they have openly possessed it for a statutory period of time, usually 7 to 20 years.

For title to be transferred by adverse possession, such possession must be "actual and exclusive, open and notorious, hostile, and continuous" for a statutory period of time. The phrase *actual and exclusive* does not require that the adverse possessor physically occupy the land at all times. Improving the land with a residence would constitute actual possession. So would clearing the land, building a fence along its boundaries, or farming it. Allowing other people to use the land without express permission would prove that the possession was not exclusive. The possessor must maintain possession in the manner of a reasonable owner. The terms *open and notorious, hostile,* and *continuous* have the same meaning in the case of adverse possession as they do in the case of a prescriptive easement.

Another important prerequisite for adverse possession in some states is that the possession be under a "claim of right." This means that the adverse possessor must have a basis for believing he or she owns the real estate claimed. A tenant who takes possession of a house while acknowledging the landlord's ownership cannot adversely possess the leased property. If a claim of right is based on a written

REAL ESTATE TODAY

LEGAL HIGHLIGHT

Adverse Possession

In 1986 Scott and Kathleen Walling bought a lot in Queensbury, New York. The next year they built a house and landscaped and installed drainage adjacent to another building lot which Paul and Denise Przybylo bought in 1989. The Przybylos built a house on their lot in 1994, but because they didn't obtain a mortgage and there was no requirement to do so, they didn't have the lot surveyed. That was a mistake.

The Wallings continued to improve the side yard, installing a buried-wire dog fence in 1998 and planting ten willow saplings in 2003. About this time relations between the families deteriorated and they began to file counter-complaints against each other in town court about barking dogs and other matters.

Finally, in 2004 the Przybylos decided to plant a row of trees on the property line to shield themselves from the Wallings, which necessitated having the property surveyed. The survey showed that they actually owned 5,800 square feet, somewhat over 0.1 of an acre, of the side yard that Walling had been using. The Wallings then claimed they had obtained title to the disputed land through adverse possession due to their open and continuous use of the property, under a claim of right, for longer than the 10-year statutory period required under New York law.

The Walling family won. New York's highest court ruled that since the Przybylos had waited 15 years after purchasing the property, and almost 10 years after moving into their house, to assert their right over the disputed parcel, they had lost it to the Wallings.

Was this fair? Many would say no, but that is the law of adverse possession. Of course, the Przybylos could have avoided this problem if they had obtained a survey when they bought their lot.

The legendary poet Robert Frost wrote that "good fences make good neighbors." So do good surveys, and one should never buy land without one.

[*Walling v. Przybylos*, 24 AD3d 1, NY Ct. of Appeals, 2006]

document, such as an invalid deed, the claim is said to be made under "color of title." Some states require that the possessor have color of title to possess land adversely, while other states reduce the number of years required for continuous possession if written color of title is present. Still other states treat all claims of right in the same manner, whether or not they are based on documents.

At times, it is hard to imagine how anyone could become confused about land ownership unless a mistake has been made in the legal description in the deed. Adverse possession today is much more common in connection with boundary disputes than with possession of entire tracts. Boundary disputes involving adverse possession are of particular importance in residential areas, as can be seen in the Legal Highlight above.

CHAPTER REVIEW

- Restrictions and limitations on ownership interests in real property take many forms. A *private restriction* is a limitation on the owner's title by some private individual or business. An encumbrance created by a governing body or public authority is a *public restriction.*

- *Covenants, conditions, and restrictions—CC&Rs*—are promises made by property owners that restrict how the property may be used. CC&Rs are intended to protect and enhance property values by preventing uses that would be incompatible with other properties.

- A *lien* is a security interest in a property held by a creditor as security for repayment of a debt or other obligation. It does not represent an ownership interest in the property. Mortgages and mechanics' liens are examples of specific liens on real property. Other claims, such as judgment liens, are more general in that they can be attached to real or personal property. If a debtor fails to satisfy a specific or general lien, the property may eventually be used to satisfy the debt.

- *Easements* are restrictions on a landowner's title in which another person or entity has the ongoing right to use someone's property for a specific purpose. When an easement exists, the property that is subject to the easement is known as the servient estate. An easement appurtenant exists when the easement's benefits are tied to another parcel of property—the dominant estate. If such benefits are held by an individual or a business without regard to the location of that individual or business, an easement in gross exists. A *license* is created by the landowner's grant of permission to use his or her property. Generally, licenses can be revoked at the landowner's whim; therefore, they are less permanent than easements.

- A *profit a prendre* is similar to an easement, but it specifically allows the holder to remove certain natural resources from the servient property.

- *Adverse possession* is the term used to describe a process by which ownership of real property can be transferred from one party to another as a result of the second party's ongoing possession of the land under certain conditions.

KEY TERMS

adverse possession	easement in gross	license
conservation easement	encroachment	lien
covenants, conditions, and restrictions (CC&Rs)	encumbrance	mechanic's lien
	express grant	mortgage
dominant estate	express reservation	mortgagee
easement	foreclosure	mortgagor
easement appurtenant	general lien	profit a prendre
easement by implication	implied grant	servient estate
easement by prescription	implied reservation	specific lien
	judgment lien	

STUDY EXERCISES

1. What is the difference between a general lien and a specific lien?

2. Suppose that Charlie decides that he is going to cheat Harry out of the money he owes Harry for installing a new air-conditioning system in Charlie's house. What steps might Harry take to collect the debt? (Do not include breaking Charlie's legs.)

3. Why would someone voluntarily allow a mortgage lien on their property?

4. Define the following terms: *easement, license,* and *encroachment.*

5. What is the difference between an easement appurtenant and an easement in gross?

6. Suppose that David sells Joan an easement to run a water line across his property to her property. Who has the dominant estate and who has the servient estate? Explain your answer. Is this an easement appurtenant or an easement in gross?

7. Suppose that David sells the above property to Tamara. She tells Joan to remove the water line from her property. Can she force Joan to remove the line?

8. What is the difference in creating an easement by grant, by reservation, or by implication?

9. Describe an easement by necessity. Describe an easement by prescription.

10. List three methods for terminating an easement.

11. What is the difference between an easement and a license? Between an easement and a profit a prendre?

12. Suppose that Cindy purchases a house and discovers that her neighbor Eleanor has several rose bushes that encroach on her lot. When Cindy asks

Eleanor to move the bushes, Eleanor becomes indignant and accuses Cindy of being unfriendly and a poor neighbor. May Cindy legally insist that the bushes be moved? Why or why not?

13. Suppose that Jack inherits his grandmother's house. He finds that the deed granted many years ago contains a restriction that the property may be sold only to someone of the Caucasian race. Could this restriction be enforced? Why or why not?

14. When Claudia decides to sell her house, she discovers that there is a restriction in her deed that prohibits putting up a For Sale sign on her lawn. "This violates my free speech," she fumes. "I'm going to sue the community association." Will she win? Why or why not?

15. Tim makes the following argument: "Even though CC&Rs limit what a property owner can do with his land, they may increase his property value." Is Tim right? Why or why not?

16. Suppose a new homeowner in the Meadow Brook Ranch development is upset because his neighbor is keeping a horse on her property. Based on the covenants for this development discussed in the Real Estate Close-Up on pages 51–52, may the upset owner demand that the horse be removed?

17. Internet Exercise: Do a Google search at *www.google.com* on the term "CC&Rs" and locate the CC&Rs for a residential development project near you. Read over the CC&Rs and comment on some of the restrictions that you think have a positive impact on the value of the homes in the development. Do any of the restrictions make owning a home in this development less appealing to you? If you can't find the CC&Rs for a project near you, search for "CC&Rs oak hollow estates section one."

CHAPTER 4

Public Restrictions on Ownership

CHAPTER PREVIEW

In addition to the private restrictions on property rights discussed in the previous chapter, governments also create limitations on the ownership of real estate. These limitations arise from governments' powers of

- taxation;

- eminent domain;

- police power; and

- escheat.

After reviewing the four powers governments have over real property, this chapter discusses some of the techniques and tools of public land-use control and examines a few of the controversies surrounding land-use policy issues. The specific topics covered are

- the history of land-use controls;

- the public land-use planning process;

- zoning and other land-use control methods; and

- the takings issue.

REAL ESTATE TODAY

LEGAL HIGHLIGHT
Mechanics of
the Property Tax
Certificate Market in
Florida

LEGAL HIGHLIGHT
What Constitutes
"Public Use"?

LEGAL HIGHLIGHT
Inverse
Condemnation

CLOSE-UP
The Smart Growth
Controversy

LEGAL HIGHLIGHT
The Strange Case
of the Incredible
Shrinking Building

LEGAL HIGHLIGHT
The Case of the
Costly Permit

LEGAL HIGHLIGHT
The Takings Issue

THE PROPERTY TAX

The first power of government over private property to be considered is the power of taxation. The government exercises this power by levying both property taxes and income taxes. We will consider the impact of income taxes later in this text and focus our attention on the property tax in this chapter.

The property tax is an important source of revenue for state and local governments. On average, property taxes account for about 75 percent of state and local government tax revenues in the United States. These revenues are used to fund education, police and fire protection, and other government services. Governments often find that property taxation provides a stable source of revenue that is not greatly affected by short-term fluctuations in business activity. And because it is tied to property that is largely immobile, the property tax is relatively easy to administer and very difficult to evade.

The Property Taxation Process

The property tax is an **ad valorem tax;** that is, it is levied as a percentage of value. It is a tax on the *value of the property,* as opposed to a tax on the *income earned from the property.* Property taxes are often expressed in **millage rates** rather than percentage rates. One *mill* is equal to one dollar of tax for every one thousand dollars of value. One *percent* is equal to one dollar of tax for every one hundred dollars of value. Stated another way, one *mill* equals $0.001, or 1/1,000 of $1. In some jurisdictions, only a portion of the market value of the property is subject to taxation, where **market value** is generally defined as the price that the property probably would bring in the market, given knowledgeable and willing buyers and sellers who act under no unusual pressures and who have a reasonable time to complete the transaction. The portion of market value subject to taxation is called the **assessed value.** The fraction used to determine assessed value from market value is called the **assessment ratio.** (Some states, such as Florida, use an assessment ratio of 1.00, which means 100 percent of the market value of property is subject to tax. Other states, such as Georgia, use an assessment ratio of 0.40, which means that only 40 percent of the market value of property is subject to tax.) Furthermore, some jurisdictions exempt certain amounts of a property's assessed value to provide tax relief for certain types of property owners (full-time residents, disabled persons, the elderly, etc.). These **exemptions** effectively shift some of the tax burden away from the properties that qualify for the special treatment toward properties that do not qualify. Subtracting the amounts of exemptions from assessed value gives the property's **taxable value.**

To see how property taxes are calculated, consider a property with a market value of $120,000 in a jurisdiction that applies an assessment ratio of 40 percent. For this property, the assessed value is $48,000 ($120,000 × 0.40 = $48,000). Suppose the property qualifies for a tax exemption of $2,500 because it is the owner's homestead. The taxable value of this property is thus $45,500 ($48,000 − $2,500

= \$45,500). If the tax rate in this jurisdiction is 25 mills (or 2.5 percent), then the property tax amount is \$1,137.50 ($45,500 \div 1,000 \times 25 = \$1,137.50$).

The following framework shows how the property tax bill for this property is calculated:

Market Value	\$120,000
multiplied by Assessment Ratio	× 0.40
equals Assessed Value	\$48,000
minus Exemptions (if any)	\$ −2,500
equals Taxable Value	\$45,500
divided by 1,000	÷ 1,000
multiplied by Millage Rate	× 25
equals Property Tax	\$1,137.50

Administering the Property Tax

From the government's perspective, the steps involved in administering the property tax are

1. property value assessment,
2. development of the budget and tax rate, and
3. tax billing and collection.

Property Value Assessment

The first step in the property taxation process is to estimate the market value for all properties within the jurisdiction, a process known as **assessment.** The government official responsible for doing so, usually called the *assessor, property assessor,* or *property appraiser,* must identify, list, and value all taxable properties in the jurisdiction. An efficient assessor maintains a complete set of maps that show each parcel of real estate and its features, as well as a system of continuing inspection of deeds and building permits in order to keep up with new construction and changes in property ownership.

After all properties have been identified, the assessor must accomplish the most difficult part of the job, that of estimating the market value of the properties within the jurisdiction. Many states use mass appraisal techniques, or statistical models, to assess the value of all properties in a jurisdiction each year. After estimating the property's market value and applying the assessment ratio and any exemptions, the assessor arrives at the property's taxable value. This value is subject to review, and the results of the review process may be appealed by the taxpayer before an appeal board or court.

Development of a Budget and Tax Rate

The next step in the property taxation process is the development of a budget and tax rate by the city council, the county commission, or other government body. The amount of revenue coming from other taxes and from nontax sources is subtracted from the total budget; the remainder must be collected in property taxes.

This amount then is divided by the total of the taxable values of all properties in the jurisdiction to determine the tax rate.

For example, suppose that the local government needs to raise $10 million in property taxes, and the total taxable value of all properties in the jurisdiction, known as the *tax digest,* is $500 million. The tax rate needed to raise these revenues is $10,000,000 ÷ $500,000,000 = 0.02.

The tax rate usually is expressed as the rate per thousand dollars of assessed value—the millage rate, where one mill equals $0.001, or 1/1,000 of $1. In the example above, 20 mills equal $20 tax per $1,000 of assessed valuation, or 2 percent.

As a matter of practice, of course, the local governing body does not merely decide what it would like to spend and then set a corresponding tax rate. It may feel constrained not to raise the present tax rate at all, to raise it only slightly, or even to lower it. In many areas, tax rate adjustments require a vote on the issue by the people in the jurisdiction.

After the tax rate is set, the taxable values are multiplied by the tax rate to obtain individual tax bills. If a house in our hypothetical locality has a taxable value of $50,000, for example, the property tax would be $1,000 (20 mills × $50,000).

Tax Billing and Collection

Tax billing and collection procedures vary widely among the states. In some, property tax bills are payable annually; in others, taxes are payable semiannually or quarterly. Some states have special taxing districts that send their tax bills at different times of the year.

If property taxes are not paid when due, the government to which the taxes are owed can place a lien on the real estate for the unpaid taxes, plus a penalty and interest. If the taxes remain unpaid for a certain period of time, which varies from state to state, the property may ultimately be sold at public auction to satisfy the tax lien. In essence, the tax sale is similar to a foreclosure sale that follows default on either a mortgage or a mechanic's lien. The Real Estate Legal Highlight on pages 75–76 demonstrates how one state (Florida) enforces property tax payments through the use of "delinquent tax certificates."

▌ POWER OF EMINENT DOMAIN

Under the power of **eminent domain,** a government can acquire property for a public use, even if the owner doesn't want to sell, as long as the owner receives **just compensation.** This power comes from the Fifth Amendment to the U.S. Constitution, which, among other things, states that property shall not be taken from any person for public uses without the payment of just compensation. Although this provision applies specifically to the federal government, it has been extended to the states through the due process clause of the Constitution's Fourteenth Amendment. In addition, state constitutions have similar provisions.

In an eminent domain proceeding, also known as a *condemnation proceeding,* the government must establish that the land is needed for a public use or benefit and that the amount of money offered to the landowner is the reasonable value of the land

Mechanics of the Property Tax Certificate Market in Florida

 This Legal Highlight describes how property taxes in Florida are collected from delinquent property owners. In essence, the state's laws allow counties to auction off any unpaid tax bill to the highest bidder. The highest bidder (usually an investment group formed for just this purpose) pays the taxes on behalf of the property owner in exchange for a "tax certificate" that represents a lien against the property and entitles the holder to receive interest on the amount paid on the owner's behalf. If the interest and taxes are not repaid to the certificate holder within two years, the holder can force the sale of the property at public auction to recover the investment and interest due. The details of this process are described below.

Under Chapter 197 of the Florida Statutes, all property taxes represent a first lien, superior to all other liens, as of January 1 of each year. Taxes are due and payable in November of the same year and are considered delinquent if unpaid on April 1 of the following year. After proper notice is provided by mail to the property owner and any lienholder of record who has previously requested notification, the tax collector is required to advertise a public sale of tax certificates on all properties in the county with delinquent taxes. This advertisement must appear in a locally circulated newspaper within 45 days of April 1 and must list each parcel for which taxes are delinquent, including owner's name, delinquent tax amount, and a property identification number. The sale is scheduled to begin on or about June 1. Prior to the sale, a property owner can preempt the sale of the certificate for the property by paying all taxes due plus 18 percent annual interest to date and proportional share of any advertising costs.

On the day advertised, the tax collector begins the sale of certificates in the order listed in the advertisement and continues day to day until each certificate is sold. Rather than bidding a dollar amount, bidders bid the interest rate they are willing to accept in exchange for paying the property taxes for the property owner. Bids start at 18 percent and go down in ¼-point increments until a low bid is determined. In the event no bidder bids on a certificate, the certificate is issued to the county with an interest rate of 18 percent. Certificates are fully transferable on payment of a nominal fee to the tax collector. In 2000, more than 21,000 such certificates were sold to investors in Palm Beach County, Florida, for a total of more than $41 million. The average interest rate on these certificates was 12.68 percent. After the sale, a property owner can redeem the certificate by paying the taxes and interest due to the tax collector. The tax collector then cancels the certificate and remits the funds to the certificate holder. If the certificate is not redeemed within two years of issuance, the holder may apply for a tax deed to be issued by the Clerk of the Circuit Court. The tax deed applicant must pay for a title search and must pay the amount required for redemption of all other outstanding tax certificates, interest, omitted taxes, and current taxes. A completed application forces the sale of the property at public auction.

At the tax deed auction, the Clerk of the Circuit Court issues a tax deed to the highest bidder. The opening bid must cover all the costs paid by the tax deed applicant plus all other costs for conducting the sale. If the property involved is a homestead property (the permanent residence of a full-time Florida citizen), the minimum bid at the tax deed auction is increased by one half of the assessed value of the property.

(continued)

REAL ESTATE TODAY

LEGAL HIGHLIGHT

Mechanics of the Property Tax Certificate Market in Florida

Anyone may bid at the tax deed auction, including the property owner and the tax deed applicant. The proceeds from the sale are used to repay the tax certificate holder, with any excess proceeds being returned to the property owner. The title granted to the winning bidder at a tax deed auction is subject only to other government liens, easements, and usual restrictions and covenants. In particular, no liens for a private debt (including mortgages) survive a tax deed sale. The winning bidder is entitled to immediate possession of the property.

being taken. The concept of public use is quite broad, going beyond the taking of land for public facilities such as roads and schools. It has been extended to include the condemnation of private land for resale to other private individuals or firms for urban renewal, as well as the enforced breakup of old Hawaiian estates to extend land ownership more widely. The concept also has been extended to include quasi-public organizations such as utility companies, railroads, and pipelines.

In the past, most of the controversy surrounding the taking of private property by condemnation has centered on the question whether compensation was adequate. If the condemning authority and the owner fail to agree on the property's value, the owner can request a trial to determine the amount of just compensation.

Inverse condemnation occurs when a property owner, seeking to force the purchase of the property, starts condemnation proceedings against the government, contending that a government action has destroyed or reduced the value of the property to such an extent that the government has effectively taken the property away from the owner. For example, suppose a highway department announces plans for a new road but delays purchasing the necessary rights-of-way. A property owner in the path of the proposed road could sue to force the highway department to purchase the land, contending that the announced plans have made it impossible to sell the land for private purposes. Or a property owner near an airport might bring legal action to force a condemnation and collect payment for damages caused by the noise of low-flying aircraft.

POLICE POWER

Under **police power,** governments have the power of regulation, which gives them the ability to protect the public health, safety, morals, and general welfare. In addition to obvious actions such as protecting against crime and health hazards, governments have also relied on these police powers to enact a variety of controls over the way landowners can use their properties.

What Constitutes "Public Use"?

 As governments have moved beyond their traditional use of the power of eminent domain to acquire land for public projects such as schools and roads to include objectives such as economic development, an extended controversy has arisen as to what constitutes "public use."

In 1946, the United States Congress established a District of Columbia Redevelopment Land Agency to redevelop blighted areas of the city. The agency began to acquire land within the designated area, including a department store owned by Berman. Berman sued, contending that condemning his property for redevelopment was not a "public use." The U.S. Supreme Court disagreed, ruling that economic redevelopment of blighted areas was a legitimate use of the power of eminent domain. [*Berman v. Parker,* 348 US 26, (1954)]

While the concept of governments acquiring property in blighted areas for redevelopment has been generally accepted, what about taking nonblighted properties to transfer land from one property owner to another to further economic development? In the early 1990s the City of Detroit took about 1,000 homes and 600 businesses in the Poletown neighborhood to make room for a General Motors plant. Although this project was bitterly contested, it was upheld in the courts. More recently, however, Wayne County, Michigan, desired to construct a business and technology park near the Detroit airport to spur economic development. It acquired all but 40 acres of the 1,300 acre site, and it sought to condemn the remainder under eminent domain. One of these

property owners was Edward Hathcock, who owned a 12-employee millwork and kitchen cabinet factory that sat in the middle of the proposed project. Although the county offered him $360,000 for the one-acre site, he declined to sell, saying that it would cost him far more to relocate. He fought the taking, contending that taking private property in order to turn it over to other private interests was not a "public use." The Michigan Supreme Court agreed, overturning the Poletown decision, and rejecting the principle that "a private entity's pursuit of profit was a 'public use' for constitutional taking proposed simply because one entity's profit maximization contributed to the health of the general economy." [*County of Wayne v. Edward Hathcock,* 684 MW2d 765, Michigan Supreme Court, (2004)]

This issue came to the U.S. Supreme Court when New London, Connecticut, attempted to take Susette Kelo's house in the Fort Trumbull neighborhood as part of a plan to redevelop some 90 acres containing 115 properties. All but 15 owners agreed to sell, and the city condemned the other homes, including Kelo's. She challenged the taking, and the case went to the U.S. Supreme Court. In a 5-4 decision, the Court ruled for the City, holding that economic development fits within the definition of public use, and thus justifies the condemnation of private property. [*Kelo v. the City of New London,* 545 US 469 (2005)]

The Kelo decision sparked a virtual firestorm of adverse public opinion, and, subsequently, a majority of state legislatures have passed laws restricting the use of eminent domain for development purposes. This is an issue that will be a lively one for many years to come.

REAL ESTATE TODAY

LEGAL HIGHLIGHT

Inverse Condemnation

The Thomas A. McElwee & Sons printing company had been located on Philadelphia's Market Street since 1954. In 2000 the Southeastern Pennsylvania Transportation Authority (SEPTA) began construction of a new rail line in the area. The Authority's vehicles and construction debris blocked McElwee's driveway so it could not be used either to receive shipments or to send out deliveries. Trucks had to park some distance away, greatly reducing productivity. Then, in September 2002 the block in which the firm was located was closed during business hours for nine months. This effectively shut down any walk-in traffic, which had constituted over 20 percent of their business. Finally, in May 2005 McElwee gave up and closed the business, with $20,000 in unpaid bills.

Thereafter, McElwee sued SEPTA in inverse condemnation, claiming a de facto taking of their business. They claimed that blocking their driveway and closing the street during business hours reduced their productivity and ability to attract business and caused severe financial harm to the business. The Pennsylvania Commonwealth Court agreed, ruling that McElwee was entitled to compensation.

The court said that a de facto taking occurs when an entity having the power of eminent domain essentially deprives the owner of a property of "beneficial use" and enjoyment of his property. This, the court said, included reasonable access to the property. In this case there was extremely limited access to the firm's driveway for the three-year construction period, and virtually no access for the time when the Authority closed the street during business hours. Extreme deprivation of use for such a lengthy period constituted more than a "temporary inconvenience" and, in fact, constituted a taking of the business for which compensation from SEPTA was required.

[*Thomas A. McElwee v. Southeastern Pennsylvania Transportation Authority*, Commonwealth Court of Pennsylvania, 2006]

The use of a particular parcel of land is affected greatly by other nearby land uses and depends heavily on public investments and the economic vitality of the surrounding neighborhood and community. It is this interdependence of land uses that creates the need for public land-use controls. Generally speaking, the use of land affects the owners of other nearby properties more than the use of any other type of private property. Conversely, financial returns for the real estate developer or investor may be greatly affected by the land uses that are permitted by governments or by the allowable intensity of land use. Consequently, the issue of public land-use controls is of vital importance to all who are concerned with real property.

The concept of planning and control of land use is not new. In fact, in this country, it dates back to the colonial era. Many early American cities were carefully planned and developed under a variety of land-use controls. One of the early controls still valid today is the English common-law concept of nuisance law, laws relating to the use of property in such a way as to harm the property of others. Most of the prohibited land uses were hazardous or noxious practices, such as the operation of a slaughterhouse or the manufacture of bricks near a residential area. In these cases, the offending activity might be declared a nuisance. The injured parties could seek an injunction to force the polluter to stop the offending activity, or they could seek monetary damages.

Nuisance laws provided some relief to individual property owners from the worst types of injurious land uses, but they were not well suited for public land-use control because a substantial injury had to be proved before any relief could be given. As the United States rapidly urbanized around the turn of the century, municipalities increasingly turned to police power controls to regulate land uses. Most cities have found that a comprehensive general plan is necessary to effectively implement land-use controls.

THE COMPREHENSIVE GENERAL PLAN

To ensure that urban areas develop in an orderly fashion, most local governments have formulated and adopted a **comprehensive general plan** that serves as a statement of policies for the future development of the community. These policies provide a basis for the land-use control methods employed by the municipality. The policies should reflect a long-range plan that examines closely the community's predicted physical needs for 15 to 25 years in the future. It usually contains the following elements:

- An analysis of projected economic development and population change
- A transportation plan to provide for necessary circulation
- A public-facilities plan that identifies such needed facilities as schools, parks, civic centers, and water and sewage-disposal plants
- A land-use plan
- An official map

The comprehensive plan may also include other elements such as housing, redevelopment, and historic preservation. It should not be a static document but must be revised continually as conditions change.

Implementing the Comprehensive Plan

The comprehensive plan and its land-use component are implemented through several tools of land-use control. The most prominent of these is comprehensive zoning, but they also include building codes, mandatory dedication, impact fees, zoning for planned unit development, performance or impact zoning, incentive zoning, and transfer of development rights. We will consider each of these methods in turn.

ZONING

Zoning refers to the process of dividing a community's land into districts in which only certain uses of the land are allowed. For example, an area might be zoned to allow only single-family residences on lots of at least one-half acre in size, another area might be zoned to allow only commercial uses, and yet another area might allow only industrial uses of the land. The first comprehensive zoning ordinance was passed in New York City in 1916 to restrict the use and height of buildings in various districts of Manhattan. Zoning gained increasing acceptance during the 1920s, and after the constitutionality of the concept was upheld in 1926, zoning ordinances and related land-use controls were adopted in most urban areas and many rural communities of the United States.

Type of Use

The three main kinds of zoning districts classified by use are residential, commercial, and industrial. Each such district usually is divided into several subcategories. For example, there generally are several single-family districts with varying minimum sizes of lot and house. Other residential districts may permit multifamily housing. Similarly, commercial and industrial districts usually are subcategorized as neighborhood shopping districts, highway commercial districts, light industrial districts, and so on. Most zoning ordinances contain, in addition to the three main categories, such special-purpose districts as agricultural, floodplain, and historic preservation.

Intensity of Use

Within each zone, governments may specify the **intensity of use,** or the extent to which land in the zone may be used for its permitted purposes. The government can regulate intensity of use, also known as *developmental density,* in several ways, including placing restrictions on building height and bulk, specifying **minimum lot sizes,** and establishing **setback requirements.**

Height and Bulk Limitations

Height limitations regulate the maximum height of buildings in feet or stories. **Bulk limitations** control the percentage of the lot area that may be occupied by buildings. Both serve to control the volume of a structure on the land and, therefore, the intensity of use.

Floor-Area Ratio

Another measure by which building volume may be controlled is the **floor-area ratio** (FAR). The FAR is the relationship between the total floor area of a building and the total land area of the site. For example, an allowable ratio of 4 to 1 would permit a 4-story building to occupy the entire area of its lot; an 8-story building

FIGURE 4.1 │ Examples of Floor-Area Ratios

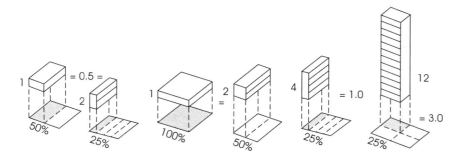

would be permitted to occupy only half of the site's surface area; while a 16-story building could occupy only one-fourth of the land area. Other FARs are illustrated in Figure 4.1.

Minimum Lot Size and Setback Requirements

The most common method of regulating development density is through provisions for a minimum lot size. Relatively large lots may be necessary for public health reasons if public sewer and water systems are not provided. However, requirements of very large minimum lot sizes may run into court challenges on the basis that they deprive the owner of reasonable use or are designed to exclude various groups.

Zoning ordinances generally provide for setback of buildings from the street and minimum size of side yards in residential districts. Such restrictions also may be applied to commercial and industrial districts, but this is less common.

Some Innovative Zoning Issues

Traditional zoning has been criticized for being inefficient, for being subject to poor administration and even corruption, and for having little relationship to planning goals. Some attack it for its flexibility, charging that true separation of uses seldom is achieved because zoning boards submit to developer pressure to grant extensive rezonings. Others attack zoning for its rigidity, charging that its inflexible requirements stifle good design and foster inefficiency and rising costs. A few have come to the conclusion that zoning controls should be abolished, while others have attempted to improve the zoning process. The latter movement has led to some innovative techniques, including zoning for planned unit development, performance or impact zoning, incentive zoning, and transferable development rights.

Planned Unit Development

Zoning for **planned unit developments** (PUDs) can avoid some of the failings of traditional zoning practices. Generally, many bulk and use regulations may be waived to permit greater flexibility of design. For example, lot sizes may be reduced to permit greater densities, and setback and side-yard requirements may be waived to permit attached housing. Convenience shopping also may be permitted within the development. In return, the community should receive the advantages of preservation of natural features, community recreation and open space, greater housing choice, safer streets and pedestrian ways, reduced need for automobile travel, and lower costs.

Performance Zoning

Performance zoning, often known as **impact zoning,** is a technique to relate permitted uses of land to certain performance standards, usually to protect the environment. Such performance standards, particularly industrial-use standards related to noise, smoke, smell, and the like, sometimes are quite detailed.

Adoption of performance zoning generally results in simplified land-use controls. The performance standards relate land-use demands to land-use capacity, and they can be used to achieve better design and to reduce the cost of regulation as well as to protect the environment. The standards used are often related to density; open-space ratio; impervious-surface ratio (surface-water runoff); and the number of vehicle trips generated by the site.

During the past several decades, a number of municipalities in Bucks County, Pennsylvania, have adopted performance zoning ordinances that reduce the number of residential zoning districts to only one or two. A variety of housing densities is possible, however, because the number of units permitted is related to the environmental carrying capacity of each site. Although at first glance these rules seem somewhat complex, developers generally have favored the innovation because the performance standards are not subject to varying administrative interpretation and permit much greater variety in design.

Breckenridge, Colorado, has abolished zoning altogether and regulates all development through a comprehensive permit system based on performance standards. A small Victorian-era mining community in the Rocky Mountains, Breckenridge has become a major ski area in recent years, with attendant development pressure. The performance standards establish architectural guidelines to ensure that new development is compatible with the existing Victorian character of the town, prohibit certain features in a development and require others, and assign positive or negative scores for other features related to environmental impact. The development must achieve a total score of zero or better to receive a permit, but it can receive significant density bonuses if it achieves higher scores. As in Bucks County, developers generally have been pleased with the permit system because its structured nature reduces uncertainty and processing time.

Performance zoning also can aid redevelopment of an area. For example, South Pointe, a deteriorated, 250-acre, multifamily residential district on the southern tip of Miami Beach, was originally platted in small, 50-by-100-foot lots sold to individual buyers in the 1920s. Attempts to redevelop the area had met with little success until a new performance zoning ordinance was enacted that increased the minimum lot size and minimum width of lots, required 60 percent to 70 percent open space, yet increased the allowable FAR. These changes have encouraged the aggregation of the small lots and have led to substantial development.

Incentive Zoning

Closely related to performance zoning is **incentive zoning,** which encourages developers to provide certain publicly desired features in return for various incentives. For example, the San Francisco City Planning Code permits increased floor area if the developer provides a pedestrian plaza or arcade, and New York City has provided similar incentives. Other communities permit higher densities for residential developments that provide such features as open space.

Transferable Development Rights

Another creative technique of land-use regulation that has received increasing attention involves **transferable development rights.** Under a transfer system, in order to develop their property, landowners can sell part of their bundle of rights to other landowners, who then can use their own land more intensively. For example, suppose that Mrs. Johnson owns a ten-acre wooded tract that she wishes to preserve as it is. Nearby, Mr. Hite owns another ten-acre tract that he wishes to develop. Existing regulations require minimum one-acre lots in the area, so Mr. Hite could build only ten houses on his land. Mrs. Johnson, having no interest in developing her property, could sell her development rights to Mr. Hite, who then could build 20 houses on his ten acres, while Mrs. Johnson's land remained in its wooded state. Proponents of this system contend that it is more equitable than one that does not permit such transferable development rights; it enables communities to preserve floodplains, open space, and historic structures without wiping out their property values because development rights can be sold to other property owners.

The use of transferable development rights still is limited but is growing in application. Several communities in New Jersey and California are experimenting with the system in their efforts to preserve open space. A number of cities, including New York, Chicago, Denver, and Washington, are using the transfer mechanism as a means to preserve historic landmarks. FARs on such properties can be transferred to other properties to allow denser development on those sites. For example, Tiffany sold development rights over its Fifth Avenue building to Donald Trump to enable him to add more space to his Trump Tower development.

Zoning Changes

For various reasons, a property owner may seek a change in zoning or relief from some provision of the zoning ordinance. This can be accomplished through legislative, administrative, or judicial means.

Legislative Relief

If a property owner seeks a change in the property's use, he or she can request a change in zoning use classification from the local zoning authority, usually the city council or county commission. Zoning amendments generally require review by a

---

REAL ESTATE TODAY

CLOSE-UP

The Smart Growth Controversy

 Smart Growth . . . Sprawl . . . New Urbanism . . . Property Rights . . . Housing Density . . . Light Rail. These are some of the bywords tossed around in the "Smart Growth" controversy, perhaps the most contentious issue in land use today.

In earlier years, American cities were mostly pedestrian oriented, with relatively high population densities. They were limited in geographic reach to the footpower of people or horses. Then in the early years of the past century the trolley and other public transportation enabled cities to spread out, and the age of the streetcar suburb arrived. With the coming of the automobile age, this trend toward decentralization and lower-density development speeded up. Within the past few decades it has accelerated at an ever-increasing pace, leading to the cries of "Sprawl!" The question: Is sprawl an evil, or is sprawl the inevitable result of an expanding population and an essential element in "the American Dream"?

Sprawl has been blamed for a multitude of problems: traffic congestion, diminished air quality, loss of farmland, urban decay, increased cost of public infrastructure, loss of neighborliness—even the obesity crisis. The prescription according to "smart growth" advocates is to increase urban densities, restrict rural development through the imposition of urban growth boundaries, and limit road improvements in favor of public transportation, particularly light rail.

Although some elements in the smart growth agenda are widely supported, particularly redeveloping inner-core urban areas and developing infill sites, reusing "brownfields," preserving open space and farmland, and encouraging new forms of "new urbanist" design, increasingly the smart growth advocates have been defending themselves against accusations that it is an elitist, anti-opportunity movement that raises housing prices, destroys property rights, and deprives low-income households of an opportunity to pursue the American dream of home ownership. The opponents also point out that despite the claims of the smart growth advocates, such policies increase traffic congestion and air pollution. Spending on light rail transit is attacked as wasteful and inefficient.

In a practical sense, however, the smart growth movement has little power to reshape America's urban landscape in any significant way. The biggest factor influencing future land-use decisions is the nation's need to accommodate a projected 23 percent increase in population by 2020—some 64 million people. Thus, continued dispersal of the urban population appears inevitable, particularly given people's demonstrated preference for the suburban lifestyle.

Portland: The Smart Growth City

Nowhere has the smart growth model been embraced more fully than in the Portland, Oregon, metropolitan region. In 1992 Portland area voters created Metro, a "supergovernment" regional planning authority with vast powers over land use and transportation planning in three counties and 24 cities. An urban growth boundary was established that encloses 365 square miles. This boundary is not just symbolic. Growth outside the boundary is virtually nonexistent. It is common to observe high-density development on one side of a road that marks the urban growth boundary, while on the other side land use is limited to agriculture.

(continued)

REAL ESTATE TODAY

CLOSE-UP

The Smart Growth Controversy

Although Metro estimates that Portland's population will increase by 80 percent by 2040, the planned expansion of the urban growth boundary is only 6 percent. Thus, to accommodate the population increase localities within the region have been assigned mandatory population targets requiring high-density, mixed-use developments. The impact on housing costs is predictable. With restricted supply the price has increased greatly, making Portland one of the least affordable cities for home ownership in the United States.

Portland is attempting to accommodate the increasing need for transportation through the development of a 125-mile light rail network, while limiting road improvements. More than half the region's transportation dollars are being spent on this network, even though public transit accounts for only 1 percent of travel. Traffic congestion is predicted to quadruple by 2020, which Metro says will increase smog by 10 percent.

So, does Portland's "smart growth" model produce a more livable city, as its proponents claim, or is it a planning disaster, as its opponents claim? The jury is still out, but obviously "smart growth" in Portland is not producing an urban utopia.

planning commission, an advertised public hearing, and some type of justification from the applicant demonstrating that changed conditions justify the zoning change. Because zoning changes often are quite controversial, so are the hearings, with spirited and sometimes acrimonious public debate.

Administrative Relief

If a property owner seeks a relatively minor change, it sometimes can be accomplished administratively through a variance or special-use permit granted by a board of adjustments, a zoning appeals board, or some similar body. A **zoning variance** permits use to deviate slightly from a strict interpretation of the zoning ordinance to avoid placing undue hardship on an owner. For example, for a house to be constructed on an oddly shaped lot, some relief from minimum side-yard requirements may be needed.

Zoning ordinances often permit special uses within certain districts if certain conditions are met. For example, a public utility substation, church, school, or recreational facility may be permitted in a residential district if the board determines that the required conditions have been satisfied.

Variances and special-use permits can make a zoning ordinance much more reasonable and less burdensome to property owners. If not carefully controlled, however, these permits also can completely undermine the community's land-use planning efforts. Variances that change the essential character of land use within a

The Strange Case of the Incredible Shrinking Building

In New York City, developer Laurence Ginsberg applied for a building permit to construct a 31-story apartment building on Park Avenue at 96th Street. The city had established a special zoning district 150 feet on each side of Park Avenue that limited new buildings to 210 feet (18 floors), but Ginsberg based his application on a zoning map that erroneously showed the special district to extend only 100 feet from Park Avenue. He received the building permit and began construction. Later, however, the city discovered the error, canceled the permit, and issued a stop-work order on the top 12 floors. Ginsberg appealed the order and kept on building—all the way to the 31st floor. New York's highest court turned down Ginsberg's appeal, ruling that "reasonable diligence would have readily uncovered for a good-faith inquirer the existence of the unequivocal limitations of 150 feet in the original binding metes and bounds description of the enabling legislation, and that this boundary has never been changed by the [City]." The court ordered the top 12 floors removed. Ginsberg then applied, after the fact, to the city for a variance for the additional height, but this was also denied.

Finally, eight years after construction began, a 7,000-pound, hammer-wielding robot began pounding away, reducing the 31-story apartment building to 18 stories, at an estimated cost of $1 million. The developer's total losses were approximately $14 million.

[*Parkview Associates v. City of New York*, 519 N.E.2d 1372]

district often are granted with little justification. The powers of the board must be spelled out carefully to prevent such happenings.

Judicial Relief

If property owners are unhappy because the legislative or administrative relief they sought is not granted, they may appeal to the courts. An appeal is based on a contention that the zoning regulations are in some way unconstitutional or that owners were deprived of the property without due process of law because a decision was arbitrary, unreasonable, or capricious. Even with the increased aggressiveness of the judicial branch, courts are generally reluctant to substitute their judgment for that of legislative bodies, and zoning ordinances usually are upheld unless they involve clear abuses of power or are unduly restrictive.

Zoning restrictions are of great importance to real estate developers. Those who disregard them do so at their peril, as the developer in the Legal Highlight shown above found to his chagrin and financial loss.

The Case of the Costly Permit

 In 1990, the Boynton Beach, Florida, building code inspector observed Mr. Andre St. Juste performing extensive repairs to the roof of a residential rental house he owned. The inspector ordered Mr. St. Juste to stop work until he obtained a permit, and later sent him an official notice that he was violating city codes.

Mr. St. Juste ignored the notice, and several weeks later the Code Enforcement Board began fining him $200 per day. Four months later St. Juste finally applied for a building permit, but when he told the building department that the repairs would cost only $21.80, they told him he didn't need a permit because the repairs cost less than $500.

When the code inspectors learned that the repairs would actually cover more than 25 percent of the roof and cost more than $500, they again ordered St. Juste to get a permit. Again, he ignored them.

In 1992, the city made Mr. St. Juste an offer: get a permit, fix the roof, and ask the Code Enforcement Board to reduce the fines. He refused.

In 1994, the circuit court ruled that the city had made every effort to help Mr. St. Juste pass the building code, and that he owed $316,000 in fines and $20,000 in court costs. St. Juste attempted to declare bankruptcy to avoid the fines, but the judge refused to approve the bankruptcy.

Finally, in 1995 the city commissioners voted unanimously to auction off the St. Juste house to pay the fines. It was sold on the courthouse steps.

Nonconforming Uses

A **nonconforming use** is a continuing use that was legal before a zoning ordinance was passed but that no longer complies with the current zoning regulation. Such a use generally is allowed to continue for some period of time unless the nonconforming structure is substantially destroyed or abandoned. Regulations concerning nonconforming use usually do not permit the existing structure to be enlarged or substantially changed in use. They also may require that the nonconforming use be discontinued after a stated period of time, a process that is known as *amortization*. Most amortization periods for buildings are relatively long, perhaps 50 years. Most controversy has centered around more minor uses, such as nonconforming signs and billboards.

Although the courts have not been unanimous in their approval of the amortization concept, most have regarded relatively long phase-out periods, such as three to seven years, as reasonable compensation for nonconforming signs.

Building Codes

Another tool used in implementing a comprehensive land-use plan is the set of ordinances known as **building codes.** Such codes establish detailed standards for the construction of new buildings and the alteration of existing ones. Their primary purpose is to protect health and provide safety, and they are related primarily to fire prevention, quality and safety of construction, and public health safeguards.

Building codes also may be used to promote energy conservation and other public purposes. A building permit is required before construction can begin. This procedure enables local officials to ascertain that the site plan has been approved and the proposed construction complies with applicable building codes, zoning regulations, and subdivision regulations.

Subdivision Regulations

Subdivision regulations, another tool for implementing the community planning process, establish the standards and procedures for regulating the subdivision of land for development and sale. Their purpose is to protect both the community and future residents from poorly planned and executed developments.

The local planning board or another planning agency determines the standards that must be met for subdivision approval. Standards are provided for the design and construction of new streets, utilities, and drainage systems. The planning board also establishes an approval procedure, usually consisting of three distinct steps: a preapplication conference, approval of the preliminary plat, and approval of the final plat.

Preapplication Conference

The purpose of the preapplication conference is to allow the developer to meet informally with the planning board before going to the expense of preparing a formal plat. Working with a sketch plan, the planning staff can review the proposal with the developer and make suggestions for changes that may be necessary to meet the subdivision regulations. The developer also may benefit from general planning efforts of the board that may affect the development.

Approval of the Preliminary Plat

The next step is for the developer to prepare and submit a preliminary plat of the subdivision for approval. The term *preliminary plat* is misleading because all construction and mapping of the lots will be done on the basis of this plat. Detailed information is required, therefore, usually including topographic data regarding existing boundary lines, utilities, and ground elevations. Also required is the layout of the proposed subdivision, including streets, other rights-of-way or easements, lot lines and numbers, sites of special uses, and minimum building setback lines. A preliminary plat is shown in Figure 4.2.

Approval of the Final Plat

After receiving approval of the preliminary plat, the developer can stake the lots and construct streets and other required improvements. After these tasks are completed, or with the posting of a certified check or bond to guarantee completion, the developer can prepare a final plat and related documents.

FIGURE 4.2 | A Preliminary Plat

The Preliminary Plat Shall Show:

Name, location, owner, and designer

Date, north point, and graphic scale

Location of property lines, roads, existing utilities, etc.

Present zoning classification

Names of adjoining properties

Proposed utility system

Names of new streets

Dimensions, lot lines, and building setbacks

Location of proposed culverts

Contours at 5' intervals

Acreage of land subdivided

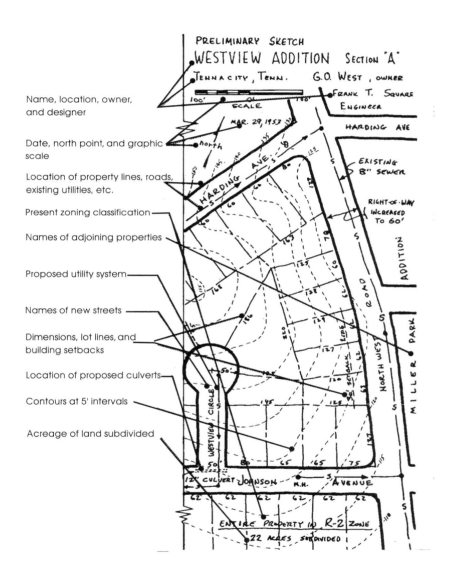

The final plat is intended to be filed in the registry of deeds and must contain all information necessary for land titles, such as exact lot lines, street rights-of-way, utility easements, and surveying monuments. A final plat is shown in Figure 4.3. The required accompanying documents usually include a certification by a licensed engineer or surveyor regarding the accuracy of the details of the plat, plans concerning utility improvements within the subdivision, and certification that the improvements have been constructed in accordance with the approved plans.

After approval by the planning board, the final plat will be recorded, and the developer then will be permitted to sell the lots in the subdivision.

Mandatory Dedication

Another method used to shape city growth is referred to as **mandatory dedication.** To obtain approval for a project, the developer often is required to dedicate parts of the property to such public purposes as rights-of-way for streets, utilities, and drainage. In some communities, developers also may be required to dedicate land for parks, open space, and schools. If the development is small, payments in lieu of dedication sometimes are required.

The mandatory dedication of land for parks and schools understandably is controversial. One view is that the need for such facilities is created by the new subdivision, while the opposing view holds that parks and schools are a general government responsibility that should be borne by the public at large. The courts are divided on the issue as well. In some cases they have upheld mandatory dedication of land for such purposes, and in other cases they have held that the denial of the right to subdivide land on the condition that the developer donate land for parks and schools is a violation of due process. In some jurisdictions, the developer is required to reserve the land for only a stated period of time, during which the municipality may purchase the property. If the land has not been purchased by the end of the period, the developer no longer is bound by the reservation.

Impact Fees

In addition to mandatory dedications, a community may also enact **impact fees** on new development to help raise the funds necessary for the expansion of public facilities. These fees are specific assessments on development; for example, $2,500 per dwelling unit or $2,000 for each 1,000 square feet of new commercial or office space. As might be expected, these fees are quite controversial, but their use by local governments is spreading rapidly.

Recent court decisions and legislation in many states have made it a necessity for governments that impose impact fees to tie them directly to the need created by the development. Otherwise, the fees may be regarded as extortion.

FIGURE 4.3 | A Final Plat

The Final Plat Shall Show:

Streets, lots, setback lines, lot numbers, and so on

Sufficient engineering data to reproduce any line on the ground

Dimensions, angles, and bearings

Monuments

Name of adjoining properties

Date, title, name, and location of subdivision

Graphic scale and true north point

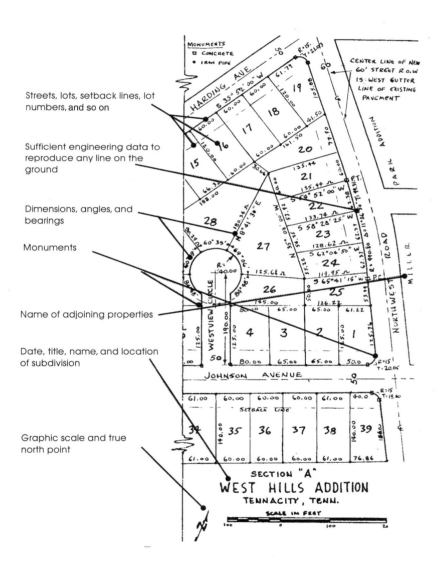

REAL ESTATE TODAY

LEGAL HIGHLIGHT

The Takings Issue

 Land-use regulations under the police power can have a great impact on the value of private property. The question as to how far these regulations can go in controlling the use of land is a very contentious one, an issue that has been fought in both legislatures and the courts.

Although the general rule is that actual or potential losses resulting from police power regulations do not require compensation, the U.S. Supreme Court has ruled that if a restriction goes "too far," it will be considered a taking. Unfortunately, in many cases the court has provided little guidance as to how far is "too far."

The Euclid Decision

Sometimes, the U.S. Supreme Court issues a decision that is truly momentous to a particular issue. *Village of Euclid v. Ambler Realty Company* (1926) was such a case, upholding the constitutionality of comprehensive zoning regulations.

Euclid, a suburb of Cleveland, adopted a comprehensive zoning ordinance in 1922. The Ambler Realty Company owned a 68-acre tract of land that it hoped to sell for industrial development. Because industrial use was precluded by the ordinance, which zoned part of the tract for single-family residential use only, Ambler Realty attacked the ordinance on the ground that it was a taking of the company's property without compensation. The district court agreed and declared the ordinance null and void.

The village appealed to the U.S. Supreme Court, which reversed the lower court by a five-to-four decision. The victory was a narrow one, with one justice changing his mind in favor of upholding the ordinance after an opinion striking down the

principle of zoning had been written but not made public. In its final decision, the court ruled that the community was not taking or destroying Ambler Realty's property for public use but was invoking a general power over private property, which was necessary for the orderly development of the community.

For better or worse, the Euclid decision changed the course of urban development in the United States. The zoning ordinances of more than 400 municipalities were upheld, and hundreds of others were soon passed. Now, almost every city with a population over 10,000 has enacted a comprehensive zoning ordinance, as have many smaller municipalities and counties. It is interesting to speculate what might have happened to the course of urban development in the United States if the one justice had not changed his vote. [*Village of Euclid v. Ambler Realty*, 272 US 365 (1926)]

Can Regulation Constitute a Taking?

In 1922 the Supreme Court ruled that a Pennsylvania law regulating the mining of coal went "too far" because it mandated that pillars of coal be left to support the ground above, and constituted a taking of the mining company's property. This has led to a series of decisions over the years attempting to define just how far is "too far."

[*Pennsylvania Coal Company v. Mahon*, 260 US 393 (1922)]

Physical Invasion

Compensation is required when the government appropriates private property. But regulation can also go so far as to result in a physical occupation of the land that calls for compensation. For example, Mrs. Jean Loretto bought a New York City apartment building that was served by a television

(continued)

The Takings Issue

cable company. A state law forced apartment building owners to provide a place on their property for TV and telephone cables. When the cable company attempted to install additional cables on Mrs. Loretto's building, however, she sued. She won, the Supreme Court ruling that this regulation constituted a physical invasion of Mrs. Loretto's property [*Loretto v. Teleprompter Manhattan CATV Corp.* 458 US 419 (1982)]

In another case, low-flying planes landing at a nearby airport passed over Mr. Causby's chicken ranch, scaring the chickens so that they flew into walls, often killing themselves. Mr. Causby was ruled eligible for compensation. [*U.S. v. Causby*, 328 US 256 (1946)]

Loss of Beneficial Use

Lucas had bought two residential lots on the Isle of Palms, a South Carolina barrier island, for $975,000. He intended to build single-family homes on the lots, as the owners of adjacent lots had done. To his dismay, however, the South Carolina legislature passed the Beachfront Management Act, which prohibited building on Lucas's lots. He sued, contending that regulation had taken his property because he was left with no economically viable use of his land. The U.S. Supreme Court agreed:

> Total deprivation of beneficial use, is, from the landowner's point of view, the equivalent of a physical appropriation . . . We think, in short that there are good reasons for our frequently expressed belief that when the owner of real property has been called upon to sacrifice all economically beneficial uses in the name of the common good, that is to leave his property economically idle, he has suffered a

taking. [*Lucas v. South Carolina Coastal Council*, 505 US 1003 (1992)]

How Far Is "Too Far?"

When governmental regulation results in a complete deprivation of the landowner's viable use of the property, as in the Lucas case, there is a taking requiring compensation. But what of regulation that reduces the economic value of a property, but still leaves the owner with an economically viable use?

In 1980, the Supreme Court upheld Tiburon, California's open-space zoning ordinance against a taking claim. The Agins family owned five acres of unimproved land overlooking San Francisco Bay that they considered "the most valuable land in California." The city subsequently enacted a zoning ordinance that restricted density on the tract to between one and five single-family residences, and the Agins sued, asserting that the city had effectively taken the property, preventing its development for residential use and completely destroying "the value of the property for any purpose or use whatever." They also sought $2 million in damages for inverse condemnation. In other words, the Agins felt the rezoning was a taking that required compensation. The Supreme Court did not agree.

In upholding the ordinance, the Court held that a zoning ordinance would constitute an unconstitutional taking only if the landowner is denied any economically viable use of the property. The Court considered the preservation of open space and the promotion of orderly development to be legitimate state interests and noted that the effects of the ordinance fell on numerous property owners, not just on the Agins. It also found that although the ordinance restricted the density of development, it did not deny the Agins "economically viable use" of the land because it could still be developed for

(continued)

The Takings Issue

residential purposes, though perhaps not at the density they desired. [*Agins v. City of Tiburon*, 447 US 255 (1980)]

Similarly, the Supreme Court upheld New York's historic preservation law against a takings challenge. The City enacted a landmarks preservation law in 1965 to establish a citywide program of identification and preservation of historic structures and sites. Designation barred any construction or alteration of a building's exterior appearance without the approval of the Landmarks Preservation Commission. Grand Central Terminal, a monumental building in the beaux-arts style that was completed in 1913, was designated as landmark under the law. Later, the Penn Central Railroad leased air rights over the terminal for a proposed skyscraper. The Landmarks Preservation Commission rejected the plan, reasoning: "To balance a 55-story office tower above a flamboyant Beaux-Arts façade seems nothing more than an aesthetic joke which would reduce the Landmark itself to the status of a curiosity."

Penn Central challenged the constitutionality of the landmarks law, contending it resulted in the taking of private property without compensation. The Court disagreed, concluding that:

The submission that appellants may establish a "taking" simply by showing that they have been denied the ability to exploit a property interest that they heretofore had believed was available for development is quite simply untenable.

Even so, the Court made it clear that preservation laws could not deprive the owner of a reasonable return from the property, but that the return need not be the highest possible return. [*Penn Central Transportation Co. v. New York City*, 438 US 104 (1978)]

Limits on Mandatory Dedications

As noted in the text, property owners are often required to dedicated land or make infrastructure improvements as a condition to obtaining developmental approvals. Here also, the Court has ruled these can go "too far."

The Nollans wanted to replace a small bungalow on their beachfront lot with a larger house. As a condition to granting a building permit, the California Coastal Commission required the donation of a ten-foot walkway easement along the beach in front of the Nollan property. The commission contended that the easement was necessary to offset the reduced "visual access" caused by the construction and to help prevent congestion of the public beaches. The Nollans contended the exaction was not related to any need to which their project contributed directly and was therefore a taking.

The Supreme Court reaffirmed the constitutionality of developmental controls and exactions, stating that the commission could have legitimately imposed conditions to protect the public's ability to see the beach, such as height and width restrictions or a ban on fences, could have required the dedication of a "public viewing spot" on the Nollans's property, or even could have prohibited the new construction altogether. However, the Court agreed with the Nollans that the requirement to dedicate the public walkway easement was not sufficiently related to the problems supposedly created by the new construction:

The lack of nexus between the condition and the original purpose of the building restriction converts that purpose to something other than what it was. The purpose then becomes, quite simply, the obtaining of an easement to serve some valid governmental purpose, but without

(continued)

The Takings Issue

payment of compensation . . . Unless the permit condition serves the same governmental purpose as the development ban, the building restriction is not a valid regulation of land use but an out-and-out plan of extortion.

This need to tie any dedication requirements more closely to actual impact of the proposed development was made clearer in the Supreme Court's decision *Dolan v. Tigard.* The Dolans owned a plumbing and electrical supply store in the city of Tigard, Oregon. They wanted to double the size of their building and add parking spaces. The planning commission approved the plans with requirement that the Dolans dedicate about a tenth of their land for flood control for the adjacent creek and about an additional 15 feet for a bike path.

The Dolans challenged the dedication requirement. In 1994 the Supreme Court decided by a five-to-four vote that requiring a dedicated easement as a condition of permission to build or expand is an unconstitutional taking unless the government can show a "rough proportionality" between the regulation and impact of the development. Do these decisions mean that local government can no longer require mandatory dedications from developers? No, but the Court has made it clear that any required dedications must be closely related to the regulatory objective. [*Dolan v. Tigard*, 114 US 2309 (1994)]

The Takings Issue

Recently, the takings battle has moved into the legislative arena, with takings assessment bills and compensation laws being introduced in many states. The takings assessment laws would require that an assessment be made for land-use regulations to analyze their impact on private property values. The compensation bills would require that private property owners be compensated if regulations reduced the value of their property by some percentage, often 25 percent. At this writing, the fate of these bills is uncertain.

The takings controversy boils down to the basic question of the nature of private property rights. Do private parties own property subject to regulations, or do they have the unlimited right to use their property as they choose? Where is the proper middle ground? This is an issue that promises to be a lively one for many years to come.

Takings

If a governmental unit acquires property for public use under the power of eminent domain, this action is a *taking,* which requires the payment of compensation, whether it involves acquisition in fee simple or only partial property rights, such as an easement. Regulation of land use under police power, on the other hand, normally does not constitute a taking. The courts have ruled, however, that if the regulation is so severe that it deprives owners of any beneficial use of their property, it may then constitute a taking and, thus, be invalid. The problem is that the courts have never defined the exact point at which regulation goes too far and becomes a taking. The increasing magnitude of land-use regulation has made this a very real issue for many property owners.

Escheat

The final power government have over private property is known as the power of **escheat.** In the very unlikely event that a landowner dies without leaving either a valid will or living relatives, the state government becomes the new owner of the property. This power prevents real estate from simply "becoming unowned." The right of the government to the land under these limited circumstances is called escheat, a concept that dates back to the medieval feudal system. The king gave land to his barons, but if they died without surviving sons, the king would reclaim the land. If a knight or servant had no male heirs, that person's land would escheat to the next higher tier in the feudal order. Today, of course, the presence of any heir, even if not a relative or the deceased landowner, will prevent the state from asserting its right of escheat.

▋ CHAPTER REVIEW

- ■ Government has four basic powers that affect real estate owners. These powers are (1) the power of taxation, (2) the power of eminent domain, (3) police power, and (4) escheat.

- ■ Property taxes are an important source of revenues for state and local governments. They provide a relatively stable source of revenue that is not subject to wide fluctuations in short-term business activity, and they are very difficult to evade because they are tied to property that is largely immobile.

- ■ The steps involved in the property taxation process are (1) property value assessment, (2) development of the budget and a tax rate, and (3) tax billing and collection.

- ■ The government's right to condemn land is founded on the power of eminent domain, as granted by the Fifth Amendment to the U.S. Constitution. Once the government establishes the right to take title to or place an easement on property for society's needs, the major issue of concern is the determination of just compensation.

- ■ The *police power* is the power of government to regulate activities to promote the public health, safety, and general welfare.

- ■ In the event that a landowner dies without heirs or a valid will, the government, through the power of escheat, becomes the owner of the property.

- ■ The *interdependence of land uses*—that is, the impact that the use of land has on other property and on the public as a whole—leads to land-use controls.

■ A *comprehensive general plan* is a statement of a community's long-range policies covering its predicted physical needs for 15 to 25 years in the future. It usually contains the following five elements: (1) an analysis of projected economic and population developments, (2) a transportation plan, (3) a public facilities plan, (4) a land-use plan, and (5) an official map.

■ The most widely employed method of regulating the use of land is comprehensive zoning. This divides land into zones and prescribes regulations relating to the type and intensity of use. Relief from zoning regulations can be sought through legislative rezoning, through administrative variance or special-use permit, or through the courts.

■ Under a system of planned unit development (PUD), many regulations are waived to permit greater flexibility of design. Lot sizes may be reduced, for example, if community open spaces are provided.

■ *Performance zoning* is a technique that relates permitted uses of land to certain performance standards. Such standards usually are intended to protect the environment.

■ *Incentive zoning,* which is closely related to performance zoning, is any type of zoning provision that encourages developers to provide certain publicly desired features in return for such incentives as increased density of land use.

■ Under the concept of transferable development rights, a landowner is able to sell part of his or her bundle of rights to another landowner, who then can use his or her own land more intensively.

■ Developers often are required to dedicate rights-of-way for public streets, utility, and drainage, and in some communities, they also may be required to dedicate land for parks, open space, and schools.

■ Building codes establish detailed standards for the construction of new buildings and the alteration of existing ones.

▊ KEY TERMS

ad valorem tax	eminent domain	intensity of use
assessed value	escheat	inverse condemnation
assessment	exemptions	just compensation
assessment ratio	floor-area ratio	mandatory dedication
building codes	height limitations	market value
bulk limitations	impact fees	millage rates
comprehensive general plan	impact zoning	minimum lot sizes
	incentive zoning	nonconforming use

performance zoning

planned unit
  developments

police power

setback requirements

subdivision regulation

taxable value

transferable development
  rights

zoning

zoning variance

STUDY EXERCISES

1. What are the desirable features of the property tax for local governments?

2. What is the tax digest?

3. Suppose a local government has a tax digest of $500 million and feels it must raise $15 million for the operation of its schools and general government. What would be the millage rate?

4. Why is the government's power of escheat so seldom used?

5. By what authority does the government have the power of eminent domain?

6. What is meant by *public use?*

7. What characteristic of real estate leads to the need for public land-use controls?

8. Contrast police power and the power of eminent domain.

9. Discuss the history of the takings issue.

10. Describe the elements usually contained in a comprehensive general plan.

11. How is zoning used to control land use and intensity of use?

12. What are mandatory dedications?

13. What is incentive zoning? Performance zoning?

14. Describe the transferable development rights concept.

15. Mack owns 25 acres of land on the edge of town on a major road that is now zoned for residential use. He decides he would like to develop this land as an office park and shopping center. What steps would he have to take to secure approval of his project?

16. Mary owns a lot on which she wishes to build her dream house. To her consternation, she finds that if the house is placed on her rather narrow lot, it will fail to meet the sideyard setback requirements by three feet. What can she do?

17. Internet Exercise: While the concept of private property rights was near and dear to the heart of America's founding fathers, there seems to be an ongoing attack on those rights by people who want more government control over property owned by individuals. Do a Google search at *www.google.com* on the words "private property rights" and look for examples of the battle around the nation. Summarize the facts of one of these battles near your location and state your personal position on this issue.

FURTHER READING

Callies, D. L., ed. *Takings: Land-Development Conditions and Regulatory Takings after Dolan and Lucas.* Chicago: American Bar Association, Section of State and Local Government Law, 1996.

Dowling, Timothy, Douglas Kendall, and Jennifer Bradley. *The Good News about Takings.* Chicago: American Planning Association, 2006.

Meltz, Robert, Dwight H. Merriam, and Richard M. Frank. *The Takings Issue: Constitutional Limits on Land Use Control and Environmental Regulation.* Washington, D.C.: Island Press, 1998.

Platt, R. H. *Land Use Control: Geography, Law and Public Policy.* Englewood Cliffs, N.J.: Prentice-Hall, 1996.

Stein, J. M., ed. *Classic Readings in Real Estate and Development.* Washington, D.C.: Urban Land Institute, 1996.

Wright, R. R. *Land Use in a Nutshell,* 3rd ed. St. Paul, Minn.: West Publishing Company, 1994.

CHAPTER 5

Deeds and Title Examination

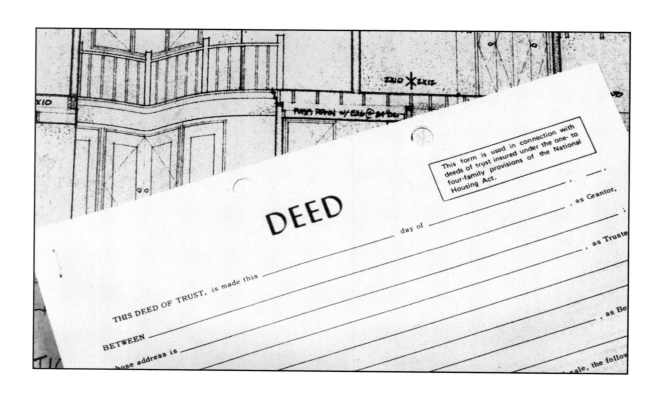

CHAPTER PREVIEW

REAL ESTATE TODAY

CLOSE-UP
Sleuthing for
Transaction Price

LEGAL HIGHLIGHT
Title Examination
through the Grantor
and Grantee
Indexes

The previous chapters in this section have described the concept of real estate ownership, including the legal rights held by real estate owners and the public and private limitations on those ownership rights. In this chapter, we first consider deeds, which are the legal documents used to convey title, or ownership, from one party to another. We then discuss the process by which parties evaluate the quality of title to a property and how grantees can protect themselves from potential defects in the title to a property.

Under the topic of deeds, we examine the necessary elements of a deed and various types of deeds, including the warranty deed, special warranty deed, bargain and sale deed, and quitclaim deed.

Under the topic of title examination, we examine the concepts of

- good and marketable title;

- insurable title;

- title perfect of record;

- chain of title;

- title search;

- title abstract;

- title opinion;

- title insurance; and finally,

- the Torrens system.

▌ DEEDS

Centuries ago in England, any person who possessed land generally was considered to be the legal owner, as possession and ownership essentially were synonymous. An owner could transfer his **title,** or legal ownership, to another person simply by going on the land in the presence of witnesses and handing the new owner a clod of earth while announcing that title was transferred. This symbolic transfer of title by delivery caused great confusion because there were no written records. The potential for fraud or forcible seizure was limitless. Therefore, in 1677, Parliament enacted a statute of frauds, which, among other things, required that all title transfers of real property be in writing. This provision has been adopted by every state in the United States with the goal of limiting the opportunities for fraudulent transactions. Thus, when title to real estate is to be transferred today, a written document called a **deed** must be given by the grantor to the new owner, the grantee.

Once the deed is written, title to real property is transferred by delivery of the deed to and its acceptance by the buyer. The delivery can be made by the seller or a person acting on behalf of the seller. Delivery of a signed deed can even be made after the seller's death if that was the seller's intent. When ownership is to be transferred, a deed must be drafted, signed by the grantor, and delivered to and accepted by the new owner.

Several elements are necessary for a deed to be valid. In addition to the basic requirement that a deed must be in writing, a valid deed must include

- identification of the parties,
- consideration given for the conveyed interest,
- legal description of the property,
- specification of the interests conveyed, and
- signatures of the proper parties.

The deed in Figure 5.1 is an example of one that was retrieved over the Internet from a county public records system (names and locations have been changed for our purposes). It will serve as a useful example in the following discussion of the necessary elements of a valid deed.

Necessary Elements of a Deed

All valid deeds must identify the parties involved in the transfer of title. The parties involved are usually, but not always, the buyer and the seller. (Sometimes property is given as a gift from one party to another.) The seller, or giver, is the **grantor** and the buyer, or receiver, is the **grantee.** In the example deed shown in Figure 5.1, the grantors are Joseph Nowak and Deborah Williamson, and the grantees are Michael Rodriguez and Nina Rodriguez.

A valid deed must involve **consideration,** something of economic value given by the grantee to the grantor in return for the property ownership. Usually, the consideration is the transaction price. Sometimes the exact amount of this consideration

FIGURE 5.1 | Warranty Deed

Prepared by and return to:
Stephanie A. McGuire, Esq.

Stephanie A. McGuire Attorney at Law
417 East Woodland Hwy.
Camden, MA 33440
369 – 983 – 0547
File number: 07.7990.01
Will Call No.:

WARRANTY DEED

This Warranty Deed made this **23rd** day of **February, 2007** between **Joseph Nowak** and **Deborah Williamson, husband and wife** whose post office address is **125 W. Dobson Avenue, Camden, MA 33440**, grantor, and **Michael Rodriguez and Nina Rodriguez, husband and wife** whose post office address is **16700 N. Sangamon Dr., Lovington, MA 33470**, grantee:

(Whenever used herein the terms "grantor" and "grantee" include all the parties to this instrument and the heirs, legal representatives, and assigns of individuals, and the successors and assigns of corporations, trusts and trustees)

Witnesseth, that said grantor, for and in consideration of the sum of TEN AND NO/100 DOLLARS ($10.00) and other good and valuable considerations to said grantor in hand paid by said grantee, the receipt whereof is hereby acknowledged, has granted, bargained, and sold to the said grantee, and grantee's heirs and assigns forever, the following described land, situate, lying and being in **Dearborn County, Massachusetts** to-wit:

> **Lots 1 through 4, inclusive, the East 25 feet Lot 5, the East 25 feet of Lot 18, and Lots 19 through 22, inclusive, all in Block 27 of the Grand Plan of Camden, Massachusetts, as revised September 7, 1937, according to the plat thereof recorded in Plat Book 2, Pages 71–78, inclusive, of the Public Records of Dearborn County, Massachusetts.**
>
> **Parcel Identification Number: 3-34-43-01-010-0027-001.0**
>
> **Subject to covenants, conditions, restrictions, easements, reservations and limitations of record, if any. Reference to these restrictions and reservations shall not operate to reimpose same.**

Together with all the tenements, hereditaments and appurtenances thereto belonging or in anywise appertaining.

To Have and to Hold, the same in fee simple forever.

And the grantor hereby covenants with said grantee that the grantor is lawfully seized of said land in fee simple; that the grantor has good right and lawful authority to sell and convey said land; that the grantor hereby fully warrants the title to said land and will defend the same against the lawful claims of all persons whomsoever; and that said land is free of all encumbrances, except taxes accruing subsequent to **December 31, 2006.**

FIGURE 5.1 | Warranty Deed *(continued)*

In Witness Whereof, grantor has hereunto set grantor's hand and seal the day and year first above written.

Signed, sealed and delivered in our presence:

_____   _____ (Seal)

Witness Name: _____   Joseph Nowak

_____   _____ (Seal)

Witness Name: _____   Deborah Willliamson

_____

Witness Name: _____

State of Massachusetts
County of Dearborn

The foregoing instrument was acknowledged before me this 23rd day of February, 2007 by Deborah Williamson and Joseph Nowak, who [_] are personally known or [_] have produced a driver's license as identification.

_____

Notary Public

[Notary Seal]

Printed Name: _____

My Commission Expires: _____

is stated on the deed, but often a nominal amount (such as "$10 and other good and valuable considerations") is mentioned in the deed as the consideration paid. This practice tends to keep the actual purchase price a secret known only to the parties involved in the transaction, but a little detective work can often reveal the transaction price. (See the Real Estate Today feature: Sleuthing for Transaction Price.)

A valid deed must include a unique description of the real estate involved in the transaction. The property must be described accurately so that there is no question about what parcel of real estate is being conveyed. A mere street address is an insufficient description in the deed because the address does not define the exact property boundaries and is subject to change. Buyers frequently discover that the street number by which their new property is known (and where mail is delivered) is not the number

> ### REAL ESTATE TODAY
> ## CLOSE-UP
>
> ## Sleuthing for Transaction Price
>
> Sometimes a little detective work is necessary to determine the transaction price from a recorded deed. The transaction price can often be discovered by closely examining the fee paid to the records office to record the document. In most counties in Florida, for example, the fee for recording a deed in the public records system is $0.70 per $100 of the transaction amount. The amount of this fee, called a **documentary stamp tax** or simply *doc stamp tax*, is stamped onto the first page of the recorded document. The party recording the deed is required to provide a sworn affidavit of the transaction amount. Thus, anyone who knows the amount of the tax and the way it is calculated can, with a little bit of algebra, determine the transaction amount for any transaction even if the deed does not specify the full amount.
>
> The example deed shown in Figure 5.1 has a computer-generated "stamp" in the top left hand corner of each page that shows the Official Record Book and Page in which the document was recorded. The stamp also shows the amount of deed documentary tax paid when the document was recorded: $4,007.50. Using the explanation of doc stamps in the previous paragraph, the documentary stamp tax for a deed recorded in this county is calculated as:
>
> $$Tax = \$0.70 \times \frac{Transaction\ Price}{\$100}$$
>
> Rearranging terms gives:
>
> $$Transaction\ Price = \frac{Documentary\ Stamp\ Tax \times \$100}{\$0.70}$$
>
> For this property transfer, therefore, the transaction price is:
>
> $$Transaction\ Price = \frac{\$4,007.50 \times \$100}{\$0.70} = \$572,500.$$

stated in other documents; at some time in the past, the number was changed. To describe the real property's precise location, the metes-and-bounds method, the rectangular survey method, and/or a reference to plats should be used. We considered each of these methods in Chapter 2. The **legal description** for the property being transferred by the deed in Figure 5.1 uses the "reference to recorded plat" method:

> Lots 1 through 4, inclusive, the East 25 feet Lot 5, the East 25 feet of Lot 18, and Lots 19 through 22, inclusive, all in Block 27 of the Grand Plan of Camden, Massachusetts, as revised September 7, 1937, according to the plat thereof recorded in Plat Book 2, Pages 71–78, inclusive, of the Public Records of Dearborn County, Massachusetts.

The legal description is accompanied by the words that actually convey the property interest. The words of conveyance should make it clear what rights are being transferred. In this example, the words of conveyance specify that the grantor has "granted, bargained, and sold . . ." the property to the grantee ". . . to have and to hold in fee simple forever."

The deed may also include promises (covenants and warranties) that the grantor is making to the grantee. These promises are the defining features of the different types of deeds we will consider in the next section of this chapter. Notice that several promises appear at the bottom of the first page of the sample deed.

As shown on the second page of the sample deed, the grantor then must sign the deed. Before a deed can be recorded, most states require that the grantor sign in the presence of one or more witnesses (who also sign the document). Notice that the grantee's signature is not required on the deed in some states. The grantors sign this deed along with two witnesses, one of whom is a public notary. Once the deed is properly signed, it can be said to have been **executed**, or subjected to all requirements that establish its validity.

Finally, the deed must be delivered to the grantee. Title to the property is not actually transferred from the grantor to the grantee until delivery has been completed. Of course, it is assumed for the purposes of this discussion that the grantee accepts the deed. Refusal to accept the deed results in an ineffective delivery. Although a transfer of title need not be recorded in the public records to be valid, the grantee must record the new deed in the county's record or deed office to be assured of protection against claims that the grantor later transferred his or her title to someone else. The public records system will be discussed in more detail later in this chapter.

Additional Elements

Although the elements just described are essential to a valid deed, the most common types of deeds contain additional elements called *covenants* and *warranties*. A *covenant* is any agreement or promise, and a *warranty* is a guarantee that the statements made are true. Traditionally, there are four covenants and one warranty: (1) covenant against encumbrances, (2) covenant of seisin or ownership, (3) covenant of quiet enjoyment, (4) covenant of further assurances, and (5) warranty forever. Whether all, some, or none of these items exist in a deed depends on the type of deed the grantor is required to give. In some states the five items are not expressly stated in the deed but are incorporated by reference to statute.

Degree of Protection

It is important to understand the degree of protection each type of deed gives to the grantee. The order in which these types of deeds will be discussed is also the order of the amount of protection provided. The warranty deed contains the greatest assurances by the grantor that the grantee will have security from nearly all potential claims. The special warranty deed limits the grantor's liability to title defects that occurred during the grantor's ownership. The bargain and sale deed simply states that the grantor has the right to convey the title involved, but all other assurances are missing. Finally, the grantor who gives a quitclaim deed does not even promise that he or she has any rights in the real estate, but conveys whatever rights the grantor does have to the grantee.

Types of Deeds

There are many kinds of deeds, each having its own special characteristics. The more common types are warranty deeds, special warranty deeds, bargain and sale deeds, and quitclaim deeds.

Warranty Deed

The warranty deed is the broadest type of all deeds. In a **warranty deed,** the grantor makes promises that cover the traditional covenants and warranty. The grantor assures the grantee that no liens or encumbrances other than those on public record exist against the property **(covenant against encumbrances),** that the grantor has a fee simple interest in the property, and that he or she is in full possession of the interest being conveyed and, thus, has the right to convey it **(covenant of seisin).** (The covenant against encumbrances does not mean that there are no encumbrances on the property but rather that if there are encumbrances, they will be listed in the deed or in public records. In many states, encumbrances that are open and visible and that benefit the land are also excluded.) The grantor also promises that the grantee's enjoyment of the property will not be disturbed by some party claiming to own or to have a lien on it *(covenant of quiet enjoyment)*. These covenants relate to the present condition of the grantor's title.

A warranty deed further assures the grantee that the grantor will execute any future documents needed to perfect the grantor's title **(covenant of further assurances).** Finally, the grantor promises to always defend the title conveyed **(warranty forever).** These latter two items relate to the grantor's duties as they might arise in the future.

In the typical residential sales transaction, the buyer should insist that the sales contract require that the seller transfer title by warranty deed. The language at the bottom of the first page of Figure 5.1 demonstrates how these covenants and warranty are spelled out in a typical warranty deed.

A warranty deed provides some protection to the purchaser concerning the acquisition of "good title" to real estate. This protection, however, may not extend to "marketability" of the title. If, for example, a neighbor has obtained an unrecorded easement by prescription (as described in Chapter 3) across the property being transferred, the grantee under a warranty deed can successfully sue the grantor for the amount by which this encumbrance has diminished the property. In this situation, the grantor would have breached the covenant of quiet enjoyment and the covenant against encumbrances. Some states have interpreted the covenants and warranties of a deed as being breached only if the grantee loses possession to another party. Obviously, under this interpretation, the existence of a prescriptive easement would not be a breach of the covenant of quiet enjoyment or the covenant against encumbrances.

Special Warranty Deed

A **special warranty deed** is similar to a warranty deed except the special warranty deed limits the extent of the grantor's warranties to events that occurred during the grantor's period of ownership. It does not protect the grantee against encumbrances that may have arisen before the grantor took title. The grantor's warrants cover only title defects that occurred during the grantor's ownership. For example, a corporation might give a special warranty deed to protect itself against any potential liabilities resulting from a foreclosure that happened before it owned the property.

Bargain and Sale Deed

A deed that implies the grantor has title to the property and the right to convey it but does not contain any express covenants as to the title's validity is called a **bargain and sale deed**. This deed is also called a **warranty deed without covenants** or a **grant deed**.

In essence, the bargain and sale deed simply specifies that the grantor "does hereby grant, sell, and convey" some interest in real property to the grantee. Notice the lack of covenants in this type of deed in comparison to the warranty deed and special warranty deed discussed above. If the sales contract fails to specify what type of deed must be delivered, the bargain and sale deed may be the only one required. If the buyers want to make certain they receive a warranty deed, this must be clearly stated in the sales contract.

Quitclaim Deed

A **quitclaim deed** transfers any interest that the grantor may have in the property described but does not imply that the grantor has any valid interest in it. (Some people mistakenly say "quickclaim" instead of "quitclaim.") The quitclaim deed is most commonly used to clear defects in the title to property. For example, suppose Bob wished to sell land he allegedly owned to David, but Clare, Bob's sister, claimed to own a one-fourth interest in the land. Before David would be willing to purchase the land, he would want Clare to give Bob a quitclaim deed that would extinguish any claim she might have had on the property. Then, David can accept a deed from Bob knowing that Clare has no claim on the property. The quitclaim deed would indicate that Clare had relinquished any claim she might have had in the property, but she would not be liable for any defects in the title. If David wished to get full clear title to the land, he typically would insist on receiving a general warranty deed from Bob, as well as the quitclaim deed from Clare.

Similarly, a quitclaim deed is sometimes used to release marital interests in a property. If Bob and Jane divorce and Jane is awarded ownership of the family home, Bob may be required to sign a quitclaim deed that releases any interest he may have in the property to Jane. The quitclaim deed would serve as evidence that Bob no longer held an interest in the property after the divorce.

The grantee who takes property under a quitclaim deed must understand that he may be receiving nothing at all of value. A person could give a quitclaim deed describing a neighbor's land, or even a university's football stadium for that matter. Under a quitclaim deed, the grantor conveys all the interests possessed without any assurances that any rights of ownership exist. If the grantor has no rights in the property, then nothing is transferred. Of course, the grantor might be guilty of fraud if he or she falsely claims ownership of the football stadium!

An example of a quitclaim deed is shown in Figure 5.2. The readability of some deeds can be sorely lacking. Handwritten deeds that contain all the necessary elements are just as valid as a nicely printed deed and accomplish the purpose of transferring property rights from the grantor to the grantee.

Deeds for Special Uses

There are several other kinds of deeds that have specific purposes. Each of these specialized deeds is named for the signer, and the warranties given, if any, depend on that signer's capacity. An *executor's deed* is an example. An executor of an estate seldom will be willing to promise that the title being transferred is free of all defects. Therefore, the executor covenants only that he or she is conveying the title held by the deceased person and that he or she has not encumbered the property in his or her capacity as executor. A grantee taking property under any such special deed must be aware that the grantor's covenants and warranties are very limited or nonexistent.

TITLE EXAMINATION

From previous discussion we now understand that deeds are documents that convey title, or legal ownership, from one party to another. In the typical real estate transaction, the buyer's chief desire is to acquire "good" title from the seller. More specifically a *good title* is one that is *marketable, insurable, perfect of record*, or some combination of these attributes.

A **marketable title** is one that is free and clear of all past, present, or future claims that would cause a reasonable purchaser to reject such title. An **insurable title** is one that a reputable title insurance company is willing to insure. And **title perfect of record** means that the public records related to the particular title involved show no defects whatsoever. This last condition usually provides the buyer with the most protection. Suppose, for example, that inspection of the seller's title reveals that years ago a deed was signed improperly by a previous title holder. Perhaps the signor left out her middle initial in her signature. A reasonable buyer might not hesitate to accept the title and a title insurance company might be willing to insure it, but the seller's title still is not perfect of record.

Any prospective grantee of real estate must take steps to discover all possible defects in the seller's title. This responsibility generally is satisfied by means of a lawyer's title opinion or by title insurance. A **title opinion** is a statement by a lawyer that summarizes the findings disclosed by a search through all public documents that may relate to the title. **Title insurance** is a policy that insures the title received by the grantee against any deficiencies that may have been in existence at the time title was transferred. Before a title insurance policy or title opinion can be given concerning a particular property, a search of the title will be performed.

FIGURE 5.2 | Quitclaim Deed

Name:
Address:
This Instrument Prepared By:
Address:
Property Appraisers Parcel Identification:
Folio Number(s):
Grantee(s): S. S. # (s)

_____Space above This Line for Processing Data_____

This Quit Claim Deed, _Executed the _____ day of _____ _____ , by_
_____ , first party, to
_____ ,
_whose post office address is _____ , second
party._
(Wherever used herein the terms "first party" and "second party" include all the parties to this instrument and the heirs, legal representatives, and assigns of individuals, and the successors and assigns of corporations, wherever the context so admits or requires.)

Witnesseth, _That the first party, for and in consideration of the sum of $ _____ ,_

_in hand paid by the said second party, the receipt whereof is hereby acknowledged, does hereby remise, release, and quit claim unto the second party forever, all the right, title, interest, claim and demand which the said first party has in and to the following described lot, piece or parcel of land, situate, lying and being in the County of _____ , state of _____ , to-wit:_

To Have and to Hold _The same together with all and singular the appurtenances thereunto belonging or in anywise appertaining, and all the estate, right, title, interest, lien, equity and claim whatsoever of the said first party, either in law or equity to the only proper use, benefit and behoof of the said second party forever._

In Witness Whereof, _the said first party has signed and sealed these presents the day and year first above written._

Signed, sealed and delivered in presence of:

_____   _____ LS
Witness Signature (as to first Grantor)   Grantor Signature

_____   _____
Printed Name   Printed Name

_____   _____
Witness Signature (as to Co-grantor, if any)   Post Office Address
                                                                          LS
_____   _____
Printed Name Co-Grantor   Signature, (if any)

                                                 _____
                                                 Post Office Address

STATE OF _____)
COUNTY OF _____)

I hereby Certify that on this day, before me, an officer duly authorized to administer oaths and take acknowledgments, personally appeared _____ known to me to be the person _____ described in and who executed the foregoing instrument, who acknowledged before me that _____ executed the same, and an oath was not taken. (Check one) ❑ Said person(s) is/are personally known to me. ❑ Said person(s) provided the following type of identification: _____ .

  NOTARY RUBBER STAMP SEAL   Witness my hand and official seal in the County and State last
                                      aforesaid this _____ day of _____, _____

                                      _____
                                      Notary Signature

                                      _____
                                      Notary Signature

Title Search

A **title search** reveals the ownership history, or **chain of title,** of a property. An examination of the chain of title might show that the seller has good title, or it could show that the seller is only one of several parties claiming to own the real estate being sold. The title search is made possible by the recording system provided by each state.

Recording System

Each state's recording statute provides that any document affecting title to real estate must be recorded. Although recording systems vary from state to state, the purpose of all such systems is to protect the potential interest holder, including the fee simple owner, the tenant, and the mortgagee. The documents related to those interests are, of course, the deed, the lease, and the mortgage. As a result of the recording requirement, anyone concerned with the validity of a real estate title can determine that validity by means of a title search.

Most states require that the recorded document be signed by the grantor. To be filed in the public record, the instrument must be witnessed and acknowledged by a notary public or another person authorized to acknowledge such documents. If this formality is not satisfied, the document cannot be recorded.

The location for the recording of real estate documents varies from state to state. State law generally creates a recorder's office in the local courthouse. The official in charge of that office may be called the clerk of the court, county clerk, recorder, or registrar of deeds.

Because the public has constructive notice of all interests that are properly recorded, any buyer or lender can determine easily whether the seller or borrower has title to the real estate he or she claims. Failure to record an interest may cause the holder to lose that interest to a subsequent good-faith purchaser because that purchaser would have no notice of unrecorded interests.

The recording requirement is the key element that creates an efficient method of transferring title to real estate. Without public records, the confusion that existed in England centuries ago still would occur. Prospective buyers or mortgagees can gain near certainty as to their predecessors' titles because of public records. To reach any level of certainty about the validity of a real estate title, the method of conducting a title search must be understood.

Although real estate title records are public and open to inspection by any interested person, real estate title searches normally should be conducted by an attorney or title examiner (sometimes called an *abstractor*) who is trained specifically in this field. A title examiner must trace the grantor's chain of title to be sure that no defects exist from previous transactions. For example, in a previous transaction involving the property, a spouse may not have signed the deed, even though both the husband and wife jointly owned the property. This type of title defect raises the possibility that the spouse who did not sign still has a legal interest in the property. This defect should be corrected before the new buyer accepts the current grantor's deed.

Assume, for example, that Otis had good and marketable title to a parcel of land. Assume further that Otis sold the parcel to Bill, but Bill failed to record the deed he received. Between the two, Bill has the superior title to the property. Assume, however, that Otis has wrongfully deeded the lot to George, who is unaware of Bill's interest. When George searches Otis's title, he will find no record that Otis previously sold the lot to Bill. Therefore, as far as George can ascertain, Bill has no right to the lot. Because George had no notice of Bill's interest and because George recorded his deed before Bill did, all states would say that George, as a good-faith purchaser, has title to the property.

Grantor and Grantee Indexes

The chain of title can be followed through **grantor and grantee indexes.** Each county in the United States maintains indexes of people or entities (grantors) who have given any interest in real estate to another and people or entities who have received such interests (grantees). For a particular property, the current owner will be listed in the grantee index. When ownership of the property is transferred, the previous owner's name will be added to the grantor index, and the new owner's name will be entered into the grantee index. The title examiner begins by tracing the property involved back through the grantee indexes to verify that the seller is, in fact, the current owner of record. Then the examiner searches the applicable grantor indexes to verify that the current owner has not granted any interest in the property to another person. Generally, a title search covers a period of 40 to 60 years.

Completing the Records Search

Merely examining the grantor and grantee indexes is not enough to ensure an accurate title search. The examiner also must check the tax records to discover whether any tax payments are delinquent. Furthermore, the examiner must search the local court records to determine whether any judgment has been awarded or any lien has been filed against the property. Only after these additional factors have been researched can the title be considered insurable or marketable. Of course, any recorded document that appears to relate to the property at issue must be checked for its legal description. Only if a tax lien or an attempted transfer by an owner concerns part or all of the property under contract does that record have to be examined.

Title Abstract

In some states, a title examination is made much easier by the use of title abstracts. A **title abstract** is a written summary of the chain of title for a given parcel of real estate. Generally, such abstracts are prepared by employees of an abstract company who are not licensed lawyers but are trained specifically to search titles. When an abstract is readily available, the buyer's attorney does not have to go through the detailed search of the grantor and grantee indexes. The attorney obtains the proper abstract, studies it, and issues a *title opinion,* an opinion to the buyer on the validity or defectiveness of the title. When abstracts are used widely, the attorney's fees in a real estate transaction may be much lower than they are when the attorney must perform the entire title examination. Title abstracting is declining in popularity, partially due to the costs of storing and maintaining the documents involved. Title insurance has supplanted the title opinion as a means of title examination in most areas of the country.

Title Insurance

The lawyer's title opinion is not the only type of protection a buyer can obtain to ensure that the seller can deliver marketable title. In many parts of the country, title insurance, which grew out of the expanded function of abstract companies or a group of lawyers, is purchased to provide protection in case the acquired title is defective. In addition to preparing abstracts or writing opinion letters, these companies or associations began to issue insurance that the title to a parcel of real estate was "good and marketable."

On receiving a request for title insurance, the title insurance company conducts its own search of the grantor's title, using public records. The company then evaluates the validity of this title and determines the risk it must take to ensure the title's marketability. The title insurance policy includes a schedule of exceptions, which might list liens, easements, or other encumbrances that appear in an examination of the public record. Often, the policy will state that all restrictions of record are excluded from coverage. In addition, the policy can exclude those defects created by any party who possesses the property at the time the policy is delivered. Other risks excluded might include defects revealed by an accurate survey of the property or defects not recorded as required. The insured party under a title insurance policy must be certain what defects are excepted from the policy and either have the seller-grantor clear the title of these defects or encumbrances before purchasing the property or protect themselves by receiving credit from the seller for existing financial liens and paying off such liens after the purchase.

In a real estate transaction, title insurance may be purchased for the buyer-grantee or for the institution (mortgagee) financing the transaction and taking a security interest in the real estate. In the typical transaction, the policy is paid for by the buyer, or mortgagor, as a condition of obtaining financing. Title insurance differs from liability, life, or property-hazard insurance in several important ways. First, the insured is charged a premium only once, and it is payable when the policy is delivered. Second, a title insurance policy protects only the named insured; therefore, when the insured transfers the title that is covered, the insurance does not protect the new owner. Third, in contrast with most types of insurance (which protect against future events), title insurance protects against past events only. The schedule of exceptions normally exempts from coverage any liens, encumbrances, or other defects that arise after the title is insured.

A title insurance policy may act as a substitute for the lawyer's title opinion letter. Indeed, the practice in many states is to purchase a title policy rather than obtain a title opinion because some people feel the title policy provides more protection at a better price. Alternatively, a title policy may be purchased as supplemental protection to the lawyer's opinion, although most would consider this redundant and a waste of money.

In essence, a title insurance company provides protection to the insured to the extent that the title was free from unknown defects when the insured acquired title. Primarily, this protection covers the possibility that the recording system has failed to disclose a proper claim to the property. For example, if a previous owner received title through a forged deed and later the true owner appeared, the title insurance company would be obligated to defend the insured's title in court, reach a monetary settlement with the lawful owner, or make good the insured's loss. In such a situation, title insurance can provide very valuable protection.

Mortgage companies usually require a title insurance policy before they will loan money to purchase the property. Although the buyer will normally have to pay for this policy as part of the costs of obtaining the loan, the policy protects only the lender. If the property owners also want title insurance to protect their interest, they must purchase a separate policy. In any case, the buyer can file suit against the seller for breach of warranty if the title turns out to be defective. The seller, however, may be insolvent and unable to pay any judgment the buyer might obtain. Legal action also involves attorney's and other expenses, as well as considerable time and inconvenience.

If a lawyer for a title abstract company has given an opinion on a title that later turns out to be defective and the defect was overlooked because of the negligence of the abstractor or the attorney, the title holder has a cause of action against the negligent party. Here again, however, recovering from a title insurance company normally will be much cheaper and less time-consuming than having to pursue a lawsuit for negligence.

The Legal Highlight on the next page demonstrates the use of the grantor and grantee indexes in title searches.

The Torrens System

The **Torrens system** of land registration provides the landowner with a title certificate similar to that used to show title to a car. To obtain the Torrens certificate of title, the purported owner must be willing to go through a legal registration proceeding. After reviewing all potential interests in the land, the judge issues a decree naming the true owner of the land and any valid claims, such as mortgages, easements, or other restrictions, against the land. The judge's decree is entered on the court's records, an original certificate of title is recorded, and a duplicate certificate is given to the landowner. To transfer title under the Torrens system, the old certificate of title is returned to the registrar, who then issues a new certificate to the new owner.

Although the Torrens system simplifies the real estate transfer process, it is permitted as an optional method of land transfer in only 12 states (Colorado, Georgia, Hawaii, Iowa, Illinois, Massachusetts, Minnesota, New York, North Carolina, Ohio, Oregon, and Washington), and even in those areas, it has been applied on a very limited basis.

Title Examination through the Grantor and Grantee Indexes

 Suppose you are thinking of buying a house from the current owner, Sarah Howell. You or your representative will want to examine the title to be sure Sarah is the true owner of the property.

By using the grantor and grantee indexes, the title examiner finds the following information. First, by looking through the grantee index, the examiner discovers that the seller, Sarah Howell, bought the house now being sold on March 28, 1984, from Charles Edwards. Again via the grantee index, the examiner finds that Edwards purchased the land on which the house sits on June 17, 1965, from J. William Martin. The examiner learns that Martin had owned the property since November 12, 1916, after inheriting it from his mother, Edith Martin. Having determined that the chain of title can be traced back more than 80 years (some states require only a 30-year *root of title*, the time period that must be examined to ensure full legal protection), the examiner must "come forward" with the title to make sure that each grantor had the right and power to transfer title. Beginning with the grantor index, the examiner searches the grantor index to see whether Mrs. Martin's executor deeded the land involved to anyone other than J. William Martin on November 12, 1916. The examiner must take similar measures to learn what Martin did with the property between November 12, 1916, and June 17, 1965.

When the examiner is satisfied that Charles Edwards received good title on June 17, 1965, she finds next that Edwards mortgaged the land to finance the construction of the house you now want to buy. A *satisfaction of that mortgage*—that is, a discharge of the obligation—was filed when Edwards sold the house and lot to Sarah Howell in 1984. Therefore, it appears that as of the date of her purchase, Sarah Howell had good, clear, marketable title. To complete the job, the examiner must check the grantor index under the name Sarah Howell from March 28, 1984, to the present. Again, the land and house were mortgaged when Sarah bought the property. Because she has not yet paid off that mortgage, at the closing the buyer will insist that a document be recorded showing that the seller has totally paid the mortgage. A mortgage satisfaction generally is filed at the same time as the deed conveying the property from the seller to the buyer.

There are two main reasons for this. First, the high initial cost of the proceeding discourages owners from having their land registered. Second, and perhaps more important, lawyers, abstractors, and title insurance companies have fought against the use of the Torrens system because land transfers under this system eliminate or greatly diminish the need for their services.

CHAPTER REVIEW

- A *deed* is a legal document that conveys title, or ownership, from one party to another. A valid deed must be written formally to include

(1) identification of the parties, (2) a legal description of the property, (3) language of conveyance in return for the consideration named, and (4) signature of the grantor. It then must be (5) delivered to and accepted by the grantee.

■ Deeds are differentiated by the covenants and warranties that the grantor makes regarding the title being transferred. Such assurances may include (1) covenant against encumbrances, (2) covenant of seisin, (3) covenant of quiet enjoyment, (4) covenant of further assurances, and (5) warranty forever. The general warranty deed, special warranty deed, bargain and sale deed (also called warranty deed without covenants or grant deed), and quit-claim deed are the most common deeds used in real estate transactions. Each has a special purpose, with which the parties involved should be familiar.

■ Title to land signifies the legal right to ownership. A buyer of real estate is concerned fundamentally with acquiring "good title." *Good title* is title that is specified as marketable, insurable, perfect of record, or any combination thereof. To protect themselves against inadvertent acceptance of defective titles, all buyers should obtain a title opinion or title insurance. Title opinions are written by lawyers after they have searched the applicable title or examined the title abstracts. Title insurance provides protection from defects in title that might be discovered after the grantee receives the property from the grantor.

■ A title search is conducted by trained personnel who examine the grantor and grantee indexes, the tax records, and the judgment records to determine whether the grantor has the right and power to grant the stated interest. An abstractor searches a title and compiles all records applicable to a piece of real estate; the resulting compilation is called an *abstract*.

■ Title insurance can be beneficial in conjunction with or in lieu of a title opinion. In essence, a title policy insures the title against any defects or claims that exist as of the date title is acquired. Title insurance does not cover potential defects or claims that come into existence after the policy is issued. Although title insurance is important in some situations, it should not be purchased automatically when a title opinion is obtained because that opinion may provide sufficient protection.

■ The Torrens system of land registration provides an alternative to the more traditional method of exchanging title to real estate by delivery of a deed. Through a legal action to register the land, the judge determines the true owner of the land and the valid claims that exist. A certificate of title is issued then, and new certificates are issued when the property is sold in the future. This registration system has not gained wide acceptance in the United States because of the high cost of the required legal proceeding and the opposition of lawyers and abstractors. Title being conveyed in a deed should be examined to determine its quality.

▌ KEY TERMS

bargain and sale deed	grant deed	title abstract
chain of title	grantee	title insurance
consideration	grantor	title opinion
covenant against encumbrances	grantor and grantee indexes	title perfect of record
covenant of further assurances	insurable title	title search
	legal description	Torrens system
covenant of seisin	marketable title	warranty deed
deed	quitclaim deed	warranty deed without covenants
documentary stamp tax	special warranty deed	warranty forever
executed	title	

▌ STUDY EXERCISES

1. What are the essential elements of a deed?
2. Describe the covenants and warranty contained in a warranty deed.
3. What are the differences between
   a. a warranty deed and a special warranty deed?
   b. a warranty deed and a bargain and sale deed?
4. Evaluate the following statement: Quitclaim deeds are useful for removing "clouds" on real estate titles.
5. How should you respond to a dear friend who says, "I'm buying a new house in a new subdivision, so I don't need to worry about a title search. No one has owned this house before."
6. What is the difference between *insurable title* and *marketable title*?
7. Discuss whether or not you think the Torrens System would be an improvement over the deed system used in most parts of the United States.
8. Internet Exercise: Visit the Web site for the public records system in your area (usually the county clerk's office) and view a few recently recorded warranty deeds and quitclaim deeds. Compare the language of these two types of deeds and explain how the warranty deed provides better protection to the grantee than does the quitclaim deed. If you can't find the Web site for your local public records system, try *http://hendryclerk.org/official records.htm* to access the records for a county in Florida.

▌ FURTHER READING

Karp, James, and Elliot Klayman. *Real Estate Law*, 6th ed. Chicago: Dearborn Real Estate Education, 2006.

CHAPTER 6

Contracts and Title Closings

CHAPTER PREVIEW

This chapter focuses on three specific types of contracts that define the agreement between parties to eventually transfer ownership in real property: sales contracts, option-to-buy contracts, and contracts for deed. Each of these types of contracts provides the rules governing the parties' rights and duties during the time between the agreement to transfer real property and the actual transfer of title using a deed.

The transfer of title occurs at the title **closing** or **settlement** of the transaction. We consider the responsibilities of the parties to the transaction to bring the transaction to a close. We also demonstrate how the funds are accounted for in a typical residential real estate closing.

Under the topic of topic of contracts, we examine

- the necessary elements of a contract;

- performance and breach of contract;

- the purpose and structure of the real estate sales contract;

- the purpose and structure of option-to-buy contracts;

- the purpose and structure of contracts for deed; and

- some contract negotiation tips and strategies.

Under the topic of title closing, we study

- the buyer's responsibilities;

- the seller's responsibilities;

- closing costs and the closing statement;

- events at closing; and

- escrow closing.

REAL ESTATE TODAY

LEGAL HIGHLIGHT
Validity of an Oral Contract

LEGAL HIGHLIGHT
Necessity to Meet "Concurrent Conditions" by Date of Closing

NECESSARY ELEMENTS OF A CONTRACT

The required elements of any valid **contract** consist of (1) an offer, (2) an acceptance, (3) consideration, (4) parties with capacity, and (5) a lawful purpose. When contracts involve real estate, there is an additional requirement that the agreement be expressed in writing to be enforceable by the court system (one exception is a lease for one year or less).

Offer and Acceptance

Before any contract can be created, one person must make an offer to another. In essence, an **offer** is a statement that specifies the position of the maker of the offer (who is called the **offeror**). The offeror states implicitly in an offer that he or she is willing to be bound by the stated position. An offer becomes a valid contract when it is accepted by the party who receives it. The receiving party is called an **offeree,** and his or her acceptance should create a contract.

An **acceptance,** which expresses satisfaction with an offer, must mirror the precise terms and conditions stated in the offer. If the terms in the purported acceptance differ from those of the offer, no contract is formed. Indeed, such an attempted acceptance becomes a **counteroffer.** With a counteroffer, the original offeror and offeree switch legal positions, and a contract may result when a counteroffer is accepted. Acceptance of a contract involving real estate is indicated by the signatures of the parties on the written document that spells out their agreement.

Consideration

The law requires that an exchange of consideration occur before a contract is enforceable. **Consideration** often is described as anything that incurs a legal detriment or the forgoing of a legal benefit. What that means, in simple terms, is that each party to a contract must give up something. In a typical real estate contract, the seller promises to give up title to the land in return for money; the buyer promises to give up money in return for title to the land.

Capacity of Parties

To have a valid contract, all parties involved must have **contractual capacity.** The law insists that all parties have the mental capability to know what the contract represents and to understand its terms. Most commonly, two categories of people are said to lack contractual capacity. First, those who have been declared mentally incompetent are protected from people who attempt to take advantage of their mental condition. Because the law often cannot distinguish people with unjust intent from those with good intentions, insane persons cannot be held to the terms and conditions of a contract. Therefore, such contracts, although binding on the competent party, are voidable, or can be rescinded, at the election of the incompetent party's guardian.

The second category of people who lack contractual capacity consists of *minors*—that is, those who have not reached the age of majority, usually 18 or 21. Although some minors (typically defined as persons younger than 18) have the intelligence to comprehend even the most complex transactions, the law provides them with protection.

Any time before a person reaches the age of majority and within a reasonable period thereafter, nearly all contracts that the minor has entered into may be voided by the minor. Certain types of contracts involving a minor's purchase of necessities—such items as food, clothing, and medical care, essential for the preservation and reasonable enjoyment of life—cannot be voided. Because real estate is seldom considered a necessity, however, minors generally lack the capacity to purchase or sell it. Therefore, when one party to a contract involving the transfer of real estate is a minor, that contract is voidable at the minor's (or his guardian's) option.

If a contract is voided, the minor and adult parties must return any consideration that was previously exchanged. Therefore, an adult must beware of buying real estate from or selling it to a minor, as such a transaction subsequently may be undone.

Lawful Purpose

A valid contract must have as its ultimate purpose some legal act or function. For example, a contract for the delivery of illegal drugs is not enforceable—at least not in the courts. Although people sometimes subsequently put real estate to an illegal use, the sale or lease of real estate seldom directly involves illegal intentions; therefore, this element of a valid contract generally is less troublesome than the other elements.

Even so, both buyers and sellers should be aware that any illegal purpose in the contract may make it void. For example, suppose a sales contract specifies the buyer's intent to utilize the property in violation of current zoning provisions. This clause may give the buyer an "out" that the seller may not recognize.

Writing Requirement

Contracts may be either implied or expressed, and expressed contracts may be oral or written. All contracts involving land or items attached to it, however, must be in writing before a court will enforce them. Contracts involving the sale of timber and crops may be oral and remain binding. The rules governing contracts for personal property are found in each state's version of the Uniform Commercial Code, a collection of laws that govern business transactions. Each state's law should be consulted regarding the requisites of such contracts.

The requirement that real estate contracts be in writing to be enforceable by the legal system is found in each state's **statute of frauds,** a law designed to prevent fraudulent practices by requiring that certain contracts, including those involving real property, be in writing and signed. We discussed this statute briefly in the previous chapter. Real estate contracts must be written to reduce the possibility that a court may be defrauded or tricked into ruling improperly when the subject matter is valuable real estate. The required writing does not have to be a formally drafted document. Indeed, any written words that indicate the parties' positions and that are signed by the parties involved satisfy the statute of frauds. For example, the words "I agree to sell my farm to Robert Harris for $50,000," written on a paper napkin, are enforceable by Harris if they are signed by the farm owner. Of course, it is assumed that the owner has only one farm; otherwise, the property designated as "my farm" is not adequately described. An adequate written description of the real property being sold is essential. Methods of legal description were discussed in Chapter 2.

Although the statute of frauds requires that contracts involving real estate be in writing, there are exceptions to this rule. Courts may, for instance, enforce an oral contract if the parties have partially performed their agreement. **Partial performance** is the fulfillment of the terms of an agreement to such an extent that the existence of the agreement may be reasonably inferred, even though no written contract exists. If a court can determine from the parties' actions what their intentions were, it may hold that a contract exists despite the lack of a written document. Generally, mere payment of some money by the buyer is not sufficient to replace a written contract.

Payment plus possession by the buyer and physical improvements made to the property, however, point to the existence of some kind of contractual understanding, and the courts often will rule in favor of such a buyer—but not always, as the buyers found in the Connecticut case described in the Legal Highlight on the next page.

BREACH OF CONTRACT

Failure to perform a required contractual obligation is called a **breach of contract.** If a party to an agreement breaches its terms, the other party has a choice of remedies, either outlined in the contract or provided by law. Let's assume the seller, who has signed a valid real estate sales contract, refuses to transfer title to the buyer. The buyer may then sue for **specific performance;** that is, ask the court to order the breaching party to perform the terms of the contract.

A suit for specific performance is possible only if the contract concerns a unique item. Because land and improvements on land are considered one-of-a-kind items, a buyer probably will be successful in obtaining an order of specific performance. As an alternative, a buyer may seek payment for any damages that result from the seller's breach. Such damages could include compensation for the buyer's loss of time and the buyer's expenses related to the sale, such as legal fees for a title search, a land survey, and a building inspection.

If the buyer refuses to perform the duties under a valid contract, the seller also has the right to sue. In many states, however, the seller's rights are limited to recovering monetary damages, including any earnest money that may have been paid by the buyer. Usually, a seller cannot seek specific performance because courts do not feel that a ready, willing, and able buyer is a unique commodity. Eventually, the courts presume, some other purchaser will be found.

Validity of an Oral Contract

The statute of frauds requires that contracts for the sale of real estate be written in order to be enforceable. Richard and Mary Kelly learned this to their sorrow. The Kellys reached an oral agreement with William Ryan to purchase his residential waterfront property in Greenwich, Connecticut, for $2,125,000 in cash. The sale was subject to securing approval from the Coastal Area Management Commission for construction on the property that would double the size of the existing house and add a tennis court. The Kellys had a wetlands survey made and site plans prepared for submission of the application. A few days later, their attorney submitted a contract to Ryan's attorney, which essentially put the oral agreement into writing. Ryan refused to sign, and the next day, he contracted to sell the property to a third party. The Kellys sued, seeking specific performance by Ryan of the oral contract. They lost.

The court ruled that:

However plain and complete the terms of an oral contract for the sale and purchase of real estate, it cannot be enforced against a party thereto unless he, or his agent, has signed a written memorandum which recited the essential elements of the contract with reasonable certainty.

Even though the Kellys had a definite oral agreement with Ryan, as the Hollywood producer Sam Goldwyn used to say, "An oral agreement isn't worth the paper it's written on." The Kellys also argued that they had made "substantial improvements" to the property on the basis of the oral agreement, thus defeating the written requirement in the statute of frauds. The court did not agree, holding that the survey and site plans, at a cost of less than $5,000, were not "substantial" to a property with a value of more than $2 million. The lesson is clear: *Never, never, never* rely on an oral contract in the sale or purchase of anything of value, particularly not in the sale or purchase of real estate.

[*Kelly v. Ryan*, Nos. CV 91 011 53 81, DV 91 011 54 38 S., Connecticut Superior Court, 1991]

CONTRACT CONTINGENCIES

The preceding discussion of remedies for a breached contract is based on the presumption that the party's nonperformance is not excused. A well-drafted contract provides that the parties will be discharged from performance in the event of certain conditions. These conditions are called **contingencies.** A common clause in residential real estate sales contracts is a **financing contingency** that allows a buyer who is not able to arrange the necessary financing within a certain time period to cancel the contract and recover any earnest money paid without further obligation. Similarly, real estate sales contracts often contain a **title contingency** that allows either party to cancel a contract if the title search reveals a problem with the seller's legal title to the property that cannot be resolved within a certain time period. Another common component of real estate sales contracts is the **inspection and repair contingency.** This clause permits the buyer to have a qualified inspector examine the property for any physical defects. If defects are found, the seller may be obligated to make repairs up to an agreed-on amount. If the cost of repairs exceeds this amount, the buyer may elect to cancel the contract. Almost any condition can be added to an agreement, as long as it does not create a contract for an unlawful purpose. Also, most courts would consider a contract that included an *unconscionable condition* (one that is shockingly unfair) to be invalid.

REAL ESTATE SALES CONTRACTS

Now that we understand the fundamental concepts behind the theory of contracts, let's consider some specific examples of contracts used in real estate transactions. Frequently encountered contracts in real estate transactions include sales contracts, option-to-buy contracts, contracts for deed, leases, listing agreements, buyer representation agreements, and property management agreements. Our focus in this section is on the real estate sales contract. **Sales contracts** provide for the eventual transfer of title to real property. *Title,* or the legal right to ownership of land, is passed by use of a deed and does not change hands until the transaction actually is closed, or brought to a successful conclusion. The sales contract's purpose is to provide the rules governing the parties' rights and duties during the time between the agreement to transfer real property and the actual transfer of title. A reasonable time period generally is necessary to allow the buyer to secure financing, check the seller's title, and obtain property insurance.

Negotiating a Sales Contract

In most real estate markets, property owners who wish to sell their properties will advertise them at a specified price through a local real estate broker or as a for-sale-by-owner deal *(FSBO,* sometimes pronounced "fizbo"). Potential buyers examine the property and decide if they are interested in purchasing it. Preliminary negotiations between buyers and sellers are very often oral, but because the ultimate agreement must be in written form, sincere negotiations usually begin with one party (either the buyer or the seller) writing his or her offer, signing it, and presenting it to the other party for review. If the other party accepts the offer and signs it, then a contract is formed as specified in the document. If the other party, however, suggests a change to the first party's offer, then the second party has essentially rejected the offer and presented a counteroffer. Perhaps the first party will accept this change and thus a deal is struck, or the other party may choose to make yet another counteroffer to the second party's counteroffer. The negotiations continue in this fashion until the parties either reach an agreement or discontinue negotiations. Keep in mind that one party must make an offer, or a counteroffer, that the other party accepts in the exact form in which it was offered before a final agreement is reached. Offers and counteroffers can be withdrawn by the offeror at any point prior to acceptance by the offeree.

Sales Contract Example

Parties to a real estate transaction are free to negotiate any legal and conscionable agreement they can reduce to written form. To ease the process of negotiating a real estate sales contract "from scratch," most states allow real estate brokers to fill in the blanks on contract forms that have been drafted by an attorney and/or approved by the state bar association. An example of such a contract form is shown in Figure 6.1. This "contract for sale and purchase" of real estate has been jointly adopted by the Florida Association of REALTORS® and the Florida Bar for use by real estate brokers who are assisting buyers and sellers to negotiate transactions in that state. Some of the details of this contract are state-specific. Most other states have a similar contract form that reflects any state-specific requirements for valid real estate contracts. This type of contract form often serves as the framework for negotiations between the parties, as well as the final agreement.

Let's consider an example to understand how this contract is used in a real estate transaction. Suppose Clay Williams is purchasing a house listed with Rodriguez Realty Company and owned by Sarah Howell. Sarah was asking $309,900 for the home, but the parties have agreed on a price of $295,000, as shown on line 16. Clay gave $10,000 as an earnest money deposit to Julio Rodriguez, the real estate broker assisting the parties in the transaction. In his capacity as the escrow agent Julio must safeguard the deposit according to the terms of the contract and state laws regulating escrow account management. Clay will borrow $236,000 from a mortgage lender and will need an additional $49,000 as the balance to close this transaction ($295,000 − $236,000 − $10,000 = $49,000). Let's consider some of the key points of this contract.

Lines 25–32: We see that when Clay made this offer to Sarah, he allowed her until June 13, 2007, to consider it. Looking ahead to line 113, we can see that Clay signed the offer on June 6, 2007, implying that he gave her one week from that date to consider it. Obviously, the time allowed to consider the offer can be important in the negotiation strategy. If she had not accepted the offer before the date specified, his offer would have been automatically withdrawn and his deposit would have been returned to him. Until his offer is withdrawn (either by Clay or automatically by time expiration), Sarah could create a binding contract by accepting the outstanding offer. Note that Sarah signed the contract (again, line 113) on June 11, 2007. Once it is accepted, an offer cannot be withdrawn because an accepted offer is a binding contract.

Lines 35–49: Clay and Sarah have agreed that Clay will apply for a mortgage loan for $236,000 that has a fixed interest rate of no more than 9 percent and a term of 30 years. Notice that if Clay's loan application is denied, he is entitled to a refund of his earnest money deposit.

FIGURE 6.1 | Contract for Sale and Purchase

THIS FORM HAS BEEN APPROVED BY THE FLORIDA ASSOCIATION OF REALTORS® AND THE FLORIDA BAR

Contract For Sale And Purchase
FLORIDA ASSOCIATION OF REALTORS® AND THE FLORIDA BAR

1* PARTIES: Sarah Howell _____ ("Seller"),
2* and Clay Williams _____ ("Buyer"),
3 hereby agree that Seller shall sell and Buyer shall buy the following described Real Property and Personal Property (collectively "Property")
4 pursuant to the terms and conditions of this Contract for Sale and Purchase and any riders and addenda ("Contract"):
5 I. **DESCRIPTION:**
6* (a) Legal description of the Real Property located in Broward _____ County, Florida: Lot 1 Block A,
7* Ridgeview Subdivision according to the plat thereof recorded in Book 2349, Page 481, in the
8* Official Records of Broward County, Florida, on May 4, 1971.
9* (b) Street address, city, zip, of the Property: 501 SE 1st Street, Fort Lauderdale, Florida, 33301
10 (c) Personal Property includes existing range(s), refrigerator(s), dishwasher(s), ceiling fan(s), light fixture(s), and window treatment(s) unless
11 specifically excluded below.
12* Other items included are: existing "GE" clothes washer and dryer in laundry room (SN 955404A and 98900D2),
13* "Jennings Spa" hot tub on patio (SN 1989084)
14* Items of Personal Property (and leased items, if any) excluded are: satellite television system (antenna and receivers)
15* chandelier in foyer
16* II. **PURCHASE PRICE** (U.S. currency) . . . . $_____295,000.00
17 **PAYMENT:**
18* (a) Deposit held in escrow by Julio Rodriguez _____ (Escrow Agent) in the amount of (checks subject to clearance) $_____10,000.00
19* (b) Additional escrow deposit to be made to Escrow Agent within _____ days after Effective Date
20* (see Paragraph III) in the amount of. . . . . $_____0.00
21* (c) Financing (see Paragraph IV) in the amount of . . . . $_____236,000.00
22* (d) Other . . . . $_____0.00
23 (e) Balance to close by cash, wire transfer or LOCALLY DRAWN cashier's or official bank check(s), subject
24* to adjustments or prorations . . . . $_____49,000.00
25 III. **TIME FOR ACCEPTANCE OF OFFER AND COUNTEROFFERS; EFFECTIVE DATE:**
26 (a) If this offer is not executed by and delivered to all parties OR FACT OF EXECUTION communicated in writing between the parties on or
27* before 6/13/2007 _____, the deposit(s) will, at Buyer's option, be returned and this offer withdrawn. UNLESS OTH-
28 ERWISE STATED, THE TIME FOR ACCEPTANCE OF ANY COUNTEROFFERS SHALL BE 2 DAYS FROM THE DATE THE COUN-
29 TEROFFER IS DELIVERED.
30 (b) The date of Contract ("Effective Date") will be the date when the last one of the Buyer and Seller has signed or initialed this offer or the
31 final counteroffer. If such date is not otherwise set forth in this Contract, then the "Effective Date" shall be the date determined above for
32 acceptance of this offer or, if applicable, the final counteroffer.
33 IV. **FINANCING:**
34* ❏ (a) This is a cash transaction with no contingencies for financing;
35* ☑ (b) This Contract is contingent on Buyer obtaining approval of a loan ("Loan Approval") within 15 days (if blank, then 30 days) after
36* Effective Date ("Loan Approval Date") for (CHECK ONLY ONE): ☑ a fixed ❏ an adjustable; or ❏ a fixed or adjustable rate loan, in the prin-
37* cipal amount of $236,000.00, at an initial interest rate not to exceed 9.00 % discount and origination fees not to exceed
38* 2.00 % of principal amount, and for a term of 30 years. Buyer will make application within 3 days (if blank, then 5 days) after
39 Effective Date. Buyer shall use reasonable diligence to: obtain Loan Approval and notify Seller in writing of Loan Approval by Loan
40 **Approval Date;** satisfy terms and conditions of the Loan Approval; and close the loan. Loan Approval which requires a condition related to
41 the sale of other property shall not be deemed Loan Approval for purposes of this subparagraph. Buyer shall pay all loan expenses. If Buyer
42 does not deliver written notice to Seller by Loan Approval Date stating Buyer has either obtained Loan Approval or waived this financing con-
43 tingency, then either party may cancel this Contract by delivering written notice ("Cancellation Notice") to the other, not later than seven (7)
44 days prior to Closing. Seller's Cancellation Notice must state that Buyer has three (3) days to deliver to Seller written notice waiving this
45 financing contingency. If Buyer has used due diligence and has not obtained Loan Approval before cancellation as provided above, Buyer
46 shall be refunded the deposit(s). Unless this financing contingency has been waived, this Contract shall remain subject to the satisfaction,
47 by Closing, of those conditions of Loan Approval related to the Property;
48* ❏ (c) Assumption of existing mortgage (see rider for terms); or
49* ❏ (d) Purchase money note and mortgage to Seller (see Standards B and K and riders; addenda; or special clauses for terms).
50* V. **TITLE EVIDENCE:** At least _____ days (if blank, then 5 days) before Closing a title insurance commitment with legible copies of instruments
51 listed as exceptions attached thereto ("Title Commitment") and, after Closing, an owner's policy of title insurance (see Standard A for terms) shall
52 be obtained by:
53* **(CHECK ONLY ONE):** ☑ (1) Seller, at Seller's expense and delivered to Buyer or Buyer's attorney; or
54* ❏ (2) Buyer at Buyer's expense.
55* **(CHECK HERE):** ❏ If an abstract of title is to be furnished instead of title insurance, and attach rider for terms.
56* VI. **CLOSING DATE:** This transaction shall be closed and the closing documents delivered on 8/4/2007 _____ ("Closing"), unless
57 modified by other provisions of this Contract. If Buyer is unable to obtain Hazard, Wind, Flood, or Homeowners' insurance at a reasonable rate
58 due to extreme weather conditions, Buyer may delay Closing for up to 5 days after such coverage becomes available.
59 VII. **RESTRICTIONS; EASEMENTS; LIMITATIONS:** Seller shall convey marketable title subject to: comprehensive land use plans, zoning,
60 restrictions, prohibitions and other requirements imposed by governmental authority; restrictions and matters appearing on the plat or otherwise

FAR/BAR-7s Rev. 7/04 © 2004 Florida Association of REALTORS® and The Florida Bar All Rights Reserved **Page 1 of 4**

FIGURE 6.1 | Contract for Sale and Purchase *(continued)*

61 common to the subdivision; outstanding oil, gas and mineral rights of record without right of entry; unplatted public utility easements of record
62 (located contiguous to real property lines and not more than 10 feet in width as to the rear or front lines and 7 1/2 feet in width as to the side
63 lines); taxes for year of Closing and subsequent years; and assumed mortgages and purchase money mortgages, if any (if additional items, see
64 addendum); provided, that there exists at Closing no violation of the foregoing and none prevent use of the Property for
65* single-family residential _____ purpose(s).
66 **VIII. OCCUPANCY:** Seller shall deliver occupancy of Property to Buyer at time of Closing unless otherwise stated herein. If Property is intended
67 to be rented or occupied beyond Closing, the fact and terms thereof and the tenant(s) or occupants shall be disclosed pursuant to Standard F.
68 If occupancy is to be delivered before Closing, Buyer assumes all risks of loss to Property from date of occupancy, shall be responsible and liable
69 for maintenance from that date, and shall be deemed to have accepted Property in its existing condition as of time of taking occupancy.
70 **IX. TYPEWRITTEN OR HANDWRITTEN PROVISIONS:** Typewritten or handwritten provisions, riders and addenda shall control all printed pro-
71 visions of this Contract in conflict with them.
72* **X. ASSIGNABILITY:** (CHECK ONLY ONE): Buyer ❑ may assign and thereby be released from any further liability under this Contract; ❑ may
73* assign but not be released from liability under this Contract; or ☒ may not assign this Contract.
74 **XI. DISCLOSURES:**
75* (a) ❑ CHECK HERE if the Property is subject to a special assessment lien imposed by a public body payable in installments which
76* continue beyond Closing and, if so, specify who shall pay amounts due after Closing: ❑ Seller ❑ Buyer ❑ Other (see addendum).
77 (b) Radon is a naturally occurring radioactive gas that when accumulated in a building in sufficient quantities may present health risks to per-
78 sons who are exposed to it over time. Levels of radon that exceed federal and state guidelines have been found in buildings in Florida.
79 Additional information regarding radon or radon testing may be obtained from your County Public Health unit.
80 (c) Mold is naturally occurring and may cause health risks or damage to property. If Buyer is concerned or desires additional information
81 regarding mold, Buyer should contact an appropriate professional.
82 (d) Buyer acknowledges receipt of the Florida Energy-Efficiency Rating Information Brochure required by Section 553.996, F.S.
83 (e) If the real property includes pre-1978 residential housing then a lead-based paint rider is mandatory.
84 (f) If Seller is a "foreign person" as defined by the Foreign Investment in Real Property Tax Act, the parties shall comply with that Act.
85 (g) **BUYER SHOULD NOT EXECUTE THIS CONTRACT UNTIL BUYER HAS RECEIVED AND READ THE HOMEOWNERS' ASSOCIA-**
86 **TION/COMMUNITY DISCLOSURE.**
87 (h) PROPERTY TAX DISCLOSURE SUMMARY: BUYER SHOULD NOT RELY ON THE SELLER'S CURRENT PROPERTY TAXES AS THE AMOUNT
88 OF PROPERTY TAXES THAT THE BUYER MAY BE OBLIGATED TO PAY IN THE YEAR SUBSEQUENT TO PURCHASE. A CHANGE OF OWNER-
89 SHIP OR PROPERTY IMPROVEMENTS TRIGGERS REASSESSMENTS OF THE PROPERTY THAT COULD RESULT IN HIGHER PROPERTY TAXES.
90 IF YOU HAVE ANY QUESTIONS CONCERNING VALUATION, CONTACT THE COUNTY PROPERTY APPRAISER'S OFFICE FOR INFORMATION.
91 **XII. MAXIMUM REPAIR COSTS:** Seller shall not be responsible for payments in excess of:
92* (a) $_____5,000.00_____ for treatment and repair under Standard D (if blank, then 1.5% of the Purchase Price).
93* (b) $_____5,000.00_____ for repair and replacement under Standard N not caused by Wood Destroying Organisms (if blank, then 1.5%
94 of the Purchase Price).
95* **XIII. HOME WARRANTY:** ❑ Seller ❑ Buyer ☒ N/A will pay for a home warranty plan issued by _____
96* at a cost not to exceed $_____.
97 **XIV. RIDERS; ADDENDA; SPECIAL CLAUSES: CHECK** those riders which are applicable AND are attached to and made part of this Contract:
98* ❑ CONDOMINIUM ❑ VA/FHA ❑ HOMEOWNERS' ASSN. ❑ LEAD-BASED PAINT ❑ COASTAL CONSTRUCTION CONTROL LINE
99* ❑ INSULATION ❑ "AS IS" ❑ Other Comprehensive Rider Provisions ❑ Addenda
100* Special Clause(s): _____
101* _____
102* _____
103* _____
104 **XV. STANDARDS FOR REAL ESTATE TRANSACTIONS ("Standards"):** Buyer and Seller acknowledge receipt of a copy of Standards A
105 through Y on the reverse side or attached, which are incorporated as part of this Contract.
106 **THIS IS INTENDED TO BE A LEGALLY BINDING CONTRACT. IF NOT FULLY UNDERSTOOD,**
107 **SEEK THE ADVICE OF AN ATTORNEY PRIOR TO SIGNING.**
108 THIS FORM HAS BEEN APPROVED BY THE FLORIDA ASSOCIATION OF REALTORS® AND THE FLORIDA BAR.
109 Approval does not constitute an opinion that any of the terms and conditions in this Contract should be accepted by the parties in a
110 particular transaction. Terms and conditions should be negotiated based upon the respective interests, objectives and bargaining
111 positions of all interested persons.
112 AN ASTERISK(*) FOLLOWING A LINE NUMBER IN THE MARGIN INDICATES THE LINE CONTAINS A BLANK TO BE COMPLETED.

113* _____ _____ _____ _____
114 (BUYER)   (DATE)   (SELLER)   (DATE)

115* _____ _____ _____ _____
116 (BUYER)   (DATE)   (SELLER)   (DATE)

117* Buyers' address for purposes of notice _____ Sellers' address for purposes of notice _____
118* 934 Jupiter St., Townsend, Florida 33440   1000 Banyan Street, Suburb, Florida 33323
119* _____ Phone   _____ Phone
120 **BROKERS:** The brokers (including cooperating brokers, if any) named below are the only brokers entitled to compensation in connection with
121 this Contract: Julio Rodriguez
122* Name: _____none_____   _____
123 Cooperating Brokers, if any   Listing Broker

FAR/BAR-7s Rev. 7/04 © 2004 Florida Association of REALTORS® and The Florida Bar All Rights Reserved **Page 2 of 4**

FIGURE 6.1 | Contract for Sale and Purchase *(continued)*

STANDARDS FOR REAL ESTATE TRANSACTIONS

124
125 **A. TITLE INSURANCE:** The Title Commitment shall be issued by a Florida licensed title insurer agreeing to issue Buyer, upon recording of the deed to Buyer, an
126 owner's policy of title insurance in the amount of the purchase price, insuring Buyer's marketable title to the Real Property, subject only to matters contained in
127 Paragraph VII and those to be discharged by Seller at or before Closing. Marketable title shall be determined according to applicable Title Standards adopted by
128 authority of The Florida Bar and in accordance with law. Buyer shall have 5 days from date of receiving the Title Commitment to examine it, and if title is found defec-
129 tive, notify Seller in writing specifying defect(s) which render title unmarketable. Seller shall have 30 days from receipt of notice to remove the defects, failing which
130 Buyer shall, within 5 days after expiration of the 30 day period, deliver written notice to Seller either: (1) extending the time for a reasonable period not to exceed 120
131 days within which Seller shall use diligent effort to remove the defects; or (2) requesting a refund of deposit(s) paid which shall be returned to Buyer. If Buyer fails to
132 so notify Seller, Buyer shall be deemed to have accepted the title as it then is. Seller shall, if title is found unmarketable, use diligent effort to correct defect(s) within
133 the time provided. If, after diligent effort, Seller is unable to timely correct the defects, Buyer shall either waive the defects, or receive a refund of deposit(s), thereby
134 releasing Buyer and Seller from all further obligations under this Contract. If Seller is to provide the Title Commitment and it is delivered to Buyer less than 5 days prior
135 to Closing, Buyer may extend Closing so that Buyer shall have up to 5 days from date of receipt to examine same in accordance with this Standard.
136 **B. PURCHASE MONEY MORTGAGE; SECURITY AGREEMENT TO SELLER:** A purchase money mortgage and mortgage note to Seller shall provide for a
137 30 day grace period in the event of default if a first mortgage and a 15 day grace period if a second or lesser mortgage; shall provide for right of prepayment
138 in whole or in part without penalty; shall permit acceleration in event of transfer of the Real Property; shall require all prior liens and encumbrances to be kept
139 in good standing; shall forbid modifications of, or future advances under, prior mortgage(s); shall require Buyer to maintain policies of insurance containing a
140 standard mortgagee clause covering all improvements located on the Real Property against fire and all perils included within the term "extended coverage
141 endorsements" and such other risks and perils as Seller may reasonably require, in an amount equal to their highest insurable value; and the mortgage, note
142 and security agreement shall be otherwise in form and content required by Seller, but Seller may only require clauses and coverage customarily found in mort-
143 gages, mortgage notes and security agreements generally utilized by savings and loan institutions or state or national banks located in the county wherein the
144 Real Property is located. All Personal Property and leases being conveyed or assigned will, at Seller's option, be subject to the lien of a security agreement evi-
145 denced by recorded or filed financing statements or certificates of title. If a balloon mortgage, the final payment will exceed the periodic payments thereon.
146 **C. SURVEY:** Buyer, at Buyer's expense, within time allowed to deliver evidence of title and to examine same, may have the Real Property surveyed and certified
147 by a registered Florida surveyor. If the survey discloses encroachments on the Real Property or that improvements located thereon encroach on setback lines, ease-
148 ments, lands of others or violate any restrictions, Contract covenants or applicable governmental regulations, the same shall constitute a title defect.
149 **D. WOOD DESTROYING ORGANISMS:** "Wood Destroying Organisms" (WDO) shall be deemed to include all wood destroying organisms required to be report-
150 ed under the Florida Structural Pest Control Act, as amended. Buyer, at Buyer's expense, may have the Property inspected by a Florida Certified Pest Control Operator
151 ("Operator") within 20 days after the Effective Date to determine if there is any visible active WDO infestation or visible damage from WDO infestation, excluding fences.
152 If either or both are found, Buyer may within said 20 days (1) have cost of treatment of active infestation estimated by the Operator; (2) have all damage inspected
153 and cost of repair estimated by an appropriately licensed contractor; and (3) report such cost(s) to Seller in writing. Seller shall cause the treatment and repair of all
154 WDO damage to be made and pay the costs thereof up to the amount provided in Paragraph XII(a). If estimated costs exceed that amount, Buyer shall have the
155 option of canceling this Contract by giving written notice to Seller within 20 days after the Effective Date, or Buyer may elect to proceed with the transaction and
156 receive a credit at Closing equal to the amount provided in Paragraph XII(a). If Buyer's lender requires an updated WDO report, then Buyer shall, at Buyer's expense,
157 have the opportunity to have the Property re-inspected for WDO infestation and have the cost of active infestation or new damage estimated and reported to Seller
158 in writing at least 10 days prior to Closing, and thereafter, Seller shall cause such treatment and repair to be made and pay the cost thereof; provided, Seller's total
159 obligation for treatment and repair costs required under both the first and second inspection shall not exceed the amount provided in Paragraph XII (a).
160 **E. INGRESS AND EGRESS:** Seller warrants and represents that there is ingress and egress to the Real Property sufficient for its intended use as described
161 in Paragraph VII hereof and title to the Real Property is insurable in accordance with Standard A without exception for lack of legal right of access.
162 **F. LEASES:** Seller shall, at least 10 days before Closing, furnish to Buyer copies of all written leases and estoppel letters from each tenant specifying the nature
163 and duration of the tenant's occupancy, rental rates, advanced rent and security deposits paid by tenant. If Seller is unable to obtain such letter from each ten-
164 ant, the same information shall be furnished by Seller to Buyer within that time period in the form of a Seller's affidavit, and Buyer may thereafter contact ten-
165 ant to confirm such information. If the terms of the leases differ materially from Seller's representations, Buyer may terminate this Contract by delivering written
166 notice to Seller at least 5 days prior to Closing. Seller shall, at Closing, deliver and assign all original leases to Buyer.
167 **G. LIENS:** Seller shall furnish to Buyer at time of Closing an affidavit attesting to the absence, unless otherwise provided for herein, of any financing statement,
168 claims of lien or potential lienors known to Seller and further attesting that there have been no improvements or repairs to the Real Property for 90 days imme-
169 diately preceding date of Closing. If the Real Property has been improved or repaired within that time, Seller shall deliver releases or waivers of construction
170 liens executed by all general contractors, subcontractors, suppliers and materialmen in addition to Seller's lien affidavit setting forth the names of all such gen-
171 eral contractors, subcontractors, suppliers and materialmen, further affirming that all charges for improvements or repairs which could serve as a basis for a
172 construction lien or a claim for damages have been paid or will be paid at the Closing of this Contract.
173 **H. PLACE OF CLOSING:** Closing shall be held in the county wherein the Real Property is located at the office of the attorney or other closing agent ("Closing
174 Agent") designated by the party paying for title insurance, or, if no title insurance, designated by Seller.
175 **I. TIME:** In computing time periods of less than six (6) days, Saturdays, Sundays and state or national legal holidays shall be excluded. Any time periods provided
176 for herein which shall end on a Saturday, Sunday, or a legal holiday shall extend to 5:00 p.m. of the next business day. **Time is of the essence in this Contract.**
177 **J. CLOSING DOCUMENTS:** Seller shall furnish the deed, bill of sale, certificate of title, construction lien affidavit, owner's possession affidavit, assignments of leases,
178 tenant and mortgagee estoppel letters and corrective instruments. Buyer shall furnish mortgage, mortgage note, security agreement and financing statements.
179 **K. EXPENSES:** Documentary stamps on the deed and recording of corrective instruments shall be paid by Seller. All costs of Buyer's loan (whether obtained
180 from Seller or third party), including, but not limited to, documentary stamps and intangible tax on the purchase money mortgage and any mortgage assumed,
181 mortgagee title insurance commitment with related fees, and recording of purchase money mortgage to Seller, deed and financing statements shall be paid by
182 Buyer. Unless otherwise provided by law or rider to this Contract, charges for the following related title services, namely title evidence, title examination, and
183 closing fee (including preparation of closing statement), shall be paid by the party responsible for furnishing the title evidence in accordance with Paragraph V.
184 **L. PRORATIONS; CREDITS:** Taxes, assessments, rent, interest, insurance and other expenses of the Property shall be prorated through the day before Closing.
185 Buyer shall have the option of taking over existing policies of insurance, if assumable, in which event premiums shall be prorated. Cash at Closing shall be
186 increased or decreased as may be required by prorations to be made through day prior to Closing, or occupancy, if occupancy occurs before Closing. Advance
187 rent and security deposits will be credited to Buyer. Escrow deposits held by mortgagee will be credited to Seller. Taxes shall be prorated based on the current
188 year's tax with due allowance made for maximum allowable discount, homestead and other exemptions. If Closing occurs at a date when the current year's mill-
189 age is not fixed and current year's assessment is available, taxes will be prorated based upon such assessment and prior year's millage. If current year's assess-
190 ment is not available, then taxes will be prorated on prior year's tax. If there are completed improvements on the Real Property by January 1st of year of Closing,
191 which improvements were not in existence on January 1st of prior year, then taxes shall be prorated based upon prior year's millage and at an equitable assess-
192 ment to be agreed upon between the parties; failing which, request shall be made to the County Property Appraiser for an informal assessment taking into
193 account available exemptions. A tax proration based on an estimate shall, at request of either party, be readjusted upon receipt of current year's tax bill.
194 **M. SPECIAL ASSESSMENT LIENS:** Except as set forth in Paragraph XI(a), certified, confirmed and ratified special assessment liens imposed by public bod-
195 ies as of Closing are to be paid by Seller. Pending liens as of Closing shall be assumed by Buyer. If the improvement has been substantially completed as of
196 Effective Date, any pending lien shall be considered certified, confirmed or ratified and Seller shall, at Closing, be charged an amount equal to the last estimate
197 or assessment for the improvement by the public body.

FIGURE 6.1 | Contract for Sale and Purchase *(continued)*

STANDARDS FOR REAL ESTATE TRANSACTIONS (CONTINUED)

198
199 **N. INSPECTION AND REPAIR:** Seller warrants that the ceiling, roof (including the fascia and soffits), exterior and interior walls, foundation, and dockage of
200 the Property do not have any visible evidence of leaks, water damage, or structural damage and that the septic tank, pool, all appliances, mechanical items,
201 heating, cooling, electrical, plumbing systems, and machinery are in Working Condition. The foregoing warranty shall be limited to the items specified unless
202 otherwise provided in an addendum. Buyer may inspect, or, at Buyer's expense, have a firm or individual specializing in home inspections and holding an occu-
203 pational license for such purpose (if required), or by an appropriately licensed Florida contractor, make inspections of, those items within 20 days after the
204 Effective Date. Buyer shall, prior to Buyer's occupancy but not more than 20 days after Effective Date, report in writing to Seller such items that do not meet
205 the above standards as to defects. Unless Buyer timely reports such defects, Buyer shall be deemed to have waived Seller's warranties as to defects not report-
206 ed. If repairs or replacements are required to comply with this Standard, Seller shall cause them to be made and shall pay up to the amount provided in
207 Paragraph XII (b). Seller is not required to make repairs or replacements of a Cosmetic Condition unless caused by a defect Seller is responsible to repair or
208 replace. If the cost for such repair or replacement exceeds the amount provided in Paragraph XII (b), Buyer or Seller may elect to pay such excess, failing which
209 either party may cancel this Contract. If Seller is unable to correct the defects prior to Closing, the cost thereof shall be paid into escrow at Closing. For pur-
210 poses of this Contract: (1) "Working Condition" means operating in the manner in which the item was designed to operate; (2) "Cosmetic Condition" means
211 aesthetic imperfections that do not affect the Working Condition of the item, including, but not limited to: pitted marcite or other pool finishes; missing or torn
212 screens; fogged windows; tears, worn spots, or discoloration of floor coverings, wallpaper, or window treatments; nail holes, scratches, dents, scrapes, chips
213 or caulking in ceilings, walls, flooring, fixtures, or mirrors; and minor cracks in floors, tiles, windows, driveways, sidewalks, or pool decks; and (3) cracked roof
214 tiles, curling or worn shingles, or limited roof life shall not be considered defects Seller must repair or replace, so long as there is no evidence of actual leaks
215 or leakage or structural damage, but missing tiles will be Seller's responsibility to replace or repair.
216 **O. RISK OF LOSS:** If the Property is damaged by fire or other casualty before Closing and cost of restoration does not exceed 1.5% of the Purchase Price, cost
217 of restoration shall be an obligation of Seller and Closing shall proceed pursuant to the terms of this Contract with restoration costs escrowed at Closing. If the
218 cost of restoration exceeds 1.5% of the Purchase Price, Buyer shall either take the Property as is, together with either the 1.5% or any insurance proceeds
219 payable by virtue of such loss or damage, or receive a refund of deposit(s), thereby releasing Buyer and Seller from all further obligations under this Contract.
220 **P. CLOSING PROCEDURE:** The deed shall be recorded upon clearance of funds. If the title agent insures adverse matters pursuant to Section 627.7841, F.S.,
221 as amended, the escrow and closing procedure required by this Standard shall be waived. Unless waived as set forth above the following closing procedures
222 shall apply: (1) all closing proceeds shall be held in escrow by the Closing Agent for a period of not more than 5 days after Closing; (2) if Seller's title is rendered
223 unmarketable, through no fault of Buyer, Buyer shall, within the 5 day period, notify Seller in writing of the defect and Seller shall have 30 days from date of receipt
224 of such notification to cure the defect; (3) if Seller fails to timely cure the defect, all deposits and closing funds shall, upon written demand by Buyer and within 5
225 days after demand, be returned to Buyer and, simultaneously with such repayment, Buyer shall return the Personal Property, vacate the Real Property and recon-
226 vey the Property to Seller by special warranty deed and bill of sale; and (4) if Buyer fails to make timely demand for refund, Buyer shall take title as is, waiving all
227 rights against Seller as to any intervening defect except as may be available to Buyer by virtue of warranties contained in the deed or bill of sale.
228 **Q. ESCROW:** Any Closing Agent or escrow agent (collectively "Agent") receiving funds or equivalent is authorized and agrees by acceptance of them to deposit
229 them promptly, hold same in escrow and, subject to clearance, disburse them in accordance with terms and conditions of this Contract. Failure of funds to clear shall
230 not excuse Buyer's performance. If in doubt as to Agent's duties or liabilities under the provisions of this Contract, Agent may, at Agent's option, continue to hold the
231 subject matter of the escrow until the parties hereto agree to its disbursement or until a judgment of a court of competent jurisdiction shall determine the rights of the
232 parties, or Agent may deposit same with the clerk of the circuit court having jurisdiction of the dispute. An attorney who represents a party and also acts as Agent
233 may represent such party in such action. Upon notifying all parties concerned of such action, all liability on the part of Agent shall fully terminate, except to the extent
234 of accounting for any items previously delivered out of escrow. If a licensed real estate broker, Agent will comply with provisions of Chapter 475, F.S., as amended.
235 Any suit between Buyer and Seller wherein Agent is made a party because of acting as Agent hereunder, or in any suit wherein Agent interpleads the subject matter
236 of the escrow, Agent shall recover reasonable attorney's fees and costs incurred with these amounts to be paid from and out of the escrowed funds or equivalent
237 and charged and awarded as court costs in favor of the prevailing party. The Agent shall not be liable to any party or person for misdelivery to Buyer or Seller of items
238 subject to the escrow, unless such misdelivery is due to willful breach of the provisions of this Contract or gross negligence of Agent.
239 **R. ATTORNEY'S FEES; COSTS:** In any litigation, including breach, enforcement or interpretation, arising out of this Contract, the prevailing party in such liti-
240 gation, which, for purposes of this Standard, shall include Seller, Buyer and any brokers acting in agency or nonagency relationships authorized by Chapter
241 475, F.S., as amended, shall be entitled to recover from the non-prevailing party reasonable attorney's fees, costs and expenses.
242 **S. FAILURE OF PERFORMANCE:** If Buyer fails to perform this Contract within the time specified, including payment of all deposits, the deposit(s) paid by
243 Buyer and deposit(s) agreed to be paid, may be recovered and retained by and for the account of Seller as agreed upon liquidated damages, consideration for
244 the execution of this Contract and in full settlement of any claims; whereupon, Buyer and Seller shall be relieved of all obligations under this Contract; or Seller,
245 at Seller's option, may proceed in equity to enforce Seller's rights under this Contract. If for any reason other than failure of Seller to make Seller's title mar-
246 ketable after diligent effort, Seller fails, neglects or refuses to perform this Contract, Buyer may seek specific performance or elect to receive the return of Buyer's
247 deposit(s) without thereby waiving any action for damages resulting from Seller's breach.
248 **T. CONTRACT NOT RECORDABLE; PERSONS BOUND; NOTICE; FACSIMILE:** Neither this Contract nor any notice of it shall be recorded in any public
249 records. This Contract shall bind and inure to the benefit of the parties and their successors in interest. Whenever the context permits, singular shall include
250 plural and one gender shall include all. Notice and delivery given by or to the attorney or broker representing any party shall be as effective as if given by or to
251 that party. All notices must be in writing and may be made by mail, personal delivery or electronic media. A legible facsimile copy of this Contract and any sig-
252 natures hereon shall be considered for all purposes as an original.
253 **U. CONVEYANCE:** Seller shall convey marketable title to the Real Property by statutory warranty, trustee's, personal representative's, or guardian's deed, as
254 appropriate to the status of Seller, subject only to matters contained in Paragraph VII and those otherwise accepted by Buyer. Personal Property shall, at the
255 request of Buyer, be transferred by an absolute bill of sale with warranty of title, subject only to such matters as may be otherwise provided for herein.
256 **V. OTHER AGREEMENTS:** No prior or present agreements or representations shall be binding upon Buyer or Seller unless included in this Contract. No mod-
257 ification to or change in this Contract shall be valid or binding upon the parties unless in writing and executed by the parties intended to be bound by it.
258 **W. SELLER DISCLOSURE:** There are no facts known to Seller materially affecting the value of the Property which are not readily observable by Buyer or which
259 have not been disclosed to Buyer.
260 **X. PROPERTY MAINTENANCE; PROPERTY ACCESS; REPAIR STANDARDS; ASSIGNMENT OF CONTRACTS AND WARRANTIES:** Seller shall main-
261 tain the Property, including, but not limited to lawn, shrubbery, and pool in the condition existing as of Effective Date, ordinary wear and tear excepted. Seller
262 shall, upon reasonable notice, provide utilities service and access to the Property for appraisal and inspections, including a walk-through prior to Closing, to
263 confirm that all items of Personal Property are on the Real Property and, subject to the foregoing, that all required repairs and replacements have been made,
264 and that the Property has been maintained as required by this Standard. All repairs and replacements shall be completed in a good and workmanlike manner,
265 in accordance with all requirements of law, and shall consist of materials or items of quality, value, capacity and performance comparable to, or better than,
266 that existing as of the Effective Date. Seller will assign all assignable repair and treatment contracts and warranties to Buyer at Closing.
267 **Y. 1031 EXCHANGE:** If either Seller or Buyer wish to enter into a like-kind exchange (either simultaneous with Closing or deferred) with respect to the Property
268 under Section 1031 of the Internal Revenue Code ("Exchange"), the other party shall cooperate in all reasonable respects to effectuate the Exchange, includ-
269 ing the execution of documents; provided (1) the cooperating party shall incur no liability or expense related to the Exchange and (2) the Closing shall not be
270 contingent upon, nor extended or delayed by, such Exchange.

Lines 50–55: Clay and Sarah have agreed that Sarah will be responsible for obtaining a title insurance policy to protect Clay's property rights from any undiscovered defects in the title. Title insurance was addressed in the previous chapter.

Line 53: The parties have set the closing date for August 4, 2007.

Lines 72-73: Clay may not assign this contract (transfer his right under this contract) to another buyer.

Lines 91-94: Sarah has agreed to pay up to $5,000 to treat and repair any termite or wood-destroying organism damage and up to $5,000 percent of the purchase price to repair any functional defects identified by qualified inspectors. To see the full impact of these clauses, refer to Standard D starting on line 149 and Standard N starting on line 199. The contract specifically states who must pay for the inspections (the buyer) and what the buyer's choices are if the cost of treating and repairing the property due to termite or wood-destroying organism damage exceeds $5,000 or the cost of repairing functional defects exceeds $5,000. Termite damage and hidden functional defects often require an expert to detect and can be quite expensive to correct. Lenders are concerned about the loss of value of the loan collateral and typically require certifications from appropriately qualified inspectors stating that the property is free of termites or functional defects before final loan approval. These clauses limit the seller's exposure to the agreed-upon amounts in each case and give the buyer a choice of paying any additional costs of treatment and repairs or canceling the contract and having any earnest money refunded.

As you can see, the contract form addresses many more details than we have outlined here. Before signing this document, Sarah and Clay should each ensure that all of the terms and conditions are acceptable. The fine print is crucial in any contract and should be read carefully. Whether the real estate sales contract is drafted by an attorney or completed by a broker, it should provide answers to any questions that arise during the time between the signing of the agreement and the closing, and the obligations of both buyer and seller. For example, a close reading of this contract will answer each of the following questions:

- When does the buyer get occupancy of the premises? (line 66)
- What actions can the buyer take if the seller's title proves to be unmarketable? (line 125)
- Whose responsibility is it to obtain and pay for a survey to detect any encroachments? (line 146)
- If an encroachment is detected in the survey, what happens? (line 146)
- Who must pay the documentary stamp tax necessary to record the deed in the public record system? (line 179)
- What happens to this agreement if the property is destroyed by fire or other casualty before the closing? (line 216)
- What actions can one party take if the other party breaches the contract? (line 242)

▌ OPTION-TO-BUY CONTRACTS

Another type of contract that is often useful in real estate transactions is the **option-to-buy contract.** Sometimes a party is interested in buying a specific property but is not yet ready to sign a sales contract. The option-to-buy contract is one way to ensure that the property will not be sold to another party before the person who holds the option to buy has made a final decision.

The *option-to-buy contract* is an agreement between a property owner and a potential buyer that states that the property owner agrees to keep an offer open for acceptance during a stated period of time. If the buyer decides to exercise the option before it expires, the owner must sell the property at the specified price. For example, an owner may state that he or she will sell the property to the option holder for $75,000 and will allow the holder to accept this offer at any time within the next six months. To ensure that the option is binding, it must be in writing and contain all of the necessary elements of a valid contract: offer, acceptance, consideration, parties with capacity, and lawful purpose.

The amount of consideration for the option depends on the circumstances. Suppose, for example, that Broker Judy Michaud is trying to assemble six properties as a tract for a shopping center. She offers Blanche, the owner of one of the six properties, an option-to-buy contract to purchase her house for $110,000, even though the property is worth only $90,000 as a residence. Blanche's property is worth the larger amount only if it can be used for the shopping center, and to achieve this, Judy must both obtain contracts from the other property owners and secure rezoning of the entire tract.

Thus, Judy offers Blanche an option contract that gives Judy the right to purchase the property for $110,000 any time in the next six months. Blanche might be happy to accept consideration of $1,000 or even less for agreeing to this arrangement because she will receive a very good price for her house if Judy is successful in putting the deal together. The consideration received by Blanche for the option granted to Judy is hers to keep, regardless of whether Judy exercises her option to buy. Thus, the consideration received by Blanche is her compensation for giving up the right to sell the property to anyone other than Judy for the next six months.

▌ CONTRACT FOR DEED

In addition to the contracts discussed thus far, real estate transactions are sometimes arranged as "installment sales," using a **contract for deed.** This arrangement stretches out the payments to the seller over time, but it allows the seller to retain legal title to the property until the agreed-on amount is paid. While making payments to the seller, the buyer typically has possession of the property as the "equitable" owner. Contracts for deed are sometimes called **land contracts** or **agreements for deed.**

The obvious question you might be asking is: How does a contract for deed differ from a mortgage? The answer is that the seller's collateral interest in the property is better protected in the event the buyer defaults on the agreement. If the buyer stops making payments, the seller is already (still) the legal owner of the property and thus can simply assert his or her ownership rights and sell the property to another buyer or keep it. Most states, however, recognize the possibility of a buyer's losing any equity he or she might have acquired in the property while making payments over time. In these states, buyers who breach a contract for deed are entitled to a refund of their equity (if any) in the property, but not interest paid. This requirement makes the contract for deed even more similar to a mortgage in these states. Regardless of whether default on the contract for deed requires that the seller refund any of the buyer's equity, buyers should realize that the seller is the legal owner of the property while a contract for deed is in place and could possibly cause other liens to be placed on the property prior to transferring title to the buyer.

Recall from the sales contract example we reviewed earlier in this chapter that the buyer, Clay Williams, is acquiring a property from Sarah Howell, the seller, in exchange for $189,000. Sarah will get all of her money at the closing and will simultaneously transfer title to Clay. At the same time, Clay will receive title from Sarah, then immediately pledge the property to the lender as collateral for the mortgage loan. If Clay and Sarah had agreed to use a contract for deed instead of the contract for sale and purchase, Sarah would hold the title to the property in her name while receiving payments over time from Clay. If Clay defaulted on the payments, Sarah's ownership rights would be clear and could easily be defended. Because the property in our example is in Florida (a state that treats contracts for deed as a mortgage document and sales contract combined), Sarah would have to foreclose on Clay just as if she held a mortgage lien on Clay's property if he should ever default on the contract terms.

SOME BASIC NEGOTIATION STRATEGIES

Many novice negotiators mistakenly approach a negotiation as if there were one pie that had to be somehow divided among the parties involved, and that every bite one party got was one less bite another party could get. In other words, some negotiators approach a negotiation as if it were a "zero-sum" game with the parties being classified as either "winner" or "loser" when the game is over. In most situations, however, the size of the pie, so to speak, is not nearly as fixed as we might assume, and all parties can ultimately benefit if the right solution can be found.

There is an old saying in real estate: "You can name the price if I can name the terms." This saying goes to the heart of what good negotiation is all about. Be willing to let the people who are most concerned about certain slices of the pie grab what they think they want, but look for creative ways to make the total pie bigger, thus ensuring yourself a sufficient slice, too!

In a typical real estate transaction, price is often viewed as the single most important factor to be resolved. Suppose a seller wants to get $1 million for the property and adamantly refuses to take one cent less. While some buyers might be discouraged by the seller's stubbornness, an astute buyer might think of another issue that can be added to the negotiation to "sweeten the deal." Perhaps the buyer will agree to the full asking price if the seller will agree to allow the buyer to pay only $850,000 immediately and make annual payments of $50,000 each for the next three years (a total of $1 million, but an interest-free loan for part of this amount). Or perhaps the seller will agree to take part of the $1 million in the form of another parcel of real estate the buyer owns and the remainder in cash or cash and a note. The potential for finding a creative solution is limitless in real estate negotiations, and those who seek solutions that make "winners" out of all parties to the negotiation are more likely to enjoy sustained success.

An important step in becoming a successful negotiator is to keep an open mind so you can better understand the other party's position. Find out what is important to the parties and try to ensure that they get what they want, while you get something you want (which may not be the same something you thought you wanted when the negotiation began). Search for common ground early in the negotiation process. With this accomplished, the remaining contentious issues may not appear nearly so large, and both parties may ultimately benefit. One of the worst mistakes a novice negotiator can make is to ignore the possibility of other ways to structure a deal that would benefit all parties involved.

TITLE CLOSINGS

When all the conditions of the sales contract have been met, the last step in the transaction process is to "close" or "settle" the transaction. In fact, a real estate transaction may involve several types of closings. The borrower and the lending institution must close the loan; the escrow agent, if one is employed, must close the escrow arrangement; and the grantor and grantee must close or transfer the title to the property involved. Generally, but not always, the various closings occur at the same meeting. Therefore, the word closing or settlement can refer to the conclusion to several different relationships. Remember that the ultimate purpose of the real estate sales process is to transfer title from the seller to the buyer. To look at closing properly, we must first examine each party's prior responsibilities.

Buyer's Responsibilities

Once the negotiations between a buyer and seller are completed and a sales contract is signed, the real estate transaction begins. Indeed, during the time period (usually 60 days) between the signing of a contract and the closing of the transaction, buyers often take on many new responsibilities, including

- obtaining financing,
- examining the title evidence,
- having the property surveyed,
- obtaining property insurance, and
- having the property inspected.

Financing the Purchase

A house is the largest financial investment the average American family makes. Very few families are able to pay cash for a home; indeed, even those who have such large amounts of cash are encouraged to borrow money because the interest paid on the loan is deductible from income taxes, and the money otherwise spent on the house is available for other forms of investment. Typically, buyers of residential real estate finance 70, 80, 90, or even 100 percent of the total purchase price. The use of borrowed funds is not limited, of course, to residential real estate. Even large corporations with access to international capital markets may choose to use significant portions of borrowed funds to acquire real estate. Lenders in the business of real estate financing have the power of foreclosure on their side and are comfortable lending money as long as they get a lien on the real estate.

Buyers' reliance on borrowed money requires that they insist on a financing contingency. A buyer who, after a good-faith effort, is unable to secure the specified financing may cancel the sales contract and have the earnest money refunded.

Under a clause conditioning the sale on the buyers' ability to obtain adequate financing, the buyers must use good faith and honesty in all attempts to borrow the required amount. They must apply for the loan within a short time after the contract is signed. They cannot delay such an attempt until there is not enough time for the lending institution to approve the loan before the closing date. If the buyers' failure to secure adequate financing is a result of their lack of good faith, the sellers can sue for damages as a consequence of the buyers' inability to close the transaction. If the money market is exceedingly tight, however, or if lenders are unwilling to risk the loan because they doubt the buyers' ability to pay, or if the loan is not approved for some reason over which the potential borrowers have no direct control, the buyers are relieved of their contractual obligation.

Failure to include in the sales contract the clause conditioning the sale on the buyers' ability to obtain financing can cause great hardship to the buyers. In that case, failure to secure adequate financing does not relieve the buyers of their contractual duties; therefore, buyers who cannot pay the purchase price at closing have breached the contract and are liable for the sellers' damages and may be required to forfeit any deposit money.

Examining the Title Evidence

Another principal responsibility of the buyer before closing is to examine the title evidence. Even though a seller may agree to pass title by general warranty deed, the buyer must check on the state of the seller's title for at least two important reasons. First, the seller's deed usually promises that there are no encumbrances other than "restrictions of record." It then becomes the buyer's responsibility to learn of any restrictions of record. Second, the sales contract normally requires that the buyer inform the seller of any defects found in the seller's title and give the seller the opportunity to correct them. As discussed in Chapter 5, title defects are discovered through a title examination.

Having the Property Surveyed

An actual survey of the property's boundaries is not always required before title can be transferred, particularly in subdivisions that have been platted. The plat in the public records normally will suffice in lieu of a survey. If there is some confusion as to the actual property lines, however, or if the lending institution requires that a survey be made to determine if any encroachments exist, the buyer usually must pay for it. Of course, the sales contract can provide that the seller bear the cost of any survey if the buyer and seller agree to this arrangement.

Obtaining Property Insurance

Again, because of the magnitude of real estate costs, most people cannot bear the risk of losing the property's value as a result of fire, vandalism, or other potential hazards. When a buyer is borrowing money to purchase real estate, the lender will require that the buyer purchase property insurance. Indeed, the lending institution will refuse to close the loan unless the borrower has provided proof that the property is insured for at least the amount of the loan.

Such proof typically is provided by a letter from the insurance company to the lender, a document often referred to as an *insurance binder.* Property insurance is indirectly vital to the title closing because the property insurance must be obtained before the loan can be completed, and the loan is crucial to the overall performance of the sales contract.

Inspecting the Property

Except in the most unusual circumstances, a buyer will have visited the real estate once or twice, or perhaps many times, before the sales contract is signed. Despite numerous visits to view the property, the prospective buyer seldom investigates thoroughly the property's mechanical systems such as the plumbing, wiring, or heating systems. At times, a buyer feels great pressure to sign a sales contract so that he or she will not lose the opportunity to buy a particular property the buyers have selected. The major utilities and appliances, if included, often remain uninspected as well.

The high cost associated with repairing any structural problems, mechanical systems, or appliances makes it extremely important that these items be in good working order. If any of these components of the property are damaged or not working properly, the buyer should know so that the offer to purchase can be adjusted accordingly.

The real estate sales contract we reviewed in the previous chapter included two specific inspection and repair clauses: termite/wood-destroying organisms and functional/mechanical defects. The buyer should inspect the premises during the time period before the closing. The seller must cooperate in allowing access to the buyer for this purpose. Although it does cost money to have someone knowledgeable inspect the major items of concern, the expense is far smaller than that of replacing the heating unit two weeks after the transaction is closed. If the inspections reveal repairs needed up to the agreed-on limit, the seller must correct the problems. Otherwise, the buyer can elect to cancel the contract.

Other Responsibilities

A buyer who is purchasing land for development purposes should investigate the zoning restrictions on the parcel involved. A sales contract for commercial land should contain a provision permitting the buyer to cancel the contract if the zoning regulations do not permit the intended use or cannot be changed to permit it by the stipulated closing date. A buyer of rental property should study the current lease's terms and conditions, as well as the schedule of rental payments. Of course, because the parties are the masters of their contracts, a sales agreement may include other duties owed by the buyer before the closing of the transaction.

Seller's Responsibilities

A seller's work, like a buyer's, really begins when a sales contract is signed. Before actually going to the closing, a seller must typically do the following:

- Prepare the required deed
- Remove all encumbrances
- Prepare papers with respect to the seller's loan
- Cooperate with inspectors

Preparing the Deed

As we discussed previously, various types of deeds can be used to transfer title, depending on the circumstances of the transaction. The sales contract always should specify the kind of deed that is to be delivered by the seller. The typical sales transaction involves a warranty deed or special warranty deed. For example, the sales contract between Clay Williams and Sarah Howell on pages 126–29 in this chapter requires that Sarah furnish a warranty deed to Clay at closing.

Removing Encumbrances

Assuming that a seller is required to present a warranty deed, he or she will covenant that the real estate is free of encumbrances other than those specified in the deed. Encumbrances that the seller may have to remove could include unrecorded claims of ownership, easements, covenants, and liens. One of the most frequently filed liens is the tax lien, resulting from the owner's failure to pay state, county, or city property taxes. Therefore, before the closing, a seller must have paid all taxes that are then due on the property.

Paying the Seller's Loan

Loans for the purchase of residential property usually are to be paid back over a period of 25 to 30 years. Because of the longevity of such loans, most owners do not complete their mortgage payments before they sell the property. Therefore, a major encumbrance on the real estate being purchased is the seller's mortgage.

Necessity to Meet "Concurrent Conditions" by Date of Closing

As illustrated in our discussion of the sale of Sarah Howell's home to Clay Williams on pages 126–29, a real estate sales contract usually creates conditions that both parties must fulfill by the closing date. These are called *concurrent conditions*. Failure to do so can void the contract, as one purchaser found to his sorrow.

On November 24, 85-year-old Lily Canham agreed to sell a 56-acre parcel of land in San Luis Obispo County, California, to real estate broker Jeffrey Pittman for $250,000. The contract called for an initial deposit of $1,000 and a further deposit of $24,000 before closing. The balance of the purchase price was to be paid by a note secured by a deed of trust on the property. The closing of escrow was to be within 30 days, and the contract provided that "time is of the essence."

About the second week of December, Canham sent a signed copy of the deed to the escrow agent, which—he pointed out—had not been notarized. When broker Pittman contacted Canham, she told him she would have the deed notarized at an escrow agent near her home. By the closing date of December 24, Canham still had

not sent the signed deed to the escrow agent, nor had Pittman tendered the $24,000, promissory note or deed of trust. There the matter rested until the following May, when Canham told Pittman she had entered into a contract with other purchasers to buy her property for $600,000. Pittman wrote her a letter demanding she sell the property to him as agreed in the earlier contract, but she refused and sold it to the other buyers. Pittman sued for breach of contract. He lost.

Under the contract, Canham was supposed to tender a signed and notarized deed by the closing date of December 24; Pittman was supposed to tender a $24,000 deposit, note, and deed of trust. The court ruled that neither party had fulfilled the concurrent conditions called for in the contract by the closing date, resulting in a "discharge of both parties' duty to perform."

"We appreciate the reluctance of a buyer to act first by placing money into escrow. But in a contract with concurrent conditions, the buyer and seller cannot keep saying to one another, 'No, you first.' Ultimately, in such a case the buyer seeking enforcement comes in second; he loses."

[*Pittman v. Canham*, 3 Cal. Rptr. 2d 340]

One of two things can happen with respect to the seller's loan at closing: It will be satisfied out of the sale's proceeds, or it will be taken over by the buyer. Whichever event occurs, the seller must have the proper papers ready at the closing. With the aid of the seller's lender and lawyer, either a certificate of satisfaction or the loan assumption papers must be prepared.

Cooperating with Inspectors

As mentioned earlier, the seller may be obligated to cooperate with the various inspectors a buyer may hire to inspect the property for termite damage or structural/functional defects in the property. Cooperation includes making the property available to the inspector and having utilities available to fully test the mechanical systems.

Other Responsibilities

If the property being sold is for a development project, the seller may have contractual duties to assist the buyer in changing the zoning restrictions. On closing a transaction involving rental property, the seller must turn over all valid leases to the buyer. In addition, the rent schedules and copies of letters to all tenants informing them of the change of ownership must be provided.

Once again, a sales contract can place special duties on both the buyer and seller, and generally, these contractual obligations must be performed before the transaction is closed. Failure to do so may void the contract, as the buyer in the Legal Highlight on the previous page discovered.

Costs at Closing

A prospective purchaser of real estate may save up money for the down payment only to learn that he or she needs more cash to cover the closing costs. The elements of closing costs vary from time to time and from location to location, but generally the buyer must pay for the following items in cash:

- Loan origination fee
- Loan discounts, or points
- Appraisal fee
- Credit report fee
- Lender's inspection fee
- Mortgage insurance premium
- Attorney or closing agent's fees
- Hazard insurance premium
- Recording fees for the mortgage he or she gives (yes, the borrower gives a mortgage in exchange for the loan)

The loan origination fee, the points, and the mortgage-guarantee insurance premium usually are based on a percentage of the loan. For example, the *loan origination fee*—the fee charged by the bank to process the loan—may be 1 percent to 3 percent of the amount of the loan. *Points* are an extra charge made by the bank; each point is 1 percent of the amount of the loan. (Points and other financing charges are discussed in Chapter 18.) The typical mortgage insurance premium is 2 percent of the amount of the loan, of which 0.5 percent is due at the closing. The other 1.5 percent is paid over a ten-year period. These types of closing costs generally total 2 percent to 6 percent of the money borrowed.

The seller also has to pay closing costs, which may include the

- real estate brokerage commission;
- attorney or closing agent's fees for preparing the deed or other documents;
- documentary stamp taxes, where required; and
- recording fees for the certificate of satisfaction of the seller's mortgage.

A seller, however, generally does not have to worry about coming up with the cash to pay for these items. Such costs simply are subtracted from the proceeds of the sale. We will examine the breakdown of the buyer's and seller's closing costs in detail in Figure 6.2.

Proration of Homeowner's Costs

Certain homeowner's costs must be prorated or shared by the buyer and seller. Such costs normally include state and local taxes, the hazard-insurance premium if that insurance policy is to be assigned to the buyer, and the monthly mortgage payment, should the buyer assume the seller's loan.

The costs of any other contracts that exist during the seller's and buyer's ownership should be prorated. For example, the cost of a pest extermination contract purchased by the seller and not canceled by the buyer must be shared. Whether this proration will appear as a credit to the seller or to the buyer depends on which party pays the amount owed. In commercial sales, the collection or payment of rents also must be prorated equitably. If the house is heated by oil, the buyer must pay the seller for the oil remaining in the storage tank, usually at the current price per gallon.

Understanding the Settlement Statement

In residential transactions involving mortgage loans, the Real Estate Settlement Procedures Act of 1974 requires that lenders fully disclose the financial details of the transaction to the buyer and seller in writing using the **HUD-1 Uniform Settlement Statement** approved by the U.S. Department of Housing and Urban Development. At the closing, the buyer and seller sign this statement, and each receives a copy. The settlement statement shown in Figure 6.2 on pages 140–41 is completed in accordance with the Howell-Williams contract presented earlier in this chapter on pages 126–29.

Although the settlement statement may appear rather complex at first glance, its purpose is to simplify and summarize the financial transactions. Page 2 of the form is a worksheet designed to help determine the seller's and buyer's closing costs. Let's use this statement to "close" the deal between Sarah Howell and Clay Williams. Sections A through I on page 1 of the statement are self-explanatory, but the other sections require a closer examination.

FIGURE 6.2 | Uniform Settlement Statement

A. **Settlement Statement**   U.S. Department of Housing and Urban Development   OMB Approval No. 2502-0265 (expires 11/30/2009)

B. Type of Loan

1. ☐ FHA 2. ☐ FmHA 3. ☑ Conv. Unins.	6. File Number:	7. Loan Number:	8. Mortgage Insurance Case Number:
4. ☐ VA 5. ☐ Conv. Ins.	01-4569b	79-999034	

C. Note: This form is furnished to give you a statement of actual settlement costs. Amounts paid to and by the settlement agent are shown. Items marked "(p.o.c.)" were paid outside the closing; they are shown here for informational purposes and are not included in the totals.

D. Name & Address of Borrower:	E. Name & Address of Seller:	F. Name & Address of Lender:
Clay Williams 1000 Banyan Street Suburb, Florida 33323	Sarah Howell 501 SE 1st Street Fort Lauderdale, Florida 33301	Realty Mortgage Co. 101 Main Street Fort Lauderdale, Florida 33301

G. Property Location:	H. Settlement Agent:	
501 SE 1st Street Fort Lauderdale, Florida 33301	B.A. Settler, Fort Lauderdale, Florida 33301	
	Place of Settlement: Broward County	I. Settlement Date: August 4, 2008

J. Summary of Borrower's Transaction		K. Summary of Seller's Transaction	
100. Gross Amount Due From Borrower		**400. Gross Amount Due To Seller**	
101. Contract sales price	295,000.00	401. Contract sales price	295,000.00
102. Personal property		402. Personal property	
103. Settlement charges to borrower (line 1400)	16,377.84	403.	
104.		404.	
105.		405.	
Adjustments for items paid by seller in advance		**Adjustments for items paid by seller in advance**	
106. City/town taxes to		406. City/town taxes to	
107. County taxes to		407. County taxes to	
108. Assessments to		408. Assessments to	
109.		409.	
110.		410.	
111.		411.	
112.		412.	
120. Gross Amount Due From Borrower	311,377.84	**420. Gross Amount Due To Seller**	295,000.00
200. Amounts Paid By Or In Behalf Of Borrower		**500. Reductions In Amount Due To Seller**	
201. Deposit or earnest money	10,000.00	501. Excess deposit (see instructions)	
202. Principal amount of new loan(s)	236,000.00	502. Settlement charges to seller (line 1400)	22,050.50
203. Existing loan(s) taken subject to		503. Existing loan(s) taken subject to	
204.		504. Payoff of first mortgage loan	113,245.00
205.		505. Payoff of second mortgage loan	
206.		506.	
207.		507.	
208.		508.	
209.		509.	
Adjustments for items unpaid by seller		**Adjustments for items unpaid by seller**	
210. City/town taxes January 1 to August 3	1,943.60	510. City/town taxes to	1,943.60
211. County taxes January 1 to August 3	2,644.50	511. County taxes to	2,644.50
212. Assessments to		512. Assessments to	
213.		513.	
214.		514.	
215.		515.	
216.		516.	
217.		517.	
218.		518.	
219.		519.	
220. Total Paid By/For Borrower	247,943.60	**520. Total Reduction Amount Due Seller**	139,883.60
300. Cash At Settlement From/To Borrower		**600. Cash At Settlement To/From Seller**	
301. Gross Amount due from borrower (line 120)	311,377.84	601. Gross amount due to seller (line 420)	295,000.00
302. Less amounts paid by/for borrower (line 220)	(247,943.60)	602. Less reductions in amt. due seller (line 520)	(139,883.60)
303. Cash ☑ From ☐ To Borrower	63,434.24	**603. Cash** ☑ To ☐ From Seller	155,116.40

Section 5 of the Real Estate Settlement Procedures Act (RESPA) requires the following: • HUD must develop a Special Information Booklet to help persons borrowing money to finance the purchase of residential real estate to better understand the nature and costs of real estate settlement services; • Each lender must provide the booklet to all applicants from whom it receives or for whom it prepares a written application to borrow money to finance the purchase of residential real estate; • Lenders must prepare and distribute with the Booklet a Good Faith Estimate of the settlement costs that the borrower is likely to incur in connection with the settlement. These disclosures are manadatory.

Section 4(a) of RESPA mandates that HUD develop and prescribe this standard form to be used at the time of loan settlement to provide full disclosure of all charges imposed upon the borrower and seller. These are third party disclosures that are designed to provide the borrower with pertinent information during the settlement process in order to be a better shopper.

The Public Reporting Burden for this collection of information is estimated to average one hour per response, including the time for reviewing instructions, searching existing data sources, gathering and maintaining the data needed, and completing and reviewing the collection of information.

This agency may not collect this information, and you are not required to complete this form, unless it displays a currently valid OMB control number.

The information requested does not lend itself to confidentiality.

FIGURE 6.2 | Uniform Settlement Statement *(continued)*

L. Settlement Charges

			Paid From Borrowers Funds at Settlement	Paid From Seller's Funds at Settlement
700. Total Sales/Broker's Commission based on price $ 295,000.00 @ 6 % = 17,700.00				
Division of Commission (line 700) as follows:				
701. $ 17,700.00	to Julio Rodriguez			
702. $	to			
703. Commission paid at Settlement				
704.				17,700.00
800. Items Payable In Connection With Loan				
801. Loan Origination Fee %				
802. Loan Discount 2 %			4,720.00	
803. Appraisal Fee 300.00 to	Harry Newstreet, Certified General Appraiser		300.00	
804. Credit Report to				
805. Lender's Inspection Fee				
806. Mortgage Insurance Application Fee to				
807. Assumption Fee				
808.				
809.				
810.				
811.				
900. Items Required By Lender To Be Paid In Advance				
901. Interest from August 4 to August 31 @$ 50.75 /day			1,420.00	
902. Mortgage Insurance Premium for months to				
903. Hazard Insurance Premium for 1 years to F.A Insurance			5,900.00	
904. years to				
905.				
1000. Reserves Deposited With Lender				
1001. Hazard insurance 2 months@$ 491.67 per month			983.34	
1002. Mortgage insurance months@$ per month				
1003. City property taxes 2 months@$ 275.00 per month			550.00	
1004. County property taxes 2 months@$ 374.00 per month			748.00	
1005. Annual assessments months@$ per month				
1006. months@$ per month				
1007. months@$ per month				
1008. months@$ per month				
1100. Title Charges				
1101. Settlement or closing fee to B.A. Settler				350.00
1102. Abstract or title search to				
1103. Title examination to				
1104. Title insurance binder to				
1105. Document preparation to B.A. Settler			100.00	100.00
1106. Notary fees to				
1107. Attorney's fees to				
(includes above items numbers:)				
1108. Title insurance to B.A. Settler				
(includes above items numbers:)				
1109. Lender's coverage $ 295,000.00			250.00	
1110. Owner's coverage $ 295,000.00				1,825.00
1111.				
1112.				
1113.				
1200. Government Recording and Transfer Charges				
1201. Recording fees: Deed $ 10.50 ; Mortgage $ 10.50 ; Releases $			10.50	10.50
1202. City/county tax/stamps: Deed $; Mortgage $				
1203. State tax/stamps: Deed $ 2,065.00 ; Mortgage $ 826.00			826.00	2,065.00
1204.				
1205.				
1300. Additional Settlement Charges				
1301. Survey to J. Almond PSM			425.00	
1302. Pest inspection to Sunbelt Termite Man, Inc.			145.00	
1303.				
1304.				
1305.				
1400. Total Settlement Charges (enter on lines 103, Section J and 502, Section K)			16,377.84	22,050.50

The first step is to enter the contract sales price on lines 101 and 401. We then turn to the "Settlement Charges" section of the statement beginning at the top of page 2 and calculate the broker's commission in lines 700–704. The broker in this transaction is entitled to $17,700 (6 percent of the $295,000). The seller is paying the commission in this transaction.

On line 802, we see that the borrower's lender is charging the borrower a loan discount fee of $4,720, or 2 percent of the loan amount of $236,000. In addition, the lender required that the buyer obtain an appraisal of the property from Harry Newstreet, a state-certified general appraiser, who charged $300 for his services.

Lines 901–1008 are often confusing the first time students see the HUD settlement statement, so let's make sure we understand these items before moving on. The topic for lines 900–905 of the settlement statement is "Items Required By Lender To Be Paid In Advance." The lender in question is the buyer's lender. This lender is funding the loan for the borrower on the fourth day of closing (August 4), but the lender will not expect the first payment on the loan from the borrower until *the first day of the first full month after origination.* Thus, the first loan payment paid by Clay Williams will occur on October 1.

Because Clay will not make a payment on September 1, the lender requires him to "prepay" the interest he will owe for the use of the lender's money during the month of August. (The payment on October 1 will cover the interest charges for the month of September.) The amount of interest due for the period August 4 through August 31 is $1,420.00. This amount is calculated by multiplying the loan amount of $236,000 by the annual interest rate (assumed to be 8 percent in this example), dividing the result by 12, then dividing that result by 31 (number of days in August) to get the daily interest amount for the month of August. We then multiply the daily interest amount (rounded to two decimal places) by 28 (the number of days Clay uses the lender's money in August) to get the prepaid interest amount for line 901.

Similarly, the lender requires that Clay deposit two months "reserve" of hazard insurance premiums and property taxes into an escrow account maintained by the lender. Each mortgage payment paid by the borrower must include these monthly amounts that will also be deposited into the borrower's escrow account maintained by the lender. This requirement ensures that when the bills from the insurance company and tax collector are received at the end of the year, the borrower will have the money on hand to pay these bills.

The lender estimates the amount of the insurance premium using the price of the first year's policy (which the borrower will have to purchase at or before the closing directly from the insurance company). For this example, the price of a full year's insurance policy is $5,900. Dividing this amount by 12 gives $491.67 as the monthly reserve amount.

The current year's property tax assessments are $3,330 for the city tax and $4,488 for the county tax. Dividing each of these annual taxes by 12 gives the monthly reserve amount. Two months' reserve of each is entered on lines 1003 and 1004 as appropriate.

On line 1101, we see that the seller is being charged a $350 fee by the title agent for handling the closing. Each party is being charged $100 for document preparation (line 1105). On line 1108, we see that the title insurance charges to the buyer and seller are $250 and $1,825, respectively. The borrower has purchased a title insurance policy to protect the lender (lender's coverage), and the seller has purchased a title insurance policy (as agreed to in the sales contract) to protect the buyer (owner's coverage).

On lines 1201–1203, the buyer and seller have each been charged $10.50 for recording fees: The buyer must pay this fee to record the mortgage for his lender, and the seller is paying the fee to record the deed she is giving to the buyer. The seller is also paying the documentary stamp tax on the deed ($2,065 = $295,000 ÷ 100 × $0.70), and the buyer is paying the documentary stamp taxes on the mortgage ($826.00 = $236,000 ÷ 100 × $0.35).

The final section shows any additional settlement charges paid by the parties. In this example, the buyer is charged with the cost of a property survey ($425) and a pest inspection ($145).

Line 1400 shows the total settlement charges for the buyer and the seller. These amounts must be posted to line 103 for the buyer and line 502 for the seller on page 1 of the settlement statement.

After entering the settlement charges to the buyer and seller, the next step is to calculate the gross amount due from the borrower, as shown on line 120. We then add up any amounts paid by or on behalf of the borrower. On line 201 we see the $10,000 earnest deposit paid by Clay, and on line 202 we see the loan proceeds he is expecting from his lender. Lines 210 and 211 are another area of some initial confusion for students, so we will consider this section in detail.

Many taxing authorities collect their taxes annually "in arrears," which simply means that they collect the money after the services have been provided. In Florida, where our example property is located, city and county governments expect to be paid at the first of each calendar year for services they provided to property owners in the prior calendar year. Because the tax bills will be addressed to Clay Williams (the buyer in our transaction) when they are sent out next year, Clay is entitled to collect from Sarah (the seller) an amount equal to the expected property taxes for the period she owned the property (January 1 through August 3 of the current tax year). The title agent simply calculates the daily tax rate based on the current year's tax bill and then prorates the amount due from the seller based on the number of days of ownership in the current tax year. In this case, the city tax for this property this year was $3,300, and the county tax was $4,488. Dividing each of these amounts by 365 days gives the daily property tax amounts for the city and county of $9.04 and $12.30 (rounded), respectively. Multiplying these amounts by 215 (the actual days Sarah was the owner of the property) gives the city and county tax amounts for which the seller should be held responsible. These amounts are entered as adjustments on lines 210 and 211 for the buyer and on lines 510 and 511 for the seller (using double-entry accounting).

The total amount paid by and for the buyer is the sum of lines 201 through 219, and the total reduction amount due the seller is the sum of lines 501 through 519. Subtracting the total amount paid by and for the borrower from the Gross Amount due from borrower gives the cash due from (or to, in certain cases) the borrower on line 303. Subtracting the reductions in the amount due the seller from the Gross amount due to seller gives the cash to (or from, in certain cases) the seller on line 603.

To summarize what this statement says, the buyer and seller agreed to transact for $295,000. The seller has an outstanding loan for $113,245 on the property that must be paid off to give the buyer good title. The buyer is borrowing $236,000 from his lender. The seller must pay certain closing expenses (title insurance coverage for the buyer, deed recording fees, deed documentary stamp taxes, the broker's commission, etc.) The buyer must pay certain closing expenses (appraisal fee, lender's title insurance coverage, recording fees on his new mortgage, taxes and stamps on his new mortgage, the survey fee, a pest inspection fee, and some prepaid items required by his lender). In addition, the buyer and seller have agreed to prorate the property taxes so both parties will pay the taxes for the time period during which each owned the property. The buyer must bring $63,434.24 to the closing, and the seller will leave the closing with $155,116.40. When the monies are distributed properly to all involved parties and the documents are recorded, the deal is officially closed.

Parties Present at the Closing

Although closings can be handled through the mail without ever having a group meeting of interested parties, the closing of a real estate sale normally is held at the offices of one of the people involved in the transaction: the real estate broker, the lending institution, the title insurance company, the seller's attorney, or the buyer's attorney. Obviously, the seller wants to be there to get his or her money, the buyer wants the deed and the keys to the doors, the broker wants the commission, the lender's representative (who may be the title company) wants signatures on the mortgage documents, and the title company and attorneys want to be paid. Usually, the appraiser, pest inspector, and surveyor are content to get their money from the closing agent after the deal is closed.

Escrow Closing

Instead of the conventional closing described above, **escrow closings** are practiced in some communities in the eastern United States and in the majority of western states. Instead of the buyer and seller coming face to face, a third party called an **escrow agent** acts as an intermediary to facilitate the closing. The escrow agent is usually an attorney, a title company, a trust company, an escrow company, or the escrow department of a lending institution.

The seller deposits a fully executed deed with the escrow agent, who then delivers the deed to the purchaser after the receipt of the purchase price. The agent then delivers the deed to the purchaser and the purchase price to the seller.

Some of the advantages of the escrow closing are (1) the seller is assured of receiving the buyer's money before title passes because the check must clear before this occurs, (2) the buyer's money will not be paid until the seller's title is acceptable and free from liens, and (3) the parties need not be present. The last is particularly advantageous if one or both of the parties reside in other areas.

◼ CHAPTER REVIEW

- ◼ A *contract* is a legal document that represents an agreement between two or more parties. The essential elements required before any contract is binding include (1) an offer, (2) an acceptance, (3) consideration, (4) parties with legal capacity, and (5) a lawful purpose. In addition, all states require that contracts involving any interest in land must be in writing and signed by the party against whom enforcement is sought.

- ◼ Failure to perform contractual duties is a *breach of contract.* Remedies available to a buyer for the seller's breach include an order for specific performance, monetary damages, or the return of the earnest money. A seller generally cannot seek the specific performance of a buyer who has breached the contract, but will probably be able to retain any earnest money paid by the buyer and may be able to seek additional damage compensation through the courts.

- ◼ Most contracts include various contingency clauses that specify that the contract may be voided in the event of certain conditions. Common examples in real estate contracts include financing contingencies, title contingencies, and inspection and repair contingencies.

- ◼ Real estate sales contracts are, in essence, gap fillers. Such contracts must govern the parties' rights between the time an agreement is reached to transfer property from one party to another and the time the transaction is formally completed, or closed.

- ◼ Several kinds of contracts may be used in a real estate transaction. Among the common types are the sales contract, the option-to-buy contract, and the contract for deed.

- ◼ The traditional real estate sales contract should consist of provisions specifying (1) the property description, (2) the purchase price and the way it is to be paid, (3) the escrow arrangement, (4) the effect on the contract of the destruction of improvements, (5) the pest-free warranty, (6) the closing date, and (7) the broker's commission, if any.

- ◼ The option-to-buy contract gives the holder the right, but not an obligation, to purchase the property at an agreed-on price on or before a specified date. While the optionee is not obligated to perform, the optionor is obligated to honor the contract terms.

- *Contracts for deed* are a combination of a sales contract and a financing arrangement: The seller holds title to the property while the buyer makes payments over time. On paying the agreed-on amount, the seller will transfer title to the buyer.

- Skilled negotiators realize that successful negotiations are not "zero-sum" games in which the parties attempt to capture all they can grab of the same pie. Keeping an open mind and looking for ways to create win-win situations are important keys for becoming a better negotiator.

- The real estate transaction is "closed" when title to real property passes from the seller to the buyer. In essence, a *closing*—or *settlement,* as it is sometimes called—includes the closing of the loan, of the escrow arrangement, and of the title.

- Between the signing of the sales contract and the closing of the deal, both seller and buyer have certain responsibilities that must be completed. The buyer must obtain an opinion about the status of the title and attempt in good faith to secure the needed financing. Among other obligations, the seller must make sure that all encumbrances are removed and obtain the type of written deed the contract requires.

- *Closing costs* are the charges incurred by the buyer and seller at the close of the transaction. Such costs to the buyer include the loan origination fee, the loan discount points, and attorney's fees. Costs to the seller may consist of the real estate brokerage commission and various recording fees. The buyer's closing costs and the down payment often must be paid in cash. The seller's closing costs are deducted from the amount due to the seller.

- At the closing, many papers are examined, signed, and exchanged by the parties. A successful closing of the transaction results in the transfer of the seller's title to the buyer.

KEY TERMS

acceptance
agreements for deed
breach of contract
closing
consideration
contingencies
contract
contract for deed
contractual capacity
counteroffer

escrow agent
escrow closings
financing contingency
HUD-1 Uniform Settlement Statement
inspection and repair contingency
land contracts
offer
offeree

offeror
option-to-buy contract
partial performance
sales contracts
settlement
specific performance
statute of frauds
title contingency

▌ STUDY EXERCISES

1. List and explain the six essential elements of a valid real estate sales contract.

2. In a contract, what is meant by *capacity?* By *consideration?*

3. Mark offered to buy Charlie's four-acre tract for $200,000, and they shook hands on the deal. Both men went to an attorney to draft the formal contract. The next day, Mark signed the written contract, but Charlie refused to do so because he had received a higher offer. What recourse, if any, does Mark have against Charlie for failing to abide by their oral agreement?

4. Suppose instead that Mark and Charlie had agreed on the deal and Mark wrote the terms of the sale on the back of an envelope, which both signed. They planned on hiring an attorney to "flesh out" the agreement and draft a more formal contract. Charlie refused to sign the formal contract, having received a higher offer. Could Mark force Charlie to carry out the contract?

5. Nell and Edward agreed that Nell would purchase Edward's house and lot. Because both parties wanted to avoid the expense of having a formal contract drafted, they signed their names below the following handwritten statement: "Nell hereby agrees to buy from Edward the house at 1023 Washington Avenue for $65,000. Closing to be within 60 days from today: September 13, 2007." Nell had planned to borrow 90 percent of the purchase price but failed to qualify for this loan. Does Nell's inability to obtain a loan excuse her from performance of the agreement as written?

6. After Kristy finished college and started working, she found a small house that she wanted to buy but could not afford. As an alternative, she agreed to lease the house with an option to buy it. To be valid, what must the option agreement include?

7. Answer the following questions based on the real estate sales contract depicted in Figure 6.1.

   a. When does the buyer get occupancy of the premises?

   b. What actions can the buyer take if the seller's title proves to be unmarketable?

   c. Whose responsibility is it to obtain and pay for a survey to detect any encroachments?

   d. If an encroachment is detected in the survey, what happens?

   e. Who must pay for the various closing costs associated with the deed?

   f. What happens to this agreement if the property is destroyed by fire or other casualty before the closing?

   g. What actions can the parties take if the other party breaches the contract?

8. From the buyer's perspective, what advantage does traditional mortgage financing offer in comparison to agreement for deed financing, even in states that treat these arrangements similarly?

9. Why might a buyer elect to use agreement for deed financing instead of traditional mortgage financing? The Hoods and the Wakeleys entered into a formal contract whereby the Hoods agreed to buy the Wakeleys' partially restored 80-year-old house. During the time period between the signing of the contract and the closing of the transaction, what things should the Hoods accomplish? What responsibilities do the Wakeleys have?

10. In a typical residential transaction, what closing costs must the buyer normally pay? Which are usually paid by the seller?

11. Property taxes for the 2005 year are due on March 31, 2006, and will be $1,875 for a property being sold on July 1, 2005. Using a 365-day year, how much should the sellers be responsible for?

12. As a part of a purchase transaction, the buyers have taken out a loan for $75,000 at 10.5 percent annual interest with monthly payments of $702. The closing date is to be March 16, but the first loan payment will not be made until May 1. At the closing, how much interest must the buyers "prepay" for the month of March?

13. Internet Exercise: Visit the Web site *www.hud.gov* and search for a document called "Buying Your Home: Settlement Costs and Helpful Information." Read the document and answer the following questions based on it.

    a. How soon after applying for a mortgage loan should the lender provide a written "good-faith estimate" of the settlement charges you will likely have to pay in association with the loan?

    b. Is the borrower entitled to a copy of the appraisal report prepared in association with your loan application?

14. Does federal law dictate whether the buyer or seller must pay for certain settlement charges in a real estate sales contract or can the parties negotiate this issue?

▌ FURTHER READING

de Heer, Robert. *Realty Bluebook,* 33rd ed. Chicago: Dearborn Real Estate Education, 2003.

Nierenberg, Gerald I. *The Art of Negotiating.* New York: The Negotiation Institute, 1988.

Siedel, George, and Robert J. Aalberts. *Real Estate Law*, 6th ed. Mason, Ohio: South-Western, 2006.

Real Estate Leases

CHAPTER PREVIEW

The previous chapter introduced the general requirements of real estate contracts with a focus on the sales contract. In this chapter, we consider another type of contract that is common in real estate markets: the lease. Real estate leases are contracts that transfer the rights of use and possession, but not ownership, of real estate between a landlord and tenant. Leases are the documents that create the leasehold estates discussed in Chapter 2.

We will consider

■ the recommended elements of a lease;

■ specific clauses in lease agreements; and

■ duties of the lessor and lessee.

REAL ESTATE TODAY

CASE STUDY
Jill Rents an Apartment

LEGAL HIGHLIGHT
Landlord's Liability for Failure to Provide Adequate Maintenance

LEGAL HIGHLIGHT
Liability of Landlords for Injuries to Guests of Tenants

LEASES

When a property owner agrees to transfer rights of use and possession (but not ownership) of the property to a tenant in exchange for rent or lease payments, the agreement is called a **lease** or **rental agreement.** Leases divide estates in land into two components: a leased fee estate and a leasehold estate.

Although some leases need not be put into written form (short-term residential leases, for example), most prudent real estate market participants know the importance of making sure the agreement between parties is clearly stated in writing to minimize misunderstandings and disputes.

A lease is a type of contract, and its basic requirements are the same as the general requirements for contracts. Through the lease contract, the landlord conveys use and possession of the property in return for the tenant's agreement to pay rent. The lease also defines the rights, duties, and liabilities of both landlord and tenant and should contain, at a minimum, the following elements:

- Names of the **lessor** (landlord) and **lessee** (tenant), both of whom must have contractual capacity to enter into the lease agreement
- Identification of the premises
- Conveyance of the premises
- Term or duration of the lease
- Amount of rent and manner of payment
- Duties and obligations of the parties
- Signatures of the parties

As in all contracts, a lease becomes valid when it is delivered and accepted. If the lease is for a term of one year or longer, it must be in writing to be enforceable in court.

Classification of Leases

Leases can be classified in several ways. Generally, they are classified by duration of term, type of use, and method of rental payment.

Duration of Term

The duration of the term of a leasehold estate determines whether it is a tenancy for a stated period, a tenancy from period to period, a tenancy at will, or a tenancy at sufferance.

A **tenancy for a stated period** conveys the property to the tenant for a stated period of time, sometimes called the **term.** The term may be for any length of time from one month to many years, although in most states a lease for longer than 99 years is regarded as a fee simple transaction. Possession of the property reverts to the landlord at the end of the term, subject to any right of renewal set forth in the lease. Some states require that long-term leases, usually for more than 1 to 3 years, be recorded in the public record to be enforceable as a contract.

A **tenancy from period to period** is of indefinite duration. The tenancy does not terminate until proper notice is given by either party. It commonly exists from month to month and is renewed automatically at the end of each month, provided the tenant has paid the rent.

A **tenancy at will** may be terminated by either party at any time. Tenant-protection statutes, however, generally require reasonable notice on the part of the landlord—usually 30 days.

A **tenancy at sufferance** is created when a tenant continues to occupy property after the expiration of the lease period. The tenant has no right to the property and remains there at the sufferance of the landlord. Even so, many states require that the tenant be given notice to quit the premises before eviction proceedings can be instituted.

Type of Use

Leases are often distinguished by the type of use to which the property will be put. For example, a lease involving property that will be used for commercial purposes may be very different from a lease involving property that will be used for residential purposes. The laws regulating the relationship between parties to leases in some states differ significantly for commercial and residential leases. Many residential leases specifically prohibit the tenant from using the property in a commercial capacity.

A **ground lease** is a long-term (usually 50 years or longer) lease involving unimproved land. The leased land is usually developed by the tenant for commercial, residential, or agricultural purposes. At the end of the lease, the land and any improvements revert to the landowner. Because such a lease makes it possible to separate the ownership of the land from the ownership of the improvements, the ground lease frequently is used as a financing device in the development of major office buildings.

For example, many Manhattan office buildings are built on leased land. Because the land often constitutes 30 percent to 40 percent of the cost of such projects, a ground lease can greatly reduce the amount of money the developer must raise. The ground lease can also offer substantial tax advantages to the lessee because lease payments are fully deductible from taxable income as an ordinary expense, whereas the cost of land cannot be *depreciated*—that is, the owners cannot reduce their taxes by stating on their tax return an amount by which the value of the land has decreased with age, as one can do in the case of buildings.

Methods of Rent Payment or Adjustment

Arrangements for rental payments between tenant and landlord can take many forms, and rental arrangements are far from uniform. Two factors that determine the form of the lease are the degree of overhead cost that is assumed by the tenant and whether the amount of rent is fixed or variable.

Under a **gross lease,** the landlord agrees to pay the real estate taxes, utilities, insurance, and all other operating expenses in connection with use of the premises.

Under a **net lease,** the tenant pays the operating expenses in addition to rent. Such a lease transfers uncertainty regarding the future cost of operating expenses to the tenant and leaves the landlord with a more definite net return. Occasionally, the tenant assumes responsibility for other costs as well, so there are net-net leases and net-net-net leases. Under a **net-net lease,** the lessee pays not only operating expenses but insurance premiums as well. Under a **net-net-net lease,** also known as the *triple-net lease,* the lessee pays operating expenses, insurance premiums, and real estate taxes.

Under a **fixed-rent lease,** the amount of the rental payment is fixed for the term of the lease. This type of rental payment is most common for short-term residential leases. In the **graduated-rent lease,** or **step-up rent lease,** the rental payment is fixed for the initial term of the lease and then is increased by specified percentages at designated intervals. This type of lease provides some protection against inflation for the landlord and also may be used for a new business or property whose income-producing ability is expected to increase in the future. This type of lease is seldom used for rental terms longer than ten years.

The **reappraisal lease** is similar to the graduated-rent lease except that the level of each rent increase is determined by a reappraisal of the property. Such leases are used most often for the long-term rental of entire buildings. For example, if a tenant leases an entire warehouse for $10 per square foot, and the property value increases by 10 percent, the rent in the following year would be $11 per square foot.

The **percentage lease** is a lease of a property used for commercial purposes under which the rent payments are based on some percentage of sales made on the premises. Usually, the stated percentage of gross sales is combined with a flat minimum rent. Such leases are found predominantly in shopping centers, particularly in the larger malls. For example, a toy store in a mall may be charged a base rent of $1,500 per month, plus 2 percent of gross sales over $50,000. If the store's December sales are $90,000, the rent will be $1,500 plus 2 percent of $40,000, for a total of $2,300. If January's sales are only $25,000, the store will pay only the base rent of $1,500.

The percentage of gross sales charged as rent will vary, depending on whether the store is a low-margin/high-volume or high-margin/low-volume outlet and on its relative importance to the shopping center. For example, an "anchor" department store almost always can negotiate more favorable lease terms than can a small merchant.

Another type of lease is known as the **index lease.** In this arrangement, lease payments are "indexed" to some measure of the cost of living, such as the Consumer Price Index. Rents are adjusted periodically to account for changes in the value of the dollar. The adjustments provide protection for the landlord against inflation and rapidly changing prices in the economy.

THE LANDLORD-TENANT RELATIONSHIP

The purpose of the lease agreement is to define the relationship between the landlord and the tenant. Thus, a well-drafted lease should address such issues as the term of the lease, rent amount, rent adjustment process (if any), limitations on use, and responsibility for maintenance, expenses, renewal provisions, and so forth.

Renewal Options

Many leases contain a **renewal option,** a provision that protects the tenant against large increases in rent. The renewal option specifies what the rent will be if the lease is renewed, usually at a higher level to protect the landlord against rising costs. Without the renewal option, the landlord can raise the rent to any level desired. The tenant then has the option of paying the higher rent or moving out.

Expenses

The lease should state clearly who pays for expenses in connection with the property, including maintenance, property taxes, insurance, and utilities. In residential leases, the landlord is usually responsible for normal maintenance to the building and for taxes and insurance on the real estate. Utilities usually are the responsibility of the tenant, as is breakage or other damage caused by the actions of the tenant. In commercial leases, it is quite common for tenants to be held responsible for some portion of the landlord's operating expenses of the property. Commercial leases often specify that tenants must pay **common area maintenance fees** (CAM fees) in addition to rent. Such leases often specify an **expense stop** that sets the maximum amount of operating expenses the landlord will pay. Above the stop, the tenants will be charged for all operating expenses that exceed the stop in proportion to the amount of space each tenant has as a percentage of the total space available in the property. Obviously, the language relating to responsibility for expenses can be a crucial part of commercial lease negotiations.

Assignment and Subleasing

It often is desirable to a tenant to be able to assign a lease or sublease to another tenant if plans change before the end of the lease term. **Assignment** means that all of the tenant's rights under a lease are transferred to the new tenant, although the lessee still is liable unless released by the landlord. **Subleasing** means transferring a portion of rights under a lease. For example, a tenant could sublease an apartment for only six months of a two-year lease term. Under a sublease clause, the landlord may reserve the right to approve of any sublessee, generally for reasons of creditworthiness. Unless the landlord consents, the tenant is not relieved of his or her obligation to pay the rent.

If rents are rising, it may be possible to sublease to another tenant at a profit, receiving rent from the sublessee and then paying the required rent under the original lease to the landlord. In a long-term commercial lease, this "leasehold interest" may be worth literally millions of dollars. If the lease contains a clause against subleasing, then subleasing is a violation of the lease agreement and can result in eviction.

Jill Rents an Apartment

Jill Jewell had just graduated from college and moved to Charlotte, North Carolina, to take a job with Amalgamated Whitzadiddle Corporation. She needed a place to live and decided to rent a duplex apartment in a nearby suburb. Let's look at the rental agreement to see what Jill agreed to do and what was promised by the landlord, Virginia Wells. (See Figure 7.1.)

Security Deposits

The lease may require that the tenant provide a **security deposit** prior to occupancy. Security deposits are intended to give the landlord protection if the tenant damages the property, moves out early, or fails to pay the rent. The landlord may also require that the tenant pay a cleaning fee at the termination of the lease, which is usually withheld from the security deposit owed to the tenant. Deposits make it essential that both landlord and tenant inspect the property *before* occupancy and note any damages that may exist.

Improvements

If a tenant makes improvements to a rented property, the tenant must recognize that unless they can be removed easily, these improvements normally become part of the real estate (fixtures) and remain with the property when the lease expires. If built-in bookcases were added to a residential property, for example, these would become a fixture and part of the property. But, added shelving to a commercial property would normally be considered a trade fixture and would remain the property of the tenant at the end of the lease. We discussed fixtures and trade fixtures in Chapter 2. Before making any improvements or adding any items to the real estate, it is wise to reach an agreement with the landlord, preferably written, as to who will own them at the termination of the lease.

Provisions of a Typical Residential Lease

FIgure 7.1 on pages 157–63 illustrates the provisions of a typical residential lease.

After identifying the parties and the property, the agreement states that the property is rented only for the purpose of a single-family residence. If Jill should open some type of business in the apartment, for example, she would be in default, and Virginia Wells would have the right to terminate the lease agreement. Jill also agrees

FIGURE 7.1 | Case: Residential Lease Example

Residential Lease for Single Family Home and Duplex
FLORIDA ASSOCIATION OF REALTORS®

(For A Term Not To Exceed One Year)

INSTRUCTIONS:

1. Licensee: Give this disclosure to the Landlord prior to your assisting with the completion of the attached Lease.

2. Licensee: As the person assisting with the completion of the attached form, insert your name in the first (5) blank "Name" spaces below.

3. Licensee: **SIGN** the disclosure below.

4. Landlord and Tenant: Check the applicable provision regarding English contained in the disclosure and **SIGN** below.

5. Licensee, Landlord and Tenant: Retain a copy for your files.

* * * * *

DISCLOSURE:

Julio Rodriguez _____ told me that he/she is not a lawyer and may not give
(Name)
legal advice or represent me in court.

Julio Rodriguez _____ told me that he/she may only help me fill out a form
(Name)
approved by the Supreme Court of Florida. Julio Rodriguez _____ may only help me
(Name)
by asking me factual questions to fill in the form. Julio Rodriguez _____ may also
(Name)
tell me how to file the form.

Julio Rodriguez _____ told me that he/she is not an attorney and cannot tell me
(Name)
what my rights or remedies are or how to testify in court.

Tenant: Landlord:

✔ _____ I can read English.   ✔ _____ I can read English.
_____ I cannot read English but this   _____ I cannot read English but this
notice was read to me by   notice was read to me by
_____   _____
(Name)   (Name)
in _____   in _____
(Language)   (Language)

_____   _____   _____
(Licensee)   (Landlord)   (Tenant)

RLHD-2 10/00

FIGURE 7.1 | Case: Residential Lease Example *(continued)*

Residential Lease for Single Family Home and Duplex
FLORIDA ASSOCIATION OF REALTORS®

(FOR A TERM NOT TO EXCEED ONE YEAR)
A BOX (☐) OR A BLANK SPACE (____) INDICATES A PROVISION WHERE A CHOICE OR DECISION MUST BE MADE BY THE PARTIES.

THE LEASE IMPOSES IMPORTANT LEGAL OBLIGATIONS. MANY RIGHTS AND RESPONSIBILITIES OF THE PARTIES ARE GOVERNED BY CHAPTER 83, PART II, RESIDENTIAL LANDLORD AND TENANT ACT, FLORIDA STATUTES. UPON REQUEST, THE LANDLORD SHALL PROVIDE A COPY OF THE RESIDENTIAL LANDLORD AND TENANT ACT TO THE TENANT(S).

1. PARTIES. This is a lease ("the Lease") between Virginia Wells
1008 8th Street, Hialeah, Florida 33225
(name and address of owner of the property)
("Landlord") and

Jill Jewell
(name(s) of person(s) to whom the property is leased)
("Tenant.")

2. PROPERTY RENTED. Landlord leases to Tenant the land and buildings located at 149 Jarnigan Drive
(street address)
Hialeah   , Florida   33225
(zip code)

together with the following furniture and appliances [List all furniture and appliances. If none, write "none."] (In the Lease, the property leased, including furniture and appliances, if any, is called "the Premises"):

The Premises shall be occupied only by the Tenant and the following persons: none

3. TERM. This is a lease for a term, not to exceed twelve months, beginning on ____ 05/01/2007
(month, day, year)
and ending ____ 04/30/2008 ____ (the "Lease Term").
(month, day, year)

4. RENT PAYMENTS, TAXES AND CHARGES. Tenant shall pay total rent in the amount of $ ____ 1,250.00 ____ (excluding taxes) for the Lease Term. The rent shall be payable by Tenant in advance
☐ in installments. If in installments, rent shall be payable
    ☑ monthly, on the ____ 1st ____ day of each month. (If left blank, on the first day of each month.)
    ☐ weekly, on the _____ day of each week. (If left blank, on Monday of each week.)
    in the amount of $_____ per installment.
☐ in full on _____ in the amount of $_____ .
(date)

Tenant shall also be obligated to pay taxes on the rent when applicable in the amount of $ ____ 0.00
☐ with each rent installment ☐ with the rent for the full term of the Lease. Landlord will notify Tenant if the amount of the tax changes.

Payment Summary
☑ If rent is paid in installments, the total payment per installment including taxes shall be in the amount of $_____ .

☐ If rent is paid in full, the total payment including taxes shall be in the amount of $_____ .

Landlord (____) (____) and Tenant (____) (____) acknowledge receipt of a copy of this page which is Page 1 of 6
RLHD-2 10/00   Approved for use under rule 10-2.1(a) of The Rules Regulating The Florida Bar

FIGURE 7.1 | Case: Residential Lease Example *(continued)*

All rent payments shall be payable to _Virginia Wells_ at
_____
(name)

1008 8th Street, Hialeah Florida 33225 .(If left blank, to Landlord at Landlord's address).
_____
(address)

☐If the tenancy starts on a day other than the first day of the month or week as designated above, the rent shall be prorated from
_____through_____in the amount of $_____and shall be due on
(date) _(date)_

_____. (If rent paid monthly, prorate on a 30 day month.)
(date)

Tenant shall make rent payments required under the Lease by (choose all applicable) ☑cash, ☑personal check, ☑money order,
☑cashier's check, or☐other_____(specify). If payment is accepted by any means other than
cash, payment is not considered made until the other instrument is collected.

If Tenant makes a rent payment with a worthless check, Landlord can require Tenant☑to pay all future payments by☑money order,
cashier's check or official bank check or☑cash or other (specify)_____,
and☑to pay bad check fees in the amount of $_____35.00 (not to exceed the amount prescribed by Florida Statutes
section 68.065).

**5. MONEY DUE PRIOR TO OCCUPANCY. Tenant shall pay the sum of $_____3,500.00 in accordance with this Paragraph
prior to occupying the Premises.** Tenant shall not be entitled to move in or to keys to the Premises until all money due prior to
occupancy has been paid. If no date is specified below, then funds shall be due prior to tenant occupancy. Any funds designated in
this paragraph due after occupancy, shall be paid accordingly. Any funds due under this paragraph shall be payable to Landlord at
Landlord's address or to _____
(name)

at _____,
(address)

First☐month's☐week's rent plus applicable taxes	$	1,250.00 due	05/01/2007
Prorated rent plus applicable taxes	$	due	
Advance rent for☑month☐week of_____April, 2008			
plus applicable taxes	$	due	
Last☑month's☐week's rent plus applicable taxes	$	1,250.00 due	5/1/2007
Security deposit	$	1,000.00 due	5/1/2007
Additional security deposit	$	due	
Security deposit for homeowner's association	$	due	
Other _____	$	due	
Other _____	$	due	

6. LATE FEES. (Complete if applicable) In addition to rent, Tenant shall pay a late charge in the amount of $_____125.00 for
each rent payment made____5____days after the day it is due (if left blank, 5 days if rent is paid monthly, 1 day if rent is paid weekly).
7. PETS. Tenant☐may☑may not keep pets or animals on the Premises. If Tenant may keep pets, the pets described in this
Paragraph are permitted on the Premises.

_____
(Specify number of pets, type(s), breed, maximum adult weight of pets.)

8. NOTICES. _____is Landlord's Agent.
All notices must be sent to:
☑Landlord _Virginia Wells_
_____
(name)

at _1008 8th Street, Hialeah, Florida 33225_
_____
(address)

☐Landlord's Agent _____
(name)

at _____
(address)

Landlord (____) (____) and Tenant (____) (____) acknowledge receipt of a copy of this page which is Page 2 of 6
RLHD-2 10/00   Approved for use under rule 10-2.1(a) of The Rules Regulating The Florida Bar

FIGURE 7.1 | Case: Residential Lease Example *(continued)*

unless Landlord gives Tenant written notice of a change. All notices of such names and addresses or changes thereto shall be delivered to the Tenant's residence or, if specified in writing by the Tenant, to any other address. All notices to the Landlord or the Landlord's Agent (whichever is specified above) shall be given by U.S. mail or by hand delivery.

Any notice to Tenant shall be given by U.S. mail or delivered to Tenant at the Premises. If Tenant is absent from the Premises, a notice to Tenant may be given by leaving a copy of the notice at Premises.

9. UTILITIES. Tenant shall pay for all utilities services during the Lease Term and connection charges and deposits for activating existing utility connections to the Premises except for __water__

_____, that Landlord agrees to provide at Landlord's expense.

10. MAINTENANCE. Landlord shall be responsible for compliance with Section 83.51, Florida Statutes, and shall be responsible for maintenance and repair of the Premises, unless otherwise stated below:

(Fill in each blank space with "Landlord" for Landlord or "Tenant" for Tenant, if left blank, Landlord will be responsible for the item):

_____ roofs   _____ windows   _____ screens

_____ steps   _____ doors   _____ floors

_____ porches   _____ exterior walls   _____ foundations

_____ plumbing   _____ structural components

_____ heating   _____ hot water   _____ running water

_____ locks and keys   _____ electrical system   _____ cooling

_____ smoke detection devices   _____ garbage removal/outside receptacles

_____ extermination of rats, mice, roaches, ants and bedbugs   _____ extermination of wood-destroying organisms

_____ lawn/shrubbery   _____ pool/spa/hot tub   _____ water treatment

_____ filters(specify)_____   _____ ceilings   _____ interior walls

Other (specify)_____

Tenant shall notify __Virginia Wells__ _____ at __1008 8th Street, Hialeah, Florida 33225__
                                    (name)   (address)

and __(305) 555-5555__ _____ of maintenance
                    (telephone number)

and repair requests.

11. ASSIGNMENT. Tenant ☐ may ☑ may not assign the lease or sublease all or any part of the Premises without first obtaining the Landlord's written approval and consent to the assignment or sublease.

12. KEYS AND LOCKS. Landlord shall furnish Tenant __1__ # of sets of keys to the dwelling __1__ # of mail box keys

_____ # of garage door openers

If there is a homeowner's association, Tenant will be provided with the following to access the association's common areas/facilities: _____ # of keys to _____

_____ # of remote controls to _____

_____ # of electronic cards to _____

_____ other (specify) to _____

At end of Lease Term, all items specified in this Paragraph shall be returned to __Virginia Wells__
                                                                                            (name)
at __1008 8th Street, Hialeah, Florida 33225__ _____ (If left blank, Landlord at Landlord's address).
                    (address)

13. LEAD-BASED PAINT. ☐ Check and complete if the dwelling was built before January 1, 1978

Lead Warning Statement

Housing built before 1978 may contain lead-based paint. Lead from paint, paint chips, and dust can pose health hazards if not managed properly. Lead exposure is especially harmful to young children and pregnant women. Before renting pre-1978 housing, Lessors must disclose the presence of known lead-based paint and/or lead-based paint hazards in the dwelling. Lessees must also receive a federally approved pamphlet on lead poisoning prevention.

Landlord (____) (____) and Tenant (____) (____) acknowledge receipt of a copy of this page which is Page 3 of 6
RLHD-2 10/00   Approved for use under rule 10-2.1(a) of The Rules Regulating The Florida Bar

FIGURE 7.1 | Case: Residential Lease Example *(continued)*

Lessor's Disclosure (initial)

_____(a) Presence of lead-based paint or lead-based paint hazards (check (i) or (ii) below):

(i) ____Known lead-based paint and/or lead-based paint hazards are present in the housing (explain).

_____

_____

(ii) ____Lessor has no knowledge of lead-based paint and/or lead-based paint hazards in the housing.

_____(b) Records and reports available to the Lessor (check (i) or (ii) below):

(i) ____Lessor has provided the Lessee with all available records and reports pertaining to lead-based paint and/or lead-based paint hazards in the housing (List documents below).

_____

_____

(ii) ____Lessor has no reports or records pertaining to lead-based paint and/or lead-based paint hazards in the housing.

Lessee's Acknowledgment (initial)

_____(c) Lessee has received copies of all information listed above.

_____(d) Lessee has received the pamphlet *Protect Your Family From Lead in Your Home.*

Agent's Acknowledgment (initial)

_____(e) Agent has informed the Lessor of the Lessor's obligations under 42 U.S.C. 4852d and is aware of his/her responsibility to ensure compliance.

Certification of Accuracy

The following parties have reviewed the information above and certify, to the best of their knowledge, that the information provided by the signatory is true and accurate.

_____ _____ _____ _____
Lessor   Date   Lessor   Date

_____ _____ _____ _____
Lessee   Date   Lessee   Date

_____ _____ _____ _____
Agent   Date   Agent   Date

14. MILITARY/U.S. CIVIL SERVICE. ☐Check if applicable. In the event Tenant, who is in the Military/U.S. Civil Service, should receive government orders for permanent change of duty station requiring Tenant to relocate away from the Premises, then Tenant may terminate the Lease without further liability by giving Landlord 30 days advance written notice and a copy of the transfer order.

15. LANDLORD'S ACCESS TO THE PREMISES. As provided in Chapter 83, Part II, Residential Landlord and Tenant Act, Florida Statutes, Landlord or Landlord's Agent may enter the Premises in the following circumstances:

A. At any time for the protection or preservation of the Premises.

B. After reasonable notice to Tenant at reasonable times for the purpose of repairing the Premises.

C. To inspect the Premises; make necessary or agreed-upon repairs, decorations, alterations, or improvements; supply agreed services; or exhibit the Premises to prospective or actual purchasers, mortgagees, tenants, workers, or contractors under any of the following circumstances:

1. with Tenant's consent; 2. in case of emergency; 3. when Tenant unreasonably withholds consent; or

4. if Tenant is absent from the Premises for a period of at least one-half a Rental Installment period. (If the rent is current and Tenant notifies Landlord of an intended absence, then Landlord may enter only with Tenant's consent or for the protection or preservation of the Premises.)

16. HOMEOWNER'S ASSOCIATION. If Tenant must be approved by a homeowner's association ("association"), Landlord and Tenant agree that the Lease is contingent upon receiving approval from the association. Any application fee required by an association shall be paid by ☐ Landlord ☐Tenant and is ☐ refundable ☐nonrefundable. If such approval is not obtained prior to commencement of Lease Term, Tenant shall receive return of deposits specified in Paragraph 5, if made, and the obligations of the parties under the Lease shall terminate. Tenant agrees to use due diligence in applying for association approval, to comply with the requirements for obtaining approval and agrees to pay any fee required by the association for procuring approval.☐ Landlord☐ Tenant shall pay the security deposit required by the association, if applicable.

Landlord (____) (____) and Tenant (____) (____) acknowledge receipt of a copy of this page which is Page 4 of 6
RLHD-2 10/00   Approved for use under rule 10-2.1(a) of The Rules Regulating The Florida Bar

FIGURE 7.1 | Case: Residential Lease Example *(continued)*

17. USE OF THE PREMISES. Tenant shall use the Premises for residential purposes. Tenant shall have exclusive use and right of possession to the dwelling. The Premises shall be used so as to comply with all state, county, municipal laws and ordinances, and all covenants and restrictions affecting the Premises and all rules and regulations of homeowners' associations affecting the Premises. Tenant may not paint or make any alterations or improvements to the Premises without first obtaining the Landlord's written consent to the alteration or improvement. Any improvements or alterations to the Premises made by the Tenant shall become Landlord's property. Tenant agrees not to use, keep, or store on the Premises any dangerous, explosive, toxic material which would increase the probability of fire or which would increase the cost of insuring the Premises.

18. RISK OF LOSS/INSURANCE.

A. Landlord and Tenant shall each be responsible for loss, damage, or injury caused by its own negligence or willful conduct.

B. Tenant should carry insurance covering Tenant's personal property and Tenant's liability insurance.

19. DEFAULTS/REMEDIES. Should a party to the Lease fail to fulfill their responsibilities under the Lease or need to determine whether there has been a default of the Lease, refer to Part II, Chapter 83, entitled Florida Residential Landlord and Tenant Act which contains information on same, and/or remedies available to the parties.

20. SUBORDINATION. The Lease is subordinate to the lien of any mortgage encumbering the fee title to the Premises from time to time.

21. LIENS. Tenant shall not have the right or authority to encumber the Premises or to permit any person to claim or assert any lien for the improvement or repair of the Premises made by the Tenant. Tenant shall notify all parties performing work on the Premises at Tenant's request that the Lease does not allow any liens to attach to Landlord's interest.

22. RENEWAL/EXTENSION. The Lease can be renewed or extended only by a written agreement signed by both Landlord and Tenant, but the term of a renewal or extension together with the original Lease Term may not exceed one year. A new lease is required for each year.

23. TENANT'S PERSONAL PROPERTY. BY SIGNING THIS RENTAL AGREEMENT, TENANT AGREES THAT UPON SURRENDER OR ABANDONMENT, AS DEFINED BY THE FLORIDA STATUTES, LANDLORD SHALL NOT BE LIABLE OR RESPONSIBLE FOR STORAGE OR DISPOSITION OF TENANT'S PERSONAL PROPERTY.

24. TENANT'S TELEPHONE NUMBER. Tenant shall within 5 business days of obtaining telephone services at the Premises, send written notice to Landlord of Tenant's telephone numbers at the Premises.

25. ATTORNEY'S FEES. In any lawsuit brought to enforce the Lease or under applicable law, the party who wins may recover its reasonable court costs and attorney's fees from the party who loses.

26. MISCELLANEOUS.

A. Time is of the essence of the Lease.

B. The Lease shall be binding upon and for the benefit of the heirs, personal representatives, successors, and permitted assigns of Landlord and Tenant, subject to the requirements specifically mentioned in the Lease. Whenever used, the singular number shall include the plural or singular and the use of any gender shall include all appropriate genders.

C. The agreements contained in the Lease set forth the complete understanding of the parties and may not be changed or terminated orally.

D. No agreement to accept surrender of the Premises from Tenant will be valid unless in writing and signed by Landlord.

E. All questions concerning the meaning, execution, construction, effect, validity, and enforcement of the Lease shall be determined pursuant to the laws of Florida.

F. A facsimile copy of the Lease and any signatures hereon shall be considered for all purposes originals.

G. As required by law, Landlord makes the following disclosure: "RADON GAS." Radon is a naturally occurring radioactive gas that, when it has accumulated in a building in sufficient quantities, may present health risks to persons who are exposed to it over time. Levels of radon that exceed federal and state guidelines have been found in buildings in Florida. Additional information regarding radon and radon testing may be obtained from your county health department.

Landlord (_____) (_____) and Tenant (_____) (_____) acknowledge receipt of a copy of this page which is Page 5 of 6

FIGURE 7.1 | Case: Residential Lease Example *(continued)*

27. BROKERS' COMMISSION. ☑ Check and complete if applicable. The brokerage companies named below will be paid the commission set forth in this Paragraph by ☑ Landlord ☐ Tenant for procuring a tenant for this transaction.

Julio Rodriguez
_____
Real Estate Licensee

_____
Real Estate Licensee

_____
Real Estate Brokerage Company

_____
Real Estate Brokerage Company

1,250.00 (one month's rent)
_____
Commission

_____
Commission

28. EXECUTION.
Executed by Landlord

_____
Landlord's Signature

_____
Date

_____
Landlord's Signature

_____
Date

Executed by Tenant

_____
Tenant's Signature

_____
Date

_____
Tenant's Signature

_____
Date

This form was completed with the assistance of:

Name of Individual: Julio Rodgriquez

Name of Business: Licensed Real Estate Broker

Address: 1287 Cypress Lane, Plantation FL 33317

Telephone Number: (954) 555-5555

Landlord (_____) (_____) and Tenant (_____) (_____) acknowledge receipt of a copy of this page which is Page 6 of 6
RLHD-2 10/00   Approved for use under rule 10-2.1(a) of The Rules Regulating The Florida Bar

to pay $850 per month rent in advance and to pay a late-payment fee if the rent is not paid on time. This agreement does not allow subletting or assignment of the apartment without the consent of Virginia.

Jill needs to be certain the apartment is in good repair before signing the agreement because she is agreeing to accept the premises in their present condition. If she thinks the apartment needs painting, for example, it is too late to demand repainting after the agreement is signed unless a written notation is made on the agreement that Virginia will paint the apartment. Jill also is agreeing to keep the premises in good repair; to pay for damages, including repair to plumbing caused by freezing; and to pay all utility bills on the property. The agreement contains no renewal provisions. If Jill wants to renew the lease after the first year, she must agree on new terms with Virginia. Because this leaves her vulnerable to future price increases or other changes in lease conditions, she might seek the inclusion of a renewal provision that would specify renewal terms.

The Rights and Obligations of Tenant and Landlord

The fundamental right of the landlord is to receive rents, while that of the tenant is to use, enjoy, occupy, and possess the leasehold premises. The tenant has the right of exclusive possession of the property during the period of the lease, known as the **covenant of quiet enjoyment,** and can use the property in any legal manner that is agreed to in the lease document. Unless exceptions are made in the lease, the landlord cannot enter the property except to abate some nuisance or prevent destruction of the property. For example, a landlord could enter a tenant's apartment without securing permission to repair a burst water pipe but not to make alterations or improvements without the tenant's prior consent. Conversely, the tenant cannot alter the leasehold premises without the permission of the landlord. The tenant has the obligation to pay the rent when due and not violate any of the lease provisions. If the tenant fails to pay the rent or violates other provisions of the lease, the landlord can move to have the tenant evicted from the premises.

Under the implied **warranty of habitability** principle, the landlord also has the obligation to maintain the premises in reasonable condition. Should a landlord fail to do so, many states have granted tenants of residential property the right to repair minor defects and deduct the cost of such repairs from rent payments. Local ordinances also require that landlords meet city and county health and safety codes.

Landlords also have the obligation to maintain common areas, such as elevators, hallways, and grounds, in a safe condition. If they do not, they may be liable for injuries that result from any defects or lapses in security.

The landlord's responsibility to protect tenants against criminal acts committed by third parties is still a murky area; nevertheless, courts are increasingly awarding tenants damages when landlords are held partially responsible because of some type of negligence (such as not repairing locks, etc.).

Many leases contain provisions giving the tenant the option of renewing the lease before its expiration. As mentioned above, this does not necessarily mean,

REAL ESTATE TODAY

LEGAL HIGHLIGHT

Landlord's Liability for Failure to Provide Adequate Maintenance

 Landlords have the duty to provide adequate maintenance on their properties, and when they do not, a tenant may collect damages for any harm that results. This the Haverford Place Apartments discovered.

Shortly after Elizabeth Stroot moved into the Haverford Place Apartments she noticed mold around the windows and in the bathroom. She attempted to remove the mold with bleach, but it kept returning. There were also leaks in Stroot's bathroom ceiling; within a few months the leaks had caused holes in the drywall, and the edges of these holes were covered with a black substance. Whenever the tenants above Stroot showered, black water ran out of the holes.

Stroot complained to the management, but she was told that the problem was caused by the upstairs tenants taking "sloppy" showers. The lessors did nothing to fix the problem, even after Stroot made an emergency call to the maintenance department complaining that the hole in the ceiling was so large that it was not just leaking, but "raining." The management still did not attempt to fix the problem, and finally the bathroom ceiling collapsed, flooding the bathroom floor. The drywall debris and the exposed ceiling area were covered with black, green, orange, and white mold, which emitted a strong, nauseating odor. When Stroot

called maintenance, she was told they could do nothing until the following day.

By the next morning Stroot, who had suffered from allergies and asthma since childhood, could not breathe and was rushed to the hospital by ambulance. During the 21 months she had lived at Haverford Place, her medical problems had increased significantly, forcing her to go to the emergency room 7 times for asthma attacks, spend 9 days as an inpatient and receive intravenous steroids 12 times.

Stroot sued for damages, and at trial several experts testified there was excessive and atypical mold growth in the apartment buildings, that it was caused by the landlord's failure to maintain the buildings, and that the high concentration of toxic mold significantly and permanently increased the severity of Stroot's asthma. The jury agreed, awarding Stroot $5,000 for property damage and $1,000,000 for personal injuries. The landlord appealed, claiming that the jury award "was so excessive as to shock the conscience." The landlord lost, the court ruling that "given the permanent nature of Stroot's injuries as well as the physical and emotional pain and suffering Stroot will have to endure for the remainder of her life," the verdict was not excessive.

[*New Haverford Partnership v. Stroot and Watson,* 772. A.2d 792, Supreme Court of Delaware]

however, that the lease can be renewed with the same terms as in the old lease, and rental rates often are raised at this time.

A lease may contain one or two distinct types of renewal clauses. If, by its terms, a lease is renewed automatically if neither party gives notice of termination,

---

REAL ESTATE TODAY

LEGAL HIGHLIGHT

Liability of Landlords for Injuries to Guests of Tenants

Dr. Thomas Luck (his real name) was attending a medical meeting in Winston-Salem, North Carolina. After the conference had ended for the day he spent the evening and night with his daughter at the Hill Top Ridge apartment complex.

During the night it began to snow, and another tenant noticed that the frozen precipitation had made the outside stairs that provided access to the apartment quite slippery, but she did not inform the management. Early the next morning, the apartment's site manager checked the weather, and finding only slush on the steps outside his own apartment, believed there was no need to clear snow or ice from the property.

Later that morning, Dr. Luck left his daughter's apartment, carrying a small bag in his left hand and a clothes bag over his shoulder. The lighting was dim and there was a light fog. When he reached the second step from the top of the exposed stairway, he hit the ice and slipped. He grabbed at the slick, ice-coated handrails, but to no avail. Dr. Luck fell down the staircase all the way to the bottom, suffering permanent injuries. He sued the apartment owners and managers, alleging that their negligence caused him to be permanently paralyzed, lose his medical practice, and suffer great financial loss.

Dr. Luck's ability to gain compensation for his losses hinged on whether he was an "invitee" or a "licensee" under North Carolina law. An invitee is someone who is invited to be on the property, such as a customer in a store, and the law affords them considerable protection against negligence by the landlord. A licensee, on the other hand, is a social guest of the owner or the tenant, and under North Carolina law only "willful or wanton conduct" on the part of the landlord will result in liability. The court ruled that although the apartment complex perhaps should have made sure that the steps were clear of ice, they were not guilty of willful or wanton conduct. As a social guest of his daughter, Dr. Luck was not entitled to recover for any alleged damages. Dr. Luck was out of luck.

[*Luck v. GWWS L. P.*, 1997 U.S. App. LEXIS 39011, U.S. 4th Circuit]

---

a negative renewal clause is involved. A lease that provides for renewal only when the tenant gives notice to the landlord that renewal is desired contains a positive renewal clause. In accordance with this latter provision, if no notice of renewal is given properly, the landlord-tenant relationship terminates at the end of the original lease period.

Most leases have a specific time period within which notice to terminate (under a negative renewal clause) or notice to renew (under a positive renewal clause) must be given. Although the landlord and tenant always may agree to whatever time period they desire, one to two months prior to the expiration of the lease is very common.

State Statutes Affecting the Landlord-Tenant Relationship

In addition to the agreed-on lease terms, the relationship between a landlord and tenant may be further defined by state laws that regulate the relationship. For example, state laws dictate the eviction process that landlords must follow for removing tenants who have violated the lease agreement, including the nonpayment of rent. Similarly, state laws may specify how long the landlord has to return any security deposit at the end of a lease, assuming the tenant has not damaged the landlord's property. Laws such as these vary dramatically from state to state. To view the actual statutes, visit the Web site at *www.nolo.com* and follow the links to your state.

CHAPTER REVIEW

- A *lease* is a contract that conveys use and possession of a property from the landlord to the tenant in return for the tenant's agreement to pay rent.

- The four types of leasehold estates in regard to duration of term are (1) tenancy for a stated period, (2) tenancy from period to period, (3) tenancy at will, and (4) tenancy at sufferance.

- A *ground lease* is a lease of land to the exclusion of any improvements. Such leases frequently are used as a financial device in the development of major office buildings.

- In a *gross lease*, the landlord agrees to pay the overhead expenses that arise in connection with the use of the premises. In a *net lease*, the tenant pays the operating expenses.

- Rental payments can be fixed or variable under a lease. In a *graduated-rent lease*, the payment is increased by specified percentages at stated intervals, while under a *reappraisal lease*, the level of each rent increase is determined by a reappraisal of the property. A *percentage lease* is a lease of property used for commercial purposes under which the rental payments are based on some percentage of sales made on the premises.

KEY TERMS

assignment	fixed-rent lease	lessee
common area maintenance fees	graduated-rent lease	lessor
	gross lease	net lease
covenant of quiet enjoyment	ground lease	net-net lease
	index lease	net-net-net lease
expense stop	lease	percentage lease

reappraisal lease

renewal option

rental agreement

security deposit

step-up rent lease

subleasing

tenancy at sufferance

tenancy at will

tenancy for a stated
period

tenancy from period to
period

term

warranty of habitability

STUDY EXERCISES

1. Define the following terms: *lease, lessor, lessee, tenancy for a stated period, tenancy from period to period, tenancy at will, tenancy at sufferance.*

2. What is the difference between a *gross lease* and a *net lease*?

3. Define the following terms: *percentage lease, graduated-rent lease, ground lease, reappraisal lease,* and *index lease.*

4. What is the difference between subleasing and assignment? When is subleasing desirable for the existing tenant?

5. What do the terms *covenant of quiet enjoyment* and *warranty of habitability* mean?

6. Do expense stops limit the expenses paid by the landlord or the tenant?

7. Based on the Legal Highlight involving Dr. Luck on page 166, are landlords liable for injuries suffered by guests of tenants?

8. What purpose do security deposits serve from the lessor's perspective?

9. What is the difference between a negative renewal clause and a positive renewal clause?

10. Al's Shoe Store has a percentage lease that requires a base rent of $2,000 per month, plus 2 percent of gross sales over $10,000. What will the rent be when the monthly gross sales are $18,000?

FURTHER READING

Bogart, Daniel, and Celeste Hammond. *Commercial Leasing: A Transactional Primer*. Durham, N.C.: Carolina Academic Press, 2007.

Stewart, Marcia, and Ralph Warner. *Leases and Rental Agreements*. Berkeley, Calif.: Nolo Press, 2007.

PART TWO

Real Estate Service Industries

Real Estate Brokerage

CHAPTER PREVIEW

Real estate brokers are trained specialists who assist individuals, firms, and other entities in their real estate transactions for compensation. A real estate broker's specialized knowledge is extremely valuable to those who purchase and sell real property infrequently and may not be familiar with the complexities of real estate transactions. To ensure that those who call themselves real estate brokers are competent to perform the task, each state has adopted professional licensing laws that regulate the real estate brokerage profession.

The objective of this chapter is to describe the typical real estate sales process, then consider numerous aspects of the real estate brokerage business, including

- the difference between real estate brokers and sales associates;

- state licensing and regulation of brokers and sale associates;

- the legal nature of agency relationships;

- the role of real estate brokers in real estate transactions;

- types of listing agreements, namely the (1) exclusive-brokerage listing, (2) exclusive-right-to-sell listing, (3) open listing, (4) net listing, and (5) limited service listing;

- the buyer representation agreement;

- duties and rights of brokers, sellers, and buyers;

- termination of agency relationships;

- types of real estate brokerage firms and their characteristics; and

- issues relating to broker and sales associate compensation.

LEGAL HIGHLIGHT
The Seller's Agent's Obligations to the Buyer

LEGAL HIGHLIGHT
Fair Housing

THE REAL ESTATE SALES PROCESS

When a property owner decides to sell a property or a potential buyer decides to purchase one, real estate brokers can often provide useful assistance. The primary functions of the real estate brokerage industry are to match properties and customers and guide the buyer and seller through the complexities of real estate transactions. Both buyers and sellers of real estate need to understand the sales process, which typically involves the following steps: (1) listing, (2) marketing the property and qualifying buyers, (3) presentation and negotiations, (4) contracts, and (5) settlement or closing.

Listing Agreement

The **listing agreement** is the contract that defines the relationship between the property owner and the real estate broker. This agreement authorizes the broker to begin searching for a buyer for the specified property. Perhaps the most critical point in the listing agreement is the determination of an offering (or listing) price. Most sellers do not have adequate market information to determine the value of their property. If the offering price is priced too high, the property probably will not sell within a reasonable period of time, if at all; if it is too low, the owners will not receive as much as they should. In addition to specifying the offering price, the listing agreement usually defines the amount of compensation due to the broker for finding a buyer, how long the broker has to search for a buyer before the relationship ends, and any other details of the relationship between the property owner and the broker.

Marketing the Property and Qualifying Buyers

With the listing agreement in place, the broker will then begin marketing the property to potential buyers. Marketing techniques include a For Sale sign on the lawn, newspaper advertisements, special television advertisements, open houses, and Internet-based advertising. As responses to these advertisements are received, the broker will then deal with potential prospects directly.

In the process of searching for a buyer, the broker provides an important service for the seller: separating true prospects from casual shoppers or those who really do not have adequate financial resources to buy the property. For example, a couple earning $30,000 a year and having little available equity may be quite ready and willing to buy a $175,000 house, but they probably will be unable to pay for it. The process of examining buyers' ability to purchase the property is known as *qualifying the buyer.* Mortgage lenders also use this phrase when they determine a borrower's creditworthiness.

Presentation and Negotiations

After the broker has found a qualified and interested buyer, a period of presentation and negotiation begins. This period can last for a few hours or many months, depending on such factors as the complexity of the transaction, the extent to which the property actually meets the potential buyer's perceived needs, and, of course, price. The buyer should remember that in these negotiations the broker generally is employed by the seller and is obligated to represent the seller's interests. Accordingly, in any complicated transaction, buyers may want to employ the services of a broker to represent their interests.

Contracts and Closing

If the parties agree, a contract that spells out the details of the agreement is drawn up and signed by both seller and buyer, a process discussed in Chapter 6. Though the broker cannot provide legal advice unless he or she is a licensed attorney, the broker can assist the parties in negotiating an agreement and committing that agreement to paper. After insurance is obtained, financing is arranged, and the deed and other necessary legal papers are prepared, the transaction can be closed. At the closing, or settlement of the transaction, ownership is formally transferred to the buyer. Real estate closings were also discussed in Chapter 6. With this general discussion of the real estate sales process in mind, we now turn our attention to more specific aspects of the real estate brokerage business.

REAL ESTATE BROKERS AND SALES ASSOCIATES

In general terms, a **broker** is an intermediary who brings together buyers and sellers, assists in negotiating agreements between them, executes their orders, and receives a **commission** (or brokerage) in compensation for services rendered. The broker does not take ownership of the item being transferred from seller to buyer but merely negotiates a transaction between the parties to the transaction. A **real estate broker** is a specialized type of broker—an intermediary licensed by the state in which he or she operates—who arranges real estate sale or lease transactions for a fee or commission. A real estate associate is also a broker in the general sense but, under the laws of the state, is authorized to act only under the direction of a licensed real estate broker. In other words, sales associates can carry out only those responsibilities assigned to them by their supervising broker.

LICENSING OF SALES ASSOCIATES AND BROKERS

Although you need not hold a real estate license to conduct real estate transactions on your own behalf, a license is required if you engage in real estate activities on behalf of someone else. The license and educational requirements imposed by states generally do not constitute serious obstacles to most people who want to enter the field, and the number of brokers and sales associates in the industry tends to expand or contract with swings in demand for real estate. Most states have a Web site where the licensing requirements and application materials for various real estate occupations (brokerage, appraisal, property management, etc.) can be found.

All states and the District of Columbia require that real estate sales associates and brokers obtain a license. The license requirements vary from state to state and also depend on whether the applicant wishes to become a sales associate or a broker. Typically, an applicant for a sales associate's license must have completed high school and a basic real estate course. The most common educational requirement is a 40-hour classroom course or the college equivalent. In addition, the applicant must pass a written test given by the state real estate commission. The prospective sales associate usually needs no previous experience if educational requirements have been satisfactorily met. To obtain a brokerage license, however, the applicant usually must work for a specified period of time (usually one year or more) as a licensed sales associate, complete additional real estate educational courses, and pass a more comprehensive written test.

About half of the states now have continuing education requirements for both sales associates and brokers. The intent of these requirements is to ensure that those involved in real estate brokerage keep abreast of current developments in the field. Successful completion of the required course is a prerequisite for license renewal.

Because real estate licensing laws and regulations change from time to time, readers interested in obtaining a real estate license should contact their local realty board or state real estate commission for full details on current licensing requirements.

REAL ESTATE BROKERAGE REGULATION

In addition to licensing sales associates and brokers, the state real estate commission or a similar body is responsible for ensuring that licensees obey laws designed to protect the public from unscrupulous business practices. These include misrepresentation, fraud, and failure to comply with fair housing laws. If the commission finds a licensee guilty of an infraction, it may revoke or suspend that person's license or invoke similar penalties.

In more severe cases, a legal judgment may be brought through a lawsuit by the injured party against a licensee or firm. Because these judgments sometimes are uncollectible due to the defendant's poor financial status, roughly 40 states either require that real estate brokers be bonded or, more commonly, maintain a state-sponsored recovery fund. A portion of each real estate license fee goes into the recovery fund, available to pay uncollectible judgments against licensees.

LEGAL ASPECTS OF THE BROKER-CLIENT RELATIONSHIP

Because people have neither the time nor the knowledge to accomplish everything they want or need to do, they hire other people to assist them. This certainly is true in real estate transactions, where a specialized knowledge of markets, law, and financing is vital to the success of the transaction.

The law recognizes the relationship between an employer and an employee as that of principal and agent. The **principal** (employer) is the person who authorizes the **agent** (employee) to act on his or her behalf. The agent is a **fiduciary** of the principal, which means the agent is in a position of confidence and must perform his or her duties in the best interest of the principal. In addition to fair dealings, the principal owes the agent compensation for services, and the agent owes the principal the duties of good faith, diligence, and loyalty.

The legal relationship known as **agency** is applicable to real estate transactions in several ways. First, a seller of real estate may authorize a broker to help locate a buyer. Second, a potential buyer may engage the services of a broker to search for available properties. Third, many brokers hire sales associates to assist in locating buyers and properties. These three relationships are created from written or oral contracts. In each case, one party is the principal, and the other is the agent. The broker is the agent in the relationship with the client (either seller or buyer), and the broker is the principal in the relationship with a sales associate. The sales associate is an agent of the broker and a **subagent** of the broker's principal.

■ THE ROLE OF REAL ESTATE BROKERS

Real estate brokers and sales associates play an important role in many real estate transactions. Traditionally, real estate brokers have been hired by property owners to help locate buyers for their property. The broker's role is to advertise and market the property and assist the seller in finalizing the transaction once a buyer is found. In this situation, the broker is an agent of the seller. Brokers may also represent property owners who wish to lease their properties to tenants. Property management and leasing are discussed in Chapter 12.

Many real estate transactions involve more than one broker. Frequently, one broker (called the **listing broker**) obtains a listing agreement with the property owner, while another broker (called the **selling broker**) actually locates a buyer. The selling broker in such a transaction may represent either the buyer or the seller. If the selling broker represents the seller, he or she is an agent (subagent) of the seller. If the selling broker represents the buyer, the broker is an agent of the buyer.

Increasingly, potential buyers are hiring brokers to assist them in locating a property for purchase. As a buyer's agent, the broker's role is to identify properties that meet the buyer's specifications, then assist the buyer in negotiating a transaction for the desired property.

In some cases, a single broker is employed by both the seller and the buyer to assist in the completion of a transaction. When this broker has fiduciary duties to both parties simultaneously, the broker is known as a **dual agent.** Many states recognize the problems inherent in this type of agency relationship and have declared it illegal for a broker to attempt to work as a dual agent. To overcome this situation, some states recognize that brokers may act as a **transaction broker** and provide limited representation to both parties to a negotiation to help them close their deal without working to the detriment of either of the parties.

Most states' laws require that the broker disclose the nature of his or her agency relationship to all parties involved in the negotiations prior to entering into meaningful negotiations to avoid confusion and possible violations of the fiduciary responsibilities. The next section examines the creation of agency relationships between (1) sellers and brokers and (2) buyers and brokers.

THE CREATION OF AGENCY RELATIONSHIPS

Before a principal is bound by the acts of an agent, the agent must have actual or apparent authority to transact business on the principal's behalf. In other words, there must be evidence that the principal has authorized the agent to perform in some capacity on behalf of the principal. Real estate brokers can act as agents for either sellers or buyers because a broker may be employed by either. Listing agreements refer to the agreement between the seller and the broker when the broker is a **seller's agent.** Buyer representation agreements define the agency relationship between the buyer and the broker when the broker is a **buyer's agent.** We will examine each of these agency relationships in turn.

The Broker-Seller Relationship (Seller's Agent)

Property owners generally give real estate brokers authority to sell their property using a written document called a *listing agreement.* Because listing agreements are contractual in nature, the essential elements of a binding contract must be present. These elements are discussed more fully in Chapter 6. Only about 20 states actually require listing agreements to be in writing, but as in any transaction, a written contract always is preferable to an oral agreement to clarify the relationship established and the duties owed.

A listing agreement describes the property and states the asking price, the duties of the broker, the extent of authority granted, the duration of the agreement, and the rights of the broker to a commission. There are various forms of listing agreements and each has its own legal impact. The more common types of agreements are the exclusive-brokerage listing, the exclusive-right-to-sell listing, and the open listing. These listing agreements create certain obligations between the broker and the seller, and the extent of the obligation depends on the type of agreement.

Suppose, for example, that Sarah Howell is being transferred by her job and wants to sell her house in Fort Lauderdale, Florida. She has decided to hire Julio Rodriguez to assist her in finding a buyer and accomplishing the sale. The following paragraphs outline how the various types of listing agreements would affect the terms of this agency relationship.

Open Listing

If Sarah signs the document that appears in Figure 8.1, she grants an **open listing** to Julio Rodriguez of Rodriguez Realty. In this type of listing, the broker is only entitled to a commission if he successfully arranges a transaction. At the same time Julio is trying to find a buyer, other brokers may also have entered into open listing with the seller. The document used to create open listing agreements is often called a **commission agreement.** The document identifies the parties to the agreement, the location of the property, and the broker's compensation should he successfully close the deal.

By entering into an open listing, the seller is authorizing the broker to attempt to find a willing buyer. Nevertheless, the owner reserves the right to authorize other

FIGURE 8.1 | Commission Agreement

Commission Agreement
FLORIDA ASSOCIATION OF REALTORS®

Date _____ June 1, 2007 _____

Sarah Howell _____ ("Seller/Lessor")
agrees   that
Julio Rodriguez _____ ("Broker") may show
and will use diligent effort to:

(Check One):

☑ sell

❑ lease

Seller's/Lessor's Property located at 501 SE 1st Street, Fort Lauderdale, Florida 33301

_____ (Property),
to ANY QUALIFIED _____ (Prospect).
In the event the Property is:

(Check One):

☑ sold, optioned, contracted to be sold

❑ leased

to Prospect procured by **Broker**, within ____90____ days of the date referenced above, **Seller/Lessor** agrees to pay **Broker**:

(Complete One):

❑ $ _____

☑   _____ 3.00 % of the gross purchase price of the Property.

❑   _____ % of the gross lease value of a lease executed regarding the Property.

❑   other _____.

The fee shall be paid to **Broker** by **Seller/Lessor** in the event of sale, at time of closing the sale; or in the event of lease at time of lease execution. **Broker's** fee is due if **Seller** defaults on an executed sales contract with Prospect or if **Seller** agrees with Prospect to cancel an executed sales contract

Other Provisions: _____

_____.

_____   _____
Seller/Lessor   Date

_____   _____
Seller/Lessor   Date

_____   Rodriguez Realty
Broker   Brokerage Office

_____   _____   _____
Accepted By   Title   Date

brokers to locate a potential buyer. In addition, the seller may sell her property without the aid of any broker. Under this commission agreement, Julio Rodriquez is entitled to the stated commission only if he successfully brings a buyer to Sarah. Julio will not receive any commission if either another broker or Sarah herself sells the property.

The open listing has both advantages and disadvantages for the sellers. Because they are not limited to one broker, they have greater flexibility. On the other hand, the broker does not have as much incentive to concentrate on selling the property because there is no assurance of actually earning a commission if another broker beats him to the punch. For this reason, open listings are seldom encouraged by brokers.

Exclusive-Brokerage Listing

If Sarah enters into an **exclusive-brokerage listing,** also called an *exclusive-agency listing,* the contract would be similar to the one in Figure 8.2. This listing agreement differs from the open listing in that the seller cannot authorize another broker to find a buyer without becoming obligated to pay the original broker a commission even if another broker finds a buyer for the property. Despite the limit placed on the seller's use of multiple brokers, she retains the right to sell her property on her own without becoming liable to pay Julio a commission. This type of agreement may seem most beneficial to sellers because they have one broker acting as their exclusive agent and can sell their property themselves without becoming liable for the commission. The broker may not be totally dedicated to marketing the property, however, because he or she could lose all rights to the commission on a sale-by-owner transaction.

Exclusive-Right-to-Sell Listing

Another popular type of listing agreement that is probably the most preferred type of listing agreement from the broker's perspective is called an **exclusive-right-to-sell listing.** In an exclusive-right-to-sell listing agreement, the owner authorizes the broker to search for a buyer for the property and agrees to pay the broker a commission even if property is sold by anyone while the listing agreement is active, including the owner. This agreement gives the broker the best guarantee of ultimately receiving a commission on the sale of the property. An example of an exclusive-right-to-sell listing is provided in Figure 8.3.

Net Listing

A type of listing used very infrequently today, and illegal in many states, is the **net listing.** In this agreement, the seller is guaranteed a specified amount of money, while the broker receives the remainder of the sales price. This type of listing obviously invites fraud because there is an incentive for the broker to deceive the seller about the fair-market value of the property and thus obtain a larger commission.

FIGURE 8.2 | Exclusive-Brokerage Listing Agreement

Exclusive Brokerage Listing Agreement
FLORIDA ASSOCIATION OF REALTORS®

1* This Exclusive Brokerage Listing Agreement("Agreement") is between
2* Sarah Howell _____ ("**Seller**") and

3* Julio Rodriguez _____ ("**Broker**").

4   **1. AUTHORITY TO SELL PROPERTY: Seller** gives **Broker** the right to be the EXCLUSIVE BROKER in the sale of the real and
5* personal property (collectively "Property") described below, at the price and terms described below, beginning the __1st__ day of
6* _____June_____, __2007__, and terminating at 11:59 p.m. the __31st__ day of _____August_____, __2007__ ("Termination
7   Date"). **Seller** reserves the right to sell the Property directly to a buyer without the assistance of any real estate licensee and, if
8   successful, does not owe **Broker** a commission. Upon full execution of a contract for sale and purchase of the Property, all rights
9   and obligations of this Agreement will automatically extend through the date of the actual closing of the sales contract. **Seller** and
10 **Broker** acknowledge that this Agreement does not guarantee a sale. This Property will be offered to any person without regard
11 to race, color, religion, sex, handicap, familial status, national origin or any other factor protected by federal, state or local law.
12 **Seller** certifies and represents that he/she/it is legally entitled to convey the Property and all improvements.

13 **2. DESCRIPTION OF PROPERTY:**
14*   **(a)** Real Property Street Address: 501 SE 1st Street, Fort Lauderdale Florida 33301 _____
15* _____
16* Legal Description: Lot 1, Block A, Ridgeview Subdivision, Broward County FL _____
17* _____ ❑ See Attachment _____
18* **(b)** Personal Property, including appliances: washer, dryer, hot tub _____
19* _____
20* _____ ❑ See Attachment _____
21* **(c)** Occupancy: Property ❑ is ☑ is not currently occupied by a tenant. If occupied, the lease term expires _____.

22 **3. PRICE AND TERMS:** The property is offered for sale on the following terms, or on other terms acceptable to **Seller**:
23*   **(a)** Price: _____$304,900.00_____
24*   **(b) Financing Terms:** ☑ Cash ☑ Conventional ☑ VA ☑ FHA ❑ Other _____
25*   ❑ **Seller** Financing: **Seller** will hold a purchase money mortgage in the amount of $_____ with the
26*   following terms: _____
27*   ❑ Assumption of Existing Mortgage: Buyer may assume existing mortgage for $_____ plus an
28*   assumption fee of $_____. The mortgage is for a term of _____ years beginning in _____, at
29*   an interest rate of _____% ❑ fixed ❑ variable (describe) _____
30*   Lender approval of assumption ❑ is required ❑ is not required ❑ unknown. Notice to **Seller**: You may remain liable for an
31   assumed mortgage for a number of years after the Property is sold. Check with your lender to determine the extent of
32   your liability. **Seller** will ensure that all mortgage payments and required escrow deposits are current at the time of closing
33   and will convey the escrow deposit to the buyer at closing.
34*   **(c) Seller Expenses: Seller** will pay mortgage discount or other closing costs not to exceed _____0_____% of the purchase
35   price; and any other expenses **Seller** agrees to pay in connection with a transaction.

36 **4. BROKER OBLIGATIONS AND AUTHORITY: Broker** agrees to make diligent and continued efforts to sell the Property until
37 a sales contract is pending on the Property. **Seller** authorizes **Broker** to:
38   **(a)** Advertise the Property as **Broker** deems advisable in newspapers, publications, or other media; place appropriate
39   transaction signs on the Property, including "For Sale" signs and "Sold" signs (once **Seller** signs a sales contract); and use
40   **Seller's** name in connection with marketing or advertising the Property;
41   **(b)** Obtain information relating to the present mortgage(s) on the Property.
42   **(c)** Place the Property in a multiple listing service ("MLS"). **Seller** authorizes **Broker** to report to the MLS this listing
43   information and price, terms and financing information on any resulting sale for use by authorized Board / Association
44   members, MLS participants and subscribers; and
45*   **(d)** (Check if applicable) ❑ Use a lock box system to show and access the Property. A lock box does not ensure the
46   Property's security; **Seller** is advised to secure or remove valuables. **Seller** agrees that the lock box is for **Seller's** benefit and
47   releases **Broker**, persons working through **Broker** and **Broker's** local Realtor Board / Association from all liability and
48*   responsibility in connection with any loss that occurs. ❑ Withhold verbal offers. ❑ Withhold all offers once
49   **Seller** accepts a contract for sale and purchase of the Property.

50* **Seller** (____) (____) and **Broker/Sales Associate** (____) (____) acknowledge receipt of a copy of this page, which is Page 1 of 3 Pages.

EBLA-4x   Rev. 10/06   © 2006   Florida Association of REALTORS®   All Rights Reserved

FIGURE 8.2 | Exclusive-Brokerage Listing Agreement *(continued)*

51   **5. SELLER OBLIGATIONS:** In consideration of **Broker's** obligations, **Seller** agrees to:
52   **(a)** Cooperate with **Broker** in carrying out the purpose of this Agreement, including referring immediately to **Broker** all
53   inquiries from real estate licensees regarding the Property's transfer, whether by purchase or any other means of transfer.
54   **(b)** Provide **Broker** with keys to the Property and make the Property available for **Broker** to show during reasonable times.
55   **(c)** Inform **Broker** prior to leasing, mortgaging or otherwise encumbering the Property, and immediately upon **Seller**
56   entering into a sales contract with a buyer procured by **Seller.**
57   **(d)** Indemnify **Broker** and hold **Broker** harmless from losses, damages, costs and expenses of any nature, including
58   attorneys' fees, and from liability to any person, that **Broker** incurs because of **Seller's** negligence, representations,
59   misrepresentations, actions, or inactions, the use of a lock box or the existence of undisclosed material facts. This clause will
60   survive **Broker's** performance and the transfer of title.
61   **(e)** Perform any act reasonably necessary to comply with FIRPTA (Internal Revenue Code Section 1445).
62   **(f)** Make all legally required disclosures, including all facts that materially affect the Property's value and are not readily
63   observable or known by the buyer. **Seller** certifies and represents that **Seller** knows of no such material facts (local
64* government building code violations, unobservable defects, etc.) other than the following: _____
65* _____
66   **Seller** will immediately inform **Broker** of any material facts that arise after signing this Agreement.
67   **(g)** Consult appropriate professionals for related legal, tax, property condition, environmental, foreign reporting requirements
68   and other specialized advice.

69   **6. COMPENSATION: Seller** will compensate **Broker** as specified below for procuring a buyer who is ready, willing and able to
70   purchase the Property or any interest in the Property on the terms of this Agreement or on any other terms acceptable to
71   **Seller. Seller** will pay **Broker** as follows (plus applicable sales tax):
72* **(a)** ____6____% of the total purchase price OR $_____, no later than the date of closing specified in the
73   purchase contract. However, closing is not a prerequisite for **Broker's** fee being earned.
74* **(b)** _____ ($ or %) of the consideration paid for an option, at the time an option is created. If the option is exercised,
75   **Seller** will pay **Broker** the paragraph 6(a) fee, less the amount **Broker** received under this subparagraph.
76* **(c)** _____ ($ or %) of gross lease value as a leasing fee, on the date **Seller** enters into a lease or agreement to lease,
77   whichever is soonest. This fee is not due if the Property is or becomes the subject of a contract granting an exclusive right to
78   lease the Property.
79   **(d)** **Broker's** fee is due in the following circumstances: **(1)** If any interest in the Property is transferred, whether by sale, lease,
80   exchange, governmental action, bankruptcy or any other means of transfer, with the assistance of any real estate licensee. **(2)** If
81   **Seller** refuses or fails to sign an offer at the price and terms stated in this Agreement, defaults on an executed sales contract or
82* agrees with a buyer to cancel an executed sales contract. **(3)** If, within ____90____ days after Termination Date ("Protection
83   Period"), **Seller** transfers or contracts to transfer the Property or any interest in the Property to any prospects with whom **Broker**
84   or any other real estate licensee communicated regarding the Property prior to Termination Date. However, no fee will be due
85   **Broker** if the Property is relisted after Termination Date and sold through another broker.
86* **(e)** Retained Deposits: As consideration for **Broker's** services, **Broker** is entitled to receive ____50____% of all deposits
87   that **Seller** retains as liquidated damages for a buyer's default in a transaction, not to exceed the paragraph 6(a) fee.

88   **7. COOPERATION WITH OTHER BROKERS: Broker's** office policy is to cooperate with all other brokers except when not in
89* **Seller's** best interest: ☑ and to offer compensation in the amount of ____3____% of the purchase price or $_____ to
90   Buyer's agents, who represent the interest of the buyers and not the interest of the Seller even if compensated by **Seller** or
91* **Broker** in a transaction; ☑ and to offer compensation in the amount of ____3____% of the purchase price or $_____
92* to a broker who has no brokerage relationship with the Buyer or **Seller;** ☑ and to offer compensation in the amount of
93* ____3____% of the purchase price or $_____ to transaction brokers for the Buyer; ❑ None of the above (if this is
94   checked, the Property cannot be placed in the MLS.)

95   **8. BROKERAGE RELATIONSHIP: Seller** authorizes **Broker** to operate as (check which is applicable):
96* ❑ single agent of **Seller.**
97* ☑ transaction broker.
98* ❑ single agent of **Seller** with consent to transition into a transaction broker.
99* ❑ nonrepresentative of **Seller.**

100 **9. CONDITIONAL TERMINATION:** At **Seller's** request, **Broker** may agree to conditionally terminate this Agreement. If **Broker**
101 agrees to conditional termination, **Seller** must sign a withdrawal agreement, reimburse **Broker** for all direct expenses incurred
102* in marketing the Property and pay a cancellation fee of $_____1,000.00__ plus applicable sales tax. **Broker** may void the
103 conditional termination and **Seller** will pay the fee stated in paragraph 6(a) less the cancellation fee if **Seller** transfers or
104 contracts to transfer the Property or any interest in the Property during the time period from the date of conditional termination
105 to Termination Date and Protection Period, if applicable.

106* **Seller** (____) (____) and **Broker/Sales Associate** (____) (____) acknowledge receipt of a copy of this page, which is Page 2 of 3 Pages.

EBLA-4x   Rev. 10/06   © 2006   Florida Association of REALTORS®   All Rights Reserved

FIGURE 8.2 | Exclusive-Brokerage Listing Agreement *(continued)*

107 **10. DISPUTE RESOLUTION:** This Agreement will be construed under Florida law. All controversies, claims and other matters
108 in question between the parties arising out of or relating to this Agreement or the breach thereof will be settled by first
109 attempting mediation under the rules of the American Mediation Association or other mediator agreed upon by the parties. If
110 litigation arises out of this Agreement, the prevailing party will be entitled to recover reasonable attorneys' fees and costs,
111 unless the parties agree that disputes will be settled by arbitration as follows:
112* **Arbitration:** By initialing in the space provided, **Seller** (_____) (_____), Listing Associate (_____) and Listing Broker (_____)
113 agree that disputes not resolved by mediation will be settled by neutral binding arbitration in the county in which the Property
114 is located in accordance with the rules of the American Arbitration Association or other arbitrator agreed upon by the parties.
115 Each party to any arbitration or litigation (including appeals and interpleaders) will pay its own fees, costs and expenses,
116 including attorneys' fees, and will equally split the arbitrators' fees and administrative fees of arbitration.

117 **11. MISCELLANEOUS:** This Agreement is binding on **Broker's** and **Seller's** heirs, personal representatives, administrators,
118 successors and assigns. **Broker** may assign this Agreement to another listing office. Signatures, initials and modifications
119 communicated by facsimile will be considered as originals. The term "buyer" as used in this Agreement includes buyers,
120 tenants, exchangors, optionees and other categories of potential or actual transferees.

121* Date: _____ **Seller's Signature:** _____ Tax ID No: __ __ __ - __ __ - __ __ __ __

122* Home Telephone: _____ Work Telephone: _____ Facsimile: _____

123* Address: _____

124* Date: _____ **Seller's Signature:** _____ Tax ID No: __ __ __ - __ __ - __ __ __ __

125* Home Telephone: _____ Work Telephone: _____ Facsimile: _____

126* Address: _____

127* Date: _____ **Authorized Listing Associate or Broker:** _____

128* Brokerage Firm Name: _____ Telephone: _____

129* Address: _____

130* | Copy returned to **Customer** on the __1st__ day of _____June_____, _2007_ by: ❑ personal delivery ❑ mail ❑ E-mail ❑ facsimile. |

131* **Seller** (_____) (_____) and **Broker/Sales Associate** (_____) (_____) acknowledge receipt of a copy of this page, which is Page 3 of 3 Pages.

FIGURE 8.3 | Exclusive-Right-to-Sell Listing Agreement

Exclusive Right of Sale Listing Agreement
FLORIDA ASSOCIATION OF REALTORS®

1   This Exclusive Right of Sale Listing Agreement ("Agreement") is between
2*   Sarah Howell _____ ("**Seller**") and

3*   Julio Rodriguez _____ ("**Broker**").

4   **1. AUTHORITY TO SELL PROPERTY: Seller** gives **Broker** the EXCLUSIVE RIGHT TO SELL the real and personal property
5*   (collectively "Property") described below, at the price and terms described below, beginning the ___1st___ day of
6*   _____June_____, _2007_, and terminating at 11:59 p.m. the __31st__ day of _____August_____, _2007_
7   ("Termination Date"). Upon full execution of a contract for sale and purchase of the Property, all rights and obligations of this
8   Agreement will automatically extend through the date of the actual closing of the sales contract. **Seller** and **Broker**
9   acknowledge that this Agreement does not guarantee a sale. This Property will be offered to any person without regard to
10   race, color, religion, sex, handicap, familial status, national origin or any other factor protected by federal, state or local law.
11   **Seller** certifies and represents that he/she/it is legally entitled to convey the Property and all improvements.
12   **2. DESCRIPTION OF PROPERTY:**
13*   **(a)** Real Property Street Address: _501 SE 1st Street, Fort Lauderdale, Florida 33301_____
14*   _____
15*   Legal Description: _Lot 1, Block A, Ridgeview Subdivision, Broward County, Florida_____
16*   _____ ❑ See Attachment _____
17*   **(b)** Personal Property, including appliances: _washer, dryer, hot tub_____
18*   _____
19*   _____ ❑ See Attachment _____
20*   **(c)** Occupancy: Property ❑ is ☑ is not currently occupied by a tenant. If occupied, the lease term
21*   expires_____.
22   **3. PRICE AND TERMS:** The property is offered for sale on the following terms, or on other terms acceptable to **Seller**:
23*   **(a) Price:** _____$304,900.00_____
24*   **(b) Financing Terms:** ☑ Cash ☑ Conventional ☑ VA ☑ FHA ❑ Other _____
25*   ❑ **Seller** Financing: **Seller** will hold a purchase money mortgage in the amount of $_____ with the
26*   following terms: _____
27*   ❑ Assumption of Existing Mortgage: Buyer may assume existing mortgage for $_____ plus an
28*   assumption fee of $_____. The mortgage is for a term of _____ years beginning in _____, at
29*   an interest rate of _____ % ❑ fixed ❑ variable (describe)_____.
30*   Lender approval of assumption ❑ is required ❑ is not required ❑ unknown. Notice to **Seller**: You may remain liable for an
31   assumed mortgage for a number of years after the Property is sold. Check with your lender to determine the extent of your
32   liability. **Seller** will ensure that all mortgage payments and required escrow deposits are current at the time of closing and
33   will convey the escrow deposit to the buyer at closing.
34*   **(c) Seller Expenses: Seller** will pay mortgage discount or other closing costs not to exceed ___0___ % of the purchase
35   price; and any other expenses **Seller** agrees to pay in connection with a transaction.
36   **4. BROKER OBLIGATIONS AND AUTHORITY: Broker** agrees to make diligent and continued efforts to sell the Property
37   until a sales contract is pending on the Property. **Seller** authorizes **Broker** to:
38   **(a)** Advertise the Property as **Broker** deems advisable in newspapers, publications, computer networks, including the
39   Internet and other media; place appropriate transaction signs on the Property, including "For Sale" signs and "Sold" signs
40   (once **Seller** signs a sales contract); and use **Seller's** name in connection with marketing or advertising the Property;
41   **(b)** Obtain information relating to the present mortgage(s) on the Property.
42   **(c)** Place the property in a multiple listing service(s) (MLS). **Seller** authorizes **Broker** to report to the MLS/Association of
43   Realtors® this listing information and price, terms and financing information on any resulting sale. **Seller** authorizes **Broker**,
44   the MLS and/or Association of Realtors® to use, license or sell the active listing and sold data.
45   **(d)** Provide objective comparative market analysis information to potential buyers; and
46*   **(e)** (Check if applicable) ❑ Use a lock box system to show and access the Property. A lock box does not ensure the
47   Property's security; **Seller** is advised to secure or remove valuables. **Seller** agrees that the lock box is for **Seller's** benefit
48   and releases **Broker**, persons working through **Broker** and **Broker's** local Realtor Board/Association from all liability and
49*   responsibility in connection with any loss that occurs. ❑ Withhold verbal offers. ❑ Withhold all offers once **Seller** accepts a
50   sales contract for the Property.
51   **(f)** Act as a transaction broker.
52   **5. SELLER OBLIGATIONS:** In consideration of **Broker's** obligations, **Seller** agrees to:
53   **(a)** Cooperate with **Broker** in carrying out the purpose of this Agreement, including referring immediately to **Broker** all
54   inquiries regarding the Property's transfer, whether by purchase or any other means of transfer.
55   **(b)** Provide **Broker** with keys to the Property and make the Property available for **Broker** to show during reasonable times.
56   **(c)** Inform **Broker** prior to leasing, mortgaging or otherwise encumbering the Property.

57*   **Seller** (____) (____) and **Broker/Sales Associate** (____) (____) acknowledge receipt of a copy of this page, which is Page 1 of 3 Pages.

ERS-11tbx   Rev. 10/06   © 2006   Florida Association of REALTORS®   All Rights Reserved

FIGURE 8.3 | Exclusive-Right-to-Sell Listing Agreement *(continued)*

58   **(d)** To indemnify **Broker** and hold **Broker** harmless from losses, damages, costs and expenses of any nature,
59   including attorney's fees, and from liability to any person, that **Broker** incurs because of (1) **Seller's** negligence,
60   representations, misrepresentations, actions or inactions, (2) the use of a lock box, (3) the existence of undisclosed material
61   facts about the Property, or (4) a court or arbitration decision that a broker who was not compensated in connection with a
62   transaction is entitled to compensation from **Broker**. This clause will survive **Broker's** performance and the transfer of title.
63   **(e)** To perform any act reasonably necessary to comply with FIRPTA (Internal Revenue Code Section 1445).
64   **(f)** Make all legally required disclosures, including all facts that materially affect the Property's value and are not readily
65   observable or known by the buyer. **Seller** represents there are no material facts (building code violations, pending code
66* citations, unobservable defects, etc.) other than the following: _____
67* _____
68   **Seller** will immediately inform **Broker** of any material facts that arise after signing this Agreement.
69   **(g)** Consult appropriate professionals for related legal, tax, property condition, environmental, foreign reporting
70   requirements and other specialized advice.
71   **6. COMPENSATION: Seller** will compensate **Broker** as specified below for procuring a buyer who is ready, willing and able
72   to purchase the Property or any interest in the Property on the terms of this Agreement or on any other terms acceptable to
73   **Seller**. **Seller** will pay **Broker** as follows (plus applicable sales tax):
74* **(a)** _____ **6**% of the total purchase price OR $_____, no later than the date of closing specified
75   in the sales contract. However, closing is not a prerequisite for **Broker's** fee being earned.
76* **(b)** _____ ($ or %) of the consideration paid for an option, at the time an option is created. If the option is exercised,
77   **Seller** will pay **Broker** the paragraph 6(a) fee, less the amount **Broker** received under this subparagraph.
78* **(c)** _____ ($ or %) of gross lease value as a leasing fee, on the date **Seller** enters into a lease or agreement to lease, whichever
79   is soonest. This fee is not due if the Property is or becomes the subject of a contract granting an exclusive right to lease the Property.
80   **(d) Broker's** fee is due in the following circumstances: (1) If any interest in the Property is transferred, whether by sale, lease,
81   exchange, governmental action, bankruptcy or any other means of transfer, regardless of whether the buyer is secured by
82   **Broker, Seller** or any other person. (2) If **Seller** refuses or fails to sign an offer at the price and terms stated in this
83   Agreement, defaults on an executed sales contract or agrees with a buyer to cancel an executed sales contract. (3) If, within
84* ____ **90** ____ days after Termination Date ("Protection Period"), **Seller** transfers or contracts to transfer the Property or any
85   interest in the Property to any prospects with whom **Seller, Broker** or any real estate licensee communicated regarding the
86   Property prior to Termination Date. However, no fee will be due **Broker** if the Property is relisted after Termination Date and
87   sold through another broker.
88* **(e) Retained Deposits:** As consideration for **Broker's** services, **Broker** is entitled to receive ____ **50** ____% of all deposits
89   that **Seller** retains as liquidated damages for a buyer's default in a transaction, not to exceed the paragraph 6(a) fee.
90   **7. COOPERATION AND COMPENSATION WITH OTHER BROKERS: Broker's** office policy is to cooperate with all other
91* brokers except when not in **Seller's** best interest: ☑ and to offer compensation in the amount of ____ **3** ____% of the
92* purchase price or $_____ to **Buyer's** agents, who represent the interest of the buyers, and not the interest of **Seller**
93* in a transaction; ☑ and to offer compensation in the amount of ____ **3** ____% of the purchase price or $_____
94* to a broker who has no brokerage relationship with the **Buyer** or **Seller**; ☑ and to offer compensation in the amount of
95* ____ **3** ____% of the purchase price or $_____ to Transaction Brokers for the **Buyer**; ❑ None of the above (if this is
96   checked, the Property cannot be placed in the MLS).
97   **8. BROKERAGE RELATIONSHIP:**

TRANSACTION BROKER NOTICE

98* As a transaction broker, _____ and its associates, provides to you a limited
99   form of representation that includes the following duties:
100 **1.** Dealing honestly and fairly;
101 **2.** Accounting for all funds;
102 **3.** Using skill, care, and diligence in the transaction;
103 **4.** Disclosing all known facts that materially affect the value of residential real property and are not readily observable to the buyer;
104 **5.** Presenting all offers and counteroffers in a timely manner, unless a party has previously directed the licensee otherwise
105 in writing;
106 **6.** Limited confidentiality, unless waived in writing by a party. This limited confidentiality will prevent disclosure that the seller will
107 accept a price less than the asking or listed price, that the buyer will pay a price greater than the price submitted in a written
108 offer, of the motivation of any party for selling or buying property, that a seller or buyer will agree to financing terms other than
109 those offered, or of any other information requested by a party to remain confidential; and
110 **7.** Any additional duties that are entered into by this or by separate written agreement.
111 Limited representation means that a buyer or seller is not responsible for the acts of the licensee. Additionally, parties are
112 giving up their rights to the undivided loyalty of the licensee. This aspect of limited representation allows a licensee to
113 facilitate a real estate transaction by assisting both the buyer and the seller, but a licensee will not work to represent one
114 party to the detriment of the other party when acting as a transaction broker to both parties.

115*
116 _____   _____   _____
     Date   Signature   Signature

117* **Seller** (____) (____) and **Broker/Sales Associate** (____) (____) acknowledge receipt of a copy of this page, which is Page 2 of 3 Pages.

ERS-11tbx   Rev. 10/06   © 2006   Florida Association of REALTORS®   All Rights Reserved

FIGURE 8.3 | Exclusive-Right-to-Sell Listing Agreement *(continued)*

118 **9. CONDITIONAL TERMINATION:** At **Seller's** request, **Broker** may agree to conditionally terminate this Agreement. If
119 **Broker** agrees to conditional termination, **Seller** must sign a withdrawal agreement, reimburse **Broker** for all direct expenses
120* incurred in marketing the Property and pay a cancellation fee of $_____1,000.00 plus applicable sales tax. **Broker** may
121 void the conditional termination and **Seller** will pay the fee stated in paragraph 6(a) less the cancellation fee if **Seller** transfers
122 or contracts to transfer the Property or any interest in the Property during the time period from the date of conditional
123 termination to Termination Date and Protection Period, if applicable.
124 **10. DISPUTE RESOLUTION:** This Agreement will be construed under Florida law. All controversies, claims and other matters in
125 question between the parties arising out of or relating to this Agreement or the breach thereof will be settled by first attempting
126 mediation under the rules of the American Arbitration Association or other mediator agreed upon by the parties. If litigation arises out
127 of this Agreement, the prevailing party will be entitled to recover reasonable attorney's fees and costs, unless the parties agree that
128* disputes will be settled by arbitration as follows: **Arbitration:** By initialing in the space provided, **Seller** (____) (____), Listing
129 Associate (____) and Listing Broker (____) agree that disputes not resolved by mediation will be settled by neutral binding
130 arbitration in the county in which the Property is located in accordance with the rules of the American Arbitration Association or other
131 arbitrator agreed upon by the parties. Each party to any arbitration or litigation (including appeals and interpleaders) will pay its own
132 fees, costs and expenses, including attorney's fees, and will equally split the arbitrators' fees and administrative fees of arbitration.
133 **11. MISCELLANEOUS:** This Agreement is binding on **Broker's** and **Seller's** heirs, personal representatives, administrators,
134 successors and assigns. **Broker** may assign this Agreement to another listing office. Signatures, initials and modifications
135 communicated by facsimile will be considered as originals. The term "buyer" as used in this Agreement includes buyers,
136 tenants, exchangors, optionees and other categories of potential or actual transferees.
137* **12. ADDITIONAL TERMS:** _____
138* _____
139* _____
140* _____
141* _____
142* _____
143* _____
144* _____
145* _____
146* _____
147* _____
148* _____
149* _____
150* _____
151* _____
152* _____
153* _____
154* _____

155* Date: _____ **Seller's Signature:** _____ Tax ID No: __ __ __ - __ __ - __ __ __ __
156* Telephone #'s: Home_____ Work_____ Cell_____ Fax:_____
157* Address:_____ E-mail: _____
158* Date: _____ **Seller's Signature:** _____ Tax ID No: __ __ __ - __ __ - __ __ __ __
159* Telephone #'s: Home_____ Work_____ Cell_____ Fax:_____
160* Address:_____ E-mail: _____
161* Date: _____ **Authorized Listing Associate or Broker:** _____
162* Brokerage Firm Name: _____ Telephone: _____
163* Address: _____

164* | Copy returned to **Customer** on the __1st__ day of _____June_____, _2007_ by: ❑ personal delivery ❑ mail ❑ E-mail ❑ facsimile. |

165* **Seller** (____) (____) and **Broker/Sales Associate** (____) (____) acknowledge receipt of a copy of this page, which is Page 3 of 3 Pages.
ERS-11tbx Rev. 10/06 © 2006 Florida Association of Realtors® All Rights Reserved

Limited-Service Listing

A relatively new type of listing agree is starting to become more popular in many markets around the United States. In a **limited-service listing** the broker agrees to place the property on the multiple listing service (MLS), an arrangement in which participating brokers make their listings available to other members. The broker provides minimal support to the seller, but this type of listing allows property owners to advertise their properties for sale on the MLS, which is only available to paying members. An example of a limited-service agreement is provided in Figure 8.4.

The Broker-Buyer Relationship (Buyer's Agent)

When a potential buyer hires a broker to assist in locating a property for purchase, the relationship between the broker and the potential buyer should be clearly specified in a written document referred to as a **buyer representation agreement.** As in the case of listing agreements, buyer representation agreements must contain the essential elements of a contract. In addition, the document should specify the type of property desired, the duties and obligations of the buyer and seller, and the terms by which the broker will be paid for services rendered. A sample buyer representation agreement is provided in Figure 8.5.

Types of Buyer Representation Agreements

Similar to the different types of listing agreements discussed earlier, buyer representation agreements may specify that the broker has an exclusive-right-to-represent or that the arrangement is an "open" one. Under an exclusive right to represent, as in Figure 8.5, the broker is entitled to a commission if the potential buyer purchases a property with or without the assistance of the broker. In an open arrangement, the broker is entitled to a commission only if the buyer purchases a property identified and suggested by the broker. If the buyer finds a property without the broker's assistance, no commission is due.

Compensating the Buyer's Broker

Structuring the compensation to a buyer's broker properly is an important aspect of the buyer representation agreement. In many cases, the agreement calls for a retainer fee at the time the contract is signed, with a commission due if a property is purchased. The commission is either a fixed fee or is calculated as a percentage of the transaction amount. If the property is identified through the MLS, the buyer's broker will receive a "commission split" from the listing agent. Typically, the compensation due from the buyer is reduced by this amount. Because the compensation due the broker is calculated as a percentage of the purchase price, one might question whether the broker will negotiate aggressively for the lowest price possible on behalf of the buyer. Fortunately, the fiduciary responsibility owed to the principal precludes the agent from engaging in this type of behavior.

FIGURE 8.4 | Limited-Service Listing Agreement

Limited Service Listing Agreement
FLORIDA ASSOCIATION OF REALTORS®

1 This Limited Service Listing Agreement ("Agreement") is between

2* Sarah Howell _____ ("**Seller**") and

3* Julio Rodriguez _____ ("**Broker**").

4 **1. AUTHORITY TO SELL PROPERTY: Seller** gives **Broker** the Exclusive Right to Sell the real and personal
5 property (collectively "Property") described below, at the price and terms described below, beginning the
6* __1st__ day of _____June_____, __2007__, and terminating at 11:59 p.m. the __31st__ day of ___August___,
7* __2007__ ("Termination Date"). Seller certifies that Seller is legally entitled to convey the Property and all
8 improvements. This Property will be offered to any person without regard to race, color, religion, sex, handicap,
9 familial status, national origin or any other factor protected by federal, state or local law.

10 **2. DESCRIPTION OF PROPERTY:**
11*   **a)** Real Property Street Address: 501 SE 1st Street, Fort Lauderdale Florida 33301 _____
12* _____
13*   **b)** Legal Description: Lot 1, Block A, Ridgeview Subdivision, Broward County Florida. _____
14* _____
15*   **c)** Personal Property, including appliances: washer, dryer, hot tub _____
16* _____ ❏ See Attachment

17 **3. PRICE AND TERMS:** The property is offered for sale on the following terms, or on other terms acceptable to
18 **Seller:**
19*   **a) Price:** _____ $304,900.00 _____
20*   **b) Financing Terms:** ☑ Cash ☑ Conventional ☑ VA ☑ FHA ❏ Other _____

21 **4. BROKER OBLIGATIONS AND AUTHORITY:**
22   **a) Seller** authorizes **Broker** to place the property in a multiple listing service (MLS), to offer compensation to
23   cooperating brokers, and to post a For Sale sign on the property.
24   **b) Seller** authorizes **Broker** to report to the MLS/Association of Realtors this listing information and price, terms
25   and financing information on any resulting sale. **Seller** authorizes **Broker**, the MLS and/or Association of
26   Realtors to use, license or sell the active listing and sold data.
27*   **c) Broker** shall act as a ❏ Single agent of **Seller;** ❏ Single agent of **Seller** with consent to transition to
28*   transaction broker; ☑ Nonrepresentative; ❏ Transaction broker
29   **d)** In addition, **Seller** authorizes **Broker** to perform the following:
30* _____
31* _____
32* _____

33 **5. SELLER OBLIGATIONS:**
34   **a) Seller** shall indemnify **Broker** and hold Broker harmless from losses, damages, costs and expenses of any
35   nature, including attorney's fees and from liability to any person, that **Broker** incurs because of (1) **Seller's**
36   negligence, representations, misrepresentations, actions or inactions, (2) the use of a lock box, (3) the existence
37   of undisclosed material facts about the Property, or (4) a court or arbitration decision that a broker who was not
38   compensated in connection with a transaction is entitled to compensation from Broker. This clause will survive
39   **Broker's** performance and the transfer of title.
40* **Seller** (_____) (_____) and **Broker/Sales Associate** (_____) (_____) acknowledge receipt of a copy of this page, which is Page 1 of 2 Pages.

LSLA-1x   Rev. 10/06   © 2006   Florida Association of REALTORS®   All Rights Reserved

FIGURE 8.4 | Limited-Service Listing Agreement *(continued)*

41 **b) Seller** shall make all legally required disclosures, including all facts that materially affect the Property's value
42 and are not readily observable or known by the buyer. **Seller** represents there are no material facts (building
43* code violations, pending code citations, unobservable defects, etc.) other than the following: _____
44* _____
45 Seller will immediately inform Broker of any material facts that arise after signing this Agreement.

46 **6. COMPENSATION:**
47 **Seller** agrees to compensate **Broker** for performing the responsibilities delineated in Paragraph 4(a)
48* $_____ **$500.00** or _____% ❑ of list price or ❑ purchase price on _____ (date)
49 regardless whether the property sells and no matter who sells the property, whether by **Broker**, **Seller** or other
50 real estate licensee.

51 (Check and complete if applicable)
52* ❑ **Seller** shall pay **Broker** $_____ or ____**3**____% of the total purchase price at closing should a
53 broker who participates in the MLS in which compensation was offered by Broker, sell the Property.
54* ❑ **Seller** shall pay **Broker** $_____ or _____% ❑ of list price or ❑ purchase price at closing for
55 any other services specified in this Agreement.

56* **7. ADDITIONAL TERMS:** _____
57* _____
58* _____
59* _____
60* _____
61* _____

62* Date: _____ **Seller:** _____ Tax ID No: __ __ __ - __ __ - __ __ __ __
63* Telephone #'s: Home _____ Work _____ Cell _____ Fax _____
64* Address: _____ E-mail: _____

65* Date: _____ **Seller:** _____ Tax ID No: __ __ __ - __ __ - __ __ __ __
66* Telephone #'s: Home _____ Work _____ Cell _____ Fax _____
67* Address: _____ E-mail: _____

68* Date: _____ **Authorized Listing Associate or Broker:** _____
69* Brokerage Firm Name: _____ Telephone: _____
70* Address: _____

71* | Copy returned to **Seller** on the _____ day of _____, _____ by: ❑ personal delivery ❑ mail ❑ e-mail ❑ fax |

72* **Seller** (_____) (_____) and **Broker/Sales Associate** (_____) (_____) acknowledge receipt of a copy of this page, which is Page 2 of 2 Pages.
LSLA-1x Rev. 10/06 © 2006 Florida Association of REALTORS® All Rights Reserved

FIGURE 8.5 | Exclusive Buyer Brokerage Agreement

Exclusive Buyer Brokerage Agreement
FLORIDA ASSOCIATION OF REALTORS®

1. **PARTIES:** _____ ("**Buyer**") grants

_____ ("**Broker**")

Real Estate Broker   /   *Office*

the exclusive right to work with and assist **Buyer** in locating and negotiating the acquisition of suitable real property as described below. The term "acquire" or "acquisition" includes any purchase, option, exchange, lease or other acquisition of an ownership or equity interest in real property.

2. **TERM:** This Agreement will begin on the _____ day of _____, _____ and will terminate at 11:59 p.m. on the _____ day of _____, _____ ("Termination Date"). However, if **Buyer** enters into an agreement to acquire property that is pending on the Termination Date, this Agreement will continue in effect until that transaction has closed or otherwise terminated.

3. **PROPERTY: Buyer** is interested in acquiring real property as follows or as otherwise acceptable to **Buyer** ("Property"):

    (a) Type of property: _____

    (b) Location: _____

    (c) Price range: $_____ to $_____ .

    ❑ **Buyer** has been ❑ pre-qualified ❑ pre-approved by _____

    for (amount and terms, if any) _____

    (d) Preferred terms and conditions: _____

_____

_____

_____

4. **BROKER'S OBLIGATIONS:**
    (a) Broker Assistance. Broker will
      * use **Broker's** professional knowledge and skills;
      * assist **Buyer** in determining **Buyer's** financial capability and financing options;
      * discuss property requirements and assist **Buyer** in locating and viewing suitable properties;
      * assist **Buyer** to contract for property, monitor deadlines and close any resulting transaction;
      * cooperate with real estate licensees working with the seller, if any, to effect a transaction. **Buyer** understands that even if **Broker** is compensated by a seller or a real estate licensee who is working with a seller, such compensation does not compromise **Broker's** duties to **Buyer**.
    (b) Other Buyers. Buyer understands that **Broker** may work with other prospective buyers who want to acquire the same property as **Buyer**. If **Broker** submits offers by competing buyers, **Broker** will notify **Buyer** that a competing offer has been made, but will not disclose any of the offer's material terms or conditions. **Buyer** agrees that **Broker** may make competing buyers aware of the existence of any offer **Buyer** makes, so long as **Broker** does not reveal any material terms or conditions of the offer without **Buyer's** prior written consent.
    (c) Fair Housing. Broker adheres to the principles expressed in the Fair Housing Act and will not participate in any act that unlawfully discriminates on the basis of race, color, religion, sex, handicap, familial status, country of national origin or any other category protected under federal, state or local law.
    (d) Service Providers. Broker does not warrant or guarantee products or services provided by any third party whom **Broker**, at **Buyer's** request, refers or recommends to **Buyer** in connection with property acquisition.

FIGURE 8.5 | Exclusive Buyer Brokerage Agreement *(continued)*

5. BUYER'S OBLIGATIONS: Buyer agrees to cooperate with **Broker** in accomplishing the objectives of this Agreement, including:
(a) Conducting all negotiations and efforts to locate suitable property only through **Broker** and referring to **Broker** all inquiries of any kind from real estate licensees, property owners or any other source. If **Buyer** contacts or is contacted by a seller or a real estate licensee who is working with a seller or views a property unaccompanied by **Broker**, **Buyer** will, at first opportunity, advise the seller or real estate licensee that **Buyer** is working with and represented exclusively by **Broker**.
(b) Providing **Broker** with accurate personal and financial information requested by **Broker** in connection with ensuring **Buyer's** ability to acquire property. **Buyer** authorizes **Broker** to run a credit check to verify **Buyer's** credit information.
(c) Being available to meet with **Broker** at reasonable times for consultations and to view properties.
(d) Indemnifying and holding **Broker** harmless from and against all losses, damages, costs and expenses of any kind, including attorney's fees, and from liability to any person, that **Broker** incurs because of acting on **Buyer's** behalf.
(e) Not asking or expecting to restrict the acquisition of a property according to race, color, religion, sex, handicap, familial status, country of national origin or any other category protected under federal, state or local law.
(f) Consulting an appropriate professional for legal, tax, environmental, engineering, foreign reporting requirements and other specialized advice.

6. RETAINER: Upon final execution of this Agreement, **Buyer** will pay to **Broker** a non-refundable retainer fee of $_____ for **Broker's** services ("Retainer"). This fee is not refundable and ❑ will ❑ will not be credited to **Buyer** if compensation is earned by **Broker** as specified in this Agreement.

7. COMPENSATION: Broker's compensation is earned when, during the term of this Agreement or any renewal or extension, **Buyer** or any person acting for or on behalf of **Buyer** contracts to acquire real property as specified in this Agreement. **Buyer** will be responsible for paying **Broker** the amount specified below plus any applicable taxes but will be credited with any amount which **Broker** receives from a seller or a real estate licensee who is working with a seller.
(a) Purchase or exchange: $_____ or _____% (select only one) of the total purchase price or other consideration for the acquired property, to be paid at closing.
(b) Lease: $_____ or _____% (select only one) of the gross lease value, to be paid when **Buyer** enters into the lease. If **Buyer** enters into a lease-purchase agreement, the amount of the leasing fee which **Broker** receives will be credited toward the amount due **Broker** for the purchase.
(c) Option: Broker will be paid $_____ or _____% of the option amount (select only one), to be paid when **Buyer** enters into the option agreement. If **Buyer** enters into a lease with option to purchase, **Broker** will be compensated for both the lease and the option. If **Buyer** subsequently exercises the option, the amounts received by **Broker** for the lease and option will be credited toward the amount due **Broker** for the purchase.
(d) Other: Broker will be compensated for all other types of acquisitions as if such acquisition were a purchase or exchange.
(e) Buyer Default: Buyer will pay **Broker's** compensation immediately upon **Buyer's** default on any contract to acquire property.

8. PROTECTION PERIOD: Buyer will pay **Broker's** compensation if, within _____ days after Termination Date, **Buyer** contracts to acquire any property which was called to **Buyer's** attention by **Broker** or any other person or found by **Buyer** during the term of this Agreement. **Buyer's** obligation to pay **Broker's** fee ceases upon **Buyer** entering into a good faith exclusive buyer brokerage agreement with another broker after Termination Date.

9. EARLY TERMINATION: Buyer may terminate this Agreement at any time by written notice to **Broker** but will remain responsible for paying **Broker's** compensation if, from the early termination date to Termination Date plus Protection Period, if applicable, **Buyer** contracts to acquire any property which, prior to the early termination date, was found by **Buyer** or called to **Buyer's** attention by **Broker** or any other person. **Broker** may terminate this Agreement at any time by written notice to **Buyer**, in which event **Buyer** will be released from all further obligations under this Agreement.

10. DISPUTE RESOLUTION: Any unresolveable dispute between **Buyer** and **Broker** will be mediated. If a settlement is not reached in mediation, the matter will be submitted to binding arbitration in accordance with the rules of the American Arbitration Association or other mutually agreeable arbitrator.

11. ASSIGNMENT; PERSONS BOUND: Broker may assign this Agreement to another broker. This Agreement will bind and inure to **Broker's** and **Buyer's** heirs, personal representatives, successors and assigns.

FIGURE 8.5 | Exclusive Buyer Brokerage Agreement *(continued)*

12. BROKERAGE RELATIONSHIP: Buyer authorizes **Broker** to operate as (check which is applicable):
❏ single agent of **Buyer.**
❏ transaction broker.
❏ single agent of **Buyer** with consent to transition into a transaction broker.
❏ nonrepresentative of **Buyer.**

13. SPECIAL CLAUSES: _____

_____

_____

_____

_____

_____

14. ACKNOWLEDGMENT; MODIFICATIONS: Buyer has read this Agreement and understands its contents. This Agreement cannot be changed except by written agreement signed by both parties.

Date: _____   **Buyer:** _____   Tax ID No: __ __ __ - __ __ - __ __ __ __

                          Address: _____

                          Zip: _____ Telephone: _____ Facsimile: _____

Date: _____   **Buyer:** _____   Tax ID No: __ __ __ - __ __ - __ __ __ __

                          Address: _____

                          Zip: _____ Telephone: _____ Facsimile: _____

Date: _____   **Real Estate Associate:** _____

Date: _____   **Real Estate Broker:** _____

DUTIES AND RIGHTS UNDER AGENCY RELATIONSHIPS

Once any principal-agent relationship is established, each party owes the other the duties of loyalty, good faith, and diligence in fulfilling the conditions promised. These duties are not a matter of choice but are created by state laws that govern the agency relationship. In addition to their legal responsibilities, successful real estate brokers and sales associates know that ethical business practices are critical to continued professional success. For example, the National Association of REALTORS®, the largest trade organization for real estate brokers and sales associates, holds its members to high ethical standards. In general, these standards require fair dealings with clients, customers, and the public. The National Association of REALTORS® has state and local associations in many areas of the country and is the largest membership organization in the real estate industry, with more than 1 million members. The Web site for this organization (*www.realtor.org*) provides a wealth of information for real estate practitioners, consumers, and students. The following sections examine the broker's, seller's, and buyer's legal duties to one another in detail.

The Broker's Duties

Real estate brokers and sales associates assume a fiduciary role when they are hired by either a seller or a buyer. A *fiduciary* is a person who occupies a position of trust and confidence in relation to another person or his or her property. Therefore, brokers must protect their clients' best interests at all times. A breach of a fiduciary's duties may occur as a result of negligence, fraud, misrepresentation, or failure to follow instructions. **Fraud** is present if a broker, (1) with the intention to mislead, (2) makes a false statement material to a transaction that (3) is justifiably relied on by a client, resulting in (4) injury to the client. The elements of **misrepresentation** are the same as for fraud except that the *intention* to mislead need not be present.

Seller's Agent's Duties to Seller

After a listing agreement is signed, the broker's job is to locate a willing and able buyer. Of course, the broker must do so honestly, diligently, and in good faith while following any instructions given by the owner and looking out for the owner's interests. The broker must also keep the seller informed at all times and communicate any and all offers received to the seller.

Seller's Agent's Duties to Buyers

When the broker is an agent of the seller, the broker must look out for the seller's best interests. Even so, the broker must be careful not to misrepresent the property to a potential buyer. Courts are increasingly holding that the broker must go farther, having a responsibility to disclose any negative factors that might adversely affect the property's value. Suppose, for example, that the foundation of the house has settled, necessitating repairs. In addition, the basement has been subject to flooding

The Seller's Agent's Obligations to the Buyer

The Strassburgers owned a 3,000-square-foot home in Diablo, California, located on a one-acre lot and complete with a swimming pool and large guest house. They listed their home with Valley Realty, which sold the property to the Eastons for $170,000. Unfortunately for the Eastons, however, they were not aware that part of the property was on filled land that already had been subject to earth slides.

Shortly after moving in, the Eastons became painfully aware of this fact when massive earth movement cost them a portion of their driveway and caused the foundation of the house to settle, the walls to crack, and the doorways to warp. Estimates to repair the damage and avoid recurrence ranged as high as $213,000. The Eastons sued the Strassburgers and Valley Realty for damages,

charging misrepresentation. In a landmark decision that has had lasting implications for the real estate brokerage industry, they won.

The court held that although there was no evidence that the broker intentionally misled the buyers by deliberately giving false information, he had an "affirmative duty" to the buyers to conduct "a reasonably competent and diligent inspection of the property listed for sale and to disclose to prospective purchasers all facts materially affecting the value or desirability of the property that such an investigation would reveal." Because the broker did not do this, he was liable for part of the assessed damages of $197,000. As a result of this case, brokers are held responsible for disclosing information about the condition of the property to buyers.

[*Easton v. Strassburger*, 199 Cal. Rptr. 383, Cal. App. 1 Dist., 1984]

in extremely wet weather. The broker has the responsibility to inform any interested buyer that these problems exist and that additional repairs to correct them may be necessary in the future. The Legal Highlight above illustrates the liability brokers may face if they do not furnish adequate information to a prospective buyer.

If a buyer gives a broker any money as deposit on a potential purchase, these funds must be kept separate from the broker's personal and other business funds and cannot be used for the broker's benefit. For example, any use of "earnest money" by the broker for anything other than the buyer's instructed purposes is improper and illegal. The money must be deposited in an escrow account and must not be "commingled" with the broker's personal or other business funds.

Buyer's Agent's Duties to Buyers

When a buyer representation agreement is in place, the broker is a fiduciary of the buyer. The broker must act diligently and in good faith to find a property that matches the buyer's criteria. Failure to attempt to locate a property for the buyer would violate the terms of the buyer representation agreement. Although normally still splitting a commission paid by the seller, the buyer's broker's loyalties must lie with the buyer. The broker has the responsibility of advising the buyer, negotiating the lowest price, and otherwise assisting the buyer in closing the transaction.

Buyer's Agent's Duties to Sellers

Even though a buyer's broker is a fiduciary of the buyer, the broker must treat sellers fairly, honestly, and with due care. Failure to do so is a violation of the "fair dealings" requirement imposed on state-licensed real estate agents.

Fair Housing

In all situations, the broker also must be careful not to violate federal **fair housing laws,** which prohibit housing discrimination based on sex, race, color, religion, national origin, disabilities, or familial status. In the past, some brokers have engaged in the practice of **steering**—that is, channeling minority prospects only to minority neighborhoods. Other unscrupulous brokers have engaged in **blockbusting**—using scare tactics to drive down home prices when minority owners begin moving into an area.

The Civil Rights Act of 1866 provides that "All citizens of the United States shall have the same right, in every State and Territory, as is enjoyed by white citizens thereof to inherit, purchase, lease, sell, hold and convey real and personal property." In 1968, the U.S. Supreme Court ruled that this law prohibits "all racial discrimination, private as well as public, in the sale or rental of property." More recently, the Fair Housing Act of 1988, enforced by the U.S. Department of Housing and Urban Development, was enacted to, among other things, provide civil penalties ranging from $10,000 to $50,000 plus actual and compensatory damages against individuals who engage in discriminatory practices. Americans who feel their rights have been violated should file a complaint immediately with the Office of Fair Housing and Equal Opportunity at HUD. The law means what it says, as the broker in the Legal Highlight on the next page discovered. Most states have similar laws.

Disclosure of Agency Relationship

Most states have enacted laws and regulations that require that real estate brokers and sales associates disclose the nature of any agency relationships at the first substantive contact with clients and customers. In many states, this disclosure must be made in writing and acknowledged by the parties involved. In the past, many buyers have purchased property with the mistaken belief that one of the brokers involved in the transaction represented their best interests. Unless a buyer representation agreement is executed, buyers should not assume that the broker is working exclusively to benefit them.

Fair Housing

 Landlords may wish to remove a tenant for some reason, but they must be very careful they do not violate the fair housing laws. This the owners of the Boulder Meadows mobile home park and the Sabre Village apartments learned to their sorrow.

Barbara Saville had lived in Boulder Meadows for eight years when she received a notice of eviction, asserting that she had failed to maintain her home and lot site as required in her ground lease agreement. She responded with a letter explaining that she had a medical condition resulting in dizziness and seizures when performing physical labor. Boulder Meadows then commenced another attempt to evict Ms. Saville.

Because she was unable to maintain the property, Saville then arranged to provide free rent to a caretaker to live in her home in return for performing the required maintenance work. Boulder Meadows responded by issuing another notice of eviction for violation of a covenant requirement that prohibited anyone other than persons listed on the lease agreement from living on the premises. Saville responded to this demand by delivering a letter to Boulder Meadows requesting a reasonable accommodation for her disability under state and federal fair housing laws. Boulder Meadows refused, and this case went to court.

The court ruled that Boulder Meadows was required to provide reasonable accommodation for Saville's disability, noting that allowing the caretaker to remain would have provided this. They ordered Boulder Meadows to provide maintenance of Saville's lot without any charge, given the company was receiving revenue in excess of $3 million per year from the park. They also awarded Saville $150,000 in damages for increased stress and humiliation caused by the park's failure to provide reasonable accommodation as required by the fair housing laws. [*Boulder Meadows v. Saville*, Colorado Court of Appeals]

When Elmo Green moved into the Sabre Village apartments he was the only African American tenant. Racial discrimination appeared to be evident from the outset: Green was forced to pay a double deposit and was placed in a unit that was isolated from other buildings in the complex. Later, the apartment management laid sod in every other yard but his. One day Green came home to find police and management in and around his apartment, managers saying they saw someone in the unit they didn't recognize. The man was Green's brother, who was baby-sitting his five-year-old son. Shortly after that the management removed Green's air-conditioning and screen doors. At trial, a former employee testified that management had told him at the time, "We're going to let that n____ sweat in that box."

The jury awarded Green $715,000 in damages, finding that the owners of Sabre Village were guilty of racial discrimination in housing practices, forcible entry, and trespassing. [*Green v. Sabre Village*, Callaway County, Missouri Circuit Court, 2004]

TERMINATION OF AGENCY RELATIONSHIPS

In the typical agency relationship in real estate, the relationship ends when a transaction occurs as specified in the listing agreement or buyer representation agreement. For example, if an open listing created the relationship, the relationship terminates on a sale, whether that sale is completed by the listing broker, another broker, or the owner. In an exclusive-brokerage listing agreement, it is understood that the agreement ends with the sale, whether the real estate is sold by the listing broker or by the owner.

If a transaction does not occur, the time period provided in the listing agreement governs the duration of the agency relationship. At the expiration of that term, the relationship terminates. Some states do not require a stated termination date for a listing agreement. In such cases, the agency relationship lasts for a reasonable time. A "reasonable" time is generally considered to be three months for residential property and six months for commercial property. The determination of a reasonable time period often must be made by a court; therefore, absence of a specific term in the agency agreement may result in expensive litigation.

A third way the agency relationship between a broker and owner ends is by mutual agreement. Some circumstances make it more beneficial to all parties to relieve the broker of his or her duties to locate a buyer and to relieve the owner of his or her duties to the broker. Such an agreement may occur before the expiration of the agency agreement's term. Provisions for early termination should be specified in the agreement.

Even without the consent of the agent, many states allow the principal to revoke at any time the listing agreement that established the agency relationship. Revocation of an open or exclusive-brokerage listing is looked upon less harshly than revocation of an exclusive-right-to-sell listing. Of course, the principal who breaches the agreement is liable to the broker for damages, although the determination of an agent's damages may be difficult.

Of course, if either party to the agency relationship breaches his or her duties, the other party is relieved of further liability under the listing agreement. For example, if a broker fails to keep the seller fully informed of negotiations, the seller can list the property with another broker or sell it without a broker even if the original listing agreement was an exclusive-right-to-sell listing. The owner's revocation of the listing agreement releases the broker from all duties to locate a buyer.

Because the agreement that created the principal-agent relationship is a contract between the parties, loss of contractual capacity by either party terminates the relationship. Such loss of capacity may occur as the result of the death or insanity of either the principal or the agent. Destruction of improvements on the listed property or the property's seizure by the government under the power of eminent domain also terminates the agency relationship. A broker is under no obligation to seek a buyer for a house that has been destroyed in a hurricane, for example, and a seller is not obligated to pay a commission for one that has been condemned for a highway right-of-way.

In summary, there are at least seven means by which the broker-owner agency relationship can be terminated:

1. A transaction occurs.
2. The term of the agreement expires.
3. The parties agree to termination.
4. One party breaches his or her duties.
5. One party becomes contractually incapacitated.
6. A listed property's improvements are destroyed.
7. A listed property is taken by the government under the power of eminent domain.

TYPES OF BROKERAGE FIRMS

Real estate markets, particularly markets for single-family homes, are local in nature, and real estate brokerage firms traditionally have been small, one-office businesses that operated only in their local markets. For the most part, the real estate brokerage industry is still made up of small firms. Increasingly, however, the real estate brokerage market in most larger communities is dominated by large, multi-office firms, often part of regional or national organizations.

Many real estate brokers and brokerage firms specialize in one type of real estate transaction. Some brokers, for example, act only as buyer's brokers, while others serve only as seller's brokers. Many brokers limit their activities to the owner-occupied residential market; apartment leasing; vacant land sales; or commercial, industrial, or retail properties. Concentrating one's efforts on a smaller market segment allows some brokers to finely tune their skills to the needs of their clients and customers and ultimately increase their productivity.

Franchises

One way the smaller real estate brokers compete with the large regional and national firms is by becoming part of a franchise chain, such as Century 21 or Better Homes & Gardens. Franchisees pay an initial fee plus a percentage of their annual gross. For this, they receive the advantages of sales and management training programs, a referral network, and, perhaps of most importance, name recognition. Just as families moving to an area recognize McDonald's and Domino's Pizza, they also often recognize real estate franchise chains. Consumers should recognize, however, that most of these firms are independently owned and operated, and the quality of service can vary.

Desk Fee Arrangements

Increasingly, brokerage firms are organizing the brokers and sales associates who work in the firm in a "desk fee" arrangement. Brokers or sales associates who wish to work with other members of the firm pay a monthly fee for the right to occupy space in the office. The firm provides phone service, cooperative advertising, and other resources that are shared by the members of the firm. In some cases, the members must also share a portion of their commissions earned with the other members of the firm.

Multiple Listing Services

Multiple-Listing-Service Clause

Another way the smaller broker is able to compete with larger firms is by becoming part of a **multiple listing service** (MLS). If another broker sells the property, the listing broker still receives a portion of the commission. While the MLS is particularly valuable to the small broker, who otherwise might not have enough properties to sell, the service is also usually an advantage to the seller because all members of the MLS offer the property for sale and may reach many more potential buyers.

The MLS is an arrangement in which participating brokers make their listings available to all other members. The members agree that they will share information about properties they are trying to sell and agree to share (not necessarily equally) the commission being paid by the seller if another member finds a buyer for the property.

Suppose a seller has agreed to pay the listing broker a 6 percent commission. If the broker is a member of the MLS and offers to split the commission on a 50-50 basis with any other member broker who locates a buyer, each broker will receive 3 percent of the transaction price. If the listing broker finds a buyer without the assistance of another broker, of course, the listing broker would receive the full 6 percent commission.

BROKER AND SALES ASSOCIATE COMPENSATION

As discussed above, a real estate broker or sales associate receives a commission for services rendered in connection with the transaction. Normally, the commission is determined by a percentage of the gross transaction amount, though it can also be a flat fee. Usually, no commission is paid until the transaction is completed. In some cases, however, the broker may receive an advance fee, or a fee may be paid for performance of specific services, such as consultation and advice or appraisal of property. The commission amount varies with the type of property sold. Commissions on single-family homes typically range from 2 to 6 percent. Large commercial properties usually carry a lower percentage commission, in the range of 1 to 5 percent, while commissions on unimproved land generally range from 6 to 10 percent.

Of course, real estate brokerage commissions cannot be set by agreement among brokers without violating antitrust statutes but must be negotiated between broker and client. Even discussion between brokers concerning the level of commissions is an antitrust violation and a criminal offense. Nevertheless, like other prices, commission rates tend to be relatively uniform, although lower rates can be negotiated, particularly in a "sellers' market."

When more than one broker is involved in a transaction, the commission usually will be split among the selling broker, the listing broker, and the firms that employ the brokers. Each broker typically receives half of the commission amount specified in the listing agreement. The brokers may then be obligated to split their commissions with their respective firms and, possibly, their sales associates. Of course, if the selling and listing broker were the same person, he or she would collect both commissions.

Compensation for Sales Associates

State laws require that sales associates must work under the direction of a broker. Compensation for sales associates is often based on a percentage of the commissions earned for the broker. The actual percentage will vary from firm to firm and from sales associate to sales associate on the basis of such factors as the prevailing practice in the area, the degree of advertising and other support provided by the broker, and the sales record of the associate. In general, the portion of the total commission going to the sales associate will increase with his or her level of sales.

▌ CHAPTER REVIEW

- ■ Two characteristics of real estate markets—the complexity of transactions and buyers' limited knowledge of the markets—have led to the establishment of various real estate service activities, including real estate brokerage, property management, and appraisal.

- ■ The steps in the real estate sales process are (1) listing, (2) marketing the property and qualifying buyers, (3) presentation and negotiations, (4) contracts, and (5) settlement or closing.

- ■ A *real estate broker* is an intermediary who arranges real estate sale or lease transactions for a fee or commission. A real estate sales associate must work through a broker and can carry out only those responsibilities assigned by the broker.

- ■ All states and the District of Columbia require that brokers and sales associates be licensed and meet mandatory education or experience requirements. Failure to obtain the proper license prohibits the collection of any commission.

- ■ The primary functions of the real estate brokerage industry are to match properties with buyers and to guide the buyer and seller through the complexities of real estate transactions.

■ Real estate brokers' relationships with sellers and buyers are governed by the law of agency. The broker or sales associate serves as an agent for either the seller or the buyer, who is the principal. A principal authorizes his or her agent to perform certain functions on behalf of the principal. In a typical real estate transaction, the principal (seller) grants the agent (broker) express authority as stated in the listing agreement.

■ The broker-seller relationship is created on the establishment of a listing agreement, usually written. Such an agreement specifies the parties, describes the property, states the asking price, and provides the governing terms. The traditional types of listing agreements include (a) the open listing, (b) the exclusive-brokerage listing, (c) the exclusive-right-to-sell listing, and (d) the limited-service listing. Net listing agreements are used infrequently today because of the possibility of fraud.

■ The broker-buyer relationship is created on the establishment of a buyer representation agreement, usually written. Such an agreement identifies the parties, describes the property desired, and establishes the broker's right to compensation. These agreements can be open or exclusive.

■ A broker or sales associate has the duty to act honestly and diligently on the principal's behalf. Complete loyalty is owed to the party the agent represents.

■ Federal fair housing laws prohibit housing discrimination based on a buyer's or (lessee's) sex, race, color, religion, national origin, disabilities, or familial status.

■ A commission is earned when the conditions of the agreement have been satisfied. In a listing agreement, the commission is due when the broker procures a ready, willing, and able buyer or when the transaction is actually completed. In a buyer representation agreement, the commission is due when the buyer contracts to purchase a property.

■ The agency relationship terminates when a transaction occurs, when the term provided in the agreement expires, when both parties consent to termination, when either party breaches its conditions, when either party becomes incapacitated, when the property is destroyed or heavily damaged, or when the property is condemned by the government under the power of eminent domain.

■ A real estate broker or sales associate normally receives a commission when the transaction is completed successfully but no salary or other fee until that time. The commission normally is stated as a percentage of the gross sales price, and it varies with the type of property sold.

KEY TERMS

agency

agent

blockbusting

broker

buyer representation
agreement

buyer's agent

commission

commission agreement

dual agent

exclusive-brokerage
listing

exclusive-right-to-sell
listing

fair housing laws

fiduciary

fraud

limited-service listing

listing agreement

listing broker

misrepresentation

multiple listing service

net listing

open listing

principal

real estate broker

seller's agent

selling broker

steering

subagent

transaction broker

STUDY EXERCISES

1. What characteristics of real estate have led to the establishment of the real estate brokerage industry?

2. Discuss the difference between the function of a real estate broker and that of a real estate sales associate.

3. What is the difference between an open listing and exclusive-brokerage listing? How does an exclusive-brokerage listing differ from an exclusive-right-to-sell listing?

4. What is a net listing? Why is it illegal in most states?

5. What is the difference between fraud and misrepresentation?

6. What are blockbusting and steering? Why are these practices illegal?

7. What impact do you think the Internet has had on the real estate brokerage business? Take a look at *Realtor.com* and *Loopnet.com* for insights.

8. What document is used to create a relationship between a broker and a buyer who wishes to have the broker work in his or her best interest?

9. Would the compensation to a broker be the same if he or she assists a seller using a limited-service listing agreement as opposed to an exclusive-right-to-sell listing agreement? Why or why not?

10. Joe desires to sell his house. He lists the property with Johnny White, a real estate broker. In this case, who is "principal" and who is the "agent"? What duties does Johnny owe to Joe? What duties does he owe to any potential buyer?

11. Suppose that Johnny shows the house to Janice, who asks him to negotiate on her behalf with Joe. If he does so, what is he guilty of? What must he do to protect his right to a commission on this sale if he grants her request?

12. Sylvia listed her house for sale at $105,000 with the Keg Realty Company, and Keg began to show the property. A prospective buyer looked at Sylvia's house, liked it, and gave a written offer for her asking price—$105,000. Having some second thoughts about selling, Sylvia claimed that this particular buyer could not afford her house and refused to accept the offer. If there is no evidence that the buyer is in financial difficulty, does Keg Realty have any claim against Sylvia?

13. Real estate broker Molly Smith has listed a house for sale that is located in a floodplain and has been flooded on several occasions. Does Molly have an obligation to make these facts known to prospective buyers?

14. Suppose that Molly knows about the potential floodplain problem but tells a potential purchaser that the house is not in the floodplain. Of what is she guilty? Would the buyer have a claim against her?

15. Suppose that Molly fully informs the potential buyer about the floodplain problem, but he still buys the house. Later his house is flooded, and he sues Molly for not telling him that houses in floodplains can be flooded. Does he have a legitimate claim?

16. Visit the Web site for the National Association of REALTORS® at *www.realtor.org* and explore the many resources there that are available to help members of the organization do their jobs better. Summarize one of the resources there and offer any ideas you have about how the resource could be improved.

FURTHER READING

de Heer, Robert. *Realty Bluebook,* 33rd ed. Chicago: Dearborn Real Estate Education, 2003.

Real Estate Appraisal

What is the property worth? This question is central to decision making in almost every aspect of real estate. Sellers want to know what their properties should bring in the marketplace, and buyers want to know what their potential purchases are worth in comparison with other properties in the market. Mortgage lenders want to know that the value of a property being pledged as security for a debt is at least as much as the loan amount. Tax assessors, insurance adjusters, and right-of-way agents also must obtain estimates of value in order to collect property taxes, pay insurance claims, and compensate landowners for eminent domain takings.

Arriving at reliable estimates of property values requires an in-depth understanding of the factors that influence value, as well as the methods available for estimating value. A thorough understanding of the process appraisers use to estimate value is beneficial to all real estate market participants, and it is absolutely necessary for anyone who hopes to make a career in the appraisal profession. The objectives of this chapter are to

- discuss the regulatory environment surrounding the appraisal profession;

- define the concept of value;

- define some of the basic principles underlying the appraisal process;

- describe the steps in the appraisal process;

- review the basic techniques appraisers use to arrive at value estimates; and

- demonstrate the appraisal process for a single-family home.

APPRAISAL REGULATORY ENVIRONMENT

Even though almost all individuals, businesses, and other organizations use real estate in their normal activities, few have the expertise necessary to evaluate real estate market conditions and arrive at sound estimates of property value. As a result, many real estate decision makers often must seek the services of real estate appraisers who possess the skills and knowledge necessary to accurately estimate property value. To ensure that people engaged in appraisal services do so in a competent and professional manner, all states have established minimum education and experience requirements for obtaining an appraisal license or certification.

Prior to 1989, few states regulated the appraisal industry and no specific license was required to perform appraisals. In that year, Congress passed the **Financial Institutions Reform, Recovery, and Enforcement Act** (FIRREA). Among other things, FIRREA established a federal regulatory hierarchy for the appraisal industry in an attempt to improve the reliability of appraisals in the loan approval process. Under FIRREA, appraisals for properties involved in "federally related" transactions must be performed by state-licensed or state-certified appraisers. Federally related transactions include those involving certain federal government agencies, as well as those involving institutions that are regulated or insured by federal agencies. Because most banks, savings institutions, and credit unions are federally regulated, virtually all appraisal assignments must be completed by a state-licensed or state-certified appraiser.

The **Appraisal Foundation** is a nonprofit educational organization formed by the appraisal profession in 1987. Its members consist solely of other organizations that have an interest in the promotion of professionalism in the appraisal industry. The Appraisal Foundation structure includes the **Appraisal Qualifications Board** (AQB) and the **Appraisal Standards Board** (ASB). Under FIRREA, the AQB established minimum education and experience guidelines that states must use to issue appraisal licenses and certifications (some states set even higher standards than the federal minimums). The ASB has established *Uniform Standards of Professional Appraisal Practice (USPAP)* that must be followed in federally related transactions. Many states require that all appraisals (even those not involved in federally related transactions) be performed in accordance with USPAP.

Appraiser License and Certification Guidelines from the AQB

The guidelines adopted by the AQB establish four different appraiser categories that permit the license or certificate holder to perform appraisal services in federally related transactions. These categories distinguish between residential and nonresidential assignments and the complexity of the transactions.

The first category is called **trainee appraiser.** A trainee appraiser must work under the supervision of a licensed or certified appraiser who is ultimately responsible for the work performed by the trainee. Becoming a trainee appraiser requires at least 75 hours of classroom instruction in appraisal topics. There is no experience requirement for becoming a trainee appraiser, nor is there an examination that must be passed in order to become a trainee appraiser. Generally, trainee appraisers remain in this category for no more than two years. As they gain experience, they can apply for a more advanced license or certificate.

The second category of appraisers recognized by the Appraisal Foundation is called **licensed real property appraiser.** Licensed appraisers are authorized to perform appraisals involving complex one- to four-unit residential properties in transactions of less than $250,000 and to perform appraisals for noncomplex one- to four-unit residential properties for transactions of less than $1 million. Licensed appraisers must have completed 150 hours of classroom instruction, must have passed a written examination on appraisal topics, and must have completed 2,000 hours of appraisal experience.

The Appraisal Foundation's third category of appraisers is called **certified residential appraiser.** Appraisers who hold this certification can appraise residential properties of one to four units without regard to transaction amount or complexity. These appraisers must have completed at least 200 hours of appraisal education (inclusive of the 150 hours required for becoming a licensed appraiser), must have passed an examination, and must have completed at least 2,500 hours of appraisal experience.

The most advanced category of real estate appraiser established by the Appraisal Foundation is the **certified general appraiser.** Appraisers who hold this certification can appraise any type of property. Certified general appraisers must complete a minimum of 300 hours of classroom instruction (inclusive of the 200 hours required for becoming a certified residential appraiser), must have passed an examination, and must have completed at least 3,000 hours of appraisal experience.

Uniform Standards of Professional Appraisal Practice from the ASB

The standards of practice adopted by the ASB set forth the rules appraisers must follow when developing an appraisal and reporting its results. There are ten Standards and each one has various "rules" associated with it. For example, Standard 1 requires that appraisers carefully identify the appraisal problem to be solved and the tasks necessary to reach a solution to the problem in a credible manner. The rules that accompany Standard 1 require that appraisers use recognized appraisal methods and techniques and that they apply these techniques appropriately. Furthermore, the rules stipulate what it means to "identify the appraisal problem" by specifically identifying the real estate involved and the definition of value that will be investigated. For readers who are interested in the specific rules that appraisers must follow, the 2006 edition of the *Uniform Standards of Professional Appraisal Practice* can be viewed on the Internet at *www.appraisalfoundation.org.*

WHAT IS VALUE?

The concept of *value* is a topic that has been dear to philosophers and economists for centuries, and the debate over a proper definition of value is frequently revisited in the real estate appraisal literature. Some of the questions considered by researchers include the following: What constitutes value? Is it the worth of a property to society in general or to an individual investor? Is it priced in terms of money or some intrinsic characteristic of the property? Is it value in exchange, value in use, or perhaps the cost to produce? For our purposes, we limit our concern to this question: What is it that real estate appraisers are trying to estimate? As we will see, the answer to this question is carefully defined.

Market Value

The type of value that real estate appraisers generally attempt to estimate is **market value.** The following definition, taken from the FIRREA legislation, is the most widely accepted definition of market value and is the basis for most appraisal reports.

Market value: The most probable price which a property should bring in a competitive and open market under all conditions requisite to a fair sale, the buyer and seller each acting prudently and knowledgeably, and assuming the price is not affected by undue stimulus. Implicit in this definition is the consummation of a sale as of a specified date and the passing of title from seller to buyer under five conditions whereby

1. buyer and seller are typically motivated;
2. both parties are well informed or well advised, and acting in what they consider their best interests;
3. a reasonable time is allowed for exposure in the open market;
4. payment is made in terms of cash in U.S. dollars or in terms of financial arrangements comparable thereto; and
5. the price represents the normal consideration for the property sold unaffected by special or creative financing or sales concessions by anyone associated with the sale.

Though lengthy, each portion of this definition is important to the appraiser's estimate of value. For example, the price for which one family member might sell a particular property to another could be very different from the price that could be received if the property were offered to all prospective buyers. Similarly, because the financing terms of a transaction may affect the price, the definition of market value refers to the most probable cash or cash equivalent price. Furthermore, this definition assumes that all market participants have an opportunity to consider the property and make an informed and voluntary decision about whether to purchase it. While the implications of the above definition should be always kept in mind, we will simply refer to a property's market value as its most probable selling price.

Investment Value

Market value is what the classical economists called *value in exchange,* that is, the consensus price that would be reached in a market with many buyers and sellers. Another classical value concept is "value in use," which has a modern real estate application in the concept of **investment value.** *Investment value* is defined as the worth of a property to a particular investor, based on that investor's personal standards of investment acceptability. Investment value refers to the value of a property to a specific buyer, while market value refers to the value of a property to the typical, but unspecified, buyer in the market. We will consider the topic of investment analysis in Chapter 19.

Price versus Market Value

As opposed to market value, which is an estimate of the most probable selling price, **price** is the amount actually paid for a property in a particular transaction. It is a historical fact, not a prospective concept. Because the buyer or seller may not be well informed, may not be acting prudently or may not be free from undue pressure, or may not be engaged in an "arm's-length" transaction, the price actually paid for a property may not be the same as the market value estimated by an appraiser. On the other hand, price is an accurate indicator of market value if the transaction matches the conditions described in the definition of market value.

Market Value versus Cost of Production

One of the factors influencing market value is cost of production. No rational entrepreneur will keep producing a product unless it is expected to sell for a price that is high enough to cover costs and provide a profit. Unfortunately, however, this does not mean that an entrepreneur will not make a mistake and produce a product that the market will value at less than the cost of production. Real estate developers occasionally make mistakes by misjudging markets and developing projects that will not sell at their desired price. Although costs are one indication of value, market value actually may be higher or lower than cost of production.

Other Types of Value

Although appraisers usually estimate market value, they may be asked to estimate other measures of value as well. Among these are assessed value and insurable value. **Assessed value** is the value placed on a property for property tax assessment purposes. As already has been shown in the discussion of the property tax, even though assessed value is based on market value, it is seldom a valid estimate of current market value. Property taxation is considered in Chapter 4.

Insurable value represents the amount of insurance that should be carried on the destructible portion of the real estate to compensate the owner adequately in case of loss. Because insurable value is measured using the concepts of actual cash value and replacement cost, it often differs from current market value.

SOME KEY APPRAISAL PRINCIPLES

A number of basic principles drawn primarily from economic thought are essential to the practice of appraisal, and they apply to every type of real estate appraisal assignment. Among them are the principles of anticipation, change, substitution, and contribution.

Anticipation

The current value of a property depends on the anticipated utility or income that will accrue to the property owner in the future. This is the **principle of anticipation.** Because the present value of a property depends on the expected future benefits of ownership, the appraiser must be skilled in analyzing national, regional, local, and neighborhood trends that will influence future income or utility. For example, a motel may have been very profitable in the past, but changing road patterns and other neighborhood factors may considerably reduce the property's income and, hence, its value in the future.

Change

The principle of anticipation is closely related to the **principle of change,** the notion that economic, social, political, and environmental forces are constantly causing changes that affect the value of real property. Real estate markets are dynamic rather than static, and appraisers must carefully analyze the direction and degree of change in factors affecting market values. For this reason, every value estimate must be made as of a specified date.

Substitution

The **principle of substitution** holds that a prudent buyer will pay no more for a property than the cost of acquiring an equally desirable substitute in the open market. This principle is fundamental to all three traditional approaches to real estate valuation, the sales comparison, income, and cost approaches. It supports the premise that a buyer will not pay any more for a home or other real estate improvement than the cost of reproducing the improvement on a similar site. Suppose, for example, that a lot can be purchased in a particular subdivision and a certain size and type of house constructed for a total cost of $300,000. This will tend to set the upper limit of value for existing houses of similar size and type in the subdivision unless they have some distinguishing locational feature such as an exceptional view or nearness to a golf course or lake.

Contribution

The principles of diminishing marginal utility and diminishing returns as factors of production are fundamental to economic theory. Their application in real estate appraisal is closely related to the **principle of contribution,** which states that the value of a component part of a property depends on the amount it contributes to the value of the whole. For example, tasteful landscaping may increase the value of a home much more than the cost of the improvement. An expenditure for extensive plantings of exotic shrubs, however, probably will not be recovered if the property is sold. In fact, certain improvements to a property can actually have a negative effect on value.

Suppose a homeowner builds an elaborate shrine in the dining room honoring a major league baseball team. Because the typical buyer prefers that such an item not be a part of the property, the "value" of the shrine is negative and equal to the cost of removing it, less any salvage value. The principle of contribution is an especially important consideration for real estate appraisers. Even though a property may have an expensive feature or characteristic, the contribution to market value is often less than the cost of the feature (or perhaps even negative) because the typical buyer in the market does not desire that feature in the property.

THE APPRAISAL PROCESS

Over the years, appraisers have developed a formal process to collect data, analyze the data to arrive at an estimate of value, and present their findings. The **appraisal process** is a systematic procedure employed to arrive at an estimate of value and convey that estimate to the appraisal user. Although we present the steps of this process in their general chronological order, it is important to realize that in practice, the order of consideration of these steps may need to be adjusted to match the conditions of a specific appraisal assignment. Careful consideration of each of the following six steps will lead to sound estimates of value:

1. Definition of the problem
2. Data selection and collection
3. Highest and best use analysis
4. Application of the three approaches to value
5. Reconciliation of value indications into a final value estimate
6. Report of defined value

Step 1: Definition of the Problem

The first step in the appraisal process is to define the problem at hand. The accuracy of the value estimate provided by the appraiser depends on careful specification of the appraisal assignment. The appraiser and the client must be in accord as to the

- type of value to be estimated,
- property involved,
- specific property rights being appraised,
- use of the appraisal, and
- effective date of the appraisal.

The most common purpose of an appraisal is to estimate market value, but appraisers may be asked to estimate rental value, insurable value, assessed value, or investment value. The type of value to be estimated will largely dictate the type of data that must be collected and the way they should be analyzed. It is essential, therefore, that the purpose of the appraisal and the definition of value be stated clearly.

The identification of the property to be appraised must include the location of the property, usually provided by both its street address and legal description. This description must also include any easements or encroachments that might affect value. Obviously, the physical characteristics of the property must be identified, including buildings and other improvements, the size of the parcel, its topography, soil conditions, elevation, and other physical features.

Not only the physical property but the specific property rights to be appraised must be clearly identified. These rights may be complete, as in a fee simple estate, or partial, including only such interests as air rights, the reversionary right in a leased fee, an easement, or some other type of limited property interest. The description should include limitations on these property rights, such as restrictive covenants and land-use controls.

The appraiser usually is called on to make an estimate of the current value of the property, although in some cases an appraisal is required for some date in the past. Retrospective appraisals may be required for many reasons, including a determination of inheritance taxes and insurance claims. Because the value of property changes over time, specification of an effective date for an appraisal is a necessary part of defining the problem.

Step 2: Data Selection and Collection

After defining the problem, the appraiser must identify and collect data that will permit an accurate estimate of property value. In addition to general information regarding economic, social, political, and environmental factors that may affect the value of the property being appraised, the appraiser must collect specific information regarding recent sales prices of similar properties, construction cost data, and income and expense information for the subject property and comparable properties in the market. As we will see in the remaining steps of the appraisal process, the accuracy and appropriateness of data collected for analysis are critical to the validity of the value estimate. Estimates of value based on inaccurate or inappropriate data are not reliable.

Step 3: Highest and Best Use Analysis

After determining the data requirements for an appraisal assignment and collecting the data for analysis, the next step is to analyze the property's highest and best use. **Highest and best use** is defined as that use that is found to be legally permissible, physically possible, financially feasible, and *maximally productive*. As we noted earlier, market value refers to the most probable price a property would bring in an open market transaction. Because the typical buyer in such a transaction would most probably use the property in its highest and best use, value estimates are based on the assumption that the highest and best use of the property has been identified. This follows from the recognition that competition among market participants will result in the most efficient and appropriate use of a property, even if that means changing its current use. Any estimate of market value must include a determination of the property's highest and best use.

The determination of the highest and best use of a property is of primary importance in any appraisal, although in many cases it is readily apparent. For example, if the property to be appraised is a five-year-old house in an established single-family neighborhood, the highest and best use of the property is most likely a single-family home. In other cases, however, the highest and best use of a property may be dramatically different from its current use.

Highest and best use of a property is affected by many factors, including its past and present use, land-use controls, nearby land uses, the availability or absence of utilities and transportation facilities, and recent or anticipated economic growth in the area. Analysis of highest and best use generally is easier for vacant land than for land with improvements that might require removal, so we will consider each in turn.

Highest and Best Use of Vacant Land

Suppose that a 50-acre tract of land has been planted in soybeans for some years. The value of the land in this agricultural use is $2,500 per acre. In the past, farming represented the highest and best use of the tract because the site was located several miles from a small city. More recently, the city has begun expanding because increased business and manufacturing activity there has led to population growth. These factors, combined with road improvements and the extension of water and sewer lines, have led to a change in the highest and best use of the site. In fact, there may be several legally permissible and financially feasible uses for it. One developer believes there is sufficient demand for a low-density, single-family residential subdivision and is willing to pay $30,000 per acre. Another developer wishes to build an apartment complex and is willing to pay $120,000 per acre. The second developer must believe that using the land for an apartment complex is more profitable than using it for single-family homes. Assuming both of these uses are legally permissible and physically possible, the highest and best use of this parcel is for an apartment complex because it results in the highest land value.

Highest and Best Use of Land with Improvements

In the example above, the determination of highest and best use was simplified by the fact that the land was vacant. Suppose, however, that a one-acre lot and the house on it are worth $175,000 as a single-family home. Under the current zoning ordinances, if the land were vacant, it could be sold for $80,000 as a single-family home site, or for $150,000 for a commercial activity. If vacant, the highest and best use of the site is clearly commercial, but because the property is worth more in its current use, its highest and best use still is residential. If the value of the site for commercial use increases above its value in residential use (plus the cost of demolition), however, it would be advantageous to tear down the existing house and change the use to commercial. The highest and best use of this property may change quickly if the existing improvements begin to deteriorate rapidly as a result of age or other factors. Although identifying a property's highest and best use can be a difficult task, appraisers must understand the manner in which the property would be used by the typical buyer in order to estimate its most probable selling price.

Step 4: Application of the Three Approaches to Value

In the traditional appraisal process, the appraiser normally considers three approaches to value. Each of these approaches is intended to replicate the thought processes of the typical buyer in order to estimate a property's most probable selling price in an open market transaction. Because we will consider the details of each of these approaches in the following sections of this chapter, we provide only brief descriptions here.

In the **sales comparison approach,** appraisers compare similar properties that have been sold recently in open market transactions with the subject property. The prices of these comparable properties provide an indication of the value of the subject property. Of course, every property is unique, and any differences between the comparable properties and the subject property must be taken into consideration.

In the **cost approach,** appraisers arrive at an estimate of the market value of a property by estimating its cost of production. Estimating value using this approach involves (1) estimating the value of the site as though it were vacant, (2) estimating the cost to produce the improvements, (3) subtracting depreciation, and (4) adding site value. There are numerous techniques for estimating the value of vacant land, with the most preferred method being the sales comparison approach. Estimating production cost requires knowledge of construction methods and current prices of materials and labor. The estimate of production cost is based on constructing a new structure, so the appraiser must subtract any depreciation that exists in the subject property. Adding the site value to the depreciated cost of the improvements provides an indication of market value.

In the **income approach,** appraisers estimate market value by estimating the income that the property is expected to generate, then converting the income stream into a present value estimate. The techniques used to relate income expectations to market value estimates include gross income multiplier analysis, net income capitalization, and discounted cash-flow analysis.

Step 5: Reconciliation of Value Indications into a Final Value Estimate

Although the three approaches described above should theoretically lead to identical value estimates, the realities of real estate markets usually result in a different estimate of value from each approach. Large differences between the value indications suggest that one or more of the approaches may not be appropriate for estimating a particular property's market value. To arrive at a final estimate of value, appraisers must reconcile the estimates obtained from each approach. Reconciliation of the three approaches requires considerable judgment on the part of the appraiser.

In most appraisal situations, the appraiser may feel that one of the approaches provides a better indication of value than the others and will therefore give more emphasis to that approach in the reconciliation step. For example, if an appraiser is estimating the market value of a church building, the sales comparison approach might not be appropriate if sales of church buildings are infrequent in the market. Similarly, the income approach may not be appropriate because such properties are not considered income producing. The lack of data required to implement these approaches in this situation may lead the appraiser to place more emphasis on the value estimate provided by the cost approach. In all cases, the appraiser must determine the weight given to the value indicated by each approach using his or her professional judgment. The appropriate weight depends on the amount and quality of available data, as well as the relevance of the approach to the problem at hand. When all of the approaches are relevant to some degree, appraisers often use a weighted average of the three value estimates to arrive at a final value estimate.

Step 6: Report of Defined Value

After reaching an estimate of value, the appraiser must convey the information to the client, normally in a written report. This report describes the data considered as well as the methods and reasoning used in arriving at the final value estimate. Any assumptions used in the analysis must be clearly stated and defended.

When the property involved is a single-family home and the function of the appraiser is to verify property value for loan approval purposes, the appraiser's analysis and conclusion must be reported in a format acceptable to the lender. Because lenders often sell their loans in the secondary mortgage market, the secondary market participants dictate the format of the appraisal report. Fannie Mae and Freddie Mac have jointly approved a Uniform Residential Appraisal Report (URAR) form for loans sold in the secondary mortgage market. (An example of the URAR form is shown in the case study at the end of this chapter.) Similar forms are used for other types of property, including vacant land and small income properties. For more complex appraisal assignments, the analysis and conclusions are usually presented in a narrative report format. Narrative appraisal reports may exceed several hundred pages for large-scale income properties.

Now that we understand the general process appraisers use to estimate property value, we can take a closer look at the specific techniques used in each of the three approaches to value: the sales comparison approach, the cost approach, and the income approach.

∎ THE SALES COMPARISON APPROACH

Perhaps the best single indication of the value of any good is the price that similar goods are selling for in the marketplace. This is the basis of the sales comparison approach to the valuation of real property. This technique has tremendous intuitive appeal because it closely resembles the process most buyers go through when selecting a property for purchase. The procedure involves comparing the subject property with similar properties that have sold relatively recently or are currently offered for sale, then using the sale prices of these properties to gain insight into the market value of the subject property.

Because individual parcels of real estate all have unique characteristics, close comparisons are difficult. In addition, sales data may be very sketchy or nonexistent for specialized properties. Nevertheless, when data are available, the sales comparison approach generally is considered the best method for estimating the value of real property. It is particularly valuable in appraising single-family homes in active markets.

The sales comparison approach involves two steps: (1) collection of data on sales of similar properties and (2) adjustment of the sales data to make them reflect the subject property as accurately as possible in regard to physical and locational characteristics, financing arrangements, conditions of the sale, and market conditions at the time of the sale.

Comparable Sales Data

The selection of "comparables," recently sold of properties that are roughly similar to the subject property, is critical to the market value estimate. The appraiser must take great care that the sales selected are truly representative and not distorted in some way. For example, the price that results from a voluntary sale to a mortgage lender in lieu of foreclosure probably would not be representative of the property's market value, nor would the price that results from a sale from one family member to another.

Generally, three to six comparable sales are considered adequate. The information on each transaction should include the date of sale, price, financing terms, location of the property, and a description of its physical characteristics and improvements. Deed records can provide information regarding location and date of sale, and where available, deed tax stamps may also give some indication of sales price. More definitive price and property characteristics may be provided by the buyer or seller, brokers, title and abstract companies, multiple listing services, or specialized financial report services.

Adjustment of Sales Data

After data on comparable sales have been gathered, they must be adjusted to make them reflect the subject property as accurately as possible. The appraiser may make lump-sum adjustments by evaluating all of the differences between the comparable sale and the subject property that are considered important. For example, the appraiser may conclude that on the basis of a comparable sale of $75,000, the subject property should sell for $80,000 because of its more desirable location and better quality construction. A refinement of this lump-sum approach is to evaluate the individual elements that may affect value. In any case, the following elements of comparison must be evaluated for potential differences between the subject property and the comparable properties.

Elements of Comparison

Six different elements of comparison must be considered in the sales comparison approach. The first two elements of comparison are *property rights conveyed* and *conditions of sale.* If analysis of these two elements identifies significant differences between the subject property and any potentially comparable property, the sale price of such a comparable provides little insight into the market value of the subject property and it should be eliminated from further consideration.

For example, if the subject property involves a fee simple absolute estate and a comparable property was sold as a life estate, the subject property is almost certainly worth more than the comparable. Therefore, the sale price of the comparable property will not give a reliable indication of the value of the subject property. In most cases, appraisers prefer to eliminate properties with inconsistent property rights from further analysis. Similarly, if a potentially comparable property's transaction price is not the result of arm's-length negotiation between informed parties, the sale price of the comparable property will not provide a valid indication of the market value of the subject property. The definition of market value is explicit in defining the conditions of sale for the subject property. In general, appraisers assume that the subject property will be sold in a competitive and open market under all conditions necessary for a fair sale.

Another element of comparison addresses the *financing terms* in a comparable sale. As required by the definition of market value, the market value of the subject property is estimated in terms of cash or financial arrangements comparable to cash. If the transaction of a comparable property involves unique financial arrangements that may have affected the sale price, the sale price of the comparable must be adjusted to reflect this difference. For example, if a seller provides a mortgage loan with a below-market interest rate to the buyer, it is likely that the buyer would pay a higher price for the property. Because the financing terms in this transaction are more favorable than those generally available in the market, the price of the comparable must be adjusted downward to accurately reflect the value of the subject property. The amount of adjustment primarily depends on the interest savings provided to the buyer by the below-market financing.

Another important consideration is the fact that local market conditions are subject to change over time as a result of changing economic, political, social, and environmental factors. This element of comparison is frequently referred to as *market conditions.* A property that sold four months ago or even a week ago may sell for more or less today as a result of changing market conditions. Therefore, appraisers must adjust the sales prices of comparable properties to reflect differences in market conditions between the time of sale and the effective date of the appraisal. If conditions have improved such that a sale of a comparable property in today's market would result in a higher price, then the price of the comparable should be adjusted upward to provide a valid indication of the subject property's current market value.

Yet another element of comparison involves differences in the *locational characteristics* of the subject and comparable properties. Most people are familiar with the old saying among real estate investors that the three most important factors affecting real estate values are "location, location, and location." Though simplistic, this statement embodies a certain amount of wisdom. Because real estate values are dramatically influenced by local market factors, properties located in the same neighborhood are considered the most comparable to each other. A *neighborhood* can be defined as a geographic area containing complementary land uses. For some properties, the boundaries that define a neighborhood are quite expansive, while others are more compact. Even within the same neighborhood, one site may be preferable to another due to access and proximity to shopping and schools, traffic volume on the surrounding streets, and numerous other factors. Consideration of locational characteristics is a critical step in the adjustment process.

The final element of comparison reflects differences in *physical characteristics* between the subject property and the comparable properties. Though the possibilities are endless, some commonly encountered differences include the size of the property (land area and improvements), number and size of the rooms, type of construction, quality of construction, interior design, architectural style, and numerous special features. If the comparable properties possess physical characteristics that differ from the subject property, appropriate adjustments must be made to the sale prices of the comparable properties to ensure that the price is indicative of the subject property's market value.

When the adjustments for each of these elements of comparison are complete, the adjusted sales prices for the comparables give an indication of the value of the subject property. Again, the steps involved in this approach mirror the steps a potential buyer might go through when comparing alternative properties and making a purchase decision. The example presented below demonstrates the logic behind the sales comparison approach using "matched pair analysis" to determine the appropriate adjustment amounts.

Applying the Sales Comparison Approach

Consider the problem of estimating the value of a vacant lakefront lot in a residential subdivision. The lot under consideration measures 80 by 120 feet. Three similar vacant lots in this subdivision have sold recently in transactions resulting from arm's-length negotiations for the transfer of fee simple absolute estates, and all sale

TABLE 9.1 | Sales Comparison Market Data Grid

| | Subject | Comparables | | |
		#1	#2	#3
Sales price	—	$30,100	$32,500	$21,600
Size in square feet	9,600	10,200	11,900	9,600
Price per square foot	—	$2.95	$2.73	$2.25
Date of sale	Current	– 2 weeks	– 1 year	– 6 months
Adjustment for changing market conditions	—	+ $0	+ $0.22	+ $0.11
Adjusted price per square foot	—	$2.95	$2.95	$2.36
Location	Lake	Lake	Lake	Interior
Adjustment for location	—	+ $0	+ $0	+ $0.59
Adjusted price per square foot	—	$2.95	$2.95	$2.95

Indicated value of subject property: 9,600 square feet × $2.95 = $28,320

prices reflect cash-equivalent financing terms. The significant differences between these properties are date of sale, lot size, and location of the lot relative to the lake. Comparable number one measures 85 by 120 feet and is also located on the lake. It sold for $30,100 two weeks ago. Comparable number two is a lakefront lot measuring 85 by 140 feet. This lot sold one year ago for $32,500. Comparable number three sold six months ago for $21,600. It is an interior lot measuring 80 by 120 feet.

A good way to organize and analyze sales comparison data is through a market data grid such as the one shown in Table 9.1. Because the lots differ in terms of size, we can simplify our analysis by first calculating the sale price per square foot. After adjusting the sale prices of each comparable for differences in market conditions since the sale date, we can then multiply the adjusted price per square foot by the size of the subject property to arrive at an estimate of value for the subject property.

To determine the adjustment necessary to account for changing market conditions, notice that comparables 1 and 2 are both lakefront properties, but comparable 2 sold approximately one year later than comparable 1. Because we eliminated the size difference by calculating price per square foot, the only difference between comparables 1 and 2 is the date of sale. The difference in price for these properties suggests that property values have increased by approximately $0.22 per square foot over the past year. Because the effective date of the appraisal is today, we must estimate the price the comparables would bring if offered for sale under current market conditions. Thus, we adjust the price per square foot of comparable 2 upward by $0.22. Assuming the change in property values has been constant over the past year, we can also adjust the sale price of comparable 3 upward by half of this amount, or $0.11, to account for changing market conditions over the past six months.

After adjusting for changing market conditions, the only remaining difference between the subject property and any of the comparables is location of the lots relative to the lake. Our subject property is a lakefront lot, as are comparables 1 and 2. Comparable 3, however, is an interior lot. Just as we determined the adjustment for changing market conditions by comparing the sale prices of two of the comparables that differed only in terms of their sale date, we can determine the appropriate adjustment for location by comparing the sale price of comparable 3 with the sale prices of the other comparables. The higher sale prices of the first two comparables suggest that lake frontage adds approximately $0.59 per square foot to property values in this neighborhood. Adding this amount to the price per square foot of comparable 3 results in a value indication from each of the comparables of $2.95. Multiplying this amount by 9,600 square feet yields $28,320. Thus, we conclude that this amount is an estimate of the current market value of the subject property, after adjustments for differences in market conditions, lot size, and location.

Although this example refers to vacant land, the same procedure can be applied to improved residential and nonresidential properties. We will apply this approach to a single-family home in the case study at the end of the chapter. Of course, it is unlikely that all of the comparable properties will provide an identical indication of value. Also, the appropriate unit of comparison is not always price per square foot. The primary consideration in this approach to value is to correctly determine the appropriate amount and direction of adjustments for each element of comparison. In most situations, the adjustments are much more detailed than those described here. Furthermore, the data available from sales of comparable properties may be insufficient to provide a valid value estimate. Without adequate data, the sales comparison approach is not reliable.

THE COST APPROACH

In addition to having existing properties to choose from, a potential buyer of a home or other real property improvement usually has the alternative of buying a similar site and constructing a new building. Generally, therefore, site value plus production costs of the improvements tend to set the upper limit to value. In this sense, the principle of substitution is the basis of the cost approach to value. There are four key steps in the cost approach, including (1) estimating the value of the site as though it were vacant, (2) estimating the cost to produce the improvements, (3) subtracting depreciation, and (4) adding site value.

The indicated value of the property is the cost to produce the building, less the estimated accrued depreciation, plus the value of the site and site improvements. Subtracting accrued depreciation is necessary because the cost estimate is based on constructing a new, identically designed building using current prices for materials and labor. The subject property is most likely not new, and if it were constructed new, any design flaws would be corrected. Estimating the accrued depreciation for a property is often the most difficult step of the cost approach.

Estimating Site Value

The first step in the cost approach is to estimate the value of the site. Land values are usually estimated by the sales comparison approach, as demonstrated above, though other techniques are sometimes used. The cost of site improvements such as grading, landscaping, and paving must be added to arrive at a total value for the site.

Estimating Production Cost

The second step in the cost approach is to estimate the production cost of the improvements. Production cost estimates are based on either *reproduction cost* or *replacement cost*. Reproduction cost refers to the cost of constructing an exact replica of the subject property's improvements, while replacement cost refers to the cost of constructing an equally functional improvement, rather than an exact duplicate. Using replacement cost as the basis for this approach simplifies the cost-estimating procedure when the property being appraised contains design elements or materials that are out-of-date and would, therefore, not be included if the building was constructed today.

Estimating production cost requires specialized knowledge regarding construction methods, so appraisers frequently rely on engineering and architectural experts for accurate cost estimates. Professional cost-estimating companies publish cost manuals or provide computerized cost programs that assist appraisers in this task. In practice, construction costs can be estimated by obtaining actual expenditure data on the subject property, by collecting data on other similar projects in the area, or through data services that collect and distribute cost data on various types of construction. Methods used in estimating production costs include the comparative-unit method, the segregated-cost method, and the quantity-survey method. Of these methods, the quantity-survey method is the most detailed.

The *comparative-unit method* employs the known costs of similar structures, typically measured in dollars per square foot, to derive an estimate of the cost to produce a subject property's improvements. For example, a typical warehouse might cost $32.15 per square foot to construct. If the subject property contains 50,000 square feet, its cost is estimated at $1,607,500. This approach does not separately identify the individual components that make up the building, but it can be fairly accurate for properties with uniform construction.

In the *segregated-cost method,* the unit costs for various building components are used to arrive at a cost estimate. If the cost of building finished exterior walls on a warehouse is $5.52 per square foot, and the subject property has 10,700 square feet of exterior walls, then the cost of this component would be approximately $59,000. The cost of each major component of the building (walls, roof, flooring, plumbing, etc.) is estimated separately, then all costs are added together for a final cost estimate. This method is more comprehensive than the comparative-unit method, but less detailed than the quantity-survey method.

The *quantity-survey method* is the most comprehensive method, and is therefore more accurate when correctly applied. In this method, the quantity and quality of all materials and all categories of labor are identified separately, then costs for each of these items are totaled to arrive at a final cost estimate. For example, the number of sheets of plywood, gallons of paint, the amount of piping, hours of electricians' labor, and all other materials or labor needed to construct the building must be identified and the costs of each estimated. The quantity-survey method provides the most detailed cost estimate, but it is time-consuming and not used frequently in the appraisal process.

Estimating Accrued Depreciation

Structures wear out over time. They also may become obsolete or unprofitable because of technological innovation or economic change. Therefore, unless the subject property's improvements are new, appraisers must estimate **depreciation**—the amount by which the value of a building has declined since it was built, as a consequence of physical deterioration, functional obsolescence, and economic obsolescence.

Physical deterioration may result from ordinary wear and tear, weathering from the elements, vandalism, or neglect. Physical deterioration should be minimal in new buildings and can be prevented or minimized by proper maintenance and quality construction. Appraisers often estimate the effective age of the improvements, then use the ratio of effective age to useful life to measure physical deterioration. For example, a 15-year-old house with normal maintenance might exhibit 25 percent physical deterioration if its useful life is 60 years.

Many properties suffer their greatest loss in value from the effects of obsolescence, both functional and economic. **Functional obsolescence** is a loss in value that occurs because the property has less utility or ability to generate income than a new property designed for the same use. This sort of depreciation results from factors inherent in the property itself. It may occur because of changes in technology or in tastes, which would cause a new building to be constructed quite differently from the way the existing structure was built. For example, buildings using asbestos insulation now suffer a large penalty. To a lesser extent, so do outmoded, multistory factory buildings and poorly designed houses with small, dark rooms. An increasingly important issue faced by appraisers is the difficulty of estimating the value of environmentally contaminated parcels.

Economic (or external) **obsolescence** is a loss in value resulting from factors outside the property that affect its income-producing ability or other degree of use. For example, suppose that a well-designed and well-constructed motel in good physical condition is located in an area that is bypassed by a new highway. The resulting

TABLE 9.2 | Summary of Cost Valuation of an Apartment Property

Estimated production cost		$594,000
Depreciation		
Physical deterioration: cost of repairs (roof repair, painting, exterior caulking)	$4,680	
Miscellaneous physical deterioration (3% of reproduction costs)	17,820	
Functional obsolescence (screen between swimming pool and apartment to reduce noise from pool)	4,000	
Economic obsolescence	0	
Production cost less depreciation		567,500
Estimated site value		150,000
Total value indicated by cost approach		$717,500
Rounded		$718,000

decline in traffic may greatly decrease the income-producing ability of the property and hence its value. Economic obsolescence also may occur because of changes in consumer expenditure patterns, population movements, adverse legislation, or neighborhood change.

Applying the Cost Approach

To demonstrate the steps involved in the cost approach, consider a two-year-old apartment building. To estimate its value by this approach, we must estimate the value of the site, the production cost of the improvements, and the accrued depreciation resulting from physical deterioration and economic and functional obsolescence. Suppose the appraiser estimates these items as shown in Table 9.2. The land value is estimated as $150,000 using the sales comparison approach. Estimated production cost for the two-year-old building is $594,000.

Even though the buildings are almost new, the appraiser still determines that there should be some allowance for depreciation. A minor roof repair is necessary ($4,680), and there is some miscellaneous physical deterioration that requires attention ($17,820). In addition, the appraiser judges that the swimming pool has been placed too close to apartment number 11, resulting in some minor functional obsolescence that could be eliminated by building an appropriate screening wall ($4,000). Because the property is relatively new, the appraiser determines that no allowance is necessary for economic obsolescence. Depreciation from all causes in the amount of $26,500 is subtracted from the estimated reproduction costs to yield a depreciated building value of $567,500. Adding this amount to the site value provides an indication of value by the cost approach of $717,500, which the appraiser rounds to $718,000.

THE INCOME APPROACH

The income approach to value is based on the principle of anticipation, which implies that purchasers buy properties in expectation of receiving future benefits. In general, the value of any income-earning asset can be thought of as the sum of the present value of the expected future returns to the owner, including both periodic cash flows from operations and cash flows from the eventual sale of the asset. The same logic is valid for any income-producing asset, whether it be the goose that lays golden eggs, a savings certificate from a financial institution, common stock, or income-producing real estate such as an apartment complex, a shopping mall, an office complex, or an industrial building. The income approach in real estate appraisal involves two basic steps: (1) estimating future income and (2) converting the income estimate into a present value estimate.

Appraisers employ many different techniques to convert future income into present value estimates. Each of these techniques has been developed to replicate the thought processes of the typical buyer in a market. We consider two these techniques here: gross income multiplier analysis and net income capitalization.

Gross Income Multiplier

All techniques used in the income approach to value are based on the idea that market participants demand investment returns in exchange for purchasing income properties. Furthermore, competition between market participants results in a relatively stable relationship between income and value in most real estate markets. When this relationship can be measured or quantified, appraisers can use it to estimate market values. One "rule-of-thumb" measure of the relationship between gross income and market value is the **gross income multiplier,** or GIM.

$$\text{Gross Income Multiplier} = \frac{\text{Value}}{\text{Gross Income}}$$

The GIM is an estimate of the prevailing relationship between prices investors are willing to pay for properties and the gross income the properties are expected to produce. To calculate the GIM for a market, appraisers collect information about properties that have recently sold in the market, then divide the price of each property by its gross income. Of course, the properties used to estimate the GIM for a market must truly be comparable to the subject property. Gross income is defined as the total amount of revenue the property is expected to generate annually.

For example, consider a property that is expected to generate $10,000 per year in gross income. If that property is sold in an arm's-length transaction for $100,000, the GIM for this property is 10: 100,000 ÷ 10,000. To use this measure to estimate the value of a similar property that is expected to generate $9,000 per year in gross income, we multiply $9,000 by 10 to get a market value estimate of $90,000. By observing market transactions, appraisers can measure the relationship between income and value using GIM, then use the multiplier to estimate market value of the subject property.

Because the GIM technique ignores the expenses of operating an income property, it is most appropriate when the expenses of the comparable sales are similar to the expenses of the subject property. When expenses differ across properties, a more detailed technique is required. The net income capitalization technique described below is an alternative technique that recognizes the variability in operating expenses across similar properties.

Net Income Capitalization

The net income capitalization technique recognizes that the value of an income property depends on "net" rather than "gross" income, as discussed above. In this technique, net income is converted into a present value estimate using a **capitalization rate** rather than a multiplier. The relationship between value and net income is measured as shown below:

$$\text{Capitalization Rate} = \frac{\text{Net Income}}{\text{Value}}$$

For example, consider a property that recently sold in an arm's-length transaction for $1 million. If this property is expected to generate net income of $100,000 annually, the implied *capitalization rate* for this property is 10 percent. To estimate the value of a similar property that is expected to generate $105,000 in net income (gross income minus expenses), we can rearrange the capitalization rate formula as follows:

$$\text{Value} = \frac{\text{Net Income}}{\text{Capitalization Rate}}$$

$$\text{Value} = \frac{\$105,000}{0.10}$$

Dividing net income by 10 percent provides a market value estimate of $1,050,000 for this property. By observing market transactions, appraisers can determine the capitalization rate that best represents the relationship between net income and value, then use this measure to estimate the value of a subject property based on its net income. The accuracy of this technique, of course, depends on accurate estimates of the subject property's net income and the capitalization rate.

Applying the Appraisal Process in a Single-Family Home Appraisal

 Consider a hypothetical single-family home owned by Harold and Gladys Stewart. Suppose that an agreement has been reached between the Stewarts and Frank and Elizabeth Barr. The Barrs have agreed to purchase the property for $120,000. The Barrs plan on borrowing 90 percent of the purchase price, using a mortgage loan from a local lender. As part of the loan approval process, the lender requires that an appraisal be performed by a qualified real estate appraiser to verify that the property value supports the requested loan amount. The following discussion describes the steps the appraiser will take to apply the appraisal process to this property.

Defining the Problem

The appraiser selected to perform the assignment for the Barrs' lender is Michelle Tipton, a state-certified appraiser. Michelle has ten years' experience in the appraisal industry and is qualified to perform appraisals on all types of properties. Her fee for this appraisal assignment is $250. The cost of hiring the appraiser will be paid by the Barrs, even though the appraiser is performing the appraisal on behalf of the lender.

The Barrs and their lender will provide Michelle with the basic information she needs to begin the appraisal process. To define the appraisal problem at hand, the appraiser must know what type of value she is trying to estimate, the property rights being appraised, and the legal description of the property that is the subject of the appraisal. In this case, the purpose of the appraisal is to estimate the current market value of the property described as

All that tract or parcel of land, situated in St. Joseph, Buchanan County, Missouri, together with all improvements thereon, known as 1097 Timbers Crossing. Such property is more accurately described as Lot 3, Block G, of the Harris Billups Estate, as recorded in Plat Book 8, page 37, in the Office of the Clerk of the Circuit Court of Buchanan County, Missouri.

The property rights being appraised are those that comprise a fee simple absolute ownership interest in the subject property. All of this information will be entered in the "Subject" section of the URAR as shown in Figure 9.1.

Selecting and Collecting the Data

After defining the appraisal problem, the appraiser begins selecting and collecting the data she will need to estimate the value of the subject property. She begins by personally inspecting the property to familiarize herself with its neighborhood, as well as the physical characteristics of the site and improvements.

As indicated in the "Neighborhood" section of Figure 9.1, the property is located in an urban area that is more than 75 percent developed, has a stable growth rate, stable property values, and supply and demand conditions that appear to be in balance. In addition, Michelle notes that the age of homes in this neighborhood ranges from new to 50 years old, and that prices range from $70,000 to $155,000. Single-family homes make up approximately 85 percent of all properties in this area, with 2–4-family structures, 4-or-more-family structures, and commercial uses accounting for 5 percent each. Michelle believes that a change in land use in this neighborhood is not likely in the near future. Michelle also defines the boundaries of the neighborhood and its characteristics, and provides

(continued)

Applying the Appraisal Process in a Single-Family Home Appraisal

additional comments about the market conditions in the subject neighborhood as shown on the report.

In the "Site" section of the URAR, the appraiser reports the site dimensions, size of the site, whether the property is a corner lot, the zoning classification, zoning compliance, utilities available to the site, off-site improvements, and other site-related information. Notice that this section requires that the appraiser identify the highest and best use of the site. Of course, if the appraiser determines that the highest and best use of the site is not single-family residential, then the URAR form should not be used to report the value estimate.

The site in this example is rectangular (80 feet by 120 feet), is zoned for residential use, and has access to public electricity, water, and sewer. The property is not on a corner, and the street is asphalt. The site appears to be well-drained, has adequate landscaping, and has an asphalt driveway. The property is not located in a flood zone as defined by the Federal Emergency Management Agency (FEMA).

The appraiser will also note the major characteristics of the improvements on the site as shown in the "Description of Improvements" section of Figure 9.1. The single-family detached house located on this site is a one-story, ranch-style home built with concrete block and stucco (CBS) on a concrete slab foundation. The roof is asphalt shingles, with typical gutters and downspouts. The windows are awning type with screens. The house consists of a living room, dining room, kitchen, a family room, three bedrooms, two bathrooms, and a laundry room. The size of the home is 1,950 square feet. The interior walls are plaster, with wooden doors and trim. The floors are covered in carpet and vinyl tile. The house is served by a central heating and cooling unit that operates on electricity. The house has no attic storage, but it does have a small concrete patio and an open porch. As is typical in this market, kitchen equipment includes a refrigerator, range, and washer/dryer. The house has a two-car carport of 430 square feet.

The URAR also has a designated section for the appraiser to comment on any additional features of the property, the overall condition of the improvements, and any adverse environmental conditions that might affect property value. In this example, the appraiser finds no unusual factors that should be noted.

Now that the appraiser is familiar with the property, she must now collect the specific information she will need to apply the three approaches to value. For the cost approach, the information required includes construction cost data and a site value estimate. For the sales comparison approach, she must identify comparable properties that have sold recently in the subject property's neighborhood. For the income approach, she must obtain information about the income-earning ability of the subject property and the relationship between income and value that prevails in the market. We will consider each of these approaches in detail.

Applying the Cost Approach

To complete the first step in the cost approach, Michelle uses the sales comparison approach to estimate the value of the site as if it were vacant. Her estimate of the site value is $32,000. Second, Michelle consults a residential construction cost-estimating guide and finds that this type of dwelling costs approximately $58 per square foot to produce. The appliances, porch, and patio cost approximately $2,500, and the carport costs $11 per square foot. Because the house is 15 years

(continued)

Applying the Appraisal Process in a Single-Family Home Appraisal

old, Michelle determines that depreciation from all sources is approximately 25 percent of the total production cost. Finally, she estimates the value of site improvements (asphalt driveway and average landscaping) at approximately $2,200. All of this information is summarized in the "Cost Approach" section of the URAR.

CHAPTER REVIEW

■ Real estate appraisers are specialists who possess the skills and knowledge necessary to estimate property value. The appraisal industry is subject to state regulation as a result of the Financial Institutions Reform, Recovery, and Enforcement Act of 1989, which requires that appraisals for property involved in "federally related" transactions be performed by state-licensed or certified appraisers.

■ The Appraisal Foundation, through its Appraiser Qualifications Board and Appraisal Standards Board, implements the minimum guidelines for the four different appraiser categories and the professional standards of practice appraisers must follow when performing appraisal tasks.

■ The type of value that appraisers most often estimate is market value, or a property's most probable selling price in well-defined situations.

■ Four key principles underlying appraisal practice are
    1. anticipation,
    2. change,
    3. substitution, and
    4. contribution.

■ The six steps in the appraisal process include
    1. definition of the problem,
    2. data selection and collection,
    3. highest and best use analysis,
    4. application of the three approaches to value,
    5. reconciliation, and
    6. reporting the defined value.

FIGURE 9.1 | Applying the Appraisal Process in a Single-Family Home Appraisal

Uniform Residential Appraisal Report
File No. 2007-1098

The purpose of this summary appraisal report is to provide the lender/client with an accurate, and adequately supported, opinion of the market value of the subject property.

SUBJECT

Property Address 1097 Timbers Crossing City St. Joseph State MO Zip Code 94334
Borrower Barr Owner of Public Record Stewart County Buchanan
Legal Description Lot 3, Block G, Harris Billups Estate, Plat Book 8, P. 37
Assessor's Parcel # 0223-0300471 Tax Year 2007 R.E. Taxes $ 1,207.10
Neighborhood Name Harris Billups Estates Map Reference Census Tract
Occupant [X] Owner [ ] Tenant [ ] Vacant Special Assessments $ [ ] PUD HOA $ [ ] per year [ ] per month
Property Rights Appraised [X] Fee Simple [ ] Leasehold [ ] Other (describe)
Assignment Type [X] Purchase Transaction [ ] Refinance Transaction [ ] Other (describe)
Lender/Client Barber Savings Association Address 4390 N. Main, St. Joseph MO 94330
Is the subject property currently offered for sale or has it been offered for sale in the twelve months prior to the effective date of this appraisal? [X] Yes [ ] No
Report data source(s) used, offering price(s), and date(s). Local MLS listing at $124,900

I [X] did [ ] did not analyze the contract for sale for the subject purchase transaction. Explain the results of the analysis of the contract for sale or why the analysis was not performed.
Contract terms are typical for this market.

CONTRACT

Contract Price $ 120,000 Date of Contract 10/15/2007 Is the property seller the owner of public record? [X] Yes [ ] No Data Source(s) public records
Is there any financial assistance (loan charges, sale concessions, gift or downpayment assistance, etc.) to be paid by any party on behalf of the borrower? [ ] Yes [X] No
If Yes, report the total dollar amount and describe the items to be paid. $

Note: Race and the racial composition of the neighborhood are not appraisal factors.

NEIGHBORHOOD

Neighborhood Characteristics		One-Unit Housing Trends		One-Unit Housing		Present Land Use %	
Location [X] Urban [ ] Suburban [ ] Rural		Property Values [ ] Increasing [X] Stable [ ] Declining		PRICE	AGE	One-Unit	85 %
Built-Up [X] Over 75% [ ] 25-75% [ ] Under 25%		Demand/Supply [ ] Shortage [X] In Balance [ ] Over Supply		$(000)	(yrs)	2-4 Unit	5 %
Growth [ ] Rapid [X] Stable [ ] Slow		Marketing Time [ ] Under 3 mths [X] 3-6 mths [ ] Over 6 mths		70 Low	50	Multi-Family	5 %
Neighborhood Boundaries West of Lyans Ave, North of Brookline, East of SFCE Rail tracks, South				155 High	1	Commercial	5 %
of Binderville Road				120 Pred.	25	Other	%

Neighborhood Description An area of mostly single-family homes showing good maintenance levels. The presence of 5% commercial utilization is limited to the main throroughfares and does not adversely affect the subject's value or marketability.

Market Conditions (including support for the above conclusions) Supply and demand for housing in this neighborhood appears to be in balance. Mortgage money is readily available at typical terms.

SITE

Dimensions 80 x 120 (subject to survey) Area 9600 Sq.Ft. Shape Rectangular View residential
Specific Zoning Classification R1-1 Zoning Description Single family residential
Zoning Compliance [X] Legal [ ] Legal Nonconforming (Grandfathered Use) [ ] No Zoning [ ] Illegal (describe)
Is the highest and best use of the subject property as improved (or as proposed per plans and specifications) the present use? [X] Yes [ ] No If No, describe.

Utilities	Public	Other (describe)		Public	Other (describe)	Off-site Improvements—Type	Public	Private
Electricity	[X]		Water	[X]		Street Asphalt	[X]	
Gas	[X]		Sanitary Sewer	[X]		Alley		

FEMA Special Flood Hazard Area [ ] Yes [X] No FEMA Flood Zone FEMA Map # FEMA Map Date
Are the utilities and off-site improvements typical for the market area? [X] Yes [ ] No If No, describe.
Are there any adverse site conditions or external factors (easements, encroachments, environmental conditions, land uses, etc.)? [ ] Yes [X] No If Yes, describe.

IMPROVEMENTS

GENERAL DESCRIPTION	FOUNDATION	EXTERIOR DESCRIPTION materials/condition	INTERIOR materials/condition
Units [X] One [ ] One with Accessory Unit	[X] Concrete Slab [ ] Crawl Space	Foundation Walls	Floors wood/carpet
# of Stories 1	[ ] Full Basement [ ] Partial Basement	Exterior Walls cbs/good	Walls drywall/good
Type [X] Det. [ ] Att. [ ] S-Det./End Unit	Basement Area sq. ft.	Roof Surface shingl/goode	Trim/Finish wood/good
[X] Existing [ ] Proposed [ ] Under Const.	Basement Finish %	Gutters & Downspouts typical/good	Bath Floor vinyl/good
Design (Style) Ranch	[ ] Outside Entry/Exit [ ] Sump Pump	Window Type awning/good	Bath Wainscot
Year Built 1992	Evidence of [ ] Infestation	Storm Sash/Insulated no	Car Storage [ ] None
Effective Age (Yrs) 15	[ ] Dampness [ ] Settlement	Screens yes/good	[ ] Driveway # of Cars
Attic [ ] None	Heating [X] FWA [ ] HWBB [ ] Radiant	Amenities [ ] WoodStove(s) #	Driveway Surface
[ ] Drop Stair [ ] Stairs	[ ] Other [ ] Fuel	[ ] Fireplace(s) # [ ] Fence	[ ] Garage # of Cars
[ ] Floor [X] Scuttle	Cooling [X] Central Air Conditioning	[X] Patio/Deck [X] Porch open	[X] Carport # of Cars 2
[ ] Finished [ ] Heated	[ ] Individual [ ] Other	[ ] Pool [ ] Other	[ ] Att. [ ] Det. [ ] Built-in
Appliances [X] Refrigerator [X] Range/Oven	[ ] Dishwasher [ ] Disposal [ ] Microwave	[X] Washer/Dryer [ ] Other (describe)	

Finished area above grade contains: 7 Rooms 3 Bedrooms 2 Bath(s) 1,950 Square Feet of Gross Living Area Above Grade
Additional features (special energy efficient items, etc.). ceiling fans (4)

Describe the condition of the property (including needed repairs, deterioration, renovations, remodeling, etc.). The subject property shows average condition on the interior and exterior. The property exhibits typical appeal for the neighborhood. No functional or external obsolescence observed.

Are there any physical deficiencies or adverse conditions that affect the livability, soundness, or structural integrity of the property? [ ] Yes [X] No If Yes, describe.

Does the property generally conform to the neighborhood (functional utility, style, condition, use, construction, etc.)? [X] Yes [ ] No If No, describe.

Freddie Mac Form 70 March 2005 Produced using ACI software. 800.234.8727 www.aciweb.com Page 1 of 6 Fannie Mae Form 1004 March 2005 1004_05 033005

For more information about appraisal forms, and for the most up-to-date versions of the forms, visit the Fannie Mae Web site at *www.efanniemae.com*.

FIGURE 9.1 | Applying the Appraisal Process in a Single-Family Home Appraisal *(continued)*

Uniform Residential Appraisal Report

File No. 2007-1098

There are **5** comparable properties currently offered for sale in the subject neighborhood ranging in price from $ 119,900 to $ 149,900

There are **7** comparable sales in the subject neighborhood within the past twelve months ranging in sale price from $ 115,000 to $ 145,000

FEATURE	SUBJECT	COMPARABLE SALE NO. 1	+(-) $ Adjustment	COMPARABLE SALE NO. 2	+(-) $ Adjustment	COMPARABLE SALE NO. 3	+(-) $ Adjustment
Address	1097 Timbers Crossing St. Joseph	1244 NE 34 Street		1297 NE 34 Street		1539 Ne 38 Street	
Proximity to Subject		1 block southwest		1 block south		5 blocks northeast	
Sale Price	$ 120,000	$ 119,000		$ 126,500		$ 121,000	
Sale Price/Gross Liv. Area	$ 61.54 sq. ft.	$ 63.47 sq. ft.		$ 65.89 sq. ft.		$ 61.58 sq. ft.	
Data Source(s)		MLS, public records		MLS, public records		MLS, public records	
Verification Source(s)		broker		seller		buyer	
VALUE ADJUSTMENTS	DESCRIPTION	DESCRIPTION	+(-) $ Adjustment	DESCRIPTION	+(-) $ Adjustment	DESCRIPTION	+(-) $ Adjustment
Sale or Financing Concessions		VA	-1,000	conventional		conventional	
Date of Sale/Time	10/15/2007	8/07		9/07		7/07	
Location	Urban	similar		similar		similar	
Leasehold/Fee Simple	Fee Simple	Fee Simple		Fee Simple		Fee Simple	
Site	9600 Sq. Ft.	Corner, Average		Corner/Average		Inside/Average	
View	residential	commercial	+2,000	Residential		Residential	
Design (Style)	Ranch	Ranch		Ranch		Ranch	
Quality of Construction	Average	similar		similar		similar	
Actual Age	15+/- Years	16		14		16	
Condition	average	similar		similar		similar	
Above Grade Room Count	Total 7 / Bdrms. 3 / Baths 2	Total 7 / Bdrms. 3 / Baths 2		Total 7 / Bdrms. 3 / Baths 2		Total 7 / Bdrms. 3 / Baths 2	
Gross Living Area	1,950 sq. ft.	1,875 sq. ft.	+1,125	1,920 sq. ft.		1,965 sq. ft.	
Basement & Finished Rooms Below Grade							
Functional Utility	Average	similar		similar		similar	
Heating/Cooling	FWA C/Air	similar		similar		similar	
Energy Efficient Items							
Garage/Carport	2 Car Carport	2 car carport		2 car garage	-5,000	2 car carport	
Porch/Patio/Deck	Patio/Deck, Porch	similar		similar		similar	
Fence	none	none		wood privacy	-1,000	non	
Net Adjustment (Total)		[X]+ []- $ 2,125		[]+ [X]- $ 6,000		[X]+ []- $ 0	
Adjusted Sale Price of Comparables		Net Adj. 1.8% Gross Adj. 3.5% $ 121,125		Net Adj. -4.7% Gross Adj. 4.7% $ 120,500		Net Adj. 0.0% Gross Adj. 0.0% $ 121,000	

I [X] did [ ] did not research the sale or transfer history of the subject property and comparable sales. If not, explain

My research [ ] did [X] did not reveal any prior sales or transfers of the subject property for the three years prior to the effective date of this appraisal.

Data source(s) public records

My research [ ] did [X] did not reveal any prior sales or transfers of the comparable sales for the year prior to the date of sale of the comparable sale.

Data source(s) public records

Report the results of the research and analysis of the prior sale or transfer history of the subject property and comparable sales (report additional prior sales on page 3).

ITEM	SUBJECT	COMPARABLE SALE NO. 1	COMPARABLE SALE NO. 2	COMPARABLE SALE NO. 3
Date of Prior Sale/Transfer				
Price of Prior Sale/Transfer				
Data Source(s)				
Effective Date of Data Source(s)				

Analysis of prior sale or transfer history of the subject property and comparable sales

Summary of Sales Comparison Approach. All comparables utilized are of similar style single family homes in the same neighborhood as the subject property. The adjusted prices range from $120,500 to $121,125.

Indicated Value by Sales Comparison Approach $ 121,000

Indicated Value by: Sales Comparison Approach $ 121,000   Cost Approach (if developed) $ 124,400   Income Approach (if developed) $ 121,125

This appraisal is made [X] "as is," [ ] subject to completion per plans and specifications on the basis of a hypothetical condition that the improvements have been completed, [ ] subject to the following repairs or alterations on the basis of a hypothetical condition that the repairs or alterations have been completed, or [ ] subject to the following required inspection based on the extraordinary assumption that the condition or deficiency does not require alteration or repair:

Based on a complete visual inspection of the interior and exterior areas of the subject property, defined scope of work, statement of assumptions and limiting conditions, and appraiser's certification, my (our) opinion of the market value, as defined, of the real property that is the subject of this report is $ 121,000 as of **September 4, 2007**, which is the date of inspection and the effective date of this appraisal.

FIGURE 9.1 | Applying the Appraisal Process in a Single-Family Home Appraisal *(continued)*

Uniform Residential Appraisal Report

File No. 2007-1098

ADDITIONAL COMMENTS

COST APPROACH TO VALUE (not required by Fannie Mae)

Provide adequate information for the lender/client to replicate the below cost figures and calculations.

Support for the opinion of site value (summary of comparable land sales or other methods for estimating site value) Sales of vacant residential lots in the neighborhood of the subject property range from $30,000 to $32,000 for lots measuring 9,600 square feet.

ESTIMATED [X] REPRODUCTION OR [ ] REPLACEMENT COST NEW	OPINION OF SITE VALUE .... = $		32,000
Source of cost data Marshall Valuation Services	Dwelling 1,950 Sq. Ft. @ $ 58.00 .... = $		113,100
Quality rating from cost service Good Effective date of cost data 10/31/07	Sq. Ft. @ $ .... = $		
Comments on Cost Approach (gross living area calculations, depreciation, etc.)	appliances, patio, porch		2,500
Estimated remaining economic life of 45 years or original	Garage/Carport 430 Sq. Ft. @ $ 11.00 .... = $		4,730
economic life of 60 years. Depreciation estimated at 25%.	Total Estimate of Cost-New .... = $		120,330
	Less	Physical	Functional	External	
	Depreciation 30,083	$0	$0	= $ (	30,083)
	Depreciated Cost of Improvements .... = $		90,247
	"As-is" Value of Site Improvements .... = $		2,200
Estimated Remaining Economic Life (HUD and VA only) -15 Years	INDICATED VALUE BY COST APPROACH .... = $		124,400

INCOME APPROACH TO VALUE (not required by Fannie Mae)

Estimated Monthly Market Rent $ 1,275 X Gross Rent Multiplier 95.00 = $ 121,125 Indicated Value by Income Approach

Summary of Income Approach (including support for market rent and GRM) Comparable homes are availabe for rents ranging from $1,100 to $1,300 per month. Sale prices of these homes indicates GRM of 95.

PROJECT INFORMATION FOR PUDs (if applicable)

Is the developer/builder in control of the Homeowners' Association (HOA)? [ ] Yes [ ] No Unit type(s) [ ] Detached [ ] Attached

Provide the following information for PUDs ONLY if the developer/builder is in control of the HOA and the subject property is an attached dwelling unit.

Legal name of project

Total number of phases	Total number of units	Total number of units sold
Total number of units rented	Total number of units for sale	Data source(s)

Was the project created by the conversion of an existing building(s) into a PUD? [ ] Yes [ ] No If Yes, date of conversion.

Does the project contain any multi-dwelling units? [ ] Yes [ ] No Data source(s)

Are the units, common elements, and recreation facilites complete? [ ] Yes [ ] No If No, describe the status of completion.

Are the common elements leased to or by the Homeowners' Association? [ ] Yes [ ] No If Yes, describe the rental terms and options.

Describe common elements and recreational facilities.

Freddie Mac Form 70 March 2005

Produced using ACI software, 800.234.8727 www.aciweb.com
Page 3 of 6

Fannie Mae Form 1004 March 2005
1004_05 033005

■ In the sales comparison approach to value, appraisers compare the subject property with similar properties that have sold recently. After adjusting for differences in the appropriate elements of comparison, the prices of these "comparables" provide an indication of the value of the subject property.

■ In the cost approach, appraisers estimate value by estimating a property's cost of production. The four steps in the cost approach are

1. estimate the value of the site,

2. estimate the cost to produce the improvements,

3. estimate accrued depreciation and subtract depreciation from production cost, and

4. add site value.

■ In the income approach, appraisers estimate value by forecasting the future income that is expected to be generated by the property, then converting that forecast into a present value. Techniques include gross income multiplier analysis, net income capitalization, and discounted cash-flow analysis.

KEY TERMS

Appraisal Foundation	economic obsolescence	physical deterioration
appraisal process	Financial Institutions	price
Appraisal Qualifications Board	Reform, Recovery, and Enforcement Act	principle of anticipation
		principle of change
Appraisal Standards Board	functional obsolescence	principle of contribution
	gross income multiplier	principle of substitution
assessed value	highest and best use	sales comparison approach
capitalization rate	income approach	
certified general appraiser	insurable value	trainee appraiser
certified residential appraiser	investment value	
cost approach	licensed real property appraiser	
depreciation	market value	

STUDY EXERCISES

1. Provide a justification for the federal government's decision to establish minimum education requirements and standards of practice for appraisers.

2. How many hours of experience are required for each of the categories of appraisers under the AQB criteria?

3. Based on the most widely accepted definition, what is *market value?*

4. Define the following concepts: *value in exchange, value in use, investment value.*

5. Does the concept of market value reflect the perceptions of the typical buyer in a market or a specific buyer? What is the difference?

6. Under what conditions is price equivalent to market value?

7. In what circumstances is it possible for the production cost of a property to exceed its market value?

8. Define the following terms: *assessed value, insurable value.*

9. List and define the four key appraisal principles discussed in the chapter.

10. Outline the steps in the appraisal process.

11. What issues must be considered in step 1 of the appraisal process?

12. Define the concept of highest and best use. Why is this an important step in the appraisal process?

13. Consider a property that is worth $45,000 as a vacant commercial site. The property is improved with a single-family residence. As such, the property is worth $35,000. If it costs $5,000 to demolish the structure, what is the value of the site? What is the value of the structure? What is the highest and best use of this property?

14. List the steps involved in each of the three approaches to value.

15. Why is reconciliation a necessary step in the appraisal process?

16. List the six elements of comparison in the sales comparison approach.

17. Consider a vacant lakefront lot measuring 90 by 120 feet in a residential subdivision. Three similar vacant lots have sold recently. Comparable number one measures 85 by 120 feet and is also located on the lake. It sold for $35,000 one week ago. Comparable number two is also on the lake, and it measures 85 by 120. It sold one year ago for $30,000. Comparable number three sold six months ago for $31,000. It is a hillside lot that offers an exceptional view. The lot measures 80 by 120 feet. Complete the market data grid provided on the next page to estimate the value of the subject property.

Sales Comparison Market Data Grid

| | Subject | Comparables | | |
		#1	#2	#3
Sales price	—	$35,000	$30,000	$31,000
Size in square feet	10,800	10,200	10,200	9,600
Price per square foot	—			
Date of sale	Current	– 1 week	– 1 year	– 6 months
Adjustment for changing market conditions		—		
Adjusted price per square foot	—			
Location	Lake	Lake	Lake	Hillside
Adjustment for location	—			
Adjusted price per square foot	—			
Indicated value of subject property:				

18. Define the following terms:
    a. *accrued depreciation,*
    b. *physical deterioration,*
    c. *functional obsolescence,* and
    d. *economic obsolescence.*

19. Consider the example discussed in Table 9.2. If the actual market value of the land was $190,000, and the cost to reproduce the structures was $610,000, what market value would be indicated by the cost approach?

20. Define the following concepts: *gross income multiplier, capitalization rate.*

21. An investor is considering the purchase of a 11,000-sq. ft. warehouse that is expected (based on comparable properties) to command $8.40 per square foot in annual rents. The two comparable warehouses have recently sold in the market. Comparable 1 measures 12,000 sq. ft. and sold recently for $450,000. Comparable 2 measures 8,600 sq. ft. and sold recently for $322,500. Compute the gross income multiplier that is implied by these transactions and estimate the value of the subject property.

22. Suppose the investor in the previous problem is concerned that the subject property may be more expensive to operate than the comparable properties. Analysis of the operating expenses for each of the properties reveals the following net income estimates:

Subject Property	$52,400
Comparable 1	$65,600
Comparable 2	$47,000

Compute the capitalization rate implied by these transactions to estimate the value of the subject property by the net income capitalization technique.

FURTHER READING

The Appraisal of Real Estate, 12th ed. Chicago: The Appraisal Institute, 2001.

Property and Asset Management

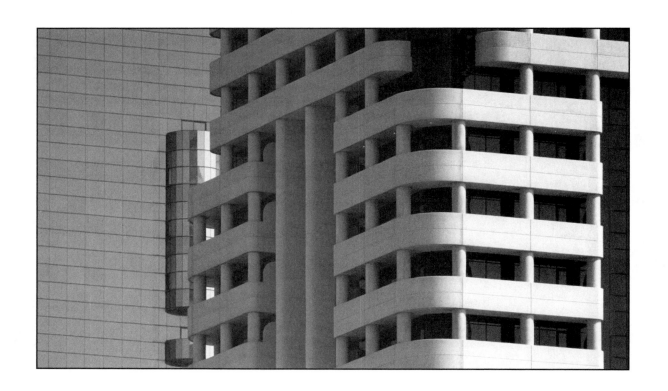

CHAPTER PREVIEW

As discussed throughout this text, the characteristics of real estate resources and transactions imply that specialized knowledge is needed for successful decision making regarding real estate. Just as real estate brokers, salespersons, and appraisers provide a valuable service to buyers and sellers, property managers and asset managers also provide an important service to property owners. This chapter explores several issues related to the business of property management, including

- the role of the property manager in investment real estate;
- the property management agreement and the manager's compensation;
- the functions of the property manager, including
    - administration,
    - marketing and advertising,
    - tenant selection,
    - lease negotiation,
    - move-in inspections,
    - property maintenance,
    - rent collection,
    - move-out inspections, and
    - security deposit returns;
- and the role and function of asset managers.

REAL ESTATE TODAY

CLOSE-UP
Green Acres Shopping Center—A Property Management Success Story

THE ROLE OF THE PROPERTY MANAGER

While many property owners are quite capable of managing their own properties, others may find they have neither the ability nor the desire to cope with the complexities of managing rental properties. Day-to-day operating decisions for most income-producing properties require specialized skills that many real estate investors do not have. Whether the owner chooses to wear the hat of the property manager or to hire a professional, the goal of the property manager is unchanged: to manage properties efficiently with the objective of securing the highest net return for the property owner over the property's useful life. When an owner hires a professional, the **property manager** acts as an agent for the property owner with respect to the leasing, marketing, and overall operation of the property. In many cases, the property manager is also a licensed real estate broker, though some states issue a separate license to property managers.

Consider an investor who purchases a small shopping center. Unless that investor is experienced in shopping center management, a property manager may be required to handle the center's operations. For example, the property manager will be responsible for marketing space in the center to potential tenants, negotiating the lease agreement, collecting rents, addressing tenant concerns, coordinating the property maintenance program, bookkeeping, and paying the property expenses such as utilities, property insurance, property taxes, and employee salaries. Having a trained professional to handle these tasks improves the likelihood that the investment will prove successful.

Property managers may be hired by the property owner as employees or independent contractors, or they may work for a property management firm that has contracted with the property owner to provide management services. Many successful property managers hold designations such as the Institute of Real Estate Management's Certified Property Manager (CPM) or Accredited Resident Manager (ARM). Managers can be awarded these designations only after meeting the education and experience requirements established by the awarding organization. Some states regulate the property management profession by requiring that managers obtain a license from the state after completing educational and experience requirements.

THE MANAGEMENT AGREEMENT

The **management agreement** establishes an agency relationship between the owner of a property and the property manager. To clarify each party's duties and responsibilities, this agreement should be written. The document should specify the powers, obligations, and compensation of the manager, and it should set the term of the agreement.

Powers of the Manager

As the agent of the owner, the property manager has the power to set rents; to execute, extend, and cancel leases; to make settlements with tenants; to collect rents;

to spend money on behalf of the property (a power generally limited to some maximum dollar amount beyond which the owner's approval is necessary); and to hire, fire, and supervise personnel to operate the property.

Just as the manager has the power to act on behalf of the owner, he or she also has the obligation to carry out those functions in a professional manner. Because the manager has a fiduciary relationship with the owner, many management agreements require that the agent and his or her employees be bonded.

Compensation

If the property manager is employed directly by the property owner, the most common form of compensation is a fee based on a percentage of the property's gross income. The fee ranges from approximately 4 percent to 10 percent, depending on such factors as the size of the project, the responsibilities of the manager, and the competitiveness of the local market. If the property manager is an employee of a property management firm, the manager's compensation is usually a fixed salary. The management company contracts with the property owner to provide management services for a fee. In the past, fee schedules often were established by the local real estate associations, but this practice now would be considered a violation of the antitrust laws.

When a property owner hires a property manager, the parties should carefully outline their agreement to avoid confusion and disputes. Because property managers serve as a fiduciary of the property owner, the relationship between owners and managers is an agency relationship. We saw the legal issues involved with agency in Chapter 8 concerning real estate brokerage. Being a fiduciary means that the manager must always work in the best interest of the principal in the agency relationship. Though some states allow oral management agreements, we recommend, as always, that such an important contract be put into written form. Figure 10.1 shows a typical management agreement document from the Florida Association of REALTORS®.

In the sample property management agreement shown on pages 238–40, the manager (broker) is being authorized to identify a tenant for the property, enter into a lease on the landlord's behalf, manage relations with the tenant (including rent collection and eviction, if necessary), and manage the property repair orders. Additional duties, of course, can be added to the manager's responsibilities. The owner in this agreement is agreeing to compensate the property manager as agreed to in the document. Notice that the compensation is broken down into five major categories: securing a tenant, managing tenant relations, managing the property, supervising property repairs, and other duties as agreed. Compensation may be in the form of a stated dollar amount, an hourly rate, a percentage of the transaction (rent) amount, or any combination of the above.

FIGURE 10.1 | Exclusive Property Management Agreement

Exclusive Property Management Agreement
FLORIDA ASSOCIATION OF REALTORS®

This Exclusive Property Management Agreement ("Agreement") is between
Virginia Wells _____ ("Owner") and
Julio Rodriguez _____ ("Broker")
1. **AUTHORITY TO MANAGE PROPERTY: Owner** gives **Broker** the EXCLUSIVE RIGHT TO MANAGE the real and personal property (collectively "Property") described below beginning the ___1st___ day of _____January_____, ___2007___ ending at 11:59 p.m. the ___31st___ day of _____December_____, ___2008___, except that either party may terminate this Agreement by giving ___30___ calendar days written notice to the other party by certified mail. **Owner** certifies and represents that he/she has the legal authority and capacity to lease the Property and improvements.
2. **DESCRIPTION OF PROPERTY:**
    (a) **Real Property:** Street Address: _149 Jarnigan Road, Hialeah Florida 33225_
    _____
    (b) **Legal Description:** ❏ See **Addendum** _____, Legal Description of Real Property.
       ☑ Lot 7, Block G of the Freedom Subdivision, Miami-Dade County, Florida
    (c) **Personal Property,** including appliances: ❏ See **Addendum** _____, Inventory.
       ❏ _____
    _____
    (d) **Type of Property** (single family home, warehouse, etc.): _single-family house_
    (e) **Occupancy:** Property ❏ is ☑ is not currently occupied by a tenant. If occupied, the lease term expires _____.
3. **BROKER OBLIGATIONS AND AUTHORITY: Broker** will use due diligence to manage, operate and lease the Property in accordance with this Agreement.
    (a) **Tenant Matters: Owner** authorizes **Broker** to (check if applicable):
       ☑ Secure a tenant for the Property, see **Addendum** _____, Exclusive Right to Lease Agreement.
       ☑ Enter into a lease/contract to lease on **Owner's** behalf (**Owner** must execute special power of attorney).
       ❏ Complete and sign the lead-based paint/hazards certification on **Owner's** behalf (for Property built before 1978).
       ☑ Manage tenant relations, including negotiating renewals of existing leases; collecting, holding and disbursing rents and other amounts due or to become due to **Owner**; handling tenant requests and negotiations; terminating tenancies and signing and serving appropriate notices on behalf of **Owner**; initiating and prosecuting eviction and damages actions on behalf of **Owner**; and procuring legal counsel when necessary to protect **Owner's** interests and rights in connection with the Property.
    (b) **Property Maintenance: Owner** understands that Florida law requires licensed professionals in the construction trades to perform relevant repairs on rental properties unless the repairs can be made for under $1,000 and are not of a life/safety concern. Additionally, **Owner** understands that when **Broker** acts as the **Owner's** agent Florida law provides the **Broker** may contract for repairs, maintenance, remodeling or improvement of the Property with a certified or registered contractor when labor and materials together do not exceed $5,000. Subject to these limitations set by law, **Owner** authorizes **Broker** to (check if applicable):
       ☑ Maintain and repair interior, exterior and landscaping of Property, including making periodic inspections; purchasing supplies; and supervising alterations, modernization and redecoration of Property. **Broker** will obtain prior approval of **Owner** for any item or service in excess of $_____1,000.00_____, except for monthly or recurring expenses and emergency repairs which, in **Broker's** opinion are necessary to prevent the Property from becoming uninhabitable or damaged, to avoid suspension of services required to be provided by law or lease, or to avoid penalties or fines to be imposed by a governmental entity.
       ☑ Enter into contracts on **Owner's** behalf for utilities, public services, maintenance, repairs and other services as **Broker** deems advisable.
       ☑ Hire, discharge and supervise all labor and employees required for the operation and maintenance of the Property, and to arrange for bonding for employees who will handle cash on behalf of **Owner** and **Broker**.
    (c) **Other Matters: Owner** authorizes **Broker** to (check if applicable):
       ❏ Make payments on **Owner's** behalf, including (check all that apply):
          ❏ mortgage $_____ per _____ to _____
          _____
          ❏ insurance $_____ per _____ to _____
          _____
          ❏ property taxes $_____ per _____ to _____
          _____ and special assessments as made.
          ❏ condominium or homeowners' association dues $_____ per _____ to _____ and assessments as made.

Owner (____) (____) and **Broker/Sales Associate** (____) (____) acknowledge receipt of a copy of this page, which is Page 1 of 3 Pages.

FIGURE 10.1 | Exclusive Property Management Agreement *(continued)*

❑ charges for repairs, materials, equipment, labor and attorneys' fees and costs.
❑ state and local sales and service taxes.
☑ Maintain accurate records of receipts, expenses and accruals to **Owner** in connection with managing the Property. **Broker** will render to **Owner** itemized financial statements (how often) _____
_____
and will promptly remit to **Owner** the balance of receipts less disbursements and accruals for future expenses.
❑ Other Duties: See **Addendum** _____, entitled _____.
4. **OWNER OBLIGATIONS:** In consideration of the obligations of **Broker**, **Owner** agrees:
   (a) To cooperate with **Broker** in carrying out the purpose of this Agreement.
   (b) To provide **Broker** with the following keys to the Property (specify number): unit __2__ / building access __2__ / mailbox _____ / pool _____ / garage door/opener _____ / other _____
   (c) To provide complete and accurate information to **Broker** including disclosing all known facts that materially affect the value of the Property (see **Addendum** _____, entitled _____). If the Property was built in 1977 or earlier, **Owner** will provide **Broker** with all information **Owner** knows about lead-based paint and lead-based paint hazards in the Property and with all available documents pertaining to such paint and hazards, as required by federal law. **Owner** understands that the law requires the provision of this information to **Broker** and to prospective tenants before the tenants become obligated to lease the Property. **Owner** acknowledges that **Broker** will rely on **Owner's** representations regarding the Property when dealing with prospective tenants.
   (d) To carry, at **Owner's** sole expense, public liability, property damage and worker's compensation insurance adequate to protect the interests of **Owner** and **Broker**. Said insurance will name both **Broker** and **Owner** as insured parties, and will specifically cover the indemnity and hold harmless provision of subparagraph 4(h). **Broker** will not be liable for any error of judgment or mistake of law or fact or for any loss caused by **Broker's** negligence, except when the loss is caused by **Broker's** willful misconduct or gross negligence. **Owner** will carry insurance as follows:
      (1) Perils of fire, lightning, wind, hail, explosion, smoke, riot, aircraft, vehicles, vandalism, and burglary on the contents of the Property in the amount of $_____ 500,000.00 .
      (2) "At Risk" protection on the building in the amount of $_____ 500,000.00 , and on rental income in the amount of $_____ 25,000.00 .
      (3) Liability for personal injury and property damage in the amount of $_____ 1,000,000.00 ($500,000 minimum).
   (e) To inform **Broker** before conveying or leasing the Property.
   (f) Upon termination of this Agreement, to assume obligations of all contracts that **Broker** entered into on **Owner's** behalf.
   (g) To pay all amounts billed by **Broker** for authorized expenditures within __30__ calendar days after written notice of the expense is placed in the mail by **Broker**. If **Owner** fails to promptly reimburse **Broker**, **Owner** authorizes **Broker** to reimburse itself out of rents collected, if applicable.
   (h) To indemnify and hold harmless **Broker** and **Broker's** officers, directors, agents and employees from all claims, demands, causes of action, costs and expenses, including reasonable attorneys' fees at all levels, and from liability to any person, to the extent based on (1) **Owner's** misstatement, negligence, action, inaction or failure to perform the obligations of this contract or any lease or agreement with a vendor; (2) the existence of undisclosed material facts about the Property; (3) **Broker's** performance, at **Owner's** request, of any task beyond the scope of services regulated by Chapter 475, F.S., as amended, including **Broker's** referral, recommendation or retention of any vendor; or (4) services or products provided and expenses incurred by any vendor. This subparagraph will survive **Broker's** performance and the transfer of title.
   (i) To reasonably inspect the Property before allowing the tenant to take possession and to make the repairs necessary to transfer a reasonably safe dwelling unit to the tenant.
   (j) To exercise reasonable care to repair dangerous defective conditions upon notice of their existence by the tenant, after the tenant takes possession.
5. **COMPENSATION: Owner** agrees to compensate **Broker** as follows, plus any applicable taxes on **Broker's** services:
   (a) For securing a tenant, see **Addendum** _____, Exclusive Right to Lease Agreement.
   (b) For managing tenant relations, a fee of:
      ❑ _____% of the gross lease value   ❑ __15__% of rent due in each rental period
      ❑ $_____   ❑ other _____
      The above fee is to be paid (when, how) monthly from rent receipt _____
   (c) For managing the Property, a fee of:
      ❑ $_____ to be paid (when, how) _____
      ❑ __5__% of rent due in each rental period to be paid (when, how) monthly from rent receipt _____
      ❑ other _____
   (d) For supervising alterations, modernization, redecorating, or repairs above and beyond normal refurbishment of the Property, a fee of ❑ $_____ per hour OR ❑ _____ to be paid (when, how) _____.
   (e) **Other:** ❑ See **Addendum** _____, Attachment to Property Management Agreement.

Owner (_____) (_____) and **Broker/Sales Associate** (_____) (_____) acknowledge receipt of a copy of this page, which is Page 2 of 3 Pages.

FIGURE 10.1 | Exclusive Property Management Agreement *(continued)*

6. DISPUTE RESOLUTION: This Agreement will be construed under Florida law. All disputes between **Broker** and **Owner** based on this Agreement or its breach will be mediated under the rules of the American Arbitration Association or other mediator agreed upon by the parties. Mediation is a process in which parties attempt to resolve a dispute by submitting it to an impartial mediator who facilitates the resolution of the dispute but who is not empowered to impose a settlement on the parties. The parties will equally divide the mediation fee, if any. In any litigation based on this Agreement, the prevailing party will be entitled to recover reasonable attorneys' fees and costs at all levels, unless the parties agree that disputes will be settled by arbitration as follows:

   Arbitration: By initialing in the space provided, **Owner** (_____) (_____), Listing Associate (_____) and Listing Broker (_____) agree that disputes not resolved by mediation will be settled by neutral binding arbitration in the county in which the Property is located in accordance with the rules of the American Arbitration Association or other arbitrator agreed upon by the parties. The arbitrator may not alter the Contract terms. Each party to any arbitration or litigation (including appeals and interpleaders) will pay its own fees, costs and expenses, including attorneys' fees at all levels, and will equally split the arbitrators' fees and administrative fees of arbitration.

7. ATTORNEYS' FEES: In any action between **Owner** and a tenant in which **Broker** is made a party because of acting as an escrow agent under this Agreement, or if **Broker** interpleads escrowed funds, **Broker** will recover reasonable attorneys' fees and costs, to be paid out of the escrowed funds and charged and awarded as court costs in favor of the prevailing party.

8. MISCELLANEOUS. This Agreement is binding on **Broker's** and **Owner's** heirs, personal representatives, administrators, successors and assigns. Signatures, initials, documents referenced in this Agreement, counterparts and modifications communicated electronically or on paper will be acceptable for all purposes and will be binding.

9. ADDITIONAL CLAUSES: _____

_____

_____

_____

_____

Broker advises Owner to consult an appropriate professional for related legal, tax, property condition, environmental, foreign reporting requirements and other specialized advice.

Date: _____   Owner: _____   Tax ID/SSN: _____

Date: _____   Owner: _____   Tax ID/SSN: _____
Home Telephone: _____   Work Telephone: _____   Facsimile: _____
Address: _____
                                    E-mail: _____

Date: _____   Authorized Licensee or Broker: _____
Home Telephone: _____   Work Telephone: _____   Facsimile: _____
Address: _____
                                    E-mail: _____

> Copy returned to **Owner** on the __1st__ day of _____January_____, 200_7 by: ❑ personal delivery ❑ mail ❑ facsimile

Owner (_____) (_____) and **Broker/Sales Associate** (_____) (_____) acknowledge receipt of a copy of this page, which is Page 3 of 3 Pages.

▮ FUNCTIONS OF A PROPERTY MANAGER

The property manager may be involved in virtually all aspects of the operation of a rental property. Whether the property manager is the owner of the property or an agent of the owner, the functions of a property manager include

- administration,
- marketing and advertising,
- tenant selection,
- lease negotiation,
- move-in inspections,
- property maintenance,
- rent collection,
- move-out inspections, and
- security deposit returns.

We will consider each of these functions in turn.

Administration

Part of a property manager's function is to handle the day-to-day administrative concerns of the property. Administration refers to record keeping, report generation, paying the property's bills, monitoring the employees, and generally overseeing the property's operations. The exact administrative activities of the property manager vary with the type of property and the breadth of the property management agreement.

Marketing and Advertising

Leases are perishable commodities: They expire. Rental space, therefore, must be marketed continually so new tenants can be found to take the place of those who leave. Lease periods range from one day for hotel and motel rooms to several years for commercial property. (Residential apartments may be leased for perhaps six months or a few years.) The general objective of marketing is to maximize income. This usually means to maximize occupancy rates and rental price schedules. The two obviously are in conflict, however, and a balance must be found in order to maximize income. One can ensure a rental unit's occupancy for three years, for example, by granting a three-year lease, but the income derived from the unit may be greater if it is rented to three successive tenants for one year each—if, at the end of each year, market conditions provide a tenant willing and able to pay a higher rent. The property manager must understand the market in which he or she is operating in order to make the right decision.

Choosing the correct marketing strategy is important to the success of any rental project. This is an area where the property manager's experience and expertise can be of tremendous value to the owners. A clear marketing strategy is essential. What types of tenants are sought? Will the project attempt to stress some price advantage, location, design, or other marketing feature? Unless a clear strategy is carried over into tenant selection, rent schedules, and the physical character of the project, it will be impossible for the property to reach its maximum potential.

The purpose of advertising a rental property is to find a tenant, and the type of advertising that is appropriate varies from market segment to market segment. For example, a property manager seeking a tenant for a vacant unit in a trailer park might use very different advertising methods from those secured by a manager seeking a tenant in a Class A office building. The key to "good" advertising is using the advertising tool that will attract the best tenants to that particular property type. Examples of advertising tools include

- signs on the property,
- neighborhood flyers,
- bulletin boards,
- Internet sites,
- listing the property with leasing companies,
- newspaper ads, and
- "open house" days or weekends.

Tenant Selection

If the advertising campaign is effective, potential tenants will respond and express an interest in leasing the property. Property managers must carefully evaluate each tenant to ensure that accepting this tenant is consistent with the overall objective of the manager: maximizing the return to the property owner. Of course, no property manager should discriminate against potential tenants in any way that violates fair housing laws or laws protecting disabled persons, but other tenant characteristics should certainly be considered in the tenant selection process.

In the case of residential property, for example, the 1988 Fair Housing Act prohibits anyone from refusing to rent to someone because of their race, color, national origin or ancestry, religion, sex, familial status (including children younger than 18 living with parents or legal custodians, pregnant women, and people securing custody of children younger than 18), or physical disability. Discrimination charges under this act are investigated by the U.S. Department of Housing and Urban Development. In addition to this federal requirement, many states and some counties and cities impose additional restrictions on how residential landlords can screen potential tenants. Various state- and city-level antidiscrimination laws address educational status, sexual preference, occupation, medical status, and age.

The tenant mix is also important for nonresidential properties. The objective usually is to achieve a variety of tenants that will complement and enhance the image the project is seeking. For example, a coin-operated laundry would not be a desirable tenant in an upscale shopping center where relatively expensive goods were sold in boutiques, but it might be quite complementary to other stores in a small neighborhood center.

To evaluate prospective tenants on valid grounds, property managers should request from each tenant a completed tenant application that collects information regarding the applicant's financial resources (including employment and income status), credit history, and references from prior landlords. In his book *The Landlord's Troubleshooter,* Robert Irwin strongly recommends that more emphasis be placed on the reference (or lack thereof) provided by the applicant's landlord before the current one. The current landlord may be anxious for the tenant to leave and may give a glowing recommendation to speed the tenant's departure. The landlord prior to the present one is likely to give a more honest recommendation.

Lease Negotiation

Even before the advertising and tenant selection processes begin, the property manager should decide the acceptable conditions of the lease agreement. Obviously, the rent amount is a key issue, but there are many other factors that should be resolved in a well-written lease. Examples of issues to be addressed include the following:

- What is the amount of the security deposit?
- What day will rent be due each month?
- What day will the rent be considered late each month?
- What is the nature of the tenancy (tenancy for a stated period, tenancy from period to period, or tenancy at will, as discussed in a previous chapter)?
- Is the lease renewable? At what rent level?
- What items will the tenant be responsible for maintaining?
- What is the permitted use of the property?
- How many people may occupy the property?
- Who is responsible for maintaining insurance on the property?
- Can the tenant sublease the property to others?
- Do local laws require that the landlord make any safety or health disclosures to the tenant (asbestos, lead-based paint, radon, etc.)?
- Are pets allowed? How many? What kind? How big?

As we discussed in Chapter 6 on contracts, being a good negotiator requires being open to new ways of structuring a deal to benefit all parties. Of course, there are some issues that managers must hold firm to or risk violating their overall objective: maximizing return to the property owner.

Move-in Inspections

When a lease agreement is in place, the next step before turning over the keys to the property is for the manager and tenant to perform a move-in inspection. This inspection is critical because it will be the basis for any claim the manager may make against the tenant's security deposit at the end of the lease. Any existing damage to the property should be carefully documented, and both the manager and the tenant should sign the document. With this strategy, the tenant can be held responsible for any additional damages (beyond normal wear and tear) that might be discovered during the lease period or on termination of the agreement. Some property managers use photographs and videotape to document property condition at the start and finish of a lease agreement.

Property Maintenance

Though some leases require that the tenant take care of any property repairs, the manager is usually responsible for ensuring that the repairs are done promptly and correctly. Some larger properties may have a property maintenance staff, while smaller properties will use local repair contractors (plumbers, roofers, electricians, etc.) on an as-needed basis. The manager must shop for the needed professionals carefully to get the best price and performance for the property owner. Failure to address minor repairs may lead to even more costly repairs in the future.

Physical management is divided into two categories: (1) maintenance designed to conserve the property and (2) rehabilitation and renovation designed to make the project more competitive in a changing market.

A program of continuing maintenance is essential to continued economic viability. Owners and managers who fail to give proper attention to landscaping, redecorating, and other items of general maintenance will soon find their project no longer competitive in the marketplace. Even if a project is well maintained, it may be necessary, after a time, to conduct extensive renovations to keep it viable. For instance, an older shopping center may benefit greatly from a new facade and redesigned landscaping and parking areas.

Rent Collection

One of the most arduous tasks facing a property manager is rent collection. Sooner or later, every manager must deal with a tenant who is "late with the rent." If a tenant does not pay the rent on the due date stated in the lease agreement, the manager should take the following actions simultaneously:

- Discuss the issue with the tenant and determine when the rent will be paid
- Begin the eviction process

In most cases, tenants will offer an excuse for why they have not paid their rent as required. A "tough" manager will respond that the rent always must be paid on

Green Acres Shopping Center—A Property Management Success Story

 When Frank Brookins took over the management of the Green Acres Shopping Center, it was in real trouble. Built 20 years earlier in typical neighborhood strip-shopping-center style, two-thirds of its approximately 60,000 square feet were vacant. The center was showing its age, and the main tenant, a grocery store, had moved out, leaving its 16,000-square-foot space empty. The tenant mix was less than desirable. For example, a "game" room had become well known to local police for the drug activity that allegedly occurred there. The center obviously was not generating an acceptable return for its owners, and its marketability was low.

Frank's first task was to improve the appearance of the center. He was helped by a storm and the local government. The storm tore the outdated turquoise facade off the building, and the insurance settlement provided the monies to replace it and repaint the center. The local government bought right-of-way for widening the road in front of the center, and these monies paid for a new sign with a time and temperature display to give the center some identity. The ugliness of the black-top parking lot was broken by the construction of islands filled with shrubs and trees. Although these improvements were relatively inexpensive, they vastly improved the attractiveness of the center.

The next task was to improve the tenant mix and to fill the empty spaces. The key was securing a tenant for the black hole formerly occupied by the supermarket. Mr. Brookins learned that the state's nursing school was unhappy with its current location. Although this would be a somewhat unconventional tenant for a neighborhood shopping center, the 100 students would provide a ready market for restaurants and other potential tenants. The catch was that the state required that the owner provide building improvements equal to about three years' rent, although it would sign only a one-year lease. Even so, the owner took the plunge.

With the nursing school as an anchor, two restaurants and other stores soon followed, one replacing the game room whose lease was not renewed. Currently the center is fully leased, and it is generating three times the gross income it did just five years earlier, with consequent increase in value.

"Successful property management depends on constant attention to detail," explains Mr. Brookins. "Every morning I am there making sure the parking lot is clean, the plants maintained, and that the center is ready for customers. That's what keeps tenants happy, creates value for the owners, and provides good commissions for me."

time and that there are no acceptable excuses for late rent. The manager will explain that if the tenant cannot afford to pay the rent on time, then the tenant cannot afford to occupy these premises. What does a "reasonable" manager do? Exactly the same things. If the tenant is persistent in paying rent late, the manager should either renegotiate the lease agreement to change the date rent is due or should evict the tenant for violating the original lease agreement. Of course, if a tenant refuses to pay the rent, the manager has no choice but to evict the tenant.

Most states have landlord-tenant laws that regulate the eviction process. Managers must follow these laws precisely to avoid denying a tenant "due process." Most states require that landlords give tenants a written notice stating that eviction will begin in a certain number of days (usually three to seven) if the rent is not paid in full before the time expires. After the time period expires, the landlord must file a lawsuit asking a court for possession of the premises from the tenant. If the landlord prevails in the suit, the tenant is evicted. **Eviction** means the tenant's rights of use and possession are terminated by the court, and the tenant will be forcibly removed (if necessary) from the property by a court officer (sheriff). Managers may not use threats or intimidation tactics to encourage tenants to vacate a property. Managers must follow the process for eviction prescribed by state and local laws.

Move-Out Inspections

On termination of the lease agreement, the manager should inspect the premises with the tenant to determine if the tenant is responsible for any damage to the property. As mentioned earlier, having a carefully documented "move-in inspection" makes the "move-out inspection" go more smoothly.

Security Deposit Returns

After the inspection is completed, the manager is legally obligated to return any unused security deposit to the tenant. The **security deposit** is money collected from the tenant prior to granting occupancy that protects the landlord from damages the tenant may cause or from failure to pay rent as agreed. If any of the deposit is retained for damages, most states require that the landlord give the tenant a written explanation of all charges. Most states set a time limit on how long the landlord has after the lease terminates to return any deposits due to the tenant.

Administrative Management

Administrative management—the keeping of records and the preparation of reports—is one of the vital, if not very glamorous, functions of a property manager. Accurate records and accounts are vital to the efficient management of income property. The manager needs such records in order to report receipts and disbursements to the owner, to file tax and other reports required by government agencies, and as a source of data on which to base management decisions and reports.

Rent Schedules

The establishment of rent schedules is a continuing function of marketing that requires extensive knowledge of market conditions. If rents are set too low, the project may achieve full occupancy but still not maximize income. If rents are set too high, vacancies may increase to such an extent that total income will be reduced.

■ THE ROLE AND FUNCTION OF ASSET MANAGERS

The preceding discussion has focused on the role of the property manager when the property is operated as income-producing real estate. Another type of property manager, known as the **asset manager,** is increasingly becoming common in the real estate market.

Almost every business firm must own or lease real estate as a part of its operation, even if the firm's primary line of business is not real estate–related. Often, the company's exposure to the real estate market is quite substantial, and a professional real estate manager is needed to manage the company's real estate assets. In this situation, persons assigned to this task are known as *corporate real estate asset managers.* The tasks of an asset manager are often more complicated than those of a traditional property manager because the asset manager must operate within the framework of meeting the company's overall objective in its primary line of business. Corporate real estate asset managers are real estate specialists who provide a wide range of real estate services for their companies, even though the company may not be "in the real estate business."

The asset manager has four major functions, including (1) management, (2) acquisition, (3) financing, and (4) disposition of corporate real estate assets.

Management

The management function of the real estate asset manager goes beyond facility management to include the strategic decisions involving the real estate needs of the firm. The asset manager can aid operating units in planning, acquiring and financing facilities, often improving the return on the firm's real estate that might otherwise be underutilized.

Acquisition

Few top business executives possess the specialized skills needed in planning for their real estate needs or in site selection. A professional real estate asset manager can assist in targeting space requirements and design features. He or she can also aid the site selection process, considering the complex factors involved with locating various types of facilities. The asset manager also serves as the firm's negotiator in reaching a final agreement when it comes to leasing or buying additional space.

Financing

The first issue in financing a new facility is the question of whether it is in the company's best interest to lease or purchase the property. This decision involves many factors, including the general financial status of the firm and whether the facility required is a special-purpose building. The firm might decide to build the structure needed, then immediately sell it to an investor and simultaneously lease it back. This strategy, known as **sale-and-leaseback,** frees up the firm's capital for use in its primary line of business. If ownership is the chosen alternative, the asset manager assists in deciding what type of financing will best fit the objectives of the firm.

Disposition

Another important part of the corporate asset manager's job is to redeploy or divest property that is no longer needed by the firm. This may occur because of reduced operations and consolidations or because the facilities have become surplus owing to the acquisition of new ones. Disposition may involve the property's sale or lease to another firm, renovation for another use, or exchange for another property.

CHAPTER REVIEW

- Professional property managers are trained to manage properties efficiently with the objective of securing the highest net return for the property owner over the property's useful life. The property manager acts as an agent for the property owner with respect to the leasing, marketing, and overall operation of the property.

- Property management encompasses three functions: (1) administrative management (the collection of rents, the keeping of records, and the preparation of reports), (2) marketing (the leasing of rental space in the manner most profitable for the owner in the long term), and (3) physical management (maintenance designed to conserve the property and rehabilitation and renovation designed to make the project more competitive in a changing market).

- The management agreement identifies the powers and obligations of the property manager and the compensation he or she is to be paid. The agreement also specifies the time period for which the relationship will exist.

- The usual form of compensation for property managers is a fee based on a percentage of gross income from the property.

- Corporate real estate asset managers are real estate specialists who provide a wide range of real estate services for their company, even though the company may not be "in the real estate business." The asset manager has four major functions, including (1) management, (2) acquisition, (3) financing, and (4) disposition of corporate real estate assets.

KEY TERMS

asset manager	management agreement	sale-and-leaseback
eviction	property manager	security deposit

STUDY EXERCISES

1. What is the primary objective of a property manager?

2. What are the general functions of a property manager?

3. What is the legal relationship between the property manager and the owner? What document creates this relationship?

4. What purpose do security deposits serve from the lessor's perspective? What does an asset manager do? How do these tasks differ from the traditional property manager's?

5. Describe the strategy known as *sale-and-leaseback*.

6. If a tenant fails to pay the rent on time, can the manager or landlord disconnect the utilities to encourage the tenant to cough up the dough?

7. Under what circumstances can a private property owner refuse to accept a tenant because of his or her gender, or race, or religion?

8. Why should a property manager carefully document the physical condition of the property at the beginning of a lease?

9. Define the concept of *eviction*.

FURTHER READING

Kyle, Robert C. *Property Management,* 7th ed. Chicago: Dearborn Real Estate Education, 2005.

O'Mara, Martha A. *Strategy and Place: Managing Corporate Real Estate and Facilities for Competitive Advantage.* New York: The Free Press, 1999.

PART THREE

Real Estate Market Analysis

Residential Land Uses

CHAPTER PREVIEW

The process of real estate development is one that requires extensive knowledge and practice of all aspects of real estate: legal, financial, and markets. Because of the special characteristics of real estate improvements—large size, long life, and long gestation period—success in real estate development is in large part determined by the accuracy of forecasts of long-term market potential for the project.

This chapter and Chapter 13 examine the real estate development process. In this chapter, we focus on residential land development, while Chapter 13 deals with various types of commercial development.

Residential development takes various forms: single-family and multifamily dwellings, primary and secondary homes, custom-built and factory-built houses. Whatever form a development is to take, successful developers must study carefully the market for the type of housing they contemplate and analyze carefully the financial feasibility of the proposed project.

The topics to be covered in this chapter are

■ types of residential development, including (1) single-family detached houses, (2) single-family attached houses, (3) multifamily residences, (4) manufactured homes, and (5) second homes;

■ time-sharing;

■ market and feasibility analysis; and

■ financial feasibility analysis.

REAL ESTATE TODAY

CLOSE-UP
Fairview Village

CLOSE-UP
Do "Green" Buildings Sell?

CLOSE-UP
Five Historic New Towns: Savannah, Riverside, Radburn, Levittown, and Reston

CLOSE-UP
Highlands Falls Country Club

CLOSE-UP
Milford Hills Saga

TYPES OF RESIDENTIAL DEVELOPMENT

Although the single-family home on its own lot remains the ideal of most American families, other forms of single-family dwellings are becoming increasingly popular. Multifamily residences, too, take various forms. The five principal types of residential development are

1. single-family detached houses,
2. single-family attached houses,
3. multifamily residences,
4. manufactured homes, and
5. second homes.

Single-Family Detached Houses

The single-family house separated from any adjoining house with at least some open land on all four sides remains the dwelling type most sought after by American families. Many will accept a very basic house on a very small lot simply to attain this goal. The reason often given is that the detached house provides more privacy than an attached dwelling, though this is not always the case, especially if lots are small. Nevertheless, because of this perception, detached houses often have the best resale value.

Single-Family Attached Houses

The attached row house is a form of housing that goes back to colonial times. This type of dwelling, on its own fee simple lot but sharing common walls with its neighbors, was quite common in cities of the East and in San Francisco.

The first association of homeowners who owned streets and parkland in common was founded in Boston in 1826. Louisburg Square, which contains 18 row houses and a common park on a 2.3-acre site on Beacon Hill, remains a very desirable residential area even today.

The rise of the suburbs shortly after the turn of the 20th century led to the domination of the detached house. The suburban form of the row house, the town house, was a rarity until the 1960s; the overwhelming majority of such dwellings have been built since 1970. For projects that are owner-occupied, almost all have used the condominium form of ownership, with a community association managing common areas.

The single-family attached dwelling has several advantages over the detached project. Clustering requires less road frontage and shorter utility lines, resulting in lower development costs per unit. The higher density of houses also permits lower land costs, further reducing cost per unit. This type of development also can result in less adverse ecological impact, with more of the site being left in its natural state and with more useful open space. A frequent complaint in conventional subdivisions is "I have to spend my weekends cutting all that grass, but there's no place for the kids to play." In a well-designed single-family attached project, yard maintenance by the homeowner is reduced greatly or eliminated, and there is a place for the children to play.

Single-family attached housing can be of several types, including the town house, the plex, and the patio house.

Town Houses

The **town house** is similar to the old row house. Each unit has its own front door that opens to the outdoors, but it shares one or both side walls with adjacent houses. Although the town house has no side yards, it may have front and rear yards. Town houses may front on the street or may be built in a series of five to ten units fronting on a common area.

Plexes

The **plex** shares the characteristics of the town house and the single-family detached house. Each building in a plex contains two or more units, each with its own outside entrance. A duplex is for two families; a triplex, for three families; a quadruplex, for four families; and so on.

Patio or Zero-Lot-Line Houses

The **patio house,** or zero-lot-line house, is very similar to the detached house except that construction is from lot line to lot line, with an outdoor living area in an interior garden court.

The garden court is normally enclosed by the house or by the house and walls. Although small compared to the yard of the usual single-family detached house, the secluded area provides a great deal of privacy. The houses are usually one story, are often L-shaped, and may have one small side yard to provide passage to the rear court area.

Multifamily Residences

Although the single-family home is still preferred by most families, it is too expensive for an increasing portion of the population. Multifamily housing may be the best alternative for such families, as well as for young couples who lack the down payments necessary to purchase their own homes, "empty nesters" who no longer need or desire as large a home as they did when their children lived with them, and single-person households. Where land prices are extremely high, rental or owner-occupied apartments may be the only feasible type of new housing available.

Fairview Village

While the debate over "smart growth" and "new urbanism" goes on, a few such developments have demonstrated there is a definite market for this type of environment. Fairview Village is perhaps the most outstanding example.

Rick Holt is an experienced developer who had a vision and a mission—to demonstrate there was a profitable market for an "urban village" rather than a typical suburban subdivision. He bought 96 acres of land previously zoned industrial located in Fairview, a small community located on the eastern edge of the Portland, Oregon, metropolitan area. The city had no "center." For example, the city hall was located in an old Grange Hall—so Holt worked with the city to incorporate a new city hall, branch library, post office, community church, pedestrian-oriented shopping area, and elementary school into the plan for his village. It also included an office building, day care center, and gym, as well as 600 residential units. The residences encompass single-family detached homes ranging from $150,000 to $300,000, attached town homes, duplexes, and apartments, many above the retail shops, and even above the library. Although the residential density is much higher than in a traditional subdivision, the inclusion of miniparks and walking trails creates a feeling of ample open space and a sense of community. The trails also make it feasible to walk to shopping and other community activities.

Fairview Village has been a success in every way. It has received wide acclaim for its innovative design, and it has also been a financial success for its developers.

Ownership Alternatives: Condominiums and Cooperatives

As noted in Chapter 2, many potential homeowners look to condominiums and cooperatives as ownership alternatives. To review these concepts very briefly, the owner of a condominium (condo) holds title in fee simple to the particular unit occupied and shares ownership in common areas such as recreational facilities, lobbies, and parking lots. The owner of a cooperative (co-op) owns stock in a corporation that actually holds title to the property, but the individual has the right to live in a particular apartment. The condominium, which in the United States is a relatively recent development, is far more common than the older cooperative form; most cooperatives are located in New York City. Almost all condos and co-ops are attached or multifamily units.

Condominiums and cooperatives offer several economic advantages to the buyer when contrasted with renting. Like other homeowners, the owner of a condo or co-op can deduct property taxes and mortgage interest from taxable income for income tax purposes. Second, and perhaps of even greater importance, condominium

Do "Green" Buildings Sell?

 Increasing environmental awareness in recent years combined with greatly increased energy costs has led to a movement towards "green" buildings that use less energy and are more environmentally sound. This is an admirable goal, but will it sell in the marketplace?

The Solaire, a 27-story glass-and-brick luxury apartment building at Battery Park City in New York City's financial district, has been recognized for its many "green" features. It was designed to consume 35 percent less energy, reduce peak demand for electricity 65 percent, and require 50 percent less potable water than conventional residential high-rise buildings. A storm water catchment system provides irrigation to both a rooftop garden and a green roof. An on-site black water treatment and reuse system supplies the cooling tower and the building's toilets with water. The building also incorporates an advanced heating and air-conditioning system fueled by natural gas and free of ozone-depleting refrigerants. Multi-level humidification and ventilation systems supply filtered fresh air to each residential unit.

While these features are quite impressive, how would they fare in the marketplace? Quite well, as it turned out. The leasing agents quickly found that the green elements were extremely attractive to prospective renters, even surpassing the building's great location and luxury features. Prospective tenants liked the reduced utilities costs and the healthier interior air. Its 293 units were leased within five months of its opening in 2003 at a 10 percent premium in rents, and rents have risen 15 percent since the building's opening.

or cooperative ownership serves as a hedge against potential inflation, enabling the owner to accumulate an equity position. Conversely, of course, it also exposes the owner to potential declines in housing prices.

The demand for condos and co-ops has increased during the past several decades, primarily in response to demographic trends and rapidly rising home prices. Many first-time buyers were forced out of the single-family detached market, but they still could afford a condominium or cooperative. The market was also helped by the growth in the number of households, by the smaller size of families and the increase in single-member households, by growing preference for in-town living, and by increasing commuting costs.

Besides these demographic trends, economic factors affecting the rental market have also helped increase the popularity of condos and co-ops. Owners of rental property have been caught in a serious cost squeeze. Operating costs in many cities have increased far more rapidly than rents, and in cities with rent controls, the squeeze has been much worse. This has led to a large number of conversions from rental units to condominiums and cooperatives. The large-scale trend began in Chicago, then spread rapidly across the country.

Manufactured Homes

A **manufactured home,** or *mobile home,* is a dwelling that is manufactured in a factory and then moved to a particular site. The traditional image of mobile homes has been that of cheap, tacky, and high-density housing in sleazy "shantytown" trailer parks. Unfortunately, in the past, much of this reputation was richly deserved. In contrast to the resale value of conventional site-built houses, which has generally appreciated, the value of a mobile home generally fell each year. This caused many lenders to treat mobile homes as personal property, much like automobiles, and to provide only relatively short-term, high-interest installment loans. In many areas, it was impossible to obtain a single mortgage that would cover the purchase of both a mobile home and its site. Opposition to mobile-home developments led many communities either to zone them out completely or to limit them to generally undesirable or rural areas.

The image is changing, however, because the design and construction of manufactured homes has been greatly improved. With the introduction of new materials and designs, the "oversized aluminum shoebox" has been replaced by a structure much closer to a conventional house in appearance. Part of this process has been the trend toward wider units and the double-wide and triple-wide units that are assembled on site into 24-foot-wide to 36-foot-wide homes. Construction quality also has improved tremendously with the introduction of required national construction standards.

The economies of scale and the controlled construction environment give manufactured homes a definite price advantage over conventional site-built homes. Although direct comparisons are difficult because conventional homes usually contain more luxury features, U.S. Department of Commerce data show that the average price of a multisection manufactured home is about $40 per square foot, compared to over $90 for the average site-built home.

These factors, plus the trend toward owner-occupied manufactured-home subdivisions instead of rental parks, have led lenders to liberalize financing and make it more comparable to that for conventional homes. In the past, mobile homes were considered personal property and were financed with 10-year to 15-year consumer installment loans that generally carried an interest rate approximately 2 percentage points above conventional mortgage rates. Today, however, owners of manufactured homes located permanently on their lots can obtain 30-year, FHA-insured mortgages.

Second Homes

By their very nature, second homes are very different from primary homes, and second-home markets are quite different from primary-home markets. The principal

Five Historic New Towns:
Savannah, Riverside, Radburn, Levittown, and Reston

 Although we tend to think of large-scale planned developments and "new towns" as being relatively recent developments, they are not. This Close-Up examines five historic examples: Savannah, Georgia, a new town from the colonial era; Riverside, Illinois, a railroad suburb begun in the 1870s; Radburn, New Jersey, a 1920s "city for the motor age"; Levittown, New York, which introduced mass home building; and Reston, Virginia, one of the most successful of recent years.

Savannah, Georgia

Quite a few cities in this country were planned communities, including New Haven, Philadelphia, Detroit, Williamsburg, Mobile, New Orleans, and, of course, Washington, D.C. One of the most innovative was Savannah, Georgia, planned in 1730s by James Oglethorpe. His basic unit was a ward, consisting of 48 lots grouped around public squares. For over 100 years the city expanded by adding such cellular units until there were 26 squares.

Savannah became an economic backwater when the cotton economy collapsed, protecting most of the old plan from redevelopment until its historic and economic potential was realized. Two of the squares were destroyed to make way for a road, and one was covered over by a hideous parking garage. The remainder, with their homes restored, make Savannah one of the unique cities of the United States.

Riverside, Illinois

Adoption of the rectangular survey system for the western lands stretched the grid system across the country, and almost all new communities were laid out in this fashion. A notable exception was Chicago's most famous suburb, Riverside. Riverside was designed in 1869 by the nation's leading landscape architect, Fredrick Law Olmsted, who rejected the conventional grid pattern and developed a curvilinear street system. Open parkland straddled the Des Plaines River, and a park surrounding the railroad station provided a focus for the town government and business activities. The railroad made commuting the ten miles to Chicago feasible and allowed the town to develop as a bedroom community.

Over 130 years after it was first developed, Riverside is still an outstanding town that contains the best features of "modern" planning. It also remains an economically viable community in which property values bring a premium.

Radburn, New Jersey

Radburn, New Jersey, was designed as a "city for the motor age." It was originally conceived as a town for 25,000 residents located on 1,300 acres in then-rural Bergen County. Ten miles from mid-Manhattan, Radburn was designed as a series of "superblocks." Traffic was routed around these neighborhoods, and houses were located on cul-de-sacs, oriented toward interior parks of four to six acres. A system of pedestrian walkways and underpasses achieved complete separation of vehicular and pedestrian traffic.

The Great Depression, which hit only five months after the first houses were completed in May 1929, aborted Radburn's growth, and only 150 acres, containing two superblocks, were developed according to the original plan. Even so, Radburn is a viable community today and has served

(continued)

Five Historic New Towns:
Savannah, Riverside, Radburn, Levittown, and Reston

as a planning example for developments in many countries, particularly in recent years.

Levittown, New York

Following World War II, there was tremendous pent-up demand for housing, particularly among the returning veterans. William Levitt, who was already an experience mass builder of war-time housing, bought 1,000 acres of potato farms on Long Island and set out to build a new town, Levittown.

Levitt's homes won no awards for architectural excellence. They were 750 square foot, two-bedroom Cape Cods on 60 by 100 foot lots. The houses were built in assembly line fashion, with specialized crews for each step of the process. For example, one man's sole job was to bolt washing machines to the floor. Using these techniques, Levitt was able to turn out 30 to 40 houses a day, and sell them for only $7,990. Even in 1951, this was a very attractive price, and he ended up selling 17,400 homes in Levittown.

Many predicted that Levittown would turn into instant slum, but the town has since surprised many of its critics. The modest standardized houses have been modified over the years to reduce the sameness, and the saplings that were set out fifty years ago are now mature large trees. The homes, which sold for about $8,000, now sell for an average of near $155,000, some reaching more than $200,000.

Reston, Virginia

Reston was the first of the modern new towns in the United States and owed much of its inspiration to Radburn. The town was begun in the early 1960s by Robert E. Simon, who used his initials in naming the town. Simon purchased 6,750 acres of Virginia countryside near Washington, D.C., and planned a complete city for approximately 70,000 residents.

Reston was officially dedicated in May, 1966, just in time to have its sales severely affected by the tight-money conditions accompanying the Vietnam War buildup. Land development requires relatively large up-front investment before sales generate adequate cash flow. In a large undertaking such as Reston the up-front costs were massive, and the sales slowdown forced Simon to sell Reston to Gulf Oil Company, which already had made an investment in Reston and had the financial resources to sustain a long-term development.

Reston has met Simon's original vision and has been a financial success, even if not for him. The town now has a population of about 60,000. Six of the village centers have been completed, along with the town center which serves as Reston's "downtown." Reston straddles the Dulles Technology Corridor and is the home of three Fortune 500 companies, the National Wildlife Association, a regional governmental center, and the U.S. Geological Survey.

reason for owning a second home is the desire to use it for leisure-time enjoyment, and certain amenities are ordinarily the main factors in its location: beaches, mountains, golf courses, tennis courts, ski lifts, and so on.

Most second-home owners occupy their dwellings for only a small portion of the year, often because of the seasonal nature of many resorts but also because the owners are unable to get away from their jobs or other responsibilities for extended periods. Hence, many units are bought at least partially for their investment potential and rented for much of the year. As landlords, owners enjoy various tax benefits, including depreciation allowances and deduction of maintenance costs, but changes in tax laws and regulations have greatly reduced potential tax advantages in recent years. For example, there are limits on the time the owner can occupy the dwelling and still claim it as rental property.

Because ownership of a second home is so expensive, many buyers in recent years have turned to resort **time-sharing,** a concept discussed in Chapter 2. Under time-sharing, a single dwelling is sold to a number of buyers, each of whom receives exclusive ownership of the dwelling for a specified time period each year. Like other forms of fee simple ownership, this ownership interest can be willed, leased, or sold.

The time-sharing concept of vacation property first appeared in the 1960s, and today there are about 1,600 timeshare resorts in the United States. Over three million consumers own time-share units.

MARKET AND FEASIBILITY ANALYSIS

We have covered in previous chapters some of the factors that determine the demand for housing at the national, regional, and neighborhood levels. All such factors must be considered when analyzing the market for a particular project. Both developers and lenders need to know what the market will be for a project in order to determine its feasibility. Essentially, they must determine what market conditions have been in the recent past and which factors that would affect the market for the project are likely to change in the near future. The steps in such a market analysis are

1. delineation of the market area;
2. analysis of recent economic trends in the local market area;
3. determination of possible changes in demand factors, such as employment, disposable income, population, household characteristics, and the **absorption rate** (the number of units that are being absorbed by the market); and
4. analysis of the potential supply, including other possible competing projects.

CLOSE-UP

Highlands Falls Country Club

It was not an outstanding golf club community or real estate development. In fact, the Highlands Falls Country Club was a failure. Located near the western North Carolina mountain resort town of Highlands, the club was first opened as the nine-hole Skylake golf course in the 1960s. It was a shoestring operation, with golfers depositing their greens fees in an honor box, where the money was picked up at the end of the day. Several developers worked on the project, the last adding nine more holes and a clubhouse. By 1980, there were about 85 homes, but the sales were slow and the project's mortgage was foreclosed.

The mortgage on the Highlands Falls Country Club was held by two real estate investment trusts. They had to decide whether the development could be made economically viable.

Not only was Highlands Falls Country Club a failed project with a poor reputation, it also came with about 85 very disgruntled and suspicious existing homeowners. Thus, the new development firm was faced with the daunting task of not only developing a high-quality golf club that could yield a development profit but also handling a near revolt of existing club members. It was no small task.

Noted golf architect Joe Lee completely redesigned the golf course, building several new holes and combining others to create longer ones, and the entire course was refurbished. While this made Highlands Falls a much better and more challenging golf course, it also made some of the old club members unhappy because they preferred the shorter course. A tennis and swim center was added, and extensive additions and renovations were made to the clubhouse.

The developer worked very hard to upgrade the image of Highlands Falls, but this was a slow, uphill process. Both the members and the community had seen too much mediocre development and failure in the past. Rumors persisted that the club would soon be foreclosed again. Gradually, however, the sweeping physical facility improvements, increasing lot and home sales, and small but important touches such as extensive landscaping and masses of flowers turned the country club's image around.

Today, Highlands Falls Country Club has a deserved reputation as one of the premier clubs in an area of very exclusive golf courses. Lots, which in 1980 ranged in price from $10,000 to $15,000, now range from $80,000 to $300,000, with one exceptional view lot selling for $650,000. There are now more than 375 homes in the development, with only a few lots available. Club memberships, which in 1984 sold for only $1,100, now sell for $45,000. Home prices range from about $340,000 for some of the older homes to $2 million for some of the newer ones.

The story of the Highlands Falls Country Club shows that even a failed development can be turned into an outstanding and profitable one if the basic elements for success are present and the project is managed by a knowledgeable developer with sufficient resources and a sincere desire to create a quality development.

Delineation of the Market Area

To begin with, the project's *market area*—that is, the extent of the housing submarket in which it will compete—must be described. The market area is determined largely by employment opportunities and commuting ranges. In smaller communities, of course, all of the local employers will be within the market area, but local workers also may commute to jobs in nearby communities.

In larger urban areas, the analyst must determine the extent of employment available within relevant commuting ranges. Public transportation facilities can extend the commuting range and expand the market area.

Analysis of Recent Trends

What has been the demand for housing within the market area during the past few years, and what economic factors lie behind recent trends? What are the vacancy rates for local rental housing and the absorption rates for new owner-occupied units? Such data usually are available and are essential for an analysis of the market potential of a new project.

Determination of Future Demand

After past and present housing market conditions have been determined, the most important part of the analysis remains—the estimation of future demand. How much unfulfilled demand remains in the market? What changes in the economic base or in national or regional economic conditions will affect demand in the local area? Are new transportation facilities or other public facilities being completed that will influence demand? The developer must analyze such factors carefully to make a reasonably accurate estimation of potential demand for the project.

Of course, not even the most keen and careful analyst can always accurately prophesy the future. Indeed, one would need almost supernatural powers to totally forecast the impact on real estate of the interactions of international political and economic intrigues, tax changes coming from Congress or state and local governments, the expansion or contraction plans of large corporations, and the complexity of business locational decisions.

Analysis of Future Supply

Many developers correctly analyze demand factors but then court disaster by ignoring competitive projects. One of the primary characteristics of real estate improvements is their long gestation period, and developers must estimate both demand and supply conditions during that period.

Suppose, for example, there is a potential demand for 500 new apartment units in a community within the next two years. If three developers respond to this potential demand by constructing three 500-unit complexes, it is impossible that each will be successful in the short run unless the market expands more than anticipated. At best,

Milford Hills Saga

 The Milford Hills saga is an interesting tale, and one that incorporates many of the varied aspects of real estate development we have studied in this book. (This example is based on a true case.)

When Charles and Becky Barr moved to Lower Nowhere they wanted privacy and place for their dog Puddy to run. They were able to achieve these objectives by buying 56 acres on the edge of town and building their home in the middle of it. After enjoying the land for 35 years, however, they wanted to retire, sell the land, and spend their retirement years elsewhere.

Charles and Becky's economic objective, of course, was to get the maximum value for their house and land. This was a much more complex problem than merely selling a house in a subdivision. It involved determining the highest and best use of the property, possibly securing a zoning change to enable them to sell the property for this use, and then finding a developer-buyer.

Although the area was undeveloped when the Barrs built their house, in the intervening years their land had become an island of greenspace surrounded by residential subdivisions, a school, and a church. As might be expected, the residents of these new subdivisions had come to enjoy the Barrs' open space and didn't want to see it developed, particularly at a higher density than the two units per acre permitted by the Rowan County zoning ordinance.

The Land Planning Process
Much of the Barr land was heavily wooded, with steep slopes and two small rocky-bottom streams.

Not only did these features create natural beauty for the property, they also made the land unfeasible for a half-acre, "cookie-cutter" subdivision. In fact, Mr. Barr's preliminary investigations convinced him that it would not be feasible to develop more than 75 conventional lots on the property. Both good development practices and practical economics called for a conservation subdivision on the property. In other words, the homes would be clustered on relatively small lots, with large areas left in permanent open space.

Because Rowan County did not have provisions for conservation subdivisions in its zoning code, it was necessary for the Barrs to apply for a Planned Development. Because this type of zoning required specific plans, the Barrs hired land planner Ron Meislar. After going through several iterations, he and the Barrs agreed on a plan that clustered 125 homes within a 22.5 acre "building envelope." The remainder of the land, 34 acres, approximately 60 percent of the total land, would be left in permanent open space. Mr. Barr named the development after the area where he grew up, Milford Hills.

Dealing with the Neighborhoods
The Barrs knew their land would be much more valuable if they could secure a zoning change to permit their proposed development. They were also realistic enough to know that the plan had little chance of approval without neighborhood support. Accordingly, they held a number of meetings over a 12-month period with small groups of neighborhood leaders to explain details of the plan and to gain their input.

(continued)

Milford Hills Saga

The Conservation Easement

At one of the meetings the view was expressed that although the open space was desirable, there was no guarantee it would not be disturbed and possibly developed in the future. When Mr. Barr proposed putting a large portion of the open space in a conservation easement, this gained immediate neighborhood support. Thus, working with the Yadkin River Land Trust, the Barrs agreed to place 24 acres in a conservation easement. The terms of the easement limited use of this area to walking trails and prohibited cutting any of its large hardwood trees. The agreement did permit an easement for a sewer line, as this was the only way to tie in with the county's sewerage system.

The conservation easement gave the adjoining homeowners significant benefits, providing them with open space area they knew would remain undisturbed forever. The conservation easement also provided significant benefits for the Barrs. Not only did it gain vital neighborhood support for their rezoning effort, it improved the marketability of the property and also provided tax benefits.

The Rezoning Process

After two years of formulating the land plan and gaining neighborhood support, and spending more than $20,000 on the planning effort, the Barrs applied to Rowan County for a Planned Development. The planning staff suggested a few changes, and these were incorporated into the plan. They then recommended to the Planning Commission that the plan be approved. At the public meeting, a number of nearby neighbors spoke in favor of the plan, expressing the view that although they would naturally prefer the land to remain undeveloped,

they felt the conservation subdivision was a "best-case" alternative. Only two people spoke in opposition. The Planning Commission praised the plan and voted unanimously to recommend approval by the County Commission.

At this point the Barrs were introduced to the ugly side of land planning politics. One of the county commissioners who was aspiring to be elected mayor decided to oppose the plan for perceived political advantage. He organized a public meeting to try to organize neighborhood opposition. Happily for the Barrs, however, this effort backfired and helped solidify support from residents who felt the plan was as good as they were likely to get and who wanted to secure the benefits of the proposed conservation easement. They worked to inform other residents, and Mr. Barr hand-delivered a copy of the plan to 185 nearby neighbors so they would know exactly what was being proposed.

These efforts bore fruit. At the public hearing, another commissioner who was opposed to any new development joined in trying to defeat the plan. Despite this, in a close vote the County Commission voted to approve it.

Selling the Land

With approval of the Planned Development zoning, the Barrs were no longer simply selling a house and 56 acres. Now they were selling 56 acres and the right to develop a 125-unit conservation subdivision. It was no longer necessary for a potential developer to spend a year or more in the uncertain process of trying to secure a rezoning while interest and other costs kept accumulating.

(continued)

Milford Hills Saga

The Barrs signed a six-month exclusive-listing agreement with broker Frank Glover to sell the property for $900,000. This worked out at $5,600 per unit plus $200,000 for the existing house. The house could be used as a clubhouse for the development, or sold as a residence.

Mr. Glover prepared a comprehensive sales package that included the developmental plan, a copy of a letter from the county engineer stating that water and sewer capacity was adequate to serve the development, and other supporting documents. He sent this package to commercial brokers in the area, as well as potential developers. He also placed an advertisement in an area business magazine to try to attract buyers from outside the immediate Lower Nowhere locale.

The old adage that "real estate is easy to buy but hard to sell" proved true for the Milford Hills project. Unlike stocks, bonds, or other financial instruments, real estate markets can grind very slowly, particularly for complex properties. Ten months after placing the property on the market the Barrs had received several serious expressions of interest, but nothing that resulted in a sales contract. They did receive three "letters of intent," but quickly learned these meant little or nothing. The potential buyer was merely expressing interest, but this expression of interest was not binding in any way.

Then a local developer, Mr. Mayer, presented a sales contract to Mr. Glover. He offered $562,500, or $4,500 per unit for the land but did not want to buy the house. The Barrs would be forced to sell this separately. Mr. Mayer also wanted five months to close on the property, and his contract provided him the opportunity to withdraw if he did not secure what he considered to be adequate financing. The Barrs rejected this offer.

Mr. Tom White, a developer in a nearby area, was seeking to find suitable land for a residential development in Rowan County. His broker earlier had received a sales package on the Milford Hills development from Mr. Glover. He presented this to Mr. White, and he felt Milford Hills might be what he was looking for.

After conducting market and financial feasibility studies, Mr. White offered the Barrs $800,000 for the property, with a 120-day closing date. This offer was contingent on the Barrs's securing an updated letter from Rowan County verifying that adequate water and sewer capacity was available for the development and providing a Phase 1 Environmental report certifying there were no environmentally hazardous materials on the property. It was also contingent upon Mr. White's being able to secure a development loan.

The Barrs countered with a price of $850,000 and a deposit of $15,000 earnest money that would go to them in the event that Mr. White did not close on the property for any reason other than the contingency factors. Mr. White came back with a revised offer of $825,000, and the Barrs accepted. The closing took place in late December in the office of attorney Bill Berryfield.

Market Analysis

To determine the feasibility of the Milford Hills project, and before he made his offer to the Barrs, Mr. White conducted a market analysis study. Although Milford Hills would be the first conservation subdivision in the Lower Nowhere area, he determined there was a strong market for single-family houses

(continued)

REAL ESTATE TODAY

CASE STUDY

Milford Hills Saga

in the $160,000–$185,000 range. From this study he felt it would be feasible to sell 40 homes a year at an average price of $175,000. From this sales price he felt that the value of each lot was $30,000.

Developmental Analysis

Mr. White then had his engineer, Bevan Barringer, make an estimate of the expenditures that would

be necessary to develop the Milford Hills project. (See Table 11.1.) Assuming that land and house could be purchased for $825,000, the following table shows that total developmental expenses would be $2,287,050, compared to an assumed lot sales yield of $3,750,000. In addition, there would be interest expense on the development loan.

vacancy rates in the local market probably will rise to a high level, and the general profitability of all complexes will be reduced, or perhaps will be nonexistent, resulting in foreclosure and failure.

The second step in the analysis—determining what lies behind recent trends—sometimes is not given enough emphasis, much to the subsequent regret of the developer. Suppose that housing markets in a particular community have been very tight during the past five years; that is, there has been excess demand. Without proper analysis, this might indicate a continuing strong demand for housing in the next few years.

On more thorough investigation, however, the developer might determine that the tight market conditions resulted from an influx of workers to a major new

TABLE 11.1 | Milford Hills Project—Projected Development Expenses

Purchase of Land and House	$825,000
Clearing, Grubbing, Grading, and Drainage	368,550
Curb, Gutter, and Paving	516,900
Water Mains and Sanitary Sewer	357,500
Landscaping, Entrance Signs, and Nature Trail	86,100
Engineering, Permits, and Survey	133,000
Total	$2,287,050

TABLE 11.2 | Milford Hills Development—Pro Forma Cash Flow Statement

	Quarter					
	1	2	3	4	5	6
Sale of Lots			$300,000	$300,000	$300,000	$300,000
Use of Funds:						
Land and House	$825,000					
Clearing, Grading, etc.		$275,000				93,880
Curb, Gutter, Paving		350,000				166,900
Water and Sanitary Sewer		268,125				89,375
Landscaping, Entrance			50,000			36,100
Engineering, Surveying	65,000	68,000				
Interest Expense		22,250	46,841	41,762	35,306	28,688
Net Cash Flow	(890,000)	(983,625)	203,159	258,238	264,694	(114,913)
Cumulative Cash Flow	(890,000)	(1,873,625)	(1,670,466)	(1,412,228)	(1,147,534)	(1,262,447)

	Quarter					
	7	8	9	10	11	12
Sale of Lots	$300,000	$450,000	$450,000	$450,000	$450,000	$450,000
Use of Funds:						
Land and House						
Clearing, Grading, etc.						
Curb, Gutter, Paving						
Water and Sanitary Sewer						
Landscaping, Entrance						
Engineering, Surveying						
Interest Expense	31,561	24,850	14,221	3,327		
Net Cash Flow	268,439	425,150	435,779	446,673	450,000	450,000
Cumulative Cash Flow	(994,008)	(569,858)	(133,079)	313,594	763,594	1,213,594

manufacturing plant, which now operates at its designed level. Unless growth occurs in either the plant or some other part of the community's economic base, the absorption rate—and, therefore, absolute demand for new housing—will decline.

The analyst also must carefully evaluate potential demand in the particular submarket at which the project is aimed. For example, it may be that the new plant mentioned above caused a significant expansion in demand for rental housing. The future demand for this segment of the market may decline, even though demand in other segments may expand, if the new workers move out of the rental units to owner-occupied houses.

FINANCIAL FEASIBILITY ANALYSIS

In addition to a market analysis, the developer should conduct a financial feasibility analysis of the proposed project. Such an analysis may be quite sophisticated in the case of a large and complicated development or relatively simple for a small one. In either case, the purpose is to determine—on paper, at least—the probable success of the project.

Finally, bank financing, which is usually essential, also helps to reduce the developer's risk because a large amount of the developer's own or company funds are not involved. On the other hand, any delays can be quite expensive when the interest-rate meter is running. For example, if the site improvements cannot be constructed as rapidly as the developer anticipates or if the houses do not sell as rapidly as expected, the result could be a greatly reduced profit or even default on the loan.

THE IMPORTANCE OF MARKET ANALYSIS

If the three most important factors in real estate are "location, location, and location," it should be clear to the readers of this book that the three most important factors in real estate development are "the market, the market, and the market." Real estate developers who forget this lesson usually fail; those who carefully and correctly analyze the market usually succeed.

CHAPTER REVIEW

- The five principal types of residential development are (1) single-family detached houses, (2) single-family attached houses, (3) multifamily residences, (4) manufactured homes, and (5) second homes.
- The single-family detached home has dominated the housing markets for the past 50 years and remains the most sought after type of dwelling. Escalating land costs and growing environmental and energy concerns have made this type of housing less attractive than it once was, however.

- Types of attached housing include (1) the town house, (2) the plex, and (3) the patio house.

- Condominium and cooperative ownership of multifamily and attached housing is increasing because of the economic benefits of such ownership, favorable demographic trends, and the declining profitability of rental housing.

- Manufactured or mobile homes gradually are moving toward greater acceptance by consumers, financial institutions, and communities. As a result of improvements in design and quality, the availability of financing, and the rising cost of conventional housing, manufactured homes probably will capture an increasing share of the single-family market.

- Amenities are the primary factors leading to the purchase of a second home. Because most buyers cannot occupy their units for much of the year, many units are purchased for their investment potential.

- Time-sharing enables buyers to purchase the use of a second home for a specific time period each year. Buyers thus protect a large portion of their future vacation costs from inflation and benefit from any appreciation in the value of their interest.

- The steps in analyzing the market for a residential project are (1) delineation of the market area, (2) analysis of recent trends in the local market area, (3) determination of possible changes in the demand factor of the project, and (4) analysis of the potential supply, including other possible competing projects.

- The market area is determined largely by employment opportunities within the relevant commuting range.

- The market analyst essentially determines what market conditions have been in the recent past and which factors that would affect the market for the project are likely to change in the near future.

- The developer should conduct a financial feasibility analysis that projects the probable cash flow and profit or loss of a proposed project.

▌ KEY TERMS

absorption rate	patio house	time-sharing
manufactured home	plex	town house

▎ STUDY EXERCISES ─────────────────────────────

1. What are the five principal types of residential developments?

2. What are the differences between condominium and cooperative owner-ship? What are some of the advantages of these types of ownership over renting?

3. What are the three types of single-family attached housing? What are the differences among the three?

4. What are the three types of multifamily residential housing? What are the differences among the three?

5. Discuss some of the factors that are leading to greater acceptance of manu-factured or mobile homes.

6. What are the principal reasons for owning a vacation home, and how do they differ from the reasons for owning a principal residence?

7. Discuss the use of time-sharing in the marketing of vacation homes.

8. Describe the steps in analyzing the market for a residential project.

9. What factors determine the market for a residential project?

10. Describe the process of financial feasibility analysis for a proposed residen-tial project.

▎ FURTHER READING ─────────────────────────────

Arendt, Randall G. *Conservation Design for Subdivisions: A Practical Guide to Creating Open Space Networks.* Washington, D.C.: Island Press, 1996.

Bohl, Charles C. *Place Making.* Washington, D.C.: Urban Land Institute, 2002.

Bookout, Lloyd W. *Value by Design: Landscape, Site Planning, and Amenities.* Washington, D.C.: Urban Land Institute, 1994.

Daniels, Tom, and Katherine Daniels. *The Environmental Planning Handbook.* Chicago: American Planning Association, 2003.

Ewing, Reid. *Best Development Practices: Doing the Right Thing and Making Money at the Same Time.* Chicago: Planners Press, 1996.

Katz, Peter. *The New Urbanism: Toward an Architecture of Community.* New York: McGraw-Hill, 1994.

Miles, Make E., Marc A. Weiss, and Gayle Berens. *Real Estate Development: Principles and Process.* Washington, D.C.: Urban Land Institute, 2000.

Schmitz, Adrienne (ed.). *Multifamily Housing Development Handbook.* Washington, D.C.: Urban Land Institute, 2000.

CHAPTER 12

Home Purchase Decisions

CHAPTER PREVIEW

Buying a home is the most important investment decision that the average U.S. family ever makes. Too often, however, it is made with the buyer at a distinct disadvantage and without the complete information needed to make the best choice at the most favorable terms. By now, you should be far better informed about real estate transactions than the usual homebuyer because you already know the basic principles of real estate. This chapter covers four topics specifically related to buying a home:

CASE STUDY
The House That
Came Off the
Mountain

1. The rent-or-buy decision

2. How much home you can afford

3. Choosing the right property

4. The negotiation, purchase, and closing process

■ THE RENT-OR-BUY DECISION ————————————————

Everyone needs a place to live, and housing expense is a dominant portion of most families' budgets. A major question facing these families is the rent-or-buy decision.

Should you rent, or should you buy? That depends on a great number of factors, many of which are not economic. For example, many families derive great satisfaction from owning their own homes; to others, the responsibility of home ownership is a psychological burden.

To make the correct economic decision, you really need an all-seeing crystal ball that accurately reveals the future. What will happen to home prices in the future? Will they rise, making your investment in a home more valuable? How much will they rise? Or will home prices fall, making your investment an unwise decision? What will happen to income tax laws that affect the deductions you can take for mortgage interest and property taxes? If these deductions are reduced or eliminated, home ownership will be relatively less desirable than renting. How long will you live in the home? Will your work require that you move within a relatively short time, or will you remain in the home for many years? Will you and your spouse continue to live in marital bliss, or will you split, making your home just one more thing to fight over?

We could go on and on conjuring up more and more imponderables, but let's try to analyze the rent-or-buy decision based on some reasonable assumptions regarding the future. Suppose that Carlos and Mary Mallory, a financially successful young couple, are pondering the purchase of a home. They currently live in an apartment, which costs them $1,000 per month plus utilities, but they have found a $180,000 house they like. They can finance the home with a down payment of $36,000 and a 30-year, 7.5 percent, $144,000 mortgage. In addition to the down payment, closing costs on the loan will add $3,800 to the required investment.

Monthly payments for principal and interest on the mortgage will be $1,006.87, plus another $230 per month for property taxes and $80 for property insurance—a total of $1,316.87. The first year's interest charges will be approximately $10,755, and property taxes will total $2,760. These two items are deductible from taxable income, and for their analysis, Carlos and Mary assume a marginal federal and state tax rate of 30 percent. This means they can save $4,055 in income taxes during the coming year, or $337.88 per month, if they purchase the house. This reduces their after-tax monthly payment on the new home to $978.99, approximately the amount they currently pay in rent.

Of course, home ownership also entails additional maintenance expenses, but because the house is new, Carlos and Mary believe these will be relatively minor during the analysis period.

(The amount of income tax savings depends on many factors. With their assumed income of $79,200, the Mallorys are entitled to a standard deduction of $6,000. Until their itemized deductions exceed this amount, they gain no tax advantage. Let us assume that the Mallorys pay $4,000 in state income taxes, but they have no additional deductions other than the $2,760 in property taxes and $10,755 in mortgage

TABLE 12.1 | The Mallorys' Home Ownership Analysis

Assumptions

1. House will cost $180,000. It will appreciate 3 percent annually over five years. House will sell for $208,669 in five years.
2. Real estate sales commission will be 6 percent of sales price.
3. House will be financed by a down payment of $36,000 and a 30-year, 7.5 percent, $144,000 mortgage. Financing costs will be $3,800.

Sales price after five years	$208,669
Sales commission	−12,520
Net sales receipts	196,140
Loan repayment	−136,249
Cash to Mallorys	59,900
Cash after taxes	$55,055

Return on investment of $39,800 = 8.6% annually
After-tax return on alternative investment = 4.3% annually

interest. Under these assumptions, the tax savings would be only $3,245 annually, not $4,055, as assumed above. If they live in a state with no state income tax, the tax savings would be even less; however, if they have other allowable deductions, such as charitable contributions or unreimbursed employee expenses, their income tax savings from buying the house could equal or exceed the assumed $4,055. Life is not simple!)

Their jobs may require that the Mallorys move sometime in the next several years, but they do not know when that might occur or whether it will be necessary or desirable at all. This is one of the uncertainties that make the rent-or-buy decision difficult. For this analysis, however, the Mallorys assume they will move after five years.

The next question is what will happen to home prices. This, of course, is a critical assumption. Carlos and Mary initially assume a 3 percent annual growth rate, but recognize that they must also analyze other possibilities.

Given these assumptions, the Mallorys arrive at the analysis summarized in Table 12.1. At a 3 percent annual rate of appreciation, the home can be sold for $208,669 in five years, or $196,149 after deducting a 6 percent real estate sales commission. From the mortgage loan repayment schedule in Table 12.2, we find that the principal of the mortgage has been reduced by only 5.4 percent, leaving a balance of $136,249.

After paying off the loan, the Mallorys would be left with $59,900, which would represent a 8.6 percent annual return on their $39,800 initial investment.

The Mallorys also would benefit from another federal income tax break for homeowners. Profit on the sale of a principal residence up to $250,000 for individuals and $500,000 for married couples filing jointly is excluded from taxable income, and a taxpayer can claim this exemption every two years. In our example, Carlos and Mary would have a profit on the sale of their home of $16,149, but no income taxes would be due.

TABLE 12.2 | Mortgage Loan Repayment Schedule

Year	6%	7.5%	9%
1	1.2	0.9	0.7
2	2.5	1.9	1.4
3	3.9	3.0	2.2
4	5.4	4.1	3.1
5	6.9	5.4	4.1
6	8.6	6.7	5.2
7	10.4	8.3	6.4
8	12.2	9.7	7.6
9	14.2	11.4	9.0
10	16.3	13.2	10.6
15	28.9	24.6	20.7
20	46.0	41.1	36.5
25	69.0	65.1	61.2
30	100.0	100.0	100.0

Alternative Investment

We must not forget that if Carlos and Mary do not buy the home, they can invest the $39,800 elsewhere. They might buy Amalgamated Whitzadiddle stock, which could be worth 100 times their initial investment. But Amalgamated Whitzadiddle might also go bankrupt, leaving their investment worthless. For simplicity, let's suppose the Mallorys invest the money very conservatively in U.S. government savings bonds, an investment that pays 6 percent annually, with income taxes on the interest not due until the bonds are cashed. This investment yields a 4.3 percent after-tax annual rate of return on the Mallorys' $39,800 investment—considerably less than the yield on the investment in the home.

Impact of Inflation or Deflation on Home Prices

Suppose, however, that Carlos and Mary purchase the home just before a period of rapid inflation, during which home prices rise 10 percent annually. Under this assumption, the Mallorys' house could be sold for $289,892 at the end of five years, yielding a profit of $92,498 after the sales commission and giving the Mallorys

$136,249 in cash after they repay the loan. This would yield a 27.9 percent annual return on their investment of $39,800.

In this type of inflationary situation, it would be extremely likely that the cost of renting an apartment would also rise rapidly. If the cost of renting their apartment should rise at this assumed 10 percent annual rate, the Mallorys' $1,000-per-month apartment would cost $1,600 per month in five years. On the other hand, if they buy the house and finance the purchase with a fixed-rate mortgage, the mortgage payment would not rise. This is another factor that makes home ownership more advantageous in inflationary times.

Now, let's make the pessimistic but often realistic assumption that home prices decline by 3 percent annually during the five-year analysis period. Under this grim scenario, the Mallorys could sell their house for only $154,572 in five years, leaving them with $9,049 after paying a real estate brokerage commission and repaying the mortgage. This means they would lose $30,751 of their $39,800 investment—a decidedly negative return.

Are Carlos and Mary likely to experience a 10 percent annual increase in the value of their home during the analysis period? Probably not. Are they likely to experience a 3 percent annual decline? Probably not. But these extremes set realistic parameters for their analysis.

Impact of Mortgage Interest Rates

In this evaluation of the rent-or-buy decision, the Mallorys have benefited from a historically relatively low mortgage interest rate of 7.5 percent. Suppose, however, that interest rates rise considerably and the best rate they can obtain is 9 percent. This would affect the analysis in two principal ways. First, of course, the Mallorys would face much higher monthly payments for principal and interest—$1,158.66 compared with $1,006.87. This would make the total monthly payment $1,468.66, or $1,062 after taxes the first year assuming they benefit from the entire mortgage interest and property tax deduction.

In addition, as indicated in Table 12.2, the mortgage payback is much slower with the higher interest rate. If we assume our initial 3 percent annual rate of appreciation in home prices, the Mallorys will receive a lower cash return because they have a larger mortgage repayment—$138,067 compared with $136,249 with the 7.5 percent mortgage. This reduces their rate of return to only 5.9 percent annually.

Period of Ownership

Generally, because of the inflation in home prices, the longer the period of ownership, the greater the relative advantage of home ownership over renting. For example, let's return to our original assumptions for the Mallorys' rent-versus-buy analysis, with one exception.

Let's now assume that Carlos and Mary will own the home for ten years rather than five. The results of this analysis are shown in Table 12.3. The sales price of the

---

TABLE 12.3 │ The Mallorys' Rent-versus-Buy Analysis—Ten-Year Ownership Period

Assumptions

1. House will cost $180,000. It will appreciate 3 percent annually over ten years. House will sell for $241,905 in ten years.
2. Real estate sales commission will be 6 percent of sales price.
3. House will be financed by a down payment of $36,000 and a 30-year, 7.5 percent, $144,000 mortgage. Financing costs will be $3,800.

Sales price after ten years	$241,905
Sales commission	−14,514
Net sales receipts	227,391
Loan repayment	−124,985
Cash to Mallorys	$102,406

Return on investment of $39,800 = 10% annually

After-tax return on alternative investment = 4.3% annually

house would increase to $241,905, leaving the Mallorys with $88,189 in cash after paying the brokerage commission and repaying the mortgage.

This represents a 10 percent after-tax annual rate of return on their original $39,800 investment. We might also note that if apartment rents increase at the same 3 percent annual rate, in ten years, the Mallorys will pay more than $1,345 a month if they stay in their apartment.

Some Conclusions

After all this, should Carlos and Mary rent, or should they buy? That depends on what assumptions they make regarding these future imponderables. However, at least we now know the parameters for the decision. Given the history of the past several decades, homeowners have done well compared to renters because their homes have served as hedges against inflation. Although it appears that rates of inflation will be lower in future years, don't count on it.

And what will happen to present income tax breaks enjoyed by homeowners? Will proponents of a flat tax remove the deductions for mortgage interest and property taxes? Will the tax forgiveness on the profit on the sale of a principal residence be done away with? We don't know, although these tax breaks have broad support.

Of course, the Mallorys' decision may well rest on noneconomic factors. Perhaps the intangibles of owning a home are very important to the Mallorys. Perhaps they love to garden and will enjoy working on their home. If so, they may want to buy even if they feel the investment probably will not be economically profitable. Or perhaps they hate yard work and all forms of home maintenance. They might want to be able to simply call the landlord when the heating system conks out, rather than having to deal with it themselves. If so, they may even be willing to pay a premium to live in a rental unit.

TABLE 12.4 | The Mallorys' Estimated Monthly Income

Salary (gross)	$6,200
Self-employment income	500
Dividends	300
Interest on $20,000	100
Total	$7,100

▌ HOW MUCH CAN YOU AFFORD?

After working through the rent-or-buy analysis, Carlos and Mary decide that they want to further explore the option of buying a house. The next question is how much house can they afford? In other words, how big a mortgage can they expect a lender to extend, given their income and financial obligations? First, the Mallorys need to estimate their income, including gross salary, self-employment income, wages from a second job, dividends, interest, pensions, Social Security, rental income, and child support or alimony received, but excluding one-time events, such as inheritances, insurance settlements, and capital gains.

Carlos and Mary have combined gross monthly salaries of $6,200. In addition, Carlos earns an average of $500 monthly in tax work for outside clients and has done so for several years. Mary receives an average of $300 in dividends on some Amalgamated Whitzadiddle stock that she inherited from her uncle. They also receive $100 in monthly interest on $60,000 of savings and Mary's additional inheritance they have in a bank, but they would need to use almost $40,000 of this money for the down payment and closing costs if they buy the home they are considering. See Table 12.4 for a breakdown of the Mallorys' monthly income.

Next, the Mallorys calculate their monthly payments. These include items such as payments on loans for automobiles, furniture, appliances, boats or recreational vehicles, revolving credit, and student loans. Carlos and Mary's monthly payments, shown in Table 12.5, are $1,100: $450 for a car, $200 for furniture, $300 for revolving credit, and $150 for a student loan.

As noted earlier, lenders use qualifying ratios as rules of thumb to estimate maximum mortgage payments. Generally, these ratios range between 25/33 and 28/36. The first figure of both ratios is the percentage of gross income a lender will allow as a maximum monthly mortgage payment. For the Mallorys' $7,100 monthly gross income, this amount would range from the conservative 25 percent ($1,775) to the more generous 28 percent ($1,988).

The second calculation reduces this amount to account for payments on other indebtedness. Using the 33 percent conservative figure, a lender would calculate the Mallorys' maximum monthly payment as follows:

Monthly gross income	$7,100
Times 33% (one-third)	2,367
Less other monthly payments	1,100
Amount available for payment	$1,267

Using the more liberal 36 percent ratio, the maximum monthly payment could be $1,456. In other words, the Mallorys' maximum monthly payment would be reduced significantly to reflect the impact of their existing debts.

In addition to principal and interest, the typical house payment includes one-twelfth of yearly property taxes and property insurance. Thus, the $1,267 to $1,456 that Carlos and Mary have available for a monthly house payment must be reduced to reflect these items before the Mallorys can estimate the maximum mortgage they can afford. The amount of property taxes depends on several factors, including the value of the home and the community in which it is located. Property taxes for the house the Mallorys are considering would be $280 each month, with another $80 for property insurance. This means they are left with $957 to $1,146 for the actual mortgage payment.

Because the monthly payment for principal and interest on the 7.5 percent, 30-year, $144,000 loan they need to buy the house is $1,007, the Mallorys have adequate income to qualify for this loan. The fact that Mary owns the Amalgamated Whitzadiddle stock and they would still have $20,000 in the bank after expending $39,800 for the down payment and closing costs also makes them a more favorable credit risk.

▌ CHOOSING A PROPERTY

Now that Carlos and Mary know the price range of the home they can afford, they need to decide whether their chosen house is really their best buy. The search for a home has two aspects. First, they must decide on a general area in which to look, and second, they must decide on a particular property. While the decision is

TABLE 12.5 │ The Mallorys' Monthly Payments

Car	$450
Furniture	200
Appliances	0
Boat or recreational vehicle	0
Revolving credit	300
Student Loan	150
Other	0
Total	$1,100

very important, it is not one they will have to live with forever—the average first-time homebuyer moves after five years—and the decision must be based partly on the Mallorys' desires and preferences and what will appeal to prospective future buyers.

Choosing an Area

If the Mallorys buy in a small or medium-sized town, choosing an area may be quite uncomplicated. But if they live in a large metropolitan area, the choice can be quite complex. Let's suppose the latter is the case. Not only do Carlos and Mary have to decide what type of home they would like and what development they might like to live in, they must also choose a community.

The Mallorys begin their search by deciding how far they want to commute to work. Some people do not like commuting and choose residences that are close to their employment. Others will endure longer commutes to enjoy the suburban lifestyle they prefer. Carlos and Mary decide they will limit their hunt to a maximum commuting distance of 60 minutes during rush hour. Within this area, they concentrate on six basic criteria for choosing one community over another:

1. Property tax base
2. Quality of general public services
3. Available recreational facilities
4. Quality of public school system
5. Crime statistics
6. Overall quality of community

Property Tax Base and Quality of Public Services

In a metropolitan area, property tax rates and the quality of public services can vary considerably from one community to another. Other things equal, a low tax rate is desirable if it is not achieved by cutting necessary services. Both factors are important.

Available Recreational Facilities

Good public recreational facilities and established sports programs may be very important factors in locational decisions for some families. For others, they may not be important at all. Carlos and Mary, who have no children, are much more interested in access to cultural events and good shopping.

Quality of Public School System

Having no children, the Mallorys are not concerned significantly about the local school system, although they know it may be quite important in the future. In addition, they realize that quality of schools probably will be a vital consideration for potential future buyers of their home.

Crime Statistics

Carlos and Mary, like most homebuyers today, are very concerned about their security. Thus, crime statistics and the quality of the local police force are extremely important considerations in their locational decision.

Overall Quality of Community

In the final analysis, the locational decision may come down to what the Mallorys perceive as the overall quality of the community. Is it attractive? Does it control signage, or are its thoroughfares visual litter boxes? Are homes in the community well maintained? And, finally, does the community control its growth and require quality real estate development, or does mediocrity abound? The answers to these questions may be based partly on fact and partly on perception, but the quality of a community is vital to property values.

Many sources of information are available on these community factors, including real estate agents, building and real estate publications, and bankers or lenders. Another extremely good source of information is people in a neighborhood. If they respond favorably to inquiries about their area, this almost certainly indicates a desirable community.

Evaluating the Individual Home

Even more than the selection of a community or housing area, selection of an individual property is governed by personal preferences. Carlos and Mary prefer a home with traditional architecture, for example, and want large, open rooms that are good for entertaining.

If a house has a swimming pool, they will not even consider buying it because neither likes to swim, and they don't want the maintenance burden that goes with a pool. To others, a pool would be a very desirable feature.

Despite these individual preference items, all homebuyers should consider certain basic factors. The first rule is to buy a home that is less expensive than the average for the neighborhood. The more expensive homes will tend to raise its value. Conversely, never buy the most expensive home in a neighborhood. The others will drag down its value.

Also, look carefully at other factors that affect a home's investment potential. Does it have a good exterior design? Is the floor plan well arranged? Does it have convenient traffic flow? Is the home well placed on the lot? Is the lot well drained, with good landscaping?

Finally, the structural integrity of the home is extremely important, as the Case Study on the next page shows. In fact, even if the home is new, but particularly if it is not, it may be very prudent to have the home inspected by a professional. But there are many items that anyone armed with a flashlight and a bit of common sense can examine. Carlos and Mary did this with several houses they considered, covering the items discussed in the following paragraphs.

REAL ESTATE TODAY

CASE STUDY

The House That Came Off the Mountain

Why should you obtain a professional home inspection before you purchase a home? Let's look at a dramatic example.

Philip and Phyllis McDonald (not their real names) bought a mountainside house with a spectacular view in an exclusive resort area of western North Carolina. Even though the house had a 40-foot-high concrete block foundation wall on the downhill side, the McDonalds did not have the house inspected before they purchased it for $375,000. They should have!

Less than six years later, the McDonalds came up from Florida to open their summer mountain home. That night, Philip awoke to hear loud cracking noises. The next day, he had the house inspected by a local contractor and later by an engineer. Both informed him that the structure was very unsafe and could collapse at any time. They noted separated and bulging foundation walls, twisted and leaning deck supports, separation of roof sections and walls, and separation of concrete blocks throughout the basement area. The house was in such dangerous and deteriorated condition that the only practical course of action was to move out immediately and have the house demolished. The demolition cost $25,000.

The McDonalds, sadder but wiser, suffered a loss of more than $400,000. They could not recover anything from their homeowner's insurance policy because no "occurrence" caused the loss. For the same reason, they could not claim a casualty loss on their income tax return. The contractor who built the home had gone out of business, so the McDonalds were advised that legal action against him was not practical. The loss fell on them alone.

This financial tragedy could have been avoided if the McDonalds had only spent perhaps $200 to have the house inspected before they bought it, as any qualified inspector could have spotted the inadequate construction methods and the potential for disaster. This sad tale also points out the need for adequate government building codes to protect consumers.

Attic

Does inspection of the attic reveal water leaks or signs of rodent infestation? Are insulation and ventilation adequate?

Walls and Ceilings

Are there cracks in plaster walls or ceilings? Are seams in wallboard smooth and invisible?

Floors

What is the condition of the floors? Do they show signs of buckling or sagging? What is the condition of any carpets?

Roof

Does the roof show signs of wear? An asphalt roof usually lasts only 15 to 20 years, for example, and bare spots can mean it will have to be replaced soon.

Basement or Crawlspace

Are there signs of water damage under the house? If so, a professional should evaluate the problem. Is there evidence of rot or termites? Almost all lenders require an inspection by a professional from a pest control firm.

Electrical System

A professional should inspect the electrical system, but the potential buyer can check some important things on his or her own. For example, does the home have adequate electrical capacity? A modern home should have at least a 150-ampere entrance. Are there enough outlets throughout the home?

Heating and Cooling System

How old is the heating and air-conditioning system? Older units are less efficient and may need to be replaced soon. Again, the services of a professional may be necessary.

Water Supply and Waste Disposal

If the home is connected to a municipal water and sewerage system, the potential buyer need worry about only the adequacy of the household plumbing. If the home depends on a well, the water should be tested before purchase. Is the supply adequate throughout the year? How old is the pump? If the home uses a septic tank waste disposal system, this also needs to be checked by a professional. In many states, inspection by the state health department is required before the property can be sold.

Two Final Thoughts

Following these guidelines can help you make an informed decision regarding where and what home to buy. And remember—you can always find a buyer for a good home in a good location. Take the time and effort to do the job right.

Finally, remember that this home is probably not your last. Consider your future needs, but unless you are an extremely unusual buyer, you will move in a few years.

MAKING AND CLOSING THE DEAL

Carlos and Mary have now completed the preliminary steps to buying a home. They have determined how much home they can afford. They have researched communities and specific neighborhoods and developments to determine where they might like to be located. They also have learned some of the factors they should look for in a home and have thought carefully about what features are important to them.

Now they are ready to choose a property, negotiate its purchase, obtain financing, and close the deal.

In this process, always remember one thing: In the normal sales transaction, no one works for you. The real estate broker works for the seller (unless you have hired a buyer's broker); the lender works for the mortgage company; even the closing attorney, whose fee you pay, does not really look out for your interests. This does not mean that these people are dishonest or out to cheat you, but *they do not work for you.* It is not their job to look out for your interests.

The Real Estate Agent

A real estate broker or salesperson can be a valuable source of information on neighborhoods and homes for sale. He or she can also save you considerable time by narrowing your search to properties that might really fit your needs and desires. But remember, unless you hire an agent specifically to represent you, the real estate broker does not work for you. The broker works for the seller and is legally bound to represent the seller's interests, not yours. Even though the salesperson spends long hours showing you around town, taking you to lunch, and, in general, being a wonderful person, don't forget that simple fact. For example, you certainly shouldn't tell the agent that you probably would be willing to make a higher offer on a particular house. The agent is duty bound to take that information to the seller, thereby weakening your position.

As discussed earlier in Chapter 8, buyers are increasingly being represented by buyer's brokers. This may be a very good idea, particularly when you move to a community that you do not know thoroughly.

The Negotiating Process

Suppose you have found a home that fits your needs. Now comes the tricky part—negotiating a price and terms. In this process, there are two rules:

1. Set a top limit above which you will not go
2. Be prepared to walk away from the deal

If you fall in love with a home and just have to have it, you are in a very poor bargaining position. Be prepared to walk away. On the other hand, if you really have found the home of your dreams, it may be worth spending a little more to get it, rather than going through the time-consuming process of extending the search. But be certain it really is the home you want. Don't fall in love with the first thing you see.

Not everyone, and particularly not a first-time homebuyer, is an experienced and shrewd negotiator. This may be one more reason to engage an agent to represent your interests. For one thing, the buyer's broker probably knows conditions in the market better than you do. Your agent may know that the house you are considering has been on the market for some time, and the owners are eager to sell. This information may place you in position to obtain a much better deal, which may more than pay for your representative's fee.

Finally, don't forget a fundamental rule of contracts: Oral agreements are not worth the paper they are written on. Unless something is written down as part of a contract, it is *not* part of the contract. If promises or agreements are made, be certain they are contained in the written contract. If not, they are worthless.

Dealing with the Lender

Lenders sell money, and, naturally, they want to get the highest price (the interest rate) they can. You should shop as carefully for a mortgage loan as you do for a home. Don't take the first offer, and check with several lenders to find the best deal.

Also, remember that any appraisal and inspections required by the lender are to protect the lender, not necessarily you. For example, the purpose of the appraisal, which you normally pay for, is to ensure that the home has value high enough to enable the lender to be able to recover its money in case of foreclosure. The appraisal does not tell you whether the home is a good investment for you, although it certainly should help in this determination. (It is amazing how many appraisals for lending purposes arrive at values that are almost exactly the selling prices.)

The Closing Attorney or Escrow Agent

The closing attorney's or escrow agent's job is to prepare the necessary documents relating to the sale and loan and to make sure the title is in order, the requirements of the lender and the title insurance company have been met, all funds have been collected and properly disbursed, and the necessary documents have been recorded. All of this is important to the buyer, but, again, the closing agent is not paid to look after the buyer's interests. The agent does not negotiate for you, draft a purchase contract favorable to you, make certain the contract has no clauses that are unfavorable to your interests, help arrange favorable financing, or make sure that the seller fully honors his or her agreement with you. To the contrary, the closing agent's job is to see that the transaction meets legal requirements and is closed.

Perhaps we have been too forceful in warning you of the pitfalls in the sales, lending, and closing transactions when buying a home. Certainly, the intention is not to convey that real estate brokers, lenders, and attorneys are dishonest or unethical. But do remember whom they work for. If you feel you need someone to represent your interests, don't depend on these individuals; hire your own representative.

SELLING THE HOME

After six years, Carlos and Mary decided to move to another city, so they needed to sell their home. They learned that preparing the home properly for sale, setting the right asking price, and choosing the right real estate agent can make a large difference in determining how much they can gain from the sale. They also learned that while real estate is easy to buy, it sometimes is hard to sell. It is not a liquid asset, and sales involve significant transaction fees.

Preparing the House for Sale

In preparing their house for sale, Carlos and Mary had to step back and take a hard look as a potential buyer would do. Most of us tend to overlook minor things—burned out light bulbs, dingy paint, cluttered garages, the door that doesn't close just right, the leaking faucet, dirty carpets—that may turn off a prospective buyer. A "well-polished" house will normally sell much faster and for a higher price than its shabby neighbor, even though both are structurally well-maintained.

So, it makes sense to spend money on cleaning, painting, and cosmetic repairs. In particular, the kitchen and bathrooms should receive special attention, making them clean, bright, and odor free. A fresh coat of paint will probably be a wise investment, perhaps both inside and out.

Major repairs do not make economic sense, however, unless they are absolutely necessary. For example, a new roof may impress a potential buyer, but usually this won't increase the selling price enough to cover the cost.

When it comes time to actually show the house, it needs to present its best appearance. The lawn should be cut and neatly trimmed, as well as the shrubbery and flowerbeds. Clear out the clutter to make the house look more spacious.

Setting the Asking Price

Setting the right price is perhaps the most important factor in selling a home. Set it too high, and the house won't sell. Set it too low, and the house won't bring what it should in the marketplace.

A real estate agent who knows the market can be of great assistance in setting an appropriate asking price. Even so, the sellers also need to find out the sale prices of similar houses, partly to reduce their own unrealistic expectations.

One important thing to be considered is how quickly the house needs to be sold and whether the sellers are anxious to sell. Obviously, a lower price will help the house sell quicker. If time is not a critical factor, sellers can afford to be patient and perhaps get a higher price.

Choosing a Real Estate Agent

Selling a house is not a simple process, and most homeowners do not have the knowledge or experience to manage it successfully. A competent broker will help set a realistic asking price based on his or her extensive market knowledge, and will have access to many more potential buyers. Of course, this also comes at a price, typically 6 percent of the selling price, but the rate can sometimes be negotiated downward.

The Sale

How the Mallorys fared in their house sale is hard to say. Perhaps they set a realistic market price, engaged a very competent real estate broker, enjoyed a strong market, and sold their home quickly. Or perhaps they had difficulty, setting the price too high, listing with a broker who did not market the house effectively, and failing to sell as quickly and for not as much as they had hoped. Real estate home sales involve many factors.

CHAPTER REVIEW

- Important factors in the rent-or-buy decision are (1) the future of home prices, (2) the probable period of ownership, (3) the mortgage interest rate, and (4) noneconomic factors.

- Lenders will normally make a mortgage loan with a monthly payment equal to between 25 and 28 percent of monthly gross income or, if the payment is less, an amount equal to 33 to 36 percent of monthly gross income reduced by the amount of existing monthly debt payments.

- Important factors in choosing a community in which to buy a home are (1) commuting distance to work, (2) property tax base, (3) quality of general public services, (4) available recreational facilities, (5) quality of the public school system, (6) crime statistics, and (7) overall quality of the community.

- In choosing a home, it is a good rule to buy one priced lower than the average for the neighborhood. Also, the buyer should consider a home that has a good design and should carefully check the home's structural integrity.

- In the negotiating, lending, and closing process, always remember that in the normal sales transaction, no one works for the buyer, and therefore, no one really looks out for the buyer's interests.

STUDY EXERCISES

1. What are some of the important factors to consider in the rent-or-buy decision?

2. Jack and Jill Jolly are thinking about buying a home. Their combined monthly income is $5,000, and they have $30,000 savings in a bank. They also have existing debt that requires monthly payments of $350 for a car, $200 for furniture, and $250 for revolving credit. How large a mortgage loan could they expect to get if the current interest rate is 8.5 percent? How expensive a home could they buy?

3. In choosing a location and home, what factors should Jack and Jill consider?

4. Is the assertion really true that in the negotiating, lending, and closing process, no one works for the buyer? Why or why not?

Commercial and Industrial Land Uses

CHAPTER PREVIEW

Shopping centers and other buildings for retail trade, office buildings, hotels and motels, and restaurants are examples of income-producing commercial properties. Industrial property includes factory buildings and warehouses. The development of these types of properties is the focus of this chapter.

Specific topics to be discussed are

- shopping center development;

- evolution of the shopping center;

- the development process of commercial properties, including (1) market and feasibility analysis, (2) site location, (3) tenant selection, and (4) financial feasibility analysis;

- office buildings;

- industrial parks and distribution facilities; and

- hotels and motels.

REAL ESTATE TODAY

CLOSE-UP
A Brownfields Development: Stratford Crossing Retail Center

CLOSE-UP
The First Suburban Shopping Center: Country Club Plaza

CASE STUDY
Birkdale Village

CASE STUDY
The Trump Building: 40 Wall Street

CASE STUDY
The Interstate North Industrial Park

CASE STUDY
The Boiler Room Office Building: A Unique Adaptive Use

CASE STUDY
Three Luxury Adaptive Use Hotels

FIGURE 13.1 | Types of Shopping Centers

Neighborhood Shopping Center

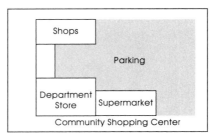

Community Shopping Center

Regional Shopping Center

Super-regional Shopping Center

SHOPPING CENTER DEVELOPMENT

The suburban shopping center is a creature of the automobile and is both a result and a cause of the suburban explosion that has taken place since World War II. As shopping centers have proliferated in suburban areas, the older **central business districts** of many cities have become economic backwaters. Others have been redeveloped, some as specialized shopping areas.

The traditional American shopping area was the central business district, an unplanned series of buildings constructed along major streets in the center of town. The modern shopping center is distinguished from the traditional commercial district by the following characteristics:

- One or more structures of unified architecture housing firms that are selected and managed as a unit for the benefit of all tenants
- A site that serves a particular trade area
- On-site parking
- Facilities for deliveries separated from the shopping area
- Single ownership and management

Although all shopping centers share these characteristics, not all shopping centers are alike. In fact, there are four major types, classified on the basis of type of tenants, size, and function: the neighborhood center, the community center, the

TABLE 13.1 | Characteristics of Shopping Center, by Type

Type	Leasing Tenant	Typical Leasable Area (Square Feet)	Range of Gross Leasable Area (Square Feet)	Typical Site Area (Acres)	Minimum Support Required (Number of People)
Neighborhood or convenience center	Supermarket or drugstore	50,000	30,000–100,000	3	2,500–40,000
Community center	Variety, discount, or junior department store	150,000	100,000–300,000	10–30	40,000–100,000
Regional center	One or more full-line department stores	400,000	300,000–750,000	30–50	150,000 or more
Super-regional center	Three or more full-line department stores	1,000,000	750,000–1,500,000	100 or more	200,000 or more

regional center, and the super-regional center. The types of shopping centers and their characteristics are shown in Figure 13.1 and listed in Table 13.1.

The *neighborhood shopping center,* sometimes called a *convenience center,* is designed to serve an area within a radius of approximately 1.5 miles and a population of 2,500 to 40,000. Its principal tenant usually is a supermarket, while the other stores largely provide convenience and shopping goods, such as pharmaceuticals, housewares, and personal services. Its **gross leasable area**—that is, the total floor area designed for the tenants' use—ranges from 30,000 to 100,000 square feet, with 50,000 square feet typical. It usually is located on about three acres of land. Generally, the neighborhood center is built in the *strip style*—that is, in basically a straight line, with stores tied together by a canopy over a pedestrian walk. Parking space is provided adjacent to the stores and off the public street.

The *community shopping center* provides a wider range of merchandise and usually is built around a junior department store, variety store, or discount store. It is designed to serve an area with a radius of approximately three to five miles and has a gross leasable area of 100,000 to 300,000 square feet located on from 10 to 30 acres.

When a discount store is the main tenant, the community shopping center sometimes is known as a **discount shopping center.**

The *regional shopping center* offers a full range of goods and services, usually has between 300,000 and 750,000 square feet of gross leasable area, and occupies between 30 and 50 acres. It is anchored by at least one full-line department store but usually has two or more. These shopping centers almost always are built as open or enclosed pedestrian malls, with the closed mall the overwhelming choice in recent years.

A *super-regional shopping center* exceeds 750,000 square feet in gross leasable area, occupies 100 acres or more, and includes at least three department stores. Most centers exceed 1 million square feet and may draw customers from more than 50 miles. Most super-regional centers are built with multiple levels to reduce walking distances for shoppers.

Variations on the major types of shopping centers include the superstore, the power center, the specialty shopping center, and the factory outlet center. The **superstore** is a very large discount store with between 60,000 and 200,000 square feet under one roof. Such stores are typified by the Wal-Mart and Target Superstores.

The **power center** is a large strip type shopping center that contains several "big box" retailers that are of a certain type: "category killers," discount department stores, and warehouse clubs. They usually have a trade area that goes far beyond the typical shopping center. Sometimes large retailers such as Wal-Mart, Target, Lowe's, and Home Depot will build very large stand-alone stores.

The **specialty shopping center** focuses on unusual market segments, usually offering high-quality and high-priced merchandise in boutique-type stores, although a number of new specialty centers focus only on discount stores.

Another type of specialty center is the **factory outlet center**, which consists of manufacturers' retail outlet facilities, where goods are sold directly to the public in stores owned and operated by manufacturers. These centers began a few years ago when manufacturers opened factory-owned stores near their plants to sell off seconds, outdated, or overproduced goods, or goods sent back unsold by retailers. Then, in the 1980s, developers began constructing shopping malls catering specifically to outlet stores. Now there are more than 300 outlet malls, some with more than 2 million square feet of space.

The locational requirements of outlet malls are similar to those of full-price centers, with the exception that factory outlet malls generally must be located on the outskirts of large market areas or major tourist resorts. This requirement appeases major retailers, who are not happy to have factory stores in their markets selling the same merchandise at cheaper prices.

A Brownfields Development: Stratford Crossing Retail Center

 There are an estimated 40,000 former industrial or other sites in this country where pollution from their former use inhibits their reuse and development. The Stratford Crossing Retail Center in Stratford, Connecticut, was built on the site of one such "brownfield."

The Raymark Corporation used the site for brake lining manufacturing operations from 1919 to 1989, leaving it substantially contaminated with asbestos, dioxin, and PCBs. It was designated as a Superfund site under a federal pollution cleanup program, and abatement work was completed prior to acquisition by The Home Depot and its development partners, Wal-Mart and Shaw's Super-markets. Even so, the developers still faced many environment challenges. They spent more than $80 million to install a ground water drainage system to remove and divert liquid contaminants or polluted ground water to a special treatment plant. Then the entire site was covered with a multilayer protective cap that included a rubber membrane, clay layer, sand, and a six-foot soil layer. This abatement system had to be carefully maintained during the construction process.

Despite these environmental challenges, the project was completed within seven months, and a former derelict site was returned to productive use. Even with the additional environment abatement costs, the developers got an attractive location at a favorable price. The town gained about 1,000 new jobs and an estimated $1 million in annual tax revenue.

EVOLUTION OF THE SHOPPING CENTER

The tremendous rise in automobile ownership during the 1920s put a strain on downtown shopping areas designed for pedestrians and public transportation. Congested streets, parking meters, and the limited curbside areas available for parking in most cities encouraged a shift to new concentrations of shopping facilities with adequate provisions for parking.

The automobile also encouraged population movement to the suburbs, and these areas on the outskirts of cities became the logical sites for the new shopping facilities. A few developers built the first true suburban shopping centers with unified architecture, a planned mix of tenants, and the essential ingredient—off-street parking. The surge in the number of centers came after World War II, with the explosion of residential suburbs.

The first suburban shopping center was Country Club Plaza in Kansas City, profiled on page 299. The first regional shopping center to contain a major full-line department store as the leading tenant was the Northgate Shopping Center in Seattle, constructed in 1950. The center contains several features that soon became familiar, including a central pedestrian mall, a truck tunnel to separate deliveries from the shopping areas, and vast seas of parking spaces surrounding the central building.

In the late 1950s, a design breakthrough was achieved when developers began to construct completely enclosed malls so that the interior climate could be controlled with air-conditioning and heating. Developers also began to expand centers vertically instead of horizontally to conserve land and protect the environment. The first enclosed mall, which also initiated the multilevel concept, was the Southdale Center near Minneapolis, opened in 1956. In the 1960s and 1970s, the enclosed multilevel mall became the dominant form of regional shopping center. There also was a trend toward larger complexes, with three or more full-line department stores.

The building of large, multilevel regional shopping centers has continued in recent years, but at a reduced pace. Major activity has centered on the expansion, redesign, and refurbishment of earlier centers, along with the building of power centers.

One other development of note is the megamall, as typified by the Mall of America in Minneapolis-St. Paul, a 4.2-million-square-foot center containing a 2.5-million-square-foot shopping mall with more than 525 specialty stores, 4 national department stores, more than 50 restaurants, 7 nightclubs, 14 movie theaters, an 18-hole miniature golf course, a roller coaster, a 7-acre Camp Snoopy theme park, a NASCAR Silicon Motor Speedway, and parking for 20,000 cars. The Mall of America attracts more than 42 million visitors a year and claims to be the nation's most visited attraction. A Phase II expansion is underway that will add another 5.6 million square feet to the center, including a 6,000 seat performing arts auditorium and a 3000,000 square foot Bass Pro Shop. This expansion will make the Mall of America the largest in the world.

THE SHOPPING CENTER DEVELOPMENT PROCESS

A developer who contemplates the construction of a shopping center must undertake several exhaustive studies if the proposed project is to have any hope of succeeding. The first task is to analyze the market to determine whether the proposed project is economically feasible. If it is, the developer then must determine the precise site that will be most likely to ensure the project's success. Having settled on a site, the developer must secure the commitments of the key anchor tenants and the proper supplementary tenants to ensure a complementary mix of shopping facilities.

Market and Feasibility Analysis

Before a developer will build a shopping center, before a lender will make a mortgage loan, and before potential anchor tenants will consider signing leases, several questions need to be answered regarding the proposed center's market and economic feasibility. Can the proposed center generate enough sales volume—and, therefore, rental income—to justify its development? Can the community absorb the proposed new retailing space? Are the population and purchasing power of the potential trade area expanding? If the market is not expanding, can the proposed center and its particular merchandising mix succeed in taking business away from existing stores or shopping centers?

A new center can do little to create business; basically, it must take business away from other retailers or capture expanded trade in a growing area. It is essential, therefore, that the developer also carefully analyze the status of the competition and the future prospects of the trade area.

Defining the Trade Area

The first step in a feasibility and market analysis is to define the **trade area**— that is, the geographic area from which the major portion of the patronage necessary to support the shopping center is to be drawn. This area will vary with the types and quality of merchandise offered. For example, families generally purchase food and sundries close to their homes, but for more expensive items, such as clothing, furniture, and major appliances, they often will drive long distances to secure a better selection or lower prices. Similarly, those seeking specialty items, such as sports equipment or high-quality cameras, also will travel longer distances to shop.

These factors are reflected in the trade areas for the various types of centers. The **primary trade area**—that is, the area that accounts for 60 to 70 percent of the center's sales—will have a radius of approximately 1.5 miles for a neighborhood shopping center, 3 to 5 miles for a community shopping center, and 8 to 10 miles for a regional shopping center. Additional shoppers may come from the **secondary trade area**—the area for a regional center that is 15 to 20 minutes' driving time from the primary trade area and that normally accounts for 15 to 20 percent of sales.

Besides the types of goods desired, the main factors that determine the size and shape of the trade area are the nature and location of competitive centers, the location of major transportation facilities, and natural barriers. For example, the defined trade area for the proposed center shown in Figure 13.2 is skewed toward the east and north because there is little or no competition in those directions. A lake forms a natural barrier in the southeast, and competitive facilities in the south and particularly the west greatly reduce the radius of the trade area in those directions.

Determining the Size of the Market

After the extent of the trade area has been determined, the next step is to calculate the size of the potential market within the trade area. Basic data can be obtained from the Census of Population and Housing and the Census of Retail Trade. They can be supplemented by other public and private data sources, such as the annual estimates of personal income by county supplied by the Bureau of Economic Analysis and the *Survey of Buying Power,* published annually by *Sales and Marketing Management* magazine.

Analyzing the Competition

After determining the current size and characteristics of the trade area's population, these data must be projected into the future. Projections are critical to the center's potential success because it is in the future that the center must compete in the marketplace.

FIGURE 13.2 | Primary Trade Area of a Proposed Shopping Center, Skewed by a Natural Barrier and Competitive Facilities

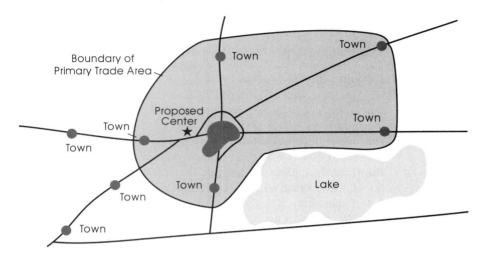

It often is tempting simply to extrapolate recent trends into the future, but this method will provide a very poor basis for decision making unless the best evidence indicates that a recent trend *will* continue. The experienced analyst or investor goes behind recent trends to find their causes and then attempts to project those trends on the basis of his or her findings.

Competitive Survey

Once the probable future purchasing power and retail purchases of the defined trade area have been estimated, the analyst must estimate the percentage of the total that can be captured by the proposed development.

One obvious step is to make a competitive survey to determine the extent and strength of existing centers in the market. It also is essential to find out what other potential competitors are planned. A market study that indicates a potential demand sufficient to support a new shopping center probably will lead to a very unsuccessful project if the developer fails to take into account another proposed new center.

Site Location

The market and feasibility analysis can substantiate the practicability of a center within the defined trade area, but it does not pinpoint the exact site, and site selection is a crucial factor in the success of a shopping center.

Several factors are important in the selection of the shopping center site, including size, shape, topography, drainage, utilities, and zoning. The most important considerations by far, however, are location and access. The neighborhood or convenience

REAL ESTATE TODAY

CLOSE-UP

The First Suburban Shopping Center: Country Club Plaza

The first suburban shopping center generally is considered to be Country Club Plaza in Kansas City, although strictly speaking, it is a shopping district rather than a shopping center. At any rate, it was the first suburban shopping area to incorporate unified architecture, common management, tenant selection, and off-street parking. It remains one of the premier urban spaces in the country, although its tenant mix has changed greatly over the years.

The J. C. Nichols Company began to develop the Country Club district shortly after the turn of the past century, when it was the extreme southern suburb of Kansas City. To the north of this area and between it and the developed portion of the city was Brush Creek Valley, a largely overgrown area that was occupied by a brick kiln, several trash dumps, and an old goat farm. In these unpromising surroundings, Nichols developed a new shopping center that featured off-street parking in what he termed "parking stations" and architecture reminiscent of that of Seville, Spain.

The first building was completed in 1923, and the center has been under almost continuous development and redevelopment since that time. It expanded greatly after World War II into a prestige shopping area containing more than 180 retail and service shops. Over the years the center has changed from a shopping center catering to general needs to a specialty center catering to high-income shoppers. For example, the last drugstore closed in 1996.

In order to remain competitive, the Plaza completed a $240 million expansion and renovation project that added 780,000 square feet of new retail and office space to the 2.8 million square feet of existing space. It was partially financed with $55 million in tax increment financing extended by the city. Under this arrangement, 100 percent of property taxes on the new buildings and 50 percent of sales and other taxes generated by the expansion will be rebated to the developer until the total reaches $55 million.

Country Club Plaza pioneered many of the concepts that are commonplace in suburban shopping centers today. Because of the high quality of its design and architecture and continuing good management that has successfully adapted the center's facilities to keep abreast of evolving marketing trends, Country Club Plaza has retained its rank as a prestige shopping center for more than 80 years.

Birkdale Village

Where separation of uses was long the rule in land-use planning and zoning, recent years have seen the rise of the mixed-use development. Birkdale Village is an outstanding example of this type.

Birkdale Village is located in the affluent and rapidly growing Lake Norman area of the Charlotte, North Carolina, region. The site has a population of approximately 55,000 within a 5-mile radius and average household income of around $110,000. Even so, to go out and essentially build a downtown on a 52-acre bare ground site was an audacious move on the part of the developers, but a very successful one.

The village is anchored at one end of a linear park with a 16-screen movie theater. On each side of the parkway are three-story buildings with retail at street level and 320 apartments above. About 60 shops and offices occupy the 285,000 square feet of retail space, along with six restaurants. Large retailers Barnes and Noble, Gap, Pier One, and Dick's Sporting Goods are located on a back street, providing this type of shopping without the typical "big box" look.

Birkdale Village has been an almost instant success. Its high-quality shops, restaurants, and community activities have attracted shoppers far beyond the usual reach of a shopping center. The Village has received a number of awards for its innovative design.

shopping center requires easy access from the supporting residential area. It usually is located on a connector street; in a planned community, it also may be located to encourage pedestrian access. The community center normally is located along a major thoroughfare, while the principal location requirement for regional and super-regional centers is easy access to major freeways and, increasingly, mass-transit facilities.

It is not necessary for shopping centers to be located far from other centers; in fact, centers located across the street from or adjacent to each other may be complementary. For example, a specialty fashion center may draw customers to an adjacent regional shopping center from competing centers in the area because the specialty center enhances the general location for shoppers. Alternatively, one center may not compete with another nearby because it handles different types of goods. For example, a convenience or neighborhood shopping center may be located near a regional center and actually benefit from this location.

Again, there is a saying among developers that there are only three important considerations in real estate development: "location, location, and location." The maxim is especially applicable in choosing a shopping center site. Selection of any but the best site not only will mean a less successful center initially; it usually will mean that a competing center eventually will be built on the best site and will use this advantage to secure the lion's share of the business.

Tenant Selection

The success of most shopping centers is contingent on the securing of key anchor tenants. For regional and super-regional centers, the anchors are major department stores; for community centers, they are junior department stores or discount stores; and for neighborhood centers, they are supermarkets or drugstores. Consequently, the negotiating strength of such firms is great, and they usually secure very favorable lease terms. Often, the major tenants in a regional center purchase land from the developer and construct their own buildings.

The major tenants are expected to attract shoppers to the supplementary tenants. These tenants must be chosen carefully to be complementary to each other and to the anchor stores. For example, men's stores—shoes, clothing, and sporting goods—tend to reinforce each other. The same principle holds for women's clothing and related shops, including food products and personal services. To yield the highest return, continuing careful attention is also crucial to ensure that the tenant mix changes when necessary to reflect new trends.

OFFICE BUILDINGS

The demand for office space in a community depends on the level of certain types of business activity and government employment. Nationally, the increasing percentage of the work force in white-collar occupations and the growth in service industries in the past several decades have added to the demand for more office space. Increased business activity in expanding areas, particularly in the Sunbelt region, has also fueled the demand for additional office space. Within cities, the growth of suburban office parks has greatly expanded the supply of office buildings in these locations.

Location of Office Activity

Office buildings traditionally have been located in downtown business districts, and in recent years, they have become the dominant form of land use in many city centers. Downtown office buildings most likely are to be used as main offices of financial institutions, corporate headquarters, attorneys' offices, and government facilities.

Most cities also have at least one secondary "uptown" office node, usually located along a major thoroughfare leading to the suburbs. Other specialized nodes may develop near government installations, shopping centers, hospitals, and universities.

Another more recent type of development is the **office park,** a community of office structures under central management and administration, usually located in the suburbs and adjacent to a major freeway. Such parks generally consist of lowrise buildings in a campuslike setting. They attract tenants in sales, manufacturing, and similar activities that do not need downtown locations. The office park's advantages are its location near suburban residential areas, with resultant reduction in commuting time, ease of parking, and a pleasant environment.

Types of Office Products

Office buildings can be classified in several ways. Building location, discussed above, is one way. Another is by number of tenants. Single-tenant buildings are very common. They range in size from a 1,000-square-foot suburban structure for a small firm or up to a one-million-square-foot skyscraper for a large corporation. They may be owner-occupied or leased from an investor.

Many office buildings, particularly the larger ones, are built by investors on a speculative basis for lease to multiple tenants. Sometimes a large company will lease a major portion of the building, which then will be named for the firm. In other cases, ownership is organized on a condominium basis, with the individual firms owning their office space and sharing ownership of the common areas.

INDUSTRIAL PARKS AND DISTRIBUTION FACILITIES

Early industrial facilities were located wherever transportation facilities, water, power, and other such features were adequate. Around the turn of the previous century, however, **industrial parks**—controlled, parklike developments designed to accommodate specific types of industry and providing all necessary utilities—came into existence. These parks provided location advantages and also avoided conflicts with other land uses.

Several planned industrial districts were pioneered in Chicago, beginning with the Original East District in 1902. These districts were served by railroads, and their success led to the establishment of other railroad-sponsored industrial districts in other parts of the country. Following World War II, the industrial-park concept spread widely. Most recent parks depend primarily on road access, but most also are served by rail facilities.

Some industrial parks contain manufacturing plants, but many allow only light manufacturing activities. Others are devoted exclusively to warehousing and distribution activities.

ANALYSIS OF INDUSTRIAL SITES

The task of determining the feasibility of developing a site for industrial use is much like that of analyzing other types of property. The basic technique is to

- determine the amount of existing or potential supply,

The Trump Building: 40 Wall Street

 Large profits in real estate investing come to those who can visualize uses or reuses that others cannot see. That was the case with flamboyant developer Donald Trump's rehabilitation of the 40 Wall Street Building.

Known as the Manhattan Company Building when it opened in May 1930, the 72-story building was briefly the tallest in the world. With its golden pyramid-shaped roof crowned by a spire, the 1.2-million-square-foot building was considered one of the most prestigious addresses in the market for more than 50 years.

In late 1982 the building and its ground leasehold was acquired by a company controlled by Philippines dictator Ferdinand Marcos and his wife Imelda. When he was driven from office, his assets in the United States were frozen, and the building was virtually ignored. Tenants began to leave, and combined with the decline in downtown Manhattan real estate following the stock market crash in 1987, the 40 Wall Street building started a long slide to being virtually worthless.

In 1989 the building and ground leasehold were auctioned off for $77 million, but the buyers soon realized their mistake and turned the building back to their lender. In 1993 another company bought the leasehold for only $8 million, but the continued depressed market convinced them that money invested in renovations would be throwing good money after bad. With ground lease payments, taxes, and operating costs continuing, the building suffered from a negative net worth. It sat virtually empty for several years.

Enter Donald Trump, who, seeing a market for a completely renovated building, purchased 40 Wall Street for $1 million. He then poured $65 million into enlarging the lobby, completely gutting the interior, lifting the ceilings, rewiring the building (including state-of-the-art telecommunication services), and providing new mechanical systems. The building was transformed from a virtually derelict property to a highly desirable Class A office building. When the market picked up in 1996, 40 Wall Street, renamed The Trump Building, quickly was leased to almost total capacity.

In 1998 Trump was able to secure a $125-million mortgage, which repaid all his renovation costs with many millions left over. At this writing the building has been placed on the market for $400 million, $330 per square foot. Because similar properties have been selling in this range, it appears that Mr. Trump will enjoy a further large gain from his foresight.

- forecast the demand for additional developed industrial acreage or building space in the general area,
- estimate the absorption rate during the analysis period, and
- compare the competitiveness of the subject site with that of other properties.

The Interstate North Industrial Park

Perhaps no aspect of real estate development has changed more in recent years than warehousing and distribution facilities. Although bulk warehouse buildings still make up a large part of the market, a new type of industrial facility has evolved, the office and distribution facility.

Interstate North, located in the northeastern part of the Atlanta metropolitan region, is an excellent example of this new type of facility. Many firms need not only to store goods for distribution but also to have office space and even showrooms in their warehouse facilities. Interstate North caters to this need, and quite successfully.

In addition to being in a major market, a distribution facility needs to be located near an Interstate highway interchange, and visibility from the highway is also an important asset. The 120-acre Interstate North site offered all these advantages, and enabled McDonald Development to convince Panasonic to build a 350,000-square-foot facility expandable to 500,000 square feet as the first firm to locate in its new industrial park. Not only did this help to provide the financing necessary to complete the park's infrastructure, it gave Interstate North prestige in attracting tenants for other buildings in the development.

The park is extensively landscaped, a necessary amenity in securing tenants who desire Class A office and showroom space in addition to their distribution facilities. The fronts of the buildings don't look like warehouses; they look like office buildings. No—these are not your father's warehouse buildings.

HOTEL, MOTEL, AND RESORT DEVELOPMENTS

The demand for lodging services comes from several sources, including pleasure travelers, business travelers, and conventioneers. The various types of lodging customers necessitate different types of facilities, although there often is considerable overlap. For example, many pleasure travelers seek easy access to and from major highways, and so do many business travelers. Pleasure travelers seek resort locations, and so do many convention groups.

The distinction between motels and hotels was quite marked in the early days of the motel. Motels usually were small structures of one or two stories offering parking space adjacent to rooms and a minimum of services. Today, many motels are almost indistinguishable from hotels, the primary distinction being that hotels generally offer a wider range of services.

Lodging facilities usually are classified as commercial hotels, highway or airport hotels, and resort hotels.

Commercial hotels cater primarily to business people and conventioneers. Their occupancy is usually relatively stable throughout the year but often drops to low

The Boiler Room Office Building: A Unique Adaptive Use

The Round Hill shopping center, a 1960s era strip center in Lake Tahoe, Nevada, was looking very tired and out of date. The main anchor, a Safeway grocery store, needed a larger and more modern building, and the entire center was simply no longer competitive. Because new commercial building sites in the environmentally sensitive Lake Tahoe area are difficult to find and the center's location was a good one, the decision was made to completely rebuild it.

The original center was heated by steam boilers located in a 3,000-square foot building from which heat was then piped to the various stores. In the rebuilt center this outdated system was replaced by package heating and air-conditioning units in the individual stores, making the boiler room building superfluous. It sat unused and unloved for about three years, its boilers and pumps slowly rusting away.

The Johnson-Perkins real estate appraisal firm needed more office space, and they were looking for a building site. Because Lake Tahoe has some of the toughest land-use regulations in the nation,

in order to build a new building, Johnson-Perkings would have had to buy transfer of development rights at a cost of about $45 per square foot for a building and $10 per square foot for the site. Not only was the old boiler room building basically quite sound, it came with the necessary development rights. The Johnson-Perkins firm decided it made economic sense to make the rather unique and unlikely conversion of the old boiler room building to first-class office space.

The first step in remodeling the building was to remove the six 12,000-pound boilers and their associated pumps and plumbing. The firm then demolished an incinerator tower, gutted the interior of the building, and cut new windows. In keeping with the rustic nature of the area, the exterior of the building featured river rock, stucco, and cedar siding. The interior included peeled-log support columns, 18-foot-tall vaulted ceilings, and cedar-finished ceilings.

The result was an office building with unique features that actually cost less than a conventional new building. The project received the South Tahoe Chamber of Commerce's award for Best Overall Remodel.

levels on weekends. Many depend heavily on convention trade and have extensive facilities to attract this type of business.

A **highway hotel,** also called an *airport hotel,* caters primarily to businesspeople or vacationers who are in transit. Such facilities range from the small highway motel that offers little more than a sparsely furnished room to elaborate facilities with extensive amenities.

Resort hotels, which are also known as *destination hotels* or *seasonal hotels,* cater to individuals or families on vacation. By definition, the hotels must be located near scenic, historic, or other attractions that appeal to pleasure travelers. To enhance their appeal further, most offer extensive facilities—golf courses, tennis courts,

REAL ESTATE TODAY

CASE STUDY

Three Luxury Adaptive Use Hotels

 In contrast to the not-so-distant past when older buildings were usually torn down to make way for "progress," many desirable older buildings are now being adapted for a new and different use. This is the case with three luxury lodging places, Richmond Hill Inn, Oheka Castle, and the Hotel Monaco.

Richmond Hill Inn

Richmond Pearson built his grand Victorian mansion known as Richmond Hill in 1889 overlooking Asheville, North Carolina, and he lived there until his death in 1923. The mansion stayed in the family for another 50 years until the house and grounds were sold for a church's retirement home. Even with the stipulation that the house must be preserved for at least ten years, its prospects appeared bleak. Before the demolition date, however, a local preservation society raised the money to move the 1.5 million-pound house to a new location 600 feet down the hill. But what to do with it?

Fortunately, Dr. and Mrs. Albert Michel saw the dilapidated mansion's potential, and following a $3 million restoration, it was opened as a luxury country inn in 1989. Since that time, five Croquet Cottages, a Garden Pavilion with 15 guest rooms, and an extensive Victorian garden have been added that, even though they are new, appear to be original outbuildings of the mansion. The inn and its restaurant have been awarded the prestigious AAA Four Diamond designation, the only such award in the area.

Oheka Castle

The Oheka saga spans years of uncertainty and controversy. The 109,000-square-foot, 126-room French chateau-style castle was built in 1917 on Long Island, New York, for *Otto Herman Kahn*, a financier and patron of the arts. The three-story mansion, the second largest house in the United States after only Biltmore House, sits on an artificially created 90-foot-high hill and was built with concrete and steel walls three to five feet thick. The entire estate originally consisted of 443 acres, which included a private 18-hole golf course, a farm, a race track, and even an airstrip.

Following Mr. Kahn's death in 1934, the house was sold to the New York City Department of Sanitation, which used it as a rest home for workers. During World War II it served as a training center for radio operators, and later it was sold to a boys' military prep school, which occupied it until 1978 when the school went bankrupt. After that, the Oheka Castle fell on hard times, the victim of vandalism and the elements. When it was purchased by Gary Melius in 1984 for $1.45 million, it was in very bad shape, and its land had been reduced to 23 acres. It took 300 trailer trucks just to carry out debris. Four hundred doors and windows had to be replaced, along with missing paneling, moldings, stair and balcony railings, balustrades, mantels, and other details. Mr. Melius sold the partially restored house to a Japanese businessman five years later for $22.5 million, but in 1993 he took back control of the building with a 114-year lease.

Mr. Melius had obviously developed a passion for Oheka, but what could be done with such a huge structure? The answer was to turn the house into a luxury inn, meeting facility, and spa. The Castle now offers 26 rooms and suites, along with function rooms that accommodate up to 400. Nightly rates range from $329 to $10,000 for the most luxurious suite.

(continued)

REAL ESTATE TODAY
CASE STUDY

Three Luxury Adaptive Use Hotels

Hotel Monaco

The Washington, D.C., General Post Office was built in two stages. The first, built in 1839–1842, was designed by Robert Mills, the principal architect of the Washington Monument. The second, designed by Thomas Walter, who designed the dome of the Capitol, was constructed in the 1850s. Later it was known as the Tariff Building, after a long-time federal government tenant. In recent years it had become a boarded-up wreck on its way to becoming a complete ruin.

A number of uses were proposed for the building, including a museum for the Smithsonian and

a federal office building. Then in 2000 the Kimpton Hotel and Restaurant Group, which specializes in so-called boutique hotels, struck a deal with the General Services Administration to lease the building for 67 years. The government took the responsibility for repairing the exterior at a cost of about $4 million, and the company spent some $35 million on the conversion.

Opened in 2002, not only is the 184-room hotel an excellent example of historic preservation, it has served as a catalyst for the transformation of the old downtown area.

swimming pools, and the like. Many are seasonal, often closing completely in the off-season or staying open to cater to convention groups.

Lodging facilities differ in several ways from other types of real estate. Their revenues are very susceptible to changes in business activity or pleasure travel, as rentals usually are from night to night rather than on the basis of the long-term leases used for other types of rental property. Conversely, rates can be adjusted quickly in periods of rapid inflation, a desirable characteristic for investors. Management is of critical importance to the success of such facilities, usually making the difference between a successful and an unsuccessful project. Even a well-designed and well-located lodging facility will have difficulty overcoming inadequate management.

CHAPTER REVIEW

- The shopping center is distinguished from the traditional commercial district by the following five characteristics: (1) one or more structures of unified architecture housing firms that are selected and managed as a unit, (2) a site that serves a particular trade area, (3) on-site parking, (4) facilities for deliveries separated from the shopping area, and (5) single ownership and management.

- There are four major types of shopping centers, classified on the basis of type of tenants and functions: (1) the neighborhood or convenience center, with a typical gross leasable area of 50,000 square feet and a supermarket or drugstore as leading tenant; (2) the community center, with a typical gross leasable area of 150,000 square feet and a variety, discount, or junior department store as leading tenant; (3) the regional center, with one or more full-line department stores and 400,000 square feet of gross leasable area; and (4) the super-regional center, with three or more full-line department stores and 1 million square feet or more of gross leasable area.

■ The factory outlet center was a development of the 1980s. These centers contain stores where goods are sold directly to the public by manufacturers.

■ So-called power centers contain a number of "big box" stores.

■ The steps involved in a feasibility and market analysis for a shopping center are (1) define the *trade area*—that is, the geographic area from which the major portion of the center's patronage will be drawn; the primary trade area (the area from which 60 to 70 percent of sales are expected to come) will have a radius of approximately 1.5 miles for a neighborhood shopping center, 3 to 5 miles for a community shopping center, and 8 to 10 miles for a regional shopping center; (2) determine the size of the market in terms of population, purchasing power, and expected sales; (3) analyze existing and potential competition; and (4) estimate the percentage of sales of the total trade area that can be captured by the proposed center.

■ Several factors are important in the selection of the shopping center site, including size, shape, topography, drainage, utilities, and zoning. Most important is location.

■ The demand for office space in a community depends on business activity and government employment.

■ Office buildings generally are located in downtown business districts, in office nodes along major thoroughfares leading to the suburbs, and in office parks.

■ A firm's selection of an industrial site is influenced by many factors, including (1) the availability of land, (2) the availability of utilities, and (3) access to major transportation facilities.

■ The steps in determining the feasibility of developing a site for industrial use are (1) determining the amount of existing or potential supply, (2) forecasting the demand for additional developed industrial acreage or building space in the general area, (3) estimating the absorption rate during the analysis period, and (4) comparing the competitiveness of the subject site with that of other properties.

■ Demand for lodging services comes from several sources, including pleasure travelers, business travelers, and conventioneers.

■ Transient hotels and motels usually are classified as (1) commercial hotels, which cater primarily to businesspeople and conventioneers; (2) highway or airport hotels, which cater primarily to businesspeople and vacationers who are in transit; and (3) resort hotels, which cater to individuals or families on vacation.

KEY TERMS

central business districts	highway hotel	resort hotels
commercial hotels	industrial parks	secondary trade area
discount shopping center	office park	specialty shopping center
factory outlet center	power center	superstore
gross leasable area	primary trade area	trade area

STUDY EXERCISES

1. What characteristics distinguish a shopping center from the traditional commercial district?

2. What are the four major types of shopping centers?

3. Describe the characteristics of (1) the neighborhood center, (2) the community center, (3) the regional center, and (4) the super-regional center.

4. Discuss the steps involved in a feasibility and market analysis for a proposed shopping center.

5. Define the *primary trade area*. What is its typical size for each of the major types of centers?

6. What factors are most important in the selection of a successful shopping center site?

7. What is a specialty shopping center? What is a discount shopping center?

8. What factors determine the demand for office space in a community?

9. What types of firms tend to lease space in downtown office locations? Why do financial institutions and attorneys often choose downtown locations?

10. Where are "office nodes" likely to develop?

11. What factors have led to the growing popularity of the suburban office park?

12. What factors determine a firm's selection of a specific industrial site?

FURTHER READING

Baltin, B., et al. *Hotel Development*. Washington, D.C.: Urban Land Institute, 1996.

O'Mara, W. P., M. D. Deyard, and D. M. Casey. *Developing Power Centers*. Washington, D.C.: Urban Land Institute, 1996.

Sabbagh, K. *Skyscraper: The Making of a Building*. New York: Penguin Books, 1989.

Schwanke, D. *Resort Development Handbook*. Washington, D.C.: Urban Land Institute, 1997.

Understanding Real Estate Market Dynamics

CHAPTER PREVIEW

CLOSE-UP
The Electronic
Revolution's Impact
on the Value of
Location

A key requirement for making effective real estate decisions is having a clear understanding of how real estate prices (values) are determined in real estate markets. This understanding is central to all aspects of real estate, including consumption and investment decisions, mortgage lending and borrowing, appraisal, brokerage, land-use policy, and, of course, development.

This chapter discusses the dynamics of owner-occupied residential real estate markets and commercial real estate markets. We will use a simple supply/demand equilibrium model to discuss how prices are determined in these two major real estate market categories. In our discussion of commercial real estate markets, we will consider the important distinction between real estate space markets (transactions between landlords and tenants regarding the use of space in exchange for rent) and the real estate asset market (transactions between developers and investors or investors and investors regarding ownership of real estate and the rights to rental income).

The objectives of this chapter are to

- use the supply and demand equilibrium model to consider how prices are determined in owner-occupied residential real estate markets;

- distinguish between real estate space markets and the real estate asset market as components of the commercial real estate market;

- examine how rents are determined in commercial real estate space markets and how prices are determined in the commercial real estate asset market;

- consider how the development industry ties commercial real estate space and asset markets together; and

- review the procedures for conducting a formal real estate market analysis.

OWNER-OCCUPIED RESIDENTIAL REAL ESTATE MARKETS

By definition, a **market** is the mechanism or arrangements through which goods and services are traded between market participants. An owner-occupied residential real estate market involves transactions of *new* and *existing* dwelling units that will be occupied by the new owners (not tenants). These markets can be further categorized by type of dwelling units and geographic location (condos in downtown Atlanta, single-family houses in a suburb of Los Angeles, townhouses in Washington, D.C., or even manufactured houses in rural Kansas).

Developers/builders/investors construct *new* dwelling units or renovate existing dwelling units when they believe they can sell those units to consumers at prices equal to or greater than the cost of constructing them (including reasonable profit). *Existing* dwelling units are typically offered for sale in this market by owners who no longer wish to own them due to employment changes, change in family size, change in financial circumstances, or even death of the owner. The dynamics of such markets are often quite complex, but they can be simplified using the familiar supply/demand equilibrium model.

Demand conditions in owner-occupied residential real estate markets can be dramatically affected by changes in total population, the number of households, individual and household income levels, changes in taste and preferences for dwelling unit designs, and the mortgage loan interest rate level. Supply conditions are sensitive to the price of developable land, the prices of construction materials and labor, and the interest rates on construction loans. The combined effects of supply and demand determine price levels in owner-occupied residential real estate markets.

The Basic Supply/Demand Equilibrium Model

In the basic supply/demand equilibrium model developed by economists, **supply** is defined as the amount or quantity of the good or service that will be offered at various prices. **Demand** is defined as the amount or quantity of the good or service that will be desired at various prices. For most goods and services, the supply increases with price, meaning that more of the good or service will be offered at higher prices. But the demand for most goods and services decreases with price, meaning that less of the good or service will be desired at higher prices. A market is said to be in **equilibrium** when the price negotiated between suppliers and demanders results in the quantity of the good or service offered by the suppliers equaling the quantity of the good or service desired by the demanders. When supply or demand conditions change, the market seeks a new equilibrium—a balanced price/quantity combination that reflects the new conditions. Economists have long used this simple model to analyze market dynamics for many different goods and services, including owner-occupied residential real estate. Let's consider a hypothetical housing market to demonstrate the model's ability to explain and predict market dynamics.

FIGURE 14.1 | Supply/Demand Equilibrium Model

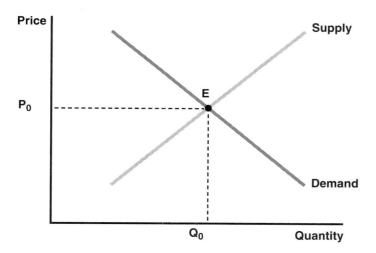

Demonstrating Market Dynamics

Suppose we interview all of the participants in a hypothetical housing market and discover the number of dwelling units offered by suppliers (builders and exist-ing-unit owners) at various prices and the number of units desired by demanders (owner-occupants) at various prices. The results of our interviews are shown graphi-cally in Figure 14.1. Notice that the demand curve is downward sloping, implying that participants in this market desire fewer dwelling units at higher prices than they do at lower prices. Also, notice that the supply curve is upward sloping, implying that participants in this market offer more dwelling units at higher prices than they do at lower prices. Note that the market is in equilibrium (E) at the price of P_0: the number of units offered equals the number of units desired. By altering the supply and demand information, we can understand how equilibrium prices will change as supply and demand conditions change in this market.

How do changes in demand affect prices in this market? Suppose that the demand for dwelling units in this market increases instantaneously from D_0 to D_1, but the supply (S_0) remains unchanged. The new demand curve (D_1) intersects with the sup-ply curve at the new, higher price of P_1 as shown in Figure 14.2. Or suppose that the demand for dwelling units in this market decreases instantaneously from D_0 to D_2, but that the supply (S_0) remains unchanged. The new demand curve (D_2) intersects with the supply curve at the new, lower price of P_2. Thus, we can say that equilibrium prices are *directly* related to changes in demand. (If demand goes up, price goes up;

FIGURE 14.2 | Demand Changes Price

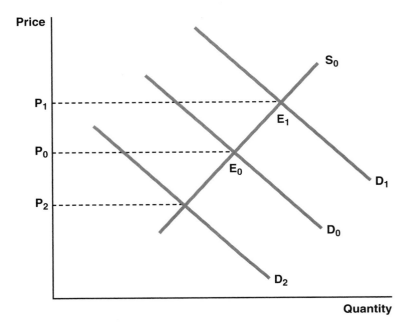

and if demand goes down, price goes down.) From this result, we know that factors that lead to increased demand in housing markets will result in price increases, other things held constant.

How do changes in supply affect prices in this market? Suppose that the supply of dwelling units in this market increases instantaneously from S_0 to S_1, as shown in Figure 14.3, but that the demand remains unchanged. The new supply curve (S_1) intersects with the demand curve (D_0) at the new, lower price of P_1. Or suppose that the supply of dwelling units in this market decreases instantaneously from S_0 to S_2, but that the demand remains unchanged. The new supply curve (S_2) intersects with the demand curve at the new, higher price of P_2. Thus, we can say that equilibrium prices are *inversely* related to changes in supply. (If supply goes up, price goes down; and if supply goes down price goes up). From this result, we know that factors that lead to increased supply in housing markets will lead to price decreases, other things held constant.

How do prices change when both supply and demand change simultaneously in this market? The answer depends on the relative magnitudes of the supply and demand changes. If both supply and demand change by the same proportionate amounts and

FIGURE 14.3 | Supply Changes Price

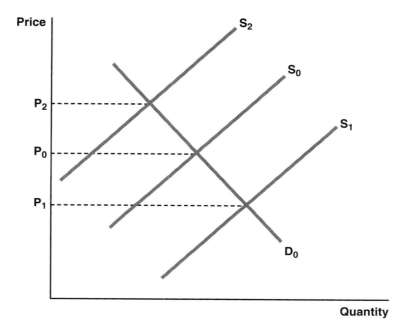

in the opposite directions, equilibrium prices will not be affected. But, if the changes in supply and demand are not equal or are in the same direction, the impact on price can be quite dramatic. Figure 14.4 shows how a small supply increase (from S_0 to S_1) and a large demand increase (from D_0 to D_1) that occur simultaneously can lead to much higher equilibrium prices (from P_0 to P_1).

▌ EXAMPLE: FORT LAUDERDALE, FLORIDA

Let's apply the supply/demand equilibrium model to a specific housing market to see how the model explains current price trends and predicts future prices.

Fort Lauderdale, Florida, is an internationally renowned tourist destination. Miles of sandy beaches along the Atlantic Ocean and perpetual sunshine make this city a favorite spot for beach lovers. In addition, much of the eastern portion of the city is crisscrossed by a series of ocean-accessible canals that connect to the Intracoastal Waterway and make it possible to dock oceangoing motor yachts and sailboats in the backyards of many single-family homes. For this reason, Fort Lauderdale is often called the "Venice of America."

FIGURE 14.4 | Simultaneous Supply and Demand Changes

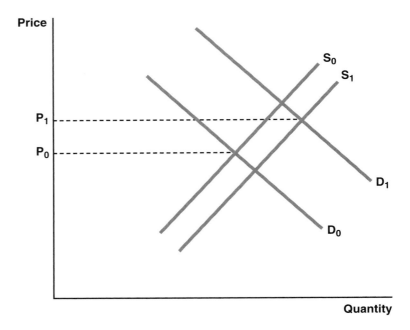

To apply the supply and demand model discussed above to the market for new, luxury homes on ocean-accessible lots in Fort Lauderdale, let's first consider the supply side of the market. The city's amenities have long been popular with wealthy retirees who were willing to pay top dollar to enjoy the Florida sun, and the city has experienced persistent population growth for most of the last 50 years. Thus, almost all ocean-accessible lots have an existing home on them, with almost no vacant lots available. The supply side consists of mostly older single-family homes that are smaller than the luxury homes of today's standards and are approaching the end of their useful lives (the houses, not the owners).

Because there are no new canals anticipated in this market, the long-run marginal cost of adding homes is upward sloping because the cost of each new, ocean-accessible luxury home includes the cost of demolition of an existing home. As more and more ocean-accessible luxury homes are built to replace the existing homes, the cost of building the next home increases even more. Over the long run, this market has a steeply sloping supply curve because the amount of land with ocean access cannot be increased.

On the demand side of this market are full- and part-time residents who have high disposable income levels or significant wealth portfolios and wish to maintain a permanent residence or vacation home in the area. Many of these full- and part-time residents are quite willing to spend several million dollars for an existing older home that they will demolish and replace with an even more luxurious home where they can dock their multi-million-dollar motor yacht or sailboat in the backyard.

The City of Fort Lauderdale recognizes the importance of attracting these big spenders and works hard to maintain the "Venice of America" image with infrastructure improvements and international marketing campaigns. The price of luxury, ocean-accessible homes in this market depends, at least to some degree, on the success of the city's efforts to maintain this image. When the number of wealthy residents (full- and part-time) increases, the demand for such homes increases. Given the shape of the supply curve, the prices of such homes increase as demand increases. As the value of the homes increases, the city's property tax base increases, enabling the city to spend even more money to attract more wealthy residents to the area (see Figure 14.4).

Between 2000 and 2007, the price of ocean-accessible homes in Fort Lauderdale skyrocketed, and the number of "teardowns" increased dramatically. Developers typically purchase two or three existing homes, tear down the structures, then combine the lots into one large lot and build a single luxury home on the combined parcels. As long as the demand continues to increase, we can expect continued price increases for homes in this market.

COMMERCIAL REAL ESTATE MARKETS

Whereas the preceding discussion focused on owner-occupied residential real estate, we now turn our attention to commercial real estate markets in which the properties generally are intended to generate rental income for the owners. We can further divide commercial real estate markets into real estate space markets (where landlords and tenants engage in transactions over the use of space) and the real estate asset market (where investors/developers engage in transactions over the ownership of real estate and the rights to receive the rents from tenants).

Real Estate Space Markets

Real estate space markets involve transactions for the rights to use land and buildings. On the demand side of this market are people, firms, and other entities that are willing to pay to use space for consumption or production purposes. The supply side of this market consists of property owners who are willing to sell such space to users. The price of use in space markets is often called *rent,* even if the user is the owner/occupant of the space.

Users of space often have specific requirements for the type of space they demand and the locations of that space. A family, for example, wants comfortable, attractive living space near shopping, education, and entertainment resources, but a manufacturing firm is likely to be more concerned with functionality and proximity to its customers or raw materials suppliers. *Suppliers* in the space market have buildings that were designed for specific uses and are fixed in their locations.

Because supply and demand are location and type-specific, real estate space markets are highly segmented. Office space in Los Angeles is clearly a different market from the warehouse space market in Texas. Prices (rents) for one type of space may be very different from rents for a different type of space in the same geographic area, and prices for the same type of space in two different geographic areas may differ dramatically.

Categories of the Real Estate Space Market

Real estate space markets can be categorized by property usage and by geographic boundaries. The major segments of the real estate space market include residential, industrial, retail, office, agricultural, and lodging. Adding geographic dimensions to these categories allows us to discuss the "highway motel market in the southeastern United States," the "warehouse market in Chicago," the "class B office market in San Antonio," or almost any other reasonable combination of location and use. Accurate analysis of a real estate space market requires an accurate market definition. Let's consider how each of the major market segments can be further subdivided in terms of property usage. As you read through these categories, keep in mind that the objective for identifying the specific market segment is to be able to analyze the factors that affect activity in that market segment.

Office Space Market

The office market is commonly divided into four subcategories: Class A, Class B, Class C, and Class D. The following distinctions are common:

- **Class A**—Buildings that will generate the highest rents per square foot due to their high quality and/or superior location.
- **Class B**—Buildings that most tenants would find desirable but are lacking certain attributes that would permit owners to charge top dollar.
- **Class C**—Buildings that offer few amenities but are otherwise in physically acceptable condition and provide cost-effective space to tenants who are not particularly image-conscious.
- **Class D**—Buildings with few amenities and poor locations and/or physical condition.

Retail Space Market

Retail space is commonly divided into five subcategories: (1) freestanding retail, (2) neighborhood centers, (3) community centers, (4) regional centers, and (5) super-regional centers. These subcategories are generally defined as follows:

- **Freestanding retail**—Single tenant buildings.

- **Neighborhood center**—Sometimes called a *convenience center,* designed to serve a relatively small trade area (1.5-mile radius) with a population of between 2,500 and 40,000 people. Its anchor tenant (primary tenant) often is a supermarket, with other stores providing convenience goods and personal services (hardware, pharmacy, hair salon, etc.). These centers usually are built in *strip style*—that is, stores placed side-by-side in a straight line or an L-shape with a covered walkway along the front for pedestrians. The neighborhood center usually is separated from the street by a customer parking area.

- **Community center**—Designed to serve a larger trade area than a neighborhood center (3- to 5-mile radius), it includes a wider variety of merchandise. Its anchor tenant is usually a discount store or junior department store. When the anchor tenant is a discount store, the center is sometimes called a *Discount Center.* These centers are usually built in strip style with large customer parking areas in front.

- **Regional center**—Designed to serve a primary trade area within a radius of 7 to 12 miles, these centers offer a full range of goods and services. Regional centers are usually designed as enclosed malls with at least one, and sometimes several, full-line department stores serving as the anchor tenants.

- **Super-regional center**—Designed to serve trade areas with a radius of more than 50 miles, these centers often exceed 1 million square feet of space and offer a tremendous range of products and services. One example of a super-regional center is the Sawgrass Mills Mall in South Florida. This mall attracts customers from all over southern Florida and also from Latin America, the Caribbean, and parts of Europe. Billed as one of the world's most popular shopping destinations and Florida's largest retail and entertainment center, Sawgrass Mills Mall features almost two miles of enclosed shopping space with more than 400 name-brand stores, pushcarts and kiosks, more than 30 restaurants, several entertainment clubs, and more than 20 movie screens.

Industrial Space Market

Industrial space is commonly divided into three categories: (1) warehouse, (2) manufacturing/production, and (3) materials processing.

The Electronic Revolution's Impact on the Value of Location

The electronic revolution of recent years has given many older buildings new, and profitable, lives as *electronic hotels*, that is, Web data centers. To the old saw of "location, location, location" has been added "location and nearness to fiber-optics lines." If a building is close to a trunk fiber-optic line and has high ceilings and wide column spacing to accommodate racks of electronics, floors capable of supporting giant DC battery arrays, and a robust electrical supply, it may be reincarnated as an electronic hotel housing equipment for multiple phone companies.

Take the vacant 264,000-square-foot warehouse for bankrupt electronics retailer Nobody Beats the Wiz in Carteret, New Jersey. The very ordinary warehouse building had one very uncommon factor in its favor—it was located within a dozen yards of a major fiber-optic line. This enabled developer Young Woo & Associates to lease it for more than $20 per square foot as a Web-hosting center, compared with $5 to $7 per square foot as a warehouse. In general, telecom hotels command rental rates several times those of comparable industrial sites and as much as 20 percent higher than nearby office space.

Another example is the seven-story Macy's Atlanta department store building. Macy's wanted to keep a presence in downtown Atlanta, but the shift of retailing to suburban shopping malls had made the store much too large. Macy's sold the building and leased back the lower three floors for its retail operation. The remaining 360,000 square feet, with its access to trunk fiber-optic lines, was converted into an electronics hotel.

The rapid growth in electronic communications has also created large demand for another former real estate liability—rooftops. The surge in mobile phone usage has forced phone companies to erect more and more antennas in urban areas, and rooftops are a viable location. Thus, rooftop space for antennas in downtown Manhattan leases for around $100 per square foot, compared to $40 for office space within the same building.

Agricultural Space Market

Agricultural space (mostly land) is commonly divided into three categories: (1) annual (seasonal) cropland, (2) perennial cropland, and (3) livestock facilities and grazing land.

Lodging Space Market

Lodging space can be divided into the following five categories: (1) highway motels, (2) convention/business hotels, (3) luxury hotels, (4) resort (destination) hotels, and (5) extended stay hotels/motels.

Residential Space Market

Residential space can be divided into (1) single-family detached homes, (2) single-family attached homes (condos, co-ops, town houses, etc.), (3) manufactured homes, and (4) multifamily apartments.

REAL ESTATE ASSET MARKETS

Whereas the real estate space market reflects transactions involving the use of space, the **real estate asset market** reflects transactions involving cash-flow rights to real estate. The term *cash-flow rights* refers to the claims to the future cash flows that the buildings and land are expected to generate. The participants in this market are concerned with the amount and timing of the cash flows a building is capable of producing rather than the building's configuration for a particular use. These market participants make their decisions about buying and selling by comparing real estate assets with other capital market assets such as stocks and bonds. As such, the real estate asset market must be regarded as part of the larger **capital market,** the market for capital assets of all types.

To understand how real estate assets compete with other capital assets, consider the chart provided in Figure 14.5. This chart divides the capital asset market into four broad categories: publicly traded equity assets, publicly traded debt assets, privately traded equity assets, and privately traded debt assets.

Public markets transactions typically involve relatively small portions of ownership rights to various capital assets. The stock market is the most obvious example of a public market. Shares of public corporations trade in huge volume on any given trading day, and observed prices reflect all currently available information about the assets.

Private markets involve transactions between individual buyers and sellers without the aid of a formal market mechanism. Private markets usually involve the sale of whole assets rather than shares of assets. Because such transactions happen less frequently than public market transactions and because the parties to the transaction may keep information private, it is generally more difficult for private market participants to determine the value of assets traded in these markets. Furthermore, the transaction costs of trading these assets are likely to be much higher than the costs of trading in the public markets.

The chart also divides the capital market into debt and equity categories. Debt assets can be thought of as rights to the future cash flows paid by a borrower on a loan. These cash flows are contractually specified according to the details of the loan agreement. As such, the debt holder is entitled to be paid before the borrower gets any cash flow from the underlying asset (the source of the cash flow). Debt assets typically have a specified maturity date.

Equity assets refer to assets that entitle their owners to the residual cash flow generated by an underlying asset (after the debt holders have been paid). Equity assets are more risky than debt assets, in general, because of their "second" priority behind debt assets. Of course, the riskier the asset, the higher the expected return.

FIGURE 14.5 | Major Types of Capital Asset Markets and Investment Products

	Public Markets	**Private Markets**
Equity Assets	Stocks REITs Mutual Funds	Real Property Private Firms Oil and Gas Partnerships
Debt Assets	Bonds MBS Money Instruments	Bank Loans Whole Mortgages Venture Debt

Capital asset vehicles based on real estate as the underlying asset take a variety of forms. In the public equity market, shares of publicly traded real estate investment trusts (REITs, pronounced "reets") trade with a volume comparable to that of shares of industrial corporations. REITs raise money from the sale of shares to investors and then use the proceeds to acquire properties and mortgages. They then manage the portfolios to maximize the return to their shareholders.

In the public debt market, investors can purchase derivative products such as mortgage-backed securities (MBSs), whose underlying assets are pools of mortgages on residential and commercial properties. As mortgage payments are made to the pool by borrowers, the money is distributed to the various investors according to the type of security they bought from the pool. In the private debt market, investors and institutions buy and sell mortgage loans that are secured by individual buildings.

Most people who think of the real estate asset market think about the private equity market that involves ownership of whole properties. The lack of complete information and infrequency of trades in the private equity real estate market make this market one of the most dynamic and interesting capital markets. Even so, the different categories of real estate asset markets are well integrated with each other and the markets for other capital assets. The prices of real estate assets in the private equity market reflect the integration of all capital markets and the competition between asset markets for investors' dollars.

Price Determinants in the Real Estate Assets Market

Real estate asset market prices are determined by three main factors: opportunity cost of capital, growth expectations, and risk. Investors make their buy/sell decisions about real estate assets by comparing the return they expect to get from real estate assets with alternative rates of return they could earn from other capital assets in the capital market. As the opportunity cost of capital goes down, investors are generally willing to put more money into real estate assets, thus driving up their prices.

FIGURE 14.6 │ The Real Estate System

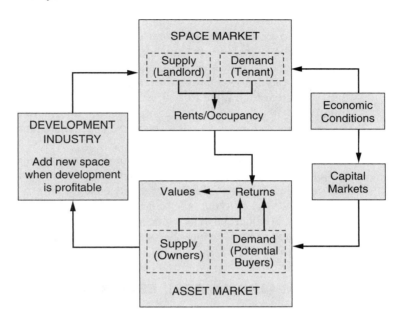

Investors are also concerned with the likely amount of growth (or decline) they expect from a property's cash flow. The cash flow a property can generate is, of course, determined in the real estate space market, as we previously discussed. The higher the expected growth rate in the space market, the more money investors will be willing to pay for property in the asset market.

Finally, the third determinant of prices in the real estate asset market is risk. Investors will evaluate how certain (or uncertain) they feel about a property's future cash flows and will prefer to pay less for a property with higher risk. Paying lower prices allows the investor to have a higher expected return for a given level of risk.

▌ TYING TOGETHER THE SPACE AND ASSET MARKETS ──────────

Now that we understand the distinctions real estate analysts make between the real estate space market and the real estate asset market, our current task is to show how these markets are interrelated. Figure 14.6 shows a simple model of "the real estate system" in terms of the development industry, the real estate asset market, and the real estate space market.

In this visual model of the real estate system, activity in the space market, the asset market, and the development industry are simultaneously determined. Influenced primarily by local economic conditions, owners/users and landlords/tenants negotiate over price (rent) levels in the space market. When demand conditions warrant, the owners/users and landlords purchase additional properties from the development industry and make them part of the available supply. At the same time, landlords and the owners/users negotiate in the capital market with potential tenants/buyers who are attracted to real estate assets by attractive risk-return combinations relative to other assets in the national or even international capital market. Potential buyers who become owners then enter the space market as landlords or owners/users, thus completing the "system."

Visualizing the real estate system in this manner can help us see how the three major components of the real estate system (development, space market, asset market) are tied together. Relatively small changes in any one component may flow through the system to the other components and can have dramatic impacts on them. A prudent commercial real estate market participant is well advised to keep this visual image in mind, especially when analyzing a real estate deal that looks much too good to be true!

■ PREPARING A COMMERCIAL REAL ESTATE MARKET ANALYSIS ————

While all of the preceding theoretical discussion is crucial to the understanding of real estate markets, how can we apply these theories to real world situations? This section of the chapter describes how to prepare a structural analysis of a real estate market. By definition, a **market analysis** is an examination of the supply and demand sides of a real estate space market segment and the balance (equilibrium) between these two sides. The goal of market analysis is to assist real estate market participants in making effective real estate decisions. Market analysis can be used to answer such questions as the following:

- How much rent should I charge tenants in this building?
- How many new units should I build this year?
- Where should I locate a new branch office for my business?
- What type of building should I build on this site?
- What are the growth prospects for this market segment?

Basic Inputs to Market Analysis

The typical real estate market analysis focuses on a few carefully chosen variables that are designed to characterize the supply and demand sides of the market segment as well as the balance between these two sides. Five of the most common inputs to a real estate market analysis are

1. vacancy rate,
2. rent or price level,
3. quantity of new construction started,
4. quantity of new construction completed, and
5. absorption of new space.

We will consider each of these variables in turn.

Vacancy rate is the measure of the amount of unoccupied space as a percentage of the total amount of space in the market. For example, a community with 50 empty rental apartments and 1,500 total rental apartments has a vacancy rate of about 3.3 percent (50 ÷ 1,500). The vacancy rate is an indicator of the balance between the supply and demand sides of the market segment. The unit of measurement used in calculating vacancy rates varies by market segment. For apartments, the typical unit of measure is "number of units," as we just demonstrated. For commercial and industrial space, the typical unit of measure is "square feet of space."

Another important indicator of the balance between supply and demand in a market segment is the rent or price level. Changes in the market rent or market price of space indicates changes in the balance between supply and demand. In residential markets, rents are often expressed as monthly rents per dwelling unit. In commercial and industrial markets, the unit of measure is more commonly the annual rent per square foot of space.

Two good indicators of the supply side conditions of a real estate space market include construction starts and completions. In residential markets, these variables are measured by the number of new homes or apartments. In commercial and industrial markets, these variables are measured in square feet of space. Construction starts and completions indicate the amount of new supply "in the pipeline" and the amount of new supply "flowing out of the pipeline," respectively. In some markets, a thorough market analysis would also need to address the amount of space being demolished to make room for new construction and the renovation of existing space.

Finally, one of the best indicators of the demand side conditions of a real estate space market is the **absorption rate. Gross absorption** refers to the total amount of new space that became occupied during a specified time period. **Net absorption** is defined as the net change in the amount of occupied space in the market segment during a specified time period.

Using Market Analysis to Look Forward

These five indicators of a space market give a good overview of the supply and demand conditions in a market and the direction of change for both the supply and demand. These five variables can be combined in some creative ways to develop a forecast for future market conditions. For example, many real estate market analysts use the concept of "months supply" to look into the future of a real estate space market. **Months supply** is calculated by the following formula:

$$\text{Months Supply} = (\text{Vacant Space} + \text{Space in Construction}) \div \text{Net Absorption per Month}$$

The months supply indicator tells us how long it will take (in months) for all the vacant space in the market to be absorbed at the current rate of absorption. A housing developer, for example, can use this measure along with an estimate of the average time it takes to complete new units to determine whether the market can support another project. In a market that is absorbing 30 housing units per month and has 30 currently vacant units and 90 units under construction, the "months supply" is four. If the developer's construction time is two months, it is likely that a new project will hit the market at a time when there is excess supply. The months supply indicator is a simple measure for looking forward in a real estate space market segment.

Professional Market Analysis Reports

Performing a thorough market analysis can be very expensive and time consuming and may require the skills of a professional market analyst. Numerous market research firms around the world offer their services to investors and consumers for a fee. Some of the big names in real estate market research include Torto Wheaton Research, LaSalle Investment Advisors, and RREEF Research. To formulate their market analysis reports, research firms examine the key "drivers" for each market segment. Examples of these drivers for various segments are described below:

- *Office:* employment in office occupations
- *Lodging:* air passenger volume, highway traffic counts, tourism receipts, number of visitors
- *Retail:* per capita income, aggregate income, wealth measures
- *Industrial:* manufacturing employment, transportation employment, shipping volume
- *Apartments:* population, household formation, local housing affordability, employment growth (blue and white collar)
- *Owner-occupied residential:* population, household formation, interest rates, employment growth, income growth

Combining the information on these key drivers with the previously described indicators allows these firms to predict future market conditions and identify investment opportunities for their clients.

CHAPTER REVIEW

- By definition, a *market* is the mechanism or arrangements through which goods and services are traded between market participants. The combined effects of supply and demand in markets determine equilibrium prices.

- Prices are generally said to be directly related to changes in demand and inversely related to changes in supply. Events that increase demand lead to increased prices, and events that decrease demand lead to decreased prices. Events that increase supply lead to decreased prices, and events that decrease supply lead to increased prices. When supply and demand change simultaneously, the resulting price depends on the relative magnitudes of the supply and demand changes.

- Commercial real estate can be divided into two types of real estate markets: the real estate space market and the real estate asset market.

- The real estate space market is concerned with transactions that involve owners/users and landlords/tenants. This market is highly segmented along lines governed by use and location.

- The real estate asset market involves transactions regarding rights to the cash flows generated by real estate assets. Participants in this market are primarily concerned with cash-flow generating ability of a property rather than its configuration for a particular use.

- The real estate asset market is a component in the larger market for all capital assets.

- Prices in the real estate asset market are primarily determined by the opportunity cost of capital, growth expectations, and risk.

- The space and asset markets are tied together by the development industry. When participants in the asset market expect high returns from real estate assets relative to other capital assets, they will purchase new construction from the development industry. The new buildings become part of the available supply in the space market. Together, the real estate space market, the real estate asset market, and the development industry form a "real estate system."

▌ KEY TERMS

absorption rate	gross absorption	real estate asset market
capital market	market	real estate space market
community center	market analysis	regional center
demand	months supply	super-regional center
equilibrium	neighborhood center	supply
freestanding retail	net absorption	vacancy rate

▌ STUDY EXERCISES

1. Use a simple graph of the supply/demand equilibrium model to show how an increase in mortgage loan interest rates might affect owner-occupied residential real estate prices (other things held constant).

2. Use a simple graph of the supply/demand equilibrium model to show how a population increase accompanied by a decrease in construction costs might affect owner-occupied residential real estate prices (other things held constant).

3. If demand in the space market declines, what is the predicted impact on prices?

4. What are the three main determinants of prices in the real estate asset market?

5. If price levels in the space market increase significantly, will that entice investors to purchase more real estate in the asset market?

6. How will the asset market and the development industry respond to an increase in demand in a space market?

7. What are the three major components of the "real estate system"?

8. Define the terms *net absorption* and *gross absorption.*

9. Calculate the months supply of warehouse space in a market that absorbed 10,000 square feet last year, has 6,000 vacant square feet, and has 3,000 square feet under construction. Would this be a good time to start a new warehouse project in this market? Why or why not?

10. Internet exercise: Visit the Web site of a major real estate research firm and compare the multifamily apartment market in your community with the national multifamily apartment market. Does the outlook for this market segment in your community look brighter or dimmer than the national outlook? Why?

▍FURTHER READING

Geltner, David M., Norman G. Miller, Jim Clayton, and Piet Eichholtz. *Commercial Real Estate Analysis and Investments*, 2nd ed. Mason, Ohio: Thomson South-Western, 2007.

Urban and Regional Economics

CHAPTER PREVIEW

As we discussed in the previous chapter, an understanding of real estate market dynamics is crucial to effective real estate decision making. The discipline of studying real estate markets at the urban and regional level is called **urban and regional economics.** In this chapter we consider some of the concepts and tools that urban and regional economists have developed for evaluating real estate markets. These tools help explain how cities grow and change and how land uses and values vary within and among urban areas. Because real estate markets are an integral component of the overall real estate system, the better we understand market dynamics, the better we can understand the overall system.

The objectives of this chapter are to define various theories and concepts from the urban economics discipline, including

- the concept of comparative advantage;

- economic base theory;

- the bid-rent curve and the concept of highest and best use;

- the concentric circle model of urban form;

- the sector growth model;

- the axial growth model;

- the multiple-nuclei growth model; and

- the neighborhood life cycle model.

REAL ESTATE TODAY

CLOSE-UP
The Rise of the "Location-Neutral" Urban Migrant

CASE STUDY
A Tale of Two Cities: Schenectady and Mooresville

CASE STUDY
A Tale of Two More Cities: The Effects of Public Infrastructure on the Development of Boston and Los Angeles

CASE STUDY
Neighborhood Revitalization

ECONOMIC FACTORS INFLUENCING THE GROWTH AND DECLINE OF CITIES

Why does one region or locality develop into a center of trade or industry while others do not? Why does the economy and population of a city or region grow or decline? What factors determine the economic growth rate of an area? The answers to these questions are closely linked to the concepts of comparative advantage and economic base.

Determinants of a Community's Comparative Advantage

Rapid economic and population growth generally results because one locale has a **comparative advantage** over another. This advantage may result from several factors. A city may grow because it has advantages in transportation facilities; advantages in the quality or quantity of other factors in the created environment; or because of natural resources, a favorable climate, or the quality or quantity of its labor force.

Transportation Facilities

Perhaps the most important factor that gives a community comparative advantage is transportation facilities. Almost all colonial cities in the United States developed around ports, either on natural harbors or along rivers. Most of the latter ports were located at important river junctions or at the *fall line,* the point at which the rivers cease to be navigable because their waters, descending from the uplands to the lowlands, form rapids and falls.

These initial natural advantages often were aided by further transportation improvements. For example, New York became the dominant port on the eastern seaboard and a world city largely because of the initial advantage it enjoyed after the completion of the Erie Canal in 1825, which provided easy access to the developing West.

Later, the advent of the railroad led to the "railroad town." A community located on a railroad enjoyed a distinct economic advantage over a town that was not, and communities at important rail junctions gained an even greater comparative advantage. The best example is Chicago, which developed into one of the nation's largest cities primarily because of its dominance as a rail center between East and West.

Because major highways have tended to follow the paths of major railroads, rail centers have also become highway centers. Similarly, many have become major air-traffic transfer points. Two of the busiest airports in the United States are those in Chicago and Atlanta, two cities that serve as transfer points, one between East and West and the other for the Southeast.

Educational Facilities

In today's technological and service-oriented economy, the quality of educational facilities is of great importance, both in providing centers for technological development and in increasing the educational quality of the labor force. These factors undoubtedly will become even more important in future years.

Created Environment

The created environment consists of such things as utilities, public services and tax levels, housing, cultural activities, and transportation and educational facilities. The quality and quantity of such factors may give a region or community a comparative advantage or disadvantage. If a community has an industrial park, for instance, it may attract additional industrial employment. Conversely, an industrial firm will not locate where adequate utilities and other services are not available.

Natural Resources

Another important factor in the location of cities is the existence of various natural resources. Denver owes its origins to the discovery of gold and silver in the nearby mountains; ample deposits of coal and iron ore greatly aided the development of Birmingham and Pittsburgh. After the resources that led to its formation have been depleted or become less of a comparative advantage, and if it is to continue to prosper, a resource-based city must develop other advantages as a center of trade and industry.

Climate

Other cities and regions owe much of their comparative advantage to their favorable climate; for those whose economy is based on tourism, this factor may be dominant. Climate has been an extremely important factor in the development of cities in Florida and California and is cited as one of the major comparative advantages of the Sunbelt. As a greater percentage of the population reaches retirement age over the coming decades, the advantage of these communities as retirement locations will also rise in significance.

Labor Force

Another important factor that may give an area a comparative advantage is the quality or quantity of the labor force. For example, the textile industry, for the most part, deserted the cities of New England for those of the Southeast following World War II, largely because the Southeast offered an ample supply of labor that was willing to work for relatively low wages. Conversely, New England cities—particularly those in Massachusetts—were able to attract a substantial portion of the expanding electronics industry because their labor forces possessed a relatively high level of education and skill.

Leadership

An intangible but critical factor in community growth and in a community's becoming a quality place to live is community leadership. In fact, many feel this is *the* most important factor in regional and area growth and quality development.

Some communities have many comparative advantages, but languish; others prosper, though they possess few natural advantages. The difference, in most cases, is the caliber of local leadership.

The Concept of an Economic Base

Specialization is both a fundamental economic concept and the primary reason for the existence of cities. In a developed economy, and even in most primitive societies, neither the individual nor the family nor the community can be wholly self-sufficient. Even solitary trappers occasionally must emerge from the wilds to sell pelts and purchase necessary supplies. Similarly, a community or region is not self-sufficient but must sell goods and services outside its borders to pay for the imports it needs.

The pelts Trapper Joe sells are "exports" for his economy, and the proceeds can be used to purchase needed supplies, "imports". Similarly, a community tends to specialize in certain activities in which it has a comparative advantage and to sell those goods and services to the rest of the world. The income from those exports can be used to import goods and services from outside the community.

In examining local economies, analysts often classify employment into two general categories: (1) **export activities,** also called *basic activities,* which produce goods and services for sale or consumption outside the area's borders, and (2) **population-serving activities,** also called *nonbasic activities,* which produce goods and services for sale or consumption within the community itself. Although it is difficult to determine with any exactness which of a community's activities are for export, they usually include most of those in the fields of agriculture, mining, manufacturing, and wholesale trade.

The population-serving activities generally include those undertaken by the construction industry, public utilities, the retail trade, finance, service industries, and government. Sometimes, however, population-serving activities are also export in nature. A regional shopping center may draw customers from far beyond the local area, a city may serve as headquarters for financial institutions serving a large region, and a large university usually attracts students far from the local area.

If export activity in a region or city expands, so will employment in the population-serving industries. Suppose that Amalgamated Whitzadidle opens a new manufacturing plant in Lower Swampville that employs 500 workers. The economic impact of the new plant will go far beyond this direct employment increase. Construction workers will be needed to build the facility and homes and apartments for individuals and families who may move to the area. Purchases of various goods and services by the manufacturing workers will give rise to additional employment in the trade and service industries. The new residents also will be purchasing and financing homes and buying insurance, thereby creating new jobs in those fields. In the same fashion, the impact of the new plant will spread throughout the local economy so that the total employment and income created will be far greater than the direct impact.

In the past, many regional analysts, planners, and appraisers have tried to quantify the relationship between changes in employment in industries that bring income

The Rise of the "Location-Neutral" Urban Migrant

We know that except for retirees and the few with independent incomes, people normally must work within commuting distance of their employment. However, with modern communications and data networks a small but increasing number of workers are employed in jobs that can be referred to as "location-neutral," not tied to any particular location. Thus, these people can choose where they want to live without regard to employment needs.

Take, for example, Greg and Kristin Shields. Greg is sales engineer and expert on the communication needs of the financial industry with telecommunications company SAVVIS. He assists sales representatives around the country, primarily through conference calls. Kristin is a program

manager with a consulting firm, doing environmental impact studies for the Corps of Engineers. Neither of these jobs requires them to be in a particular location, so they decided to move away from their suburban Washington home to a less fast-paced life in Salisbury, North Carolina. Instead of his former 45-minute commute, Greg now walks the seven blocks to his office, an office that is much less costly for his company than his former urban location. They live in a 100-year-old home in a historic district that they never would have been able to afford in their former location, where housing was much more expensive. They also benefit from other less costly small-town amenities such as membership in the local country club and boating on nearby lakes. Having location-neutral jobs has definitely enabled Greg and Kristin to enjoy a more relaxed and better lifestyle.

into a region from beyond its borders—that is, changes in the **economic base**—and changes in total employment, income, and population. To understand the potential market for real property in a community, it is essential to understand the community's industrial structure and the probable changes that will occur. If the economic base is likely to expand, demand for real property also is likely to expand. Conversely, of course, if the economic base is expected to contract, the demand for real estate also is likely to contract.

▌ THE LOCATION OF PEOPLE

Cities tend to develop in places that offer firms a comparative advantage, and exploitation of that advantage leads to growth of the economic base. People also tend to locate where they can achieve a comparative advantage, and although there are exceptions, most people live where they do because of economic opportunities. When jobs are plentiful, other factors come into play as well—personal preferences for a particular type of climate or landscape, big-city attractions or small-town tranquility,

A Tale of Two Cities: Schenectady and Mooresville

 When a community's economic base is dominated by a single industry, its economic fortunes are also dominated by the economic factors that affect that industry. Consider the cases of Schenectady, New York, and Mooresville, North Carolina.

Fifty years ago, with tens of thousands employed at General Electric and American Locomotive, Schenectady was known as "the city that lights and hauls the world." But American Locomotive closed its factory in 1969, and GE has slowly moved its manufacturing elsewhere. Median family income in 2005 was only $31,800, compared to the state average of $49,480. Additionally, median home value was only $97,100, compared to the state average of $258,900. As one would expect, with economic opportunity declining, the city's population, as in most of the old industrial cities of upper New York state, has also fallen: from 92,000 in 1950 to less than 62,000 today.

In 1980, Mooresville had a population of around 9,000 and an economy that was almost totally dominated by the textile industry. By the turn of the century, every textile mill had closed, largely due to cheaper foreign competition. The last one, a denim plant that once employed about one-fifth of the town's population, closed in 1999.

The town made a concerted and fairly successful effort to diversify its economy, but renewed employment growth came from an unlikely source—stock car racing. Lured by convenient interstate highway access, closeness to the Lowe's Motor Speedway and the Charlotte airport, and recreational opportunities offered by nearby Lake Norman, racing shops began locating in the Mooresville area in the mid-1990s. As their presence grew, agglomeration economies also developed—a large cadre of skilled mechanics, a wind tunnel for aerodynamic testing, and the NASCAR Technical Institute among them. Today, the community is home to more than 120 motor sports–related teams and suppliers with employment reaching approximately 1,500. The racing shops and the stock-car museum located there also attract many tourists, creating significant demand for area motels and restaurants. Mooresville, which now calls itself "Race City USA," has a vigorous and growing economy.

and closeness to or distance from relatives. When jobs become more scarce, such considerations tend to lose their force; people go where they can find work.

The growth of Social Security and other retirement benefits in recent years has created a large group of retirees who are relatively free to follow their locational preferences. This group has been a major factor in the population growth of such warm-weather states as Florida and Arizona. Most interstate migrants in this age group move for family or retirement reasons. Even in this age group, however, nearly 14 percent of the moves in a recent census study were made for reasons of employment.

It follows that demand for housing in a locality is very closely related to *employment demand*—that is, to the community's economic base. Indeed, most real estate activity occurs as a result of changes in the economic base. For example, industrial construction is a direct result of such changes. And indirectly—through increases in the demand for population-related activities—changes in the economic base lead to the development of shopping centers, construction of schools, and the like.

ANALYZING LOCAL REAL ESTATE DEMAND

How do these regional and community growth factors influence the local demand for real estate? The real estate analyst must have an understanding of both the current changes in the industrial structure of the community and the factors that might lead to economic changes that attract new people or cause residents to leave. Demand for existing properties is tied to the current industry mix and expected short-run changes. Long-term demand for existing properties and for new developments is related to the long-run vitality of the community's economy, which can be assessed only by an analysis of potential change.

Analysis of Short-Run Demand

Previously, we saw that although completion of new construction may add to the supply of real property improvements, the supply is largely fixed in the short run. Changes in demand in the short run most often affect vacancy rates, sales of existing properties, prices, and lease rates.

The real estate analyst attempting to ascertain possible short-term changes in local real estate markets must ask the following questions:

- What is the current supply of various types of real estate improvements?
- What is the industrial structure of the community?
- What changes have occurred in the local economy in the recent past?
- What is likely to happen to the economy in the near future?

Suppose, for example, that a city's economy is heavily dependent on the automotive industry. A decrease in demand for automobiles would have an immediate impact on employment, which would lead in turn to a decrease in consumer spending. If these conditions persist, and particularly if a major firm closes its local manufacturing facility, then housing and other real estate markets would be quite adversely affected.

Analysis of Long-Run Demand

Suppose a potential investor is considering building a new resort facility in a community or that a developer is considering building a shopping center in a city whose dominant manufacturing employer has been forced to begin massive layoffs.

In these situations, the prospects obviously would be poor in the short run. But the proposed improvements would not actually come onto the market for some time, and demand could then be quite different and favorable for the new project. In this situation, the analyst must examine additional questions:

- What are the long-run prospects for the economy of the community?
- What national or regional trends are likely to affect employment in the area?
- Are new firms likely to locate in the area, bringing additional employment?

Projecting and forecasting future employment trends is an interesting exercise that often involves sophisticated modeling techniques. In the final analysis, however, the real estate investor must carefully evaluate the assumptions that lie behind population and employment projections. While most of our discussion thus far has been targeted at how entire urban areas grow and change, the next several sections of this chapter examine land-use patterns within urban areas.

THE BID-RENT CURVE AND THE CONCEPT OF HIGHEST AND BEST USE

Why is a certain parcel of land used for a particular purpose? Why are certain parcels of land worth more than others? The answer to these questions lies in the concept of land rent. The classical economists included land as one of the three elements of production (land, labor, and capital), and rent is the return on or price of land. In theory, a particular parcel will be used in the way that yields the highest return to the owner. **Land rent** is the return that a particular parcel of land will bring in the open market.

Land rent, of course, differs from one parcel to another because the highest and best use of each parcel differs. By definition, **highest and best use** is that use of a parcel that will produce the highest return or price to the owner. Highest and best use is constrained by legal restrictions and the physical characteristics of the parcel. Over time, the highest and best use of a parcel of land may change, but the process by which one land use gives way to another is not rapid. Rather, the existing improvements will be converted to a new use over a period of time; the final conversion occurs only when the value of the land in an alternate use is great enough to pay for the site, the existing building, and its demolition.

To understand how location and use affect price, let's examine one of the classic concepts from the urban economic discipline: the **bid-rent curve.** *Bid-rent* refers to the maximum rent that a potential real estate space user would be willing to pay, or "bid," for a specified location.

Consider a simple community that consists of three different types of space users: commercial, residential, and agricultural. Each of these potential users in this community space market has its own bid-rent function that can be expressed as the

FIGURE 15.1 | Theoretical Price-Distance Relationships

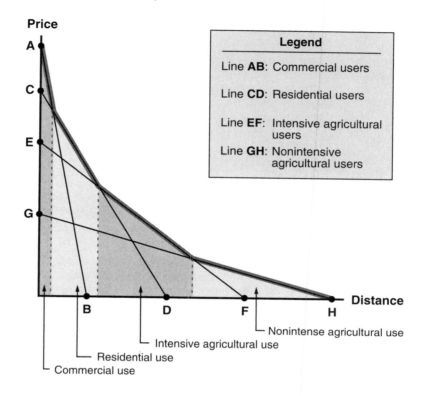

relationship between the price they would be willing to pay for locations as the distance from the center of the community increases.

Figure 15.1 shows the bid-rent functions for each of the three space users in our community. Notice that the commercial users are willing to pay the highest prices for locations closest to the center of the city. But the commercial users are not willing to pay any price for locations at distances greater than point A from the community center. Similarly, we see that residential users are willing to pay the second highest prices for locations at the center of the community, but not as much as the commercial users are willing to pay. At distances beyond the first vertical dashed line, however, the residential users are the high bidders for space. Beyond the second vertical dashed line, agricultural users are the high bidders. Looking at the "outer edge" of the curve formed by the combination of the three users' bid-rent functions gives the bid-rent curve for this community. We can see the land prices fall as distance from the city center increases, quickly at first, but more slowly as the distance increases more and more.

FIGURE 15.2 | Concentric-Circle Growth

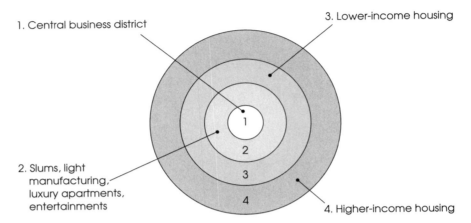

1. Central business district

3. Lower-income housing

2. Slums, light manufacturing, luxury apartments, entertainments

4. Higher-income housing

This model shows that each location has a highest and best use that is determined by its land rent. We will see this concept again in the appraisal chapter of this text.

MODELS OF URBAN GROWTH PATTERNS

A city may grow in several ways: vertically, by replacement of smaller structures with taller ones and by use of air rights to construct new buildings over existing ones; by **in-filling** of open spaces between existing structures; and horizontally, by extension of settled areas.

Of these forms of growth, the first two are applicable to already established urban areas, while the last describes the process of urban expansion. Several models have been used to explain these growth patterns, including the concentric-circle, axial, sector, and multiple-nuclei models of growth. Each model describes aspects of modern urban growth in simplified model form, and most observed growth patterns contain elements from several models.

Concentric-Circle Growth

One model of urban growth patterns resulted from the 1920s study of land uses by Ernest Burgess in Chicago. The **concentric-circle model** postulates that from a central business district, several concentric zones radiate outward. (See Figure 15.2.) In this model, zone 2, immediately bordering the central business district, was one of transition, consisting primarily of slums occupied by recent immigrants, who remained there until they were financially and socially prepared to move to better-quality residences farther from the center. The study found that this zone also contained widely contrasting development, including luxury apartment buildings, elegant restaurants, nightclubs, and theaters. Light-manufacturing facilities were located at its outer edge.

The next zone was occupied mostly by workers employed in the manufacturing activities located in zone 2. Most housing consisted of older single-family dwellings converted into multifamily use. The passage of older housing to less affluent families as it ages is referred to as **filtering,** and it is an important element in neighborhood change.

Higher-income families who could afford better housing on larger lots occupied zone 4. This zone also contained specialized commercial activities serving the affluent group. Still farther out was the limit of the commuter zone, consisting of satellite cities and suburban developments. The area beyond was given over to agricultural activities.

The concentric-circle model basically follows bid-rent theory. Users who are able to pay higher rents are located closer to the center. When considering the realism of the concentric model, we must remember that it was developed in the 1920s, when the central business district was *the* business district because the automobile had not yet influenced the creation of alternate shopping nodes. The model is also more realistic when its assumption of uniform topography is dropped.

Rivers, lakes, mountains, and other geographic features may constrain growth or make it impossible in certain directions. For example, Chicago cannot grow to the east because of Lake Michigan; and the growth of Colorado Springs to the west is constrained by Pikes Peak. Growth in the San Francisco area has been southward, down the peninsula, and largely restricted to the east because of the coastal mountain range. Urban development in the East Bay area is constrained by San Francisco Bay on the west and the Diablo Range on the east. Similarly, the form of most other urban areas has been shaped by geographic features and barriers.

Axial Growth

Transportation is a critical factor not only in the location of cities but also in the way they develop. We know that cities are often located at *transportation nodes*— that is, at the junctions of major transportation routes. They may originate near ocean or river ports, at junctions of major railroads or highways, or where various modes of transportation interconnect. These cities have a competitive edge over communities that do not enjoy such transportation advantages.

Similarly, land within an urban area that is well served by transportation facilities has a comparative advantage over land that is not. Thus, land tends to develop along major transportation routes. The result, according to the **axial model** of growth, is a star-shaped city with growth extending outward along transportation lines. (See Figure 15.3.)

The axial growth model was developed in the 1930s, before most workers had automobiles to commute to work and before trucks freed industrial facilities from

FIGURE 15.3 | Axial Growth

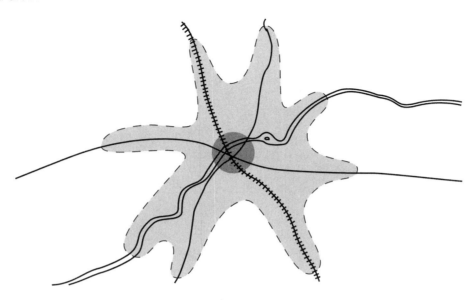

dependence on railroads. These factors, plus the construction of major beltway highways, have reduced the impact of radial transportation routes on urbanization, but they are still an important factor in urban development.

Sector Growth

Extensive studies in the 1930s of residential neighborhood change also led to the development of the **sector model** theory of urban growth by a famous geographer and real estate investor named Homer Hoyt. Hoyt found that particular types of development tended to extend in wedge-shaped sectors from the center of the city, as illustrated in Figure 15.4. For example, if expensive homes were first built in the western sector of a city, their development tended to continue outward in the same direction. The older houses in the sector would be occupied by successively lower-income groups through the filtering process and eventually might be converted into multifamily dwellings. Lower-income groups were not able to commute long distances and tended to live near their work. Thus, lower-income housing usually was located near manufacturing activities but also tended to develop in wedge-shaped patterns.

Most people's experience verifies the sector model. Consider your own hometown and how it has developed. While it won't follow the model precisely, you probably will be able to identify a number of sectors that conform to this model of urban growth.

FIGURE 15.4 | Sector Growth

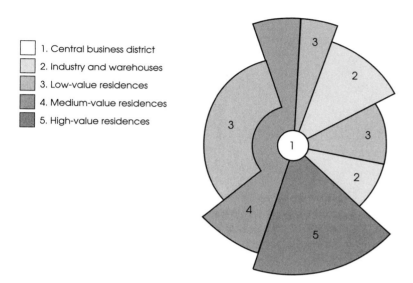

1. Central business district
2. Industry and warehouses
3. Low-value residences
4. Medium-value residences
5. High-value residences

Multiple-Nuclei Growth

The **multiple-nuclei model** of city growth takes the sector theory another step toward describing the actual growth process. It emphasizes that many commercial activities occur in clusters and that, in most cities, there is more than one center of commercial activity (see Figure 15.5). This theory of urban growth was formulated in the 1940s by researchers Harris and Ullman, after the automobile's impact on land-use dispersion had more fully developed. This theory maintains that these clusters developed because (1) certain activities require specialized facilities, (2) many similar activities benefit from close proximity to one another, (3) certain dissimilar activities are detrimental to each other, and (4) some activities must seek less desirable, lower-priced sites.

Many factors, particularly highway and communications improvement, have led to the further fragmentation of most cities' commercial activities in recent decades. Generally, the importance of the central business district has greatly declined with the growth of major suburban shopping centers and office parks. The development of such subcenters has led to a serious deterioration in the central business districts of many communities, and the question "What can we do to save downtown?" has occupied the attention of many planners and public officials.

Some downtowns, however, have experienced a revival recently as a result of concern with urban sprawl, a lessening of inner-city tensions, and public policies designed to encourage such development.

FIGURE 15.5 | Multiple-Nuclei Growth

1. Shopping and offices
2. Industry and warehouses
3. Low-value residences
4. Medium-value residences
5. High-value residences

THE IMPORTANCE OF PUBLIC FACILITIES IN THE GROWTH PROCESS

Investments in public facilities, often called **infrastructure,** play a critical role in the local development process. Transportation improvements figure prominently in the theories of urban form, but other public investments in such facilities as sewerage and water lines also are important in the local development process. Infrastructure development or the lack of it is often used as a policy tool to encourage or discourage growth.

Transportation Facilities

Until about 1870, urbanized areas were almost exclusively pedestrian cities, with commuting limited to the distance one could travel on foot or in a horse-drawn vehicle. The introduction of the streetcar and electric rail transit greatly extended commuting ranges during the next 50 years and led to axial-type development along the transit lines. The automobile era (which began around 1920), when cheap, mass-produced cars became available, expanded the size of the city even more. The automobile tended to bring more concentric-type growth, for it was not limited to a few axial routes. Freeways and other highways, however, did promote development along their routes.

Figure 15.6 illustrates the process of development that often occurs when a major freeway is constructed at the rural fringe of an urban area. In the first drawing, the

FIGURE 15.6 | The Impact of Freeway Construction on Urban Development

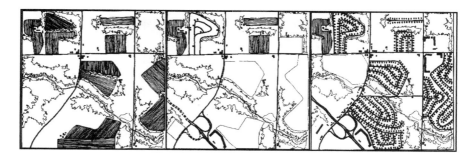

land is used primarily for farming, but there are scattered residences and some minor commercial activity at one road junction. In the second stage, the highway is under construction, and developers have recognized the area's heightened potential. Much of the farming activity has ceased, and this land has been purchased for possible future development. In the third picture, intense development is occurring.

In addition to several subdivisions, commercial strips have formed along the road near the freeway interchange. Some apartments have been constructed, and still another tract awaits development.

The beltways constructed around many large cities as part of the interstate highway program have also had a great effect on urban form. Beltways have reduced the star-shaped growth tendencies of their cities, making many areas more accessible, and have encouraged large amounts of residential and industrial development. They have also served as the sites of many shopping malls and office parks, thereby furthering the development of multiple nuclei and greatly weakening the importance of the central business district.

Water and Sewer Facilities

Water and sewer facilities are not glamorous, but they are essential to urban growth. Even in areas that have ample water, access to a municipal water system is still necessary for any type of concentrated growth. In the more arid regions, where wells are often impractical, almost any type of urban development is impossible without access to a municipal water system. Similarly, if soil and other conditions are adequate, it may be possible to serve low-density developments with septic tanks, but public sewerage is essential to high-density developments. The growth potential of a particular parcel can be influenced dramatically by its access to such facilities.

Figure 15.7 shows how the construction of a major sewer line can enhance the development potential of a particular site. The first drawing shows scattered residences along rural roads in the watershed of a creek at the edge of an urban region.

FIGURE 15.7 | The Impact of a Major Sewer Line on Urban Development

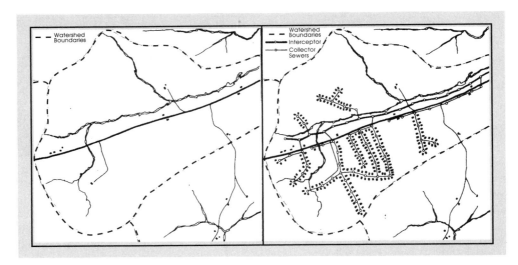

The building of the sewerage system paralleling the stream enables subdivisions to be built within this area. Because there are no sewers in the adjoining areas, intensive development cannot occur there.

THE DYNAMICS OF NEIGHBORHOOD CHANGE

Thus far, we have seen that the value of individual parcels of real estate depends, to a large extent, on national changes in demand, regional and community growth, and urban growth patterns. Let's narrow our focus a bit and consider the importance of local neighborhood changes on property values.

What Is a Neighborhood?

Location is perhaps the most important single factor in determining the value of real property. The selling prices of identical houses built in different locations within an urban area almost always vary with the character of the surrounding neighborhood.

A **neighborhood** can be defined in several ways: As an area in which types of property are similar; as a distinct geographic area or one distinguished by a conspicuous physical feature; as a *social unit*—that is, a community with religious or ethnic ties; and as a group of people with the same general level of income. All these factors

A Tale of Two More Cities: The Effects of Public Infrastructure on the Development of Boston and Los Angeles

 Boston and Los Angles offer the extremes of urban form in the United States. Boston's core goes back to the early colonial period; it later expanded along streetcar lines but remains an area of relatively high population density. Los Angeles developed in the interurban and automobile eras and has a relatively low population density.

Boston

In 1630 the Massachusetts Bay Company established a new town as capital of the colony of Massachusetts Bay on the Shawmut Peninsula, a hilly area barely connected to the mainland by a marshy narrow neck of land. By 1722 the city had a population of 15,000, and had become the center of trade for the New England area.

The colonial city developed a medieval type of street pattern that still confounds drivers in the older section. As it grew, Boston expanded outward but also in-filled to create a denser urban mass. Much of the in-filling required the swampy area to be drained and filled to create more usable land.

By 1850 the city's population of 200,000 was located almost entirely within a two-mile radius from City Hall, that is, within pedestrian range. During the next 30 years streetcars pulled by horses stretched out the existing city to an approximate 4-mile radius. The 23-year period between 1880 and 1900 was a period of rapid growth in the Boston area; electric street railroads extended the city dramatically and subways were also developed. By 1900 the population of approximately 1 million stretched in a ten-mile radius from the center. Boston had developed into two distinct sections:

(1) an industrial, commercial, and communications center packed tightly against the port; and (2) an outer suburban ring of residential, commercial, and industrial subcenters.

During the 20th century, commuter railroads, heavy-rail transit, and highways extended the urbanized area almost to the semicircular I-495, approximately 25 miles from the old port. The 46 miles contained in the city of Boston now comprise only 7 percent of the urbanized area.

Los Angeles

Los Angeles was founded in 1781 by Spanish priests as part of their effort to colonize California. With water for irrigation available from the Los Angeles River, the settlement was to serve as an agricultural village (pueblo) to furnish food to other missions and presidios (fortified settlements). The community retained its primarily agricultural orientation for over a hundred years; by 1850 it still had a population of only 1,600.

The next 30 years saw Los Angeles transformed from a Mexican pueblo to an American town and trade center with a population of over 11,000. The transcontinental railroads reached the city in the 1880s, bringing thousands of migrants and an economic boom. Population totaled over 50,000 in 1890 and 102,000 in 1900.

There are several reasons for the subsequent geographical expansion of Los Angeles as the city's population grew. Although ringed by mountains, the Los Angeles basin is essentially flat, allowing few natural barriers to expansion. The Los Angeles River provided an adequate source of water for the early settlement, but by the turn of the century it proved inadequate and an aqueduct was built to the Owens Valley, 250 miles to the

(continued)

A Tale of Two More Cities: The Effects of Public Infrastructure on the Development of Boston and Los Angeles

north. The availability of this water enabled the city to grow from 107 square miles to 440 square miles within the next 15 years. More recently, Southern California has tapped the Colorado River and the northern California area for water to serve its burgeoning population.

The city's period of rapid population growth following the arrival of the steam railroads coincided with the beginning of the trolley age. The interurban line was built to Pasadena in 1895, and over the next two decades the Pacific Electric Railway Company built a system of over one thousand miles that covered the entire basin. The "Big Red Cars" made it possible to commute long distances and helped to create a metropolis of numerous communities and basically single-family detached homes. In a classic example of axial growth, new lines, sometimes subsidized by land developers or by the development activities of the transit company growth.

The process of population dispersion was furthered by the automobile. The number of automobiles registered in the Los Angeles area mushroomed from fewer than 20,000 in 1910 to over 800,000 by 1930. In the 1940s, freeways began to replace the interurban railroads, and by 1965 the transit system had been completely abandoned. (They would love to have it back now.) The freeway system soon grew to over 600 miles, and the Los Angeles urbanized area's population totaled over 8 million.

Los Angeles is sometimes described as a collection of suburbs in search of a city, and as one observer commented, "There's no 'there' there." Fear of earthquakes restricted building heights to 150 feet until 1957 (the only exception was the City Hall), but in recent years a "there" has developed in the central city, which serves as a center of finance and commerce. Population densities are also increasing, with much of the recent residential construction consisting of multifamily dwellings. Rising fuel costs have led to proposals for a new transit system, but the low population densities have so far made such a system unfeasible except for short segments.

Sources:

Boston: Sam Bass Warner, Jr., *Streetcar Suburbs: The Progress of Growth in Boston, 1870–1900* (Cambridge: Harvard University Press, 1978). Michael P. Conzen and George K. Lewis, *Boston: A Geographical Portrait* (Cambridge: Ballinger, 1976).

Los Angeles: Howard J. Nelson and William A.V. Clark, *Los Angeles: The Metropolitan Experience* (Cambridge: Ballinger, 1976). Robert M. Fogelson, *The Fragmented Metropolis: Los Angeles, 1800-1930* (Cambridge: The Harvard University Press, 1967). Spencer Crump, *Ride the Big Red Cars: How the Trolleys Helped Build Southern California* (Costa Mesa, California: Ivans-Anglo Books, 1970).

work to create housing submarkets in which the values of properties are influenced by the same general set of outside influences.

Neighborhood Change

As do humans, neighborhoods go through a life cycle consisting of seven stages: (1) gestation, (2) youth, (3) maturity, (4) incipient decline, (5) clear decline, (6) accelerating decline, and (7) death or abandonment. Unlike the human situation, however, the process of change in neighborhoods is not inevitable. It can be arrested or reversed, and a declining neighborhood can be restored to vigorous health.

Gestation, Youth, and Maturity

In the early stages of a neighborhood's life cycle, both property values and residents' incomes generally are rising. Turnover usually is relatively low, and new residents are economically and socially similar to those already living in the neighborhood.

Incipient Decline

At some point in the process of neighborhood change, those who leave the neighborhood are replaced by less affluent families and individuals, and over time, the housing may filter down to still less affluent groups. In this stage of the life cycle, housing prices and rentals decline as more affluent families leave the neighborhood.

The process of decline may be caused by several factors. The houses simply may have reached an age where the costs of maintenance are greater than the residents can afford. There may be outside influences, such as construction of a new freeway, which make living conditions in the area less desirable and competing areas more accessible. The decline of the neighborhood may be caused by various changes in the socioeconomic characteristics of its residents or by their aging and death. Likewise, construction of more desirable dwellings in other neighborhoods may lead to a drop in demand for property in a certain area.

Clear Decline

As the housing in a neighborhood ceases to provide a reasonable return to the owners and becomes substandard by most definitions, the neighborhood enters a period of clear decline. Owners make only minimal repairs, and properties deteriorate noticeably. Financial institutions may avoid investing in the area, making rehabilitation and the introduction of new owners even more difficult. As owners try to squeeze additional income from their declining investments, housing densities and the consequent need for public services increase dramatically, though those services (schools, police protection, sanitation) may not be provided.

Accelerating Decline and Abandonment

The demise of a neighborhood often occurs quickly. Those who are able to move elsewhere do so. Only the lowest-income residents remain, and unemployment rates and the percentage of families on welfare are high. Landlords cease making repairs

Neighborhood Revitalization

Declining or even virtually abandoned neighborhoods can be revitalized and once again be a valuable asset to their communities. The Edenton Cotton Mill Village is an outstanding example.

The textile industry was a vital element in the industrialization of the southeastern United States, and many of these firms built mill villages to house their workers. With the obsolescence of many of the old mills and the general decline of the industry in the United States, most have closed, with the mill villages often being abandoned. Such was the case with the Edenton Cotton Mill in Edenton, North Carolina.

The mill, which opened in 1898, constructed more than 70 homes adjoining the mill for its workers and supervisors. When it finally closed in 1995, the 44-acre village, with 57 remaining houses and the mill building, was donated to Preservation North Carolina, which sought to restore it as a viable community and a living example of a historical southern mill village. They have succeeded.

Some of the houses had been boarded up, and the remainders were sorely in need of rehabilitation. Preservation North Carolina made some infrastructure improvements such as placing the utilities underground, and restored one of the houses as a model. A few of the houses were purchased by the former tenants, but the remainder were sold at favorable prices to others who

agreed to rehabilitate them according to restrictive covenants that ensured that the historical integrity of the village would be maintained. Because the Edenton Cotton Mill Village has been placed on the National Register of Historic Places, the buyers could receive a tax credit on their state income taxes for a portion of the rehabilitation expenses. With the success of the houses, attention then turned to the old brick cotton mill building, with its two-story windows lining all sides, a clerestory running the length of the rooftop, and a tower overseeing the entrance. The mill building was converted into 33 condominium residences.

Today, taxable property values in the old mill village have increased from $610,000 before to $12.4 million today. In addition to preserving its heritage, the community has gained an economically prosperous neighborhood.

and often abandon their buildings when they are no longer profitable. At the terminal stage, the neighborhood may be virtually abandoned—as are portions of the South Bronx in New York City—or the buildings may be demolished, allowing the neighborhood to enter a new cycle.

Neighborhood Stabilization and Rehabilitation

It must be emphasized that the process of neighborhood deterioration and decline is not inevitable. Values in many mature neighborhoods remain strong over long periods of time if the area remains competitive in housing markets. Other neighborhoods may, as a result of a conscious public policy effort or natural market forces, reverse their decline and become healthy once again.

The first people who attempt to renovate deteriorated dwellings often are young, middle-income individuals or families who desire to live in town; cannot afford housing in the established, higher-income neighborhoods; and are willing to spend the time and effort to rebuild the dwellings and social fabric of the declining neighborhood. If the process is successful, values may rise dramatically as the neighborhood becomes a desirable location for middle- or upper-income groups. This process is known as **gentrification.**

A negative aspect of gentrification is the displacement of low-income families, who often can no longer afford to live in their neighborhood.

URBAN FORM: A SYNTHESIS

The development of urban form may, at first, appear of interest only to city planners and public officials. To the contrary, the real estate investor or analyst must understand the factors that direct city growth in order to assess the potential development of a certain piece of real estate. The various theories of urban growth describe particular aspects of the growth process. Let us synthesize and summarize some of the critical growth factors so we can better understand the impact of potential urban change on the economics of the individual parcel.

Commercial Growth

Because access is so important to commercial developments, major commercial projects such as regional shopping centers are usually located near freeway interchange nodes or other major road junctions. Smaller commercial developments are also dependent on transportation access and the customer traffic it brings; therefore, they usually are located along heavily traveled roads and streets.

Due to improvements in transportation, particularly the development of the automobile and the attendant growth of highways, cities have spread out, and many commercial subcenters have been created. As a result, the central business district has declined in importance and, in many communities, has become a blighted area. Office buildings have also been moving from the central city to outlying subcenters, often in suburban office parks.

Industrial Growth

Like commercial development, industrial growth has tended to move away from the central city to the suburbs or to rural areas. Most small- and medium-sized plants, along with warehousing and other distribution facilities, are often found in industrial parks where transportation and other necessary public facilities are available. Major manufacturing facilities often locate in more rural areas, where land for expansion is more readily available and major highways or railroads provide accessible transportation.

Residential Growth

Residential development is also strongly influenced by the location of public facilities. High-density development is impossible without the provision of public water and sewerage facilities. Commuting access is important, but individuals have demonstrated that they will endure long commutes to enjoy a suburban or rural lifestyle and to escape some of the central city problems. In addition, the dispersion of employment to suburban locations in recent years has also encouraged the dispersion of residential development to these areas.

CHAPTER REVIEW

■ The reason why one locality rather than another will develop into a center of trade or industry is because that community enjoys a comparative advantage, which can result from transportation facilities or other factors of the created environment, natural resources, climate, or the quality and quantity of the local labor force.

■ A community's export activity produces goods and services for sale outside its borders. Population-serving activities produce goods and services sold within the community itself.

■ Almost all real estate market activity and development depends directly or indirectly on the location of people, and the location of people depends largely on the location of employment.

■ Because the supply of real estate is largely fixed in the short run, changes in demand most often influence vacancy rates, sales of existing property, prices, and lease rates. Over the long run, the supply can, of course, be increased, and the potential investor in a new development must carefully analyze the long-run prospects for the community's economic base.

■ Nothing is more essential to the determination of real estate values than the process of community development and neighborhood change.

■ A city may grow in several ways: (1) vertically, by replacement of smaller structures with taller ones and by use of air rights to construct new buildings over existing ones; (2) by in-filling of open spaces between existing structures; and (3) by extension of settled areas.

■ Some models that have been used to explain the peripheral growth patterns of urban areas are (1) concentric-circle growth, (2) axial growth, (3) sector growth, and (4) multiple-nuclei growth.

■ Investments in public facilities, often called the *infrastructure,* play a critical role in local development. The infrastructure includes transportation improvements, sewer systems, and water lines.

■ Because access is so important, major commercial growth tends to occur near transportation nodes, such as freeway interchanges and junctions of other major roads.

■ Industrial growth tends to occur along major highways, railroads, or both.

■ A neighborhood can be defined in several ways: (1) as an area in which types of property are similar; (2) as a distinct geographic area or one that is distinguished by a conspicuous physical feature; (3) as a *social unit*—that is, as a community with religious or ethnic ties; and (4) as a group of people with the same general level of income.

■ Neighborhoods tend to go through a life cycle, from gestation to maturity to decline, but this process can be arrested or reversed, and a declining neighborhood may be restored to economic health.

▌ KEY TERMS

axial model	filtering	multiple-nuclei model
bid-rent curve	gentrification	neighborhood
comparative advantage	highest and best use	population-serving activities
concentric-circle model	in-filling	sector model
economic base	infrastructure	urban and regional economics
export activities	land rent	

▌ STUDY EXERCISES

1. What is meant by the concept of *comparative advantage*?

2. What are some of the factors that may give a community a comparative advantage in attracting new employment?

3. Why do people locate where they do?

4. Discuss the concept of an economic base. What are export activities, and what are population-serving activities?

5. How do local real estate markets react to changes in short-run demand? To changes in long-run demand?

6. What steps might a community take when faced with declining industry or a plant that closes?

7. Discuss the concept of land rent, and explain how it tends to allocate land resources.

8. Why would we not expect to find someone growing corn on a lot in midtown Manhattan in New York City?

9. Discuss some of the models that have been used to explain growth patterns in urban areas.

10. What is meant by *infrastructure?*

11. Suppose a new freeway is completed in a relatively undeveloped suburban area. What would be some of the probable developmental impacts?

12. A new interceptor sewerage line is completed in an area that previously could be served only by septic tanks. How would this likely change residential development?

13. Discuss how improvements in public facilities influence the local development process.

14. Why have American cities tended to develop in a more multinucleated form during the past several decades?

15. Where does major commercial growth tend to occur within a community?

16. Where does industrial growth tend to occur within a community?

17. Describe the life cycle of neighborhoods.

PART FOUR

Real Estate Finance and Investment Analysis

Residential and Commercial Property Financing

CHAPTER PREVIEW

CLOSE-UP
What Is Credit
Scoring?

The economic characteristics of real estate make mortgage credit both necessary for most real estate purchasers and attractive to many lenders. As we saw in a previous chapter, a specialized legal framework for real estate financing exists whereby real estate assets can be pledged as security for a debt and, if the borrower should default on the loan, the value of the property can be used to satisfy the debt.

The objectives of this chapter are to describe the processes of obtaining financing for residential and commercial property. With respect to owner-occupied residential properties, we

- discuss the mortgage concept and U.S. mortgage practice,

- review the structure of the U.S. housing finance system and its most prominent participants,

- examine the loan origination process by considering the residential loan application procedure,

- discuss several federal regulations designed to protect residential mortgage consumers, and

- outline the underwriting guidelines used by lenders to evaluate residential loan applications.

The commercial property financing system relies on the concept of secured debt just as the housing finance system does, but there are some important differences in the way these two financing systems work. We address the following topics in the commercial property financing system:

- Sources of debt and equity capital in commercial property markets

- Underwriting criteria used by lenders to evaluate commercial property loan applications

357

UNDERSTANDING THE MORTGAGE CONCEPT

The basic factor that differentiates real estate credit from most other loans is the concept of secured debt. A borrower's promise to repay an **unsecured loan** is not backed by a lien or an encumbrance on a specific property, and if a borrower defaults, the lender's only recourse is to make a claim against the borrower's general assets. The lender's ability to collect on the defaulted debt depends on the amount and quality of those assets and the debtor's income-earning ability. It is hard to imagine financial institutions making many real estate loans on such a basis because the size of such loans is relatively large, and their duration is so long that the borrower's financial condition could change drastically before the loan is repaid.

In most cases, therefore, borrowers acquire financing for real estate purchases using **secured loans.** In this type of loan, the property being purchased is pledged as security for the debt, and a lien or other encumbrance is created on the title to the property. If the borrower is unable or unwilling to repay the debt as scheduled, the lender can take legal action to sell the specified property to recover the loan funds. This type of credit instrument makes it feasible for lenders to make relatively large, long-term loans for the purchase of real estate.

History of the Mortgage Concept

A **mortgage** is a pledge of property to secure a debt. The concept dates back to early Egyptian, Greek, and Roman times. Under early Roman law, nonpayment of a mortgage loan entitled lenders to make borrowers their slaves. Eventually, Roman law was changed to permit the unpaid debt to be satisfied by the sale of the mortgaged property.

Although the concept of pledging property to secure a debt was widespread in England by the 11th century, the Christian strictures against usury prohibited the charging of interest on loans. Instead of charging interest, Christian lenders simply took over a debtor's property and collected rents until the debt was paid. Jewish lenders, not being bound by Christian precepts, charged interest and left borrowers in possession of their property. By the 14th century, however, the charging of interest to borrowers left in possession of their property, known as **hypothecation,** became universal.

These early mortgages provided that if the borrower met all the terms of the loan and completely repaid the debt, the mortgage was then terminated, and the title was returned to the borrower. If any condition was not met, however, the borrower lost all rights to the property, including all money previously paid, and the property was sold to repay the debt. Gradually, a system developed to more equitably protect the rights of the parties to a loan secured by real estate, and many of these concepts serve as the basis for modern mortgage laws in the United States.

Modern Mortgage Concepts

U.S. courts typically consider a mortgage as a voluntary lien on real estate given to secure the payment of a debt. Borrowers remain in possession of the property, but some states recognize the lender as the owner of the mortgaged property, while others interpret a mortgage purely as a lien on the property. States that have adopted the concept of **title theory** recognize that the mortgagee (lender) has the right to possession of the mortgaged property immediately on default by the mortgagor (borrower). The property can be sold at this point, with the sale proceeds used to satisfy the debt. In **lien theory** states, however, if the mortgagor defaults, the lender must foreclose on the lien through a court action to enforce the lender's right of using the property to satisfy the debt. The property will then be sold (usually by the court) and the funds received from the sale will be used to extinguish the debt. In both title and lien theory states, any proceeds from a foreclosure sale in excess of the loan amount and any costs of sale must be returned to the borrower. In the normal course of a mortgage, the question of title versus lien theory is irrelevant. Only if the borrower defaults will the property be sold to satisfy the debt.

U.S. MORTGAGE PRACTICE

Although practice varies somewhat from state to state, the obligation secured by a mortgage generally is acknowledged by a **promissory note**—that is, a written promise to pay money owed. The promissory note document contains the names of the borrower and lender, the amount of the debt, the interest rate and repayment terms, reference to the security instrument, and other details of the loan agreement. The promissory note makes the borrower personally liable for the debt. If the borrower violates the terms of the promissory note, the lender can then take steps to foreclose on the debt. Figure 16.1 contains an example of a promissory note.

TYPICAL PROVISIONS OF A PROMISSORY NOTE

While much of the language in this sample promissory note is self-explanatory, a few items deserve special emphasis. Section 4 of the note is a **prepayment clause.** The borrower in this note has the right to prepay any or all of the principal any time before it is due without penalty. Section 5 specifies a late charge for overdue payments, classifies any late payment as a default on the terms of the agreement and, in the event of default, permits the lender to accelerate the full amount of principal that has not been paid and any interest that is owed on that amount. This last item is known as an **acceleration clause.** Section 6 makes all those who sign this note "jointly and severally liable" for the debt. Thus, the lender can demand payment from one or all of the borrowers at its option. Section 7 of this note contains a **due-on-sale clause.** In the event the borrower sells or transfers all or any part of the property secured by the mortgage associated with this note, the lender may, at its option, require immediate payment of all amounts owed.

FIGURE 16.1 | Promissory Note

February 5   , 2007   St. Joseph   ,   Missouri
                                  (City)   (State)

1097 Timbers Crossing
(Property Address)

1. **Borrower's Promise To Pay**

    In return for a loan that I have received, I promise to pay U.S. $ 108,000 (this amount is called "principal"), plus interest, to the order of the Lender. The Lender is First Savings Bank .

    I understand that the Lender may transfer this Note. The lender or anyone who takes this Note by transfer and who is entitled to receive payments under this Note is called the "Note Holder."

2. **Interest**

    Interest will be charged on unpaid principal until the full amount of principal has been paid. I will pay interest at a yearly rate of 8.00 %.

3. **Payments**

    (A) Time and Place of Payments

    I will pay principal and interest by making payments every month.

    I will make my monthly payments on the 1st day of each month beginning on April 1, 2007.

    I will make these payments every month until I have paid all of the principal and interest and any other charges described below that I may owe under this Note. My monthly payments will be applied to interest before principal. If, on April 1, 2037 , I still owe amounts under this Note, I will pay those amounts in full on that date, which is called the maturity date.

    (B) Amount of Monthly Payments

    My monthly payment will be in the amount of U.S. $ 792.47 .

4. **Borrower's Right To Prepay**

    I have the right to make payments of principal at any time before they are due. A payment of principal only is known as a "prepayment." When I make a prepayment, I will tell the Note Holder in writing that I am doing so. I may make a full prepayment or partial prepayments without paying any prepayment charge. The Note Holder will use all of my prepayment to reduce the amount of principal that I owe under this Note. If I make a partial prepayment, there will be no changes in the due date or in the amount of my monthly payment unless the Note Holder agrees in writing to those changes.

5. **Borrower's Failure To Pay as Required**

    (A) Late Charge for Overdue Payments

    If the Note Holder has not received the full amount of any monthly payment by the end of five calendar days after the date it is due, I will pay a late charge to the Note Holder. The amount of the charge will be 10 % of my overdue payment of principal and interest. I will pay this late charge promptly, but only once on each late payment.

    (B) Default

    If I do not pay the full amount of each monthly payment on the date it is due, I will be in default.

    (C) Notice of Default

    If I am in default, the Note Holder may send me a written notice telling me that if I do not pay the overdue amount by a certain date, the Note Holder may require me to pay immediately the full amount of principal which has not been paid and all the interest that I owe on that amount. That date must be at least 30 days after the date on which the notice is delivered or mailed to me.

FIGURE 16.1 | Promissory Note *(continued)*

(D) No Waiver by Note Holder

Even if, at a time when I am in default, the Note Holder does not require me to pay immediately in full as described above, the Note Holder will still have the right to do so if I am in default at a later time.

(E) Payment of Note Holder's Costs and Expenses

If the Note Holder has required me to pay immediately in full as described above, the Note Holder will have the right to be paid back by me for all of its costs and expenses in enforcing this Note to the extent not prohibited by applicable law. Those expenses include, for example, reasonable attorney's fees.

6. Obligations of Persons under this Note

If more than one person signs this Note, each person is fully and personally obligated to keep all of the promises made in this note, including the promise to pay the full amount owed. The Note Holder may enforce its rights under this Note against each person individually or against all of us together. This means that any one of us may be required to pay all of the amounts owed under this note.

7. Uniform Secured Note

This Note is a uniform instrument with limited variations in some jurisdictions. In addition to the protections given to the Note Holder under this Note, a Mortgage, Deed of Trust, or Security Deed (the "Security Instrument"), dated the same date as this Note, protects the Note Holder from possible losses which might result if I do not keep the promises which I make in this Note. That Security Instrument describes how and under what conditions I may be required to make immediate payment in full of all amounts I owe under this Note. Some of those conditions are described as follows:

Transfer of the Property. If all or any part of the Property or any interest in it is sold or transferred without Lender's prior written consent, Lender may, at its option, require immediate payment in full of all sums secured by the Security Instrument. If Lender exercises this option, Lender shall give Borrower notice of acceleration. The notice shall provide a period of not less than 30 days from the date the notice is delivered or mailed within which Borrower must pay all sums secured by the Security Instrument. If Borrower fails to pay these sums prior to the expiration of the period, Lender may invoke remedies permitted by the Security Instrument.

Witness the Hand(s) and Seal(s) of the Undersigned

_____   (Seal) - Borrower

_____   (Seal) - Borrower

The promise to repay the debt is secured by a pledge of property as specified in the mortgage document or other security instrument, which typically contains the names of the mortgagor and mortgagee, a description of the property involved, reference to the promissory note, and various provisions common to the mortgage arrangement. Figure 16.2 contains an example of a mortgage document.

Typical Provisions of a Security Instrument

The language of the security instrument, in this case a mortgage, is intended to provide the mortgagee with protection against financial losses resulting from default on the promissory note. The uniform covenants referred to in the security instrument represent promises between the borrower and lender regarding the repayment of the debt, provisions for maintaining the property and keeping insurance premiums and property taxes current, the lender's right to inspect the property, and numerous other issues. If the borrower fails to meet the terms of either the promissory note or the security instrument, the lender may foreclose on the debt, as described below.

UNDERSTANDING THE FORECLOSURE PROCESS

When a borrower fails to make payments or defaults on other terms of the mortgage agreement, the mortgagee can begin foreclosure proceedings to enforce its rights. **Foreclosure** refers to the process of seizing control of the collateral for a loan and using the proceeds from its sale to satisfy a defaulted debt. Usually, however, the mortgage holder will attempt to work out some type of alternative payment program to avoid the sale of the collateral. Not only is this practice much better for the lender's community relations efforts, it also avoids the time-consuming, expensive, and generally unprofitable foreclosure process. Foreclosure is, for the most part, an avenue of last resort.

Types of Foreclosure

Specific foreclosure laws vary from state to state, though there are three general types of foreclosure proceedings. In states that recognize **judicial foreclosure,** the mortgagee must request a court-ordered sale of the property after proving that the borrower has defaulted on the terms of the agreement. Some states allow **nonjudicial foreclosure.** In this situation, the security instrument (either a mortgage or deed of trust) grants the power of sale to the lender should the borrower default. Finally, a few states recognize **strict foreclosure,** whereby the lender receives title to the property immediately on default by the borrower. The lender can then dispose of the property by sale or keep it as satisfaction of the debt.

Regardless of the specific type of foreclosure recognized, most states require that the lender return any proceeds from a foreclosure sale in excess of the loan amount and certain fees to the borrower. On the other hand, some states permit the mortgagee to pursue a **deficiency judgment** against the mortgagor if the proceeds are insufficient to satisfy the debt. If the courts grant the judgment, the borrower is held responsible for the remaining amount of debt after the foreclosure sale. Other states do not allow deficiency judgments, and lenders must accept the proceeds of the sale as satisfaction of the debt.

Alternative Security Instruments

The cumbersome foreclosure process is simplified in many states through the use of a security instrument similar to a mortgage called a **deed of trust** or *trust deed.* The deed of trust is executed at the time the loan is originated to convey title to a third party, called the *trustee.* The trustee's title to the property lies dormant as

FIGURE 16.2 | Mortgage

This Mortgage ("Security Instrument") is given on February 5 , 2007 . The mortgagor is Frank L. and Elizabeth M. Barr ("Borrower"). This Security Instrument is given to First Savings Bank which is organized and existing under the laws of the State of Missouri , and whose address is 220 Las Olas Boulevard , St. Joseph, Missouri ("Lender"). Borrower owes Lender the principal sum of U.S.$ 108,000 . This debt is evidenced by Borrower's note dated the same date as this Security Instrument, which provides for monthly payments, with the full debt, if not paid earlier, due and payable on April 1, 2037. This Security Instrument secures to the Lender (a) the repayment of the debt, with interest, evidenced by the note, (b) the payment of all other sums necessary to protect the security of this Security Instrument, and (c) the Borrower's covenants and agreements under this Security Instrument and the note. For this purpose, Borrower does hereby mortgage, grant, and convey to Lender the following described property located in Buchanan County, in the State of Missouri :

Lot 3, Block G of the Harris Billups Estate, as recorded in Plat Book 8, page 37, in the Office of the Clerk of the Circuit Court of Buchanan County, Missouri, which has the address of 1097 Timbers Crossing (Property Address); together with all improvements now or hereafter erected on the property, and all easements, appurtenances, and fixtures now or hereafter a part of the property. All replacements and additions shall also be covered by this Security Instrument.

Borrower Covenants that Borrower is lawfully seised of the estate hereby conveyed and has the right to mortgage, grant, and convey the Property and that the Property is unencumbered, except for encumbrances of record. Borrower warrants and will defend generally the title to the Property against all claims and demands, subject to any encumbrances of record.

This Security Instrument implicitly contains all uniform covenants permitted by laws of the applicable jurisdictions to constitute a uniform security interest covering real property.

By signing below, Borrower accepts and agrees to the terms and covenants contained in this Security Instrument and in any rider(s) executed by Borrower and recorded with it.

_____   (Seal) - Borrower

_____   (Seal) - Borrower

long as the borrower, or *trustor,* meets the terms of the debt. In the event of default, however, the trustee sells the property to pay off the debt to the lender, who is the *beneficiary* of the trust.

Another financing device that simplifies the foreclosure process is the **land contract,** or contract for a deed. While not a mortgage in the technical sense, land contracts establish an obligation to transfer title from a seller to a buyer at some future date based on an agreed-on payment schedule. The seller retains ownership of the property until the buyer has paid a certain percentage of the purchase price, sometimes 100 percent. The contract gives the buyer *equitable ownership,* that is, the right to use the property while making payments, but legal ownership is retained by the seller. If the buyer defaults on the contract, the seller already has ownership of the property and no foreclosure is necessary.

Because the buyer has fewer rights under a land contract than under a mortgage or deed of trust, the land contract is used almost exclusively when financing cannot be easily obtained in other ways. For example, individual subdivision lots often can be financed through the use of a land contract with a very small down payment paid to the seller. Such loans usually are unobtainable from traditional mortgage lenders. Because the seller is the legal owner until the land contract is satisfied, buyers who use land contracts should make certain that the contract is carefully written to prevent the seller from encumbering the property before legal ownership is transferred.

Some Final Thoughts Related to Foreclosure

If a borrower is unable or unwilling to continue making payments on a mortgage debt and foreclosure is imminent, it may be possible to sell the mortgaged property rather than default. If the loan contains a due-on-sale clause, the mortgagor must repay the debt if the property can be sold. In many cases, the satisfaction of the debt and the sale of the property occur simultaneously, with the proceeds of any sale first being applied to the debt. If no due-on-sale clause is imposed, however, the borrower may sell the property "subject to" the existing mortgage, whereby the buyer begins making the required payments to the lender. In this type of transfer, the original borrower remains personally liable for the debt should the buyer subsequently default on the loan.

Another method of transferring mortgaged property is known as *assumption.* In this situation, the original borrower sells the property and the buyer assumes responsibility for the debt. Whether the original borrower remains personally liable for the debt should the buyer default depends on the terms of the loan. Finally, if foreclosure is imminent and a buyer cannot be found, a borrower who can no longer meet the obligations of a loan may attempt to transfer title to the property to the lender. Lenders may willingly accept a **deed in lieu of foreclosure** to avoid the expenses of a lengthy foreclosure process.

STRUCTURE OF THE U.S. HOUSING FINANCE SYSTEM

The residential lending process begins when a potential borrower contacts a mortgage lender in the hopes of acquiring a loan, either to finance the purchase of a property or to refinance property currently owned. The process of creating a new loan agreement between borrower and lender is known as **loan origination.** In essence, the borrower is purchasing the use of the lender's funds over time by paying interest to the lender. Therefore, *loan origination* refers to the transactions that occur between borrower and lender in the **primary mortgage market.** When existing loans are sold by originators to investors or from one investor to another, these transactions are said to occur in the **secondary mortgage market.** This market greatly increases the flow of mortgage funds between regions of the country. In the primary mortgage market, demand for loans depends on potential borrowers' desires and abilities to qualify for a loan, while the supply of loans depends on mortgage lenders' willingness to provide debt capital to the borrowers. As with all markets, the price of mortgage capital (the interest rate) depends on the relative supply and demand for the product at any given point in time. Obviously, these two markets are dependent on each other, and together serve as the foundation of the U.S. housing finance system.

The **U.S. housing finance system** is defined as the arrangements and institutions that facilitate the financing of owner-occupied residences in the United States using the mortgage concepts discussed above. The many facets of our current system evolved over many years, but its roots lie in New Deal legislative actions taken by the federal government in the wake of massive defaults on owner-occupied housing during the Great Depression of the 1930s. During this time period, the stock market and banking industry were in a virtual state of collapse, new construction was at a standstill, and unemployment was rampant.

The housing market was particularly hard hit during the Depression era owing to the reduction in available mortgage credit. As a matter of national policy, the federal government took steps to provide a steady flow of funds to the housing sector and to shield it from future depressions. The results of these and subsequent actions by the federal government have had a tremendous impact on the current status of our nation's housing finance system. To understand this system requires a review of the history of the government's role in the mortgage market. We begin with a discussion of the Federal Housing Administration.

Federal Housing Administration

Prior to 1929, most residential mortgages were short-term, interest-only loans: although the interest rate was fixed, regular payments covered interest only for the term of the loan, and the entire principal was due at the end of the term. During the Depression, many borrowers could not repay their debts when the loans came due, and if lenders refused to refinance the loans, default was almost unavoidable. Without intervention from the federal government, the future of the housing market looked dismal at best. New construction had virtually ceased, and many existing short-term, interest-only mortgages were already in default.

In response to the economic crisis, the **Federal Housing Administration** (FHA) was created in 1934 to, among other things, restore confidence in the mortgage market. As a federal agency, the FHA had a dramatic impact on the housing finance system. The FHA helped establish rigorous borrowing and lending standards that reduced lenders' risk and promoted the use of long-term, fully amortizing loans that were more consistent with household budgets than the interest-only loans that were prevalent at the time. (The distinction between these loan types is fully explored in Chapter 18.) In addition, the FHA established a mortgage insurance program to cover losses to lenders who originated these loans using the approved borrowing and lending standards.

Instead of lending money directly to borrowers, the primary role of the FHA in the housing finance system is to act as an insurance company for private lenders (banks, mortgage companies, savings associations, etc.) who originate loans for home purchases, repairs, and improvements. To participate in its most popular program today, the 203(b) program, borrowers purchase mortgage insurance from the FHA on behalf of the lender by paying an initial fee of 2.25 percent of the loan amount at the time of origination, followed by an annual fee of ½ of 1 percent of the original loan amount for the full term of the loan, up to 30 years. (Notice that the upfront cost can be added to the loan amount—the borrower need not pay the money in cash to obtain the insurance.) If a borrower defaults on an **FHA-insured loan,** the insurance premiums collected from borrowers are used to protect the lender from losses resulting from foreclosure. In return for reducing the lender's risk in this manner, borrowers can receive a loan for as much as 97 percent of the value of the property at an affordable interest rate. Although anyone is eligible to apply for an FHA-insured loan, the maximum loan amount available depends on the location of the property. In general, the maximum FHA loan amount for a single-family residence is 95 percent of the median house price in the community. In most high cost areas, the maximum FHA loan amount in 2007 was $362,790. Loans for larger amounts are not eligible for FHA insurance.

The success of the FHA in the 1930s and beyond greatly standardized the mortgage lending process in the United States and reduced lenders' risk exposure from mortgage loans. Life insurance companies with policy reserves and other financial institutions with funds to invest were especially attracted to these standardized mortgages, which resulted in much needed capital flows into depressed areas of the country. Many mortgage bankers began actively originating FHA-insured loans in capital-deficit areas and selling them to investors such as life insurance companies who were in search of high-yielding, relatively safe investments. With the help of other government and nongovernment initiatives in the mortgage industry, the secondary mortgage market expanded rapidly as many other types of investors were attracted to mortgage investments.

Private Mortgage Insurance

Insurance against mortgage default was not unheard of in the mortgage market even before 1929. In fact, numerous **private mortgage insurance** (PMI) companies existed in the United States prior to the collapse of the real estate market. The high number of loan defaults, however, caused a complete failure of the private mortgage insurance industry during the Depression. Not until the establishment of the Mortgage Guaranty Insurance Corporation (MGIC) in 1957 would PMI reappear in the U.S. mortgage market. Since then numerous PMI companies have been established, and PMI is once again an important aspect of the mortgage industry.

There are several reasons borrowers may choose to use PMI rather than FHA insurance. First, PMI is available for loan amounts much larger than the maximum FHA-insured loan. Second, the cost of PMI is generally less than the cost of FHA mortgage insurance because the annual premiums are based on the current loan balance. Third, many lenders allow the borrower to cancel the PMI when the balance on the loan falls below 80 percent of the value of the property. Only FHA-insured loans originated after January 1, 2001, allow borrowers to cancel the mortgage insurance premium when the loan balance falls below 78 percent of the price of the home at origination.

Federal National Mortgage Association (Fannie Mae)

To increase liquidity in mortgage investments and further stimulate the flow of funds between geographic areas with excess capital and areas with excess demand, Congress decided that a formal secondary market was needed in which mortgages originated in one area could easily be sold to investors in other areas. Only by attracting sufficient capital from the investment community would mortgage markets be able to meet the demand for mortgage funds at prices borrowers could afford. Congress created the **Federal National Mortgage Association** (FNMA) in 1938 to buy mortgages from lenders and to serve as a clearinghouse for the secondary mortgage market. **Fannie Mae,** as the agency became known, was originally established as a government agency to (1) operate a secondary market for FHA-insured loans and (2) provide FHA-insured loans to low-income borrowers in remote areas who would not otherwise have access to the mortgage market.

Over time, Congress altered the role of Fannie Mae, and in 1968, the agency was converted into a private corporation, wholly owned by investors. Today, the company is traded on the New York Stock Exchange under the symbol FNM and has more than 250,000 shareholders. Fannie Mae is the third largest corporation in the United States in terms of total assets. Fannie Mae has two primary lines of business. First, the company buys residential mortgages from loan originators, earning a spread between the yield on the mortgages and the company's cost of debt. Second, Fannie Mae also receives pools of mortgage loans from lenders and exchanges them for *mortgage-backed securities* that the company guarantees. These securities are very liquid (much more liquid than whole mortgage loans) and are traded through securities dealers on Wall Street. The company earns a fee for guaranteeing the mortgage-backed securities it sells to investors.

Even though Fannie Mae is a private entity, the federal government continues to influence its operations. Today, one-third of the board of directors of the corporation is appointed by the president of the United States, and the U.S. Treasury is authorized to lend the corporation money if necessary to ensure its smooth operation in the secondary mortgage market. Fannie Mae serves as a clearinghouse for FHA-insured loans, as well as loans guaranteed by the Department of Veterans Affairs and PMI companies.

Department of Veterans Affairs Loan Guarantee Program

Another important government agency in the development of the housing finance system has been the Veterans Administration, now the Department of Veterans Affairs. Immediately after World War II, the Veterans Administration (VA) began to guarantee mortgage loans on a large scale as part of the so-called GI Bill of Rights. Congress passed legislation at the end of the war that allowed veterans to obtain mortgage loans for home purchases with little or no down payment and low interest rates. The VA loan program guarantees the payment of a mortgage loan made by a private lender to a qualified veteran should the borrower default. Unlike FHA-insured loans, however, **VA-guaranteed loans** do not require that the borrower pay premiums for the insurance. Much of the housing boom that occurred during the postwar period is attributed to the tremendous number of VA-guaranteed loans originated to provide housing for returning veterans. Although the program has changed in many respects since its inception, the VA loan guarantee program continues to account for approximately 10 percent of new loans originated each year. As of 2007, VA loan guarantees are available for loans up to $203,000 with no down payment required from the borrower.

To be eligible for a VA-guaranteed loan today, the applicant must be a veteran who served on active duty and was discharged under conditions other than dishonorable during World War II and later periods. World War II (September 16, 1940, to July 25, 1947), Korean conflict (June 27, 1950, to January 31, 1955), Vietnam era (August 5, 1964, to May 7, 1975), and Gulf war era (August 2, 1990, to the present) veterans must have at least 90 days' service. Veterans with service only during peacetime periods and active duty military personnel must have had more than 180 days' active service. Veterans of enlisted service that began after September 7, 1980, or officers with service beginning after October 16, 1981, must in most cases have served at least two years. Reservists and National Guard members who were activated on or after August 2, 1990 (during the Persian Gulf conflict), served at least 90 days, and received honorable discharge are eligible. Members of the Selected Reserve, including National Guard, who are not otherwise eligible but who have completed six years of service and have been honorably discharged or have completed six years of service and are still serving may be eligible. The specific rules regarded eligibility can be found on the Department of Veterans Affairs Web site at *www.va.gov.*

The cost of obtaining a VA-guaranteed loan varies according to the borrower's status as a veteran and the amount of down payment the borrower is making to the lender. A basic funding fee of 2 percent must be paid to the VA by all but certain exempt veterans. A down payment of 5 percent or more will reduce the fee to 1.5 percent, and a 10 percent down payment will reduce it to 1.25 percent. A funding fee of 2.75 percent must be paid by all eligible Reserve/National Guard individuals. A down payment of 5 percent or more will reduce the fee to 2.25 percent, and a 10 percent down payment will reduce it to 2 percent. The funding fee for loans to refinance an existing VA home loan with a new VA home loan to lower the existing interest rate is 0.5 percent. Veterans who are using entitlement for a second or subsequent time who do not make a down payment of at least 5 percent are charged a funding fee of 3 percent. For all VA home loans, the funding fee may be paid in cash or it may be included in the loan.

Government National Mortgage Association (Ginnie Mae)

The reorganization of Fannie Mae in 1968 led to the creation of a new federal agency, the **Government National Mortgage Association** (GNMA), now known as **Ginnie Mae.** When Fannie Mae became a privately owned corporation, it no longer provided special assistance loans directly to borrowers. To fill this void, Ginnie Mae was organized as a vehicle for providing subsidized loans to borrowers through various FHA loan programs. For example, a lender can originate a home mortgage for a lower-income borrower at a below-market interest rate, then sell that loan to Ginnie Mae for full market value. After purchasing the loans, Ginnie Mae can either sell them for a loss or hold them in its own portfolio. Losses are paid for by funds appropriated by the Department of Housing and Urban Development, Ginnie Mae's primary agency.

In 1970, Ginnie Mae introduced a payment guarantee program aimed at expanding the supply of funds for the mortgage market. Under this program, which was (and is) backed by the full faith and credit of the U.S. government, Ginnie Mae guaranteed the timely payment of principal and interest on mortgages insured by other federal agencies to investors. That is, if an investor bought mortgages insured by FHA, Ginnie Mae guaranteed that payments from the borrowers would occur as scheduled. This guarantee, combined with the insurance against default provided by FHA, made mortgages a very attractive investment for investors who did not wish to be concerned with late payments from borrowers. Thanks to this program, many new types of financial instruments were developed that allowed investors to invest in the mortgage market without directly holding mortgages. Referred to collectively as *mortgage-backed securities,* these instruments have proven to be highly effective at attracting investment funds to the mortgage market.

Mortgage-backed securities (MBS) are securities issued in the secondary mortgage market by mortgage holders to investors who wish to invest indirectly in the mortgage market. The mortgage holders combine loans made to many different borrowers into "mortgage pools," then sell securities that are "backed" by the underlying mortgages. In other words, the payments made by the borrowers into the mortgage pool are used to pay back the holder of the mortgage security with interest. Proceeds from the sale of these securities allow mortgage holders to originate new mortgages to borrowers. Investors who wish to commit their funds to the mortgage market can do so by purchasing a variety of MBS, including securities known as *pass-through certificates, mortgage-backed bonds, pay-through bonds,* and *collateralized mortgage obligations.* Although the specific details of these securities are beyond the scope of this text, it is important to note that the creation of MBS is often credited with the dramatic inflow of capital to the mortgage market that occurred in the 1970s and continues today. About 20 percent of the MBS issued by Fannie Mae (and Freddie Mac, discussed next) are held by foreign investors. About 22 percent are held by depository institutions. The remainder is held by life insurance companies, mutual funds, hedge funds, and other types of investors.

Federal Home Loan Mortgage Corporation (Freddie Mac)

Another important action taken by the federal government designed to increase the flow of funds to the mortgage market was the creation of the Federal Home Loan Mortgage Corporation (FHLMC) in 1970. During this time, the secondary market was well established for FHA-insured and VA-guaranteed loans, but no secondary market was in place for **conventional loans.** *Conventional loans* are those that are not insured by government agencies, either because their loan-to-value ratio is lower than 80 percent or because they carry PMI. Congress authorized the FHLMC, or

Freddie Mac, as it is now called, to operate a secondary market for conventional loans similar to the one provided by Fannie Mae and Ginnie Mae for FHA and VA mortgages. Freddie Mac is now a major player in the market for all types of mortgages and competes directly with Fannie Mae to purchase mortgages and sell mortgage-backed securities.

Office of Federal Housing Enterprise Oversight

Fannie Mae and Freddie Mac are often call **government-sponsored enterprises** (GSEs) because of their close relationship with the federal government. One important aspect of that relationship is the ability of both companies to borrow money directly from the federal government at very low interest rates. The government watches over the operations of the GSEs through the **Office of Federal Housing Enterprise Oversight** (OFHEO). The mission of the OFHEO is to promote housing and a strong national housing finance system by ensuring the safety and soundness of Fannie Mae and Freddie Mac.

Now that we understand the basic structure of the housing finance system of the United States, we can begin a closer look at the participants who operate within it and account for the tremendous volume of mortgage market activity.

▌ MORTGAGE MARKET PARTICIPANTS

At the end of 2007, the total amount of mortgage debt outstanding in the United States was slightly more than $13.5 trillion, with about 77 percent of that amount secured by one- to four-family structures. The system by which this large amount of capital is committed to mortgage loans on the national level involves numerous government and quasigovernment agencies and many private entities. Table 16.1 shows mortgage debt outstanding by type of mortgage and by type of holder in the United States from 2000 through 2007.

Mortgage Originators and Investors

Who are the mortgage originators and investors? The most visible suppliers in the primary mortgage market include mortgage bankers, mortgage brokers, commercial banks, savings associations, and credit unions. **Mortgage bankers** originate about half of all residential mortgage loans in the United States each year. Although we typically think of a banker as someone who accepts deposits from savers and then lends that money to borrowers, mortgage bankers do not accept deposits from savers. Instead, they borrow money from commercial banks, then use these funds to originate new loans to mortgage borrowers. Mortgage bankers then sell the loans they originate to Fannie Mae or Freddie Mac in the secondary market, but they may continue to service the loan (collect and process payments) for a fee on behalf of the investor. The revenues to mortgage bankers include origination fees charged to applicants, servicing fees paid by investors, and the spread between the price of borrowed funds and loaned funds.

TABLE 16.1 | Mortgage Debt (in billions of dollars)

	2000	2001	2002	2003	2004	2005	2006	2007
Total Mortgages	6,785.1	7,473.7	8,352.7	9,353.4	10,656.4	12,112.9	13,337.2	13,548.9
By Type of Property								
Home	5,118.6	5,649.5	6,381.8	7,183.1	8,257.2	9,387.0	10,288.1	10,426.3
Multifamily residential	404.2	446.2	484.7	555.4	608.5	679.1	729.1	740.9
Commercial	1,171.1	1,282.0	1,382.9	1,509.8	1,680.2	1,931.9	2,200.1	2,260.7
Farm	91.1	96.0	103.4	105.1	110.4	114.9	119.9	121.0
By Holder of Debt								
Household sector	4,937.1	5,444.6	6,152.7	7,011.2	8,017.7	9,098.4	9,940.1	10,069.7
Nonfinancial corporate business	1,764.7	1,943.5	2,103.5	2,237.5	2,508.2	2,870.0	3,245.6	3,331.6
Nonfarm noncorporate business	365.9	418.7	450.3	507.1	553.5	637.6	755.2	788.9
State and local governments	1,307.6	1,428.8	1,549.8	1,625.3	1,844.3	2,117.5	2,370.5	2,421.6
Federal government	76.9	75.8	76.3	73.8	75.4	77.8	81.5	82.3
Commercial banking	1,660.1	1,789.8	2,058.3	2,255.8	2,595.3	2,956.6	3,403.0	3,378.6
Savings institutions	723.0	758.0	781.0	870.2	1,057.0	1,152.7	1,074.0	1,117.2
Credit unions	124.9	141.3	159.4	182.6	213.2	245.6	276.6	279.8
Other insurance companies	1.6	1.9	2.0	2.1	2.4	2.7	3.5	3.6
Life insurance companies	235.9	243.0	250.0	260.9	273.3	285.5	303.8	304.4
Private pension funds	11.9	9.8	10.3	10.2	10.0	9.8	9.5	9.3
State and local govt. retirement funds	22.1	21.0	21.1	20.4	19.5	19.4	21.3	˙22.1
Government-sponsored enterprises	264.3	297.5	357.3	463.3	478.4	477.2	479.5	480.6
Agency- and GSE-backed mortgage pools	2,493.2	2,831.8	3,158.6	3,489.1	3,542.2	3,677.0	3,964.5	4,075.5
ABS issuers	610.0	710.8	796.4	968.4	1,423.7	2,114.3	2,542.6	2,624.2
Finance companies	238.1	258.4	330.8	370.3	476.0	541.4	594.4	581.9
REITs	18.7	18.0	29.8	49.6	118.8	159.4	171.0	173.2

Closely related to mortgage bankers are **mortgage brokers.** Mortgage brokers typically do not lend funds directly to borrowers but simply act as brokers between loan applicants and lenders. Unlike bankers, brokers typically do not continue to service the loans they sell. Mortgage brokers' revenues are dependent on the origination fees charged to borrowers. In general, neither mortgage bankers nor mortgage brokers intentionally hold mortgage loans in a portfolio for their own benefit.

Commercial banks are private financial institutions that are organized to accept deposits from individuals and businesses and to loan these funds to all types of borrowers. Although residential mortgage lending is a small part of most commercial banks' business, commercial banks held approximately 24 percent of all outstanding mortgage debt in the United States as of 2003. Commercial banks use their own funds to originate mortgage loans in the primary market and to buy loans in the secondary mortgage market. They provide mortgages on residential and income-producing properties, as well as construction loans for developers and lines of credit for mortgage bankers.

Savings institutions have a long history of providing capital for housing purchases. The first savings institution (thrift) was founded in 1831 with the goal of accepting deposits from savers and loaning those funds to residential borrowers. Since that time, the original intent behind these institutions has remained largely unchanged, but the thrift industry has undergone dramatic cycles of growth and decline. Even after the collapse of many thrifts during the 1980s, these institutions continue to play a major role in the housing finance system. Thrifts continue to originate many new loans, both for their own portfolios and for sale in the secondary market. In 2007, savings institutions held approximately 8.2 percent of all outstanding mortgage debt in the United States.

Credit unions are an important source of consumer loans and a savings institution for many Americans. Members of a specific industry or community can join a credit union and enjoy access to their deposits through checking or savings accounts. Because profits are returned to the members, the yield available to credit union members on their deposits is slightly higher than that of other thrift institutions. Most credit unions originate mortgages only for their own portfolios, though some do sell their loans in the secondary mortgage market.

Although the participants discussed above originate the bulk of all new mortgage loans, many of them do not hold all of the loans in their own portfolios, but instead sell them to other investors in secondary mortgage market transactions. As shown in Table 16.1, about 30 percent of all mortgage debt in the United States is held by mortgage pools as of 2007.

UNDERSTANDING THE MORTGAGE LOAN ORIGINATION PROCESS

Now that we understand the legal and institutional characteristics of the mortgage market, we turn our attention to the mortgage loan origination process. We begin by reviewing the Fannie Mae/Freddie Mac Uniform Residential Loan Application, then consider borrower and property qualification criteria as well as various federal laws and rules that regulate the mortgage lending industry.

Fannie Mae/Freddie Mac Uniform Residential Loan Application

Because most of the mortgage loan originators we discussed above want to have the option of selling their loans in the secondary market, the origination process is fairly standardized throughout the United States. In fact, the two principal secondary market participants, Fannie Mae and Freddie Mac, have jointly approved an application form to be used with any loan that may eventually wind up in their secondary markets. The information solicited from the applicant by this form is then evaluated by the lender to reach a decision regarding loan approval or denial. A sample Uniform Residential Loan Application form is shown in Figure 16.3.

Information Required from Borrower

The information required to complete the Uniform Residential Loan Application is divided into various categories. Section 1 of the form asks the borrower to describe the type of mortgage requested, including the loan amount, interest rate, and term. Section 3 requests information on the borrower(s). Because most residential loans are made to married couples, both husband and wife must disclose their names, ages, Social Security numbers, present addresses, and former addresses for the past two years. In Section 4, applicants are required to disclose information regarding their employment history, including employer names, addresses, and telephone numbers. Proof of this information may be required in the form of check stubs, W-2 forms, and other documents. For self-employed borrowers, applicants must submit tax returns for at least two years prior to the application, as well as profit and loss statements prepared by an accountant.

Section 5 contains various questions about facts that may affect the borrowers' creditworthiness. Applicants must disclose information regarding their present and proposed monthly housing expenses. Section 6 requires that borrowers fully disclose their assets and liabilities, including real estate owned, stocks, bonds, life insurance policies, checking and savings accounts, credit cards, other outstanding loans, and alimony and child support obligations. In Section 7, the borrowers must disclose the details of the real estate transaction for which the loan will be used, including the purchase price of the property. By signing the application, the borrowers acknowledge that the purpose of the application is to acquire a loan to be secured by the real estate described in the application. In addition, the borrowers promise that the information provided in the application is true, and authorize the lender to verify its accuracy. The application also requests certain information that is used by the government to monitor lender activities, and requires that the lender's representative sign the application.

Duties of the Originator

Upon receiving a completed Uniform Residential Loan Application, the lender has various duties to the borrower as determined by federal lending regulations. These regulations are intended to provide protection to mortgage consumers. Important federal legislation to participants in the mortgage lending industry includes the

FIGURE 16.3 | Uniform Residential Loan Application

Uniform Residential Loan Application

This application is designed to be completed by the applicant(s) with the Lender's assistance. Applicants should complete this form as "Borrower" or "Co-Borrower," as applicable. Co-Borrower information must also be provided (and the appropriate box checked) when ☐ the income or assets of a person other than the "Borrower" (including the Borrower's spouse) will be used as a basis for loan qualification or ☐ the income or assets of the Borrower's spouse will not be used as a basis for loan qualification, but his or her liabilities must be considered because the Borrower resides in a community property state, the security property is located in a community property state, or the Borrower is relying on other property located in a community property state as a basis for repayment of the loan.

I. TYPE OF MORTGAGE AND TERMS OF LOAN

Mortgage Applied for:	☐ VA ☑ Conventional ☐ Other (explain): ☐ FHA ☐ USDA/Rural Housing Service	Agency Case Number	Lender Case Number

Amount $ 108,000	Interest Rate 8.00 %	No. of Months 360	Amortization Type: ☑ Fixed Rate ☐ GPM ☐ Other (explain): ☐ ARM (type):

II. PROPERTY INFORMATION AND PURPOSE OF LOAN

Subject Property Address (street, city, state, & ZIP) No. of Units: 1
1097 Timber Crossing, St. Joseph, Missouri

Legal Description of Subject Property (attach description if necessary) Year Built: 83
Lot 3, Block G of the Harris Billups Estate, Plat Book 8, p. 37

Purpose of Loan ☑ Purchase ☐ Construction ☐ Other (explain): ☐ Refinance ☐ Construction-Permanent

Property will be: ☑ Primary Residence ☐ Secondary Residence ☐ Investment

Complete this line if construction or construction-permanent loan.

Year Lot Acquired	Original Cost $	Amount Existing Liens $	(a) Present Value of Lot $	(b) Cost of Improvements $	Total (a + b) $ 0.00

Complete this line if this is a refinance loan.

Year Acquired	Original Cost $	Amount Existing Liens $	Purpose of Refinance	Describe Improvements ☐ made ☐ to be made Cost: $

Title will be held in what Name(s)	Manner in which Title will be held	Estate will be held in: ☐ Fee Simple ☐ Leasehold (show expiration date)

Source of Down Payment, Settlement Charges and/or Subordinate Financing (explain)

III. BORROWER INFORMATION

	Borrower	Co-Borrower
Name (include Jr. or Sr. if applicable)	Frank L. Barr	Elizabeth M. Barr
Social Security Number	000-00-0000	000-00-0000
Home Phone (incl. area code)	791-954-0723	791-954-0723
DOB (MM/DD/YYYY)	03/01/1973	06/07/1974
Yrs. School	16	16

Borrower: ☑ Married ☐ Unmarried (include single, divorced, widowed) ☐ Separated Dependents (not listed by Co-Borrower) no. 0 ages

Co-Borrower: ☑ Married ☐ Unmarried (include single, divorced, widowed) ☐ Separated Dependents (not listed by Borrower) no. 0 ages

Present Address (street, city, state, ZIP) ☐ Own ☑ Rent 4 No. Yrs.
103 Wilson Street
St. Joseph, Missouri

Present Address (street, city, state, ZIP) ☐ Own ☑ Rent 4 No. Yrs.
103 Wilson Street
St. Joseph, Missouri

Mailing Address, if different from Present Address

Mailing Address, if different from Present Address

If residing at present address for less than two years, complete the following:

Former Address (street, city, state, ZIP) ☐ Own ☐ Rent _____ No. Yrs.

Former Address (street, city, state, ZIP) ☐ Own ☐ Rent _____ No. Yrs.

IV. EMPLOYMENT INFORMATION

	Borrower	Co-Borrower
Name & Address of Employer	ABC Corp. 444 A Street St. Joseph, Missouri ☐ Self Employed	Intense Corp. 1301 Walker Drive St. Joseph, Missouri ☐ Self Employed
Yrs. on this job	5.0	4.0
Yrs. employed in this line of work/profession	8.0	7.0
Position/Title/Type of Business	Manager, Human Resources	Consultant, Advertising
Business Phone (incl. area code)	(791) 838-2591	(791) 847-3965

If employed in current position for less than two years or if currently employed in more than one position, complete the following:

	Borrower	Co-Borrower
Name & Address of Employer	☐ Self Employed	☐ Self Employed
Dates (from – to)		
Monthly Income	$	$
Position/Title/Type of Business		
Business Phone (incl. area code)		

Name & Address of Employer	☐ Self Employed	☐ Self Employed
Dates (from – to)		
Monthly Income	$	$
Position/Title/Type of Business		
Business Phone (incl. area code)		

FIGURE 16.3 | Uniform Residential Loan Application *(continued)*

V. MONTHLY INCOME AND COMBINED HOUSING EXPENSE INFORMATION

Gross Monthly Income	Borrower	Co-Borrower	Total	Combined Monthly Housing Expense	Present	Proposed
Base Empl. Income*	$ 3,100.00	$ 2,500.00	$ 5,600.00	Rent	$ 600.00	
Overtime	200.00	325.00	525.00	First Mortgage (P&I)		$ 793.00
Bonuses			0.00	Other Financing (P&I)		
Commissions			0.00	Hazard Insurance		50.00
Dividends/Interest			0.00	Real Estate Taxes		90.00
Net Rental Income			0.00	Mortgage Insurance		45.00
Other (before completing, see the notice in "describe other income," below)			0.00	Homeowner Assn. Dues		0.00
			0.00	Other:		
Total	$ 3,300.00	$ 2,825.00	$ 6,125.00	Total	$ 600.00	$ 978.00

* Self Employed Borrower(s) may be required to provide additional documentation such as tax returns and financial statements.

Describe Other Income *Notice:* Alimony, child support, or separate maintenance income need not be revealed if the Borrower (B) or Co-Borrower (C) does not choose to have it considered for repaying this loan.

B/C		Monthly Amount
		$

VI. ASSETS AND LIABILITIES

This Statement and any applicable supporting schedules may be completed jointly by both married and unmarried Co-Borrowers if their assets and liabilities are sufficiently joined so that the Statement can be meaningfully and fairly presented on a combined basis; otherwise, separate Statements and Schedules are required. If the Co-Borrower section was completed about a spouse, this Statement and supporting schedules must be completed about that spouse also.

Completed ☑ Jointly ☐ Not Jointly

ASSETS Description	Cash or Market Value	Liabilities and Pledged Assets. List the creditor's name, address and account number for all outstanding debts, including automobile loans, revolving charge accounts, real estate loans, alimony, child support, stock pledges, etc. Use continuation sheet, if necessary. Indicate by (*) those liabilities which will be satisfied upon sale of real estate owned upon refinancing of the subject property.		
Cash deposit toward purchase held by: R.E. Broker	$ 4,000.00			
		LIABILITIES	Monthly Payment & Months Left to Pay	Unpaid Balance
List checking and savings accounts below		Name and address of Company	$ Payment/Months	$
Name and address of Bank, S&L, or Credit Union First Bank -- Checking 123 Elm Street St. Joseph, Missouri		Hardy Credit 3423 S. 3rd Street San Jose, CA	$120/11	1,200.00
		Acct. no.		
Acct. no. 222222	$ 3,300.00	Name and address of Company	$ Payment/Months	$
Name and address of Bank, S&L, or Credit Union First Bank -- Savings 123 Elm Street St. Joseph, Missouri		Proposed Loan	978/360	108,000.00
		Acct. no.		
Acct. no. 27328	$ 21,800.00	Name and address of Company	$ Payment/Months	$
Name and address of Bank, S&L, or Credit Union				
		Acct. no.		
Acct. no.	$	Name and address of Company	$ Payment/Months	$
Name and address of Bank, S&L, or Credit Union				
		Acct. no.		
Acct. no. 35358	$	Name and address of Company	$ Payment/Months	$
Stocks & Bonds (Company name/number & description) Olde Discount	$ 18,300.00			
		Acct. no.		
Life insurance net cash value Face amount: $	$	Name and address of Company	$ Payment/Months	$
Subtotal Liquid Assets	$ 47,400.00			
Real estate owned (enter market value from schedule of real estate owned)	$ 20,000.00	Acct. no.		
Vested interest in retirement fund	$	Name and address of Company	$ Payment/Months	$
Net worth of business(es) owned (attach financial statement)	$			
Automobiles owned (make and year) Ford '92 Nissan '97	$ 4000 11000	Acct. no.		
Other Assets (itemize)	$	Alimony/Child Support/Separate Maintenance Payments Owed to:	$	
		Job-Related Expense (child care, union dues, etc.)	$	
		Total Monthly Payments	$ 1,098.00	
Total Assets a.	$ 82,400.00	Net Worth (a minus b) ➤ $ -26,800.00	Total Liabilities b.	$ 109,200.00

FIGURE 16.3 | Uniform Residential Loan Application *(continued)*

VI. ASSETS AND LIABILITIES (cont.)

Schedule of Real Estate Owned (If additional properties are owned, use continuation sheet.)

Property Address (enter S if sold, PS if pending sale or R if rental being held for income)	Type of Property	Present Market Value	Amount of Mortgages & Liens	Gross Rental Income	Mortgage Payments	Insurance, Maintenance, Taxes & Misc.	Net Rental Income
Lot 7, Becker Drive	land	$ 20,000	$ 0	$ 0	$ 0	$ 0	$ 0
Totals		$	$	$	$	$	$

List any additional names under which credit has previously been received and indicate appropriate creditor name(s) and account number(s):

Alternate Name	Creditor Name	Account Number

VII. DETAILS OF TRANSACTION

a. Purchase price	$ 120,000
b. Alterations, improvements, repairs	0
c. Land (if acquired separately)	0
d. Refinance (incl. debts to be paid off)	0
e. Estimated prepaid items	1,200
f. Estimated closing costs	5,000
g. PMI, MIP, Funding Fee	
h. Discount (if Borrower will pay)	
i. Total costs (add items a through h)	126,200
j. Subordinate financing	
k. Borrower's closing costs paid by Seller	
l. Other Credits (explain)	
m. Loan amount (exclude PMI, MIP, Funding Fee financed)	108,000.00
n. PMI, MIP, Funding Fee financed	
o. Loan amount (add m & n)	108,000
p. Cash from/to Borrower (subtract j, k, l & o from i)	18,200

VIII. DECLARATIONS

If you answer "Yes" to any questions a through i, please use continuation sheet for explanation.

	Borrower Yes	Borrower No	Co-Borrower Yes	Co-Borrower No
a. Are there any outstanding judgments against you?	☐	☑	☐	☑
b. Have you been declared bankrupt within the past 7 years?	☐	☑	☐	☑
c. Have you had property foreclosed upon or given title or deed in lieu thereof in the last 7 years?	☐	☑	☐	☑
d. Are you a party to a lawsuit?	☐	☑	☐	☑
e. Have you directly or indirectly been obligated on any loan which resulted in foreclosure, transfer of title in lieu of foreclosure, or judgment? (This would include such loans as home mortgage loans, SBA loans, home improvement loans, educational loans, manufactured (mobile) home loans, any mortgage, financial obligation, bond, or loan guarantee. If "Yes," provide details, including date, name and address of Lender, FHA or VA case number, if any, and reasons for the action.)	☐	☑	☐	☑
f. Are you presently delinquent or in default on any Federal debt or any other loan, mortgage, financial obligation, bond, or loan guarantee? If "Yes," give details as described in the preceding question.	☐	☑	☐	☑
g. Are you obligated to pay alimony, child support, or separate maintenance?	☐	☑	☐	☑
h. Is any part of the down payment borrowed?	☐	☑	☐	☑
i. Are you a co-maker or endorser on a note?	☐	☑	☐	☑
j. Are you a U.S. citizen?	☑	☐	☑	☐
k. Are you a permanent resident alien?	☑	☐	☑	☐
l. Do you intend to occupy the property as your primary residence? If "Yes," complete question m below.	☑	☐	☑	☐
m. Have you had an ownership interest in a property in the last three years?	☑	☐	☑	☐
(1) What type of property did you own—principal residence (PR), second home (SH), or investment property (IP)?	IP		IP	
(2) How did you hold title to the home—solely by yourself (S), jointly with your spouse (SP), or jointly with another person (O)?	SP		SP	

IX. ACKNOWLEDGMENT AND AGREEMENT

Each of the undersigned specifically represents to Lender and to Lender's actual or potential agents, brokers, processors, attorneys, insurers, servicers, successors and assigns and agrees and acknowledges that: (1) the information provided in this application is true and correct as of the date set forth opposite my signature and that any intentional or negligent misrepresentation of this information contained in this application may result in civil liability, including monetary damages, to any person who may suffer any loss due to reliance upon any misrepresentation that I have made on this application, and/or in criminal penalties including, but not limited to, fine or imprisonment or both under the provisions of Title 18, United States Code, Sec. 1001, et seq.; (2) the loan requested pursuant to this application (the "Loan") will be secured by a mortgage or deed of trust on the property described herein; (3) the property will not be used for any illegal or prohibited purpose or use; (4) all statements made in this application are made for the purpose of obtaining a residential mortgage loan; (5) the property will be occupied as indicated herein; (6) any owner or servicer of the Loan may verify or reverify any information contained in the application from any source named in this application, and Lender, its successors or assigns may retain the original and/or an electronic record of this application, even if the Loan is not approved; (7) the Lender and its agents, brokers, insurers, servicers, successors and assigns may continuously rely on the information contained in the application, and I am obligated to amend and/or supplement the information provided in this application if any of the material facts that I have represented herein should change prior to closing of the Loan; (8) in the event that my payments on the Loan become delinquent, the owner or servicer of the Loan may, in addition to any other rights and remedies that it may have relating to such delinquency, report my name and account information to one or more consumer credit reporting agencies; (9) ownership of the Loan and/or administration of the Loan account may be transferred with such notice as may be required by law; (10) neither Lender nor its agents, brokers, insurers, servicers, successors or assigns has made any representation or warranty, express or implied, to me regarding the property or the condition or value of the property; and (11) my transmission of this application as an "electronic record" containing my "electronic signature," as those terms are defined in applicable federal and/or state laws (excluding audio and video recordings), or my facsimile transmission of this application containing a facsimile of my signature, shall be as effective, enforceable and valid as if a paper version of this application were delivered containing my original written signature.

Borrower's Signature	Date	Co-Borrower's Signature	Date
X		X	

X. INFORMATION FOR GOVERNMENT MONITORING PURPOSES

The following information is requested by the Federal Government for certain types of loans related to a dwelling in order to monitor the lender's compliance with equal credit opportunity, fair housing and home mortgage disclosure laws. You are not required to furnish this information, but are encouraged to do so. The law provides that a lender may discriminate neither on the basis of this information, nor on whether you choose to furnish it. If you furnish the information, please provide both ethnicity and race. For race, you may check more than one designation. If you do not wish to furnish ethnicity, race, or sex, under Federal regulations, this lender is required to note the information on the basis of visual observation or surname. If you do not wish to furnish the information, please check the box below. (Lender must review the above material to assure that the disclosures satisfy all requirements to which the lender is subject under applicable state law for the particular type of loan applied for.)

BORROWER	☐ I do not wish to furnish this information.	CO-BORROWER	☐ I do not wish to furnish this information.
Ethnicity:	☐ Hispanic or Latino ☑ Not Hispanic or Latino	Ethnicity:	☐ Hispanic or Latino ☑ Not Hispanic or Latino
Race:	☐ American Indian or Alaska Native ☐ Asian ☑ Black or African American ☐ Native Hawaiian or Other Pacific Islander ☐ White	Race:	☐ American Indian or Alaska Native ☐ Asian ☑ Black or African American ☐ Native Hawaiian or Other Pacific Islander ☐ White
Sex:	☐ Female ☑ Male	Sex:	☑ Female ☐ Male

To be Completed by Interviewer This application was taken by: ☑ Face-to-face interview ☐ Mail ☐ Telephone ☐ Internet	Interviewer's Name (print or type) Bob Interviewer	Name and Address of Interviewer's Employer First Savings Bank St. Joseph, Missouri
	Interviewer's Signature	
	Interviewer's Phone Number (incl. area code) 954-761-0264	

Equal Credit Opportunity Act (Regulation B); the Consumer Credit Protection Act (Regulation Z); the Real Estate Settlement Procedures Act; the Flood Disaster Protection Act; and the Fair Credit Reporting Act.

Equal Credit Opportunity Act

The **Equal Credit Opportunity Act** has influenced the mortgage lending industry since 1974. Under this act, applicants must be notified within 30 days of application that their loan request has either been approved or denied, or determined to be incomplete. In addition, the act prohibits lenders from discriminating against borrowers on the following bases: race, color, religion, national origin, sex, marital status, age, whether all or part of an applicant's income is derived from public assistance programs, or whether the applicant has exercised any right under the Consumer Credit Protection Act.

Consumer Credit Protection Act

Title I of the **Consumer Credit Protection Act** is frequently referred to as *Regulation Z,* or the *Truth-in-Lending law.* Under this regulation, lenders are required to disclose the full details of the loan to the applicant within three business days of application, including exactly how much the loan will cost. The goal of the Truth-in-Lending requirement is to permit borrowers to shop for the best deal among competing lenders. Specifically, lenders are required to inform applicants of the total finance charges associated with the loan and the annual percentage rate (APR) of interest. In the event the loan is to be used to refinance a property already owned by the applicant, Regulation Z requires that the lender inform the borrower of the right to rescind the loan within three business days of origination. The APR is the effective annual interest rate that the borrower will pay after all fees and charges are taken into consideration. The APR is often quite different from the stated interest rate used to determine the payments on the loan. By comparing the APRs of various lenders, a consumer can determine which lender is offering the best deal and thereby make an informed decision about the loan.

Real Estate Settlement Procedures Act

The **Real Estate Settlement Procedures Act** (RESPA) is another important source of regulation in the mortgage lending industry. This act applies to federally related mortgage loans, and it creates several different duties for mortgage lenders following a residential mortgage loan application. First, RESPA requires that lenders provide borrowers with a copy of a special information booklet prepared by the U.S. Department of Housing and Urban Development (HUD). The information contained in *Buying Your Home: Settlement Costs and Helpful Information* is designed to describe and explain the settlement costs borrowers are likely to incur when purchasing a home using mortgage financing.

Second, RESPA requires that lenders provide borrowers with a "good-faith estimate" of the settlement costs associated with the loan within three business days of the application. We examined these costs and the loan "closing" process in detail in a previous chapter. Third, the act prohibits kickbacks or referral fees paid to parties who refer a borrower to the lender. Fourth, the act gives the applicant the right to request and receive a copy of any appraisal report used to evaluate the property that serves as security for the debt. Although the borrower is typically charged a fee for the appraisal, the report technically belongs to the lender, not the borrower. Fifth, RESPA requires the use of the HUD-1 Uniform Settlement Statement by the settlement agent at the loan closing. As we saw in a previous chapter, this settlement statement shows line-by-line costs that will be incurred as a result of the pending real estate transaction, and a copy of this completed form must be made available to both the buyer and seller. Furthermore, the act establishes the borrower's right to inspect this statement one day prior to the actual closing. At that time, the lender must accurately disclose all known closing costs and must provide a good-faith estimate of all uncertain closing costs that will be charged to the borrower. To enforce this right, the borrower must make a written request to the lender on or before the business day prior to settlement. Sixth, RESPA requires that lenders disclose whether the loan is expected to be sold in the secondary market. If the loan is sold, the lender is required to disclose this information to the borrower within 15 days of transfer. While borrowers can do little to stop the transfer of their loan, it is important that they know who their loan servicer is and how to contact the new servicer after a transfer.

Finally, RESPA limits the amount of money a lender can require that the borrower deposit to cover such recurring expenses as property taxes, hazard-insurance premiums, and other periodic assessments. In addition to the principal and interest payments due from a borrower each month, lenders may also require that a borrower's loan payment include reserve payments to be deposited into an escrow account. As the property tax bill or insurance premiums come due, the lender simply pays the bill from the funds in the escrow account. Having the money on deposit ensures that payment will be made promptly, thus protecting the lender's interest in the collateral for the loan. If these bills are not paid, the property could be destroyed without a current insurance policy, or a tax lien that has priority over the lender's lien or encumbrance could be placed on the property. Both of these events could significantly diminish the protection provided to the lender by the mortgage concept. RESPA limits the amount of reserves that the lender can collect at closing to one-sixth of the annual property taxes and insurance.

Flood Disaster Protection Act

The remaining federal legislation that regulates the mortgage lending industry includes the **Flood Disaster Protection Act** and the Fair Credit Reporting Act. The Flood Disaster Protection Act requires that lenders disclose to borrowers whether the property they are purchasing lies within a flood hazard area. If so, the lender must require that the borrower obtain flood insurance if it is available. Flood insurance is generally only available through the Federal Emergency Management Administration's (FEMA) National Flood Insurance Program. This act puts the burden of notifying borrowers that their properties are subject to damage from flooding squarely on the shoulders of the lenders.

Fair Credit Reporting Act

The **Fair Credit Reporting Act** primarily affects credit reporting agencies, but it also affects the users of information obtained from these agencies. The act requires that lenders obtain permission before investigating an applicant's credit history and handle the applicant's credit information with due care. If an applicant's loan request is denied based on information contained in a credit report, the lender must notify the applicant of this fact and provide the borrower with the name, address, and telephone number of the credit agency that supplied the information.

Mortgage Underwriting

Once the application for a mortgage loan has been received from the applicant, the lender must evaluate the applicant's creditworthiness as well as the suitability of the property as security for the debt. From the lender's perspective, lending money to a borrower is an investment in the borrower's willingness and ability to repay the debt under the terms of the agreement. As discussed earlier, the property can be used to satisfy the debt (through the foreclosure process) if the borrower is unable or unwilling to abide by the terms of the loan. The process of evaluating the risk of an applicant and a property in order to make a decision regarding a loan application is known as **underwriting.** We consider the underwriting process for borrowers and properties separately.

Qualifying an Applicant

To evaluate an applicant's creditworthiness, lenders typically examine the applicant's sources of income, net worth, and credit history, then perform a risk assessment. The sources of income that are considered relevant include wages or salary, self-employment, rent, interest, investment, and commission, as well as child support, alimony, separate maintenance income, retirement, pension, disability, and welfare benefits. Note that disclosure of information regarding child support, separate maintenance income, and alimony is not required if the applicant does not wish for this information to be considered as an income source. The Uniform Residential Loan Application described previously is used to provide information on these sources of income to the lender, and the lender must verify the accuracy of this information. Similarly, the application provides information regarding assets and liabilities that determine the applicant's net worth, which can be verified with permission of the applicant. Lenders also obtain permission to request an up-to-date residential mortgage credit report. This report, which is required if the lender intends to sell the loan in the secondary market, contains information about outstanding judgments, liens, or divorce proceedings; a list of similar credit inquiries within the previous 90 days; and all available credit information for the past seven years from at least one national credit reporting agency. If any of this information reasonably suggests that the borrower will not be able or willing to repay the proposed debt, the lender can deny the loan application subject to the regulations imposed by the Fair Credit Reporting Act.

Qualifying the Property

In addition to collecting and verifying information on the borrower's creditworthiness, the lender must also collect and verify information regarding the property being pledged as security for the debt. First, the person pledging the property must in fact be the legal owner of the property. As we discussed in a previous chapter, verifying the ownership or title to real estate requires careful inspection of the public records. If there are defects in or "clouds" on the title to the property involved, the lender will reject the loan application. To protect their interests in the property, lenders typically require that borrowers purchase title insurance or obtain a title opinion from an attorney. In general, loans originated without title insurance cannot be sold in the secondary mortgage market.

Besides verifying the applicant's right to pledge the property as security, the lender also has incentive to verify that the value of the property supports the requested loan amount. If the value of the property is less than the amount of the debt, borrowers may be unwilling to meet their obligations. If the lender is faced with foreclosing on the loan in this situation, the sale of the property will likely not result in sufficient proceeds to satisfy the debt. Therefore, the lender may require an appraisal of the property's value before granting final approval for the requested loan amount. After receiving the appraisal report from a qualified appraiser, the lender must review the appraisal report to verify its acceptability. If the loan involved will be sold in the secondary mortgage market, the appraiser's conclusions must be presented on the Uniform Residential Appraisal Report form that is accepted by Fannie Mae and Freddie Mac. We examined the topic of real estate appraisal in a previous chapter.

Risk Assessment

In addition to evaluating a borrower's residential mortgage credit report and the title and value of the pledged property, the lender must consider other factors when making the underwriting decision. Although no absolute rules exist to determine whether a borrower will be able to meet the obligations of a requested loan, there are guidelines that lenders use in the underwriting process. While each lender establishes its own guidelines, the secondary market participants (primarily Fannie Mae and Freddie Mac) provide general guidelines for loans they are willing to buy from loan originators. Because most lenders want to be able to sell their loans in this market, these guidelines are well-accepted in the lending industry. Fannie Mae and Freddie Mac guidelines fall into three categories: loan-to-value ratios, down payment sources, and income ratios.

Loan-to-Value Ratio Guidelines

The **loan-to-value ratio,** or LTV ratio, is determined by dividing the requested loan amount by the lesser of the sale price or the appraised value of the property. Generally expressed as a percentage amount, higher LTV ratios imply greater risk. For example, suppose a lender provides $95,000 to a borrower who purchases a $100,000 house (LTV ratio of 95 percent). Because the borrower has little equity in the property, default is more likely if the value of the property should fall below the loan amount. If default does occur and the property is sold through the foreclosure process, it is doubtful that the proceeds of the sale will be sufficient to cover the loan balance, past-due interest, and the expenses of sale. If the LTV ratio was only 50 percent, however, there is a much lower probability of default. If the borrower should default, the proceeds from the property sale should be sufficient to protect the lender. As a general guideline, all loans with an LTV ratio of 80 percent or higher must carry PMI, FHA mortgage insurance, or a VA loan guarantee to be acceptable in the secondary mortgage markets. While most conventional loans have a maximum LTV ratio of 95 percent even with PMI, some FHA-insured loans may have LTV ratios of up to 98.75 percent, and VA-guaranteed loan LTV ratios may be as high as 100 percent.

Down Payment Source Guidelines

The second category of guidelines refers to sources for the borrower's down payment or equity for a home purchase. In general, secondary market guidelines require that funds used for the down payment be provided primarily by the borrower rather than from outside sources. By requiring that borrowers use their own personal funds for the down payment, the borrower is likely to be more diligent in meeting the obligations of the loan. In most conventional loans with LTV ratios above 80 percent, at least 5 percent of the purchase price must represent the borrower's personal investment in the property. The remaining 15 percent could be a gift from an outside source, such as a family member or employer, but never a loan. If the LTV ratio is less than 80 percent, however, the entire down payment amount can be a gift from an outside source. Lenders who intend to sell a loan in the secondary market must verify that the down payment meets or exceeds this requirement by documenting its sources.

The down payment source requirements are applied differently for FHA and VA loans. Some FHA loan programs permit the borrower to contribute only 3 percent of the purchase price from personal savings, with the other 2 percent in the form of a gift from an outside source. Other FHA loan programs allow the entire down payment amount to be a gift to the borrower from outside sources. Many VA-guaranteed loans do not require a down payment at all, but the borrower is required to pay a funding fee that decreases as the down payment amount increases.

Income Ratio Guidelines

Income ratios compose the third category of underwriting guidelines. These ratios are designed to assess borrowers' abilities to repay the mortgage as specified in the loan documents. Two income ratios that are considered by secondary market participants and the various guaranteeing and insuring entities are the **mortgage debt ratio** (front-end ratio) and the **total debt ratio** (back-end ratio).

The *mortgage debt ratio* (MDR) is defined as the percentage of a borrower's gross monthly income that is required to meet monthly housing expenses. *Monthly housing expenses* refers to principal and interest payments, hazard insurance, property taxes, mortgage insurance, homeowners' association fees, and any payments on existing or proposed second mortgages on the property. In general, the MDR must not exceed 28 percent on a conventional loan. For example, consider a loan applicant whose gross monthly income is $5,000. The applicant is applying for a loan with monthly payments of $965. Monthly payments for hazard insurance, property taxes, and mortgage insurance total $210. No second mortgages exist, and the home is not part of a homeowners' association. The MDR for this applicant is 23.5 percent ($1,175 \div 5,000 \times 100$), which is well below the maximum ratio allowed.

The *total debt ratio* (TDR) is defined as the percentage of a borrower's gross monthly income that is required to meet monthly contractual expenses. Contractual expenses include housing expenses as defined above, any revolving credit payments, payments on any installment loans with more than 10 remaining payments, and any alimony or child support. Notice that while applicants are not required to provide information regarding alimony and child support as an *income source,* they must disclose this information if it represents an *expense.* As a guideline for conventional loans, total payments for all of the items listed above must not exceed 36 percent of a borrower's gross income. Continuing the example discussed above, if the applicant has an outstanding car loan that requires monthly payments of $280 and child support payments of $500 per month, the TDR would be 39.1 percent ($1,995 \div 5,000 \times 100$). In this case, the applicant would not qualify for the loan under this guideline.

When assessing the risk of a mortgage loan application, lenders calculate both of these ratios to verify that the borrower is capable of repaying the debt and meeting other contractual obligations. Borrowers must qualify under both ratios simultaneously to receive approval. While these ratios have evolved from years of experience with millions of loans, there are possible mitigating circumstances that will allow a lender to deviate from these guidelines. Such circumstances include a demonstrated ability to allocate a higher percentage of income to housing expenses, a low LTV ratio, a spotless credit report, large net worth, or other similar factors. In addition, the ratio limits specified above apply to conventional loans only. For FHA-insured loans, the ratio limits are 29 percent for the front-end ratio, and 41 percent for the back-end ratio. VA-guaranteed loans use a more detailed income standard, and sometimes allow back-end ratios as high as 45 percent.

The Underwriting Decision

The final step in the loan origination process is for the lender to render an underwriting decision. As mentioned above, the Equal Credit Opportunity Act requires that lenders reach their decision for completed applications within 30 days. With modern technology, most underwriting decisions can be made in minutes instead of days. If the loan is approved, the lender notifies the borrower of acceptance and, in most cases, issues a letter of commitment. If the loan is for home purchase rather than a refinancing, then the real estate closing process can occur as planned. If the lender denies the credit application, the lender must notify the applicant, give the reason for the credit denial, and provide a statement of nondiscrimination that is consistent with the provisions of the Equal Credit Opportunity Act.

Subprime Loans

It is important for us to recognize that many borrowers do not meet the lending guidelines discussed above, but many of them are still able to obtain **subprime mortgage loans.** The cost of subprime loans (interest rate) is typically much higher than the rate available to prime borrowers. In addition, the terms of the loan are often different from typical prime loans. (We will discuss a variety of mortgage types in Chapter 18.) Subprime lending grew dramatically between the years 2000 and 2006. Total subprime loans outstanding in year 2000 were around 5 percent of all outstanding mortgage debt. By year 2006, this percentage exceeded 20 percent of all outstanding mortgage debt.

Rapid housing price appreciation is one factor that led to increased subprime lending. Housing price appreciation offset some of the risk of lending to subprime borrowers. Even though the borrowers did not meet the prime lending guidelines, the value of the collateral (houses) behind the loans was increasing rapidly and lenders knew that they could ultimately use that collateral to satisfy the debt in the event of borrower default. Another major factor that led to increased subprime lending was the higher yields available to investors who purchased securities backed by these loans. Many investors saw the increased yields available and invested heavily in this market. The downturn in housing markets around the nation in 2005 led to increased mortgage defaults and lenders could not depend on the collateral values to satisfy the debts. This then led to the financial distress for some of the investors who had invested heavily in subprime loans through the primary and secondary mortgage markets.

SOURCES OF CAPITAL IN COMMERCIAL PROPERTY MARKETS

Who are the debt and equity investors in commercial property markets? Unlike residential markets, in which most equity capital is provided by households who are seeking a place to live, capital in commercial property markets is provided by investors who are seeking investment returns rather than personal use of the properties. Some of these investors provide equity capital to the market (through their down payments), and other investors provide debt capital by lending money to equity investors. The returns available through debt and equity investments in commercial properties attract individuals, pension funds, life insurance companies, commercial banks, and investment companies that are formed specifically to invest in commercial real estate.

Individual Investors

Many commercial properties are owned by individual investors (sometimes called "mom and pop" investors) who invest in relatively small-scale commercial properties as a means of diversifying their investment portfolios, which often include a variety of other asset classes (stocks, bonds, insurance policies, etc.). Individual investors often use a portion of their total wealth portfolio in conjunction with money borrowed from commercial property lenders to purchase properties that are expected to provide investment returns through property value appreciation and cash flow from rental operations to tenants. In addition to direct ownership, mom and pop investors may "hold a mortgage" on a property (provide debt capital) to other equity investors. Mom and pop investors are an important source of capital in many local real estate markets and should not be ignored as critical components of such markets.

Life Insurance Companies

Life insurance companies also invest debt and equity capital in commercial properties. A typical life insurance company sells insurance policies that have expected payouts (on death of the customers) many years into the future. The insurance company invests the proceeds from the policy sales to ensure that funds will be available to pay the eventual policy claims. Commercial real estate is an attractive investment vehicle for many life insurance companies because the assets are durable, long-lived, and provide an acceptable expected rate of return. Insurance companies invest in commercial properties by purchasing properties directly (as equity investors) and also by providing mortgage funds to borrowers seeking to purchase properties.

Pension Funds

Pension funds represent another important participant in the equity and debt capital markets. Pension funds accumulate contributions made by the fund participants over their working lives. As the contributions are received, the fund managers invest the money with the objective of increasing the income stream that will be available to the fund participant when the participant retires. Some examples of large pension funds in the United States include those operated by labor unions, private corporations, and state and local employment systems such as the California State Teachers Retirement System (CALSTERS), California Public Employees Retirement System (CALPERS), and Teachers Insurance Annuity Association (TIAA).

Since the 1980s, pension funds have increased their involvement in commercial property markets and now are a major source of capital in both the debt and equity markets. With plenty of cash on hand, many pension funds invest directly in commercial properties, often on an all-cash basis, while others prefer to underwrite mortgage loans on commercial properties for equity investors. In either case, the investment horizon for pension funds is quite long (the working life of the participants) and thus well matched to the relatively long and durable nature of commercial real estate investment opportunities. In general, investment returns to pension funds are not subject to federal income taxes at the fund level, though the participants may be taxed on the income they receive during their retirement years.

Pension funds may manage their own investments in commercial properties and mortgages, but they often seek the services of an investment management firm to identify properties for investment and to provide portfolio and property management services. In some cases, several different pension funds will combine their money into a commingled real estate fund, or CREF, that is managed by a professional

What Is Credit Scoring?

 While most of us are aware that our credit history is a critical consideration when we apply for a loan, many people may not realize how their credit history is evaluated by a potential lender. Credit bureaus maintain surprisingly detailed databases regarding our financial affairs, including loan and account balances, payment activity, bankruptcy filings, and even denied credit and life insurance applications. Potential lenders review these records before approving loan requests in an effort to assess how likely applicants are to pay their obligations.

Many lenders place significant emphasis on an applicant's "credit score." Credit scores are calculated by the major credit bureaus for everyone with a credit history in an effort to simplify detailed credit history records. The formulas used in calculating the scores are intended to rank credit histories in terms of the probability that borrowers will be delinquent with their payments. Loan applicants with higher credit scores are viewed more favorably than those with lower scores. For example, scores calculated using one popular formula range from 300 to 900, with most consumers falling between 500 and 800. Scores above 700 are considered good, while scores in the 600 range are considered marginal.

The exact details of the formulas used to calculate credit scores are proprietary and are not released to the public. The scores used by the three main credit bureaus (Equifax, Experian, and Trans Union) are calculated using a system developed by Fair, Isaac & Co., a California data-management and consulting firm. Scores calculated using this system are determined by 30 different factors available in a standard credit report. The factors relate to the applicant's delinquency history, the level of indebtedness, the length of the applicant's credit history, the number of recent inquiries regarding the credit history, and the types of credit the applicant has outstanding. Through years of research, these factors have proven to be very predictive when it comes to evaluating whether an applicant will repay the debt according to the terms of the loan agreement. Credit scores make it easier and faster to evaluate loan requests, and they are growing in popularity with mortgage lenders.

Because lenders rely heavily on credit bureau reports when evaluating loan applications, it is important that your credit record is accurate and up to date. Many financial planners recommend that consumers check their credit records annually by contacting the three main credit bureaus and requesting a credit report. Federal law requires the credit bureaus to give each person one free copy of their credit report (but not their credit score) each year. You can review your reports for errors and omissions and ensure that your credit history is accurate. In addition to correcting errors, you can enter in your credit record a statement of up to 100 words explaining the circumstances of any negative information.

To request your free credit report, visit *www.annualcreditreport.com.*

management company. In some cases, these individual CREF participants may sell or buy additional shares of the CREFs as needed to adjust the proportion of real estate held in their total investment portfolios.

Real Estate Investment Trusts

Real estate investment trusts (REITs) are another increasingly important participant in the commercial property equity and debt capital markets. REITs sell shares of stock (units) to investors through public and private markets, then use the proceeds to invest in commercial properties, either as equity or debt investors. In 1990, the total amount of capital invested in publicly traded REITs was approximately $8.7 billion. By the end of 2000, that amount had increased to approximately $138.7 billion and by the end of 2006 that amount had increased to $438.1 billion. Publicly traded REITs provide an opportunity for even the smallest investors to participate in commercial real estate markets.

REITs are not subject to firm-level taxation as long as the firm meets certain Internal Revenue Service requirements. Most important, the firm must distribute at least 95 percent of its taxable income each year to its shareholders (who are then taxed on this income as dividends). Because of this requirement, REITs have little opportunity to grow through the use of retained earnings. Instead, REITs must issue additional shares of stock or borrow from lenders to significantly increase their holdings.

Commercial Banks

Commercial banks are another important source of capital in commercial property markets. Commercial banks are divided into three broad categories: community banks (less than $500 million in assets), regional banks (more than $500 million in assets), and money center banks (the ten largest banks in the United States). Most banks attempt to match the maturity structure of their liabilities (deposits that could be withdrawn) with their assets (loans and investments). The spread between the interest rate paid on deposits and the yields earned on loans and investments represents profit to the bank. Because their investment funds are subject to withdrawal by the bank's customers, commercial banks tend to be more involved in development and construction financing and less involved in long-term mortgage lending or direct property ownership.

CMBS

An important recent advance in the commercial property financing system has been the increase in securitization of commercial mortgages. As discussed previously in this chapter regarding residential mortgages, commercial mortgages can be divided into financial securities that represent claims on the cash flows to the mortgage holder. These financial securities are called **commercial mortgage-backed securities** (CMBS).

To understand how CMBS work, consider a commercial bank or investment banking firm that has expertise in evaluating commercial property mortgage applications but does not wish to tie up its money in long-term mortgage loans. That bank may be able to originate several loans to commercial property investors, then pool those loans together and sell "shares" of the pool to other investors who want to invest in mortgage loans but do not have expertise in originating these loans. The bank that puts the pool together creates different types of securities that entitle the security purchasers to different components of the cash flow coming into the pool over time from the mortgage borrowers. One security class, for example, might be entitled to all of the cash flows for the first five years of the life of the loans, at which time this security class will be retired and the next class will be entitled to the cash-flow stream. Investors who might otherwise not have been interested in purchasing mortgage investments will be attracted to the different CMBS that match their investment preferences and horizons. Given the dramatic increase in residential mortgage securitization that occurred during the 1980s and 1990s, CMBS are expected to become an increasingly important component of the commercial financing system over the next several years.

COMMERCIAL FINANCING UNDERWRITING CRITERIA

Unlike residential mortgage underwriting criteria that rely heavily on the borrower's personal ability to earn sufficient income to repay the debt, commercial property lenders are much more concerned with the property's ability to generate sufficient income to repay the debt. Lenders typically require that a property's expected *net operating income (NOI)*, defined as gross income less operating expenses, be 15 percent to 20 percent higher than the payments required to service the debt. This underwriting criterion is often called the **debt coverage ratio,** or DCR. The DCR is calculated by dividing the NOI by DS, where NOI represents the expected net operating income from the property (rent collections less operating expenses) and DS represents the debt service (payments on the mortgage). A lender who requires a DCR of 1.2 is, in essence, requiring that the property's expected net operating income be 20 percent larger than its mortgage payments. The lender can be fairly confident that mortgage payments will be made as scheduled as long as the actual NOI is at least 80 percent of the expected amount.

In addition to the DCR, commercial property lenders also look closely at the LTV ratios. As we saw in our discussion of residential mortgages, the larger the LTV ratio, the riskier the loan is from the lender's perspective. In residential mortgages, FHA insurance, VA guarantees, and PMI allow the borrower to purchase residential property with high LTV ratios and relatively small down payment amounts. Because no such mortgage insurance or guarantees are typically available for commercial property mortgages, the LTV ratios on commercial loans are much lower (70 percent is common) than the LTV ratios for residential mortgages (where 95 percent or more is quite common). Lower LTV ratios imply that larger down payment percentages are necessary for commercial property purchases.

CHAPTER REVIEW

- A specialized legal framework has evolved for loans in which real estate is pledged as security for a debt, though the details of the mortgage concept vary slightly from state to state. Most real estate loans involve a promissory note, which makes the borrower personally liable for the debt, and a security instrument, such as a mortgage or deed of trust, which enables the lender to foreclose on the property if the borrower defaults on the loan.

- Loans are originated to borrowers in primary mortgage markets, and many loans are subsequently sold to investors in secondary mortgage market transactions. The primary and secondary mortgage markets, and the participants in those markets, have evolved into an efficient system for providing housing financing in the United States.

- Some of the more prominent participants in the housing finance system include the Federal Housing Administration, the Veterans Administration, Ginnie Mae, Fannie Mae, Freddie Mac, private mortgage insurers, mortgage bankers, mortgage brokers, commercial banks, savings institutions, and credit unions.

- To ensure that investors are willing to accept such loans, lenders employ a standardized loan application process and rigorous underwriting criteria. Fannie Mae and Freddie Mac have jointly approved an application form to be used with any loan that may eventually wind up in their secondary markets. This form solicits information about the borrower, the property, and the details of the transaction.

- The underwriting decision involves careful consideration of the borrower's ability and willingness to repay the debt, as well as the suitability of the property as collateral. Lenders evaluate an applicant's employment history, income sources, net worth, and previous credit history to assess the risk of the loan application.

- Using the general guidelines for risk assessment proposed by Fannie Mae and Freddie Mac, lenders can screen out high-risk applicants and feel confident that their lending decisions are made on a sound basis. These guidelines fall into three categories: loan-to-value ratios, down payment sources, and income ratios.

- Borrowers who do not meet the "prime" lending guidelines can often obtain financing from subprime lenders, but the cost such loans is typically higher than prime loans.

- Mortgage market consumers are protected against discrimination, fraud, and misrepresentation by various federal regulations that govern lender activity, including the Equal Credit Opportunity Act (Regulation B), the Consumer Protection Act (Regulation Z), the Real Estate Settlement Procedures Act, the Flood Disaster Protection Act, and the Fair Credit Reporting Act.

■ The participants in the commercial property financing system include individual investors, life insurance companies, pension funds, real estate investment trusts, commercial banks, and commercial mortgage-backed securities investors.

■ Commercial property lenders look closely at the debt coverage and the LTV ratio when evaluating the risk of a commercial property loan application.

▎ KEY TERMS

acceleration clause

commercial bank

commercial mortgage-backed securities

Consumer Credit Protection Act

conventional loans

credit unions

debt coverage ratio

deed in lieu of foreclosure

deed of trust

deficiency judgment

due-on-sale clause

Equal Credit Opportunity Act

Fair Credit Reporting Act

Fannie Mae

Federal Housing Administration

Federal National Mortgage Association

FHA-insured loan

Flood Disaster Protection Act

foreclosure

Freddie Mac

Ginnie Mae

Government National Mortgage Association

government-sponsored enterprises

hypothecation

judicial foreclosure

land contract

lien theory

loan origination

loan-to-value ratio

mortgage

mortgage-backed securities

mortgage bankers

mortgage brokers

mortgage debt ratio

nonjudicial foreclosure

Office of Federal Housing Enterprise Oversight

prepayment clause

primary mortgage market

private mortgage insurance

promissory note

Real Estate Settlement Procedures Act

savings institutions

secondary mortgage market

secured loan

strict foreclosure

subprime mortgage loans

title theory

total debt ratio

underwriting

unsecured loan

U.S. housing finance system

VA-guaranteed loan

▌ STUDY EXERCISES

1. Define the following terms: *secured loan, mortgage, hypothecation, promissory note, due-on-sale clause, prepayment clause, acceleration clause, mortgage broker, total debt ratio, mortgage debt ratio,* and *subprime loan.*

2. In what manner can a land contract simplify the foreclosure process?

3. Identify the parties involved in a deed of trust.

4. In states that permit their use, when would a deficiency judgment be in order?

5. Why is PMI generally less expensive than FHA insurance?

6. How does FHA mortgage insurance differ from VA loan guarantees?

7. What is meant by the term *conventional loan*?

8. List the five major types of mortgage originators.

9. List the nine factors that mortgage lenders may *not* use to discriminate against loan applicants as defined by the Equal Credit Opportunity Act.

10. Under the Equal Credit Opportunity Act, how long does a lender have to either accept or reject a completed loan application?

11. What is the general intention behind the Truth-in-Lending law? List three requirements under this regulation.

12. Why does the APR not equal the stated interest rate on a loan? Which rate is usually higher?

13. List seven requirements lenders must observe in conjunction with RESPA.

14. What requirement is imposed on mortgage lenders by the Flood Disaster Protection Act?

15. List three requirements imposed on mortgage lenders by the Fair Credit Reporting Act.

16. What is contained in a residential mortgage credit report?

17. List the three categories of risk assessment guidelines used by mortgage lenders.

18. Consider a borrower who has gross annual income of $48,000 and is applying for a mortgage that requires monthly payments of $1,040. Taxes and insurance premiums for the pledged property total $1,200 per year. The borrower has no other outstanding loans on the property, but she has 24 monthly payments of $260 on her car loan. Based on the MDR and TDR limits for a conventional loan, does she qualify for the loan? Could she qualify for an FHA-insured loan based on the appropriate MDR and TDR guidelines?

19. What is the maximum LTV ratio permitted by secondary mortgage markets on conventional mortgages that do not carry PMI?

20. Why do commercial banks typically limit their involvement in the commercial property financing system to short-term loans?

21. Has the total capitalization of REITs increased or decreased in recent years? Why?

22. Suppose a commercial property loan application has a debt coverage ratio of 0.95. What does this say about the property's ability to cover its debt service payments?

▌ FURTHER READING

Clauretie, Terrence M., and G. Stacy Sirmans. *Real Estate Finance*, 4th ed. Mason, Ohio: Thomson South-Western, 2006.

Kolbe, Phillip T., Gaylon E. Greer, and Henry G. Rudner, III. *Real Estate Finance*. Chicago: Dearborn Real Estate Education, 2003.

Risk, Return, and the
Time Value of Money

An understanding of basic financial concepts is essential for all real estate market participants. Real estate lending and borrowing decisions, value estimation, and investment analysis all require knowledge of the relationship between risk and return, "time value of money" principles, and financial decision rules. The purpose of this chapter is to consider each of these concepts and demonstrate their role in the financial framework of real estate. Some readers are already familiar with these concepts, but for others they represent an unexplored frontier. For the first group, many topics considered in this chapter will serve as a review. The second group will want to study the material quite carefully and make certain they master the concepts before moving on to subsequent topics. In all cases, it is helpful to think of the topics discussed in this chapter as tools that market participants should have at their disposal as they engage in real estate decision-making situations.

The topics considered in this chapter include

- the relationship between risk and return,

- the six time value of money formulas, and

- the net present value and internal rate of return financial decision rules.

THE RELATIONSHIP BETWEEN RISK AND RETURN

Financial decision making is defined as the process of comparing the expected benefits from a proposed course of action with the expected costs arising from that course of action. In the case of real estate investment decisions, for example, investors must compare the purchase price of the property with the after-tax cash flows they expect to receive from the property over the holding period.

Rather than dollar amounts, investment returns are frequently expressed as a percentage **rate of return**—that is, $100 profit on an investment of $1,000 represents a 10 percent rate of return. Because the returns from an investment opportunity are expected to be realized in future time periods, and because the future is uncertain, it would be imprudent for an investor to make decisions without recognizing that the actual rate of return from a particular investment may vary significantly from initial expectations. Uncertainty about the actual rate of return an investment will provide over the holding period is known as **risk.** Because most of us are risk-averse rather than risk-seeking (we view higher levels of risk negatively), risk is an additional cost that must be considered when evaluating an investment opportunity.

For financial decision makers to accept an investment, they must expect to receive a sufficient return to justify its cost. Thus, in addition to considering the revenues and operating expenses resulting from a property investment, real estate investors must consider the risk that the expected rate of return from pursuing that investment may deviate from initial expectations. A riskier investment must promise a higher rate of return than less risky investment opportunities. If not, prudent decision makers would prefer a less risky investment that earns the same level of return. Therefore, a positive relationship exists between risk and investors' required rates of return. This general relationship is depicted graphically in Figure 17.1.

The upward sloping line in the figure illustrates the required rate of return demanded by investors at various levels of risk. As the level of risk increases, so does the required rate of return. The point at which the risk/return line intersects the vertical axis is known as the *risk-free rate.* This point indicates the rate of return that investors are willing to accept for investments that pose no risk. Although one can argue that there is no such thing as a perfectly risk-free investment, the return available from investing in U.S. government securities, such as Treasury bills, is generally considered the risk-free rate because there is virtually no danger that the federal government will default on its obligation to pay its debts. Even though an investment is risk-free, investors require a return that compensates them for giving up use of their funds over time. As we proceed to the right along the risk/return line, it is immediately apparent that higher risk implies higher required rates of return.

Types of Risk

Uncertainty about future returns from an investment opportunity arises from a variety of factors, but most risk can be characterized as business risk, financial risk, purchasing power risk, or liquidity risk. **Business risk** is the uncertainty arising from changing economic conditions that affect an investment's ability to generate returns.

FIGURE 17.1 | Relationship Between Risk and Return

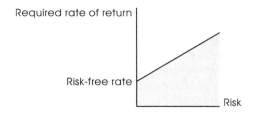

Financial risk is uncertainty associated with the possibility of defaulting on borrowed funds used to finance an investment. **Purchasing power risk** (inflation risk) arises from the possibility that the amount of goods and services that can be acquired with a given amount of money will decline. Thus, returns from an investment may be less valuable in real terms when they are received. **Liquidity risk** is the possibility of loss resulting from not being able to convert an asset into cash quickly should the need arise. Real estate is often considered less liquid than other investment assets such as stocks or bonds, which can be traded almost immediately at the current market price. In general, investors' required rates of return are a combination of the returns required for each of these risk types *and* the risk-free rate of return.

The Time Value of Money

Another important consideration in financial decision making is the "timing" of the expected benefits and costs associated with investment opportunities. Even if risk is minimal, decision makers must recognize that delaying returns until some future time represents an added cost of an investment. As we saw above, investors require a rate of return for any investment whose benefits are expected to occur in the future, even if there is no risk. In other words, a dollar in the hand today is worth more than a dollar to be received in the future because it can either be consumed immediately or put to work earning a return in another investment opportunity. This is known as the **time value of money principle.** To use this principle effectively in decision-making situations, investors must be able to convert future values into present values and present values into future values. The next section of this chapter presents six techniques for accomplishing these conversions while simultaneously accounting for the risk associated with an investment choice.

TIME VALUE OF MONEY FORMULAS

There is an old saying that "a bird in the hand is worth two in the bush," and a dollar in the hand is certainly worth more than one to be received sometime in the future. Thus, if given a choice today between receiving $5 immediately or $5 one year from now, we would choose the first option. If the choice were between $5 immediately or $15 one year from now, however, the decision becomes more complicated. Which of these options is the better one *right now?* The answer depends on two issues: risk and the time value of money. As we discussed above, both of these issues are incorporated into the decision-making process by specifying an appropriate required rate of return. A variety of time value of money formulas exist that allow us to address the choices described above, as well as more involved investment decisions. After we consider the intuition behind the first two formulas, we will describe how two popular models of financial calculators (Hewlett Packard 10B and Texas Instruments BAII PLUS) can be used to conduct time value of money analysis.

The first formula we will consider is used to find the future value of a lump sum. This formula allows decision makers to determine what an amount of money in hand today will be worth some time in the future if it increases at a constant rate each period.

Future Value of a Lump Sum

Suppose an investor buys 10 acres of vacant land today for $70,000. If land values are expected to increase at the rate of 10 percent per year, what will the land be worth at the end of three years? In one year, the land is worth $70,000 plus 10 percent of $70,000. Written algebraically, the value of the land in one year is

$$\$70,000 + (0.10 \times \$70,000) = \$77,000$$

This equation can also be written as

$$\$70,000(1 + 0.10) = \$77,000$$

In two years, the land is worth $77,000 plus 10 percent of $77,000, or

$$\$77,000(1 + 0.10) = \$84,700$$

At the end of three years the original investment of $70,000 is worth

$$\$84,700(1 + 0.10) = \$93,170$$

As shown here and in Table 17.1, the investment has grown from $70,000 to $93,170, for a total increase of $23,170 over three years. The rate of growth is 10 percent annually, but the total growth is 33.1 percent ($23,170 ÷ $70,000 = 0.331). This example demonstrates the concept of **compound interest,** which means that during any given period, interest is earned not only on the original investment, but also on the interest previously earned. Thus, as in this example, after the first year the value of the land increases by 10 percent of the previous year's value where this value includes the initial investment plus increases during prior years. Note that multiplying the growth rate by the number of periods (10 percent × 3 = 30 percent) does not provide the total percentage change in value because such a calculation ignores interest earned on previously earned interest. The *total* percentage change in value is 33.1 percent.

TABLE 17.1 | Future Value of a Lump Sum

Year	Present Amount	×	(1+ *i*)	=	Future Amount
0	$70,000				
1	$77,000		(1.10)		$77,000
2	$84,700		(1.10)		$84,700
3	$93,170		(1.10)		$93,170

If the investor is concerned only with the value of the land at the end of three years, as opposed to each year's value, we can simplify this problem greatly. The value of $70,000 invested today at 10 percent interest for three years is worth $93,170.

$$70,000(1 + 0.10)(1 + 0.10)(1 + 0.10) = \$93,170$$

Equivalently, we can write the future value of $70,000 invested at 10 percent for three years as follows:

$$70,000(1 + 0.10)^3 = \$93,170$$

Writing the calculation in this manner leads to the formal specification of the concept of the **future value of a lump sum.** Equation (1) below is used to find the future value of a known present value when the future amount is to be received in a lump sum at a particular time *n*.

$$FV = PV(1 + i)^n \qquad \textbf{(1)}$$

where *FV* is the future value we are seeking to determine, *PV* is the initial value, *i* is the rate of return per period, and *n* is the number of periods.

Present Value of a Lump Sum

The converse of the above problem requires a *present value calculation*—that is, what is the value today of a sum to be received some time in the future? Suppose there is a parcel of land that an investor believes will be worth $93,170 in three years. If the investor requires a 10 percent annual rate of return on investments with comparable risk, how much would he or she be willing to pay for the land today? The **present value of a lump sum** is given by solving equation (1) to move *PV* on the left side of the equality sign as shown in equation (2):

$$PV = \frac{FV}{(1 + i)^n} \qquad \textbf{(2)}$$

where PV is the present value we are seeking to determine, FV is the known future value, i is the required rate of return per period, or discount rate, and n is the number of periods.

Applying the present value of a lump sum formula to this investment problem reveals that the present value of $93,170 to be received three years in the future is $70,000.

$$PV = \frac{\$93,170}{(1 + 0.10)^3}$$

Note that the equations for present value and future value are mathematically reverse operations, the key difference being the variable that we are trying to find. If we know the present amount, we can find the future amount using the future value formula. Conversely, if we know the future amount, we can find the present amount using the present value formula. In solving time value of money problems, it is often helpful to recognize that when calculating present values we are looking "backward" in time, and when calculating future values, we are looking "forward" in time. The process of finding present values is known as **discounting**, and the process of finding future values is known as **compounding.**

Both time and the rate of return enter into present value calculations. The farther into the future the money will be received, the lower the present value. Also, the greater the rate of discount is, the lower the present value. The opposite is true for future value calculations. The longer a present amount is allowed to grow, the greater the future value. And, the greater the rate of growth is, the greater the future value.

Using Financial Calculators and Computer Spreadsheets to Solve for Present and Future Values

While the formulas presented above are relatively simple, we soon consider four other formulas that can become quite cumbersome to work with. We believe that students should work through these formulas to establish an understanding of how to use basic financial concepts in real estate decision making, but we also know that more efficient methods exist for working with time value of money formulas once a base level of knowledge is established.

For many years, financial analysts used cumbersome tables that listed time value of money factors for various values of i and n. These tables were a grand improvement over pencil and paper, but today such tables have been replaced by relatively inexpensive financial calculators and computer spreadsheet programs such as Microsoft Excel. Instead of laboriously working through these formulas or selecting the appropriate factor from a table and multiplying it by the appropriate present or future amount, we need only understand how to press a few keys on these wonderful devices. Spending time memorizing the formulas is not necessary for most readers of this text, but learning how to use financial calculators and computer spreadsheets is a worthwhile endeavor.

Using Your Financial Calculator

We encourage you to learn how your calculator works by first solving the problems using the formulas presented here, then by referencing the manual that came with your calculator to "plug in the numbers" and arrive at the answers. Doing so will ultimately give you confidence in your ability to use the calculator in more complex decision-making situations. The user's manual can be very useful for learning how your calculator operates!

Here are some tips for helping you solve the problems in this chapter using your calculator. First, recognize that each calculator manufacturer uses slightly different keys to solve time value of money problems, but there is some degree of uniformity. Almost all financial calculators have keys labeled *PV, FV, I/Y* or *I/YR,* and *n* or *N.* These buttons correspond to the notation used in equations (1) and (2) above and in the other equations we will consider shortly.

Second, all of the problems considered in this chapter require that your calculator be set in "END" mode. If the screen displays the word "BEGIN" or "BGN," you will not be able to calculate the correct answer.

Third, it is important that you know how to correctly change your calculator's settings to reflect the correct number of periods per year over which payments or compounding will be performed. For example, most mortgages involve monthly payments (12 periods per year), while most investment decisions are based on annual cash flow totals (1 period per year). Most calculators will have a *P/Y or P/YR* key where the periods per year can be set appropriately.

Fourth, it is important that you know how to completely clear your calculator's memory registers so it is not using "old" information from a previous calculation. In most calculators, clearing the screen is *not* equivalent to clearing the memory registers. Clearing the memory registers is a second or even a third step. Consult your calculator's user manual to be sure you can clear the memory completely between problems.

Fifth, with most calculators you will notice that the screen displays a negative sign in front of the final answer of most time value of money problems. The negative sign is a result of the algorithm used by the calculator to solve the time value of money formulas, and it should not be a great cause for concern. Just remember that if you enter a positive value in your calculator for a present value, then calculate future value, your calculator will always give you a negative future value. Similarly, if you enter a negative present value, the calculator will always give you a positive future value. If you enter both a present value and a future value and ask your calculator to solve for *n* or *i*, either the *PV* or *FV* must be entered with a negative sign or the calculator will not be able to solve the equation. The same is true for other time value of money calculations we consider next. The negative sign indicates an outflow of money, while the positive sign indicates an inflow.

Using Microsoft Excel

A computer spreadsheet program like Microsoft Excel also can be a valuable tool when considering time value of money problems like those encountered in real estate investment and financial analysis situations. Excel has financial functions available that work in much the same way as a financial calculator. The syntax for these functions is straightforward. For example, to calculate the present value of $93,170 to be received in three years at 10 percent interest, simply type the following entry into a blank Excel spreadsheet cell:

$$= pv \ (0.10,3,-93170).$$

The spreadsheet will display $70,000.

Notice the extra comma in the function syntax. This comma tells Excel that this is a present value of a lump sum problem rather than a present value of annuity problem (to be discussed shortly). Also, notice the negative sign on the future value. Like most financial calculators, Excel will return a negative number in most time value of money calculations if all of the "inputs" are positive numbers. The negative sign in the syntax converts the negative number into a positive number. And, if you are trying to use Excel to solve for n or i in a time value of money problem, either the PV or the FV (but not both) must have a negative sign or Excel will not be able to solve the equation. To learn more about each of the many financial functions that are incorporated into Microsoft Excel, consult the Excel help screen by clicking on "help" or pressing the F1 key.

Applying the Present Value Formula to Cash-Flow Streams

Up to this point we have focused our attention on finding the value of present and future lump sum amounts. In many real estate investments, however, the project generates flows of cash to the investor throughout the life of the investment. Consider an investment that promises to pay $500 in one year, $1,000 in two years, and $1,500 in three years. If your required rate of return is 10 percent, how much would you be willing to pay for this investment? To solve this problem, first recognize that we know three future amounts. Applying the present value formula to each of these amounts with the proper values for the exponent n, then adding the three results, yields the total present value of this stream of cash flows. The present value of this stream at a discount rate of ten percent is

$$PV = \frac{500}{(1 + 0.10)^1} + \frac{1,000}{(1 + 0.10)^2} + \frac{1,500}{(1 + 0.10)^3} = \$2,407.96$$

Thus, if we invested $2,407.96 in this project, we would earn exactly our required 10 percent rate of return.

In the event the stream of cash flows extends over many years, calculating the present value by repetition of the present value of a lump sum formula can be time consuming. (We describe how to use the "cash flow" features of financial calculators and Microsoft Excel to solve this type of problem later in this chapter.) If the periodic cash flows are a series of equal amounts, however, the problem is greatly simplified. Such a series of equal cash flows is called an **annuity**.

Present Value of an Annuity

Consider an investment that promises to pay $1,000 at the end of each year for three years. The required rate of return is 10 percent. What is the present value of this stream of payments? Applying the present value of a lump sum formula three times and then adding the results yields

$$PV = \frac{1,000}{(1+0.10)^1} + \frac{1,000}{(1+0.10)^2} + \frac{1,000}{(1+0.10)^3} = \$2,486.85$$

While this calculation is certainly valid, it can be cumbersome when a large number of future cash flows are involved. Fortunately, there is a simpler method. Because the amounts in each period are equal, we can use the **present value of an annuity** formula shown in equation (3).

$$PVA = A \left[\frac{1 - \dfrac{1}{(1+i)^n}}{i} \right] \tag{3}$$

where A is the amount each period (the annuity), i is the discount rate per period, and n is the number of periods. Applying this equation to the present problem yields

$$PVA = 1,000 \left[\frac{1 - \dfrac{1}{(1+0.10)^3}}{0.10} \right] = \$2,486.85$$

Using a financial calculator to solve this problem is quite simple using the *PMT* key to enter the annuity amount.

Financial Calculator Solution: *PMT* = 1,000, *N* = 3, *i* = 10, *PV* =?

Microsoft Excel Solution: = PV(0.10,3,-1000)

The following example demonstrates the use of the present value of annuity concept in a real estate context: calculating the outstanding balance on a mortgage loan. Suppose you are a lender entitled to receive payments of $16,274.54 from a borrower once per year for the next seven years. If the interest rate on this loan is 10 percent annually, what is the outstanding balance on this loan today? In other words, what is the stream of payments (an annuity) worth to you today at a required rate of return of 10 percent? To find the answer, apply the formula to the annuity amount.

$$PVA = 16,274.54 \left[\frac{1 - \dfrac{1}{(1+0.10)^7}}{0.10} \right] = \$79,231.28$$

Future Value of an Annuity

In some instances, particularly in personal finance, we are interested in finding the future value of equal payments received over time. In this type of problem, we could apply the future value formula described above to each payment individually using the proper exponent n and then add the results of each calculation, but this can be simplified by using the future value of an annuity formula.

Consider the following example. Suppose you invest $100 at the end of each year for the next five years in an interest-earning bank account paying 10 percent interest per year. How much money would you have in the account at the end of five years?

The first payment will be deposited one year from today and will earn interest for four years. The second deposit will earn interest over three years, and so on for the third and fourth deposits. Note that the fifth payment will not earn any interest, because it will only be deposited at the end of the fifth year. We can solve for the future value at the end of five years using the future value factor for each of the five deposits:

$$FV = 100(1 + 0.10)^4 + 100(1 + 0.10)^3 + 100(1 + 0.10)^2 \\ + 100(1 + 0.10)^1 + 100(1 + 0.10)^0 = \$610.51$$

To solve this problem quickly, however, we can use the **future value of an annuity** formula given in equation (4).

$$FVA = A\left[\frac{(1+i)^n - 1}{i}\right] \tag{4}$$

In this example,

$$FVA = 100\left[\frac{(1 + 0.10)^5 - 1}{0.10}\right] = \$610.51$$

Sinking Fund Payments

The next time value of money principle, the sinking fund payment formula, is algebraically equivalent to the future value of an annuity formula. The important difference is that the unknown variable is not the future value of the stream of payments, but the amount of each payment required to accumulate the future amount.

Suppose, for example, that you wish to buy a home but do not have the required down payment of $20,000. You decide that you will save that much over the next five years by making equal, annual deposits into a savings account paying 10 percent annually beginning one year from today. How much must you deposit each year to accumulate $20,000? This type of problem is known as a *sinking fund problem*—that is, how much must you "sink" into the account each year to accumulate the desired amount in the future? Just as we solved the future value formula [equation (1)] to get present value on the left side of the equality sign in equation (2), we can also solve equation (4) for the annuity A. To avoid possible confusion, we replace the variable A with the symbol SFP to represent "sinking fund payment." These manipulations of the FVA formula provide equation 5, the formula for finding **sinking fund payments.**

$$SFP = FVA\left[\frac{i}{(1+i)^n - 1}\right] \qquad (5)$$

Applying the sinking fund formula to this problem shows that you must deposit $3,275.95 into the account each year for five years to accumulate $20,000 at 10 percent interest.

$$SFP = 20,000\left[\frac{0.10}{(1+0.10)^5 - 1}\right] = \$3,275.95$$

Financial Calculator Solution: $FV = 20,000$, $N = 5$, $i = 10$, $PMT = ?$

Microsoft Excel Solution (notice the "extra" comma): $= PMT(0.10,5,,-20000)$

Mortgage Payments

The sixth and final time value of money formula to be considered is the mortgage payment formula. This formula is used to calculate payments due on a "fully amortizing" loan. Because we will consider the concept of amortization in greater detail in Chapter 18, our discussion here is limited to using this formula to calculate mortgage payments.

Suppose you wish to borrow $100,000 to buy a parcel of real estate. A mortgage company is willing to lend the money at 10 percent interest, provided that you amortize the debt with annual payments over the next ten years. How much will your payments be? Notice the similarity between this problem and the one we examined during our discussion of the present value of annuities. In both examples, we know the interest rate and the number of periods. In the present value of annuity problem, we know the amount of the annuity, but we do not know the present value. In this problem, we know the present amount, but we do not know the amount of the payment or, in other words, the annuity. Because the problems are identical except for the unknown variable, we can solve equation (3) to move the annuity (variable A) to the left side of the equality sign. To avoid confusion, we then rename A to PMT to represent mortgage payment. This results in the **mortgage payment** formula:

$$PMT = PVA \left[\frac{i}{1 - \dfrac{1}{(1+i)^n}} \right] \qquad (6)$$

Why does the symbol PVA appear in the formula for mortgage payments? The answer to this question is simple, but very important. From the lender's point of view, a mortgage is an investment in the borrower's ability to repay the debt. In return for giving the borrower cash today, the lender will receive an annuity for n periods into the future. The lender is willing to give the borrower the present value of that annuity today in the form of a loan. To the borrower, the present value of the series of future payments represents the loan amount. Thus, the loan amount, or the remaining amount outstanding, can always be thought of as the present value of an annuity, where the annuity is the future mortgage payments. Applying equation (6) to the problem at hand shows the annual mortgage payment the lender will require for a ten-year loan of $100,000 at 10 percent interest.

$$PMT = 100,000 \left[\frac{0.10}{1 - \dfrac{1}{(1 + 0.10)^{10}}} \right] = \$16,274.54$$

Financial Calculator Solution: PV = 100,000, N = 10, i = 10, PMT = ?

Microsoft Excel Solution: = PMT(0.10,10,-100000)

Monthly Compounding

We now have developed the six time value of money formulas, but in each of the examples used thus far we have dealt with annual time periods. In many instances, however, the compounding and discounting periods in real estate problems are semi-annually, quarterly, or even monthly. For example, almost all residential mortgage loans call for monthly payments. The preceding analysis remains valid for periods of any length, but with one word of caution: Time and interest must always be measured in the *same unit*—that is, if we wish to solve for a monthly mortgage payment, we must use a monthly interest rate.

Suppose, for example, we wish to calculate the monthly payment required to amortize a $100,000 loan at 12 percent annual interest for 30 years. The number of compounding periods becomes 360 (12 times 30), and the periodic interest rate becomes 1 percent (12 percent divided by 12). Substituting these numbers into the formula for finding the mortgage payment yields a monthly payment of $1,028.61.

$$PMT = 100,000 \left[\frac{0.12/12}{1 - \dfrac{1}{(1+0.12/12)^{360}}} \right] = \$1,028.6$$

We can generalize each of the six formulas to account for any compounding period by "dividing i by m and multiplying n by m," where m is simply the number of compounding or discounting periods per year, i is the annual interest or discount rate, and n is the number of years. Applying this rule restates the six time value of money formulas as follows:

$$FV = PV(1 + i/m)^{nm}$$

$$PV = \frac{FV}{(1 + i/m)^{nm}}$$

$$PVA = A \left[\frac{1 - \dfrac{1}{(1+i/m)^{nm}}}{i/m} \right]$$

$$FVA = A \left[\frac{(1+i/m)^{nm} - 1}{i/m} \right]$$

$$SFP = FVA \left[\frac{i/m}{(1+i/m)^{nm} - 1} \right]$$

$$PMT = PVA \left[\frac{i/m}{1 - \dfrac{1}{(1+i/m)^{nm}}} \right]$$

Most financial calculators can be set to automatically convert the time value of money formulas for any compounding or discounting frequency. Of course, you can do this manually by dividing the interest rate and multiplying the number of years by the number of compounding or discounting periods per year before pressing the appropriate keys, but you must enter all the decimal places (without rounding) to avoid getting the wrong answer. (Dividing 10 percent by 12, for example, will yield 0.01 if your calculator is set to display only two decimal places, but the value to eight decimal places is 0.00833333, which is a very different number from 0.01.) In Microsoft Excel, remember to divide the annual interest rate by 12 and to multiply the number of years by 12 to get the correct answers.

FINANCIAL DECISION RULES: NPV AND IRR

Now that we understand the concept of risk and the time value of money formulas, we will examine a framework for making decisions concerning investment choices. This framework compares the benefits of an investment to its costs, including risk and the time value of money. The key concept is **net present value** (NPV), which is the difference between how much an investment is worth to an investor and how much it costs. Suppose an investment promises to pay you a stream of cash flows that has a present value of $10,000. If the asking price of this investment is $9,000, the investor obviously would decide to buy it. In this case, the net present value is $1,000 ($10,000 – $9,000).

The question is this: How do we determine the present value of the stream of cash flows? We discount the cash flows at the proper discount rate, which is the rate of return we require to compensate for the risk of the investment. If the stream occurs in uneven amounts, we use the present value of a lump sum formula to discount each cash flow. If the stream is an annuity, we can simplify the calculations by using the present value of an annuity formula. The appropriate discount rate to use is one that accounts for the risk of the investment opportunity, usually determined by comparing the rates of return on alternative investment choices of similar risk. Formally, we can define net present value as follows:

NPV = Present Value of Cash Inflows – Present Value of Cash Outflows

In decision-making situations, we use the NPV concept as part of the following **NPV decision rule.** If the NPV of an investment is greater than or equal to zero, we choose to invest because the investment is worth at least as much as it costs, given our required rate of return. If NPV is less than zero, we choose not to invest because we would not be earning our required rate of return. Remember that the required rate of return reflects both the time value of money and the risk of the investment opportunity. We can take this rule a step farther and say that if faced with several alternative investment choices, we should accept the one with the highest positive NPV, because it will increase our wealth more than the others.

This leads us to another important concept in financial decision making. If the net present value of an investment is greater than or equal to zero, we must be earning at least our required rate of return. In fact, if NPV equals zero, the rate of return on the investment is exactly equal to the required rate. If NPV is not zero, what rate are we earning? We can define the **internal rate of return** (IRR) of an investment as the discount rate, which makes NPV exactly equal to zero. To determine an investment's IRR, we can search a variety of discount rates by trial and error until we find one that makes NPV equal zero. (Finding algebraic solutions to complex IRR problems generally is not feasible.) This rate will be the internal rate of return on the investment. Fortunately, most financial calculators (and Microsoft Excel) have a feature that allows automatic searches for the internal rate of return for a series of cash flows.

The definition of IRR provides another rule for financial decision making that states that if the IRR is greater than or equal to our required rate of return, we choose to invest: Otherwise, we forgo the investment opportunity. While the IRR rule and the NPV rule are based on the same principles, the NPV rule is generally the best choice to use because IRR calculations may yield multiple discount rates that set NPV equal to zero. When our objective is to determine the rate of return provided by an investment, however, the IRR calculation is extremely useful. The following example demonstrates the NPV rule and the IRR rule.

NPV and IRR Decision Rule Example

Suppose you are faced with making a decision about whether to invest $10,000 today in a risky real estate investment. In return for your investment, you expect to receive the following stream of cash flows: year one, $100; year two, $1,600; year three, $1,800; year four, $450; year five, $12,500. You believe other investment opportunities with similar risk offer a 12 percent rate of return. What are the NPV and IRR of this investment? Should you invest? We can find the NPV of this investment by applying the NPV definition:

$$NPV = PV \text{ of Cash Inflows} - PV \text{ of Cash Outflows}$$

$$NPV = \frac{100}{(1 + 0.12)^1} + \frac{1,600}{(1 + 0.12)^2} + \frac{1,800}{(1 + 0.12)^3} + \frac{450}{(1 + 0.12)^4} + \frac{12,500}{(1 + 0.12)^5}$$
$$- 10,000 = \$24.82$$

Because the NPV is greater than zero, the investment is worth more than it costs and we should choose to accept this opportunity. Likewise, we know that the IRR must be greater than our required rate of return, simply because NPV is positive. To determine the IRR of this investment, we apply different discount rates in the above calculation until NPV becomes exactly zero. In this problem, the IRR is 12.0646 percent.

Financial Calculator Solution: *CF0* = -10,000, *CF1* = 100, *CF2* = 1,600, *CF3* =1,800, *CF4* = 450, *CF5* = 12,500, *NPV* = ?, *IRR* = ?

Microsoft Excel Solution: Enter the following cash flows in contiguous cells (for example, A1 through F1): -10,000, 100, 1,600, 1,800, 450, 12,500. Then, in a blank cell, enter =NPV(0.12,B1:F1)+A1.

Notice that the NPV function in Excel assumes that all cash flows inside the parentheses begin one year from today. If the first cash flow happens at the start of the investment (as is most often the case) rather than one year from the start of the investment, omit it from the cell range inside the NPV function and subtract it from Excel's NPV calculation as shown here. To solve for the IRR, make the following entry into another blank cell in the spreadsheet =IRR(A1:F1).

CHAPTER REVIEW

- All financial decisions can be thought of as a comparison of the expected benefits from a particular course of action and the costs of pursuing it. In addition to the purchase price, however, prudent investors consider the costs of an investment resulting from uncertainty about those future benefits and forgoing the use of the investment capital over time (risk and the time value of money).

- Because most people are risk-averse rather than risk-seeking, there is a positive relationship between risk and return. The greater the risk of an investment, the greater the investor's required rate of return.

- The six time value of money formulas are useful tools for evaluating financial choices whose risky cash flows are distributed over time. These formulas allow calculation of the present value of a lump sum, the future value of a lump sum, the present value of an annuity, the future value of an annuity, sinking fund payments, and mortgage payments.

- By definition, *net present value* is the present value of cash inflows minus the present value of cash outflows. If the net present value of an investment opportunity is negative, the investment is not worth its cost and should therefore be rejected by the investor.

- The *internal rate of return* is defined as that discount rate which sets net present value equal to zero. This is the actual return that is provided by an investment opportunity. If the IRR is less than the investor's required rate of return, the investment should be rejected by the investor.

KEY TERMS

annuity	future value of an annuity	present value of an annuity
business risk	internal rate of return	
compounding	liquidity risk	purchasing power risk
compound interest	mortgage payment	rate of return
discounting	net present value	risk
financial risk	NPV decision rule	sinking fund payment
future value of a lump sum	present value of a lump sum	time value of money principle

STUDY EXERCISES

1. Define the following concepts: *risk, business risk, financial risk, purchasing power risk, liquidity risk.*

2. Describe the "risk/return relationship."

3. What is the time value of money principle?

4. Joe Saver deposits $5,000 in the Granite City Savings and Loan. To what value will his money accumulate in five years if the account pays 5 percent interest compounded annually? (Future Value of a Lump Sum)

5. How much should Joe be willing to pay today for an investment that is expected to pay $5,000 ten years in the future if he requires a 10 percent rate of return? (Present Value of a Lump Sum)

6. Define the following terms: *compound interest, compounding, discounting.*

7. Joe is offered the opportunity to receive $5,000 each year for ten years. How much would he be willing to pay for this future income stream if he desires a 10 percent return? (Present Value of an Annuity)

8. Joe expects to receive $5,000 each year for the next ten years beginning one year from today. If he deposits each payment into an account earning 8 percent interest annually, what will the balance of the account be when the last payment is deposited? (Future Value of an Annuity)

9. Joe hopes to accumulate $200,000 with ten annual deposits into a savings account earning 6 percent interest annually. What amount must Joe deposit each year to achieve his objective? (Sinking Fund Payment)

10. Harold and Helen purchase a $180,000 house using a down payment of $15,000 and a fixed rate mortgage for $165,000. The annual interest rate on the loan is 10 percent and the term is 30 years. What monthly payment is necessary to amortize this loan?

11. Define the following terms: *net present value, internal rate of return, NPV decision rule, IRR decision rule.*

12. An investor is considering purchasing a small retail property at a price of $820,000. The investor has established a required rate of return of 14 percent. Based on the following cash flow forecast, what is the NPV of this investment opportunity? Cash flows: year 1 = 100,000; year 2 = 120,000; year 3 = 110,000; year 4 = 140,000; year 5 = 950,000. Should the investor purchase this property?

13. What is the internal rate of return for the investment in question 12?

14. Bill and Ami borrowed $220,000 at 9 percent interest using a fixed rate mortgage with a maturity of 25 years. Answer the following questions about their loan.

   a. What is the monthly payment necessary to amortize this loan?

   b. If the loan required annual payments instead of monthly, what would the annual payment be?

   c. Multiply the answer in part (a) by 12. Why does this amount not equal the answer in part b?

Mortgage Mechanics

CHAPTER PREVIEW

Now that we have a basic understanding of the time value of money, we can turn our attention to the mechanics of mortgage loans. In this chapter, we investigate the process of amortization in contrast to "interest-only" loans. We also consider how the internal rate of return can be used to determine the effective interest rate on a mortgage loan. Finally, we examine several alternatives to the fixed-rate mortgage that may be encountered in today's mortgage market, including the two-step mortgage and the adjustable-rate mortgage.

The topics considered in this chapter include

■ loan amortization,

■ prepayment,

■ refinancing,

■ discount points,

■ effective interest rates, and

■ alternatives to the fixed-rate mortgage.

▌ MORTGAGE MECHANICS

Because most real estate investments involve long-term commitments of relatively large amounts of money, most real estate transactions involve long-term mortgage financing from a third party. Understanding the mechanics of mortgage financing is an important financial concept for students of real estate and real estate practitioners. In this section of the chapter, we explore mortgage mechanics in detail. Our first tasks are to distinguish between amortizing loans and interest-only loans and to fully explore the concept of amortization.

Interest-Only versus Amortizing Loans

As we discussed in Chapter 16, most loans used to finance real estate purchases prior to the 1930s were short-term, interest-only loans. In these loans, the borrower must pay interest on the full loan amount each period, and when the loan term expires, the borrower must repay the loan in one lump sum. During the Depression era, many borrowers could barely afford to make the required interest payments on these loans, much less repay the loan balance when the loan matured. One of the most successful activities of the Federal Housing Administration was the promotion of long-term, amortizing loans for home financing rather than short-term, interest-only loans. Amortizing loans are much easier to budget for most borrowers, and when combined with mortgage insurance, they are much less risky for most lenders. Amortizing loans are the dominant loan type in the housing finance industry. To fully understand the process of amortization, it is often useful to first understand how the payment streams differ between interest-only loans and amortizing loans.

Interest-only loans require that the borrower pay interest each period during the loan term, then repay the full loan amount in one lump sum at the end of the loan term. In contrast, **amortizing loans** require equal periodic payments composed of both interest and principal. As payments in this type of loan are made, the balance of the loan is gradually reduced to zero by the end of the loan term. Interest-only loan payments are calculated by multiplying the periodic interest rate by the loan amount. Amortizing loan payments are calculated using the mortgage payment formula, one of the six time value of money formulas discussed in the previous chapter.

The difference in payment streams between an amortizing loan and an interest-only loan is illustrated in Figure 18.1. Repayment of a five-year, $1,000 interest-only loan carrying a 10 percent interest rate requires a $100 interest payment for each of the first four years. At the end of the fifth year the entire principal amount of $1,000 is due plus $100 interest. (This much larger final payment is often referred to as a **balloon payment.**) The same $1,000 loan can be amortized by five annual payments of $263.80. Notice that although the periodic payments are higher for the amortizing loan, the payment is the same in each period. There is no balloon payment at the end of the loan because the loan balance is gradually reduced by the periodic payments. Also, notice that the total amount of interest paid to the lender ($500) is higher in

FIGURE 18.1 | Repayment of Five Year, $1,000 Fully Amortizing Loans and Interest-Only Term, Each Carrying 10 Percent Annual Interest

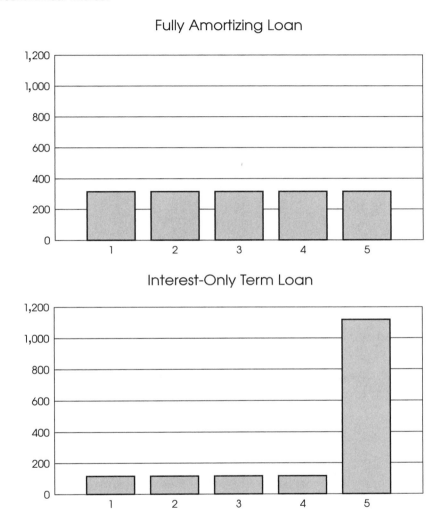

the interest-only loan, because none of the principal is repaid until the final payment. In the amortizing loan, part of the principal is repaid with each payment, so the total interest paid is less ($319).

TABLE 18.1 | Amortization Schedule for a $100,000 Loan at 10 Percent Annual Interest for Ten Years

Year	Payment PMT	Interest I_t	Principle P_t	Amount Outstanding AO_t
0	—	—	—	$100,000.00
1	$16,274.54	$10,000.00	$6,274.54	93,725.46
2	16,274.54	9,372.55	6,901.99	86,823.47
3	16,274.54	8,682.35	7,592.19	79,231.28
4	16,274.54	7,923.13	8,351.41	70,879.87
5	16,274.54	7,087.99	9,186.55	61,693.32
6	16,274.54	6,169.33	10,105.21	51,588.11
7	16,274.54	5,158.81	11,115.73	40,472.38
8	16,274.54	4,047.24	12,227.30	28,245.08
9	16,274.54	2,824.51	13,450.03	14,795.05
10	16,274.54	1,479.40	14,795.05	00.00
Total	$162,745.40	$62,745.40	$100,000.00	

Note: Component items may not add to totals due to rounding.

Understanding the Amortization Process for an Annual Payment Loan

An **amortization schedule** can be developed for any amortizing loan. A loan amortization schedule describes the payments in each period, the interest and principal contained in each payment, and the amount outstanding in each period. Table 18.1 shows an amortization schedule for a $100,000, ten-year, annual payment loan at 10 percent interest. Figure 18.2 plots the periodic payments and the interest and principal components of each payment. Note that while the payment amount is constant over the life of the loan, the portion going to interest decreases with each payment as the balance owed falls. Conversely, the portion going to payment of principal increases at an increasing rate over the life of the loan. Also, the loan balance decreases slowly in the earlier years of the loan and more rapidly as the loan approaches maturity.

Understanding the amortization process requires careful consideration of the principal and interest components of each payment as well as the changing loan balance over time. Table 18.1 shows that $10,000 of the first year's payment on the above loan goes for interest, while only $6,274.54 is used to reduce the principal owed. With the loan balance reduced to $93,725.46, interest for the second year

FIGURE 18.2 | Amortization of a $100,000 Loan over Ten Years at 10 Percent

Fully Amortizing Loan

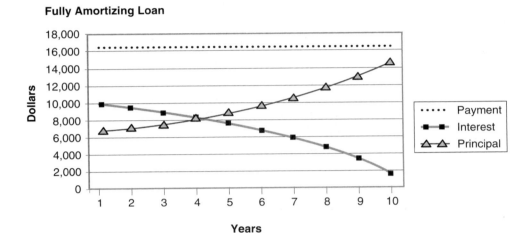

drops to $9,372.55, while the principal component of the payment rises to $6,901.99. The process continues until the last year, when interest is only $1,479.51 and principal is $14,795.05. The total amount of principal repaid equals the original loan amount, $100,000, and the total interest paid is $62,745.40. If the loan had been an interest-only loan, the borrower would have paid a total of $200,000 to the lender: $100,000 interest and $100,000 principal.

From this example we can establish several principles regarding the amortization of real estate mortgage loans:

- With a level, constant payment, the portions of each payment going to interest and principal vary greatly over time.

- The interest portion of each payment decreases at an increasing rate over time.

- The principal portion of each payment increases at an increasing rate over time.

- The amount outstanding declines to zero at the end of the loan term.

Being able to construct an amortization table is a valuable tool in many real estate decision-making situations. While most financial calculators and computer spreadsheet software packages have built-in amortization functions, we believe it is instructive for students to be able to construct a simple table "manually." To construct an amortization table, begin by calculating the periodic payment required to amortize the loan using the mortgage payment formula we discussed in Chapter 17. Rather than solving the equation directly, you could also enter the necessary information into your financial calculator or Microsoft Excel. Because the payments on this type of loan are the same in each period, this calculation need only be done once. To complete the amortization schedule, proceed down the rows of the table, one row at a time, by calculating the interest due, subtracting interest from the payment to get principal for the period, and then subtracting the principal paid in the period from the previous year's balance to get the new balance for the period.

These steps, for the first two years of the loan in Table 18.1, are shown below. As you can see, each year's principal, interest, and amount outstanding are found in the same manner. The following notation will prove useful as we consider more complicated aspects of mortgage mechanics: PMT = mortgage payment, I_t = interest due in period t, i = periodic interest rate, P_t = principal paid in period t, and AO_t = amount outstanding at the end of period t.

Amortization: Period One

$$I_t = AO_{t-1} \times i \qquad\qquad 10,000.00 = 100,000 \times 0.10$$
$$P_t = PMT - I_t \qquad\qquad 6,274.54 = 16,274.54 - 10,000$$
$$AO_t = AO_{t-1} - P_t \qquad 93,725.46 = 100,000 - 6,274.54$$

Amortization: Period Two

$$I_t = AO_{t-1} \times i \qquad\qquad 9,372.55 = 93,725.46 \times 0.10$$
$$P_t = PMT - I_t \qquad\qquad 6,901.99 = 16,274.54 - 9,372.55$$
$$AO_t = AO_{t-1} - P_t \qquad 86,823.47 = 93,725.46 - 6,901.99$$

Understanding the Amortization Process for a Monthly Payment Loan

At the risk of beating the proverbial dead horse, let's see how the amortization process works for a monthly payment loan. Table 18.2 shows the first year of an amortization schedule for a $100,000, 10-year, monthly payment loan at 10 percent annual interest. Figure 18.3 plots the periodic payments, and the interest and principal components of each payment. Just as we saw with the annual payment loan, the payment amount is constant over the life of the monthly payment loan, but the portion going to interest decreases with each payment as the balance owed falls. Conversely, the portion going to payment of principal increases at an increasing rate over the life of the loan. Also, the loan balance decreases slowly in the earlier years of the loan and more rapidly as the loan approaches maturity.

UNDERSTANDING THE FIXED-RATE MORTGAGE: PREPAYMENT

Now that we have explored the concept of amortization, we can take a closer look at other mechanics of mortgage loans. The most common mortgage loan is the **fixed-rate mortgage,** in which the interest rate is fixed at the time of origination. We have already seen how this type of loan is amortized by the payment that is calculated using the mortgage payment formula, and we now examine the concepts of prepayment, refinancing, discount points, origination fees, and effective interest rates.

TABLE 18.2 | Amortization Schedule for a $100,000 Loan at 10 Percent Annual Interest for Ten Years

Year	Payment	Interest	Principle	Amount Outstanding
0	0	0	0	$100,000.00
1	$1,321.51	$833.33	$488.17	93,725.46
2	1,321.51	829.27	492.24	99,019.58
3	1,321.51	825.16	496.34	98,523.24
4	1,321.51	821.03	500.48	98,022.76
5	1,321.51	816.86	504.65	97,518.11
6	1,321.51	812.65	508.86	97,009.25
7	1,321.51	808.41	513.10	96,496.15
8	1,321.51	804.13	517.37	95,978.78
9	1,321.51	799.82	521.68	94,457.10
10	1,321.51	795.48	526.03	94,931.07
11	1,321.51	791.09	530.42	94,400.65
12	1,321.51	786.67	534.84	93,865.82

For a variety of reasons, borrowers may decide to extinguish an outstanding mortgage loan by repaying the loan balance before the end of the loan term. Because all loans require "repayment," we use the word **prepayment** to indicate that the loan is repaid before its full term has expired. Based on historical evidence, many residential borrowers "prepay" their loans after five to seven years. Because the loan balance declines with each payment due to amortization, it is important that we be able to calculate the amount outstanding on a loan at any point in time. To simplify the calculations, we assume that all prepayments occur on a payment date, rather than between payment dates.

Consider a fixed-rate mortgage with the following characteristics: loan amount of $133,000, 30 years to maturity, an annual interest rate of 7.5 percent, and monthly payments of $929.96 (rounded to the nearest penny). Assume the borrower decides to sell the collateral and buy a new property. The loan contract contains a due-on-sale clause, so the borrower must "prepay" the loan if the property is sold. If the borrower prepays at the end of month 60, what is the amount outstanding on this loan at the time of prepayment?

To answer this question, we could construct an amortization schedule for the first 60 months of this loan. Fortunately, there is a less time-consuming method that uses the "annuity" concept to answer this question. Recall that an annuity is a series of equal payments over time. Obviously, the remaining payments on a mortgage

FIGURE 18.3 | Dollars/Months

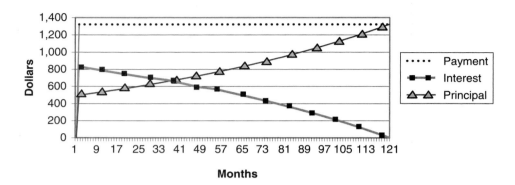

Months

meet our definition of an annuity. If we want to find the amount outstanding on a mortgage loan on any payment date, we simply need to calculate the present value of the remaining payments by discounting them at the interest rate on the loan. We can find the present value of an annuity (or amount outstanding at month 60, AO_{60}) using the appropriate formula or calculator keystrokes. First, find the monthly payment amount, then calculate the present value of the 300 payments remaining at the end of month 60. In this example, we know the payment is $929.96 and we can find the amount outstanding at the end of month 60 as follows (AO_{60} = $125,841.83).

$$PVA = A \left[\frac{1 - \dfrac{1}{(1+i/m)^{nm}}}{i/m} \right]$$

$$AO_{60} = 929.96 \left[\frac{1 - \dfrac{1}{(1+0.075/12)^{300}}}{0.075/12} \right] = \$125,841.83$$

Financial Calculator Solution
Clear the memory registers, set the periods per year to 12, then enter
$PMT = -929.96$, $N = 300$, $I/Y = 7.5$, and solve for PV.

Microsoft Excel Solution
Enter =PV(0.75/12,300,-929.96).

Using the present value of an annuity formula (see equation [3] in Chapter 17) to determine the amount outstanding on a loan is useful in many different situations. For example, how can we determine the amount of principal repaid during the sixth year of a loan? First, find the amount outstanding at the end of month 60 (300 payments remaining) as shown above. Second, find the amount outstanding at the end of month 72 (288 payments remaining). Then, subtract AO_{72} from AO_{60} to get $1,781.81.

$$AO_{72} = 929.96 \left[\frac{1 - \frac{1}{(1 + 0.075/12)^{288}}}{0.075/12} \right] = \$124,060.02$$

$$P_{61 \text{ through } 72} = AO_{60} - AO_{72} = \$125,841.83 - \$124,060.02 = \$1,781.81$$

Financial Calculator Solution
Clear the memory registers, set the periods per year to 12, then enter $PMT = -929.96$, $N = 288$, $I/Y = 7.5$, and solve for PV to get AO_{72}.

Microsoft Excel Solution
Enter =PV(0.075/12,288,-929.96) to get AO_{72}.

Taking this idea a step farther, we can also find the amount of interest paid in the sixth year by subtracting the principal paid in that year from total payments. In this example, total payments in any one year amount to $11,159.52. Subtracting the principal amount of $1,781.81 leaves $9,377.71 as interest paid in payments 61 through 72.

$$PMT_{61 \text{ through } 72} = \$929.96 \times 12 = \$11,159.52$$

$$I_{61 \text{ through } 72} = PMT_{61 \text{ through } 72} - P_{61 \text{ through } 72} = \$11,159.52 - \$1,781.81 = \$9,377.71$$

This technique of finding the amount outstanding is also useful when we are interested in determining the amount of interest or principal contained in any one monthly payment. How much interest is contained in payment number 61? We know that interest is paid on the outstanding balance after the last payment was made, so we multiply AO_{60} by 0.075 x 12 (the previous balance multiplied by the monthly interest rate) to determine the interest contained in payment number 61.

$$I_{61} = AO_{60} \times i$$
$$= \$125,841.83 \times 0.075/12$$
$$= \$786.51$$

To find the principal contained in payment 61, we use the following relationship: $P_t = PMT - I_t$. In this case, $P_{61} = 929.96 - 786.51 = \$143.45$.

$$P_{61} = PMT_{61} - I_{61}$$
$$= \$1929.96 - \$786.51$$
$$= \$143.45$$

UNDERSTANDING THE FIXED-RATE MORTGAGE: REFINANCING

In many cases, borrowers may find that the interest rate on an outstanding loan is substantially higher than rates available on new mortgages in the market. If the rate on the existing loan is higher than the market interest rate, the borrower can reduce total borrowing costs by refinancing the loan amount at the prevailing market rate. **Refinancing** involves retiring the existing loan with the proceeds of a new loan for the same property. The borrower may obtain the new loan from the same or a different lender. A reduction in borrowing cost can be obtained by either reducing the payment amount or reducing the number of payments required to amortize the loan.

Consider the loan described in the previous example. At the end of 60 months, suppose that current interest rates are at 6 percent and the borrower will replace the old loan with a new loan with the same number of months remaining. We can calculate the payment on the new loan as follows.

$$PMT = \$125,841.83 \left[\frac{0.06/12}{1 - \dfrac{1}{(1 + 0.06/12)^{300}}} \right]$$

$$= \$810.80$$

Financial Calculator Solution
$P/Y = 12$, $PV = 125841.83$, $N = 300$, $I/Y = 6$, $PMT = ?$

Microsoft Excel Solution
Enter =PMT(.06/12,300,-125841.83)

If the borrower obtains a new loan for the same amount for 25 years, the monthly payments will be $810.80. Subtracting the new payment from the old payments shows that the borrower's monthly payment amount will be reduced by $119.16. Over the remaining 25 years (300 months) of the loan, refinancing this loan at the lower interest rate will provide interest savings of $35,748.00.

On the other hand, if the borrower wishes to take advantage of the lower interest rates available in the market and is comfortable making the payments of $929.96, refinancing can reduce the remaining term of the loan. We can determine the number of monthly payments of $929.96 at 6 percent annual interest (instead of 7.5 percent) required to amortize the loan by solving the following equation for the exponent N. While the algebra may look daunting, the problem can be solved easily with a financial calculator or Microsoft Excel.

Financial Calculator Solution
$P/Y = 12$, $PMT = -929.96$, $PV = 125841.83$, $I/Y = 6$, $N = ?$

Microsoft Excel Solution
Enter =NPER(0.06/12,–929.96,125841.83)

In this problem, if the borrower refinances the loan amount of $125,841.83 at 6 percent annual interest, but continues making payments of $929.96 each month, the number of monthly payments required to repay this debt falls from 300 to 227. (The last payment made will be for less than the full amount.) Thus, refinancing the loan at a lower interest rate, but keeping the payments at the same level, reduces the time required to retire the debt by 73 months.

$$\$929.96 = \$125,841.83 \left[\frac{0.06/12}{1 - \dfrac{1}{(1 + 0.06/12)^N}} \right]$$

$$N = 226.34$$

Financial Calculator Solution
$P/Y = 12$, $PMT = -929.96$, $PV = 125841.83$, $I/Y = 6$, $N = ?$

Microsoft Excel Solution
=NPER(0.06/12,-929.96,125841.83)

UNDERSTANDING THE FIXED-RATE MORTGAGE: DISCOUNT POINTS AND EFFECTIVE INTEREST RATES

Another important aspect of mortgage financing is the use of discount points and origination fees to increase the lender's yield on the loan. The charges represent additional income to the lender and, therefore, additional cost of borrowing to the borrower. When expressed as a percentage of the loan amount, the charges are called **discount points.** By definition, one discount point is equal to 1 percent of the loan amount. When expressed as a dollar amount, the charges are generally classified as **origination fees.** These charges cover the lender's cost of processing the loan application, obtaining credit reports, and other costs associated with loan origination.

Of course, the lender could simply increase the interest rate on the loan, but many choose to charge these fees at the time of origination rather than throughout the term of the loan.

From the borrower's perspective, discount points and other fees result in an effective interest rate that may be substantially higher than the stated interest rate on the loan. The term **effective interest rate** refers to the actual cost of borrowing funds from a lender, expressed as an annual rate, after consideration of discount points and origination fees. Comparing one loan with another requires careful consideration of the effective interest rate. The calculations presented here are similar to those used by lenders to calculate the annualized percentage rate, or APR, which must be disclosed to all loan applicants under Regulation Z (see Chapter 16).

The table below shows a sample of interest rates and discount points offered by competing lenders. The quotes are based on a $100,000, 30-year loan for an owner-occupied, single-family home. Which loan provides the lowest effective interest rate? The answer to this question requires use of the internal rate of return (IRR) concept discussed previously in Chapter 17.

Lender	Interest Rate	Points %
Loan Shack	7.875	0.50
Marley Lenders	7.625	1.00
First Bank	8.000	0.00
Spider Savings	7.250	3.50

To determine which loan provides the lowest effective interest rate, we first must calculate the payments required under each loan. Notice that payments are based on the full loan amount of $100,000. In three of these loans, borrowers must pay "points" to the lender at the time of origination. Therefore, the net amount disbursed by the lender at origination is determined by subtracting the fee from the loan amount. Using the definition of discount points and the mortgage payment calculations described earlier, the cash flows for each loan are seen in the table below.

Lender	Cash Flow at Origination	Cash Flow in Periods 1–360
Loan Shack	− $99,500	$725.07
Marley Lenders	− 99,000	707.79
First Bank	− 100,000	733.76
Spider Savings	− 96,500	682.18

The effective interest rate for each of these loans is equivalent to the IRR of the cash flow stream. We can find the IRR of the cash flows in each loan using our financial calculators or Microsoft Excel as shown below for the Spider Savings loan.

Financial Calculator Solution

$CF0 = -96500$, $CF1 \ldots CF360 = 682.18$, IRR = ?

(Some calculators report the monthly IRR. Multiply by 12 to convert to annual.)

Microsoft Excel Solution

Put the cash flow amounts in 361 contiguous cells (A1=–96500, A2=682.18, A3=682.18, . . . ,A361=682.18).

In a blank cell, enter =irr(A1:A361,.10/12)*12.

Notice that Excel needs a starting "guess" in some IRR problems to find the solution in a reasonable amount of time.

Repeating this calculation for each of the loans provides the effective interest rates shown below. Notice that the effective interest rate on the loan from First Bank is the same as the stated interest rate because there are no points involved. The answer from our calculators (7.9999 percent) is slightly less than the stated rate because we rounded the payment amount to the nearest penny. As seen in the table below, of all four loans, the loan from Spider Savings provides the lowest effective interest rate, in spite of the large amount of points charged at origination.

Lender	Stated Interest Rate	Points %	Effective Interest Rate
Loan Shack	7.875	0.50	7.9275
Marley Lenders	7.625	1.00	7.7287
First Bank	8.000	0.00	7.9999
Spider Savings	7.250	3.507	7.6123

Discount points and origination fees can have a dramatic impact on effective interest rates if the borrower prepays the loan. As we mentioned earlier, most loans are prepaid within five to seven years. To determine the effective interest rate when a loan is prepaid, we must calculate the amount outstanding on the loan at the time of prepayment. To demonstrate the effect of discount points and prepayment on effective interest rates, assume that the loan from Spider Savings is prepaid at the end of month 60. What is the effective interest rate on the loan? To answer this question, first find AO_{60} for each loan as described earlier, then enter the cash flows into your financial calculator or Microsoft Excel. The solutions to the effective interest rate for the loan from Spider Savings are shown on the next page.

Financial Calculator Solution

1. Find AO_{60} = \$94,379.29 by finding the present value of the remaining 300 payments of \$682.18 at the stated annual interest rate of 7.25 percent:
   P/Y = 12, PMT = 681.19, N = 300, I/Y = 7.25, PV = ?

2. Find IRR using cash flows of: $CF0$ = −96500, $CF1$ = 682.18, . . .,
   $CF59$ = 682.18, $CF60$ = 682.19 + 94379.29 = 95061.47, IRR = ? (Multiply by 12 if your calculator doesn't do this automatically).

Microsoft Excel Solution

1. Find AO_{60} = \$94,379.29 by entering the following in a blank cell:
   =pv(.06/12,300,-682.18)

2. Put the cash flow amounts in 61 contiguous cells (A1=−96500, A2=682.18, A3=682.18, . . . ,A60=681.18,A61=682.18+94379.29=95061.47).

3. In a blank cell, enter irr(A1:A61,.10/12)*12. Notice that Excel needs a starting "guess" in some IRR problems to find the solution in a reasonable amount of time.

As you can see, prepaying a loan with high origination costs can increase the effective interest rate considerably. Prepaying the Spider Savings loan at the end of five years raises the effective interest rate to 8.1253 percent, which is significantly above the stated interest rate of 7.250 percent. Notice that the loan from First Bank has an effective interest rate of 8 percent, regardless of prepayment. Furthermore, you should also realize that the earlier you prepay a loan with discount points, the greater the effective interest rate. When shopping for a new mortgage among competing lenders, you should consider how long you expect to keep the loan before making a final choice.

ALTERNATIVES TO THE FIXED-RATE MORTGAGE

In addition to shopping for the best deal on a mortgage by comparing effective interest rates resulting from discount points or origination fees, borrowers may also wish to consider various alternatives to the fixed-rate mortgage. Several alternative mortgage types are available, including *two-step mortgages* and *adjustable-rate mortgages*. The distinguishing feature of each of these loans is that the payments are not necessarily the same in each period. In the two-step mortgage, the payment amount is re-established once during the life of the loan, usually at the end of year five or year seven. Payments in an adjustable-rate mortgage change more frequently, usually at the end of each year. Lenders are able to offer these loans at lower initial interest rates because the borrower is assuming some of the risk of future interest rate increases. If the general interest rate in the economy increases, the lender's yield on the outstanding loan amount increases as well. Borrowers who are willing to accept this additional risk enjoy a lower initial interest rate. Borrowers who plan on prepaying the loan before it matures find this type of loan, as well as the adjustable-rate loan discussed below, especially attractive. The tools we have developed in earlier sections help us understand the mechanics of these alternative loan types.

Understanding the Mechanics of Two-Step Mortgages

Two-step mortgages (also known as *reset mortgages*) are a relatively new type of loan in the residential lending market. Initial payments on this type of loan are calculated using the mortgage payment formula. At the end of five or seven years, depending on the contract terms, the payment is recalculated for the remaining balance and term of the loan based on the prevailing interest rate. The prevailing interest rate is usually defined as the yield on ten-year Treasury bonds (or some other readily available national or international interest rate) plus 2 percentage points. In other words, the interest rate is "indexed" to the Treasury bond yield with a "margin" of 2 percent. Because the new interest rate may be higher or lower than the original interest rate, the payment amount changes accordingly.

This loan is advantageous to borrowers because the interest rate used to determine the initial payments is lower than the interest rate on a fixed-rate mortgage. Borrowers who do not expect to hold their loans for the full term find the two-step mortgage especially attractive. Even if the loan is held to maturity, the borrower is protected against large payment changes by an interest rate "cap" that typically limits the increase in the interest rate to a maximum of 5 percentage points. The following example demonstrates the payment stream required in a typical two-step mortgage.

Two-Step Mortgage Example

Consider a 30-year, two-step mortgage for $110,000. This type of loan is common in the subprime lending market discussed in Chapter 16. Borrowers are attracted to this type of loan because the initial rate is lower than the rate on a fixed-rate loan, but the rate is subject to increase (sometimes by large amounts) after some initial period (1 to 7 years). Most subprime borrowers who opt for this type of loan are hoping to improve their credit rating during the initial period or hoping that interest rates will decline when the adjustment occurs.

In this example, suppose the initial interest rate is 6 percent, but the loan contract requires that the interest rate be adjusted at the end of year 7 to 2 percentage points above the ten-year Treasury bond yield. The maximum increase in the interest rate is capped at a 5 percentage point increase over the initial rate. (In some subprime loans, the margin is as high as 6 percent and there is no cap on the increase over the initial rate.) At the end of year 7 , the 10-year Treasury yield is 6.9 percent. Assuming the loan is held to maturity, monthly payments are determined as follows.

First, calculate the payment due in months 1 through 84 using the loan amount of $110,000, 6 percent interest, and 30 years. The payment amount is $659.51. Second, find the amount outstanding at the end of month 84 ($98,603.32). Third, determine the new interest rate of 8.9 percent by adding the margin and the current Treasury yield. Notice that the new interest rate is 2.9 percentage points above the initial rate, which is well within the limits of the interest rate cap. Finally, calculate the payment due in months 84 through 360 using the current loan balance, 23 years, and the new interest rate of 8.9 percent. The new payment is $840.69.

Financial Calculator Solution

1. Find monthly payment during first 84 months of $659.51: $P/Y = 12$, $PV = 110000$, $I/Y = 6$, $N = 360$, $PMT = ?$

2. Find $AO_{84} = \$98,603.99$: $PMT = -659.51$, $N = 276$, $I/Y = 6$, $PV = ?$

3. Find new monthly payment for remaining 276 months of $840.69: $PV = -98603.99$, $I/Y = 8.9$, $N = 276$, $PMT = ?$

Microsoft Excel Solution

1. Find monthly payment during first 84 months of $659.51 by entering =pmt(.06/12,360,-110000)

2. Find $AO_{84} = \$98,603.99$ by entering =pv(.06/12,276,-659.51)

3. Find new monthly payment for remaining 276 months of $840.69 by entering =pmt(.089/12,276,-98603.99)

Understanding the Mechanics of Adjustable-Rate Mortgages

Adjustable-rate mortgages are a common type of loan in both residential and commercial lending. As with two-step mortgages, the interest rate on an adjustable-rate mortgage (ARM) is subject to change as the general interest rate level in the economy changes. The key difference is that the rate changes more than once during the term of the mortgage. In fact, most ARMs require annual rate adjustments, though some require adjustments every three or five years. In general, the initial interest rate on an ARM is lower than the rate on fixed-rate or two-step mortgages, which makes this an attractive loan type for many borrowers. Of course, ARM borrowers must be confident that they can afford the payment increases that are likely to occur over the life of the mortgage.

ARM interest rates are indexed to some general interest rate in the capital market. The most common index for residential ARMs is the one-year Treasury bill. The contract interest rate in any year of an ARM is defined as the index rate plus a margin of 2 or 3 percentage points. In the first year of an ARM, some lenders offer a "teaser" that reduces the margin by 1 or 2 percentage points. At each adjustment period, the contract interest rate is adjusted and the payments are recalculated. To protect borrowers (and lenders) against large payment changes, most ARMs have two types of interest rate caps. Annual caps limit the change in the contract interest rate to 2 percentage points above the prior year's contract rate, and lifetime caps establish a maximum and minimum contract rate that is within 5 percentage points of the initial contract rate. In many ARM loans, the caps "work" in both directions and thus may limit both increases and decreases in the interest rate.

ARM Example

Consider a 30-year ARM loan for $110,000. The interest rate is indexed to the one-year Treasury bill yield, with a margin of 2 percentage points. The lender offers a teaser of 1 percentage point for the first year. The loan requires annual rate adjustments, with an annual cap of 2 percentage points and a lifetime cap of 5 percentage points. We can use the following assumptions regarding the T-bill yield to determine the payment stream for the first four years of this loan.

Time	T-Bill Yield %	Margin %	Teaser %	Contract Rate %	Payment $
At origination	4	2	−1	5	590.50
At end of first year	5	2	0	7	728.43
At end of second year	3	2	0	5	593.34
At end of third year	6	2	0	7	724.83

For each year, calculate the monthly payment using the current loan amount, remaining years, and the contract interest rate. Finding the current loan amount is accomplished by finding the amount outstanding at the end of each year. Notice that the teaser rate reduces the contract rate in the first year to 5 percent, and that the annual cap limits the contract rate at the end of the third year to 7 percent.

Financial Calculator Solution

1. Find the first year's payment amount of $590.50: $P/Y = 12$, $PV = -110000$, $I/Y = 5$, $N = 360$, $PMT = ?$

2. Find the amount outstanding (balance) of $108,376.40 at the end of the first year: $PMT = 590.50$, $I/Y = 5$, $N = 348$, $PV = ?$

3. Find the second year's payment amount of $728.43: $PV = -108376.40$, $I/Y = 7$, $N = 348$, $PMT = ?$

4. Find the amount outstanding (balance) of $107,183.75 at the end of the second year: $PMT = 728.43$, $I/Y = 7$, $N = 336$, $PV = ?$

5. Etc.

Microsoft Excel Solution

1. Find the first year's payment amount of $590.50 using =pmt(.05/12,360,-110000)

2. Find the amount outstanding (balance) of $108,376.40 at the end of the first year using =pv(.05/12,348,-590.50)

3. Find the second year's payment amount of $728.43 using pmt(.07/12,348,-108376.40)

4. Find the amount outstanding (balance) of $107,183.75 at the end of the second year using =pv(.07/12,336,-728.43)

5. Etc.

CHAPTER REVIEW

- In contrast to interest-only loans, amortizing loans require the periodic payment of both principal and interest. The balance outstanding on the loan decreases gradually through amortization of the principal.

- The amount outstanding on an amortizing loan at any regular payment date can be determined by finding the present value of the remaining payments. This rule is useful when faced with prepayment and refinancing decisions.

- The effective interest rate on a loan can be much higher than the stated contract rate, especially if the lender charges discount points or origination fees. One discount point means that the borrower must pay 1 percent of the loan amount at the time of origination. The internal rate of return provides a measure of the effective interest rate for loans that charge discount points or origination fees.

- Alternatives to the fixed-rate mortgage include two-step mortgages and adjustable-rate mortgages. In both of these types of loans, the interest rate is subject to change over time which can cause adjustments in the payment amount. The borrower accepts some of the risk of future interest rate changes in exchange for a lower initial interest rate.

KEY TERMS

adjustable-rate mortgages	discount points	origination fees
amortization schedule	effective interest rate	prepayment
amortizing loans	fixed-rate mortgage	refinancing
balloon payment	interest-only loan	two-step mortgages

▌ STUDY EXERCISES

1. Define the following terms: *interest-only loan, amortizing loan, balloon payment.*

2. Construct an amortization schedule for a loan with the following characteristics. Loan amount = $10,000; term = 5 years; interest rate = 8 percent; annual payments.

3. Ron borrows $3,000,000 to purchase a warehouse. The annual interest rate on the loan is 8.25 percent, and the term of the loan is 15 years. Answer the following questions about this loan:

   a. What is the monthly payment necessary to amortize this loan?

   b. What is the balance on the loan at the end of month 36?

   c. How much interest will Ron pay in month 37?

   d. How much principal will Ron pay in month 37?

   e. How much principal will Ron pay in the fourth year of this loan (payments 37 through 48)?

4. Suppose the loan in question 3 required 2 discount points at the time of origination.

   a. If Ron keeps this loan for the full term, 180 months, what is his effective interest rate?

   b. If Ron prepays the loan at the end of month 48, what is his effective interest rate?

5. Suppose Ron refinances the loan at the end of month 48 at the prevailing interest rate in the market (8 percent). Rather than reducing his monthly payment, however, Ron decides to keep making the same monthly payments.

   a. How many months must Ron continue to make the payments on this new loan?

   b. By how many months has Ron shortened the term of the loan with this strategy?

6. Consider a 30-year, two-step mortgage for $335,000. The initial interest rate is 5.5 percent, but the loan contract calls for a rate adjustment at the end of year 5. The new rate will be 2 percentage points above the ten-year Treasury bond yield. The interest rate is capped at 5 percentage points above the initial interest rate. If the T-bond yield is 7.5 percent at the time of the adjustment, what will the payments be for the last 25 years of this loan?

7. Consider a 30-year ARM for $335,000. The loan is indexed to the one-year T-bill yield, which is currently at 5.25 percent. The margin is 2 percentage points, and the teaser is 1.5 percent. The contract rate adjusts once at the end of each year, but the loan has annual and lifetime interest rate caps of 2 and 5 percentage points, respectively. The caps work in both directions and may limit both increases and decreases in the interest rate. Answer the following questions assuming that the actual T-bill yields for the first four years of this loan are the same as those shown below.

Time	T-Bill Yield %	Margin %	Teaser %	Contract Rate %
At origination	5.25	2	−1.5	?
At end of first year	6.50	2	0.0	?
At end of second year	7.75	2	0.0	?
At end of third year	4.25	2	0.0	?

a. What is the monthly payment during months 1 through 12?

b. What is the amount outstanding at the end of month 12?

c. What is the monthly payment during months 13 through 24?

d. What is the amount outstanding at the end of month 24?

e. What is the monthly payment during months 25 through 36?

f. What is the amount outstanding at the end of month 36?

g. What is the monthly payment during months 37 through 48?

8. A prospective homebuyer can afford to make monthly loan payments of no more than $475. If the best rate she can obtain on a mortgage is 10 percent (for a 25-year term), what is the maximum amount she can borrow?

9. Congratulations! You won the sweepstakes. The sweepstakes rules entitle you to a choice of one of the following prizes. Using the concept of present value, which choice is the most valuable to you if your opportunity rate is 8 percent?

   Choice A: $40,000 per year for the next 20 years

   Choice B: $25,000 today, plus $35,000 per year for the next 25 years

   Choice C: $200,000 today, plus $12,000 per year for the next 40 years

10. Nikki's mortgage requires her to pay $1,230 per month for the next 180 months. The balance on her loan is $130,000. What is the annual interest rate on Nikki's loan?

FURTHER READING

www.fanniemae.com
www.freddiemac.com

Analyzing Income-Producing Properties

One of the most exciting aspects of the real estate industry is investment in income-producing properties. History is filled with the names of people who have made, and sometimes lost, fortunes through real estate investments. The primary question to be considered in this chapter is this: "How do investors decide whether to invest in a particular project?" Successful investment decision making requires careful analysis of the risks and returns offered by an investment opportunity.

The objective of this chapter is to describe the analysis methods successful investors use to make real estate investment decisions. In general, this process involves (1) evaluating a project's competitive environment, (2) forecasting the cash flows that are expected to accrue to the investor, and (3) making a final decision about whether to proceed with the project. Our focus throughout this chapter is on decision-making situations facing equity investors who are considering investing in existing income properties. In this chapter we

- discuss the advantages and disadvantages of real estate investment;

- review the concepts of investment and wealth maximization; and

- discuss how investors compare the costs and benefits of investment opportunities using net present value, the internal rate of return, and the discounted cash flow model for both "buy-and-holds" and "flips."

ADVANTAGES OF REAL ESTATE INVESTMENT

What makes real estate an attractive investment category? While there are numerous motivations for pursuing real estate investments, investors often cite cash flow from operations, the possibility of value appreciation, portfolio diversification, and the ability to use financial leverage as the major incentives for pursuing real estate projects.

Cash Flow from Operations

For many investors, the primary attraction of real estate investments is the **operating cash flow** generated by income-producing properties. The source of this cash flow is the rent paid by tenants for the use of space in the property. Because real estate is a durable asset, most properties are capable of generating rental revenue for many years into the future. From this revenue, the investor must pay the property's operating expenses, debt service, and income taxes. Operating expenses typically include utilities, maintenance, property management, insurance, and property taxes. Debt service includes principal and interest payments on any outstanding mortgage debt. Income taxes are due on any taxable income generated by the property. Investors refer to the annual operating cash flow that remains after these items are paid as **after-tax cash flow** from operations. Often referred to by its acronym, ATCF, this cash flow represents the money the investor puts in his or her pocket at the end of each year of the investment holding period.

Appreciation

Another motivation for investing in income-producing real estate is the possibility of **appreciation** in property value over the investment holding period. While investment properties do not always increase in value, investors generally choose properties whose values are expected to grow at the rate of inflation or greater. Furthermore, changing market conditions can improve a property's competitive position in a market, allowing it to command higher rents and thereby increase its value to investors. When an investor sells an income-producing property, the proceeds from the sale, less selling expenses, are used to retire any outstanding mortgage debt and to pay any income taxes due as a result of the sale. To the investor, the sum of money that is generated by the sale of an investment is known as **after-tax equity reversion,** or ATER. The term *equity reversion* refers to the return of funds originally invested in the property, plus any change in the value of the investor's investment in the property.

Portfolio Diversification

Another important motivation for investing in real estate is the diversification real estate adds to a portfolio. Combining real estate investments with investments in stocks and bonds allows investors to develop a diversified portfolio. Diversification allows investors to maximize their investment returns while spreading their risk exposure across different types of investments. Such a strategy provides protection against an economic downturn in any one sector of the economy. In addition, many people are attracted to the security offered by investments in tangible assets that are under their personal control.

Financial Leverage

Real estate investors are also attracted to real estate because it allows the use of **financial leverage,** or "other people's money." The real estate finance industry makes debt capital readily available to most investors, with many lenders willing to provide 70 percent or more of the funds necessary to purchase investment properties. By borrowing additional investment funds from lenders, investors can control more real estate with less of their own funds. The use of borrowed funds has the effect of leveraging, or magnifying, the returns on funds invested by the investor. The benefits of leverage come at a price, however, because investors face increased risk. If the project fails to generate sufficient revenue to satisfy the debt service payments, the project may be forced into foreclosure.

Example of Financial Leverage

To understand the impact of leverage on an equity investor's rate of return, consider the following example. Lou Lever has $100,000 to invest. He can (1) purchase a $100,000 property without using any borrowed funds or (2) use the $100,000 to make a 10 percent down payment on a $1,000,000 property and borrow $900,000 at 11 percent annual interest on an interest-only loan. If each of the two properties provides a 15 percent return before debt service and income taxes are considered, the second is clearly more advantageous owing to the effects of financial leverage. To see why, calculate Lou's rate of return on his equity investment for both properties.

If Lou follows the first strategy, he would earn $15,000, or 15 percent, on his equity investment of $100,000. If he follows the second strategy, Lou would earn $51,000. This amount is calculated by first determining the total return on the investment (0.15 × $1,000,000 = $150,000), then subtracting the interest due on the borrowed funds (0.11 × $900,000 = $99,000). As a percentage of his equity investment of $100,000, the $51,000 ($150,000 – $99,000) reflects a 51 percent rate of return.

As you can see, financial leverage can greatly magnify the rate of return on equity. If the property in the second strategy provides an overall return of 18 percent instead of 15 percent, Lou's rate of return on equity would jump to 81 percent; an overall return of 20 percent would balloon Lou's return to 101 percent.

Of course, the magnification of the return on equity also works in the opposite direction. If, for example, the property provides a return of only 5 percent overall, then Lou would suffer a negative rate of return on equity of 49 percent (0.05 × $1,000,000 – 0.11 × $900,000 = –$49,000). The ability of leverage to magnify returns on equity implies that leverage increases risk. The additional risk comes from the fact that Lou has a fixed liability (interest on the debt) that he must satisfy each year. If the property's earnings are insufficient to cover the debt service, Lou stands to lose cash out of his pocket to keep the investment alive.

As a rule, financial leverage will increase the investor's return on equity as long as the cost (interest rate) of the borrowed funds is less than the overall return on the investment. If the interest rate exceeds the overall return, then financial leverage will reduce the return on the investor's return on equity, possibly causing it to be negative.

Disadvantages of Real Estate Investment

Though there are numerous advantages to investing in real estate, the disadvantages must not be ignored. For example, even with borrowed funds, real estate investments often require relatively large capital requirements. Large-scale properties such as office buildings and shopping centers are often beyond the resources of individual investors. In addition, investing in real estate is risky, and the risk exposure may not be suitable for every investor.

In the preceding discussion we saw how financial leverage could increase the risk of an investment. Another aspect of real estate risk comes from the lack of liquidity that real estate investments have in comparison with other types of investments. Liquidity refers to the ability to convert an asset into cash quickly without having to accept a low price. For example, stocks are considered a liquid asset because an investor who wishes to sell a portfolio of common stocks can do so by simply calling a stockbroker. The broker will immediately sell the shares at the current market price. Real estate investors should anticipate that selling a property quickly may mean that the property will sell at a lower price than could otherwise be obtained.

Real estate investors also face the risk of changing economic conditions that may affect the rents they are able to charge to tenants and the value of investment properties. Successful investors spend considerable time and effort evaluating the markets in which their properties compete to understand how changing market conditions affect the risk exposure of their portfolios.

Weighing the benefits and costs of a real estate investment opportunity requires a high degree of knowledge about the characteristics of real estate markets and transactions, as well as careful consideration of the risks involved in real estate investment. The next section takes a closer look at the process that real estate investors use when making the investment decision.

▌ FINANCIAL DECISION MAKING

As we discussed in Chapter 17, all financial decisions involve a comparison of the expected benefits from a proposed course of action with the expected costs arising from that course of action. In this context, **investment** is defined as present sacrifice in anticipation of expected future benefit. Based on this definition, the decision to continue your education is an investment, as is a decision to place money in a savings account for future use. If you do not expect the benefits of these activities to be greater than the sacrifices you must make, you would choose not to engage in them. Similarly, real estate investment decisions require a comparison of the benefits a project is expected to generate with the sacrifices one must make in order to engage in the project.

The Wealth Maximization Objective

In order to make investment decisions, investors must define their criteria for determining the acceptability of alternative projects. Some investors pursue projects that will generate income, while others are more interested in the appreciation potential that real estate offers. Other investors are in search of projects that provide tax-sheltering benefits, or those that have minimum management concerns. Although each investor has different interests, tastes, and preferences, the ultimate goal of all investors is to accept those projects that will maximize their wealth. Investors who pursue a **wealth maximization objective** will choose only those projects that offer expected benefits in excess of the costs of pursuing them and, if faced with a choice between two or more projects that increase wealth, wealth-maximizing investors will choose the project in which benefits exceed costs by the largest amount.

The NPV Rule

To evaluate the impact a project will have on wealth, investors use the net present value decision rule and the internal rate of return decision rule discussed in Chapter 17. We will review each of these rules in turn.

Recall that **net present value** (NPV) is defined as the present value of cash inflows less the present value of cash outflows. The conversion of future cash flows into present values is accomplished by discounting the future cash flows at the investor's required rate of return. The **required rate of return** reflects both the time value of money and the risk of the investment opportunity.

Investors use the NPV of a particular project as a decision rule by evaluating its sign (positive or negative). If the NPV of an investment is greater than or equal to zero, the investor should choose to invest because the investment is worth at least as much as it costs, given the investor's required rate of return. If NPV is less than zero, the investor should choose not to invest.

Taking this rule one step further, if we are faced with several alternative investment choices, we should accept the one with the highest positive NPV because it will increase our wealth more than the others. To use this rule in investment analysis, we must estimate the cash flows associated with an investment opportunity, then convert the cash flows into present values using the appropriate discount rate. The following example demonstrates the NPV decision rule.

Using the NPV Rule

Consider an investor who is facing a choice between two alternative investments. The investor has performed a detailed analysis of both projects' competitive environments and has developed the cash-flow forecasts shown below. He believes that both projects are equally risky, and that the level of risk of the projects suggests an annual required rate of return of 15 percent for both projects. Which project should the investor choose?

	Project A	Project B
Initial investment	$90,000	$80,000
Cash flow in year one	10,000	9,100
Cash flow in year two	11,100	10,000
Cash flow in year three	12,000	11,000
Cash flow in year four	12,000	11,000
Cash flow in year five	120,000	104,000

Given that the investor's objective is to choose the project that increases his wealth by the greater amount, he should calculate the NPV of each project and choose the one with the higher NPV. These calculations are shown below:

Project A

$$NPV = \frac{10,000}{(1.15)^1} + \frac{11,000}{(1.15)^2} + \frac{12,000}{(1.15)^3} + \frac{12,000}{(1.15)^4} + \frac{120,000}{(1.15)^5} - 90,000 = \$1,501$$

Project B

$$NPV = \frac{9,100}{(1.15)^1} + \frac{10,000}{(1.15)^2} + \frac{11,000}{(1.15)^3} + \frac{11,000}{(1.15)^4} + \frac{104,000}{(1.15)^5} - 80,000 = \$703$$

Both projects result in a positive NPV, which suggests that both are good projects that will result in a wealth increase to the investor above and beyond the cost of pursuing them. Because the NPV of project A is greater than the NPV of project B, the investor should choose A. By doing so, the investor expects to receive a return of 15 percent, plus a wealth increase of $1,501.

Using the IRR Rule

The internal rate of return decision rule also provides us with a "yes or no" decision about whether to proceed with an investment opportunity. Notice that in project A, above, the investor's required rate of return was 15 percent. Because the net present value is greater than zero, and because its NPV is larger than project B's NPV, the investor should choose to accept this project. But what rate of return does the investor expect to earn? Obviously, the investor expects to earn some rate above 15 percent. To find the exact return the investor expects to earn, we can define the **internal rate of return** (IRR) of an investment as the discount rate that makes NPV exactly equal to zero. To determine an investment's IRR, we can search a variety of discount rates by trial-and-error until we find one that makes NPV equal zero. This rate will be the IRR on the investment. Fortunately, most financial calculators and computer spreadsheet software packages allow automatic searches for the IRR for a series of cash flows.

To use the IRR as a financial decision-making rule, we simply compare the IRR of an investment opportunity with our required rate of return. If the IRR is greater than or equal to our required rate of return, we choose to invest; otherwise, we forgo the investment opportunity. While the IRR rule and the NPV rule are based on the same principles, the NPV rule is generally the best choice to use because IRR calculations may yield multiple discount rates that set NPV equal to zero. Furthermore, the NPV rule should be used when forced to choose between mutually exclusive projects such as those described above. When our objective is to determine the rate of return provided by an investment, however, the IRR calculation is extremely useful.

Real estate investors can use these decision rules to evaluate individual projects and to decide whether to pursue them. Applying the rules, however, requires a forecast of the cash flows that the investor expects to receive during the investment holding period. The discounted cash flow model described below provides a systematic framework for calculating the expected NPV and IRR of real estate investment opportunities on an "after-tax" basis.

▌ THE DISCOUNTED CASH FLOW MODEL

The NPV and IRR decision rules provide a sound basis for defining the suitability of an investment opportunity by identifying its impact on the investor's wealth. Using these rules, we know that a "good" investment is one that is worth more than it costs, assuming all benefits and sacrifices are identified correctly. To put the decision rules into practice, real estate investors often rely on the following **discounted cash flow model.**

$$NPV = \sum_{t=1}^{T} \frac{ATCF_t}{(1+i)^t} \frac{ATER_t}{(1+i)^T} - initial\ equity$$

In this model, *ATCF* is the annual after-tax cash flow from operations, *ATER* is the after-tax equity reversion realized on the sale of the property at the end of the holding period, *i* is the investor's required rate of return, *T* is the expected number of years the property will be held, and *initial equity* is the difference between the purchase price and any debt used to finance the purchase. Understanding the model requires careful consideration of the components of ATCF and ATER. The following example describes each of these concepts in detail.

Applying the Discounted Cash Flow Model

To illustrate some of the issues involved in real estate investment analysis, consider the decision facing Susan Adrep, an advertising account executive who is considering adding real estate to her investment portfolio. Susan became interested in buying an income-producing property several months ago. She has discussed her interests with her accountant, local lenders, other real estate investors, and several different real estate brokers. Because this is her first real estate investment, she has decided to focus on smaller residential properties located in her neighborhood. After looking at several properties that are currently available in the market, Susan feels that one property, a four-unit apartment building, deserves further consideration.

The property is located on a quiet street between a commercial district and an area containing single-family homes. Property values in this area have been increasing at approximately 3 percent per year over the past ten years. The eight-year-old building was well-constructed and the owner has maintained the property in excellent condition. The owner is moving to another city and has decided to sell the property rather than manage it as an absentee owner.

John Block, a local real estate broker, has agreed to market the property for the owner at a firm asking price of $455,000. John provides Susan with a summary of the rental income and operating expenses for the past several years. In addition, Susan talks with several lenders and learns that a 25-year, monthly payment mortgage loan can be obtained at 7 percent interest for 75 percent of the property value. Based on this information, as well as her own analysis of local market conditions, Susan develops the following forecast for income and expenses for her first year of ownership of the property.

	Year 1
Rent ($1,325 per unit per month)	$63,600
Annual rent increases	3.5 percent
Operating expenses	
Maintenance and repairs	4,550
Insurance	3,975
Property taxes	11,375
Property management services	5,520
Total	$25,420
Annual operating expense increase	3.5 percent

The question Susan faces is whether this property is a suitable investment for her portfolio. To make a decision about buying the property, Susan must identify the sacrifices she must make to acquire the property and compare those sacrifices with the benefits she expects to receive from this investment.

The sacrifices facing Susan Adrep in this project include the initial equity contribution she must make at the time of purchase and the risk she will be exposed to as a result of her decision to invest. **Initial equity** is the purchase price of a project less any debt that is used to complete the purchase. **Risk** is defined as the possibility that the actual benefits provided by the investment will deviate from the investor's initial expectations. The benefits Susan expects to receive from pursuing this opportunity include the net cash flows that will occur during the investment holding period. Susan plans to hold this property for five years, beginning January 1 and ending December 31 five years later.

TABLE 19.1 | After-Tax Cash Flows from Operations for Year 1

	Potential Gross Income	PGI	$63,600
−	Vacancy and Credit Losses	− VCL	3,180
=	Effective Gross Income	= EGI	$60,420
−	Operating Expenses	− OE	25,420
=	Net Operating Income	= NOI	$35,000
−	Debt Service	− DS	28,943
=	Before-Tax Cash Flow	= BTCF	$6,057
−	Income Tax (calculated below)	− Tax	279
=	After-Tax Cash Flow	= ATCF	$5,778

Tax Calculations

	Net Operating Income	NOI	$35,000
−	Interest Expense	− Int	23,722
−	Cost Recovery Allowance (depreciation)	− CRA	10,280
=	Taxable Income	= TI	$998
×	Ordinary Tax Rate	× OTR	0.28
=	Income Tax	= Tax	$279

Expected benefits from real estate investments are typically divided into two categories: after-tax cash flows from operations and after-tax equity reversion. The first category refers to income received each year of the investment holding period, and the second category refers to income that is realized when the property is sold. Because income taxes are an important consideration in any investment strategy, Susan must consider their impact on the income she expects to receive from this investment.

Forecasting ATCF

To forecast the after-tax cash flows from operations for the investment opportunity under consideration by Susan, we use the relationships shown in Table 19.1. We will consider the second category of cash flows in real estate investments, after-tax equity reversion, in the next section.

The starting point for estimating annual cash flows from operations in a real estate investment is **potential gross income** (PGI). PGI is the total income potential of the investment, assuming all leasable space is rented and all rents are collected. Investors must have knowledge of the expected rent for the space in the property to estimate PGI. The source of this knowledge is usually a survey of rental rates for similar space in other properties in the marketplace. For the property Susan is considering, the PGI in the first year of her holding period is expected to be $63,600 ($1,325 rent per unit × 12 months × 4 units). Susan also believes that rents will increase at 3.5 percent per year for the next five years, which is her anticipated holding period.

Calculating Net Operating Income

Because some of the PGI may not be received as a result of vacancies or uncollected rents, an allowance for these items should be deducted from PGI in the form of **vacancy and credit losses** (VCL). The forecasted allowance of VCL (often expressed as a percentage of PGI) depends on observations of historic data, comparable properties, and general market conditions. For new properties, the vacancy rate may be quite high during the initial leasing period, and older properties in declining areas may experience high credit losses from faltering tenants. Susan believes that 5 percent of PGI is a reasonable allowance for the property she is considering, so the VCL in year one is expected to be $3,180 (63,600 × 0.05). Subtracting VCL from PGI results in **effective gross income** (EGI), or the actual amount of rental revenue expected to be received each year.

With revenues accounted for, the next step is to subtract **operating expenses** (OE) from EGI to determine **net operating income** (NOI). OE includes any expenditures made in the operation of the investment property such as maintenance costs, management fees, property taxes, insurance premiums, and utility fees. NOI is the amount of revenue left after paying the expenses of operation, but before paying the mortgage payments and income taxes on the investment. In this case, Susan feels that OE for year one will be $25,420, resulting in NOI of $35,000. She also believes that these expenses will increase by 3.5 percent each year.

Debt Service

Susan now must consider the impact of financing on this investment opportunity. Using the mortgage payment formula described in Chapter 14, Susan calculates the monthly payment required to amortize a 25-year loan for $341,250 ($455,000 × 0.75) at 7 percent annual interest. Multiplying this amount, $2,411.88 × 12 gives **debt service** (DS) of $28,943. Subtracting DS from NOI results in the **before-tax cash flow** (BTCF) of $6,057. Because taxes are a real expense, however, the analysis must be based on *after-tax cash flow* (ATCF). To calculate the annual income tax consequence of Susan's investment, we must first determine the **taxable income** (TI) generated by this project.

Taxable Income

Two items that require careful consideration when determining TI in most real estate investments are (1) interest expense and (2) cost recovery allowances. Considering interest expense (Int) first, notice that we subtracted the debt service from NOI to get BTCF. DS, however, also includes principal repayments, which are not tax-deductible. Therefore, BTCF is not the same as TI. To determine TI, we subtract only the interest component of DS from NOI. Recall from the discussion of amortizing loans in Chapter 18 that the amount of interest in each payment is reduced as

TABLE 19.2 | Amortization Schedule

Year	Debt Service	Interest	Principal	Amount Outstanding
0	0	0	0	$341,250
1	$28,943	$23,722	$5,220	336,030
2	28,943	23,345	5,598	330,432
3	28,943	22,940	6,003	324,429
4	28,943	22,506	6,436	317,993
5	28,943	22,041	6,902	311,091

the loan balance declines. Developing an amortization schedule for the loan used to finance a property investment allows us to determine the amount of interest paid each year. To construct an amortization schedule, the mortgage payment is calculated by the mortgage payment formula, then each payment is separated into interest and principal components. If payments are made more frequently than once each year, annual totals are necessary. An amortization schedule for Susan's loan is shown in Table 19.2. Interest in year one totals $23,722.

The second item to consider when calculating TI is the amount of the **cost recovery allowance** (CRA). Income tax laws allow CRAs (also known as *depreciation deductions*) that provide investors with a means of recovering their original capital investment without paying taxes on this amount until the property is sold. Nonresidential and residential property improvements have depreciable lives of 39 and 27.5 years, respectively. Land is not depreciable under current tax laws, so the amount of the purchase price attributable to improvements must be identified separately.

To determine the annual CRA, we divide the value of the improvements by the appropriate depreciable life. Assuming that the value of the building alone is $295,000, the annual CRA is $10,727 ($295,000 ÷ 27.5). Under current tax laws, however, an investor must make some additional calculations to determine the CRA during the first and last years of ownership. As a rule, the investor is presumed to have purchased the property in the middle of the month in which the property was purchased or sold, regardless of the actual day of the month the transaction occurs. For example, if an investor buys a property in January, the CRA for the first year of ownership is 11.5 ÷ 12 of the annual amount. Similarly, if the investor sells the property in July of a later year, the CRA is 6.5 ÷ 12 of the annual amount for the last year of ownership.

In the example being considered here, we can assume that Susan buys the property in January of year one and sells the property in December of year five. The cost recovery allowances in those two years will be $10,280 ($10,727 × 11.5 ÷ 12). For

TABLE 19.3 | After-Tax Cash Flows from Operations

	Year 1	Year 2	Year 3	Year 4	Year 5
Potential Gross Income	$63,600	$65,826	$68,130	$70,514	$72,982
– Vacancy	3,180	3,291	3,406	3,526	3,649
= Effective Gross Income	$60,420	$62,535	$64,723	$66,989	$69,333
– Operating Expenses	25,420	26.310	27,231	28,184	29,170
= Net Operating Income	$35,000	$36,225	$37,493	$38,805	$40,163
– Debt Service	28,943	28,943	28,943	28,943	28,943
= Before-Tax Cash Flow	$6,057	$7,282	$8,550	$9,863	$11,221
– Income Tax (calculated below)	279	603	1,071	1,560	2,196
= After-Tax Cash Flow	$5,778	$6.680	$7,479	$8,302	$9,025
Tax Calculations					
Net Operating Income	$35,000	$36,225	$37,493	$38,805	$40,163
– Interest Expense (from amortization table below)	23,722	23,345	22,940	22,506	22,041
– Cost Recovery Allowance (depreciation)	10,280	10,727	10,727	10,727	10,280
= Taxable Income	$998	$2,153	$3,826	$5,572	$7,842
× Ordinary Income Tax Rate	0.28	0.28	0.28	0.28	0.28
= Income Tax	$279	$603	$1,071	$1,560	$2,196

years two, three, and four, the full deduction of $10,727 is used. In this example, subtracting interest and CRA from NOI yields TI in year one of $998.

Income Taxes

Annual **income taxes** are calculated by multiplying TI by the investors' ordinary income tax rate. Susan faces an ordinary income tax rate of 28 percent. Therefore, the taxes from operations in year one are $279 ($998 × 0.28). (In the event that TI is a negative number, which is sometimes the case in real estate investments, the tax loss may be used to offset TI from other investments in the investor's portfolio, or carried forward. (A full discussion of the tax implications of real estate investment is beyond the scope of this text.) Subtracting taxes from BTCF yields ATCF in year one of $5,778.

These calculations are repeated for each year of the investment holding period as shown in Table 19.3. Thus far in her analysis of this property, Susan knows that she must invest $113,750 (purchase price minus the loan amount) in return for annual cash flows from operations shown in the table for years one through five. Susan must now forecast the cash flow she will receive at the end of year five from selling the property.

TABLE 19.4 | After-Tax Equity Reversion

	Gross Selling Price	$502,357
−	Selling Expenses	30,141
=	Net Selling Price	$472,215
−	Mortgage Payoff (amount outstanding)	311,091
=	Before-Tax Equity Reversion	$161,125
−	Capital Gain Tax (calculated below)	12,592
=	After-Tax Equity Reversion	$148,532
	Capital Gain Tax Calculations	
	Net Selling Price	$472,215
−	Book Value (purchase price less cost recovery allowances)	$402,258
=	Capital Gain	$69,958
×	Capital Gain Tax Rate	0.18
=	Capital Gain Tax	$12,592

Forecasting ATER

The second source of cash flow in real estate investments to be considered comes from the sale of the property at the end of the holding period. *After-tax equity reversion* (ATER) is the term used to represent the after-tax cash flow to the investor when the property is sold. The relationships involved in the calculation of ATER for Susan's investment opportunity are presented in Table 19.4.

The starting point in determining the ATER is forecasting a future sale price. **Gross selling price** is the estimated transaction price that will be negotiated between the buyer and the seller at the time of the transaction. To estimate the selling price, Susan assumes that the value of her property will increase by about 2 percent each year. If it is worth $455,000 at the time of purchase, and increases in value by 2 percent annually, it will sell for approximately $502,357 at the end of five years.

From this amount, Susan subtracts $30,141 (6 percent of gross selling price) for expenses she expects to incur during the sale, including such items as brokerage commissions and attorney fees. The difference between the sale price and selling expenses gives **net selling price** of $308,950. Subtracting the mortgage payoff amount (amount outstanding at the end of year five from the amortization schedule) of $311,091 from the net selling price gives the **before-tax equity reversion** (BTER) of $161,125.

The next step is to calculate the **capital gain** on the sale for tax purposes. The capital gain on an investment is defined as net selling price less the **book value,** where book value is defined as the purchase price less all CRA claimed in previous years. (Notice how the CRA provisions of the tax code defer income tax payments until the sale of the asset.) In this example, the book value of the property to this investor is $402,258. Therefore, the capital gain is $69,958. Current IRS tax rules provide a **capital gain tax rate** that is lower than ordinary income tax rates for most investors. For Susan, the capital gain tax rate is 18 percent. We can calculate Susan's **capital gain tax** by multiplying the capital gain by 18 percent to get $12,592. ATER is determined by subtracting capital gain tax from the BTER. Based on these calculations, Susan expects to receive an ATER of $148,532.

Now that we have carefully estimated ATCF and ATER for Susan's investment opportunity, we can apply the discounted cash flow model and decide whether she should proceed with this project. Given a loan amount of $341,250 and a purchase price of $455,000, the equity required to buy this property is $113,750. Assume that Susan believes a required rate of return of 10 percent reflects the risk of the investment as well as the time value of money over the holding period. Using the estimated ATCF for each year of the holding period and the estimated ATER, Susan calculates NPV as follows:

$$NPV = \frac{5,778}{(1 + 0.10)^1} + \frac{6,680}{(1 + 0.10)^2} + \frac{7,479}{(1 + 0.10)^3} + \frac{8,302}{(1 + 0.10)^4} + \frac{9,025}{(1 + 0.10)^5}$$

$$+ \frac{148,532}{(1 + 0.10)^5} - 113,750 = \$6,143$$

Based on the NPV and IRR decision rules, Susan should choose to purchase this property. While there is no guarantee that this property will be a profitable investment, the discounted cash flow model provides a systematic process for analyzing investment choices and evaluating them with the objective of maximizing investor wealth. The accuracy of the technique depends on the quality of the information used to develop the cash-flow forecasts and on the appropriate evaluation of the risk of the investment when formulating a required rate of return.

Another Type of Real Estate Investment: Property Flipping

The above discussion focuses on analysis of the "buy-and-hold" real estate investment strategy. Another popular way for entry-level investors to get involved in real estate investments is known as **property flipping**. Whereas buy-and-hold investors count on income produced by the property during the holding period as well as appreciation in property value that is captured upon sale of the property, flip investors rely on the increase in property value as a result of property improvement during a very short holding period.

There are many variations of property flipping investment, but a common strategy of flippers is to identify a house or other property that has a current market value below the market value of other properties in the neighborhood, buy that property at the lowest possible price, then spend funds to update the property to bring its value up to the value of other properties, then sell it for a profit in excess of the original purchase price and the funds expended to improve it. This type of flipping can also be thought of as a redevelopment project.

The same tools we used to analyze a buy-and-hold investment opportunity can easily be used to consider flips. The NPV and IRR decision rules are the recommended tools for evaluating a flipping opportunity. Let's consider the following example of a property flip.

Suppose you find a neighborhood in which houses are typically selling for around $325,000. You find a house that is in need of updating and repair that can be purchased for $265,000 including all acquisition costs. You estimate (perhaps with the help of qualified contractors) that updates and repairs will cost $40,000 and your research indicates that you will be able to sell the renovated property for $320,000 net of all disposal costs (broker fees, etc.). Further suppose that you approach a lender who agrees to provide a short-term, non-amortizing loan at 10 percent annual interest with a maximum loan balance of 70 percent of the estimated market value upon completion of the redevelopment project from the sale proceeds of $320,000. The interest on this loan will accrue during the development period and must be paid (along with the original loan balance) upon sale of the property. The maximum term of this loan is six months. How do you decide if this flip opportunity is a worthwhile investment if your required rate of return is 18 percent annually?

Subtracting the cost of purchasing the property, the cost of renovating the property, and the interest cost on the loan from the ultimate selling price gives the expected profit on the flip. Of course, the cash flows (in and out) in this deal occur over time, so we must incorporate time value of money into our analysis. Let's assume for this example that the purchase occurs on January 1. We have to pay 30 percent of the purchase price in the amount of $96,000 ($320,000 × 0.30 = $96,000) on this date. Notice that the down payment is based on the expected sale price, not the actual purchase price. This condition of the loan ensures that the loan amount (not including interest) does not exceed 70 percent of the value of the property.

Based on the work that needs to be done to the property, we expect to pay the contractors who do the work $20,000 on February 1, $15,000 on March 1, and $5,000 on April 1. Our lender will give us these funds at the times we pay the contractors for their work. We need to know how the loan balance grows during the renovation period. The timeline for the loan balance is as follows.

Date	Loan Balance (including accrued interest)	
January 1	$169,000.00	($265,000 − $96,000 = $169,000)
February 1	$190,408.33	($169,000 × (1 + 0.10/12) + $20,000 = 190,408.33)
March 1	$206,995.07	($190,408.33 × (1 + 0.10/12) + $15,000 = $206,995.07)
April 1	$213,720.03	($206,995.07 × (1 + 0.10/12) + $5,000 = $213,720.03)
May 1	$215,501.03	(213,720.03 × (1 + 0.10/12) = $215,501.03)

We forecast that we will sell the property on May 1 for $320,000. The timeline for our cash flows is as follows:

Date	Cash Flow
January 1	−$96,000
February 1	0
March 1	0
April 1	0
May 1	$104,498.97 ($320,000 − $215,501.03 = $104,498.97)

Solving for the NPV at our annual required rate of return of 18 percent gives $2,457.28 as shown below. The monthly IRR of this investment opportunity is 2.14 percent and the annualize IRR is 25.7 percent.

$$NPV = -96,000 + 104,498.97 / (1 + 0.18/12)^4 = \$2,457.28$$

Both the NPV and IRR decision rules suggest that this is an opportunity we should pursue.

While this rate of return looks impressive, flippers must keep in mind that there are risks to flipping. The flippers might not be able sell the property for as much as they expect, or they may discover that the time to sell the property is longer than they expect which would cause them to incur additional interest expense. Experience and good market research helps flippers properly evaluate the risk of the flip and determine their required rate of return for the given risk level.

CHAPTER REVIEW

■ Investing in real estate is one of the most exciting aspects of the real estate industry. To be a successful real estate investor requires considerable knowledge about all of the topics addressed in this text. In addition, investors must have a clear understanding of the criteria they should use when evaluating an investment opportunity.

■ Advantages of investing in income-producing properties include cash flow from operations, appreciation in property value, portfolio diversification, and financial leverage. Disadvantages include relatively large capital requirements, risk, and the lack of liquidity of real estate investments.

■ The net present value decision rule provides a basis for sound financial decision making that is consistent with the objective of wealth maximization. To apply this rule to real estate investment opportunities, we must develop a forecast of the expected cash flows the projects are likely to generate.

■ The discounted cash flow model is the recommended framework for making real estate investment decisions. By forecasting the cash flows that are likely to result from operating the property during each year of the holding period and the cash flow that will result when the property is sold, we can calculate the expected net present value of an investment opportunity. Using the net present value rule, we can then make a decision about whether the project is expected to increase our wealth.

■ Estimating after-tax cash flow requires estimates of potential gross income, vacancy and credit losses, operating expenses, mortgage amortization, and a thorough understanding of income tax rules regarding real estate investment. Estimates of after-tax equity reversion are obtained by subtracting selling expenses, taxes due on sale, and the amount outstanding on any loans from the sale price of the property. Converting these cash flows into present value is accomplished by discounting them at the rate of return that reflects the time value of money and the risk of the investment opportunity.

■ If the present value of after-tax cash flow and equity reversion exceed the equity required, then the net present value is positive, and the investor should choose to accept the project.

■ The same tools used to evaluate "buy-and-hold" properties can be used to analyze other types of real estate investment, including property flips.

KEY TERMS

after-tax cash flow

after-tax equity reversion

appreciation

before-tax cash flow

before-tax equity reversion

book value

capital gain

capital gain tax

capital gain tax rate

cost recovery allowance

debt service

discounted cash flow model

effective gross income

financial leverage

gross selling price

income taxes

initial equity

internal rate of return

investment

net operating income

net present value

net selling price

operating cash flow

operating expenses

potential gross income

property flipping

required rate of return

risk

taxable income

vacancy and credit losses

wealth maximization objective

STUDY EXERCISES

1. What are the attractions of real estate as an investment?

2. What are the disadvantages of real estate as an investment?

3. Explain the logic behind the net present value decision rule and the internal rate of return decision rule.

4. Why do you suppose the depreciable life for residential investment properties is shorter than that of nonresidential properties? How does this fact influence an investor's decisions?

5. A real estate broker is offering an apartment building for sale that has the following characteristics:

    a. The asking price is $3.5 million, with the land valued at $500,000.

    b. The 160 apartment units rent for $450 per month with rent expected to increase by 4 percent per year starting in year two.

    c. Vacancy and bad debt allowance is 6 percent of the potential gross income.

    d. Operating expenses are expected to be 32 percent of effective gross income each year.

    e. The real estate agent estimates that the value of the property will be $4.4 million at the end of the five-year investment horizon.

    f. A 12 percent, 20-year mortgage for $2 million is available with monthly payments.

    g. The investment horizon is five years, beginning January 2007 and ending December 2012. The investor's ordinary income tax rate is 28 percent and his or her capital gain tax rate is 15 percent. The investor has several profitable real estate investments and can utilize any tax losses. The appropriate discount rate for this investment (the required rate of return) is 18 percent.

    Calculate the relevant cash flows for this investment and apply the NPV and IRR rules to decide whether to pursue this project.

6. Suppose the property in the flip example on pages 447–48 sells for only $315,000 and instead of selling on May 1 sells on June 1. Taking into consideration the addition accrued interest, what is the expected return to the investor (annualized IRR)?

■ FURTHER READING ──────────────────────────────────────

Jaffe, A.J., and C.F Sirmans. *Fundamentals of Real Estate Investment,* 3rd ed. Englewood Cliffs, N.J.: Prentice-Hall, 1995.

Kolbe, Phillip T., and Gaylon E. Greer. *Investment Analysis for Real Estate Decisions,* 6th ed. Chicago: Dearborn Real Estate Education, 2003.

A

absorption rate the number of units capable of being absorbed by the market over a given time period.

acceleration clause clause in a promissory note that permits the lender to demand payment in full of any unpaid principal and any interest due in the event of default.

acceptance an expression of satisfaction with an offer.

accrued depreciation loss in value from any cause.

actual cash value the cost of replacing an insured item minus the amount by which the item has depreciated in value since it was new.

adaptive use use of a building in a manner different from the use for which it was originally designed.

adjustable-rate mortgage a loan whose interest rate is periodically adjusted based on the current interest rate environment.

ad valorem tax a tax levied as a percentage of the value of the taxed item.

adverse possession the acquisition of property as a result of "actual and exclusive, open and notorious, hostile and continuous" possession under a claim of right for a statutory period of time.

after-tax cash flow annual operating cash flow that remains after expenses, debt service, and taxes have been paid.

after-tax equity reversion the amount of money generated by the sale of an investment after taxes have been paid and any debts extinguished.

agency a legal relationship between a principal and an agent.

agent the party authorized to conduct business on the principal's behalf.

agreements for deed a type of seller financing in which the borrower/buyer makes payments to the seller/lender until an agreed-upon amount has been paid and the seller/lender then delivers the deed to the buyer.

air lot property that does not actually touch the ground.

airport hotel a hotel near an airport that caters to business travelers.

air rights property rights associated with the space above the surface of the earth.

alienable a property owner's right to transfer interests owned in a property during his or her lifetime.

amortization the process of gradually retiring a loan or other asset; also, the requirement that a nonconforming use be discontinued after a stated period of time.

amortization schedule a table showing the breakdown of principal and interest paid over the life of a mortgage.

amortizing loan a loan whose balance is gradually retired by periodic payments.

annuity a series of equal amounts, received one at the end of each period, for a specified number of periods.

anticipation the idea that the current value of a property depends on the anticipated utility or income that will accrue to the property owner in the future.

appraisal an estimate of value.

Appraisal Foundation a nonprofit educational organization formed by the appraisal profession in 1987.

appraisal process a systematic procedure employed to arrive at an estimate of value and convey that estimate to the appraisal user.

Appraisal Qualification Board under FIRREA, established minimum education and experience guidelines that states must use to issue appraisal licenses and certifications.

Appraisal Standards Board set forth the rules appraisers must follow when developing an appraisal and reporting its results.

appreciation increase in property value of a property for tax purposes.

assessed value the estimated value of a property for tax purposes.

assessment the process of estimating the market value for all properties within a property tax jurisdiction.

assessment ratio the fraction used to determine assessed value from market value.

asset manager a company executive charged with management of the firm's real estate facilities and activities.

assignment the act of passing all of one's rights and responsibilities under a legal agreement to a third party.

axial model a model of urban growth patterns based on transportation routes.

B

balloon payment a lump sum payment due on a specified date in the future.

bargain and sale deed a deed that simply states that the grantor has title to the property and the right to convey it but does not contain any express covenants or warranties to the title's validity.

base lines east-west lines used as reference points in the rectangular survey system.

before-tax cash flow annual operating cash flow that remains after expenses and debt service have been paid.

before-tax equity reversion the amount of money generated by the sale of an investment before taxes have been paid.

bid-rent curve theoretical relationship between distance and land rent.

blockbusting the illegal practice of encouraging property owners to sell their homes when minorities begin moving into an area.

book value value of a property as stated on the company's books.

breach of contract failure to perform a required contractual obligation.

broker an intermediary who brings together buyers and sellers, assists in negotiating agreements between them, executes their orders, and receives compensation for services rendered.

building codes regulations that establish standards for the construction of new buildings and the alteration of existing ones.

bulk limitations zoning regulations that control the percentage of lot area that may be occupied by buildings.

business owner's policy an insurance policy for small and medium-sized businesses.

business risk uncertainty arising from changing economic conditions that affect an investment's ability to generate returns.

buyer representation agreement the legal agreement between a buyer and a broker hired to represent the buyer's interests.

buyer's agent a broker who is legally obligated to represent a buyer's interests.

C

capacity legal ability to understand and accept the terms of a contract.

capital gain the amount calculated as net sale proceeds less original purchase price plus all depreciation deductions taken in previous years.

capital gain tax taxes assessed on capital gains.

capital gain tax rate   a preferential tax rate given to long-term investors.

capitalization rate   the relationship between income and value, where the capitalization rate equals net operating income divided by property value.

capital market   the market for capital assets of all types.

cash on cash return   the amount calculated by dividing the amount of equity invested in a property by an estimate of annual before-tax cash flow (BTCF ÷ equity).

CC&Rs   convenants, conditions, and restrictions.

central business district   an unplanned series of buildings constructed along major streets in the center of town.

certified general appraiser   an appraiser who is certified by the state to perform appraisals on all property types.

certified residential appraiser   an appraiser who is certified by the state to perform residential appraisals regardless of complexity.

chain of title   ownership history of a specific property.

change   the idea that economic, social, political, and environmental forces are constantly causing changes that affect the value of real estate.

chattel   personal property.

closing   the settlement of a real estate transaction.

closing costs   costs associated with closing a real estate transaction.

closing statement   a worksheet showing the sources and uses of funds in a real estate transaction.

coinsurance   the joint assumption of risk by two or more parties.

commercial bank   private financial institutions organized to accept deposits from individuals and businesses and to loan these funds to all types of borrowers.

commercial hotel   a hotel that caters primarily to businesspeople and conventioneers.

commercial mortgage-backed securities   traded securities that have commercial mortgages as their collateral and source of cash flow.

commission   the compensation received by a broker for services rendered.

commission agreement   an agreement between a seller and a broker for the payment of a commission if the broker is successful in locating a buyer for the seller's property.

common area maintenance fees (CAM fees)   costs of maintaining the common areas of a commercial property that are typically passed through to tenants.

community   an area containing properties of similar type. It also can be defined by reference to geographical area; to social, religious, or ethnic ties; or to income group.

community center   designed to serve an area within a 3- to 5-mile radius with a wider variety of merchandise than a neighborhood center.

community property   theory under which all property acquired during a marriage is considered to be equally owned by the husband and wife, regardless of the financial contribution each spouse actually made to the property's acquisition.

community shopping center   a shopping center containing between 100,000 and 300,000 square feet of gross leasable area that is designed to serve an area within a 3- to 5-mile radius.

comparative advantage   the advantage one locale has over another because of transportation facilities, created environment, natural resources, or its labor force.

compounding   the process of converting present amounts into future amounts.

compound interest   interest earned on a principal amount plus any interest previously earned.

comprehensive general plan   a statement of land-use policies that shape the future development of a community.

comprehensive zoning   division of a community's land into specific land-use districts to regulate the use of land and buildings and the intensity of various uses.

concentric-circle model   a model of urban growth patterns based on concentric zones surrounding a central business district.

concurrent estate   ownership interests held jointly by two or more owners.

condominium   a form of joint ownership whereby the property owners own their individual units separately but share ownership of common areas; a building owned in this manner.

condominium declaration   legal document that describes the individual units and common areas of a property owned as a condominium, creates an association to govern the property, and sets forth restrictions on use.

conservation easement   a type of negative easement that prevents specific uses of the real estate by the owner, generally used to protect open space.

consideration   anything that incurs legal detriment or the forgoing of a legal benefit.

Consumer Credit Protection Act   the Truth-in-Lending law.

contingencies   terms of a contract that may result in the contract being canceled if certain events occur.

contingent remainder   a remainder interest that has conditions attached that can prevent the remainderman from receiving a present interest in the property.

contract   a legal device used by two or more persons to indicate they have reached an agreement.

contract for deed   an arrangement that stretches out payments to the seller over time while allowing the seller to retain legal title until the debt is paid.

contractual capacity   the mental ability to understand what a contract represents and the meaning of its terms.

contribution   the idea that the value of a component part of a property depends on the amount it contributes to the value of the whole.

conventional loan   mortgage loans not insured or guaranteed by a government agency but that may carry private mortgage insurance.

cooperative   a form of joint ownership whereby the property owners own shares of stock in a corporation that owns the property and are entitled to occupy space within the building.

cost approach   a method used to estimate value by implementing the following steps: (1) estimate the value of the site as though it were vacant, (2) estimate the cost to produce the improvements, (3) subtract accrued depreciation, and (4) add site value to the estimated depreciated cost of the improvements.

cost recovery allowance   a deduction from taxable income provided to investors under the IRS code that allows investors to recover their initial investment in the property and delay taxes on this amount until the sale of the property in the future.

counteroffer   a response to an offer that represents a new offer.

covenant   a promise or guarantee made by a grantor in a deed.

covenant against encumbrances   an assurance made by the grantor that no liens or encumbrances other than those of public record exist against the property.

covenant of further assurances   an assurance made by the grantor that the grantor will execute any future documents needed to perfect the grantee's title.

covenant of quiet enjoyment   an assurance made by the grantor that no other party will disturb the grantee claiming to own the property or to have a lien on it; a promise from the lessor that the tenant has the right of exclusive possession of the property during the term of the lease.

covenant of seisin   an assurance made by the grantor that he or she is in full possession of the interest being conveyed by a deed and thus has the right to convey it.

covenants, conditions, and restrictions (CC&Rs) private techniques for restricting land use.

credit union   credit institution designed to serve a specific industry or community.

D

debt coverage ratio   calculated by dividing net operating income by debt service (NOI ÷ DS).

debt service   total amount paid to lenders to service outstanding debt.

deed   a written document that evidences ownership.

deed in lieu of foreclosure   a process by which a borrower transfers ownership of a mortgaged property to the lender rather than face foreclosure.

deed of trust   a security instrument that conveys title to the property pledged as collateral to a trustee until the loan is repaid.

defeasible estate   an estate that can be lost should some event or stated condition come to pass.

deficiency judgment   a judgment against a borrower following a foreclosure that permits the lender to recover any shortfall between the sale price and the balance of the loan.

demand   the amount or quantity of the good or service that will be desired at various prices.

depreciation   the amount by which the value of a building has declined since it was built as a consequence of physical deterioration, functional obsolescence, and economic obsolescence.

depreciation deduction   a noncash deduction permitted by the Internal Revenue Service (IRS) for capital recovery.

descendible   a property owner's right to transfer interests owned in a property to legal heirs should the owner die without a valid will.

devisable   a property owner's right to transfer interests owned in a property via a will.

direct losses   costs of replacing or repairing property destroyed or damaged.

discounted cash flow model   model used by investors to judge the suitability of a real estate investment.

discounting   the process of converting future amounts into present amounts.

discount point   1 percent of the loan amount.

discount shopping center   a community shopping center that contains a discount store as the main tenant.

documentary stamp tax   a fee charged by the public records authority to record a document in the records system.

dominant estate   the property benefited by the existence of an easement appurtenant.

dual agency   a legal relationship that exists when an agent is legally obligated to represent the best interests of two competing principals.

dual agent   an agent who attempts to work in the best interest of two parties on opposing sides of a transaction.

due-on-sale clause   a clause in a promissory note that requires the borrower to repay all amounts due immediately upon transferring the property to a new owner.

E

easement   a right given to another party by a landowner to use a property in a specified manner.

easement appurtenant   an easement with clearly identifiable dominant and servient estates.

easement by implication   an easement created from the factual circumstances even though an easement is not expressly created.

easement by prescription   a method of creating an easement as a result of "actual and exclusive, open and notorious, hostile and continuous" use for a statutory period of time.

easement in gross   an easement with only a servient estate.

economic base   employment in industries that bring income into a region from beyond its borders.

economic obsolescence   loss in value resulting from factors outside the property that affect its income-producing ability or degree of use.

effective gross income   potential gross income less vacancy and credit losses.

effective interest rate   the actual cost of borrowed funds expressed as an interest rate.

eminent domain the government's power to take private property for public use upon payment of just compensation.

encroachment an unauthorized invasion or intrusion of a fixture, building, or another improvement onto another person's property.

encumbrance restriction or limitation on ownership rights.

Equal Credit Opportunity Act act that prohibits discrimination in mortgage lending.

equilibrium when the price negotiated between demanders and suppliers results in the quantity of the good or service offered by suppliers equaling the quantity of the good or service as desired by the demanders.

escheat the government's right to own real estate following the owner's death in the absence of a valid will or legal heirs.

escrow agent a third party who facilitates a real estate closing.

escrow closing a closing using an escrow agent.

estate in land ownership interests in real property.

estate in severalty term used to describe ownership interests without regard to the number of owners.

estate pur autre vie when a life tenant is someone other than the person whose life the life estate is tied to.

eviction when a tenant is forced to vacate the premises for failing to adhere to the terms of the rental agreement.

exclusive-agency listing a listing agreement that guarantees the broker's right to a commission if the property is sold by any licensed real estate broker or salesperson.

exclusive-brokerage listing an agreement between a property owner and a single broker authorizing that broker to seek a buyer for the property in exchange for compensation.

exclusive-right-to-sell listing a listing agreement that guarantees the broker's right to a commission if the

property is sold by the seller or any licensed real estate broker or salesperson.

executed process of placing one's signature on a legal document.

executor's deed a special use deed used by the executor of an estate to transfer ownership without any assurances regarding the quality of title being transferred.

exemption an amount that is subtracted from taxable value to provide tax relief for certain types of property owners.

expense stop a limit on the amount of operating costs to be borne by the landlord in a commercial lease agreement.

export activities activities that produce goods and services for sale or consumption outside an area's borders.

express grant method of expressly creating an easement on a grantor's property.

express reservation method of expressly creating an easement on a grantee's property.

F

factory outlet center a shopping center consisting of retail outlet facilities where goods are sold directly to the public in stores owned and operated by the manufacturers.

Fair Credit Reporting Act law regulating credit reporting agencies.

fair housing laws laws that protect the rights of certain citizens in housing transactions.

Fannie Mae *See* Federal National Mortgage Association.

Federal Housing Administration an agency that was created by the federal government in 1934 to act as an insurance company for private mortgage lenders.

Federal National Mortgage Association an agency that was created by the federal government in 1938 to buy mortgages from lenders and to serve as a clearinghouse for secondary mortgage markets. Also known as Fannie Mae.

fee interest time-share a type of concurrent estate that splits ownership of a property over time across joint owners.

fee simple absolute estate the fullest and most complete set of ownership rights one can possess in real property.

FHA-insured loan a loan insured against default by the Federal Housing Administration.

fiduciary a person who is obligated to act in the best interest of another.

filtering the passage of housing to less affluent families as the housing ages.

Financial Institution Reform, Recovery, and Enforcement Act (FIRREA) law that established a regulatory framework for appraisers.

financial leverage the use of borrowed funds with the intention of magnifying investment returns.

financial risk uncertainty associated with the possibility of defaulting on borrowed funds used to finance an investment.

financing capacity the ability of a potential borrower to incur debt.

financing contingency a clause in a sales contract that permits the cancellation of the contract if the buyer cannot successfully obtain financing for the purchase of the property according to the terms specified in the sales contract.

fixed-rate mortgage a loan with a fixed interest rate over the loan term.

fixed-rent lease a lease contract that stipulates a fixed rent amount for the period of the lease.

fixture an item that was once personal property but has become part of the real estate.

flipping *See* property flipping.

Flood Disaster Protection Act law establishing the federal flood insurance program.

floor-area ratio relationship between the total floor area of a building and the total area of a site.

foreclosure the process of seizing control of the collateral for a loan and using the proceeds from its sale to satisfy a defaulted debt.

fraud a false statement made with the intention to mislead, that is material to a transaction, that is justifiably relied on by a client, and that results in injury to the client.

Freddie Mac Federal Home Loan Mortgage Corporation.

freehold estate ownership interests in real property.

freestanding retail a retail building not located in a shopping center.

functional obsolescence loss in value that occurs because a property has less utility or ability to generate income than a new property designed for the same use.

future value of a lump sum $FV = PV(1 + i)^n$

future value of an annuity

$$FVA = A\left[\frac{(1-i)^n - 1}{i}\right]$$

G

garden apartment a two-story or three-story building with a density of 10 to 20 units per acre.

general lien a security interest on all property owned by an individual.

general warranty deed the deed that offers the most protection to the grantee, complete with all relevant covenants and warranties.

gentrification the process of neighborhood rehabilitation causing value to rise dramatically as it becomes a desirable location.

gestation period the time between conception of the idea for a development project and its completion and entry into the available supply.

Ginnie Mae *See* Government National Mortgage Association.

Government National Mortgage Association a government organization that provides subsidized loans for certain mortgage borrowers. Also known as Ginnie Mae.

government-sponsored enterprises organizations such as Fannie Mae and Freddie Mac, which are authorized and supported by the U.S. government to operate a secondary mortgage market for residential loans.

graduated-rent lease a lease contract that stipulates scheduled rent increases over the period of the lease.

grant deed a type of deed that transfers ownership of property to the grantee.

grantee the party who receives a freehold estate in real property from a grantor.

grantor the party who transfers a freehold estate in real property to a grantee.

grantor and grantee indexes an index of grantors who have given an interest in real estate to another and people who have received such an interest (grantees).

gross absorption the total number of units or square footage absorbed by the market in a specified period of time.

gross income multiplier the relationship between income and value, where the gross income multiplier equals value divided by gross income.

gross leasable area the total floor area of a building designed for the tenants' use.

gross lease a lease contract stipulating that the landlord will pay all operating expenses, taxes, and insurance for the property during the period of the lease.

gross rent multiplier the relationship between rent and value, where the gross rent multiplier equals value divided by gross rent.

gross selling price the selling price before any deductions.

ground lease a long-term lease for vacant land.

H

height limitation regulations governing the maximum height of a building in feet or stories.

highest and best use that use, found to be legally permissible, physically possible, and financially feasible, that results in the highest land value; that use of land most likely to result in the greatest long-term economic return to the owner.

highrise apartment apartment buildings containing more than eight stories.

highway hotel a motel that caters primarily to businesspeople and vacationers who are in transit.

homeowner's policy an insurance policy that provides coverage of losses from fire and other perils, personal liability, medical payments, and theft.

housing finance system the arrangements and institutions that facilitate the financing of residential buildings.

HUD-1 Uniform Settlement Statement a settlement form approved by the Department of Housing and Urban Development.

hypothecation the practice of leaving borrowers in possession of their property while repaying a loan with interest.

I

impact fees fees charged to developers to raise funds for expansion of public facilities needed as a result of the new development.

impact zoning a technique to relate permitted uses of land to certain performance standards.

implied grant a method of implicitly creating an easement on a grantor's property.

implied reservation a method of implicitly creating an easement on a grantee's property.

incentive zoning a practice used by communities to encourage developers to provide certain publicly desired features in their developments in exchange for relaxed enforcement of the zoning code.

income approach   a method used to estimate value by discounting or capitalizing the expected future income that is expected to accrue to the property owner.

income tax   taxable income multiplied by the tax rate.

index lease   a lease in which rent payments are adjusted based on changes in the cost of living.

indirect losses   additional living expenses or loss of business income suffered before a damaged property is restored.

industrial park   controlled, parklike developments designed to accommodate specific types of industry.

in-filling   a method of city growth where open spaces between structures are filled in with new structures.

infrastructure   investment in public facilities such as roads, schools, etc.

inheritable freehold estate   an ownership interest that passes to heirs upon the death of the owner.

initial equity   purchase price of a project less a debt that is used to complete the purchase.

inspection and repair contingency   clause in a real estate contract that permits the buyer to have a qualified inspector examine the property for any physical defects that the seller may be obligated to repair.

insurable title   a title in real estate that a reputable title insurance company is willing to insure. An insurable title most frequently is one without major defect.

insurable value   an estimate of value for insurance purposes.

insurance binder   temporary evidence of insurance.

intensity of use   extent to which land in a particular zone may be used for its permitted purposes.

interest-only loan   a nonamortizing loan that requires periodic payments of interest and a single balloon payment of the principal at the end of the loan term.

interim use   temporary use of a property until such time that conditions are favorable to convert it to another use intended to be permanent.

internal rate of return   the discount rate that sets net present value exactly equal to zero.

inverse condemnation   a lawsuit initiated by a property owner to force the government to purchase a property whose value has been diminished by a governmental action.

investment   present sacrifice in anticipation of expected future benefit.

investment value   the worth of a property to a particular investor, based on that investor's personal standards of investment acceptability.

IRR decision rule   if the internal rate of return is greater than or equal to the required rate of return, accept the investment.

J

joint tenancy   joint ownership in which all owners have an equal, but undivided, interest in a property.

judgment lien   a lien placed on property to settle a judgment from a lawsuit.

judicial foreclosure   a court-ordered sale of the property following default by the mortgagor.

just compensation   the amount that must be paid a landowner when property is taken under eminent domain.

L

land contract   a contract that establishes an obligation to transfer title from a seller to a buyer at some future date based on an agreed-upon payment schedule.

land rent   the return that a parcel of land will bring in the open market.

lease   a legal agreement between lessor and lessee.

leased fee estate   the property owner's interest when the property is leased.

leasehold estate   a tenant's rights to use and possess (but not own) a property as defined in a lease agreement.

legal description   specific language that uniquely identifies a parcel of real estate.

lessee   the person who receives a leasehold interest in a property from the lessor.

lessor   the person who gives a leasehold interest in a property to a lessee.

liability insurance   insurance that protects the insured against lawsuits brought in response to supposed acts of negligence that result in injury or loss of property to the public.

license   a revocable personal privilege to use land for a particular purpose.

licensed real property appraiser   a person licensed by the state to perform noncomplex residential appraisals.

lien   a claim on a property as security for a debt or fulfillment of some monetary charge or obligation.

lien theory   a concept adopted by some states that recognizes that the mortgagee must foreclose on the property through a court action to acquire possession in the event of default.

life estate   an ownership interest in real property that normally ends upon the death of a named person.

life tenant   the person who holds the present interest in a life estate (may or may not be the person whose life the estate is tied to).

limited-service listing   an agreement between a property owner/seller that authorizes a broker to perform certain tasks to seek a buyer for the property.

liquidity risk   possibility of loss resulting from not being able to convert an asset into cash quickly should the need arise.

listing agreement   the legal agreement between a broker and a property owner that authorizes the broker to attempt to sell the property.

listing broker   the broker who negotiates the listing agreement with the seller.

littoral proprietor   owner of land that adjoins navigable bodies of water.

loan origination   the process of creating a new loan agreement between a borrower and a lender.

loan-to-value ratio (LTV ratio)   the ratio obtained by dividing the loan amount by an estimate of property value.

M

management agreement   a legal agreement authorizing a property manager to conduct business on behalf of the landlord.

mandatory dedication   a requirement that developers donate property to the community for public use as a condition for obtaining development approval.

manufactured home   a dwelling unit that is manufactured in a factory and then moved to a particular site.

market   set of circumstances and arrangement through which buyers and sellers exchange goods and services.

marketable title   a title free and clear of all past, present, and future claims that would cause a reasonable purchaser to reject such title.

market analysis   vacant space plus space in construction divided by net absorption per month.

market value   the most probable price that a property should bring in a competitive and open market under all conditions requisite to a fair sale, the buyer and seller each acting prudently and knowledgeably, and assuming the price is not affected by undue stimulus. Implicit in this definition is the consummation of a sale as of a specified date and the passing of title from seller to buyer under conditions whereby

1. buyer and seller are typically motivated;
2. both parties are well informed or well advised and acting in what they consider their best interests;
3. a reasonable time is allowed for exposure in the open market;
4. payment is made in terms of cash in U.S. dollars or in terms of financial arrangements comparable thereto; and
5. the price represents the normal consideration for the property sold unaffected by special or creative financing or sales concessions by anyone associated with the sale.

mechanic's lien   a claim on a property held by a supplier of materials or labor for nonpayment of a debt.

metes-and-bounds description a legal method for describing the exact boundaries of a property; *metes* refers to the distances and *bounds* refers to the directions of the property's boundaries.

midrise apartment apartment building consisting of four to eight stories.

mill one one-thousandth, or 0.001.

millage rate the tax rate imposed on property owners, expressed as the dollars of tax for each $1,000 of property value.

mineral rights ownership rights associated with minerals that may be located below the surface of the earth.

minimum lot sizes the minimum lot size allowed by zoning or other land-use regulations.

misrepresentation a false statement that is material to a transaction, that is justifiably relied upon by a client, and that results in injury to the client.

months supply the number of months required to absorb the current supply.

monument a visible marker, either a natural or an artificial object used to establish the lines and boundaries of a survey.

mortgage a contract by which real property is pledged as security for a loan.

mortgage-backed securities securities issued by mortgage holders to investors who wish to invest indirectly in the mortgage market.

mortgage banker firms that borrow money from commercial banks to originate new loans to mortgage borrowers.

mortgage broker firms that act as brokers between loan applications and lenders.

mortgage debt ratio the percentage of a borrower's gross monthly income that is required to meet housing expenses.

mortgagee the lender in a mortgage loan transaction.

mortgage life insurance a diminishing term life insurance policy whose amount is keyed to the outstanding mortgage balance.

mortgage payment

$$PMT = PVA \left[\frac{i}{1 - \dfrac{1}{(1+i)^n}} \right]$$

mortgagor the borrower in a mortgage loan transaction.

multiple listing service (MLS) an arrangement in which brokers share their listings with other brokers in exchange for a share of the commission generated by a transaction.

multiple-nuclei model a model of urban growth patterns that emphasizes more than one center of commercial activity.

N

negative renewal clause a clause in a lease contract that automatically renews the lease in the event neither party desires to terminate the agreement.

neighborhood a geographic area containing complementary land uses in which property values tend to move together.

neighborhood center a shopping center intended to serve customers from a specific geographic area.

net absorption the amount of space rented to tenants or sold to buyers after taking into consideration space vacated by tenants or owners.

net lease a lease that stipulates that the lessee will pay operating expenses for a property during the lease period.

net listing a listing agreement in which the broker is entitled to receive as commission any amount above a base price.

net-net lease a lease that stipulates that the lessee will pay operating expenses and insurance for the property during the lease period.

net-net-net lease a lease that stipulates that the lessee will pay operating expenses, insurance, and property taxes for the property during the lease period.

net operating income   annual operating cash flow that remains after expenses have been paid.

net present value   present value of inflows minus present value of outflows.

net sales proceeds   proceeds from sale after selling expenses have been paid.

net selling price   the difference between the sales price and selling expenses.

nonconforming use   a use of land that does not conform to the current land-use controls imposed by the government.

nonjudicial foreclosure   a situation in which the security instrument grants the lender power of sale should the borrower default.

NPV decision rule   if the net present value is greater than or equal to zero, accept the investment.

nuisance   the use of property in such a way as to harm the property of others.

O

offer   a statement that specifies the position of its maker (offeror) and indicates that the offeror is willing to be bound by the conditions stated.

offeree   the receiving party in a contact.

offeror   the party making the offer in a contract.

Office of Federal Housing Enterprise Oversight   a federal agency that oversees the operations of government-sponsored enterprises in the mortgage market.

office park   a community of lowrise office structures under central management and administration, usually located in the suburbs and adjacent to a major freeway.

open listing   a listing agreement in which a broker is entitled to receive a commission only in the event the broker procures a buyer for the property.

operating cash flow   rent paid by tenants for the use of space in a property.

operating expense ratio   defined as operating expenses divided by effective gross income (OE ÷ EGI).

operating expenses   the direct expenses of a property.

option-to-buy contract   a contract that gives one party the right, but not an obligation, to purchase a property within a specified time horizon at a specified price.

origination fees   fees charged by lenders in the origination process.

P

partial performance   fulfillment of the terms of an agreement to such an extent that the existence of the agreement may be reasonably inferred.

patio house   a detached house with at least one wall that touches the property line.

percentage lease   a lease for a property used for commercial purposes under which the rental payments are based on some percentage of sales made on the premises.

performance zoning   regulations that restrict land-use based on the environmental carrying capacity of the site.

personal articles floater policy   an insurance policy that insures specific personal property items for specific amounts.

personal excess liability policy   an insurance policy that insures against disastrous liability claims involving a home, automobile, or boat.

personal property   movable items such as cars, clothing, books, and so on.

personal property replacement cost endorsement   an insurance policy that allows the holder to recoup the full replacement cost of stolen or damaged goods rather than the actual cash value of the goods.

physical deterioration   loss in value that occurs from ordinary wear and tear, vandalism, or neglect.

planned unit development   a type of zoning that may allow waivers of certain bulk and use regulations.

plat   a detailed land survey drawing, usually prepared by a professional surveyor, that shows the features of a property and its legal description.

plex   a form of attached housing containing two or more units, each with its own outside entrance.

police power   the government's power to regulate the way private property is used to protect the health, safety, morals, and general welfare of the public.

policy   a contract providing insurance coverage.

population-serving activities   activities that produce goods and services for sale or consumption within an area's borders.

positive renewal clause   a clause on a lease that states that if no notice of renewal is given properly, normally one to two months prior to the expiration of the lease, the lease terminates at the end of the lease period.

possibility of reversion   the future interest that follows a qualified fee determinable estate.

potential gross income   the total income potential of an investment, assuming all space is leased and all rents are collected.

power center   a large strip-style shopping center that is anchored by one or more "big box" retailers, along with smaller shops.

power of termination   the future interest that follows a qualified fee conditional estate.

premium   the consideration paid for an insurance policy.

prepayment   early repayment of principal.

prepayment clause   a clause in a promissory note that determines the borrower's right to prepay any or all of the principal before it is due.

prescriptive easement   an easement created when someone other than the owner uses the land "openly, hostilely, and continuously" for a statutory time period.

present value of a lump sum

$$PV = \frac{FV}{(1 + i)^n}$$

present value of an annuity

$$PVA = A\left[\frac{1 - \dfrac{1}{(1 + i)^n}}{i}\right]$$

price   actual amount paid for a property in a particular transaction.

primary mortgage market   transactions that occur between a borrower and a lender.

primary trade area   the geographic area immediately surrounding a shopping center that typically accounts for 60 percent to 70 percent of the center's sales.

principal   the person who authorizes an agent to conduct business on his or her behalf.

principal meridians   north-south lines used as reference points in the rectangular survey system.

principle of anticipation   the anticipated utility or income that will accrued to the property owner in the future.

principle of change   the notion that economic, social, political, and environmental forces are constantly causing changes that affect the value of real property.

principle of contribution   the principle that the value of a component part of a property depends on the amount it contributes to value of the whole.

principle of substitution   the principle that holds that a prudent buyer will pay no more for property than the cost of acquiring an equally desirable substitute.

prior appropriation doctrine   theory that states that the first person to use a body of water for some beneficial economic purpose has the right to use all the water needed, even though landowners who later find a use for the water may be precluded from using it.

private mortgage insurance (PMI)   nongovernment insurance that provides protection for the lender against the borrower's default.

profit a prendre   a nonpossessory interest in real property that permits the holder to remove specified natural resources from a property.

promissory note   a written promise to pay money owed.

property   an object that can be owned or possessed.

property flipping   the process of buying properties, renovating them to some degree, and reselling them with the goal of making a profit.

property manager   a person authorized by a property owner to manage the property on his or her behalf.

proprietary lease   a co-op lease that gives the owner the right to occupy a specific unit.

purchasing power risk   uncertainty associated with the possibility that the amount of goods and services that can be acquired with a given amount of money will decline.

Q

qualified estate   an estate that can be lost should an event or stated condition come to pass.

qualified fee conditional estate   an estate that a court may rule has been terminated should some condition be violated.

qualified fee determinable estate   an estate that terminates automatically should some condition be violated.

qualified fee estate   type of ownership in which the owner's rights can be lost in the future.

quitclaim deed   a deed used to transfer any interest a grantor may or may not have in a property, without implying that the grantor has a valid interest to convey.

R

range lines   north-south lines that run parallel to principal meridians in the rectangular survey system.

rate of return   the percentage return from a property.

real estate   land and structures that are attached to it.

real estate asset market   the market in which ownership of investment properties is traded between buyers and sellers.

real estate broker   an individual licensed by a state to represent others in real estate transactions in exchange for compensation.

real estate investment trusts (REITs)   publicly traded companies that own and manage real estate portfolios.

real estate salesperson   an individual licensed by a state to assist real estate brokers in arranging real estate transactions in exchange for compensation.

Real Estate Settlement Procedures Act (RESPA)   law regulating the closing procedures in a real estate loan.

real estate space market   market in which occupancy of investment properties is purchased by tenants from owners.

real property   the legal interests associated with the ownership of real estate.

reappraisal lease   a lease that stipulates that the rent will be adjusted periodically as the value of the building changes, as determined by an appraisal.

rectangular survey system   a grid-based system used to legally describe the location of a property.

refinancing   the process of obtaining a new loan and using the proceeds to repay an existing loan.

regional center   a shopping center that contains between 300,000 and 750,000 square feet in gross leasable area and contains at least one full-line department store.

remainder   the future interest associated with a life estate held by someone other than the grantor.

remainderman   the party who holds the remainder interest associated with a life estate.

renewal option   a clause in a lease agreement that defines the parties' agreement regarding renewal of the lease upon termination.

rental agreement   contract between a landlord and a tenant authorizing the tenant to use and occupy space under certain terms and conditions.

replacement cost   the estimated cost of replacing the property being appraised with a property built at today's prices, by current construction methods, and with the same usefulness as the one being appraised.

reproduction cost   the cost of constructing an exact replacement of the property being appraised with the same or similar materials, at today's prices.

required rate of return   a minimum acceptable rate of return.

residential mortgage credit report a standardized credit report used in the underwriting process for residential loans.

resort hotel a hotel that caters to individuals or families on vacation.

restrictive covenant limitations placed on a property by a landowner or previous landowner that prevents the property from being used in certain ways.

reversion the future interest associated with a life estate held by the grantor.

right of first refusal the right of a person to have the first opportunity to either purchase or lease real property.

right of reentry the landlord's reversionary right to reoccupy the property at the expiration of the lease.

right of survivorship the right of surviving joint owners to automatically divide the share owned by a deceased owner.

right to use time-share a form of leasehold estate that permits the holder to use a property for a certain period each year.

riparian rights doctrine theory that permits landowners whose land underlies or borders non-navigable bodies of water to use all the water needed as long as the use does not deprive other landowners who are also entitled to use some of the water.

risk the chance of loss; also, the uncertainty about the actual rate of return an investment will provide over the holding period.

S

sale-and-leaseback an arrangement whereby a property owner sells the property to an investor and immediately leases the property back from the investor.

sales comparison approach a method used to estimate value by comparing the property to other properties that have recently sold for known prices.

sales contract a contract providing for the transfer of property.

savings institution firms that receive deposits from savers and loaning those funds to residential borrowers.

secondary mortgage market transactions involving mortgages that occur between investors.

secondary trade area the area outside the primary trade area that typically accounts for 15 percent to 20 percent of sales at a shopping center.

section 1-square-mile rectangles that divide townships into 36 equal areas of 640 acres each.

sector model a model of urban growth in which types of development tend to extend outward in wedge-shaped sections from the center of the city.

secured loan a loan for which a specific item has been pledged as collateral.

security deposit an amount required by a lessor in advance of occupancy as security against potential damages caused by the lessee.

seller's agent a real estate broker who is obligated to represent the best interest of the seller.

selling broker the broker who actually locates a buyer for a property.

servient estate the property burdened by the existence of an easement appurtenant or easement in gross.

setback a common land-use regulation that requires a certain amount of space between improvements on a property and the property lines.

setback requirements the amount of distance between the property border and the location of the structure.

settlement closing of a real estate transaction.

sinking fund payment

$$SFP = FVA\left[\frac{i}{(1+i)^n - 1}\right]$$

specialty shopping center a shopping center that focuses on unusual market segments and usually offers high-quality, high-priced merchandise in boutique-type stores.

special warranty deed similar to a general warranty deed, except the covenants and warranties apply only to events that occurred during the grantor's period of ownership.

specific lien a security interest that relates only to a specific parcel of real estate.

specific performance a requirement that the terms of a contract be exactly complied with.

statute of frauds a law designed to prevent fraudulent practices involving contracts.

steering the illegal practice of steering potential homebuyers into certain areas to influence the racial or ethnic composition of the areas.

step-up rent lease a type of rental agreement in which the rent is scheduled to increase over time according to an agreed-upon schedule.

strict foreclosure a situation in which the lender is entitled to immediate ownership of the property should the borrower default.

strip shopping center a neighborhood shopping center built in a straight line, with stores tied together by a canopy over a pedestrian walk.

subagent an agent of an agent of a principal.

subdivision regulations the standards and procedures that regulate the subdivision of land for development and sale.

subleasing the act of transferring a portion of the leasehold estate to a third party.

subprime mortgage loans a type of loan made to borrowers with less than stellar credit histories or other issues that prevent the borrower from obtaining the most favorable loan terms.

substitution the idea that a prudent buyer will pay no more for a property than the cost of acquiring an equally desirable substitute in the open market.

super-regional shopping center a shopping center that exceeds 750,000 square feet of gross leasable area and includes at least three department stores.

superstore a very large discount store with between 60,000 and 150,000 square feet under one roof.

supply the amount or quantity of the good or service that will be offered at various prices.

T

taxable income income subject to taxation.

taxable value assessed value for property taxes less exemptions.

tenancy at sufferance a leasehold estate that defines a tenant's rights to occupy the property against the wishes of the lessor.

tenancy at will an informal leasehold estate of indeterminable length that may last as long as the parties agree.

tenancy by the entirety a form of concurrent estate in which a husband and wife can own property jointly.

tenancy for a stated period a leasehold estate that has definite starting and ending dates.

tenancy from period to period a leasehold estate that continues to automatically renew each period unless terminated by either party.

tenancy in common a form of concurrent estate in which each owner has an undivided interest in the property.

term the length of time a landlord and tenant agree to maintain their relationship involving rental property.

test of adaptability test to determine whether an item of personal property has become a fixture. An item that has been specifically adapted to the real estate is generally considered a fixture.

test of attachment test to determine whether an item of personal property has become a fixture. An item that has been permanently attached to the real property and could not be removed without damage to the land or building is generally considered a fixture.

test of intent of the parties evidence, usually written, showing that the parties intended the item of personal property to become a fixture.

time-sharing a form of concurrent estate that splits ownership of a property across owners and across time.

time value of money principle a dollar in hand is worth more than a dollar to be received in the future because it can either be consumed immediately or put to work to earn a return.

title the legal right to ownership.

title abstract a written history of a property's chain of title.

title contingency a clause in a sales contract that cancels the contract if the seller cannot provide clear title to the buyer.

title insurance an insurance policy that protects property owners and lenders against undiscovered defects in a property's chain of title.

title opinion an attorney's opinion of the quality of title for a specific property.

title perfect of record a property for which there are no defects.

title search the process of verifying the quality of title.

title theory a concept adopted by some states that recognizes that the mortgagee has the right to immediate possession of mortgaged property in the event of default.

Torrens system a system of land registration used by a few states as an alternative to grantor/grantee indexes.

total debt ratio the percentage of a borrower's gross monthly income required to meet monthly contractual expenses.

town house a form of attached housing in which each unit has its own front door but shares one or two walls with adjacent units.

township a 36-square-mile area formed by township and range lines in the rectangular survey system.

township lines east-west lines that run parallel to base lines in the rectangular survey system.

trade area the geographic area from which the major portion of the patronage necessary to support the shopping center is to be drawn.

trade fixture personal property used in a trade or business.

trainee appraiser a beginning appraiser who must work under the supervision of a licensed or certified appraiser who is responsible for the work of the trainee.

transaction broker a broker who provides limited representation to a seller or buyer in a real estate transaction.

transferable development rights the right to sell one's ability to develop a property to another property owner who desires a more intense use of the second property.

transfer of development rights a system whereby landowners can sell their development rights to other property owners so the other property owners can use their property more intensely.

two-step mortgage a loan whose interest rate is adjusted once during the term of the loan.

U

underwriting process of evaluating the risk of a loan applicant and the property being pledged in order to make a decision regarding the loan application.

unsecured loan a loan for which no specific item has been pledged as collateral.

urban and regional economics the study of the economics of urban and regional growth.

U.S. housing financial system the system of financing mortgages in the United States.

V

vacancy and credit losses revenues not received due to vacancy in the property or uncollectible rents.

vacancy rate the percentage of units vacant in a property.

VA-guaranteed loans a loan in which the lender is protected from the borrower's default by a guarantee of repayment from the Department of Veterans Affairs.

variance permission granted by a government for a landowner to use the property in a manner not ordinarily permitted.

vested remainder a remainder interest when the remainderman is guaranteed ownership of the property at some time in the future.

voidable capable of being rescinded, as a contract entered into by a minor or by a person who has been declared insane.

W

warranty a promise or guarantee made by a grantor in a deed.

warranty deed a deed that transfers title from a grantor to a grantee and obligates the grantor to certain promises specified in the document or by reference to statute.

warranty deed without covenants a warranty deed that omits some or all of the promises typically made by the grantor to the grantee.

warranty forever an assurance made by the grantor to always defend the title conveyed to the grantee.

warranty of habitability an assurance made by a lessor that the property is fit for its intended use.

water rights the right to withdraw water from the land.

wealth maximization objective the investment objective of investors.

Z

zoning the process of dividing a community's land into districts in which only certain uses of the land are allowed.

zoning variance administrative relief that allows an owner to deviate slightly from a strict interpretation of the zoning ordinance.

Time Value of Money Tables

This appendix presents the time value of money tables (often called *capitalization tables*) for interest rates of 6, 8, 10, 12, and 14 percent.

TIME VALUE OF MONEY AT 6%

Periods	Future Value Factors	Future Value of Annuity Factors	Sinking Fund Factors	Present Value Factors	Present Value of Annuity Factors	Mortgage Constant
1	1.060000	1.000000	1.000000	0.943396	0.943396	1.060000
2	1.123600	2.060000	0.485437	0.889996	1.833393	0.545437
3	1.191016	3.183600	0.314110	0.839619	2.673012	0.374110
4	1.262477	4.374616	0.228592	0.792094	3.465106	0.288592
5	1.338226	5.637093	0.177396	0.747258	4.212364	0.237396
6	1.418519	6.975319	0.143363	0.704960	4.917324	0.203363
7	1.503630	8.393838	0.119135	0.665057	5.582381	0.179135
8	1.593848	9.897468	0.101036	0.627412	6.209794	0.161036
9	1.689479	11.491316	0.087022	0.591898	6.801692	0.147022
10	1.790848	13.180795	0.075868	0.558395	7.360087	0.135868
11	1.898299	14.971643	0.066793	0.526787	7.886875	0.126793
12	2.012196	16.869941	0.059277	0.496969	8.383844	0.119277
13	2.132928	18.882138	0.052960	0.468839	8.852683	0.112960
14	2.260904	21.015066	0.047585	0.442301	9.294984	0.107585
15	2.396558	23.275970	0.042963	0.417265	9.712249	0.102963
16	2.540352	25.672528	0.038952	0.393646	10.105895	0.098952
17	2.692773	28.212880	0.035445	0.371364	10.477260	0.095445
18	2.854339	30.905653	0.032357	0.350344	10.827603	0.092357
19	3.025600	33.759992	0.029621	0.330513	11.158117	0.089621
20	3.207135	36.785591	0.027185	0.311805	11.469921	0.087185
21	3.399564	39.992727	0.025005	0.294155	11.764077	0.085005
22	3.603537	43.392290	0.023046	0.277505	12.041582	0.083046
23	3.819750	46.995828	0.021278	0.261797	12.303379	0.081278
24	4.048935	50.815577	0.019679	0.246978	12.550358	0.079679
25	4.291871	54.864512	0.018227	0.232998	12.783356	0.078227
26	4.549383	59.156383	0.016904	0.219810	13.003166	0.076904
27	4.822346	63.705766	0.015697	0.207368	13.210534	0.075697
28	5.111687	68.528112	0.014593	0.195630	13.406164	0.074593
29	5.418388	73.639798	0.013580	0.184557	13.590721	0.073580
30	5.743491	79.058186	0.012649	0.174110	13.764831	0.072649
31	6.088101	84.801677	0.011792	0.164255	13.929086	0.071792
32	6.453387	90.889778	0.011002	0.154957	14.084043	0.071002
33	6.840590	97.343165	0.010273	0.146186	14.230230	0.070273
34	7.251025	104.183755	0.009598	0.137911	14.368141	0.069598
35	7.686087	111.434780	0.008974	0.130105	14.498246	0.068974
36	8.147252	119.120867	0.008395	0.122741	14.620987	0.068395
37	8.636087	127.268119	0.007857	0.115793	14.736780	0.067857
38	9.154252	135.904206	0.007358	0.109239	14.846019	0.067358
39	9.703507	145.058458	0.006894	0.103055	14.949075	0.066894
40	10.285718	154.761966	0.006462	0.097222	15.046297	0.066462
41	10.902861	165.047684	0.006059	0.091719	15.138016	0.066059
42	11.557033	175.950545	0.005683	0.086527	15.224543	0.065683
43	12.250455	187.507577	0.005333	0.081630	15.306173	0.065333
44	12.985482	199.758032	0.005006	0.077009	15.383182	0.065006
45	13.764611	212.743514	0.004701	0.072650	15.455832	0.064701
46	14.590487	226.508125	0.004415	0.068538	15.524370	0.064415
47	15.465917	241.098612	0.004148	0.064658	15.589028	0.064148
48	16.393872	256.564529	0.003898	0.060998	15.650027	0.063898
49	17.377504	272.958401	0.003664	0.057546	15.707572	0.063664
50	18.420154	290.335905	0.003444	0.054288	15.761861	0.063444

TIME VALUE OF MONEY AT 8%

Periods	Future Value Factors	Future Value of Annuity Factors	Sinking Fund Factors	Present Value Factors	Present Value of Annuity Factors	Mortgage Constant
1	1.080000	1.000000	1.000000	0.925926	0.925926	1.080000
2	1.166400	2.080000	0.480769	0.857339	1.783265	0.560769
3	1.259712	3.246400	0.308034	0.793832	2.577097	0.388034
4	1.360489	4.506112	0.221921	0.735030	3.312127	0.301921
5	1.469328	5.866601	0.170456	0.680583	3.992710	0.250456
6	1.586874	7.335929	0.136315	0.630170	4.622880	0.216315
7	1.713824	8.922803	0.112072	0.583490	5.206370	0.192072
8	1.850930	10.636628	0.094015	0.540269	5.746639	0.174015
9	1.999005	12.487558	0.080080	0.500249	6.246888	0.160080
10	2.158925	14.486562	0.069029	0.463193	6.710081	0.149029
11	2.331639	16.645487	0.060076	0.428883	7.138964	0.140076
12	2.518170	18.977126	0.052695	0.397114	7.536078	0.132695
13	2.719624	21.495297	0.046522	0.367698	7.903776	0.126522
14	2.937194	24.214920	0.041297	0.340461	8.244237	0.121297
15	3.172169	27.152114	0.036830	0.315242	8.559479	0.116830
16	3.425943	30.324283	0.032977	0.291890	8.851369	0.112977
17	3.700018	33.750226	0.029629	0.270269	9.121638	0.109629
18	3.996020	37.450244	0.026702	0.250249	9.371887	0.106702
19	4.315701	41.446263	0.024128	0.231712	9.603599	0.104128
20	4.660957	45.761964	0.021852	0.214548	9.818147	0.101852
21	5.033834	50.422921	0.019832	0.198656	10.016803	0.099832
22	5.436540	55.456755	0.018032	0.183940	10.200744	0.098032
23	5.871464	60.893296	0.016422	0.170315	10.371059	0.096422
24	6.341181	66.764759	0.014978	0.157699	10.528758	0.094978
25	6.848475	73.105940	0.013679	0.146018	10.674776	0.093679
26	7.396353	79.954415	0.012507	0.135202	10.809978	0.092507
27	7.988061	87.350768	0.011448	0.125187	10.935165	0.091448
28	8.627106	95.338830	0.010489	0.115914	11.051079	0.090489
29	9.317275	103.965936	0.009619	0.107327	11.158406	0.089619
30	10.062657	113.283211	0.008827	0.099377	11.257783	0.088827
31	10.867669	123.345868	0.008107	0.092016	11.349799	0.088107
32	11.737083	134.213537	0.007451	0.085200	11.434999	0.087451
33	12.676050	145.950620	0.006852	0.078889	11.513888	0.086852
34	13.690134	158.626670	0.006304	0.073045	11.586934	0.086304
35	14.785344	172.316804	0.005803	0.067634	11.654568	0.085803
36	15.968172	187.102148	0.005345	0.062625	11.717193	0.085345
37	17.245626	203.070320	0.004924	0.057986	11.775179	0.084924
38	18.625276	220.315945	0.004539	0.053690	11.828869	0.084539
39	20.115298	238.941221	0.004185	0.049713	11.878582	0.084185
40	21.724522	259.056519	0.003860	0.046031	11.924613	0.083860
41	23.462483	280.781040	0.003562	0.042621	11.967235	0.083562
42	25.339482	304.243523	0.003287	0.039464	12.006699	0.083287
43	27.366640	329.583005	0.003034	0.036541	12.043240	0.083034
44	29.555972	356.949646	0.002802	0.033834	12.077074	0.082802
45	31.920449	386.505617	0.002587	0.031328	12.108402	0.082587
46	34.474085	418.426067	0.002390	0.029007	12.137409	0.082390
47	37.232012	452.900152	0.002208	0.026859	12.164267	0.082208
48	40.210573	490.132164	0.002040	0.024869	12.189136	0.082040
49	43.427419	530.342737	0.001886	0.023027	12.212163	0.081886
50	46.901613	573.770156	0.001743	0.012321	12.233485	0.081743

TIME VALUE OF MONEY AT 10%

Periods	Future Value Factors	Future Value of Annuity Factors	Sinking Fund Factors	Present Value Factors	Present Value of Annuity Factors	Mortgage Constant
1	1.100000	1.000000	1.000000	0.909091	0.909091	1.100000
2	1.210000	2.100000	0.476190	0.826446	1.735537	0.576190
3	1.331000	3.310000	0.302115	0.751315	2.486852	0.402115
4	1.464100	4.641000	0.215471	0.683013	3.169865	0.315471
5	1.610510	6.105100	0.163797	0.620921	3.790787	0.263797
6	1.771561	7.715610	0.129607	0.564474	4.355261	0.229607
7	1.948717	9.487171	0.105406	0.513158	4.868419	0.205406
8	2.143589	11.435888	0.087444	0.466507	5.334926	0.187444
9	2.357948	13.579477	0.073641	0.424098	5.759024	0.173641
10	2.593742	15.937425	0.062745	0.385543	6.144567	0.162745
11	2.853117	18.531167	0.053963	0.350494	6.495061	0.153963
12	3.138428	21.384284	0.046763	0.318631	6.813692	0.146763
13	3.452271	24.522712	0.040779	0.289664	7.103356	0.140779
14	3.797498	27.974983	0.035746	0.263331	7.366687	0.135746
15	4.177248	31.772482	0.031474	0.239392	7.606080	0.131474
16	4.594973	35.949730	0.027817	0.217629	7.823709	0.127817
17	5.054470	40.544703	0.024664	0.197845	8.021553	0.124664
18	5.559917	45.599173	0.021930	0.179859	8.201412	0.121930
19	6.115909	51.159090	0.019547	0.163508	8.364920	0.119547
20	6.727500	57.275000	0.017460	0.148644	8.513564	0.117460
21	7.400250	64.002499	0.015624	0.135131	8.648694	0.115624
22	8.140275	71.402749	0.014005	0.122846	8.771540	0.114005
23	8.954302	79.543024	0.012572	0.111678	8.883218	0.112572
24	9.849733	88.497327	0.011300	0.101526	8.984744	0.111300
25	10.834706	98.347059	0.010168	0.092296	9.077040	0.110168
26	11.918177	109.181765	0.009159	0.083905	9.160945	0.109159
27	13.109994	121.099942	0.008258	0.076278	9.237223	0.108258
28	14.420994	134.209936	0.007451	0.069343	9.306567	0.107451
29	15.863093	148.630930	0.006728	0.063039	9.369606	0.106728
30	17.449402	164.494023	0.006079	0.057309	9.426914	0.106079
31	19.194343	181.943425	0.005496	0.052099	9.479013	0.105496
32	21.113777	201.137767	0.004972	0.047362	9.526376	0.104972
33	23.225154	222.251544	0.004499	0.043057	9.569432	0.104499
34	25.547670	245.476699	0.004074	0.039143	9.608575	0.104074
35	28.102437	271.024368	0.003690	0.035584	9.644159	0.103690
36	30.912681	299.126805	0.003343	0.032349	9.676508	0.103343
37	34.003949	330.039486	0.003030	0.029408	9.705917	0.103030
38	37.404343	364.043434	0.002747	0.026735	9.732651	0.102747
39	41.144778	401.447778	0.002491	0.024304	9.756956	0.102491
40	45.259256	442.592556	0.002259	0.022095	9.779051	0.102259
41	49.785181	487.851811	0.002050	0.020086	9.799137	0.102050
42	54.763699	537.636992	0.001860	0.018260	9.817397	0.101860
43	60.240069	592.400692	0.001688	0.016600	9.833998	0.101688
44	66.264076	652.640761	0.001532	0.015091	9.849089	0.101532
45	72.890484	718.904837	0.001391	0.013719	9.862808	0.101391
46	80.179532	791.795321	0.001263	0.012472	9.875280	0.101263
47	88.197485	871.974853	0.001147	0.011338	9.886618	0.101147
48	97.017234	960.172338	0.001041	0.010307	9.896926	0.101041
49	106.718957	1057.189572	0.000946	0.009370	9.906296	0.100946
50	117.390853	1163.908529	0.000859	0.008519	9.914814	0.100859

TIME VALUE OF MONEY AT 12%

Periods	Future Value Factors	Future Value of Annuity Factors	Sinking Fund Factors	Present Value Factors	Present Value of Annuity Factors	Mortgage Constant
1	1.120000	1.000000	1.000000	0.892857	0.892857	1.120000
2	1.254400	2.120000	0.471698	0.797194	1.690051	0.591698
3	1.404928	3.374400	0.296349	0.711780	2.401831	0.416349
4	1.573519	4.779328	0.209234	0.635518	3.037349	0.329234
5	1.762342	6.352847	0.157410	0.567426	3.604776	0.277410
6	1.973823	8.115189	0.123226	0.506631	4.111407	0.243226
7	2.210681	10.089012	0.099118	0.452349	4.563757	0.219118
8	2.475963	12.299693	0.081303	0.403883	4.967640	0.201303
9	2.773079	14.775656	0.067679	0.360610	5.328250	0.187679
10	3.105848	17.548735	0.056984	0.321973	5.650223	0.176984
11	3.478550	20.654583	0.048415	0.287476	5.937699	0.168415
12	3.895976	24.133133	0.041437	0.256675	6.194374	0.161437
13	4.363493	28.029109	0.035677	0.229174	6.423548	0.155677
14	4.887112	32.392602	0.030871	0.204619	6.628168	0.150871
15	5.473566	37.279715	0.026824	0.182696	6.810864	0.146824
16	6.130394	42.753280	0.023390	0.163121	6.973986	0.143390
17	6.866041	48.883674	0.020457	0.145644	7.119631	0.140457
18	7.689966	55.749715	0.017937	0.130039	7.249670	0.137937
19	8.612762	63.439681	0.015763	0.116106	7.365777	0.135763
20	9.646293	72.052442	0.013879	0.103666	7.469444	0.133879
21	10.803848	81.698736	0.012240	0.092559	7.562003	0.132240
22	12.100310	92.502584	0.010811	0.082642	7.644646	0.130811
23	13.552347	104.602894	0.009560	0.073788	7.718434	0.129560
24	15.178629	118.155241	0.008463	0.065882	7.784316	0.128463
25	17.000064	133.333870	0.007500	0.058823	7.843139	0.127500
26	19.040072	150.333934	0.006652	0.052521	7.895660	0.126652
27	21.324881	169.374007	0.005904	0.046893	7.942554	0.125904
28	23.883866	190.698887	0.005244	0.041869	7.984423	0.125244
29	26.749930	214.582754	0.004660	0.037383	8.021806	0.124660
30	29.959922	241.332684	0.004144	0.033378	8.055184	0.124144
31	33.555113	271.292606	0.003686	0.029802	8.084986	0.123686
32	37.581726	304.847719	0.003280	0.026609	8.111594	0.123280
33	42.091533	342.429446	0.002920	0.023758	8.135352	0.122920
34	47.142517	384.520979	0.002601	0.021212	8.156564	0.122601
35	52.799620	431.663497	0.002317	0.018939	8.175504	0.122317
36	59.135574	484.463116	0.002064	0.016910	8.192414	0.122064
37	66.231843	543.598690	0.001840	0.015098	8.207513	0.121840
38	74.179664	609.830533	0.001640	0.013481	8.220993	0.121640
39	83.081224	684.010197	0.001462	0.012036	8.233030	0.121462
40	93.050970	767.091420	0.001304	0.010747	8.243777	0.121304
41	104.217087	860.142391	0.001163	0.009595	8.253372	0.121163
42	116.723137	964.359478	0.001037	0.008567	8.261939	0.121037
43	130.729914	1081.082615	0.000925	0.007649	8.269589	0.120925
44	146.417503	1211.812529	0.000825	0.006830	8.276418	0.120825
45	163.987604	1358.230032	0.000736	0.006098	8.282516	0.120736
46	183.666116	1522.217636	0.000657	0.005445	8.287961	0.120657
47	205.706050	1705.883752	0.000586	0.004861	8.292822	0.120586
48	230.390776	1911.589803	0.000523	0.004340	8.297163	0.120523
49	258.037670	2141.980579	0.000467	0.003875	8.301038	0.120467
50	289.002190	2400.018249	0.000417	0.003460	8.304498	0.120417

TIME VALUE OF MONEY AT 14%

Periods	Future Value Factors	Future Value of Annuity Factors	Sinking Fund Factors	Present Value Factors	Present Value of Annuity Factors	Mortgage Constant
1	1.140000	1.000000	1.000000	0.877193	0.877193	1.140000
2	1.299600	2.140000	0.467290	0.769468	1.646661	0.607290
3	1.481544	3.439600	0.290731	0.674972	2.321632	0.430731
4	1.688960	4.921144	0.203205	0.592080	2.913712	0.343205
5	1.925415	6.610104	0.151284	0.519369	3.433081	0.291284
6	2.194973	8.535519	0.117158	0.455587	3.888668	0.257158
7	2.502269	10.730491	0.093192	0.399637	4.288305	0.233192
8	2.852586	13.232760	0.075570	0.350559	4.638864	0.215570
9	3.251949	16.085347	0.062168	0.307508	4.946372	0.202168
10	3.707221	19.337295	0.051714	0.269744	5.216116	0.191714
11	4.226232	23.044516	0.043394	0.236617	5.452733	0.183394
12	4.817905	27.270749	0.036669	0.207559	5.660292	0.176669
13	5.492412	32.088654	0.031164	0.182069	5.842362	0.171164
14	6.261349	37.581065	0.026609	0.159710	6.002072	0.166609
15	7.137938	43.842414	0.022809	0.140097	6.142168	0.162809
16	8.137249	50.980352	0.019615	0.122892	6.265060	0.159615
17	9.276464	59.117601	0.016915	0.107800	6.372859	0.156915
18	10.575169	68.394066	0.014621	0.094561	6.467420	0.154621
19	12.055693	78.969235	0.012663	0.082948	6.550369	0.152663
20	13.743490	91.024928	0.010986	0.072762	6.623131	0.150986
21	15.667578	104.768418	0.009545	0.063826	6.686957	0.149545
22	17.861039	120.435996	0.008303	0.055988	6.742944	0.148303
23	20.361585	138.297035	0.007231	0.049112	6.792057	0.147231
24	23.212207	158.658620	0.006303	0.043081	6.835137	0.146303
25	26.461916	181.870827	0.005498	0.037790	6.872927	0.145498
26	30.166584	208.332743	0.004800	0.033149	6.906077	0.144800
27	34.389906	238.499327	0.004193	0.029078	6.935155	0.144193
28	39.204493	272.889233	0.003665	0.025507	6.960662	0.143665
29	44.693122	312.093725	0.003204	0.022375	6.983037	0.143204
30	50.950159	356.786847	0.002803	0.019627	7.002664	0.142803
31	58.083181	407.737006	0.002453	0.017217	7.019881	0.142453
32	66.214826	465.820186	0.002147	0.015102	7.034983	0.142147
33	75.484902	532.035012	0.001880	0.013248	7.048231	0.141880
34	86.052788	607.519914	0.001646	0.011621	7.059852	0.141646
35	98.100178	693.572702	0.001442	0.010194	7.070045	0.141442
36	111.834203	791.672881	0.001263	0.008942	7.078987	0.141263
37	127.490992	903.507084	0.001107	0.007844	7.086831	0.141107
38	145.339731	1030.998076	0.000970	0.006880	7.093711	0.140970
39	165.687293	1176.337806	0.000850	0.006035	7.099747	0.140850
40	188.883514	1342.025099	0.000745	0.005294	7.105041	0.140745
41	215.327206	1530.908613	0.000653	0.004644	7.109685	0.140653
42	245.473015	1746.235819	0.000573	0.004074	7.113759	0.140573
43	279.839237	1991.708833	0.000502	0.003573	7.117332	0.140502
44	319.016730	2271.548070	0.000440	0.003135	7.120467	0.140440
45	363.679072	2590.564800	0.000386	0.002750	7.123217	0.140386
46	414.594142	2954.243872	0.000339	0.002412	7.125629	0.140339
47	472.637322	3368.838014	0.000297	0.002116	7.127744	0.140297
48	538.806547	3841.475336	0.000260	0.001856	7.129600	0.140260
49	614.239464	4380.281883	0.000228	0.001628	7.131228	0.140228
50	700.232988	4994.521346	0.000200	0.001428	7.132656	0.140200

INDEX

CHAPTER 1   Why Study Real Estate?

Courtesy of Chris Joith, Atlanta, Georgia.   page 9

CHAPTER 2   Property Rights and Legal Descriptions

The Empire State Building design is a trademark of ESBC.   page 28
Courtesy of Charles Floyd.   page 40
Courtesy of Charles Floyd.   page 41
Courtesy of Charles Floyd.   page 43

CHAPTER 6   Contracts and Title Closings

Florida Association of REALTORS®. Reprinted with permission.   pages 126–29

CHAPTER 7   Real Estate Leases

Florida Association of REALTORS®. Reprinted with permission.   pages 157–63

CHAPTER 8   Real Estate Brokerage

Florida Association of REALTORS®. Reprinted with permission.   page 177
Florida Association of REALTORS®. Reprinted with permission.   pages 179–81
Florida Association of REALTORS®. Reprinted with permission.   pages 182–84
Florida Association of REALTORS®. Reprinted with permission.   pages 186–87
Florida Association of REALTORS®. Reprinted with permission.   pages 188–90

CHAPTER 10   Property and Asset Management

Florida Association of REALTORS®. Reprinted with permission.   page 238–40

CHAPTER 13   Commercial and Industrial Land Uses

Country Club Plaza. Photo provided by Highwoods Properties.   page 299

Birkdale Village, Owned and Managed by Developers Diversified Realty, *www.ddr.com.*   page 300

CHAPTER 15   Urban and Regional Economics

Photos courtesy of Preservation North Carolina.   page 350